MEDIATION

Principles Process Practice

Dedication

Za moji roditelji

MEDIATION

Principles Process Practice

Laurence Boulle
BA, LLB, LLM, PhD

Miryana Nesic
BA, BEcon, LLB (Hons), BCL (Oxon)

Butterworths
London, Dublin, Edinburgh
2001

United Kingdom	Butterworths, a Division of Reed Elsevier (UK) Ltd, Halsbury House, 35 Chancery Lane, LONDON WC2A 1EL and 4 Hill Street, EDINBURGH EH2 3JZ
Australia	Butterworths, a Division of Reed International Books Australia Pty Ltd, CHATSWOOD, New South Wales
Canada	Butterworths Canada Ltd, MARKHAM, Ontario
Hong Kong	Butterworths Hong Kong, a Division of Reed Elsevier (Greater China) Ltd, HONG KONG
India	Butterworths India, NEW DELHI
Ireland	Butterworth (Ireland) Ltd, DUBLIN
Malaysia	Malayan Law Journal Sdn Bhd, KUALA LUMPUR
New Zealand	Butterworths of New Zealand Ltd, WELLINGTON
Singapore	Butterworths Asia, SINGAPORE
South Africa	Butterworths Publishers (Pty) Ltd, DURBAN
USA	Lexis Law Publishing, CHARLOTTESVILLE, Virginia

© Reed Elsevier (UK) Ltd 2001

A CIP Catalogue record for this book is available from the British Library.

ISBN 0 406 92747 2

Typeset by B & J Whitcombe, Nr Diss, Norfolk, IP22 2LP
Printed and bound in Great Britain by Hobbs the Printers Ltd, Totton, Hampshire

Visit Butterworths LEXIS *direct* at: http://www.butterworths.com

FOREWORD

Mediation has been practised in China and other Eastern countries for many centuries as the normal means of dispute resolution; but it has only recently been adopted in the Western world. Having taken root in the United States of America it is now spreading throughout the common law world as an alternative to the traditional practice of oral adversarial trials.

Its introduction in this country is of very recent origin, particularly in commercial disputes, but its use is growing apace and I believe that in the not too distant future mediation will play as large a part in dispute resolution as any other method. A grasp of the principles and practice of mediation will become an essential element in the training of every lawyer.

I commend this book most warmly to those who wish to start or continue their education in the art of mediation. It commences with a lucid explanation of the principles, continues with a discussion of the process and concludes with a wide-ranging and scholarly review of the present and growing use of mediation in the United Kingdom.

The likely reaction of the courts to the issues raised by mediation is discussed in Chapter 12; I find myself in agreement with the authors' conclusions. In particular I hope that our courts will uphold agreements to mediate, for it has been my experience that many of those who entered the process as sceptics have departed as converts – and with a settlement!

This book is a timely and admirable contribution to mediation practice in this country. Not only does it instruct the uninitiated but it is also of real value to practising mediators. I have blushed as I have recognised some of my own errors so clearly described and so firmly castigated. I extend my congratulations and thanks to the authors.

The Right Honourable Lord Griffiths, MC

January 2001

PREFACE

This book deals with aspects of the modern mediation process. Part I considers the theories of mediation, its principles and objectives, and its place within modern conflict management systems. Part II deals with the process and conduct of mediation, with particular reference to the functions, techniques and skills of mediators. Part III provides an overview of mediation practice in the UK to December 2000 and refers to anticipated future developments, which are occurring at an increasing rate. At the time of printing, for example, Professor Walker's study of family information meetings (www.open.gov.uk/lcd/family/fla/flapt2.htm) and Professor Davis's research of publicly-funded family mediation (www. legalservices.gov.uk/misl/news/Mediation Full Research Report) were released, and the Government has announced its intention to repeal the Family Law Act 1996, Part II. The experiences of other jurisdictions, like Australia and the US, are referred to throughout the book.

This book is aimed at those who are learning about mediation in academic institutions, those who are being exposed to it in mediation training workshops, those who are involved in its practice in its many forms and guises, and those who are developing and advancing the field of dispute resolution.

To some extent, mediation is a practice in search of theory. It has its foundations in several disciplinary areas and it has yet to develop its own explanatory theories. An author writing on the subject can approach it from differing perspectives. In this work the subject-matter is approached mainly, but not exclusively, from a legal perspective; it acknowledges the 'shadow of the law' which hangs over all mediations, even though the shadow is sometimes faint. The legal focus is responsible for the choice of material, the descriptive content and the form of analysis. The topics dealt with in Parts I and II would have a very different complexion if dealt with from the disciplinary perspectives of psychology, social work, economics or management.

Despite its legal orientation, this book's sources and authorities are not the traditional legal sources of statutes and case law. Given the confidentiality of most mediations, there are not many accessible case studies on the subject. The book draws its inspiration from the literature, from survey studies of mediation, including a survey of UK law firms conducted by the authors, from the accepted 'customs' of mediation practice, from the authors' personal experience as teachers, trainers and practitioners of mediation, from insights of colleagues and others within this field here and abroad, and from a critical reflection on practice and theory.

Among those to whom this UK edition owes a debt of gratitude are Lord Woolf, whose vision has provided a spark to the development of mediation; Justice Coleman, whose leadership has encouraged mediation in some of the largest and most complex commercial disputes; Lord Griffiths, whose robust mediation style is challenging 'classical' notions of mediation practice; and the Lord Chancellor's Department for kick-starting the debate on a number of important issues relating to the development and practice of mediation. Special thanks are due to David Shapiro, whose mediation experience over several decades has provided UK practitioners with valuable lessons in mediation practice, and whose feisty promotion of mediation has inspired without exception.

Miryana would also like to express her gratitude to those who have given her encouragement and support, without which this UK edition would not have been completed, including her parents, Arandel and Diane Nesic, whose frequent phone calls across the many miles served as timely reminders that work on 'the book' had to be done; Justice Byrne of the QLD Supreme Court, with special thanks for a decade of mentoring; Virginie Claeys at the Law Society, whose friendship never waned despite devoting so many of her weekends to scouring the internet for mediation references; Alison Newman at Barclays Bank, who kept Miryana employed despite her absences to work on 'the book'; and her CEDR Mediation Faculty colleagues for pearls of wisdom and their sense of humour. In the Australian edition of this book, Laurence acknowledged the support and assistance of colleagues at the Dispute Resolution Centre at Bond University and many others in the mediation movement who provided advice and inspiration over the last decade. This indebtedness remains. In addition, thanks are due to Laurence's many students in dispute resolution subjects who continue to be a source of stimulation, insight and wisdom. As always, Laurence makes particular acknowledgment of the support and care of Philippa, Mark, Sarah and Jonathon Boulle.

Special thanks are due to those who have read and commented on this book, namely, David Shapiro, Tony Willis and Lord Griffiths. Thanks are also due to many others who have directly or indirectly assisted in the preparation of the book. Research assistance was provided by Ludwick von Moltke, Mauritsz de Kort, Betty Chan, Claire Fleming, Michael Thomson and Peter Binder. Useful information was provided by almost 250 UK law firms, in response to the authors' survey in 2000, and although the anonymity of responses was assured, their comments are quoted throughout the book and have provided the book with richness. The authors also acknowledge the wealth of information provided by the organisations listed in the Schedule to this book; the Law Societies of England & Wales, Scotland and Northern Ireland; the Lord Chancellor's Department, the Office of Law Reform and the Scottish Executive; CMS Cameron McKenna and Dr Mays at the Robert Gordon University. Special thanks are due to the courts, that provided information, and in some cases access to their ADR records and statistics, including the Court of Appeal, the Commercial Court, the Patents Court and the Technology and Construction Court. Finally, a great debt of gratitude is owed to Lesley Page, whose nimble fingers typed the drafts of this edition and whose sense of humour never failed us. She was assisted in the final stages by Simone Goulton.

To all our students, workshop and seminar participants, and the many practitioners who have worked with us in cultivating the field of mediation, may your mediation poppies grow tall and strong.

CONTENTS

TABLE OF CASES

E

F

G

H

TABLE OF ABBREVIATIONS

AC	Appeal Cases
ACSR	Australian Companies and Securities Reports
ADRJ	Australian Dispute Resolution Journal
ADRLJ	ADR Law Journal (UK)
ALJ	Australian Law Journal
All ER	All England Law Reports
ALR	Australian Law Reports
BCL	Building and Construction Law Journal (Australia)
BCLC	Butterworths Company Law Cases
Build LR	Building Law Reports
Cal 3d	California Reports, 3rd Series
Cal App 4th	California Appeal Reports, 4th Series
Ch	Chancery
Ch D	Chancery Division
CLR	Commonwealth Law Reports
CLSR	Computer Law and Security Reports
Con LR	Construction Law Reports
ECJ	European Court of Justice
EHRR	European Human Rights Reports
EIPR	European International Property Review
EPLJ	Environmental and Planning Law Journal
F 2d	Federal Reports, 2nd Series (USA)
Fam	Family Division
FCA	Federal Court Australia
FLR	Federal Law Reports (Australia)
FLR	Family Law Reports
FSR	Fleet Street Reports
HL Cas	House of Lords Cases
ICCLR	International Company and Commercial Law Review
ICL Rev	International Construction Law Review
ILT	Irish Law Times
JPN	Justice of the Peace Notes of Cases
KB	King's Bench
LIJ	Law Institute Journal
Ll LR	Lloyd's List Law Reports
Lloyd's Rep	Lloyd's Reports
LRC	Law Reform Commission (New South Wales)
LT	Law Times
Misc 2d	Misc Reports, 2nd Series (New York)
Mo J Dispute Resol	(Missouri) Journal of Dispute Resolution
My & K	Mylne & Keen's Chancery Reports
NLJ	New Law Journal
NSWLR	New South Wales Law Reports
NSWSC	New South Wales Supreme Court
NW 2d	North Western Reporter, 2nd Series (USA)

P & CR	Property, Planning & Compensation Reports
P 2d	Pacific Reporter, 2nd Series (USA)
PD	Probate Division
PIQR	Personal Injury and Quantum Reports
QB	Queen's Bench
QBD	Queen's Bench Division
QCA	Queensland Court of Appeal
Qd R	Queensland Reports
QSC	Queensland Supreme Court
RPC	Reports of Patent Cases
SMULR	Southern Methodist Law Review
SW 2d	South Western Reporter, 2nd Series (USA)
TASRMPAT	Resource Management and Planning Appeal Tribunal of Tasmania
TLR	Times Law Reports
WAR	Western Australian Reports
Web JCLI	Web Journal of Current Legal Issues
WLR	Weekly Law Reports

Part I — Principles

1

Introduction to Mediation

Mediation is a decision-making process in which the parties are assisted by a third party, the mediator; the mediator attempts to improve the process of decision-making and to assist the parties reach an outcome to which each of them can assent.

Defining Mediation

Difficulties in defining mediation

Mediation is not easy to define.[1] It does not provide a single analytical model which can be neatly described and distinguished from other decision-making processes. The drafters of the Uniform Mediation Act in the United States made the same observation as they encountered problems in defining mediation in a way that does not also encompass other processes, such as early neutral evaluation, fact-finding, facilitation, and family counselling.[2]

There are many reasons for this difficulty of definition. One is the flexibility and open interpretation of terms such as 'voluntary' and 'neutrality' which are often used in the definition of mediation, but which can never provide certainty and clear boundary lines. A second reason is that mediation has yet to develop a coherent theoretical base and an accepted set of core features which enable it to be differentiated from rival processes. A third reason is that the term mediation is used in different senses by different users; factors such as economics, politics and self-interest cause people to define and describe mediation for their own partisan purposes. Finally, there is wide diversity in the practice of mediation. It is used for different purposes, it operates in different social and legal contexts, and mediators have great differences in their background, training, levels of skill and operational style.

---

1   On some of the difficulties with definitions see G Tillet *The Myths of Mediation*, 1991; G Kurien 'Critique of Myths of Mediation' (1995) 6 *ADRJ* 43; and S Silbey 'Mediation Methodology' (1993) 9 *Negotiation Journal* 349.
2   See Proposed Uniform Mediation Act by the US National Conference of Commissioners on Uniform State Laws, December 1999, in particular, the Reporter's Working Notes for section 1(2) that defines 'mediation'. The drafters eventually approached the question of definition by providing three characteristics to distinguish mediation from other dispute resolution processes: first, a mediator is not aligned with a disputant; secondly, the mediator assists the disputants with their own negotiated dispute resolution and has no authority to make a binding decision. The drafters emphasised negotiation in order to exclude adjudicative processes. Thirdly, the mediator is appointed by an appropriate authority or engaged by the disputants. Section 1(4) defines 'mediator'.

Some of the problems of definition are a result of the contrasts between 'private mediation', on one hand, and various forms of 'institutionalised mediation' (mediation connected to the courts or required by statute), on the other. Private mediations are well-resourced, have few time limitations, and are often, though not always, conducted by well-qualified mediators who can exploit the system's potential to the full. Some forms of institutionalised mediation have none of these features and the process can be 'poor, short and nasty'.[3] Descriptions of mediation tend to have the former in mind and to disregard the latter.

In contemporary UK, mediation is still in the 'defining phase' of its development. As important as any theoretical definitions are *working definitions*. These are emerging from the actual practice of mediation, the intentions of those who promote it, and the attitudes and beliefs of mediation educators and trainers. What high-status mediators do, and are known to do, in their practices, also influences the way mediation is defined. The process is being fashioned and shaped in the contrasting circumstances of commercial and family disputes, of private and agency-based services, of fee-for-service and free services, of lawyer and non-lawyer mediators, and both with and without the use of professional advisers. There is sometimes talk of the 'orthodox mediation process' or the 'standard model of mediation' or 'classical mediation', with other versions being regarded as adaptations to, deviations from, or vulgarisations of the norm. However, while there are clearly some limits to what can be classified as mediation, it is premature to insist on such a narrow orthodoxy as is implied by these phrases.

In the UK the concept of 'alternative dispute resolution' ('ADR') has not acquired a universally agreed definition. The glossary to the Civil Procedures Rules ('CPR'), operating in England and Wales, describes ADR as a 'collective description of methods of resolving disputes, otherwise than through the normal trial process'. That definition includes arbitration, a topic of debate in the UK.[4]

Approaches to defining mediation

There are two approaches to defining the practice of mediation, as there are to defining the practices of lawyering, counselling or medicine. Some writers, practitioners and academics define the process in ideal terms, which emphasise certain values, principles and objectives. This can be referred to as the *conceptualist approach*. Conceptualist definitions have a high normative content and might not reflect what actually happens in mediation practice. Folberg and Taylor provide a conceptualist definition of mediation, namely that mediation is:

> '[T]he process by which the participants, together with the assistance of a neutral person or persons, systematically isolate disputed issues in order to develop options, consider alternatives, and reach a consensual settlement that will accommodate their needs.'[5]

---

3   T Hobbes *Leviathan*, Everyman Edition, 1962, at p 65.

4   Compare, for example, P Naughton QC 'ADR Comes in from the Cold' (1995) *New Law Journal* 145 where the author explains that, as early as 1995 in the UK, arbitration was considered to fall outside the ambit of the definition of ADR.

5   J Folberg and A Taylor *Mediation: a comprehensive guide to resolving conflict without litigation*, Jossey-Bass, San Francisco, 1984, at p 7. The authors are alert to the definitional problems. For other well-used definitions, see C Moore *The mediation process: practical strategies for resolving conflict*, Jossey-Bass, San Francisco, 1996, at p 15; and H Astor and C Chinkin *Dispute Resolution in Australia*, Butterworths, Sydney, 1992, at p 61.

In the UK a common conceptualist definition of mediation is that mediation is a form of facilitated negotiation by a neutral third party, who guides the parties to a consensual solution to their problem.[6] Despite wide endorsement, such definitions have many questionable elements and a number of internal tensions.[7] There are many instances in which mediation does not systematically isolate the issues in dispute and consider options for its most effective resolution – it merely involves incremental bargaining towards a compromise solution. Mediation can sometimes have very little to do with accommodating 'needs', and more to do with the quick and efficient disposal of cases. There are also difficulties with the terms 'neutral' and 'consensual', which are dealt with later in this chapter. Other conceptualist definitions assert that mediation 'is empowering for the parties', that it 'reflects an alternative philosophy of conflict management', or that it strives to 'improve relationships between the parties'. Again, these goals are aspired to and achieved in some mediations, but in others they are neither in evidence nor are they contemplated by those involved. It is misleading to include without qualification such factors in the definition of mediation.

The second approach is to define mediation not in terms of an idealised concept or theory, but in terms of what actually happens in practice. This can be referred to as the *descriptive approach*. Descriptive definitions have a low normative content because they accept that within the wide diversity of mediation practice the values, principles and objectives of the conceptualists are often overlooked or overridden. One descriptive approach defines mediation as:

'. . . a process of dispute resolution in which the disputants meet with the mediator to talk over and then attempt to settle their differences.'[8]

Each of the approaches to defining mediation has its strengths and shortcomings. The strength of the conceptualist approach is that it highlights for users and practitioners the higher goals and values of mediation which differentiate it from other decision-making processes. The main shortcoming of this approach is that it tends to pass off as *descriptive* those elements of mediation which are *prescriptive*; this is an ideological and not an empirical approach to the definition of mediation.

The strengths of the descriptive approach are that it is based on actual practice, and reflects reality. Its main shortcoming is that there is such variety and diversity in the practice of mediation that this approach provides a very superficial and unhelpful definition. It also produces a value-free definition of mediation which overlooks its underlying philosophy.

---

6   See G Davis and M Roberts *Access to Agreement: a Consumer Study of Mediation in Family Disputes*, Open University Press, Milton Keynes, 1988; K Mackie 'Negotiation and Mediation: from Inelegant Haggling to Sleeping Giant' in K Mackie (ed) *A Handbook on Dispute Resolution*, Routledge, London, 1991; Centre for Dispute Resolution *Model Mediation Procedure Guidance Notes*; and Lord Woolf *Access to Justice: Interim Report*, Lord Chancellor's Department, London, June 1995.
7   F Astill *On alternative significances of definition in dispute resolution*, Paper presented at Australasian Law Teachers' Conference, Canterbury, New Zealand, October 1993.
8   M Roberts 'Systems or selves? Some ethical issues in family mediation' (1992) 10 *MQ* 11.

Do definitions matter?

As an exercise in semantics, some aspects of the definitional debate are esoteric and unproductive. However, definitions are significant in several practical and political ways. Definitions of mediation are important in practical terms: because governments may provide funding for 'mediation' programmes, some 'mediators' may enjoy an immunity from liability for negligence, and there are developing codes of conduct and ethical standards which apply to 'mediators'. There are also good marketing reasons for defining and limiting the concept, in that mediation still requires explanation and justification in terms of what it does and does not do. Appropriate definitions benefit both the users of mediation services and those who advise them on and refer them to mediation. Politically the definitional debate is significant in that different professions and organisations tend to define mediation in terms of the self-interests of their members. Thus a 'social work' definition might imply that it is necessary for mediators to have counselling skills, while a 'legal' definition could imply that knowledge of the law is essential. While the mediation terrain is being claimed by competing groups of service-providers, the particular definition of mediation which prevails is politically significant.

This work's approach to the definitional question

This book deals with the definitional issue in the following ways:

(a) It acknowledges that mediation can be defined both in terms of operational features and in terms of an underlying philosophy.

(b) It defines mediation in terms of a limited set of core elements, that is, features which are common to most practices carried out in the name of mediation.

(c) It enumerates some of the normative objectives of mediation which are pursued in only some forms of mediation practice. This is followed by an inventory of some of the variable features of mediation.

(d) Reference is made to the uses of mediation, since the purpose for which it is used contributes to mediation's definition.

(e) Attention is given to some of the disputed definitional features of mediation.

(f) At the end of this chapter, reference is made to four paradigm models of mediation, which are used as a source of reference throughout the work.

(g) In the following chapter, the underlying principles of mediation, as assumed in conceptualist approaches, are critically analysed.

Core, Secondary and Variable Features of Mediation

Core features

The core features of mediation are derived from the definition on the first page of this book, namely:

- it is a decision-making process;

- in which the parties are assisted by a third person, the mediator;[9]
- who attempts to improve the process of decision-making; and
- to assist the parties reach an outcome to which each of them can assent.

The conspicuous feature of this definition is its emphasis on *decision-making*, as opposed to dispute resolution. There are several reasons for this emphasis. As is shown below, mediation is not always used for resolving disputes, or even in the context of a dispute. Even when it is used in relation to a dispute, and the parties come to a decision, it cannot always be said that the dispute has been 'resolved', in the sense that the parties subjectively accept that it has come to an end. It is therefore both inaccurate and misleading to define mediation in terms of the resolution of disputes.[10] The focus on decision-making also has to do with the image and acceptability of mediation. For many parties who are unsure about the mediation process, the idea of making decisions may be less threatening than the idea that they will have to resolve a dispute, which has connotations of struggle, compromise, victory and defeat. Decision-making has none of these connotations and may be a reassuring notion for some parties entering mediation.

In all cases in which mediation is used, the parties have the opportunity for making decisions. This is the primary objective of the process. When parties to a mediation do not reach a settlement on the substantive issues, they can still make decisions on procedural issues, for example on where to take the problem next. In essence, mediation is a form of assisted decision-making. This emphasis makes it clear that mediators do not impose binding decisions on the parties,[11] and leaves open the question of what is entailed in the 'assistance' which they provide. When it is used with the purpose of resolving disputes, mediation is sometimes reduced to the narrower notion of 'assisted negotiation', that is, the mediator helps the disputing parties to negotiate with each other, but does not negotiate with them himself or herself.

Secondary objectives of mediation

Besides its principal objective of decision-making, mediation has a number of secondary objectives. These are shaped by the underlying values and principles of

---

9 This may seem trite. However, many counsellors and lawyers at mediation training courses claim that they have been 'practising as mediators for years'. This may indicate a certain style of practice, but it cannot constitute mediation. See H Brown and A Marriott *ADR Principles and Practice* (2nd edn), Sweet & Maxwell, London, 1999, at p 149.

10 Dispute settlement may be a more appropriate term, as when there is an unwilling compromise between two disputants: see G Tillet *Resolving conflict—a practical approach* (2nd edn), Oxford University Press, 1999, at pp 4–6.

11 C Richards 'The Expertise of Mediating' [1997] *Family Law* 52; Academy of Experts *Resolving your Dispute by Mediation*; and Law Society of England and Wales *Code of Practice for Civil/Commercial Mediation* and *Code of Practice for Family Mediation*. The Law Society's Practice Information on the Codes (at Annex 22A and 22B of the *Guide to the Professional Conduct of Solicitors* (8th edn), Law Society Publishing) provides that the objectives of mediation are to involve a neutral who has no authority to make any decisions with regard to the issues, but who assists the parties by negotiation, without adjudication.

mediation, which are dealt with in the following chapter.[12] These objectives are not always achieved in practice, nor are all mediators necessarily conversant with them. However, even where there is no definitive decision-making, mediation may be successful in achieving some lesser objectives. These secondary objectives are to:

- bring clarity to the situation by identifying and defining which matters do or do not require decisions to be made;
- overcome or reduce communication problems between the parties so that they can more clearly perceive and understand what each other means and feels;
- identify and acknowledge the various parties' needs and interests, whether substantive, procedural or psychological;
- promote constructive and efficient negotiations which focus predominantly on the parties' needs and interests, and which broaden the search for options and settlement alternatives;
- reduce anxiety and other negative effects of the problem situation and to be empowering for the parties so that informed and rational decision-making can take place;
- encourage the parties to take charge of their own decisions and to accept responsibility for the consequences of those decisions;
- reduce tension and improve, or at least not lead to a deterioration in, relationships between the parties; and
- provide the parties with a model, and some skills and techniques, for future decision-making without third party assistance.

Variable features

The core features of mediation listed above are relatively few in number. There is a much higher number of variable features of mediation, some of which are:

- the degree to which the parties enter into it consensually, are influenced to participate, or are compelled to take part by the legislature, courts or contract;
- the extent of the parties' choice of mediator or mediators;
- the qualifications, expertise and skills of the mediator;
- the independence and neutrality of the mediator;
- the extent and nature of the mediator's interventions, particularly as regards recommending, advising, influencing or persuading the parties;[13]
- the mediator's responsibility towards the parties, towards outsiders, and towards standards of fairness and reasonableness;
- the degree to which any settlement is of the parties' own, consensual making;[14]

---

12 A Taylor 'Toward a comprehensive theory of mediation' (1981) 19 *Conciliation Courts Review* 1; and M Anstey *Practical peacemaking—a mediator's handbook*, Juta & Co, Kenwyn, South Africa, 1993, at p 2.

13 M Palmer and S Roberts *Dispute processes: ADR and the primary forms of decision making*, Butterworths, London, 1998 who point out that mediation conceals a wide range of degrees of intervention.

14 See S Moody 'An Overview of ADR in Scotland' in Moody and Mackay (eds) *Green's Guide to ADR in Scotland*, Sweet & Maxwell, 1995, at p 6; Academy of Experts *Guidelines for Mediation*; ADR Group *Professional Code of Conduct*; Commercial Mediation Centre *Mediator's Code of Conduct*; and INCORE (Initiative on Conflict Resolution and Ethnicity) *Mediation in Practice*.

- the extent to which the process has a therapeutic or educative function;
- the degree of confidentiality of the process;
- the extent and nature of the rules and procedures followed;
- the extent to which past controversies are canvassed and future interests are taken into account;
- the extent to which any settlement outcome reflects how a court may determine the matter; and
- the legal status of any settlement outcome.[15]

These variables indicate why many aspects of mediation cannot be confined by a black and white definition. Confidentiality is often regarded as one of the cornerstones of mediation, but in practice different degrees of confidentiality may apply to different situations. Some mediations are confidential in all respects, but there are many situations in which all or part of what is said will not remain confidential because of the wishes of the parties, the nature of what is disclosed, countervailing principles and policies, or the orders of a court.[16] It is therefore misleading to define mediation without qualification as a confidential system.

Another example of variation relates to the choice of mediator. Some parties have an unrestricted choice of mediator, others have a mediator imposed on them, others have a constrained choice or power of veto, and others have a choice only of the method used for appointing the mediator. It is thus inaccurate to define mediation as a process in which the parties choose their own mediator.

The mediation abacus

The mediation abacus on page **10** represents some of the variable features of mediation.[17] The beads on the abacus symbolise the fact that there are many dimensions on each variable: the beads can be moved along the rows and rest at any point, as the circumstances dictate.

The Uses of Mediation

Mediation can be used for the following purposes:

To define problems or disputes

Mediation can be used for the sole purpose of defining which issues are in dispute and which are not. This process is sometimes referred to as 'scoping'[18] and is regarded as an appropriate role for mediation in some planning and environmental disputes. Once

---

15 C McEwen and R Maiman 'Small Claims Mediation in Maine: An Empirical Assessment' (1981) *Maine Law Review* 237; C Menkel-Meadow 'For and Against settlement: uses and abuses of the mandatory settlement conference' (1985) *UCLA Law Review* 485.

16 On the limits of confidentiality, see Chapter 12.

17 The mediation abacus was developed over time by J Wade and S Gribben. A version is included in J Wade, S Gribben and L Boulle 'Mediation—the terminological debate' (1994) 5 *ADRJ* 204.

18 M I Jeffrey 'Accommodating negotiation in environmental impact assessment and project approval processes' (1987) 4 *EPLJ* 244.

The Mediation Abacus

Consensual entry	←●————→	Compulsory entry
Party choice of mediator	←——●———→	Mediator imposed on parties
Mediator qualified	←————●—→	Mediator with no qualifications
Independent, neutral mediator	←——●———→	Mediator an interested insider
Low intervention by mediator	←————————●→	High intervention by mediator
Non-evaluative mediator	←●——————→	Evaluative mediator
Outcome consensual	←————————●→	Mediator influences outcome
Therapeutic/educational function	←●—————→	Settlement function only
High degree of confidentiality	←———●———→	Low degree of confidentiality
Rigid rules and procedures	←————————●→	Flexible rules and procedures
Agreement legally binding	←————————●→	Agreement not legally binding
Deals with past and future factors	←———●———→	Deals only with present issues

Some factors which influence the variables:

- Resources of parties (time, funds, expertise)
- Degree of hostility between parties
- Mediator's experience and preferences
- Bargaining strengths of parties
- Facilities/amenities available
- Needs and wishes of parties

the problem has been adequately defined, it can be referred to other methods of dispute resolution, such as litigation or a public inquiry. Scoping has the advantage of allowing the parties to define the problem in the knowledge that there will be no pressure at this stage to compromise their interests. The mediation may involve the parties setting the outer boundaries of the outcome, regardless of the decision of an external body such as a court. This form of mediation can be called *scoping mediation*.[19]

To settle disputes

Much mediation takes place in the context of a dispute between two or more parties where the process is used in an attempt to settle the dispute.[20] A dispute involves an overt and contested claim between two or more parties over competing interests, principles or processes. As is shown below, even where the dispute is not settled by mediation, the process may contribute to the management of the dispute in other ways, but the main objective is to bring the dispute to an end through the parties' joint decision-making. This can be called *dispute settlement mediation*.

To manage conflict

Mediation can be used to manage conflict even where it is known that the conflict will continue. Here 'conflict' refers to an ongoing series of disputes of severe intensity which have occurred over an extended period of time. Mediation can serve to contain the conflict by establishing appropriate rules, structures and processes for communication and interaction, even where there is little goodwill between the parties. By regulating the parties' conduct in the short term, mediation can provide an opportunity for the dispute to be dealt with through other methods in the long term.[21] An example of such a situation would be a parenting dispute between 'warring' former spouses where there are irreconcilable differences in religion and culture. Mediation could assist the parties to manage these differences in practical ways without needing to resolve the value differences between them. This form of mediation can be called *conflict containment mediation*.

To negotiate contracts

Mediation can be used in the process of contract formation.[22] Negotiating parties may use a mediator to assist in:

---

19 Thus an insurer may agree to pay a minimum amount and the claimant may agree not to take more than a maximum amount, and if the court judgment is outside these parameters then the maximum or minimum, whichever is applicable, will apply. Also see the section on Environmental Disputes in Chapter 8.

20 The term 'settle' is used instead of 'resolve'. Settle implies a formal termination of the overt conflict between parties, whereas resolve could imply a full emotional and cognitive acceptance that the matter has been finalised. It has often been observed that many disputes are never resolved at the psychological and emotional levels.

21 W Faulkes 'The dispute resolution industry—defining the industry and establishing competencies' (1994) 5 *ADRJ* 285 at 287.

22 R Buckley 'The applicability of mediation skills to the creation of contracts' (1992) 3 *ADRJ* 227. Also see the section on Commercial Contracts in Chapter 8.

- establishing a positive climate;
- identifying interests and priorities;
- improving communications;
- managing destructive emotions;
- brainstorming options;
- formulating proposals;
- narrowing options; and
- noting and recording agreements.

Here mediation is used not to assist in settling existing disputes, but to manage procedures during the negotiations, to resolve the terms of a contract and to provide ways of dealing with disputes should they arise during the future contractual relationship between the parties. The mediator acts as a facilitator, by assisting all parties, not any one party. This may be referred to as *transactional mediation*.[23] Areas in which transactional mediation is used include acquisitions, joint ventures, strategic alliances and pre-nuptial agreements.[24]

In a reported US case, transactional mediation was used in the negotiations leading up to the formalisation of a joint venture between General Motors and Toyota to establish a motor vehicle manufacturing plant in California. Although the parties were agreed in principle on the joint venture, there were two main obstacles, being opposition from the Workers' Union and Toyota's requirement that it should have freedom to run the plant as it saw fit. A former United States Secretary of Labor was appointed as a settlement mediator, and achieved a resolution of all the obstacles, following seven months of mediation. The co-operative nature of the imminent venture, the good faith expectation between the parties entering into the venture and the long term nature of the venture were powerful incentives to use a mediation in this capacity.[25] In one UK example, settlement mediation was used to resolve environmental issues, which were providing the stumbling block to a deal.

To formulate policy

Mediation can be used where a public authority is required to determine policy, standards or procedures in rules and regulations. Here the process serves to allow affected parties specifically, and interested members of the public generally, to participate in and influence the policy-making process. The mediation may produce the final policy, or its decisions may be referred to a government body with the ultimate authority to draft the regulations.[26] In some countries environmental, health and safety

---

23 Some parties, or their lawyers, may prefer to refer to it as assisted or facilitated negotiation, but it is essentially similar to mediation.
24 For a more detailed discussion of the role of mediators in this context, see M Hager and R Pritchard 'Hither the deal mediators' (1999) 10 (10) *ICCR* 291; and R P Buckley 'The applicability of mediation skills to the creation of contracts' (1992) *Australian Dispute Resolution Journal* 227.
25 J Reikert 'ADR in Australian Commercial Disputes: Quo Vadis?' (1990) *Australian Dispute Resolution Journal* 31.
26 One of the authors acted in a mediation in which different interest groups within an industry attempted to negotiate a proposal to amend parts of a statute. The responsible minister agreed beforehand to seek Cabinet endorsement of the mediated proposal, for subsequent ratification by parliament.

standards are developed through this process, which is referred to as regulatory-negotiation, or reg-neg.[27] This can be referred to as *policy-making mediation.*

To prevent conflicts

Both transactional mediation and policy-making mediation involve elements of conflict prevention. More generally, mediation can be used to assist parties to anticipate problems, grievances and difficulties and to plan processes for dealing with them when they arise. This can be referred to as *preventative mediation.* It has many potential applications in large public and private sector organisations.[28]

Other functions

Mediation can serve a number of subsidiary purposes, for example as an educational tool. It can directly and indirectly educate and train the parties in a method and style of decision-making which can be used in the future. This role can be very important in an environment where conflict is common and the parties' general dispute resolution skills are limited.[29] Where successful, it can develop the parties' confidence in managing their own affairs. There have also been suggestions that one goal of mediation is the growth of the parties. This approach sees mediation as a transformation process during which the parties develop empowerment and recognition.[30] Mediation also has potential as a managerial tool, where management comes to rest increasingly on consent rather than on authority.[31] Some parties use mediation as a filtering mechanism in the litigation process, that is, to evaluate the other side's facts, arguments and witnesses in order to assess how to proceed with the matter. It can be used to 'negotiate' the facts, in the sense of developing a common version of historical reality. Mediation is one part of a growing problem-solving industry which is examining and developing systems, methods and techniques of decision-making, dispute resolution and problem-solving.

The focus in this work

Despite the many potential uses of mediation, the main focus in this book is on *dispute settlement mediation.* The term 'dispute resolution' is used synonymously with 'dispute settlement'. Therefore, unless indicated otherwise, it is assumed in this work that mediation is used with the primary objective of assisting the parties to make their own decisions in order to settle or resolve matters in dispute between them.

---

27 L Susskind and G McMahon 'The theory and practice of negotiated rulemaking' (1985) 3 *Yale Journal of Regulation* 133; and D Pritzker 'Regulation by consensus: negotiated rulemaking in the United States' (1994–1995) 1 *CDRJ* 217.

28 See the section on Dispute Management in Chapter 10.

29 For example, see K Pringle 'Aboriginal mediation: one step towards empowerment' (1996) 7 *ADRJ* 253.

30 J Antes et al 'Is a stage model of mediation necessary?' (1999) 16 *Mediation Quarterly* 287 at 291.

31 A Acland *A sudden outbreak of common sense*, Hutchinson, London, 1990 at p 15.

Unresolved Issues of Definition

There are at least five areas in which conceptualist definitions of mediation are problematic, in that they gloss over uncertain or disputed features of the process. These five areas are encapsulated in the italicised words in this hypothetical conceptualist definition:

> 'Mediation is a *voluntary* system in which a *neutral* mediator controls a *process* but does not intervene in the *content* of a dispute and which leads to *consensual* outcomes for the parties.'

Definitions such as this are partly influenced by idealised notions of mediation and are used in the promotion and marketing of mediation. It simplistically attributes to mediation five features, without acknowledging their problematic nature. The five disputed features are interrelated and are dealt with here by way of the open-ended questions which follow.

Does entry into and participation in mediation have to be voluntary?

Many commentators define mediation as a voluntary process for all parties. It is said that 'voluntarism is an essential component of mediation',[32] that it 'is the foremost tenet of good mediation'[33] and that it provides the process with legitimacy.[34] 'Voluntary' is contrasted with 'mandatory' or 'coercive', as these terms apply, for example, in the litigation process where parties might be compelled to attend, to participate and to comply with the outcome, on pain of sanctions if they do not do so. The emphasis on the term 'voluntary' in mediation is justified in terms of the 'alternative' character of mediation; if mediation was not an optional process, so the argument goes, it would no longer constitute an alternative system of dispute resolution. The voluntarism is also held to underpin other values and principles of mediation, such as its participatory nature and the emphasis on self-determination for the parties. Moreover, once the parties have entered into mediation, voluntarism requires them to be able to withdraw from the process at any stage before settlement. If a party in a mediation does not wish to continue with mediation, the process must be discontinued at least as regards that party,[35] although from a practical point of view

---

32 R Ingleby 'Compulsion is not the answer' (1992) 27 *Australian Law News* 17 at 18. The voluntarism is often said to extend to mediators, denoting that they have the discretion to decline to mediate or to terminate a mediation.

33 T Terrell 'Rights and Wrongs in the Rush to Repose: on the Jurisprudential Dangers of Alternative Dispute Resolution' (1987) 36(2) *Emory Law Journal* 541 at 551; and P Adler 'Resolving public policy conflicts through mediation: the Water Roundtable' (1990) 1 *ADRJ* 69 at 78. C Moore *The mediation process: practical strategies for resolving conflict*, Jossey-Bass, San Francisco, 1996, at pp 15, 19–20, defines mediation as a voluntary process, but acknowledges that there may be significant pressure on parties to try it.

34 On which, see Chapter 2.

35 See Law Society of England and Wales *Code of Practice for Civil/Commercial Mediation*; and, in relation to family mediation, see, for example, UK College of Family Mediators *Code of Conduct*.

it may not be possible to continue the mediation without the party's participation. Most rules governing mediator conduct and the standard mediation agreements produced by UK mediation organisations provide that a party can withdraw from a mediation without having to give reasons.[36] In family mediation, a mediator can usually bring a mediation to an end if he or she believes that a participant is unable or unwilling to participate freely in the process or if there is a fear of violence or abuse to any participant in the process or fear of harm to the children of a participant in the process.[37]

In dealing with this topic it is necessary to explore the dimensions of the concept of voluntarism. Wolski[38] identifies four dimensions, namely voluntary entry into and participation in mediation, the absence of settlement pressures, a mutually acceptable outcome, and the ability to accept or reject a particular outcome. Here the first of these dimensions is relevant. There may be situations in which mediation is not voluntary in that there is a requirement to take part in the process before a party is entitled to a court hearing or before other benefits can be obtained. The merits of these requirements are dealt with shortly. There are other situations in which mediation, while not being mandatory in the above sense, is also not voluntary in the sense of its being selected through the free and informed consent of both parties. It is possible to see that there are gradations of voluntariness, such that mediation is neither completely voluntary nor completely mandatory, but falls somewhere on a spectrum between the two. This is shown by the following examples:

(a) A court may suggest that parties go through mediation before the matter is heard and resolved by it.[39] Even where a court merely inquires about the possibility of mediation, it becomes non-voluntary if the parties, or their lawyers, feel pressured into responding affirmatively to the inquiry in order to maintain the support of the court.[40]

(b) Large organisations may influence and persuade members, employees or those contracting with them to participate in mediation, for example, through mediation clauses in contracts.[41] There is evidence to show that there is little spontaneous demand for mediation[42] and that where mediation is most used, the parties experience at least some influence or pressure from a wider community to enter the process.[43] The pressuring community could include family, friends, voluntary associations or large organisations.

(c) The majority of people who need mediation are suffering from some kind of loss and, as such, are often emotionally vulnerable. The decision to mediate

---

36 See, for example, ADR Group *Agreement to Mediate*. Compare with the requirements in cases of mandatory mediation: see Chapter 9.

37 See Law Society of England and Wales *Code of Practice for Family Mediation*; and UK College of Family Mediators *Code of Conduct*.

38 B Wolski 'Voluntariness, consensuality and coercion: in defence of mandatory mediation' unpublished LLM paper, Bond University, 1994.

39 See the section on Civil Justice Reforms and Courts in Chapter 7.

40 R Ingleby 'Court sponsored mediation: the case against mandatory participation' (1993) 56 *Modern Law Review* 441 at 443.

41 See the section on Enforceability of Mediation Clauses in Chapter 12.

42 See the section on UK Mediation Statistics in Chapter 9.

43 C McEwan and T Milburn 'Explaining a paradox of mediation' (1993) 9 *Negotiation Journal* 23, who point out that despite the 'reluctance' of parties to enter mediation, they tend to evaluate it highly once they have participated in the process.

may be the result of external pressures to resolve the disputes as quickly as possible. This limit to voluntariness is of particular concern in family law cases where women may still be mourning the loss of their marriage and are facing the possibility of losing their children as well.[44]

(d) Mediation is not genuinely voluntary where a party enters into mediation under threat of litigation from the other side, where it is not fully understood that participation is optional, or where litigation or other dispute resolution options are not affordable. Ironically, with respect to costs, there have been doubts that mediation does in fact reduce costs in all cases.[45] Furthermore, there is a risk of increased costs should mediation be unsuccessful, as the parties will have to bear the burden of litigation on top of the costs for the failed mediation.[46]

(e) Where mediation is a pre-condition for legal aid or a party fears cost sanctions for unreasonably refusing to mediate, the voluntariness of participation is questionable.[47]

In these situations mediation is not voluntary, to a greater or lesser degree. The situations indicate that it is not possible to draw a clear line between voluntarism and mandatoriness in relation to entry into, and continued participation in, mediation. It is simplistic to define mediation in terms of a rigid voluntary/involuntary distinction, yet this is a surprisingly common occurrence. In reality, entry into mediation is sometimes voluntary, but in other cases it is affected by differing degrees of pressure or duress. It is only in respect of the outcome that mediation is voluntary, but even then only in a limited sense, as is shown below. Although the 'ideology of voluntarism'[48] is an important legitimising element in the promotion and marketing of mediation, it cannot be taken at face value.

The concerns and potential advantages of mandatory mediation are considered in Chapter 9. Given the reality of mandatory mediation systems, there seems to be little purpose in regarding mandatory mediation as a contradiction in terms. The better approach is to focus on developing adequate safeguards to ensure that mediation works at its optimal level. This would involve the screening of cases to ensure that wholly inappropriate matters do not go to mediation, quality controls in relation to the qualifications and expertise of mediators, and monitoring and surveys of the systems over time. Other issues which require attention are the funding of mandatory mediation programmes and the amount and nature of any disclosures to courts or other authorities.[49]

---

44 R Alexander 'Family mediation: friend or foe for women?' (1997) 8 *ADRJ* 255.

45 See further P de Jersey 'ADR—a decade later: still not "mere gimmickry"', Speech delivered at the LEADR Annual General Meeting, 21 October 1998. Also see the section on Banking and Finance Disputes in Chapter 8.

46 C Down 'Crying Woolf? Reform of the adversarial system in Australia' (1998) 7 *Journal of Judicial Administration* 213 at 222–3; and K Kovach 'Costs of mediation: whose responsibility?' (1997) 15 *Mediation Quarterly* 13. Also see the section on Mediation and Efficiency in Chapter 2.

47 See Chapter 9 for a discussion of funding and mediation, and of CPR, r 44 and possible cost sanctions.

48 C McEwan and T Milburn 'Explaining a paradox of mediation' (1993) 9 *Negotiation Journal* 23 at 25.

49 See sections on suitability for mediation in Chapter 3, and on funding and reporting issues in Chapter 9.

Do mediators have to be neutral?

Definitions of mediation frequently assert that the mediator is a neutral intervener in the parties' dispute.[50] This is linked to the process/content distinction, dealt with below. The concept of neutrality has an important legitimising function for mediation, but is based more on the need to counterbalance the ideology of judicial neutrality than it is on an examination of the actual roles and behaviours of mediators.[51] It is sometimes justified in terms of the practice of mediation in traditional societies, but this is based on distorted understandings.[52] Some writers refer to neutrality as the most pervasive and misleading myth about mediation, arguing that it is neither a possible attainment nor a desirable one.[53] This is a large topic and can only be dealt with briefly in these pages.

The term 'neutrality' has several shades of meaning within the context of mediation.[54] In its broadest sense it can cover the following factors: the mediator has no direct interest in the outcome of the dispute, that is, he or she is a disinterested party; the mediator has no prior knowledge of the dispute; the mediator does not know the parties or have any prior association with them; the mediator will not, directly or indirectly, sit in judgment on the parties; the mediator will not use his or her substantive expertise to influence the decision-making; and the mediator will act even-handedly, fairly and without bias towards the parties. It is clear that in practice not all mediators are neutral in all these senses. Definitions of mediation and codes of conduct for mediators often overlook the multiple dimensions of neutrality in their characterisation of mediators as neutral facilitators.[55]

Some assistance is provided by distinguishing between neutrality in the sense of disinterestedness and neutrality in the sense of fairness. The former is referred to here as *neutrality* and the latter as *impartiality*, a distinction which is reflected in some mediator standards.[56] Neutrality relates to the mediator's background and his or her relationship with the parties and the dispute. It involves matters such as: the extent of prior contact between the mediator and the parties, prior knowledge about the specific dispute, the degree of mediator interest in the substantive outcome or in the way the mediation is conducted, and the extent of mediator expertise in the subject-matter of the dispute.[57] Impartiality, by contrast, refers to an even-handedness, objectivity and fairness towards the parties during the mediation process. It relates to such matters as time allocation, facilitation of the communication process, and avoidance of any display of favouritism or bias or adversarial conduct in word or action.

---

50 In the American literature, mediators are often referred to as 'third party neutrals'.
51 P H Gulliver *Disputes and Negotiations: a cross-cultural perspective*, Academic Press, New York, 1979.
52 See the section on Mediator Liability in Chapter 12.
53 G Tillet *Resolving conflict—a practical approach*, Sydney University Press, Sydney, 1991; and G Kurien 'Critique of Myths of Mediation' (1995) 6 *ADRJ* 43 at 52.
54 See D King 'Specialists in family law resolution' (1999) 10 *ADRJ* 63 at 65 for a discussion concerning neutrality in family law mediation; H Astor 'Rethinking neutrality: a theory to inform practice' part 1 (2000) 11 *ADRJ* 73 and part 2 (2000) 11 *ADRJ* 145.
55 See the section on Neutrality in Chapter 11.
56 On mediator standards, see the sections on Neutrality and Impartiality in Chapter 11. On this distinction, see also C Moore *The mediation process: practical strategies for resolving conflict*, Jossey-Bass, San Francisco, 1996 at p 52.
57 Although the notion of a 'neutral expert' is in some respects a contradiction in terms, consider the role of the single expert in court proceedings.

In the case of judicial and administrative bodies, both neutrality and impartiality are requirements of all decision-making. In the case of mediation, each concept has a different significance. Impartiality must be regarded as a core requirement in mediation, in the sense that its absence would fundamentally undermine the nature of the process. It is inconceivable that the parties could waive the requirement that the mediator act fairly. Neutrality, however, is a less absolute requirement and could be waived without prejudicing the integrity of the mediation process, for example in relation to a mediator's prior contact with one of the parties.[58] While impartiality must be a constant feature of mediation, the existence of neutrality will always be a question of degree.[59] This is illustrated by the following examples:

(a) Some parties choose a mediator who is interested, as opposed to dis-interested, in the outcome of the dispute.[60] In international conflicts and in disputes in traditional societies, the fact that a mediator has close relations with the parties, or direct knowledge of the situation, may be regarded by the parties as a useful basis for assisting them to reach a settlement.[61]

(b) It would be unusual for mediators not to have their own preferences for certain outcomes to disputes, and some writers argue that mediators seek to influence the course and outcome of negotiations for a variety of reasons related to their own values.[62] In some situations the mediator may have been selected with a view to using his or her judgment in 'shepherding' the parties to an appropriate outcome.

(c) Where the mediation takes place through separate meetings,[63] the mediator is in an unusually powerful position to impose his or her value preferences on the decision-making process, and research suggests that mediators are more inclined to violate the neutrality principle during separate meetings.[64]

(d) Some standards of conduct for mediators impose on them obligations to help the parties reach a fair and equitable settlement, to raise questions as to the fairness or equity of proposed settlement options, and to ensure consideration of the interests of children and other potentially affected third parties.[65] There have also been suggestions that mediators need to 'address

---

58 See the section on Neutrality in Chapter 11.

59 K Kressel et al (eds) *Mediation Research: the process and effectiveness of third party intervention*, Jossey-Bass, San Francisco, 1989, at pp 97–109, distinguish between *contractual mediation*, where the mediator is an outsider to the dispute, and *emergent mediation*, where the mediator is part of the ongoing 'relational set' of the disputants. In contractual mediation, mediators' power derives from their neutrality and impartiality. In emergent mediation it derives from their status in the community and their capacity to influence one or more of the parties and to enforce agreements reached.

60 On 'interested' and 'disinterested' mediators, see M Anstey *Negotiating Conflict: insights and skills for negotiators and peacemakers*, Juta & Co, Kenwyn, South Africa, 1991, at pp 251–2.

61 See the section on International Disputes in Chapter 8.

62 P H Gulliver *Disputes and Negotiations: a cross-cultural perspective*, Academic Press, New York, 1979 at p 203; K Kressel and D Pruitt 'Themes in the mediation of social conflict' (1985) 41 *Journal of Social Issues* 179 at 190.

63 On separate meetings, see Chapter 4.

64 G Welton et al 'The role of caucusing in community mediation' (1988) 32 *Journal of Conflict Resolution* 181.

65 B Wolski 'Voluntariness, consensuality and coercion: in defence of mandatory mediation' unpublished LLM paper, Bond University, 1994 at p 18 for references cited there;

power imbalances and appeal to moral authority'.[66] This casts them in a less neutral role in respect of some aspects of the mediation.

(e) In some mediations the mediator may have to use judgment in reporting to an outside authority, or in terminating the mediation where that is required by standards of conduct. This evaluative role violates one aspect of the neutrality principle.

(f) In some statutory settings the mediator or conciliator is required to show allegiance to the policies and principles contained in the statute and can therefore not be indifferent to the outcome of the mediation.[67]

(g) Mediators have their own indirect interests in the mediation process: success rates, reputation, return custom, development of their practice, and self-esteem.[68] Moreover, some mediators have direct interests in the outcome, for example where the mediator is a manager within an organisation and is mediating a dispute between two or more subordinates. Mediators' neutrality is limited where they have direct or indirect interests in outcomes.

Thus in the reality of mediation practice, neutrality needs to be seen as multi-dimensional, with not all dimensions present in all instances. Roberts suggests that the mediator's role is one of 'at least apparent neutrality'.[69] There is a core requirement of impartiality, but beyond this there may be many variations in regard to neutrality. It is not possible to assert as a matter of definition that mediators are always neutral.[70] However, whatever their lack of neutrality, they are required to act impartially, that is, fairly and without bias.

Is mediation based on a distinction between process and content?

Many texts on mediation define the system in terms of a process/content distinction. It is suggested that mediators control a process of decision-making, while the parties are responsible for the content and substantive outcome. As Brown and Marriott point out, the word 'neutral' is used in relation to the outcome, rather than the

---

L Boulle 'Emerging standards for lawyer mediators' (1993) 23 *Queensland Law Society Journal* 375 at 385; and see Chapters 5, 8 and 11 for standards and guidelines for mediators.

66 M McCormick 'Confronting social injustice as a mediator' (1997) 14 *Mediation Quarterly* 293. It is observed that the result would be a 'revision of the notion of impartiality'.

67 Some of the first ADR systems in Australia, for example, were established in the anti-discrimination area. See also the sections on Discrimination and Family Disputes in Chapter 8. The Banking Ombudsman, for example, would keep under review the principles of fairness and reasonableness in the Banking Code.

68 M Levitt 'Kilometer 101: oasis or mirage? An analysis of third party interest in international mediation' (1997) *Mediation Quarterly* 155.

69 S Roberts 'Mediation in family disputes' (1983) 46 *Modern Law Review* 537 at 545; S Cobb and J Rifkin 'Practice and paradox: deconstructing neutrality in mediation' (1991) 16 *Law and Social Inquiry* 3; and M Feer 'On "Toward a new discourse for mediation: a critique of neutrality"' (1992) 10 *MQ* 173.

70 A Taylor 'Concepts of neutrality in family mediation: contexts, ethics, influence and transformative process' (1997) 14 *MQ* 215.

process of mediation.[71] Mackie et al also emphasise that it is the process of mediation that is structured and influenced by the intervention of the mediator.[72] This distinction is justified in terms of both pragmatic and philosophical considerations.[73] Process intervention is said to be compatible with the parties' autonomy to make their own choices, rather than having another professional telling them, in however disguised a form, what to do; there are many other dispute resolution processes in which the parties can request a professional to intervene in the substantive content of their dispute. Process interventions empower the parties by reinforcing their ability to control matters of content. Decisions are more likely to endure over time if the parties have assumed the responsibility of making them. Process-only interventions by mediators also promote quality decisions in that the parties are the best-informed persons to define their real interests and issues. Allowing the parties control over matters of content also enables them to develop their own sense of 'fairness', which is defined by their satisfaction with the result.[74] Finally, restricting the mediator's involvement to matters of process entails fewer liability risks for mediators.[75]

The process/content distinction is a useful starting point for understanding and explaining the mediation system. Nevertheless, the distinction is unclear and misleading in several respects:

(a) Process can never be completely separate from substance. Many conventional 'procedural' interventions by mediators can affect matters of substance, for example when they assist the parties to develop an agenda, reinterpret the parties' dialogue or obstruct (or fail to obstruct) a particular negotiating behaviour.[76]

(b) Sometimes the practice of mediation involves significant interventions on matters of content. Thus parties might select a certain mediator in the expectation that, without imposing a decision, he or she will guide them to an outcome which is reasonable and within the normal range of outcomes for the particular problem, based on his or her expertise in the area of the dispute.

(c) The style of some mediators may involve direct and indirect interventions into the content of the dispute. Thus through a recurrent style of questioning, or merely through expressive body language, the mediator may be having a significant influence on the substance of the dispute, again without directly recommending a particular course of action or imposing a final decision.

(d) In some cases mediators share control of the process with the parties, by inviting their opinion or accepting their decisions on matters of organisation,

---

71 H Brown and A Marriott *ADR Principles and Practice* (2nd edn), Sweet & Maxwell, 1999, at p 129, who refer to Principles III(i) and (ii) of the Council of Europe's Recommendation No R(98)1 on Family Mediation (1998).

72 K Mackie, D Miles, W Marsh *Commercial Dispute Resolution: an ADR Practice Guide*, Butterworths, London 1995, at p 9 (2nd edition due for publication).

73 C Moore *The mediation process: practical strategies for resolving conflict*, Jossey-Bass, San Francisco, 1996 at pp 74–6.

74 R Alexander 'Family Mediation under the microscope' (1999) 10 *ADRJ* 18 at 20.

75 See the section on Mediator Liability in Chapter 12.

76 J Antes et al 'Is a stage model of mediation necessary?' (1999) 16 *Mediation Quarterly* 287 at 289–90.

changes in procedure, adjournments, and the like. Mediators do not, in all respects, control the process alone.

Observation studies of actual mediations have led some commentators to the view that the process/content distinction is difficult, if not impossible, to maintain.[77] The distinction has been referred to as illusory and dangerous.[78] However, even where it is accepted that the process/content distinction is not watertight, there is still uncertainty as to the permissible nature and extent of the mediator's interventions, as shown in the following section.

How far can mediators intervene in the dispute?

There is considerable debate as to the legitimate and appropriate degree to which a mediator can 'intervene' in a dispute. This is closely linked to the process/content debate. On one hand is the 'minimalist intervention' approach[79] which restricts the mediator to a facilitative role, in terms of bringing the parties together, providing structure and control, and assisting them to communicate and negotiate constructively. Mediators do not, in this view, intervene on the substance or merits of the dispute. The minimalist intervention approach is regarded as appropriate for competent parties with approximately equal bargaining power who are involved in a dispute the outcome of which will affect only themselves. On the other hand, the 'directive intervention' approach allows mediators to intervene more directly and actively, for example by encouraging the parties to compromise, by suggesting options for the parties' consideration, by advising them on the consequences of not settling, by being confrontationist when they reach impasses, and by otherwise influencing the actual content of the decision-making. This approach is regarded as appropriate, for example, in environmental disputes, where unrepresented parties might be affected by the outcome, or in family disputes where the children's interests need to be kept to the forefront.[80]

Another way of conceptualising the two approaches is in terms of Kolb's categorisation of mediators as 'orchestrators' and 'dealmakers'.[81] The orchestrator

---

77 R Ingleby 'Court sponsored mediation: the case against mandatory participation' (1993) 56 *Modern Law Review* 441 at 441 and 447, where he observed and analysed 14 Federal Court mediations, 25 Small Claims Tribunal hearings (a med-arb process) and 50 Family Court Order 24 conferences in Australia. See also R Berlin 'Mediation: sharing vs instructing' (1998) 53 *Dispute Resolution Journal* 48.

78 R Ingleby 'ADR's claims "unproven"' (1992) 27 *Australian Law News* 7.

79 H Brown and A Marriott *ADR Principles and Practice* (2nd edn), Sweet & Maxwell, 1999 at pp 138–40; and S Roberts 'Toward a minimal form of alternative intervention' (1986) 11 *MQ* 25.

80 See, respectively, L Susskind 'Environmental mediation and accountability problem' (1981) 6 *Vermont Law Review* 1; and D T Saposnek *Mediating child custody disputes: a systematic guide for family therapists, court counsellors, attorneys and judges*, Jossey-Bass, 1983. See Chapters 5 and 8 on considerations in family mediation; and Chapter 8 for further consideration of environmental disputes.

81 D Kolb *The Mediators*, MIT Press, Cambridge, Massachusetts, 1983, at pp 23–45. M Fulton *Commercial Alternative Dispute Resolution*, The Law Book Company, Sydney, 1989, at p 75 uses the terms 'active' and 'passive' mediation. K Kressel et al (eds) *Mediation Research: the process and effectiveness of third party intervention*, Jossey-Bass, San Francisco, 1989 at p 423, refer to the 'task-oriented' and the 'socioemotional' styles of mediation.

mediators manage the interaction between the parties but leave the development of the agreement to them, while the dealmakers actively promote and influence a settlement.

Some of the differences between the approaches are caused by the open-ended meaning of the word 'intervention' and related terms. Thus the minimalist intervention school argues that mediators should not 'advise' the parties. However, the term 'advise' is not straightforward and it can have different meanings. In a narrow sense it means to counsel or recommend, which would not be countenanced in many forms of mediation: the process is not a substitute for professional advice from lawyers, accountants or other expert advisers. In a wider sense it includes the giving of information, and in this sense of the term many forms of mediation do allow mediators to advise, although within limits.[82]

Riskin makes the distinction between 'narrow' and 'broad' facilitation and intervention, with broad facilitation being the least interventionist, and narrow intervention being the most interventionist, mediator style. According to Riskin:[83]

- Broad facilitation encourages the parties to consider their interests and develop proposals that would meet those interests.
- Narrow facilitation involves reality testing the parties' assessments of the strengths and weaknesses of their case.
- Narrow evaluation results in the mediator making assessments, predictions and proposals designed to meet the parties' interests.

Moore contributes to the interventionist debate by distinguishing between four different aspects of intervention.[84] First is the *level* of intervention, which refers to whether the mediator intervenes throughout the negotiation process or only in respect of particular deadlocks or difficulties. Second is the *target* of intervention, which refers to whether the mediator directs his or her moves at both parties or at only one, for example the more powerful or more intransigent party, or even at the parties' lawyers where they are present. Third is the *focus* of intervention, which refers to the critical situations at which mediators direct their moves. This could involve moving to change the emotional relationship between the parties; or to changing the style and process of negotiation which they are using; or to changing the content of the dispute by encouraging the consideration of a range of settlement options. Fourth is the *intensity* of intervention. All of these interventions can be justified in process terms, but can also, to varying degrees, impinge on the substantive issues in dispute and influence the outcome.

Broad evaluations or focus interventions attract the most heated debate, as evidenced by the question of whether and to what extent mediators can suggest proposals for settlement. The minimalist view is that mediators can neither impose nor propose options for settlement, as this is incompatible with the objectives and philosophy of mediation. The directive intervention view is that in appropriate circumstances, for example where the parties are unable to make any headway on their own, or where requested by all the parties to do so, mediators can suggest solutions. The Centre for

---

82 H Brown and A Marriott *ADR Principles and Practice* (2nd edn), Sweet & Maxwell, 1999, at p 19. See the section on Role of Mediators in family mediation in Chapter 5.
83 L Riskin 'Mediator Orientations: Strategies and techniques' (1994) 12(9) *Alternatives* 111 at 112–13.
84 C Moore *The mediation process: practical strategies for resolving conflict*, Jossey-Bass, San Francisco, 1996, at pp 76–7.

Dispute Resolution's Model Mediation Procedure allows a mediator to provide, in the event that no settlement is reached, a non-binding written recommendation of the terms of settlement at the request of the parties.[85] In the context of employment disputes, for example, 'dispute mediation' offered by ACAS requires the mediator to make formal non-binding recommendations, which are intended to form the basis for a settlement.

There are a number of concerns with the directive intervention approach. In the first place, mediators will be basing any proposals on a restricted view of the evidence, given the limitations of mediation in regard to both fact-finding and the disclosure of information. Second, where mediators propose settlement options it could raise natural justice concerns in respect of information disclosed in the separate meetings held with individual parties.[86] Third, the consent of the parties to an interventionist role for the mediator may well be based on a mistaken perception, developed in the separate meetings, that the mediator was sympathetic to their case. Finally, the knowledge that a mediator might eventually propose or impose a decision could affect the disclosure and candour which should characterise mediation proceedings. At the philosophical level, directive interventionism undermines two value assumptions in the mediation system.[87] High levels of intervention preclude the empowerment of the parties and their self-determination over the dispute in that instead of exercising control over their dispute they are told what to do, as in many other forms of professional practice.[88] High levels of intervention in a confidential process also carry the risk that the mediator, with relatively few forms of accountability, could abuse the situation and impose his or her own standards and predispositions on the parties. Many would argue that where mediators intervene by suggesting solutions, even if requested and consented to by all the parties, the mediators are transforming the mediation into a different kind of process.

There is little doubt, however, that in practice some mediators do intervene more actively in the dispute than the minimalist intervention approach would allow.[89]

---

85 Centre for Dispute Resolution *Model Mediation Procedure*, Clause 12.
86 On the nature and functions of separate meetings, see Chapter 4.
87 H Brown and A Marriott *ADR Principles and Practice* (2nd edn), Sweet & Maxwell, 1999, at p 139.
88 Compare the results of a survey conducted by the Singapore Mediation Centre between January 1998 and August 1999, where the conclusion was drawn that certain forms of mediator intervention in substantive issues, like assisting in the evaluation of a case and suggesting options for settlement, may not adversely affect the participants' perception of the fairness of the mediation and impartiality of the mediator. There was another possibility that could not be ruled out because the Centre did not have the benefit of studying cases where the participants did not perceive their mediation as fair or mediators as impartial; that there is no correlation between such intervention and the perception of fairness and impartiality, and that the acceptability of intervention on substantive matters depends on the way the mediators intervene, and the context of the intervention. It was noteworthy that fewer than 20% of the lawyers interviewed had experienced mediators who referred to legal authorities or standards. The full results of the survey are reported in the Singapore edition of this book: L Boulle and T Hwee Hwee *Mediation: principles, process, practice*, Butterworths, Singapore, 2000, in Chapter 11 and Annex A.
89 G Tillet *Resolving conflict—a practical approach*, Sydney University Press, Sydney, 1991, at p 12; and G Kurien 'Critique of Myths of Mediation' (1995) 6 *ADRJ* 43, at 52. In the survey by the Singapore Mediation Centre, ibid, of 186 party respondents, 78% said

Different approaches to intervention are a product of differences in mediator training (or a lack of training), differences in the professional background of mediators, personal differences in mediator style, and differences in consumer characteristics and expectations. Much also depends on the institutional setting of the mediation and the proximity of the dispute to the law. In most community mediation services, mediators are trained to be non-interventionist, in the sense of upholding the process/content distinction, of not advising the parties or recommending options, and of ensuring that outcomes are consensual. In these community settings, the users and mediators are from all walks of life and the disputes tend to have a relatively low legal content.[90]

By contrast, judges in court-based mediation systems and certain mediators who are legally qualified may adopt a more interventionist role in pointing out the respective parties' prospects of success at trial, highlighting potential difficulties if the matter were to proceed to court, and actively assisting the parties to reach a settlement. Much also depends on the type of dispute. For instance, mediators tend to be more interventionist in the case of labour mediations than in family mediations.[91] In practice the degree of mediator intervention may also vary as the mediation unfolds. Thus an initially non-interventionist approach may become more interventionist as the parties develop confidence in the mediator, and may become highly interventionist when the problem appears to be becoming intractable. The amount of intervention will also depend on many factors at play between the parties.[92] The UK experience shows that a purely facilitative approach can be perceived by parties in negative terms.[93] In some contexts, as in public sector mediations, it is recognised that the level of mediator activism should match the demands of the situation:

---

that their mediators evaluated the merits of the case, 85% had mediators who assisted them in evaluating the case, 56% had mediators who recommended a particular settlement, 89% had mediators who suggested possible options for settlement and 31% said their mediators kept silent about their views of the dispute. Of the 183 responses from lawyers, 55% said that their mediators evaluated the merits of the case, 78% said the mediators assisted in the evaluation, 47% said the mediators recommended a particular settlement, 90% said the mediators suggested possible options for settlement and 51% said the mediators kept their views of the case to themselves. The full results of this survey are reported in the Singapore edition of this book, ibid.

90   See the section on Community Mediation in Chapter 8.

91   ACAS offers conciliation, which most closely resembles the classic definition of mediation, and 'advisory mediation' which involves facilitation of joint discussions. See the section on Employment Disputes in Chapter 8 for more information. ACAS conciliators are generally regarded to be proactive, evaluating the parties' cases and helping them to reach a better understanding of the case and the options open to them: J Lewis and R Legard *ACAS Individual Conciliation: a qualitative evaluation of the service provided in industrial tribunal cases*, ACAS, 1999.

92   R Thurgood 'Mediator intervention to ensure fair and just outcomes' (1999) 10 *ADRJ* 142; L Y Lim 'An analysis of intervention techniques in mediation' (1998) 9 *ADRJ* 196.

93   The study of community mediation in Scotland by R E Mackay and A J Brown *Community Mediation in Scotland: a study of implementation*, The Scottish Office Central Research Unit, Edinburgh, 1999 provides examples of parties in community mediations who considered that more than mere listening was required in order to settle community disputes. Hazel Genn's study of the Central London County Court Mediation Pilot, (H Genn *The Central London County Court Pilot Mediation Scheme: Evaluation Report*, University College London, 1998, LCD Research Series No 5/98), also provides examples of parties in civil mediations being frustrated by mediators' refusal to intervene.

'. . . a passive style in a situation that requires a high level of activism will result in failure . . . too many mediators hold back . . . and are unwilling to propose "packages" that go beyond what the parties themselves are able to invent . . . on the other hand, an activist mediator can overwhelm . . . a group of participants . . .'[94]

It is important that a mediator explains the nature of the process and his or her role, including the degree of intervention the parties might expect, at the beginning of the process, in order to avoid any false expectations by the parties, in particular, if they believe that the mediator will solve the problem for them. Mediator codes of conduct across all disciplines urge mediators to provide this kind of explanation.[95]

Does mediation produce consensual outcomes?

Mediation is often defined in terms of the consensual nature of its outcomes. This claimed characteristic is related to that of voluntary entry into mediation, and also to the process/content distinction. Consensuality implies that mediated decisions reflect the preferences of the parties alone and not those of the mediator.[96] The mediator manages a process which assists and allows the parties jointly to come to their own decision on the merits, as they see them, without undue pressure to settle. Here consensuality is contrasted with coerciveness, in the sense of having a decision or order imposed on disputants, as occurs in the litigation system. While litigation is based on coercive adjudication by a court, so the argument goes, mediation is based on consensual decision-making by the parties.

It is again not possible to draw a clear line between consensual and imposed decisions and to restrict mediation only to the former. Many mediations do produce consensual outcomes, in particular where the mediator is relatively non-interventionist and there are few external pressures on the parties. It is also widely accepted that mediators do not have the authority to impose decisions on the parties without transforming mediation into a different process. However, the extent of consensuality in mediation outcomes is also a question of degree, as illustrated by the following situations:

(a) Mediation outcomes may not be regarded as fully consensual where sanctions can be imposed on a party who has entered mediation but has not participated 'reasonably and in good faith'. Rule 44 of the Civil Procedure Rules exposes parties to possible cost sanctions,[97] and the standard mediation agreements of some UK mediation organisations also attempt to ensure co-operation in respect of outcome by requiring the parties to participate in

---

The study of ACAS conciliation by J Lewis and R Legard *ACAS Individual Conciliation: a qualitative evaluation of the service provided in industrial tribunal cases*, ACAS, 1999, found that participants considered that a proactive approach was more effective.

94 L Susskind 'Multi-party public policy mediation: a separate breed' *Dispute Resolution Magazine*, Autumn 1997.

95 For example, ADR Group's *Professional Code of Conduct*; Commercial Mediation Centre *Mediator Code of Conduct*; UK College of Family Mediators *Code of Conduct*; Family Mediation Scotland *Code of Conduct*; and Mediation UK *Standards*.

96 J Folberg and A Taylor *Mediation: a comprehensive guide to resolving conflict without litigation*, Jossey-Bass, San Francisco, 1984, at pp 10 and 35.

97 See the sections on Civil Justice Reforms in Chapter 7, and on Cost Sanctions in Chapter 9.

mediation in good faith.[98] Examples can also be found in the Australian context where there are costs sanctions for mediation behaviour,[99] or where legal proceedings cannot be instituted before a party has acted appropriately in mediation.[100]

(b) Some writers refer to evidence that the mediation process creates its own momentum and pressures to settle.[101] The circumstances of the mediation, including the length of sessions, physical discomfort, the attitude of advisers, brinkmanship tactics, deadlines and fatigue, may produce a mediated settlement which is not consensual in the full sense of the word.

(c) Mediators use a range of techniques, including non-verbal signalling, impatience and threats of withdrawal, to induce the parties to settle where they might not otherwise have done so.[102] These pressures may be unconsciously generated by mediators' perceptions of the parties' interests, and by their own professional interests in a settlement.

(d) Some mediators might influence the terms of settlement in ways which do not reflect the parties' preferences.[103] Many procedural interventions provide mediators with subtle opportunities to influence the actual content of discussions without the parties' awareness, for example suggesting priorities in the list of issues to be negotiated, postponing discussion of particular issues, overlooking certain comments or actions by the parties, and becoming involved in the parties' dialogue in the many conventional ways adopted by mediators.[104] Because of their status and authority, the suggestions of mediators may perform a quasi-adjudicative function.[105]

(e) Some writers, although they are in a minority, define the role of the mediator as being to press all the parties towards agreement 'persistently and relentlessly'.[106] Despite having no authority to impose a decision, the mediator is trained to assist in the settlement of cases, and this tension tends to blur the line between consensual and coercive outcomes.[107]

---

98 The Commercial Mediation Centre *Mediation Rules and Procedures* take the matter one step further, by providing that if a mediation is conducted frivolously or vexatiously, the mediator can order the party who did so to pay the fee of the mediation and to reimburse the other party for reasonable costs of preparation and attendance.

99 In *Capolingua v Phylum Pty Ltd (as Trustee for the Gennoe Family Trust)* (1991) 5 WAR 137 the court declined to grant a successful defendant legal costs because of inappropriate behaviour in mediation. The imposition of costs sanctions is arguably different from withholding incentives.

100 For example, Australian Farm Debt Mediation Act 1994 (NSW).

101 S Goldberg et al (eds) *Dispute Resolution: Negotiation, Mediation and Other Processes* (2nd edn) 1992, at p 156.

102 C Moore *The mediation process: practical strategies for resolving conflict*, Jossey-Bass, San Francisco, 1996, at p 333.

103 B Wolski 'Voluntariness, consensuality and coercion: in defence of mandatory mediation' unpublished LLM paper, Bond University, 1994, at p 4.

104 See Chapter 6.

105 R Ingleby 'Court sponsored mediation: the case against mandatory participation' (1993) 56 *Modern Law Review* 441 at 445.

106 J B Stulberg *Taking charge/managing conflict*, Lexington Books, Lexington, Massachusetts, 1987, at p 105; and G Kurien 'Critique of Myths of Mediation' (1995) 6 *ADRJ* 43 at 47.

107 S Silbey and S Merry 'Mediator settlement strategies' (1986) 8 *Law and Policy* 7 at 12.

Although many mediations cannot be said to be consensual in the sense of lacking pressure to settle or being based only on the parties' mutual consent, it is possible to assert that they are consensual in a narrower sense. This relates to the parties' ability to accept or reject particular outcomes and to refuse to settle, where they are prepared to live with the consequences.[108] This is in line with the distinction drawn by some writers between 'coercion into' mediation and 'coercion in' mediation – even if the parties' participation was not voluntary, they cannot be coerced to enter a specific agreement.[109] It is only in this narrow sense that the consensuality of outcomes is a defining characteristic of mediation.

Four Models of Mediation

Because of the problems of definition and because of the diversity in mediation practice, it is useful to distinguish between four models of mediation, the *settlement*, *facilitative*, *therapeutic* and *evaluative*.[110] These are paradigm models which are not distinct alternatives to one another and which do not conform exactly to types of mediation practice. Mediations in practice might display features of two or more models. Thus a mediation may commence in the *facilitative* mode but later transform into the *evaluative* model. The notion that there are different models of mediation, and not a single analytical model, assists in dealing with some of the definitional problems in this field. Much writing on and discussion about mediation has the *facilitative* model in mind and it is sometimes referred to as 'pure mediation' or the 'classic mediation process'. In practice, however, the other three models influence and compete with *facilitative mediation*.

The characteristics of the four paradigm models are shown in the following table. They provide a frame of reference in the remainder of this work.

108　B Wolski 'Voluntariness, consensuality and coercion: in defence of mandatory mediation' unpublished LLM paper, Bond University, 1994, at p 16.

109　J Murray et al *Process of dispute resolution: the role of lawyers*, Foundation Press, New York, 1989, at p 281; and S Goldberg et al (eds) *Dispute Resolution: Negotiation, Mediation and other Processes* (3rd edn) 1999, at p 388.

110　H Brown and A Marriott *ADR Principles and Practice* (2nd edn), Sweet & Maxwell, 1999, at p 137 refer to facilitative and evaluative models; and S Roberts 'Three models of family mediation' in R Dingwall and J Eekelaar (eds) *Divorce Mediation and the legal process*, 1988, at p 144 refers to minimal intervention, directive intervention and therapeutic intervention models of family mediation.

Models of Mediation

	Settlement Mediation	Facilitative Mediation	Therapeutic Mediation	Evaluative Mediation
Also known as	Compromise mediation	Interest-based, problem solving mediation	Reconciliation, transformative mediation	Advisory, managerial mediation
Main Objective	To encourage incremental bargaining towards compromise, at a 'central' point between the parties' positional demands	To avoid positions and negotiate in terms of parties' underlying needs and interests instead of their strict legal entitlements	To deal with underlying causes of the parties' problem, with a view to improving their relationship as a basis for resolution of the dispute	To reach a settlement according to the legal rights and entitlements of the parties and within the anticipated range of court outcomes
Definition of Dispute	In terms of positions, based on parties' self-definition of the problem	In terms of parties' underlying interests—substantive, procedural and psychological	In terms of behavioural, emotional and relationship factors	In terms of legal rights and duties, industry standards or community norms
Types of Mediators	High status (lawyer, manager): no necessary expertise in the process, skills and techniques of mediation	Expertise in mediation process and techniques; no necessary knowledge of the subject matter of dispute	Expertise in counselling or social work, with understanding of psychological causes of conflict	Expertise in substantive areas of the dispute, no necessary qualifications in mediation techniques

Mediator's Main Role	Determine parties' 'bottom lines' and through relatively persuasive interventions move them in stages off their positions to a point of compromise	Conduct the process, maintain a constructive dialogue between the parties and enhance negotiation process	Use professional therapeutic techniques, before or during mediation, to diagnose and treat relationship problems	Provide additional information, advise and persuade the parties, bring professional expertise to bear on content of negotiations
Other Characteristics	Limited procedural interventions by mediator, positional bargaining by parties	Low intervention role for mediator, parties encouraged to fashion creative outcomes around mutual interests	Decision-making postponed until relationship issues have been dealt with	High intervention by mediator, less party control over outcome
Strengths	Understood by parties, culturally accepted, not difficult to do, little preparation needed	Can make most efficient use of negotiation opportunities, controlled by parties	Can lead to 'resolution' rather than just 'settlement' of dispute	Mediator's substantive expertise used, outcome within range of likely court verdicts
Shortcomings	Overlooks parties' needs and interests, can be manipulated through initial exaggerated claims, difficult to cross last gap	May not reach an outcome, can be lengthy, requires skills from parties	Could be prolonged and terminated without any agreement, confuses counselling/mediation roles	Blurs mediation/ arbitration distinction, does not teach parties skills for the future, additional responsibilities for mediator
Areas of Application	Commercial, personal injury, industrial disputes	Community, family, environmental, partnership disputes	Matrimonial, parent/adolescent, family networks, continuing relationship disputes	Commercial, personal injury, trade practices, anti-discrimination, matrimonial property disputes

2

Principles and Policies of Mediation

Mediation and the Law

Mediation as an alternative to the law

'Mediation' has been used as a form of dispute resolution for many centuries.[1] In modern western societies it is usually depicted as an 'alternative' form of dispute resolution and mediation is a prominent feature of the alternative dispute resolution ('ADR') movement. This raises the question of what it is an alternative to. Where the question is asked in the legal context, it is answered by reference to litigation. Here 'alternative' denotes qualitative differences to litigation, a set of principles and standards which can be contrasted with those under which the courts operate. In this context 'alternative' also implies a choice, in the sense of parties deliberately choosing to go into mediation because of its perceived advantages over litigation.

It can, however, be misleading to portray mediation as an alternative to litigation, which is itself such a rare method of managing disputes. Most disputes in modern society are dealt with by the parties themselves, through discussion, struggle, or avoidance. Of the relatively few disputes which are brought to lawyers, only a small proportion result in legal proceedings being instituted, and even less often does the dispute reach a court hearing. Of those cases which reach lawyers and are not resolved through litigation, some are simply not pursued any further, and others are resolved by the lawyers and parties through negotiation, compromise or agreement. Thus in terms of predominant modes of dispute settlement in modern societies, litigation is itself an 'alternative' system, in the sense that it is so rarely used. If mediation is to be depicted as an alternative at all, it should be seen as an alternative to the most frequently used methods of dealing with disputes, namely discussion, struggle and avoidance. As the majority of disputes are settled informally outside the court system, the claims of mediation should be measured against the other alternatives to litigation, including settlement on the steps of the court.[2]

---

1   J Wall and A Lynn 'Mediation: a current review' (1993) 37 *Journal of Conflict Resolution* 160 at 169 .
2   M Dewdney and R Charlton 'Editorial' (1992) 3 *ADRJ* 211. Some writers argue that 'ADR' should stand for 'appropriate dispute resolution' and that mediation should be considered a form of appropriate dispute resolution: see, for example, J Lee 'The ADR movement in Singapore' in K Tan (ed) *The Singapore Legal System* (2nd edn) Singapore University Press, Singapore, 1999, at pp 415–6.

However, although litigation is statistically insignificant as a dispute resolution method, the 'umpire' model on which it is based has deep roots in western societies.[3] Where conflict arises between two or more people, and it cannot be resolved by ignoring it, talking about it or threatening each other, there is an expectation that it should be referred to an umpire for an authoritative decision. The umpire could be a parent, manager, arbitrator or judge. As with their sports counterparts, these umpires take into account what has happened between the parties, and where this cannot be clearly established, their decision may well be wrong. Each kind of umpire has its own procedures for getting to understand the problem and its own principles and standards on which to base decisions. What they have in common is that they do not invite the disputants to play an active role in coming up with their own solution to the dispute. Mediation does provide an alternative to this whole tradition of dispute resolution, and litigation is an obvious point of reference in evaluating its underlying principles.[4]

Mediation is not regarded as an 'alternative' in many traditional societies where the absence of a state system and formal legal institutions require communally-based systems of managing conflict. In a wide range of traditional societies in Africa and Asia, 'mediation' has often been the preferred method of dealing with disputes.[5] The tribal nature of traditional societies, the kinship system, strong communal norms, religion and philosophy, and mutual dependence, encouraged systems in which third parties with high status assisted disputants to deal with their conflicts. These processes not only resolved disputes but also reinforced societal cohesion. With modernisation and the development of more formal institutions of government, these processes have been adapted and modified.

It has been suggested that mediation in modern western societies represents 'a symbolic harking back to a lost age when caring for others within a communal

---

3   On the 'umpiring' notion, see S Roberts 'Mediation in family disputes' (1983) 46 *Modern Law Review* 537 at 546.
4   Gonfors argues that mediation is only a 'true alternative' if it is provided by community-based voluntary organisations, the dispute is not referred on to a government agency if there is no settlement, and those providing the service do so with a clear ideological basis in terms of which mediation provides a well-reasoned alternative basis for thinking and acting: see M Gonfors 'Mediation – a romantic ideal or a workable alternative' in H Messmer and H U Ottoc *Restorative justice on trial – pitfalls and potentials of victim-offender mediation: international research perspectives*, Kluwer Academic Publishers, Boston, 1992, at p 421. See also W Twining 'Alternative to what? Theories of litigation, procedure and dispute settlement in Anglo-American jurisprudence' (1993) 56 *Modern Law Review* 380.
5   J Folberg and A Taylor *Mediation – a comprehensive guide to resolving conflicts without litigation*, Jossey-Bass, San Francisco, 1988, at pp 1–7; C Moore *The Mediation Process: practical strategies for resolving conflict* (2nd edn), Jossey-Bass, San Francisco, 1996, at pp 20–2; S Merry 'Mediation in non-industrial societies' in K Kressel et al (eds) *Mediation Research: the process and effectiveness of third party intervention*, Jossey-Bass, San Francisco, 1989, at p 68. For surveys of dispute resolution methods in various societies, see J Auerbach *Justice without law*, Oxford University Press, New York, 1983; S Roberts *Order and dispute: an introduction to legal anthropology*, Penguin Books, Sydney, 1979; and P Stein *Legal institutions – the development of dispute settlement*, Butterworths, London, 1984; and M Pryles (ed) *Dispute Resolution in Asia*, Kluwer Law International, The Hague, 1997. See also P Corne 'Judicial conciliation in Japan' (1993) 4 *ADRJ* 139. See further Chapter 7.

setting was of pre-eminent importance; it constitutes a reaction against the alienating and competitive style of dispute resolution fostered by an adversarial system'.[6] There is little doubt that this 'innocence regained' ideal of mediation is prevalent and has inspired and motivated many teachers, trainers and practitioners of mediation. But it is by no means universally accepted or understood in the modern mediation movement, where mediation is often promoted and developed for crass economic or political objectives. Nor is the understanding and depiction of mediation in traditional societies altogether without its myths and fictions.[7] In societies with strong community norms and cultural imperatives, mediators were usually persons of influence and prestige. In the light of the societal need to limit the disruption caused by conflict, mediation could involve high degrees of coercion, or moral persuasion, and serve to reproduce all that system's hierarchies, inequalities and power imbalances. The mediators were often regarded as 'representatives' of the community, they performed a didactic role, and they had various forms of sanction, including ridicule, ostracism, violence and supernatural intervention, which could be invoked against one or more parties. Although some contemporary mediators have claimed to be the 'spiritual descendants' of mediators in traditional societies,[8] modern mediation lays claims to values such as voluntariness and consensuality which are not all evident in communally-based systems of managing conflict.[9]

Mediation and the shadow of the law

Although mediation is presented as an 'alternative' to law and litigation, it also operates within 'the shadow of the law'.[10] This expression signifies that parties in mediation operate with a perception of how the legal system would resolve the matter, and with a sense of the time, costs and implications of a litigated outcome. It also entails that the enforceability of mediated agreements ultimately depends on judicial approval and that the bounds of confidentiality, mediator liability and mediators' ethical standards will be determined in part by legislatures and judges. In all these ways mediation is said to operate in the shadow of the law.

The extent of the law's shadow, however, varies considerably. Where a dispute has been packaged and labelled as a legal one, where lawyers have taken an active role, where each side has counsel's opinion and where the mediation is connected to the

---

6   M Thornton 'Mediation policy and the State' (1993) 4 *ADRJ* 230 at 235.

7   R Abel (ed) *The politics of informal justice*, vol 1, Academic Press, New York, 1982; P Adler et al 'The ideologies of mediation' (1988) 10 *Law and Policy* 335.

8   S Merry 'Mediation in non-industrial societies' in K Kressel et al (eds) *Mediation Research: the process and effectiveness of third party intervention*, Jossey-Bass, San Francisco, 1989, at p 68; and P Condliffe *Conflict Management – a practical guide*, TAFE Publications, Abbotsford, Victoria, 1991, at p 114.

9   As P Corne 'Judicial conciliation in Japan' (1993) 4 *ADRJ* 139 observes, in western mediation theory concession is regarded as less desirable than a creative solution, whereas in Japanese conciliation, concession is regarded as important.

10   The phrase comes from R Mnookin and L Kornhauser 'Bargaining in the shadow of the law' (1979) 88 *Yale Law Journal* 950. See also C Menkel-Meadow 'Towards another view of legal negotiations: the structure of problem-solving' (1993–4) *University of California Law Review* 754; M Eisenberg 'Private ordering through negotiation: dispute settlement and rulemaking' (1976) 89 *Harvard Law Review* 637; and H Astor and C Chinkin *Dispute Resolution in Australia*, Butterworths, Sydney, 1992, at pp 49, 69–71 and 270–1.

court system or takes place within a statutory framework, the shadow will be a strong one; the parties in mediation will be more directly influenced by the likely outcome of the dispute were it to be litigated. Where, however, it is a neighbourhood dispute with little legal content which is being mediated through a community service, the shadow will be much weaker. In a recent study of family mediators, the law was used as a benchmark for financial issues, whereas in child issues, non-lawyer mediators focused on the child's interests by adopting a counselling role. This differed from lawyer mediators, whose use of law was integral to the process.[11]

Although mediation takes place within the shadow of the law, it is also a challenge to the legal system. The contribution of the helping professions to mediation has caused lawyers who have come into contact with it to become more self-reflective, more diagnostic and less legalistic. There is evidence that the language of mediation has changed legal discourse, for example away from 'custody' and 'access' in matrimonial disputes towards 'parenting arrangements'. There is even evidence that substantive law has changed in some jurisdictions under the influence of mediation practice, for example towards an acceptance of shared 'custody' arrangements which had previously been avoided. Thus the influence between law and mediation operates in both directions.

The Value Claims of Mediation

Contrasting principles

The table on page **34** sets out some of the contrasting principles on which litigation and mediation are based. The value claims of litigation are presented in a somewhat traditional form. Modern litigation itself is changing and adapting to social and economic pressures – it is not only a matter of confrontation, treachery and bloody victory, as depicted in some stereotypes. Likewise, the value claims of mediation are presented in a somewhat idealised form. Some of the claims contained in the table are analysed here. This evaluation relates mainly to the *facilitative* model of mediation, with litigation as the point of comparison.

Procedural flexibility

Mediation is a highly flexible dispute resolution process. It can be conducted in a variety of physical settings, the procedure can be negotiated and adapted, additional participants can be involved for part of the mediation, and additional mediators can even be added if required. While mediators contribute structure to the negotiation process, it is unlikely that they would, for example, bind the parties to an agenda where they mutually wished to depart from it. Flexibility has the advantage of allowing the parties some say over what processes will suit them, of allowing for adaptability where the nature of the dispute and disputants require it, and of avoiding the possibility that technical procedural requirements will predominate. Litigation, by contrast, has a more rigid structure and there are established rules and procedures, some highly technical, which parties must comply with, both before and during the trial process.

---

11 F Myers and F Wasoff *A meeting in the middle—a study of solicitors' and mediators' divorce practice*, Scottish Executive, 2000, Chapter 4.

Contrasting Principles	
Litigation	Mediation
Rights enforcement	Interests accommodation
Value claiming	Value creating
Coercive and binding	Voluntary and consensual
Due process of law	Procedural flexibility
Privity of involvement	Widely participatory
Formality	Informality
Norm imposing	Norm creating
Consistency and precedential	Situational and individualised
Act-centred	Person-centred
Fact-oriented	Relationship-oriented
Past focus	Future focus
Professionalised	Peer-based
Public and accountable	Private and confidential
Adversarial	Collaborative

An important difference between mediation and litigation relates to what information and evidence can be used and how it can be presented and tested. In litigation this is regulated by evidential and procedural rules on relevance and reliability. In mediation there are no rules of evidence and there is no scope for cross-examination and procedural point-taking. There are only loose protocols for speaking and interacting. The disputing parties are allowed to tell their stories as they see fit and emotions can be vented without being dismissed as irrelevant.

There are inevitable limits to the flexibility potential of mediation. Thus, while it is not a rigid process, there is a surprising consistency in the different stages through which mediators guide the parties, particularly in *facilitative mediation*.[12] Some training programmes attempt to impose relatively strict protocols on prospective mediators, who are advised to move systematically through defined stages of mediation in their particular sequence.[13] This is to give effect to the process strengths

---

12 On the mediation process, see Chapter 4.
13 Fledgling mediators are exhorted to 'use the process', in recognition of its internal logic and utility.

of mediation, each stage of the process having its own rationale and justification. Therefore, despite its flexibility, mediation has more structure than unassisted negotiations: one of the contributions a mediator can make is to impose order on unstructured and confused deliberations. However, the flexibility potential, with all its benefits, remains an important feature of mediation.

Informality

The informality of mediation is closely linked to its flexibility. Here informality refers to the setting, style and tone of the mediation and the interpersonal behaviour and conduct of the participants.[14] It is informal, or potentially informal, in terms of dress and address, venue, seating, use of language and hours of attendance. Mediation lacks the ritual and mystique of the court process, which tends to enforce formality and hierarchy. There is usually little sense of hierarchy in the mediation room. Thus it is not unusual for all parties to be seated around a table or in easy chairs, for first names to be used, for the disputants to leave and re-enter the room, for refreshments to be served, and for the participants to banter and joke with one another. There is no equivalent of the contempt of court principle to bolster the 'dignity' of the mediation process.

The value of informality is that it can make the mediation process more user-friendly and less anxiety-ridden than the court process. It can be a physically and emotionally comfortable experience. Of particular significance is the use of everyday language and plain English, as opposed to the stylised forms of communication used in court. Some high status mediators impose a more formal tone on the proceedings, and some parties and their advisers stand on ceremony in terms of titles and forms of address. However, unlike the court system, the degree of formality can itself be negotiated to suit the culture of the dispute and disputants. Behaviour standards can also alter as a protracted mediation unfolds, lapsing from stiffly formal into alarmingly convivial.[15]

Party participation

The informality and flexibility of mediation allows for extensive and direct participation in the process, to the extent that mediation is sometimes referred to as a purely 'consumer-oriented' dispute settlement process.[16] Mediation is a highly

---

14 The opportunities provided by mediation to address non-legal concerns, like emotional and commercial issues, can also create informality to move the focus away from purely technical, or legal, arguments. In turn, this leads to a greater measure of control over costs: a view expressed by a number interviewees as part of Hazel Genn's study of the Central London County Court Mediation Pilot: H Genn *Central London County Court Mediation Pilot: Evaluation Report*, LCD Research Series, No 5/98.

15 See the amusing account of the mediation involving Spedley Securities Ltd in which the dress code, including that of the mediator, became progressively more casual and how beer appeared on the negotiating table late at night: M J Slattery 'The Spedley mediation from the inside' (1993) *Bar News* 23.

16 For example, M Robertson 'Is ADR part of a movement towards consumer-orientated legal services?' *ADR Bulletin*, vol 1, no 1, May 1998, at p 1.

accessible system of dispute resolution. This access and participation is available firstly to the disputants who, subject to elementary rules of decorum, can talk, negotiate and discuss options throughout the process. Mediation provides a pseudo 'day in court', an opportunity for each party to express their views about the dispute, a necessary step in resolving disputes in mediation.[17] In this way, mediation offers a unique opportunity for the parties to provide explanations and to proffer apologies.[18] Direct party participation in mediation is justified in terms of the promotion of responsibility for choices and the dignity of individuals. In family mediation, for example, parents retain control of their disagreements by being encouraged to take responsibility for decisions concerning their children. Mediation assumes that the parties themselves can make better decisions about their interests than outsiders, such as judges or arbitrators.[19] In this way, participation can eliminate a feeling by the parties that pressure was brought to bear on them to make certain decisions.[20] If parties perceive that they 'own' the process, they are likely to be more supportive of the outcome.[21] No other contemporary method of dispute resolution accommodates as much direct participation by the parties as does mediation and this 'self-determination' aspect of the process has been highly valued by parties, even where no settlement has been reached. The participation potential extends beyond the disputants as there are no technical rules of standing to deny the involvement of others. Thus by arrangement spouses, advisers, supporters, witnesses, and friends can all be present in the process and have some involvement in it.[22] It is also claimed that mediation can be used by repeat players, like the insurance industry, to achieve a structure to the dispute resolution process, which acts to their advantage, thereby extending their control not only to the outcome, but also to the nature and style of the process.[23]

The traditional model of litigation, by contrast, allows for only limited and structured participation by those parties with a legal interest in the outcome. It encourages passivity, dependence and an absence of responsibility for choices.[24]

---

17 F E A Sander and S B Goldberg 'Fitting the forum to the Fuss: A user friendly guide to selecting an ADR procedure' (1994) *Negotiation Journal* 55. Compare with the increasing tendency in the US and Australia, particularly in commercial mediations, to start the mediation with the separate sessions, missing out the initial joint session.

18 L Mulcahy et al *Mediating medical negligence claims: an option for the future?* NHS Executive, 2000, at p xvii. Compare the results of a study in family mediation (of the Hull and Humberside Family Conciliation Service) by Johnson in 1986, summarised in University of Newcastle upon Tyne Conciliation Project Unit, *Report to the Lord Chancellor's Department on the cost and effectiveness of conciliation in England and Wales*, March 1989, at p 31.

19 P Wahrhaftig 'Nonprofessional Conflict Resolution' in J Palenski and H Launer (eds) *Mediation Conflicts and Challenges*, Charles C Thomas, 1986.

20 M Rogers and C McEwan *Mediation: Law Policy & Practice*, Lawyers Co-operative, Rochester New York, 1989, at pp 234–5.

21 A Taylor 'Toward a comprehensive theory of mediation' (1981) 19 *Conciliation Courts Review* 1 at 4.

22 On the functions of the parties, see Chapter 5.

23 J Resnik 'From "cases" to "litigation"' (1991) 54(3) *University of Chicago Law Review* 5. In the case of repeat players, Robert Axelrod also discovered peculiar negotiation behaviour in the form of 'tit for tat': the opponent mimics the actions of the other unless and until the other does something unexpected. If co-operation is established between the parties, it is permanent: R Axelrod *The evolution of co-operation*, Basic books, New York, 1984.

24 G Bellow and B Moulton *The lawyering process: negotiation*, Foundation Press, Mineola, New York, 1981, at p 131.

This is also a characteristic of many professionals, who tend to translate a client's problem into the mystical jargon of the profession and remove them from its treatment and resolution.[25] Lawyers, it is argued, exaggerate the level of difficulty or effort needed to achieve a settlement.[26] Lawyers narrow or rephrase a problem to satisfy the language requirements of the law, rules of pleading and procedural rules, which makes it difficult for a client to exert any control in litigation.[27] Where there is less direct reliance on professionals, there are additional long-term benefits for clients. Mediation fosters confidence and a sense of personal competence by providing the parties with an opportunity to air their grievances.[28] The following explanation by a participant in a family mediation makes the point clearly:

'I felt for the first time that my ex-husband who had bullied me for years and who had sought to reduce me to "nothing" finally saw that I had equal rights, was given dignity via the mediation and confidence to speak out'.[29]

The process also becomes educative for the participants in that they are involved in and learn a problem-solving process which can be applied in other contexts.[30]

While all mediation allows for the direct and flexible involvement of the parties, the actual extent of their participation will depend on the variable factors. These include the approach and style of the mediator and the confidence and abilities of the parties. External factors could reduce the amount of participation, for example budgetary or time limitations might cause the mediator to deny extensive discussion and involvement where they become 'inefficient'. Another significant factor is the attitude of professional advisers. Where they act defensively in the mediation, out of ignorance or strategy, they are liable to dominate the proceedings and allow very little participation by the parties. There is extensive anecdotal evidence on the need for lawyers to allow their clients sufficient air space in the mediation process to exploit its participatory potential. Some lawyers express concerns that their clients' participation will damage their own case, but this can be avoided by extensive education about and preparation for the mediation meeting.

Person-centred

Much dispute resolution tends to be act-centred. Thus litigation attempts to ascertain what occurred historically through a range of techniques involving investigation, disclosure, testing and confrontation. The adjudicator develops a version of the

---

25 For example, J Rubin and F Sander 'When should we use agents? Direct versus representative negotiation' (1988) 4 *Negotiation Journal* 395 at 401.
26 L Lerman 'Lying to Clients' (1990) *University of Pennsylvania Law Review* 659.
27 C Menkel-Meadow 'The Transformation of Disputes by Lawyers: what the dispute paradigm does and does not tell us' (1985) *Journal of Dispute Resolution* 31 at 32; and H Genn *Central London County Court Mediation Pilot: Evaluation Report*, LCD Research Series, No 5/98, where a business person, interviewed after a mediation, complained about a solicitor's handling of litigation: 'I have prepared it all and all they do is to put it into legal jargon'.
28 R Abel 'The Contradictions of Informal Justice' in R Abel (ed) *The Politics of Informal Justice, vol 1*, Academic Press, New York 1982, at p 283.
29 L Moloney et al *Managing differences: federally-funded family mediation in Sydney – outcomes, costs and client satisfaction*, Attorney-General's Department, 1996 at p 105.
30 M Power 'Educating mediators metacognitively' (1992) 3 *ADRJ* 214 at 214–15.

historical facts, and on the basis of these findings attributes blame or culpability. While in litigation the personal circumstances of the parties might affect some aspects of the outcome, it is the impersonal attribution of blame or culpability which is the most important factor in this kind of dispute resolution.

Mediation is not well-equipped for resolving disputes of fact or arriving at a version of historic reality, unless the parties collaborate to provide it jointly. Mediators do not invite the parties to convince or persuade them as to the correct facts, and they lack mechanisms for investigating or testing the truth. Nor are the parties able to challenge or test the statements or assertions of each other in the same ways, such as disclosure or cross-examination, which are provided by the court system. In mediation there is a focus on people rather than on facts. This entails looking at the current needs and interests of the parties. 'Instead of problems being treated as abstract and decontextualised, the focus is on the particular and the relational.'[31] Mediation allows for individualised settlements based on the parties' subjective preferences. Thus in personal injury cases, damages can be agreed upon without any definite finding on the issues of liability, where this accords with the parties' needs and priorities. New forms of personal awareness have provided impetus in the development of ADR[32] and processes such as mediation have in turn contributed to them.

Relational

Besides being person-centred, mediation also has a relational focus. This signifies that its methods and philosophy are concerned with the human side of dispute settlement, including opportunity for the venting of emotions, acknowledgment of strongly-held feelings and attention to future relations between the parties. Mediation can preserve or improve relationships[33] by taking into account the real interests of the parties, by providing an accessible and participatory procedure, by modelling constructive negotiation and problem-solving techniques and by humanising the management of conflict.[34] This constitutes the 'gentler art' of reconciliation,

---

31 M Thornton 'Mediation policy and the State' (1993) 4 *ADRJ* 230.
32 Family Law Council *Discussion Paper on Family Mediation*, Canberra, 1991, at pp 2–3.
33 In a study by the Singapore Mediation Centre between January 1998 and August 1999, about 68% of the parties and 78% of the lawyers surveyed reported improvement in the relationship between the parties. 81% of the lawyers also found that their own relationship with opposing counsel improved after mediation. This finding is significant in view of the fact that the mediations conducted at the Centre are usually concluded in one day. Full survey results are reported in the Singapore edition of this book: L Boulle and T Hwee Hwee *Mediation: principles, process, practice*, Butterworths, Singapore, 2000, in Chapter 11 and Annex A.
34 Solicitors participating in the Bristol Law Society Mediation Scheme agreed to mediation in the hope that a relationship between the parties could be salvaged. This reason for take-up was also cited by a number of solicitors who had participated in the Central London County Court Mediation Pilot. See M Davies et al *Promoting Mediation*, Research and Policy Planning Unit, Report of our Study of the Bristol Law Society's mediation scheme in its preliminary phase, Research Study No 21, The Law Society, 1996, at p 26 in the case of the Bristol Scheme; and to H Genn *Central London County Court Mediation Pilot: Evaluation Report*, LCD Research Series, No 5/98 at pp vi, 107 and 139 in the case of the Central London County Court Pilot. For further information on both schemes, see Chapter 7.

rather than the confrontationist science of court battle.[35] Although litigation will ultimately settle a dispute through an adjudication, it may result in irreparable damage to relationships, as litigation carries overtures of bad faith.[36] Even arbitration is frequently incompatible with the maintenance of continuing relations.[37]

Mediation's relational features have been associated with a feminist approach to dispute resolution,[38] though the matter is not uncontroversial. Some writers argue that the values underlying mediation and other forms of ADR are more closely aligned to the 'moral voice' of women[39] and their approach to resolving conflict than are those values underlying litigation. This is based on a belief in women's focus on relationships, caring and consequences in dispute resolution, as opposed to the male emphasis on rights, rationality and abstract logic, which are considered pervasive features of the traditional legal system. Other writers[40] argue that the values associated with mediation are not a particularly female way of resolving disputes, nor are they especially responsive to female needs. This view is based partly on the power disadvantages affecting women, which, it is argued, are not redressed by the mediation process.[41] There is also a concern that the relational focus of mediation may cause women in matrimonial disputes to forego basic rights and entitlements in their attention to preserving relationships.

In relation to family mediation also, UK studies have shown that the existence of new relationships is positively associated with settlement reached in mediation.[42] 34% of respondents to the Lord Chancellor's ADR Discussion Paper cited preservation of relationships between disputants as the main benefit of mediation.[43] A CEDR/Pinsent Curtis survey of businesses in March 2000 indicated that 28% of respondents considered that mediation preserves relationships.[44]

---

35 D Bok 'A flawed system' (1983) *New York State Bar Journal* 8. For Australian survey evidence that mediation can be a factor in the improvement of relationships between the parties, see A Prior 'What do the parties think?' (1993) 4 *ADRJ* 99. For Singapore survey evidence, see fn 33 above.

36 S Macaulay 'Non-Contractual Relations in Business: a Preliminary Study' (1963) 28(1) *American Sociological Review* 55 at 64.

37 A study in the United States found that out of 78 arbitration cases in the textiles industry, in only 14 did relations resume: M Galanter 'Reading the Landscape of Disputes: What we know and don't know (and think we know) about our allegedly contentious and litigious society' 31 *UCLA Law Review* 4 at 25.

38 J Rifkin 'Mediation from a feminist perspective: promise and problems' (1994) 2 *Law and Inequality* 21; H Astor and C Chinkin *Dispute Resolution in Australia*, Butterworths, Sydney, 1992, at pp 92–5 and references cited there.

39 The phrase comes from C Gilligan's famous work *In a different voice: psychology theory and women's development*, 1982. For further references, see H Astor and C Chinkin, ibid, at pp 22–4.

40 For example, H Astor and C Chinkin, ibid, at p 95; and see Chapter 4.

41 On the issue of power, see the section on Power, at pages **70–72**.

42 For example, the study of the South East London Family Conciliation Bureau by Davis and Roberts in 1988, summarised in University of Newcastle upon Tyne Conciliation Project Unit, *Report to the Lord Chancellor's Department on the cost and effectiveness of conciliation in England and Wales*, March 1989, at p 30.

43 Lord Chancellor's Department, *ADR Discussion Paper: Summary of Responses*, August 2000, at para 8.

44 CEDR/Pinsent Curtis *Dispute Resolution Survey: initial analysis paper*, CEDR, London, March 2000.

Norm creating

All disputes are resolved in terms of norms and standards. In making their decisions, courts and arbitrators rely on legal norms, that is, the rules and principles provided by statutes and case law precedents. Administrative bodies and tribunals use legal norms, and in addition refer to policy and the public interest in making decisions. In these situations the norms are expressly articulated. In mediation the parties may not articulate the norms which have guided their outcome, but they are nevertheless present and can be inferred from the settlement.

In mediation the parties are free to depart from the rules, principles and policies which are binding on courts, arbitrators and administrative bodies.[45] The agreement can be reached in terms of their own mutual interests as these intersect at a particular moment in time. The parties may take a wider view of their interests than would an umpire or an administrator. Thus an informed plaintiff seeking damages for personal injuries suffered in a motor vehicle accident may forego some heads of damages in exchange for an early settlement, certainty, and avoiding the anxiety of cross-examination. Likewise business entities might come to a rough and ready commercial decision on past disputes, which does not reflect legal rights and obligations, so that they can include future business dealings in the settlement agreement. In developing their own norms for settling a dispute the parties can determine their own multiple interests, establish their own priorities, and trade off and package a deal in terms of their own business or social judgments and agendas. This is another manifestation of the self-determination principle, or of subjective rather than objective decision-making. Another aspect of the norm-creating nature of mediation is the flexibility of outcomes.[46] Parties may agree on outcomes which could never be available as a court remedy. Thus they may agree on one party performing a personal service for another, on a dismissed employee being re-employed in another branch of the firm, or on one party giving the other an employment reference.

There are some constraints on the ability of parties to base their mediated decisions on self-selected norms. First, an agreement cannot be illegal or against public policy, as provided for in statute and common law. Such an outcome will not be enforceable if it is ignored by a party to the agreement, or if an affected outsider challenges it through the legal process. Second, as mediation takes place 'in the shadow of the law',[47] the range of likely legal outcomes to a dispute will affect the parties' bargaining power and ultimately the settlement itself. Finally, where a third party intervenes in a dispute, whether as umpire or mediator, he or she will inevitably cause it to incline more towards the application of objective norms.[48] This is because a third party cannot fully understand or appreciate the subjective interests and concerns of the parties, and relies instead on more general and abstract standards. This also implies that the third party, whether umpire or mediator, is likely to be at least partly evaluative in dealing with the dispute.

---

45 On the other hand, while mediation is not precedent-based, it could create informal precedents for those attempting mediation in certain kinds of disputes, for example, insurance disputes or conflicts between large organisations.

46 Access to Justice Committee *Access to Justice – an action plan* (The Sackville Report), 1994, at p 278.

47 See section above, 'Mediation and the shadow of the law' at pages **32–33**.

48 V Aubert 'Competition and dissensus: two types of conflict resolution' (1963) 7 *Journal of Conflict Resolution* 26.

Future focus

While mediation focuses predominantly on the present interests of the parties, and not on past facts, it can also take account of future needs. There is no limitation on the future matters which the parties can refer to and agree on. Thus, where there has been an alleged breach of contract, mediation allows the parties to re-negotiate the whole agreement, irrespective of how the dispute over the breach is resolved, or even of whether it is resolved. Arbitration and litigation, by contrast, are retrospective exercises and cannot prescribe and enforce future cooperative action between the parties. Another way in which mediation can exploit the time dimension is by allowing provisional agreements to be 'test-driven'. Parties may commit to settlement terms for the short term which they would not agree to for the long term. During the interim period, the parties can test the feasibility and fairness of the plan, and thereafter abandon, modify or confirm it.[49] The time dimension is always a potential source of value and creativity in mediated decision-making.

Privacy and confidentiality

Mediation is often promoted in terms of the privacy of the mediation sessions and the confidentiality of what transpires there. Steps taken to ensure privacy include:

- the mediation meeting is conducted behind closed doors;
- outsiders can only observe proceedings with the parties' consent;
- no recording and transcript is normally kept;
- there is no external publicity on what transpired at the mediation; and
- any disclosure of the terms of settlement is a matter which can be negotiated.

Mediation proceedings are also conducted on a 'without prejudice' basis, which precludes the parties at a subsequent court hearing from leading evidence on what was said, and the mediator is usually bound by a confidentiality requirement.[50] These features are regarded as being conducive to frank and open negotiations, and as being beneficial to a party or parties wishing to avoid their affairs being publicised among business competitors, acquaintances or friends. So where a defendant has admitted liability and paid damages, there is no public precedent which might open the floodgates for other persons in the same situation as the plaintiff. They also contribute to finality in the dispute, as there is little evidence on which to seek a review or otherwise impeach an outcome. The parties can, of course, agree to suspend privacy and confidentiality arrangements in whole or in part.

The privacy and confidentiality of mediation contrast with the proceedings of courts and some tribunals, which are open to everyone and whose documentation is part of the public record. However, while the confidentiality of mediation is often emphasised in its promotion, it has been shown[51] that it is not a defining characteristic

---

49 In a family mediation the parties reluctantly agreed to an interim parenting plan which neither would have committed to permanently. When the mediation resumed a month later, they both expressed satisfaction with the agreement and the temporary arrangement became permanent.

50 See Chapter 12.

51 See Chapter 1.

of mediation. As a matter of law, there are limits to the confidentiality, privacy and without prejudice features of the process, and disclosure may be required in some circumstances.[52] There are also practical limitations on confidentiality: the greater the presence and participation of persons other than the disputants in mediation, the less effective the principle will be. In some situations parties may have to report back to constituents or ratifying authorities, an arrangement which can be referred to as *open mediation*. There are also policy concerns about the cloak of confidentiality which mediating parties can draw around them, and these are dealt with below.[53]

Peer-based

Some forms of mediation are peer-based, in the sense that the mediator is a member of the same group, profession or industry as the disputants. This is particularly the case with *facilitative mediation* in community mediations where mediators reflect the distribution of age, gender, race and class attributes of the community as a whole. These kinds of mediators act, in a sense, as representatives of the community in facilitating the parties' negotiations. In some cases particular care is taken by the mediation service to reflect the characteristics of the parties in the composition of a co-mediation panel.[54] Examples of this selectivity are male and female co-mediators in a matrimonial dispute or adult and adolescent mediators in a family dispute.[55] Where parties can select their own mediator, they can negotiate on his or her identity. In *evaluative mediation*, this is likely to be a person or persons with industry knowledge and experience, such as engineers or architects in building mediations. Litigation, by contrast, is a professionalised system with a legally-specialised judge or judicial officer whose identity is not contingent on the attributes of the parties before him or her. Judges and judicial officers are also generalists, with no special expertise in the area of the dispute. *Settlement mediation* inclines towards this arrangement, as evidenced by the use of retired judges or senior lawyers as mediators within this model.

Mediation and Approaches to Conflict

The mediation movement is based on distinct assumptions about the significance, diagnosis and treatment of conflict. In some respects these differ significantly from the assumptions of other dispute resolution systems.

Conflict is not necessarily a negative phenomenon

Conflict is often regarded as being symptomatic of a pathology which should be cured as quickly as possible, either through compromise or by getting someone else to fix it. If there is a problem in a contractual relationship, in a planning application,

---

52   See Chapter 12. V Vann 'Confidentiality in court-sponsored mediation: disclosure at your own risk?' (1999) 10 *ADRJ* 195.
53   See also Chapter 12.
54   On co-mediation, see Chapter 4.
55   A potential danger in this arrangement is that each party will identify the relevant mediator as their 'champion'. This inclination could be manipulated by the mediators.

or in neighbourly relations, this is perceived as a negative phenomenon which requires a 'remedy', often involving the payment of money, to 'resolve' it. In mediation, however, conflict is seen less negatively and more as a fact of life[56] which, if it is handled constructively, can have positive benefits for the parties. It can provide opportunities for introspection, for review and renewal, for the restoration of personal or commercial relationships, and for doing new business.

Mediation provides a safe forum in which conflict can be expressed and constructively managed. It legitimises the common reality of conflict, and validates the emotional experiences which accompany it. Experienced mediators do not discourage the expression of conflict, for example by asking the parties to get to the point or to avoid 'irrelevant' issues. Thus experienced mediators give 'permission' for conflict to occur, provided the mediation guidelines are not eroded.[57] It is regarded as potentially counterproductive to put the parties into separate rooms just because high emotions are being expressed. The catharsis of expressed and acknowledged emotions may be a necessary precondition for reaching a practical settlement, particularly where the disputants have not handled conflict well in the past or have been prevented by their advisers from communicating with each other before the mediation meeting.

Conflict can be diagnosed

Writers on mediation such as Moore[58] have emphasised the importance of mediators diagnosing the causes of conflict in order to develop a hypothesis regarding possible interventions. Diagnosis serves first to indicate what general form of dispute resolution system might be appropriate for a particular dispute, and second to suggest what specific interventions and approaches might be appropriate within a particular system, such as mediation. In such a complex area of human behaviour, any diagnosis can only be tentative and may have to be revised in the light of subsequent information. However, even a tentative diagnosis of conflict is a major resource for a mediator, and it can be shared with competent parties to assist their understanding of the dispute and ways of dealing with it.[59]

The table on page **44** shows possible causes of conflict and corresponding interventions which can be tried where an initial diagnosis has been made. It is based on Moore's 'circle of conflict'.[60]

As Moore points out, most conflicts have multiple causes, and require multiple interventions on a trial and error basis.[61] However, conflict should not be seen as just a murky

---

56 See D Lax and J Sebenius *The Manager as Negotiator*, Free Press, New York, 1986. An excellent monograph on conflict is J Rubin et al *Social conflict: escalation, stalemate and settlement* (2nd edn), McGraw Hill Inc, New York, 1994.

57 Sir Laurence Street refers to the need, in some mediations, for a 'controlled burn'. Bushfires are not advisable. Community mediators are advised to allow disputants to have a 'good spit'. On mediation guidelines, see Chapter 11.

58 C Moore *The Mediation Process: practical strategies for resolving conflict* (2nd edn), Jossey-Bass, San Francisco, 1996, at p 58.

59 In a planning mediation, which extended over four sessions, a developer and local government representative were informed about Moore's 'circle of conflict' and began using it as a common point of reference in dealing with their disputes.

60 C Moore, op cit, at pp 60–1.

61 Ibid, at p 58.

Conflict Diagnosis		
Conflict Category	Causes of Conflict	Possible Intervention Strategies
Goals/Objectives	Neither party can achieve their differing goals and objectives without assistance from the other	• Emphasise interdependence • Focus on mutual interests • Stress implications of non-settlement
Information/Data	Figures, data or documents incorrect, incomplete or differently interpreted	• Find, correct, supplement data • Develop objective criteria to evaluate information • Use expert to interpret data
Communication	Written or verbal communications unclear, incomplete, misunderstood, misfiled or not responded to	• Clarify past miscommunications • Make future communications constructive
Resources	Competition over fixed amounts of money, time, goods, services, or other matters of substantive value	• Attempt to expand resources • Emphasise mutual interests • Develop integrative solutions
Structural	Unequal access to authority, information, resources, time and other sources of power	• Emphasise different sources of power • Ensure fair decision-making process
Relationship/Emotional	Pattern of negative behaviour, untreated emotions, the grieving process, stereotypes, psychological problems	• Acknowledge and validate emotions • Avoid negativity through control of process
Values/Principles	Competing ideologies, world views, religious and cultural values, basic assumptions	• Focus on tangible interests • Search for overarching goals • Educate on 'live and let live'

morass. Even a tentative diagnosis assists a conflict manager in dealing with it and mediation has provided the occasion for more attention to the diagnostic requirement.

Conflict should be adequately defined before solutions are identified

Parties in conflict often 'present' the problem in simplistic terms. Thus in a dispute between landlord and tenant, the former may initially insist that the only issue is the non-payment of rent. The tenant in turn might claim that the only issue is the landlord's breach of the requirement to maintain the flat. In some dispute resolution processes, such as litigation, these might be the only questions considered and dealt with by the decision-making authority. However, further investigation of the dispute may reveal several issues other than those presented by the parties, for example, aggressive behaviour by the landlord towards the tenant's guests, the tenant's public attacks on the landlord's reputation, contrasting views on appropriate levels of noise, and the confrontational way in which lawyers intervened in previous disputes between the two.

Mediation provides an opportunity for the problem to be defined in terms of all its factors, before options for settlement are considered. In mediation training courses this two-stage sequence is symbolised by the mediation triangles. The upper triangle represents the problem-defining stage, during which the mediator takes the parties through a range of strategies designed to elicit all the parties' concerns and interests, but without considering possible solutions. The lower triangle represents the problem-solving stage of mediation, during which the mediator encourages the parties to consider a wide range of options before coming to a specific settlement package. The mediation movement has emphasised the need for the two distinct phases, in their proper sequence, for constructive dispute settlement.[62]

Constructive conflict management is an end in itself

The mediation movement regards constructive conflict management not only as a means to the end of settlement, but as an end in itself. The literature on mediation suggests that the system should be evaluated not only in terms of the final outcome. Even where the dispute is not fully resolved, mediation might provide other benefits. These could include:

- the parties discovering what each other's concerns and interests are;
- the venting of emotions in a protective environment and the consequent lowering of hostility and antagonism;
- defining the dispute more clearly by listing the issues in dispute and identifying what matters are not in dispute;
- agreeing on an order of priority for the discussion of issues in dispute;
- agreeing on what additional facts are required, what homework should be done, and what disclosures should be made within what time periods;
- identifying the influence of third parties (eg relatives, boards, lawyers);
- creating doubts about intransigent bargaining positions and generating a range of optional 'solutions';

---

62 See triangles diagram in Chapter 4.

- agreeing on procedures or methods to resolve substantive issues, eg employment of a valuer or referral to a counsellor;
- forcing the parties to confront the conflict and not abdicate responsibility for settlement decisions; and
- providing a model of constructive problem-solving for use in subsequent disputes.

Mediation can have a strong educative function: through modelling, advising, coaching and encouraging, the mediator can assist the parties to learn and develop the principles and techniques of constructive problem-solving. Some evidence of this feature of mediation is found in the matters which settle after the mediation meeting. This might be due to the progress made in the mediation.[63]

Mediation and Approaches to Negotiation

Negotiation is a normal element in the mediation process. This raises the question of whether mediation generally, or any of the four models individually, are based on specific approaches to negotiation. Negotiation is itself a form of conflict resolution but there are considerable differences in its definition and conceptualisation. After surveying some of these differences, Anstey[64] concludes that the following can be regarded as the core elements of negotiation:

(a) a verbal interactive process;
(b) involving two or more parties;
(c) who are seeking to reach agreement;
(d) over a problem or conflict of interest between them; and
(e) in which they seek as far as possible to preserve their interests, but to adjust their views and positions in the joint effort to achieve an agreement.

These core features accommodate widely different approaches to the negotiation process. Different times, places and cultures have generated very different traditions of negotiation. These traditions have been influenced by philosophy, religion, approaches to conflict, community values and business expectations. Some of the approaches to negotiation are reflected in the diagram opposite,[65] where the vertical axis represents each party's concern about how the other party comes out and the horizontal axis represents each party's concern about how they themselves come out. It portrays five paradigm negotiation situations: concessional, problem-solving, distributive, avoidance and positional.

Traditional approaches to negotiation

In individualistic secular societies the traditional approach to negotiation is called positional bargaining.[66] This is associated with situations where the parties make

---

63 In one such matter, the legal representative for one of the parties suggested that the subsequent settlement proved that the matter had not been suitable for mediation!
64 M Anstey *Negotiating conflict: insights and skills for negotiators and peacemakers*, Juta & Co, Kenwyn, South Africa, 1991, at pp 91–2.
65 Based on M Anstey, ibid, at p 113.
66 See the influential article of C Menkel-Meadow 'Towards another view of legal

Approaches to Negotiation

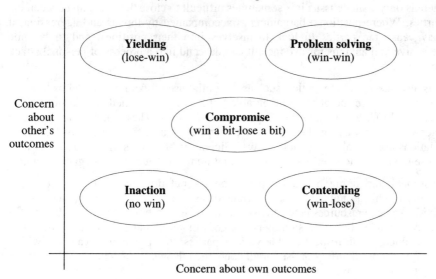

extreme opening claims and attempt to persuade, coerce or trick the other side to move closer to their initial position. Where the parties both require an outcome, they move closer to each other through a series of incremental concessions, until they reach agreement. Essentially the parties move from their initial and subsequent positions in order to find a compromise accommodation.[67] The point of compromise will be in a fairly predictable range around the mid-point between their opening claims. Positional bargaining is associated with many everyday transactions, such as buying and selling a car or making a claim against an insurer. It revolves around 'substantive issues', such as paying money, increasing leave entitlements, or rectifying building defects. It is a competitive system in that it assumes that resources are limited and that a gain for one party entails a loss for the other.[68] Positional bargaining is also known as adversarial negotiation, competitive negotiation or distributive bargaining.[69]

The positional approach to negotiation has several advantages. It is culturally understood, is compatible with other competitive activities in society, requires little preparation, is relatively easy to do, and the outcome can be predicted with some degree of accuracy. It also has many shortcomings. Positional bargaining may overlook many needs and interests which are not encapsulated in the parties' original

negotiations: the structure of problem-solving' (1993–4) *University of California Law Review* 754; and M Anstey, ibid, at pp 125–64.

67 Referred to as the 'negotiation dance' by H Raiffa *The Art and Science of Negotiation*, Belkap Press of Harvard University Press, Cambridge, Massachusetts, 1982, at pp 47–8.

68 Also known as zero-sum bargaining.

69 On the distinction between distributive and integrative bargaining, see H Raiffa, op cit, at p 33. See also J W Burton *Resolving deep-rooted conflict: a handbook*, University Press of America, Lanham, Maryland, 1987; and R Buckley 'The applicability of mediation skills to the creation of contracts' (1992) 3 *ADRJ* 227 at 235.

claims. It tends to reduce the negotiation to a single issue, usually money, and where there is only a single issue it is sometimes difficult to close the final gap between the parties. Where positional bargaining is accompanied by threats and aggression, it may cause the parties to lock themselves into their positions, and to become defensive and anxious to save face. It can descend into a process of personal attack and defence.[70]

It is also susceptible to tactics, such as the initial use of extravagant claims to make the 'compromise' point more favourable to the party concerned, and to stonewalls, threats, bluffs, tricks and other expressions of power. These tactics may result in short-term victories for the more powerful party, but at the expense of long-term relationships. Finally, it is not always efficient, in that the single issue focus may cause the parties to overlook other potential items of value at the bargaining table.

Positional bargaining has developed a poor reputation due to the above short-comings. This is not altogether warranted, as it may be an appropriate way of dividing scarce resources between two parties with no future relationship. It need not be accompanied by aggression, personal confrontation and dubious tactics.[71] It can be conducted with respect for the various parties, in a productive way, and with a satisfying sense of compromise for all concerned. However, it is not the last word in negotiation strategy.

Alternative approaches to negotiation

The shortcomings of positional bargaining have led to the development of alternative approaches to negotiation. They share the goal of making negotiation less competitive and adversarial and more cooperative and collaborative. Negotiation theory is drawn from a range of disciplines, including game theory, economics and psychology.[72] From game theory, the prisoner's dilemma shows that, when parties co-operate, they can reach an outcome favourable to both, but if one party co-operates and the other does not, the competitor exploits the co-operation and achieves a better result. When both parties fail to co-operate, however, they waste resources and will achieve only a mediocre outcome.[73] Accordingly, game theory shows that co-operation maximises individual returns.[74] Axelrod developed some basic rules to follow in order to realise the benefits of co-operation, in what he referred to as 'tit for tat':

---

70 Many studies have found that positional negotiators engage in wasteful and counter-productive adversarial, or unnecessarily compromising, behaviour. See C Menkel-Meadow 'Towards another view of legal negotiations: the structure of problem-solving' (1993–4) *University of California Law Review* 754 at p 763 and references cited there. For another study, see R Davis 'Negotiating personal injury cases: a survey of the attitudes and beliefs of personal injury lawyers' (1994) 68 *ALJ* 734.

71 M Anstey *Negotiating conflict: insights and skills for negotiators and peacemakers*, Juta & Co, Kenwyn, South Africa, 1991, at pp 126–7.

72 A useful outline of the disciplines appears in R Mnookin 'Why Negotiations Fail' (1993) 8 *Ohio State Journal on Dispute Resolution* 235 at 249.

73 R Condlin 'Bargaining in the Dark: the normative incoherence of lawyer dispute bargaining role' (1992) 51 *Maryland Law Review* 1 at 12.

74 D A Lax and J K Sebenius *The manager as negotiator: Bargaining for co-operative and competitive gain*, Free Press, New York, 1986.

- Begin negotiations co-operatively.
- Retaliate if the other side is competitive.
- Forgive the other side if it returns to co-operation.
- Be clear and consistent in the approach.[75]

While acknowledging the different, and at times competing, interests of parties, they attempt to promote problem-solving techniques which go beyond mere compromise. One of their most salient features is that they probe beneath the initial positional claims of the parties to uncover real needs and interests, and attempt to fashion creative solutions which meet as many mutual needs as possible. Chornenki considers that, in focusing on interests and needs, mediation takes the emphasis off power. In that way, Chornenki argues, mediation engages the parties in the 'power of the collective', creating order, stability and unity of direction.[76]

These approaches serve to move the dispute beyond a single issue to multiple issues. Even in apparent single-issue disputes, for example over the payment of an amount of money, there will be other issues which can be taken into account in the negotiations: the timing of payment, security, acknowledgment of the other side,[77] legal expenses, and what is disclosed publicly. By placing these matters on the negotiating table, the parties are increasing the 'resources', which they are ultimately to distribute. In well-worn words, they increase the pie before dividing it. There is a wider appreciation of the parties' psychological and procedural needs and interests and an attempt to accommodate as many of them as possible in imaginative ways.[78] These alternative approaches are known as problem-solving negotiation (the term used here), collaborative negotiation or integrative bargaining.[79]

The alternative negotiation approaches have a number of prerequisites which are not present in positional bargaining. The parties must share information, be reliable and

---

75 R Axelrod *The evolution of co-operation*, Basic books, New York, 1984. A range of examples adopt some or all of these principles. For example, the 'Untermyer Variation', developed by a New York litigator, involves a reasonable opening offer. If the other side makes an extreme counter-offer, the 'Untermyer party' would double their opening demand and continue to do so with each additional extreme counter-offer: D Shapiro 'Pushing the envelope – selective techniques in tough mediations' (2000) *ADRLJ* 117 at 120.

76 G Chornenki 'Mediating commercial disputes: exchanging "power over" with "power with"' in J Macfarlane (ed) *Rethinking disputes: the mediation alternative*, Cavendish Publishing, London, 1997, at pp 163–4.

77 In a commercial mediation a bank's representative acknowledged that the owner of a small business was not to blame for its demise, and that the owner had been a valuable customer for many years. The lawyer representing the bank estimated that the acknowledgments improved the bank's position by over £50,000.

78 Menkel-Meadow considered the problem-solving aspect of negotiation and, in particular, the need to satisfy the real or underlying needs of the parties, not just their legal needs: C Menkel-Meadow 'Lawyer Negotiations: Theories and realities – what we learn from mediation' (1993) 56 *Modern Law Review* 361 at 369. The problem-solving theory also explains the general approach of businessmen to dispute resolution. Macaulay, in his study of business disputing in America, found that businessmen rarely referred to the contracts they had entered into, when a dispute arose, but sought to negotiate a solution as if there had never been a contract: S Macaulay 'Non-contractual Relations in Business: a preliminary study' (1963) 28(1) *American Sociological Review* 55 at 61.

79 It is also known as 'win-win' negotiation. There are differences between collaborative and integrative bargaining, but for convenience they are grouped together and contrasted with competitive approaches.

honest with each other, attempt to understand and accommodate each other's interests, engage in constructive communication, and otherwise display a co-operative attitude. Williams suggests that effective negotiators need to be friendly, trustworthy and fair. Friendliness requires an avoidance of insulting, threatening or belligerent behaviour. Trustworthiness is engendered by sharing information, recognising the needs and interests of the other parties and being realistic about individual prospects of success. Fairness requires identifying common ground and communicating shared interests.[80] The alternative approaches to negotiation also assume some skills in creative problem-solving.[81] In deep-seated conflicts they require the parties to change from a bargaining to an analytical approach, to commit themselves to a wide exploration of possibilities, and to accept outside facilitation.[82] Where these various prerequisites are not present, it will be difficult to adopt problem-solving negotiation.

Interest-based bargaining

One of the most influential of the new approaches to negotiation was developed by Fisher and Ury.[83] It was called 'principled bargaining', or 'negotiating on the merits', but is referred to here as interest-based bargaining. Fisher and Ury's main goal was to devise an approach to negotiation which would achieve a 'wise agreement', that is, an agreement which 'meets the legitimate interests of each side to the extent possible, resolves conflicting interests fairly, is durable, and takes community interests into account'.[84] The negotiation approach should also be efficient and not damage the relationship between the parties. There are four defining features of this model:

(a)   People issues should be dealt with separately from substantive issues. ('Separate the people from the problem'.) Negotiating parties need to develop a working relationship involving mutual acceptance and reliability, and being unconditionally constructive. This involves acknowledging other parties' feelings, not blaming them for the situation, avoiding loss of face and treating them with respect, without necessarily conceding on the substantive issues. By keeping distinct and treating separately the personal and emotional aspects, the parties can focus clearly on the substantive problem. As Fisher and Ury put it, 'be hard on the problem but soft on the people'. This requires a range of sophisticated interpersonal and communication skills which are not necessarily a part of positional bargaining.

---

80 G Williams *Legal Negotiation & Settlement*, West Publishing Co, Minneapolis, 1983.
81 C Moore *The Mediation Process: practical strategies for resolving conflict* (2nd edn), Jossey-Bass, San Francisco, 1996, at p 73, uses the metaphor of a jigsaw puzzle which the parties are jointly putting together.
82 J Burton *The conflict series, vol 3: Readings in Management and Resolution*, St Mary's Press, New York, 1990, at p 56.
83 R Fisher and W Ury *Getting to yes: negotiating agreement without giving in* (rev edn) Hutchinson Books, Boston, 1992. See also R Fisher and S Brown *Getting together: building a relationship that gets to yes*, Business Books, Boston, 1988, for an elaboration of the earlier themes. W Ury's *Getting past no: negotiating with difficult people*, Business Books, London, 1991, deals with negotiation techniques and tactics within the same overall approach. R Fisher and D Ertel *Getting ready to negotiate: the getting to yes workbook*, Penguin Books, New York, 1995, is a guide for preparing for negotiations using the interest-based approach.
84 R Fisher and W Ury, ibid, at p 4.

(b) Parties in negotiation should focus not on their positions, but on the needs and interests which underlie those positions. This allows them to bargain 'on the merits' of the dispute, and not in terms of superficial, legally-defined, or emotional issues. While a position is the outcome which a party wants, or thinks it wants, an interest is the reason why that outcome is desired. Thus an employee requesting additional pay may be motivated by job security concerns or the need for acknowledgment and status. These underlying interests are easier to negotiate on than the positional pay claim; they could be attained in a number of different ways, whereas the pay claim can only be dealt with in one way, and could lead to an impasse. An interest focus is also likely to uncover more overlapping needs between the parties than a positional focus.

(c) Parties in negotiation should consider a wide range of options before coming to a settlement and should attempt to select those settlement options which satisfy their mutual interests.[85] This involves thinking beyond narrow legal remedies to the imaginative use of resources and to incorporating future interests. Thus in the above employment dispute, it might be in the mutual interests of all parties to recategorise a number of jobs, and even to give the disgruntled employee a specific role in relation to grievances over status. A range of specific techniques, such as brainstorming, can be used to develop the settlement options in a non-prejudicial way.

(d) Negotiation should occur independently of the subjective wills of the parties and, wherever possible, in terms of objective criteria. The objective criteria could comprise market values, an expert opinion, standards in comparative industries, or common understandings in commerce. It is easier for parties to accept an objective standard than it is to concede to the other party's demands. Another way in which individual parties can evaluate possible outcomes is in terms of their BATNA – Best Alternative To a Negotiated Agreement. This refers to the best option available to a party should it call off the negotiations, for example the likely outcome in a court determination or the terms of an agreement with an alternative party. The BATNA takes account of costs, time, anxiety and risk. A party should discontinue negotiations if it can do better elsewhere, and the BATNA attempts to provide an objective measure of when settlement through negotiation might be the pragmatic thing to do, even though it does not satisfy all objectives.

Despite the apparent simplicity of these principles, they are profound. They have had a strong influence on contemporary thinking about negotiation, and on the mediation movement. The strengths and shortcomings of the Fisher and Ury principles are considered in the wider context of problem-solving negotiation.

Strengths and shortcomings of problem-solving negotiation

The strengths of problem-solving negotiation can be summarised as follows:

- It deals with the real conflict, in that all needs and interests of the parties are considered and dealt with.

---

85 The aim is to avoid simply 'splitting the baby' or achieving a '50/50 split', an outcome which some respondents to the authors' 2000 survey, with a 30% response rate, of UK law firms, selected at random, indicated had occurred in the mediations they had experienced.

- It is efficient, in that negotiating parties look creatively at a range of options for dealing with their problem, and by looking also to future interests they avoid leaving anything of value at the negotiating table.
- It preserves relationships by acknowledging and dealing with emotional and interpersonal dimensions of conflict and taking account of future relations between the parties.
- It provides legitimate standards (objective criteria) for evaluating and accepting settlement options, without the parties appearing to be capitulating or unduly compromising.

On the other hand, problem-solving negotiation has several shortcomings, which can be summarised as follows:[86]

- It assumes that both parties are prepared to adopt this approach and that they both have the capacity to bargain creatively at the level of interests, whereas in reality many parties are not so committed or able.[87]
- It overlooks the fact that some parties have ulterior motives for taking part in negotiations, for example to exact revenge, to discover information, or for the thrill of competitive confrontation, and would have little incentive to take account of the other side's interests.
- It does not take into consideration the fact that whereas interest-based bargaining assumes a rough equality in power between the parties, in many situations one party is considerably more powerful than the other and is able to prevail through crude positional bargaining.
- It is naive to expect parties to disclose information and engage in creative options when they may still have to deal with a distributive issue at the end of the day; even in the most creative bargaining situations it will usually be necessary to distribute limited resources towards the end, and it might be difficult for both parties to emerge as winners in this distribution.
- Objective criteria may be elusive, in that no industry standard exists or the parties have competing standards of what is fair or objective; expert or legal opinions may be in conflict and may themselves contribute to the difficulties of achieving resolution.

In the light of these strengths and shortcomings, it is clear that the problem-solving approach to negotiation will be appropriate in some, but not all, situations. Where negotiations take place between strangers with no future relationship, where there is only a single issue, such as price, to be bargained over, and where the transaction costs of considering interests and options are high, positional bargaining might be the more appropriate approach. One of the functions of a mediator is to assist the parties to develop an appropriate negotiation approach for their particular circumstances.

Negotiation approaches in mediation

Much of the literature on mediation endorses problem-solving or interest-based approaches to negotiation, although the writing on negotiation generally makes little

---

86 B Wolski 'The role and limitations of Fisher and Ury's model of interest-based negotiation in mediation' (1994) 5 *ADRJ* 210 and references cited there.
87 For example, in environmental disputes, interests are often problematic. As Jurd argues, 'You can't just save half the forests. You can't save half an ecosystem, any more than you

direct reference to mediation. The influence of Fisher and Ury's thinking is found in many facets of contemporary mediation, including terminology, mediator standards and training programmes. It is at the heart of the *facilitative* model of mediation, and finds some resonance in the *therapeutic* model.

At the same time the practice of mediation often reflects positional bargaining, which is at the heart of the *settlement mediation* model and finds some resonance in the *evaluative* model. This indicates that the dominant negotiating culture is not always transformed in mediation, whether on account of the parties' insistence, the nature of the dispute, or the mediator's inability to produce any change. A party might also engage in positional negotiation with the mediator and, through the mediator, with another party.[88] Thus both positional and problem-solving negotiation are encountered in mediation practice and mediators can assist in both situations. Only the latter, however, is compatible with the philosophical underpinnings of the mediation movement. One function of mediators is to assist the parties to make the transition from positional to problem-solving negotiation where the circumstances warrant it.

Another view of negotiation in mediation describes the range of styles, from competitive to co-operative, as a shift from 'differentiation' to 'integration'. Differentiation involves the presentation by each party of their respective positions and increases the potential for conflict escalation.[89] Integration is characterised by a problem-solving or co-operative approach, involving identification of mutual interests. The progression from differentiation to integration involves three phases. The first phase requires disagreement between the parties, emphasising their extreme positions. The second phase involves identification of areas of agreement and the final phase involves determination of terms of settlement.[90]

A more complex six-phase model was developed by Gulliver.[91] In phase one the parties make decisions about the context for the negotiation and, in phase two, make their initial demands. In the next phase each party develops those initial demands and it is only in the fourth phase that parties make the shift from competitive to co-operative approaches. The next phase involves developing the negotiation range and refining the outstanding differences between the parties. The settlement is reached in phase six.[92]

Empirical studies provide support for the phase model of negotiation. Those studies show that co-operative behaviour increases in the later stages of negotiation.[93] The phase model of negotiation provides an indicator of when in a mediation the parties are likely to progress from competitive to co-operative approaches. Fisher's,

can save half a human life . . .': see H Gregorczuk 'The appropriateness of mediation in international environmental disputes' (1996) 7 *ADRJ* 47 at 57.

88 D Shapiro 'Pushing the envelope – selective techniques in tough mediations' (2000) *ADRLJ* 117 at 122.

89 J Folger and M Poole *Working through Conflict: a communication perspective*, Scott Foresman, Glenview, Illinois, 1984.

90 A Douglas *Individual Peacemaking*, Columbia University Press, New York, 1962.

91 P H Gulliver *Disputes & Negotiations*, Academic Press, New York, 1979.

92 Ibid.

93 E R Alexander 'The re-definition of cognitive conflict: Effects of various types of communication' (1979) 23 *Journal of Conflict Resolution* 120 at 138; and I Morley and G Stephenson *The Social Psychology of Bargaining*, George Allen & Unwin, London, 1977.

Williams's and Menkel-Meadow's work indicates the type of skills and factors which promote co-operative negotiation. The work of Lax and Axelrod, for instance, highlights the benefits of the co-operative approach.

There is, however, evidence in the UK to suggest that lawyers are either unaware of or do not accept the value that mediation can bring to direct negotiations between the parties or their solicitors.[94] Empirical studies in the US and UK indicate that, in the hands of lawyers, negotiation might bear little resemblance to that which is advocated in the literature.[95] UK studies show that solicitors still use litigation tactics, or positional negotiation, in mediation.[96] The principled approach to negotiation in mediation may increase as lawyers become more experienced at and comfortable with the mediation process. US commentators suggest that the way to ensure efficient and appropriate negotiation conduct in mediation is to alter solicitor codes of conduct to require them to do so.[97]

Mediation and Efficiency

A question for contemporary times would be whether, notwithstanding its normative claims, there is an economic rationale for mediation.[98] Here the focus is restricted to the issue of efficiency, which revolves around the likelihood of rational economic

---

94 See, for example, H Genn *Central London County Court Mediation Pilot: Evaluation Report*, LCD Research Series, No 5/98. She provides an example, at p 130, where a solicitor considered that the mediation was just like any other meeting that the solicitor would have had with the other side, in the particular case, with an insurance company representative. In a further example, on p 133, another solicitor felt that the mediation had been a waste of time as 'it could all have been done on the telephone'.

95 C Menkel-Meadow 'Lawyer Negotiations: Theories and Realities – what we learn from mediation' (1993) 56 *Modern Law Review* 361 at 369; H Genn *Hard Bargaining: out of court settlement in personal injury actions*, Clarendon Press, Oxford 1987; and H Kritzer *Let's make a deal: Understanding the negotiation process in ordinary litigation*, University of Wisconsin Press, Madison, Wisconsin 1990.

96 H Genn *Central London County Court Mediation Pilot: Evaluation Report*, LCD Research Series, No 5/98, at p 130 the following example is given:
    '. . . the whole thing was tactics. I start off higher . . . they start off lower . . . and we met in the middle . . . it's tactical . . . I don't think you can have a . . . cards on the table approach'.
    A further example at p 130 shows that Axelrod's 'tit for tat' approach, where parties begin by co-operating, unless and until another party defects, does not appear to be borne out by the approach of English lawyers in mediation:
    '. . . we are going to come up against these people again and if we are seen to be weak in the negotiating, they will remember that for the next time . . . so we can't drop the litigation stance . . . it's just impossible . . .'

97 R J Gilson and R H Mnookin 'Disputing through Agents: Co-operation and conflict between lawyers in litigation' (1994) 94 *Columbia Law Review* 504 at 513; and R Condlin 'Bargaining in the Dark: the normative incoherence of lawyer dispute bargaining role' (1992) 51 *Maryland Law Review* 1 at 93.

98 See J Brown and I Ayres 'Economic rationales for mediation' (1994) 80 *Virginia Law Review* 323; C Menkel-Meadow 'Lawyer Negotiations: Theories and realities – what we learn from mediation' (1993) 56 *Modern Law Review* 361; and S Shavell 'Alternative dispute resolution: an economic analysis' (1995) *Journal of Legal Studies* 1.

actors selecting mediation over alternative processes by virtue of its capacity to maximise resources while minimising costs. Mediation claims to be an efficient form of dispute resolution in at least six ways, described below:

Settlement

The first claim is that the prospect of resolution in mediation is high, as the process enables each party to assess the strengths and weaknesses of their case and to adjust unrealistically high expectations.[99] The process channels the parties' efforts into problem-solving, rather than defending claims and awaiting judgment.[100] Participation in the process also makes it more likely that a party will accept proposals made in that process.[101] This anecdotal evidence is supported by statistics in the UK. In the Central London County Court Mediation Pilot 62% of the mediated cases settled at the mediation appointment and that settlement rate remained constant between case types. The study concluded that the mediated cases had a much higher settlement rate overall than the non-mediated cases, whether or not the actual settlement occurred at the mediation appointment, suggesting that mediation promotes settlement even after an unsuccessful mediation.[102] The Centre for Dispute Resolution's statistics show a settlement rate of 85%, with the vast majority of cases being settled during the mediation itself.[103] The Solicitors' Indemnity Fund statistics showed that in 1999 80% of mediated cases were successful resolved at, or just after, mediation.[104]

In the case of family mediation, early statistics indicated a low rate of settlement. For instance, the earlier studies indicated that about 35% of cases reached full agreement and about 50% reached partial agreement.[105] More recent family mediation studies, however, support a higher rate of settlement.[106] For example, the Scottish Office Central Research Unit found in April 1999 that couples had reached agreement on all or most

---

99 M Davies, G Davis and J Webb *Promoting Mediation: Report of a study of Bristol Law Society's Mediation Scheme in its preliminary phase*, 1996 Research & Policy Planning Unit Research Study no 21, The Law Society, at p 28.

100 C Harrington 'The Politics of Participation and Non Participation in Dispute Processes' (1984) 6(2) *Law & Policy* 203 at 209.

101 Fisher, Ury and Patton *Getting to Yes: Negotiating an Agreement without giving in* (2nd edn) Houghton Mifflin, Boston, 1991, at pp 27–9.

102 H Genn *Central London County Court Mediation Pilot: Evaluation Report*, LCD Research Series, No 5/98, at p vi; and see also Centre for Dispute Resolution *Model Mediation Procedure Guidance Notes*, which confirm the Centre's experience that, even when no agreement is reached during a mediation, the parties often reach a settlement shortly afterwards as a result of the progress made during the mediation.

103 Centre for Dispute Resolution *Press Release*, 2 August 1999; and Centre for Dispute Resolution *Resolutions*, Issue no 22, at p 7.

104 Centre for Dispute Resolution *Press Release*, 2 August 1999.

105 Results of the studies conducted of the South East London Family Conciliation Bureau and Bristol Courts Mediation Project, summarised in University of Newcastle upon Tyne Conciliation Project Unit, *Report to the Lord Chancellor's Department on the costs and effectiveness of conciliation in England and Wales*, March 1989, at p 63.

106 Which has been explained by all issues mediation: see J Walker et al *An evaluation of comprehensive mediation services for divorcing couples*, Social Policy Research Findings, No 48, Joseph Rowntree Foundation, York, 1994; and I Butlin 'Outcome measures in all issues mediation' (2000) 30 *Fam Law* 212.

issues discussed in 78% of the family mediations studied.[107] A similar survey in Northern Ireland indicated an 80% settlement rate.[108] The lower family mediations in the 1970s and 1980s may be explained on the basis that parties approached conciliation with confused or erroneous expectations about the process and what it was aimed to do and on the basis that family mediation at the time was focused on child issues only.[109]

The available statistics appear to indicate that the lowest settlement rates occur in community mediation.[110] In the context of community mediation, commentators suggest that the opportunity to improve communication and relationships between members of the community and to encourage tolerance is a more important factor than settlement.[111]

In the US the Rand Report of court-based ADR in the US Federal District courts made a connection between settlement rates and timing of ADR. The Report concluded that settlement is more likely to occur when ADR takes place later in the life of a case, although the results from one district was that high settlement rates occurred even though ADR took place within 30 days of filing of defences.[112] In a Singapore study of mediation users between 1998 and 1999, a correlation between evaluative mediator behaviour and a high settlement rate was found. The mediator interventions considered by the parties to have been instrumental in achieving settlement included evaluation of the merits and recommendations of solutions.[113]

Compliance

Secondly, by involving parties in working out a solution to a problem, mediation not only enhances the prospects of reaching a settlement, and possibly maintaining

---

107 Family Mediation Scotland *Information Pack*, 1999, at p 7.

108 Northern Ireland Family Mediation Service *Report on Family Mediation Service: Client Satisfaction Questionnaire*, 1997. Compare the rate of 70% collated from statistics in Northern Ireland between 1992 and 1993, reported in G Robinson and D Devine *Family Mediation Services: Data on the Service April 1992/March 1993*, Northern Ireland Family Mediation Service, 1994.

109 University of Newcastle upon Tyne Conciliation Project Unit, *Report to the Lord Chancellor's Department on the cost and effectiveness of conciliation in England and Wales*, March 1989, at p 284. For an overview of the problems arising in 'single issue' family mediation, see B Wilson 'Mediating "single issue" disputes' (2000) 30 *Fam Law* 664.

110 39% of cases resulted in complete or partial agreement in the Community Mediation Service General Survey of 1995: C J Dignan *Community Mediation Service General Survey 1995*, University of Sheffield, Sheffield, 1995, at p 28. More recent Mediation UK statistics indicate a 50% settlement rate where only one party is referred to mediation, and an 80% settlement rate if both parties agree to participate: M Doyle *Advising on ADR: the essential guide to appropriate dispute resolution*, Advice Services Alliance, London, 2000.

111 T F Marshall 'Neighbour Disputes: Community Mediation Schemes as an alternative to Litigation' in K Mackie (ed) *A Handbook of Dispute Resolution: ADR in Action*, Routledge, London, 1991; and J Folberg and A Taylor *Mediation – a comprehensive guide to resolving conflicts without litigation*, Jossey-Bass, San Francisco, 1988.

112 RAND Corporation *An evaluation of mediation and early neutral evaluation under the Civil Justice Reform Act*, Institute for Civil Justice, 1996.

113 For full results of this study, see the Singapore edition of this book: L Boulle and

relationships, but also, it is claimed, the level of compliance with the outcome.[114] Additional reasons cited for high levels of compliance include an increased perception of fairness of outcomes reached in mediation;[115] the greater likelihood that the outcome will satisfy relevant commercial, personal or other norms;[116] and the beneficial psychological effect in cases where a party has received an admission of liability or apology.[117]

US studies on the status of mediated civil/commercial and small debt cases have provided statistical support for the anecdotal evidence.[118] UK studies in family mediation in the 1980s have not provided support for high levels of compliance,[119] although the more recent survey by the authors revealed that only 4% of respondents had concerns over issues of compliance with and enforcement of mediated settlements.

Cost savings

The third claim relates to expenditure on preparation, lawyers and experts, which can be considerably lower than for litigation. The study of the Central London County Court Mediation Pilot revealed that, amongst the respondents whose cases had settled at mediation, almost two-thirds considered that mediation had saved legal costs. Half of the plaintiffs settling at mediation believed that they had saved costs. Solicitors tended to be more likely than their clients to consider that costs had been saved. Taking all responses together, half the respondents believed that mediation had saved legal costs.[120] A study of the NHS Mediation Pilot has also

---

T Hwee Hwee *Mediation: principles, process, practice*, Butterworths, Singapore, 2000, Chapter 11 and Annex A.

114 R Abel 'The Contradictions of Informal Justice' in R Abel (ed) *The Politics of Informal Justice, vol 1*, Academic Press, New York 1982, at p 283.

115 See, for example, H Genn *Central London County Court Mediation Pilot: Evaluation Report*, LCD Research Series, No 5/98, at p 117.

116 M Galanter and J Lande 'Private Courts and Public Authority' (1992) 12 *Studies in Law Politics & Society* 393.

117 C McEwen and R Maiman 'Small Claims Mediation in Maine: an empirical assessment' (1981) 33 *Maine Law Review* 237 at 261.

118 American data shows that 70.6% of the mediation agreements surveyed with a monetary settlement were paid in full, compared to 33.8% of adjudicated results. Another 16.5% of the mediated settlements surveyed and 21.2% of judgments were partially paid: S Goldberg et al *Dispute Resolution: Negotiation, Mediation and other Processes* (2nd edn), Little Brown & Co, USA, 1992, at p 156.

119 A study of the South East London Family Conciliation Bureau (by Davis and Roberts in 1988) found that 40% of mediation settlement agreements had broken down within 18 months. In relation to the Hull & Humberside Family Conciliation Service (study by Johnson in 1986), within a period of one year, mediation settlement agreements had been changed in over half of the cases. Finally, even in the case of agreements which were being adhered to, one party or both parties had sought an improvement. See University of Newcastle upon Tyne Conciliation Project Unit, *Report to the Lord Chancellor's Department on the costs and effectiveness of conciliation in England and Wales*, March 1989, at pp 30–1 and 112. Compare with a later study: P McCarthy and J Walker *Evaluating the longer term impact of family mediation*, Joseph Rowntree Foundation, 1996.

120 H Genn *Central London County Court Mediation Pilot: Evaluation Report*, LCD Research Series, No 5/98, at pp vi and 90–1.

revealed that interviewees cited savings in cost as one of the main advantages of mediation.[121]

A Centre for Dispute Resolution/Pinsent Curtis survey of businesses in March 2000 revealed that 47% of respondents considered that mediation results in cost savings.[122] The authors conducted a survey of 700 law firms throughout the UK between December 1998 and April 2000.[123] 41% of the respondents cited cost savings as the main benefit of mediation, in particular the prospect mediation provides to avoid experts' and trial costs.

UK statistics also provide an indication of the level of the cost savings achieved in mediation. The Centre for Dispute Resolution's statistics show that business clients enjoyed an average cost saving of £44,000 per case by using mediation in 1995, and an average cost saving of £86,186 in 1998, although the highest reported cost saving by one party in the 1998 survey was £1.5m.[124] The 1998 survey indicated that the amount saved on average per successfully mediated case was £260,000.[125]

The Solicitors' Indemnity Fund calculated that in 100 mediated cases it had saved £3.5m.[126] London & Edinburgh Insurance Group calculated that, in the course of 1998, it had saved in excess of £1m in professional fees alone.[127] One English law firm has reported average savings of £45,000 for each mediated case.[128]

The authors' survey of 700 UK law firms elicited a wide range of responses in relation to the level of cost savings achieved from mediation. The responses fell within two broad categories, with 5% believing that the saving was impossible to quantify[129] and the majority, 95%, providing one of three responses:

- A minority (3%) simply referred to their cost savings as 'a lot', 'considerable', 'significant' or 'substantial'.
- A further minority (6%) referred to their cost savings in percentage terms, ranging from 30–60%, with 44% of these respondents suggesting that they had achieved at least a 50% reduction in costs.
- The majority (86%) put a figure on the level of savings achieved, as follows:
  39% saved up to £15,000;
  21% saved between £20,000 and £30,000;
  6% saved between £40,000 and £50,000;
  17% saved between £100,000 and £150,000;
  11% saved between £300,000 and £500,000;
  6% saved over £1m.

---

121 L Mulcahy et al *Mediating Medical Negligence claims: an option for the future?* NHS Executive, 2000, at p 73.
122 CEDR/Pinsent Curtis *Dispute Resolution Survey: initial analysis paper*, CEDR, London, March 2000.
123 The firms were selected at random throughout the UK. There was a 30% response rate.
124 Centre for Dispute Resolution *Resolutions*, Issue no 13, at p 4 and Issue no 22, at p 7.
125 Centre for Dispute Resolution *Resolutions*, Issue no 22, at p 7.
126 Ibid.
127 Centre for Dispute Resolution *Press Release: ADR – Rhetoric to Reality*, 17 November 1998.
128 Survey of 40 mediation cases handled by the insurance litigation department at Pinsent Curtis in Birmingham, reported in the Lawyer, 24 November 1998 'ADR's latest threat to City litigators'.
129 These respondents considered that the assessment was difficult as much depends on the

Accordingly, the authors' survey indicated that the majority of respondents (66%) considered that they had saved up to £50,000 per case, with about a quarter (28%) indicating savings of between £100,000 and £500,000, and a minority (6%) referring to savings of over £1m.

Statistics from Australia provide a useful insight into this issue. For example, higher than average savings per client have been found for legal professional negligence cases, commercial disputes and motor vehicle and industrial personal injury cases respectively.[130] American studies have also shown an increase in the percentage of mediation users saving more than US$50,000 in legal fees per mediated case.[131] US commentators suggest that an important factor in ensuring legal cost savings via mediation, in the context of commercial and civil disputes, is to ensure that litigation expenses are charged to the operating unit in which the dispute arises, rather than a central legal department, as this will provide the incentive for management to reduce their costs and improve their budgets. In comparison, the Rand Report on court-annexed ADR in US Federal District courts expressed concern that early management of cases leads to significantly increased lawyer work hours and hence litigation costs.[132]

Cost savings are not limited to civil and commercial cases or to cases involving legal representation. Community mediation is likely to be a less expensive way of resolving more complex cases which demand significant time from statutory agencies.[133]

Time savings

The fourth claim relates to time savings, involving the ability to commence a mediation without delay, the likelihood of it going ahead on the appointed day, and the potentially shorter duration of the process. Savings to the parties in a mediation are not limited to purely financial savings. Mediation can also result in savings of management time and emotion through early case preparation, evaluation and strategic decision-making.[134]

Centre for Dispute Resolution statistics for 1998 showed that 60% of parties considered that there had been significant savings, of at least one month, in management time, in the case of commercial disputes which had been successfully

---

stage reached in any litigation on foot and whether a case would have gone to trial or settled through direct negotiation in any event.

130 M Dewdney, B Sordo and C Chinkin *Continuing developments in mediation within the legal system: evaluation of the 1992/93 Settlement Week Programme*, the Law Society, New South Wales, 1994.

131 A 1997 survey of businesses indicated that 53% of respondents saved more than US$50,000 in legal fees, up from 49% in 1995: Center for Public Resources 'Survey shows ADR savings' in *Alternatives*, vol 16, no 11, December 1998, at p 176.

132 RAND Corporation *An evaluation of mediation and early neutral evaluation under the Civil Justice Reform Act*, Institute for Civil Justice, 1996.

133 C J Dignan *Community Mediation Service General Survey 1995*, University of Sheffield, Sheffield, 1995.

134 See, for example, L C Mann 'Mediation in Civil Cases' (1990) 67 *University of Detroit Law Review* 531.

mediated. One party claimed that mediation had saved 2.5 years of work on a case.[135] In the Centre for Dispute Resolution/Pinsent Curtis survey of businesses in March 2000, 37% of respondents considered that mediation offers quicker outcomes than traditional litigation.[136]

60% of respondents in the Central London County Court Mediation Pilot considered that mediation had reduced the amount of time spent on the dispute. The percentage was higher, 77%, amongst those whose cases had settled at mediation. The study also concluded that mediated settlements occurred several months earlier than non-mediated cases, although the findings suggested that settlement is less likely to occur at the extremes in the life of a case, when a case is very young or when it is very old.[137]

The authors' 2000 survey of 700 UK law firms revealed that 33% of respondents referred to time savings from mediation. The majority of these respondents (65%) referred to the saving in terms of a quicker settlement, with the remainder (35%) referring to it in terms of reduced management time in dispute resolution. Almost 20% of respondents had achieved settlement of a dispute using mediation even before issue of proceedings, with the remainder having achieved settlement in mediation following issue.

In comparison, the Rand Report of court-annexed ADR in US Federal District courts concluded that there was no strong statistical evidence that settlement time is significantly affected by mediation or early neutral evaluation.[138]

Optimal settlements

A fifth measure of efficiency relates to the parties' ability to exploit all the potential value which is at the bargaining table. A standard of efficiency is that of pareto-optimality, which refers to a situation in which no negotiating party could derive any greater benefit without it involving a loss for another party.[139] Conversely a negotiation outcome will not be pareto-optimal where one or both parties could derive additional value without affecting the position of others. One of the criticisms of positional bargaining is that, in focusing on the parties' positional claims and moving towards a point of compromise without taking account of other interests and needs, it does not result in a pareto-optimal outcome. The same criticism can be made of the *settlement* model of mediation.[140]

---

135 Centre for Dispute Resolution *Resolutions*, Issue no 22, at p 7.
136 CEDR/Pinsent Curtis *Dispute Resolution Survey: an initial analysis paper*, CEDR, London, March 2000.
137 H Genn *Central London County Court Mediation Pilot: Evaluation Report*, LCD Research Series, No 5/98, at pp vi, 47, 81 and 84.
138 RAND Corporation *An evaluation of mediation and early neutral evaluation under the Civil Justice Reform Act*, Institute for Civil Justice, 1996.
139 J Persky 'Pareto's Law' (1992) 6 *Journal of Economic Perspectives* 181.
140 Studies of lawyer negotiators have revealed inefficiencies in terms of the potential value which could be obtained from the process. See C Menkel-Meadow 'Lawyer Negotiations: Theories and realities – what we learn from mediation' (1993) 56 *Modern Law Review* 361; and R Davis 'Negotiating personal injury cases: a survey of the attitudes and beliefs of personal injury lawyers' (1994) 68 *ALJ* 734.

The *facilitative* model of mediation, incorporating problem-solving negotiation techniques, purports to be highly efficient in this fifth sense. By assisting the parties to interpret the problem in all its diversity, it allows them to take account of a wider spread of needs and interests, including procedural and psychological interests. Thus an apology offered and accepted may constitute significant value in terms of one party's self-esteem needs, and even in respect of the other's need to show remorse.[141] The mediation process itself can also be efficiency-producing, for example by enhancing the accuracy of communications between the parties, by increasing the amount and quality of information which parties disclose, and, though more controversially, by manipulating the information disclosed in separate meetings.[142] Conversely, a mediator is in a unique position to facilitate the termination of negotiations where he or she discovers that it would be inefficient to continue them.

Party satisfaction

Finally, it is claimed that party satisfaction with the mediation process is high.[143] US and Australian studies show impressive rates of party satisfaction. In particular, mediation is considered more personalised, humane and fairer than adjudication.[144] Satisfaction increases when the parties are given an opportunity to explain their case and achieve a better understanding of the other parties' points of view.[145] When solutions are tailored to the parties' needs greater party satisfaction results.[146] In a Singapore study, parties indicated that the following factors were associated with high levels of satisfaction:

● conducive environment;
● impartiality of mediators;
● assistance derived from lawyers' presence;
● fairness of process;

---

141 S Goldberg et al 'The role of apology in dispute resolution' in S Goldberg et al (eds) *Dispute Resolution: negotiation, mediation and other processes* (3rd edn) Aspen Law and Business, New York, 1999, at pp 159–62.
142 J Brown and I Ayres 'Economic rationales for mediation' (1994) 80 *Virginia Law Review* 323 at 394: 'Indirect and incomplete revelation of information is central to any economic rationale for mediation'. This raises an ethical issue of some importance.
143 There have been a number of American and Australian studies on party satisfaction:

Author	Case Type	Country
McEwen and Maiman 1981, 1982, 1984 and 1986	Civil/small claims	United States
Kelly and Duryee 1992	Family/divorce	United States
Pearson and Thoennes 1984	Family/custody	United States
Kitzmann and Emery 1993	Family/custody	United States
Chinkin and Dewdney 1992	Civil/non-small claims	Australia
Winzer and Donnelly 1988	Family	Australia

144 J Pearson 'An evaluation of an alternative to court adjudication' (1982) 7 *Justice System Journal* 420.
145 C McEwan and R Maiman 'Coercion and consent: a tale of two court reforms' (1988) 10(10) *Law & Policy* 3.
146 R Singer 'The rolling stones revisited: exploring the concept of user satisfaction as a measure of success in ADR' (1994) *Australian Dispute Resolution Journal* 77.

- mediators who understood their views;
- time and cost savings;
- no pressure to settle by others;
- evenly balanced outcome.[147]

Parties who are satisfied with the mediation process have also identified the avoidance of stress, tension and trauma associated with court hearings as significant factors determining their level of satisfaction.[148] An English study of people's perception of litigation confirms that many people find a formal court hearing intimidating and that those who fund their own cases suffer anxiety about mounting legal bills and the possibility of having to pay costs to the other party. It found that the bulk of litigants were acutely anxious, worried and distressed about the outcome of trial.[149]

American studies show that user satisfaction is consistently high in community mediation.[150] American studies have shown that, in victim offender mediation, victims experience particularly high levels of satisfaction.[151] In the case of civil and commercial mediation, Deloitte & Touche's 1993 US survey of general and outside counsel revealed high levels of satisfaction of mediation.[152] A study by McEwen and Maiman of small civil cases in Maine revealed that 66% of parties who had mediated their cases were completely or mostly satisfied with their experience, compared to only 54% of parties who had adjudicated.[153] Another American survey of business people found that executives and risk managers considered that businesses are more satisfied with out of court settlements than those brought about by trial.[154] US studies also suggest that, in the case of civil and commercial mediations, parties are willing to return to mediation even when the mediation has not helped to resolve a particular case,[155] a finding also supported by an Australian study.[156]

In a study of mediation for planning appeals in the UK, 90% of the participants in mediation expressed satisfaction with the process.[157] In a study of family mediation in the UK by Davis and Roberts, a high degree of satisfaction was found by female

---

147 Survey conducted by Singapore Mediation Centre between January 1998 and August 1999. For full results, see the Singapore edition of this book, Chapter 11 and Annex A.
148 M Dewdney, B Sordo and C Chinkin *Continuing developments in mediation within the legal system: evaluation of the 1992/93 Settlement Week Programme*, the Law Society, New South Wales, 1994.
149 J Baldwin *Monitoring the rise of the small claims unit: litigants' experiences of different forms of adjudication*, Institute of Judicial Administration, University of Birmingham, 1998.
150 C Harrington and S Merry 'Ideological Production: the making of community mediation' (1988) 22 (4) *Law & Society Review* 709.
151 See the section on Community Mediation in Chapter 8.
152 Deloitte and Touche *1993 Survey of general and outside counsel*, Deloitte and Touche, 1993, at p 1.
153 C McEwen and R Maiman (1988) 10(10) *Law & Policy* 3.
154 Gallup Organisations *Attitudes towards the liability and litigation system: a survey of the general public and business executives*, 1982, at p 198.
155 R Abel 'The Contradictions of Informal Justice' in R Abel (ed) *The Politics of Informal Justice, vol 1*, Academic Press, New York 1982, at p 283.
156 M Delaney and T Wright *Plaintiff's satisfaction with dispute resolution processes*, Justice Research Centre, Sydney, 1997, at p 71, who found that satisfaction occurred in mediation regardless of whether or not the party considered that it had 'won' the case.
157 M Welbank *Mediation in the Planning System*, DETR, London, May 2000, at p 36.

parties.[158] It has been suggested that there is a connection between satisfaction with mediation and continuing disagreement over child-related issues.[159] A Northern Ireland study found that 56.3% of the parties surveyed were satisfied with mediation, with petitioners' satisfaction levels being higher than those of respondents.[160] In a US study of divorce cases in Wisconsin, in only 28% did both parties report satisfaction, and settlements were considered to reflect the parties' relative stamina and vulnerability to the pressures of a prolonged dispute.[161] Finally, it has been suggested that, in the case of family mediation, users of all issues family mediation are likely to be more satisfied with the mediation process than users of mediation on particular issues.[162]

Although the authors' survey of UK law firms indicated that only 4% of respondents referred to party satisfaction with the mediation process as a benefit of mediation, the result is likely to have been different had the authors surveyed their clients.

These are not uncontroversial claims. Some mediations require extensive preparation, the involvement of lawyers, and even additional costs in the form of the mediator's fee. Moreover, mediations can sometimes be protracted, and where there is no settlement the system involves wasted time and expense.[163] US studies have shown that parties participating in an unsuccessful mediation are likely to be even less satisfied than those who go to trial.[164] The authors' survey of UK law firms revealed that the respondent lawyers attributed lack of success largely to poor mediator quality (17%), although a small percentage also referred to inappropriate, overly formal, proceedings as a factor (5%).

The Central London County Court Mediation Scheme found that, of those people who had participated in unsuccessful mediations, one third believed that the mediation had increased the costs of resolving the dispute.[165] The University of Newcastle upon Tyne Conciliation Project concluded, in the case of family mediations, that mediations result in a significant net addition to the overall cost of settling disputes.[166] 22% of respondents to the Centre for Dispute Resolution/Pinsent Curtis survey of businesses in March 2000 referred to the prospect of failure to reach

---

158 G Davis and M Roberts 'Mediation in the battle of the sexes' [1989] *Family Law* 306.
159 University of Newcastle upon Tyne Conciliation Project Unit, *Report to the Lord Chancellor's Department on the costs and effectiveness of conciliation in England and Wales*, March 1989, at p 222.
160 C Archbold et al *Divorce in Northern Ireland: unravelling the system*, Report to the Office of Law Reform, HMSO, 1999, at p 207.
161 H Erlanger et al 'Participation and flexibility in informal processes: cautions from the divorce context' (1987) 21 *Law & Society Review* 585.
162 P McCarthy and J Walker *Evaluating the long term impact of family mediation: report to the Joseph Rowntree Foundation*, Relate Centre of Family Studies, University of Newcastle upon Tyne, 1996. See the section on Settlement at pp **55–56**.
163 C Down 'Crying Woolfe? Reform of the adversarial system in Australia' (1998) 7 *Journal of Judicial Administration* 213 at 223.
164 S Clarke, E Ellen and K McCormick *Court-Ordered Civil Mediation in North Carolina: an evaluation*, State of Justice Institute, 1995.
165 H Genn *Central London County Court Mediation Pilot: Evaluation Report*, LCD Research Series, No 5/98, at p 91.
166 University of Newcastle upon Tyne Conciliation Project Unit, *Report to the Lord Chancellor's Department on the costs and effectiveness of conciliation in England and Wales*, March 1989, where it was found that £150 was added to the cost in cases of court-based mediation and about £250 was added to the cost as a result of an independent

a solution as the main disadvantage of mediation.[167] Similarly, 18% of respondents to the authors' survey agreed.

Apart from an increase in costs, an unsuccessful mediation may also increase the time required to reach resolution. 18% of respondents to the Centre for Dispute Resolution/Pinsent Curtis survey highlighted this time disadvantage in the event of an unsuccessful mediation.[168] The Central London County Court Mediation Pilot found that, in the cases which had not settled in mediation, one third felt that mediation had saved the amount of time, and 36% thought that mediation had increased the amount of time spent on resolving the dispute.[169] Despite this, the figures collated during the Pilot suggest that, even if agreement is not reached at mediation, the overall length of time to resolution is shorter than it would have been, on the basis of comparisons with a control sample, indicating that preparation for a mediation is unlikely to be wasted.[170] The authors' 2000 survey of UK law firms provides support, with 11% of respondents indicating that they had achieved settlement shortly after an unsuccessful mediation. Support also comes from a study of mediation users in Singapore between 1998 and 1999, where 86% of all parties surveyed reported that they believed that they had saved costs and 89% reported that they believed that they had saved time. Even in cases that were not settled, 43% of parties reported that they believed that they had saved costs and 50% believed that they had saved time.[171]

However, as a result of the potentially higher costs and greater time involved in cases where mediation is unsuccessful, mediation may not be economic for smaller claims,[172] a view shared by 12% of respondents to the authors' survey of UK law firms. Possible solutions have been suggested, in particular fixed fee[173] and 'no settlement, no fee' mediations.[174]

---

mediation. The report was made in the late 1980s and, accordingly, the figures are likely to be considerably more today. See also the section on Family Mediation in Chapter 8.
167 CEDR/Pinsent Curtis *Dispute resolution survey: initial analysis paper*, CEDR, London, March 2000.
168 Ibid.
169 H Genn *Central London County Court Mediation Pilot: Evaluation Report*, LCD Research Series, No 5/98, at p 81.
170 Ibid, at p 77.
171 Full survey results are reported in the Singapore edition of this book: L Boulle and T Hwee Hwee *Mediation: principles, process, practice*, Butterworths, Singapore, 2000, in Chapter 11 and Annex A.
172 See, for example, M Davies, G Davis and J Webb *Promoting Mediation: Report of a study of Bristol Law Society's Mediation Scheme in its preliminary phase*, 1996 Research & Policy Planning Unit Research Study no 21, The Law Society, at p 25; and Cargill's alternative dispute resolution clauses, which divert small claims to arbitration, and larger claims to mediation. Respondents to the authors' 2000 UK survey of law firms referred to the cost of venue, refreshments, mediator fees and expenses, which, when viewed against the fact that usually parties meet their own legal and other costs of preparation for and attendance at mediation (see Part II for further discussion on these issues), made mediation expensive for low value claims.
173 Dispute Mediation, a mediation organisation formed in 2000, provides fixed fee mediations (includes venue, mediator fees and expenses), with the aim of making mediation a cost-effective alternative for smaller claims; the London Mediation Service focuses on cases up to £15,000 value (for further information see the section on Mediation Organisations in Chapter 7).
174 J Fleming 'First "no settlement, no fee" offer for commercial mediation clients' *The Law*

Some suggest that mediation does not offer a better outcome, but a less stressful method of reaching an outcome.[175] Anecdotally, it is frequently suggested that mediations lead to creative settlements, not limited to legal remedies, like re-modelling a deal or making an apology. However, one US study indicates that, contrary to the expectation that creative settlements will occur in mediation, few mediated settlements involved conditions other than payment.[176] In the UK also, there is evidence to support the American findings. For example, the Central London County Court Mediation Pilot revealed that in 79% of settled cases, the settlement required the defendant to pay money to the plaintiff. In only 8% of settled cases was settlement reached on the basis of an agreement that did not involve the payment of money and, in those cases, primarily by withdrawal of the claim or counter-claim.[177] As the cases involved civil commercial cases, and since lawyers frequently attended the mediations, the result might be explained on the basis that lawyers tend to think about remedies as limited to that which would be possible if the case went to trial.[178] The authors' survey of UK law firms highlighted feelings of dissatisfaction by respondents who had achieved merely 'a 50/50 split', rather than the more creative outcome they had envisaged would be possible using mediation.

US studies show that claimants in civil cases may be able to achieve higher judgments at trial than in mediation.[179] The Central London County Court Mediation Pilot also revealed that the average settlements achieved in mediated cases were lower than those achieved amongst the sample of cases where mediation was rejected or where mediation was not offered.[180] Genn explains the findings by the fact that the majority of cases settling in mediation did so on the basis that each side would bear their own legal costs.[181] She suggests that it is possible that claimants were prepared to discount claims during mediation as a trade off for earlier settlement.[182] The authors' 2000 survey also provides support, with 11.5% of respondents indicating that their clients had achieved cost advantages using mediation, by avoiding payment of costs to the other party in accordance with the terms of the mediated settlement.

Even if the settlement reached in mediation is adequate, or better than the likely outcome at trial, both US and UK evidence suggests that plaintiffs may continue to

---

Society Gazette, 8 June 2000, at p 9. See the sections on Impartiality and Neutrality in Chapter 11 for a further consideration of the issue.

175 University of Newcastle upon Tyne Conciliation Project Unit, *Report to the Lord Chancellor's Department on the costs and effectiveness of conciliation in England and Wales*, March 1989, at p 124.

176 C McEwen and R Maiman 'Small Claims Mediation in Maine: an empirical assessment' (1981) 33 *Maine Law Review* 237, where only 12% of mediated settlements involved conditions other than payment.

177 H Genn *Central London County Court Mediation Pilot: Evaluation Report*, LCD Research Series, No 5/98, at p 65.

178 Ibid; and C Menkel-Meadow 'The Transformation of Disputes by Lawyers: what the dispute paradigm does and does not tell us' (1985) *Journal of Dispute Resolution* 31 at 33.

179 S Clarke, E Ellen and K McCormick *Court-Ordered Civil Mediation in North Carolina: an evaluation*, State of Justice Institute, 1995.

180 H Genn *Central London County Court Mediation Pilot: Evaluation Report*, LCD Research Series, No 5/98, at p 66. The study found that the average settlement in mediated claims was about £2,000 lower than in non-mediated settlements: at p vi.

181 Ibid, at pp 88 and 90.

182 Ibid, at p 66.

feel, even after a successful mediation, that they are owed the full amount of their claim.[183] These factors show that the efficiency claims still require substantiation in terms of actual mediation experiences measured against other dispute resolution processes.

Mediation and Justice

One of the concerns about mediation developments relates to their implications for justice between the mediating parties, and for the justice system as a whole. Here the point of reference is the justice system provided by law and the courts. This system is depicted as having the following features:

(a) a set of legal rules and principles;
(b) which are applied by independent courts;
(c) to all persons equally;
(d) through a process which is procedurally fair; and
(e) in which substantive outcomes are determined through the objective application of established norms of general applicability.

This depiction is somewhat idealised in that it overlooks the ambiguity of legal language, the need for discretion in its interpretation, the potential conflicts among legal rules and principles, and the complicating effects of legal formalism, technicality and ritual in the court process. It also makes unwarranted assumptions about the accessibility of court-based justice, in terms of a person's ability to afford it, their understanding of it, and their comfort levels when involved in it. Nevertheless, objectivity, rationality, regard for precedent and formal equality before the law are so firmly linked to our idea of justice '. . . that [some] disputants feel that real justice is denied them unless a bewigged judge, symbolising the majesty of the law, hands down a ruling firmly based on the ruling in a past case'.[184] Against this background is a number of persistent concerns about the justice implications of mediation, both in relation to its internal procedures and in relation to broader societal interests.[185]

The concerns about second class justice, privatised justice and procedural fairness

One of the concerns about mediation is that it provides 'second class' justice for those who cannot afford the 'first class' model, justice through the courts. Its further development will result in a 'two-track' system of justice.[186] Critics argue that the

---

183 Evidence in the United States comes from surveys of plaintiffs who were owed simple debts or who sought damages for personal injuries: M Galanter 'Quality of Settlements' (1988) *Mo J Dispute Resol* 55. The Central London County Court Mediation Pilot also found that plaintiffs continued to feel that they had been owed the full amount claimed that they had been forced to settle for less than they were entitled to: H Genn, op cit, at p 117.

184 M Thornton 'Mediation policy and the State' (1993) 4 *ADRJ* 230 at 235.

185 S Goldberg et al *Dispute Resolution: Negotiation, Mediation and other Processes* (2nd edn) Little Brown & Co, USA, 1992, at pp 11–13. See also M Fulton *Commercial Alternative Dispute Resolution*, The Law Book Company, Sydney, 1989, at p 99.

186 J Folberg and A Taylor *Mediation – a comprehensive guide to resolving conflicts*

poor and ethnic minorities are encouraged to use mediation solely to free up courts for those who can afford to pay for legal representation.[187] In Australia, for example, evidence for this view is provided by the mandatory use of mediation in legal aid offices, consumer legislation and anti-discrimination tribunals. On this track, it is argued, indigent plaintiffs, victims and complainants are forced to participate in mediation before, and in some cases instead of, their day in court. They are, it is argued, forced to compromise,[188] acknowledging weakness.[189] 10% of respondents to the authors' survey of UK law firms cited this issue as the main disadvantage of mediation. Compromise, it is argued, involves the sacrifice of rights, which represents a cost to the parties.[190] 6% of respondents to the authors' survey referred to this issue as a disadvantage of mediation. A further 9% considered that such compromise can be achieved just as well through direct negotiation. The other track provides the full trappings of formal justice, with all its sophistication and procedural safeguards, for the affluent and privileged. The caravan of judicial justice, it is felt, provides first class seats, and that of mediation justice only economy seats.

Ironically, the converse concern is also expressed, namely that the emergence of sophisticated private mediation services, based on the user-pays principle, will provide a preferred option for the affluent, because of their speed, cost savings and privacy. This will result in fewer resources being made available for free public dispute resolution systems such as the courts, which will become increasingly congested and deprived. This is the concern about 'privatised' justice.[191] It extends to apprehension that well-resourced individuals and organisations will systematically avoid the formal and public evaluation of their practices and manage their disputes confidentially, where they can manipulate smaller parties into settlements without external scrutiny. Burton refers to the problem of mediation providing 'private justice behind closed doors ... with potential for contributing to the concealment of injustice and encouraging the exploitation of the powerless'.[192]

Others suggest that mediation's insulation from public scrutiny may undermine its ability to be seen as a fair process.[193] As with criticism previously levelled at

---

without litigation, Jossey-Bass, San Francisco, 1988, at p 249; and J Auerbach *Justice without law*, Oxford University Press, New York, 1983 at p 144.

187 R Momasic 'Mediation as an alternative to adjudication – Rhetoric to Reality in the neighbourhood justice movement' in Momasic and Feeley (eds) *Common Neighbourhood Justice: Assessment of an emerging idea*, Longman, New York, 1982.

188 Although there have been instances in the UK of parties who have used the mediation process to explain why they consider they have no liability to another party.

189 In one UK insurance case, in which one of the authors had acted as legal representative, one party argued, in defence to a claim for summary judgment, that its case must have some merit since the claimant for summary judgment had suggested mediation. The judge stated that he was not prepared to make any inference from the suggestion to mediate.

190 W Twining 'Alternative to What?' (1993) 56(3) *Modern Law Review* 384; and O Fiss 'Against Settlement' (1984) 93 *Yale Law Journal* 1073.

191 J A Scutt 'The privatisation of justice: power differentials, inequality and the palliative of counselling and mediation' (1988) 11 *Women's Studies International Forum* 503; and O Fiss, ibid. See also H Astor and C Chinkin *Dispute Resolution in Australia*, Butterworths, Sydney, 1992, at pp 55–7.

192 J Burton *The conflict series, vol 3: Readings in Management and Resolution*, St Mary's Press, New York, 1990, at p 27.

193 R J MacCaun, E A Lind and T R Tyler *ADR in Trial and Appellate Courts*, Rand, Santa Monica, California, 1992, at p 100.

arbitration, mediation may become shielded from social responsibility, which is contrary to the public interest.[194] It is argued that large corporations or repeat players use mediation as it can be easily manipulated by them.[195]

The procedural fairness concern revolves around the apparent absence of any due process safeguards in mediation.[196] Critics argue that the mediation process can be abused by a party to delay or procrastinate, in order to gain time in litigation, a factor highlighted by respondents to the Lord Chancellor's ADR Consultation Paper.[197] There are concerns that mediation might be used as a tactical ploy to obtain information that might be useful subsequently at or closer to trial.[198] The authors' 2000 survey of UK law firms revealed that 16% of respondents shared these concerns. Respondents to the survey also pointed to insurers, as having a tendency to abuse mediation to put financial pressure on claimants.[199] Critics complain that parties might lie in mediation and there is no opportunity to test the truth of statements made,[200] or that parties may conceal information which may lead the other party to take a different view of a proposal.[201] Most of these concerns, however, reflect the risks inherent in any negotiation and parties make decisions with these factors in mind.

Another concern is that parties may consider themselves pressured in a mediation to compromise, a feeling shared by 5% of respondents to the authors' survey of UK law firms. This concern is more likely when there are time constraints placed on the mediation, resulting in a sense that the issues have not been properly aired. Time constraints on a mediation may even lead to anger or perceptions of assembly line treatment.[202] The Solicitors' Indemnity Fund conducted a time-capping exercise in the mediations it conducted in 1998. Of the eight cases resolved, six had settled within the three hours set by the exercise and two within five hours.[203] Time-capped

---

194 J Auerbach *Justice Without Law*, OUP, New York, 1983, at pp 112–13.
195 A Sarat 'Alternatives in dispute processing' (1976) 10(3) *Law & Policy* 339; and A Sarat and W Felstiner 'Law & Social Relations' (1988) 22 *Law & Society Review* 737.
196 J Folberg and A Taylor *Mediation – a comprehensive guide to resolving conflicts without litigation*, Jossey-Bass, San Francisco, 1988, at pp 245–50; S Charles 'Natural justice and ADR' (1986) *Law Institute Journal* 1079; G Meggs 'Issues in divorce mediation methodology and ethics' (1993) 4 *ADRJ* 198; and K E Mentzel 'Judging the fairness of mediation: a critical framework' (1990) 1 *MQ* 3.
197 Lord Chancellor's Department *ADR Discussion Paper: Summary of Responses*, August 2000, at para 11. 13% of respondents were concerned that parties might engage in mediation for the wrong reasons, in particular, as a delaying tactic or to put pressure on another party.
198 In an example of a family mediation the couple used the mediation process, ahead of hearings for protection orders, in order to 'blacken each other': University of Newcastle upon Tyne Conciliation Project Unit, *Report to the Lord Chancellor's Department on the cost and effectiveness of conciliation in England and Wales*, March 1989, at p 309. Respondents to the authors' 2000 survey of UK law firms provided a number of examples of such concerns about the use made of mediation by lawyers and experts.
199 Concerns about the tactics of insurance companies were expressed by 8% of respondents.
200 H Genn *Central London County Court Mediation Pilot: Evaluation Report*, LCD Research Series, No 5/98, at p 126.
201 R A Bush *The dilemmas of mediation practice*, National Institute for Dispute Resolution, Washington DC, 1992.
202 J Pearson 'Family Mediation' in *Court Reform Implications of Dispute Resolution*, Ohio State University, 1995, at p 65.
203 Centre for Dispute Resolution *Time-Limited Mediations*, Boughton, March 1999.

mediations were also a feature of the Central London Country Court Mediation Pilot. In most cases, however, parties need time to build trust in the mediator, exchange information and re-evaluate their expectations.[204] The presence of a co-mediator or mediator's pupil could lead to results in shorter periods of time. In a complex case a number of shorter sessions over a period of time could be appropriate.

On the other hand, parties cannot use the process to compel the production of documentation, nor to force others to attend the mediation and provide information. They do not have guaranteed time frameworks in which to prepare their case. There is not the same formal equality on which the legal process is based, as evidenced by the equal rights to present evidence, to test and rebut what the other side has presented, and to make arguments on the facts and the law. Nor does the third party have the same obligations towards fairness and natural justice as are imposed on a judge or magistrate:[205] a mediator could, for example, spend more time with one party in separate meetings than with the other.[206] There is no systemic review of mediator actions, nor are there official records and publicity to provide the basis for mediator accountability. In some contexts these fairness requirements are recognised, for example in precluding anyone who has acted as a mediator from taking any subsequent part in making a binding decision.[207] However, in most mediations there are no necessary procedural justice safeguards.

A response to these concerns is that while mediation does not uphold the principles of court-based justice, it is based on an alternative set of values in which formalism is replaced by informality of procedure, fair trial procedures by direct participation of parties, consistent norm enforcement by norm creation, judicial independence by the involvement of trusted peers, and so on.[208] This presents an alternative conceptualisation of justice. Cappelletti developed a model of 'co-existential justice' (or 'mending justice') to encapsulate the principles of mediation and other forms of ADR.[209] While all models of justice have their particular strengths, mediation justice is distinguished by its direct accessibility, in particular in comparison with the economic obstacles to legal justice, and by its responsiveness to the peculiar needs and interests of the parties. This can be a more appropriate form of justice in the 'total institutions' of modern society in which parties continue to relate after their dispute has been managed, for example in the workplace and in neighbourhood communities.[210] Moreover, skilled mediators can provide equivalent checks and

---

204 Ibid.
205 H Astor and C Chinkin *Dispute Resolution in Australia*, Butterworths, Sydney, 1992, at p 211.
206 Parties in the Central London County Court Mediation Pilot complained about the time that a mediator spends with another party in a private session: H Genn *Central London County Court Mediation Pilot: Evaluation Report*, LCD Research Series, No 5/98, at p 113.
207 For example, cases that are mediated by the Settlement Judges in the Primary Dispute Resolution Centre of the Subordinate Courts in Singapore but are not settled would not go before the same judges for adjudication as a matter of public policy and practice. This also applies to Commercial Court judges in England who provide an early neutral evaluation: see Chapter 7 for further details on UK court mediation schemes.
208 See 'The Value Claims of Mediation' at pages **33–42**.
209 M Cappelletti 'ADR processes within the framework of the world-wide access to justice movement' (1993) 56 *Modern Law Review* 282. See H Brown and A Marriott *ADR Principles and Practice* (2nd edn), Sweet & Maxwell, London, 1999, at pp 406–9.
210 M Cappelletti, ibid, at p 290.

balances to the formal safeguards, and assumptions of equality, in the court system, and can ultimately terminate the mediation if it is being abused. Parties can make use of advisers, including lawyers, and there can be a 'cooling off' period in the settlement agreement. As a final safeguard, mediation operates under the potential supervision of the law, such that extremely oppressive settlement terms could be set aside on grounds of unconscionability.

The power concern

The question of power raises two critical issues in relation to mediation. First, there is concern that certain relationships are not amenable to mediation because of the discrepancies in power between the parties. This is a policy question which is considered below. The second question concerns appropriate mediator strategies where, in the course of a mediation, one of the parties is either overpowering or disempowered. This is a practical issue which is dealt with in Part II.[211]

There are many contexts in which the issue of power imbalance is regarded as so potentially serious that it calls into question the appropriateness of mediation. The basis of the concern is that inequalities of power may be reflected in outcomes, rendering them fundamentally unfair and unreasonable. The *facilitative* model of mediation implies no mediator responsibility for a mediated outcome. It could fall outside the normal range for such disputes, as determined by the industry in question, the courts in that jurisdiction, or community standards laid down in legislation or conventional morality. This is always a prospect in unassisted negotiations. However, in most situations in which a third party intervenes in conflict, that person is a decision-maker, such as a judge or arbitrator, who decides in terms of objective principles and not in terms of who is the stronger party.[212] The question arises as to whether mediation is appropriate if it affords no further protection to weaker parties than is the case in unassisted negotiations.

There are several specific contexts in which the issue of power imbalance is regarded as highly significant. A first is gender-based power differences in areas such as matrimonial disputes. Here there is concern that because of gender-related inequalities of power in marriage and in the wider society, it is difficult for women to negotiate from a position of equality in mediation. The power differential is caused by many factors, including political, financial and psychological. It involves unequal access to resources, including lawyers, limited educational and employment opportunities, perceptions of domination and submission, high anxiety and low confidence, and unfamiliarity with negotiation techniques. These structural inequalities cannot be redressed in the mediation process, and there is concern that it is incapable of empowering women procedurally and of achieving substantive justice for them.[213] There is a concern that disempowered women in family mediations might

---

211 See Chapter 5.
212 In a recent study of family mediators and solicitors, the differences in approach were apparent: mediators focused on fairness of process, whereas solicitors focused on fairness of outcome (see F Myers and F Wasoff *A meeting in the middle—a study of solicitors' and mediators' divorce practice*, Scottish Executive, 2000, Chapter 6).
213 See for example, M Leitch 'The politics of compromise: a feminist perspective on mediation' (1986–7) 14–15 *MQ* 163; J Rifkin 'Mediation from a feminist perspective: promise and problems' (1994) 2 *Law and Inequality* 21; and N Seaman *Fair shares?*

compromise on their property entitlements, or make concessions on them in the hope of maintaining good relations. However, it would be simplistic to over-generalise on the issue of gender and power. Women will not be in the inferior bargaining position in all cases, and even if they were, the mediation emphasis on dialogue might still be a better option than the litigation emphasis on rights,[214] given the reality that no dispute resolution method can altogether mitigate power differences.

Mediation is particularly problematic in cases of domestic violence, which can result in chronic disempowerment for the victim.[215] Again, there are differences between those who argue that there can never be mediation where there is a history of domestic violence and those who argue that, subject to a range of safety precautions, victims should be able to give their informed consent to the process. The Australian National Committee on Violence Against Women has developed guidelines for use in mediating cases involving violence against women.[216] The guidelines revolve around three principles: the safety of the victim is a paramount consideration over mediated agreements; mediation should never be an alternative to legal protections and remedies; and mediation is only viable where there is free and informed consent by the victim. These principles require a range of practical precautions and techniques to be undertaken by mediators and mediation services.[217]

There are several other areas in which power imbalances can be problematic:

(a) In environmental disputes between conservation groups, on one hand, and developers, big business and government, on the other. Here the power differential is caused by structural factors, such as unequal access to resources, legal assistance, expert opinion and the news media.

(b) In anti-discrimination cases between victims of discrimination and the alleged perpetrators, particularly where the latter are large employers, educational institutions or traders, where the imbalance is caused by ignorance of the relevant standards of behaviour or legal procedures, language difficulties and precarious job security. Complainants in these matters emanate from marginal groups in society such as immigrants, non English-speakers and intellectually- or physically-impaired persons.

Barriers to equitable property settlements, Women Legal Services Network, Canberra, at p 23. A Prior 'What do the parties think?' (1993) 4 *ADRJ* 99, found no suggestion of perceived disempowerment for women in a survey of family mediations.

214 H Astor and C Chinkin *Dispute Resolution in Australia*, Butterworths, Sydney, 1992, at p 22.

215 R Field 'The use of litigation and mediation for the resolution of custody and access disputes: a survey of QLD Family Law Solicitors' (1996) 7 *ADRJ* 5 at 12, where the majority of Queensland family law solicitors surveyed believed that in situations of domestic violence, mediation is not appropriate.

216 Prepared by H Astor, 1992. See also Astor's *Position Paper on Mediation and violence against women*, prepared for the Australian National Committee on Violence against Women (NCVAW), 1991. Community Justice programmes in Australia have long had similar guidelines. The NCVAW has also prepared a booklet, *Women and Mediation*, Office of the Status of Women, Department of the Prime Minister and Cabinet, Canberra, 1992. See also T Grillo 'The mediation alternative: process dangers for women' (1991) 100 *Yale Law Review* 1545; J Rifkin 'Mediation from a feminist perspective: promise and problems' (1994) 2 *Law and Inequality* 21; and H Astor and C Chinkin *Dispute Resolution in Australia*, Butterworths, Sydney, 1992, at pp 257–60.

217 H Astor 'Elizabeth's story: mediation, violence and the legal academy' (1997)

(c) Between plaintiffs and insurers in personal injury cases,[218] between consumers and large business in fair trading disputes, and between citizens and government in administrative law issues.

These situations all pose difficulties for mediation. Where the stronger party can call on resources of power to achieve its way, it may be very difficult for the weaker party to engage in problem-solving techniques. Although mediation has the same equality assumptions as the legal system, it does not have the coercive powers to redress the imbalance. Thus a court can order the disclosure of relevant information by an employer, but a mediator cannot.

Despite the concerns, many matters are mediated where there are power differences. It is partly a function of informed choice: it is generally agreed that where the disempowered party understands the nature of the process and its constraints, he or she should be allowed the choice to participate. It is also relevant that no dispute resolution method, including litigation with its due process and equality assumptions, can ever mitigate all power differences.[219] Power is a phenomenon influenced by many factors and cannot always be translated directly into a satisfactory outcome for the power-wielder.[220] The apparently weaker party may have significant sources of power other than funds or lawyers. The apparently stronger party may be unwilling to wield its power. And finally, a skilled and aware mediator does have techniques and precautions, both before and during the mediation, to deal with some of the potential problems. Some commentators go so far as to assert that the mediation process is particularly suited to addressing and redressing power imbalances.[221]

The public interest concerns

There are a number of public interest concerns about mediation, relating to matters beyond the confines of the immediate dispute being mediated. When a court makes a decision it is not only resolving a dispute between the parties, it is also acting as the trustee of the public interest and espousing societal norms.[222] It balances competing values and authoritatively resolves important issues of policy, for example whether an employer should be liable for a worker's ill-health caused by passive

---

2 *Flinders Journal of Law Reform* 13.

218 K Burns 'Whose party is it anyway? The role of the insured in the mediation process' (1999) 1(8) *The ADR Bulletin* 102; D Alcorn 'Mediation and the psychologically injured plaintiff' (1996) 1 *Queensland University of Technology Law Journal* 162.

219 C Menkel-Meadow 'Towards another view of legal negotiations: the structure of problem-solving' (1993–4) *University of California Law Review* 754 at 835; and H Astor and C Chinkin *Dispute Resolution in Australia*, Butterworths, Sydney, 1992, at p 91. See also the classic article of M Galanter 'Why the "haves" come out ahead: speculations on the limits of legal change' (1974) 9 *Law and Society Review* 95.

220 R Fisher 'Negotiating power – getting and using influence' (1983) 27 *American Behavioural Scientist* 149; B Mayer 'The dynamics of power in mediation and negotiation' (1987) 16 *MQ* 75. See R Charlton and M Dewdney *The Mediator's Handbook: skills and strategies for practitioners*, The Law Book Company, Sydney, 1995, at p 239 for a discussion of situations where power was found not to be what it seemed.

221 For example, A Davis and R Salem 'Dealing with power imbalances in the mediation of interpersonal disputes' (1984) 6 *MQ* 17.

222 O Fiss 'Against Settlement' (1984) 93 *Yale Law Journal* 1073.

smoking at work or whether a small business in financial difficulties should be able to rescind a loan agreement on the ground that the terms assented to are oppressive. A decision of a court, moreover, acts as a standard for future community behaviour and a precedent for the resolution of subsequent disputes of a similar nature. Mediation should not be used where society requires an authoritative decision on a matter of wide community interest, for setting policy priorities or for allocating public resources. It could also deprive the legal system of important precedents which would otherwise be handed down by the courts.[223] By encouraging private compromise, and reducing the stock of precedent, it is argued that more inefficient litigation will result.[224] 4% of respondents to the authors' survey of UK law firms referred to this issue when discussing disadvantages of mediation. Commentators also argue that mediation trivialises issues by reducing the public perception of the importance of laws, which may address important rights, by placing these issues outside the legal system.[225] In the case of victim/offender mediation, there are concerns that an accused might agree to mediation, solely to impress the court in the hope that charges might be dropped or the sentence might be reduced.[226]

There is also concern that the increasing institutionalisation of mediation[227] provides more potential control for governments.[228] While community mediation programmes are justified in terms of community needs, they are subject to governmental policies and are dependent on government funding. In effect they involve a shift of dispute resolution away from the courts, the political process and community organisations, towards a system controlled by the executive arm of government. Bureaucracies do not have the institutional independence of the courts, nor are they subject to the cut and thrust of the public political process. By encouraging parties into such systems, governments could be deflecting challenges to social policy and other features of the political system and serving to maintain the social order.[229] Government control also makes inroads into the concept of mediator neutrality.

There are a number of other dimensions to the public interest concern. One relates to the protection of the interests of parties who are not present in the mediation but are directly affected by the outcome.[230] Examples would be other consumers in fair trading and product liability disputes, and children in matrimonial disputes. The mediator is not normally regarded as the trustee for these groups when settlements which may affect them are negotiated through mediation. Another public interest

---

223 L Street 'The court system and alternative dispute resolution procedures' (1990) 1 *ADRJ* 5 at 5–6.
224 M Galanter and J Lande 'Private Courts and Public Authority' (1992) 12 *Studies in Law Politics & Society* 393 at 398; and G Bryant 'Privatisation in the new market for disputes: a framework for analysis and a preliminary assessment' (1992) 12 *Studies in Law, Politics and Society* 367 at 375.
225 Woods 'Mediation: A backlash to women's progress on family law issues' (1985) 19 *Clearinghouse Review* 431 at 435.
226 R E Mackay and A J Brown *Community Mediation in Scotland: a study of implementation*, The Scottish Office Central Research Unit, Edinburgh, 1999.
227 See Chapter 13.
228 M Thornton 'Mediation policy and the State' (1993) 4 *ADRJ* 230 at 233; and A M Herriott 'ADR – a threat to democracy? (1994) 19 *Alternative Law Journal* 75.
229 R Abel (ed) *The Politics of Informal Justice, vol 1*, Academic Press, New York 1982, at p 181.
230 See the section on Enforceability of Mediated Agreements in Chapter 12.

concern relates to accountability and control in the mediation movement. These matters are dealt with in a later chapter.[231]

Judicial policy on mediation

Court-connected mediation and other institutionalised forms of the process add support to the justice claims of mediation, without allaying all the fairness and equality concerns. These expressions of judicial policy may become highly relevant when courts are asked to enforce mediation clauses in contracts or to maintain the confidentiality of the mediation process.

Competing Motivations in the Promotion of Mediation

Mediation is promoted by a vast array of individuals, professional organisations and public and private institutions.[232] Different groups are motivated by very different features of mediation in their promotion of it. Five such groups are identified below:

(a)   First are those for whom mediation is an expression of an alternative philosophy of conflict management. They promote mediation in terms of its underlying philosophy and normative objectives, for example its capacity for empowering the parties and for improving relationships.

(b)   Second are the voluntary and private users of mediation for whom questions of delay, cost and management time are important factors in dispute resolution. Mediation is seen to be able to satisfy these interests. Further, the promise of confidentiality and privacy through mediation can be attractive features for corporations in commercial disputes or insurers in personal injury disputes, although they would be unattractive features for voluntary associations in environmental disputes or local authorities in public issue disputes.

(c)   Third are governments, which in numerous countries now promote the use of mediation. Publicly, governments may promote mediation in terms of the principles and justice claims already referred to. However, the various organs of government may have other less public motivations as well. For legislatures mediation has good public relations value at a time when the formal legal system and legal profession are undergoing criticism; it appears to be a politically popular option.[233] For political executives it appears to make sense in terms of efficiency and economic rationalism; expensive courts and their infrastructure run counter to the principle of 'user pays' for private disputes.[234] For the courts, heavy case loads require more efficient forms of case management; although it has been observed that courts

---

231 On accountability and control in mediation, see Chapters 11 and 12.
232 See Chapter 7 for an outline of the various groups and individuals who are instrumental in the development of mediation in the UK.
233 M Dawson 'Non-consensual alternative dispute resolution: pros and cons' (1993) 4 *ADRJ* 173 at 173–4.
234 See M Thornton 'Mediation policy and the State' (1993) 4 *ADRJ* 230 at 235. Some American evidence disputes the view that mediation reduces court workloads: see

sometimes maintain their ADR programmes even when researchers cannot demonstrate the touted benefits of such programmes.[235]

(d) Fourth are the professional associations which promote mediation in terms of their members' interests. The current competition between professions, and the blurring of traditional professional boundaries, has prompted professional associations to investigate alternative services for those under threat from rival professions. Mediation is one such service.

(e) Finally there are the private mediation services, which promote mediation out of entrepreneurial considerations on a fee-for-service basis.

The result is a host of competing and at times conflicting motivations for the development of mediation. Government demands for efficiency are likely to manipulate mediation into forms not countenanced by those for whom it is an expression of an alternative philosophy of conflict management. This is not to suggest that government-initiated services are not worthwhile or that services developed by professional associations do not provide high-quality mediation. However, the possible conflicting motivations highlight the fact that mediation is in the crucible of politics, economics, professional interests and ideological debate. In this context it is no surprise that it takes on many shapes, forms and value orientations.

K Kressel and D Pruitt 'Themes in the mediation of social conflict' (1985) 41 *Journal of Social Issues* 179 at 398.

235 M Dawson 'Non-consensual alternative dispute resolution: pros and cons' (1993) 4 *ADRJ* 173 at 173–4.

3

Mediation as a Comparative Dispute Resolution Process

Mediation and Dispute Resolution Options

One of the major issues affecting mediation is the question of when it is appropriate as a dispute resolution method. The development of mediation in many societies in the late twentieth century is part of a broader trend affecting law and other disciplines. This trend is reflected in the alternative dispute resolution ('ADR') movement which has involved an investigation and evaluation of alternative methods of dispute resolution to those provided by the courts. Developments in ADR have been influenced by reactions against litigation and the demand for additional processes which are quicker, cheaper and otherwise more appropriate. They have been inspired by social philosophies which propose dispute management processes which are participatory, responsive and concerned with preserving relationships among those involved. However, mediation is not the only outcome of this recent phenomenon and its appropriateness must be evaluated in relation to that of other dispute resolution systems.

In broad terms, disputes can be dealt with at three levels:[1]

- *The power level:* Parties in conflict can engage in a contest of strength, through the political process, industrial action or armed conflict. These options operate at the level of power, and the dispute is resolved in favour of the more powerful party, regardless of any rights or standards.
- *The rights level:* Parties in conflict can present their dispute to an authoritative institution or individual, such as a court, parent or manager, to make a decision as to which party is in the right. This form of decision-making operates at the level of rights, in the sense that the party who has the law or other societal standards on their side will be held to prevail.
- *The interests level:* Parties in conflict can attempt, either on their own, or with varying degrees of assistance, to negotiate their way to an agreed settlement. This option operates at the level of interests, and the negotiations attempt to

---

1   W Ury et al *Getting disputes resolved: designing systems to cut the cost of conflict*, Jossey-Bass, San Francisco, 1986, at pp 3–10. Theoretically, a further form of ADR is 'avoidance', where the parties cease relations: W Felstiner 'Influences of Social Organisation on Dispute Processing' (1974) 9 *Law & Society Review* 69.

advance and reconcile the parties' interests as far as possible. Depending on the context of the negotiations, rights and power may not be of major importance at this level.

Each level of dispute management has its advantages and shortcomings.[2] As a general proposition it can be said that the interests approach is less costly and more beneficial for disputants than a rights approach, which in turn is less costly and more beneficial than a power approach. Where a dispute resolution system focuses on interests, it is likely to involve lower transaction costs, greater satisfaction with outcomes, less strain on relationships and a lower likelihood of the dispute recurring. However, some circumstances may not be conducive to interest-based resolutions, for example where questions of discrimination or civil liberties are at issue, and in these cases the rights approach may be needed. Likewise some questions of policy on issues such as abortion, land rights, or the decriminalisation of drugs are difficult to resolve at the rights or interests levels and have to be resolved through formal or informal power contests.

Mediation is one of the processes which operates at the interests level. It is considered here in relation to other processes which operate at the rights or interests levels.[3]

Mediation and other Dispute Resolution Processes

Mediation and negotiation

Negotiation is sometimes referred to as a 'primary' dispute resolution process.[4] This indicates that it cannot be reduced into constituent elements, and that it is itself an element in other dispute resolution processes, including mediation. It also implies that negotiation is often the most obvious, accessible and immediate way of dealing with conflict, whether between two parties or among many. Most negotiations, whether between business enterprises, between individuals and government, or among neighbours, involve the parties themselves dealing directly with the problem through traditional procedures of bargaining, compromise and adjustment. Negotiation is an infinitely flexible process as regards formality, time, party participation, focus and outcomes, though outcomes are sometimes influenced by legal and social standards.[5] There are also many different approaches and techniques which can be adopted in negotiation.[6]

Where negotiation takes place between the parties alone it can be referred to as *unassisted negotiation*. In some situations experts, lawyers or specialist negotiators

---

2 W Ury et al, ibid; and H Astor and C Chinkin *Dispute Resolution in Australia*, Butterworths, Sydney, 1992, at pp 30–53.
3 See Chapter 7 for a discussion of courts and mediation.
4 On the elements of negotiation, see Chapter 2.
5 M Eisenberg 'Private ordering through negotiation: dispute settlement and rulemaking' (1976) 89 *Harvard Law Review* 637 at 650–1.
6 On approaches to negotiation, see Chapter 2.

also participate in the process as partisan advisers and resource persons for the respective parties; this can be termed *supported negotiation*.[7] In other situations outsiders are involved, not in a partisan capacity but so as to facilitate the negotiations, which can be referred to as *assisted negotiation*. Mediation is the main form of assisted negotiation.

The difference between mediation and unassisted negotiation is found in the involvement of an additional person, the mediator, who is not an immediate party to the dispute. Whether the mediator has been invited by the parties to intervene, or has been appointed by an authority, his or her role is essentially to assist, as opposed to support, the disputants in their negotiations. As is shown in this book, the forms of assistance can differ greatly. However, whereas negotiation has no standard structure, all forms of mediation provide some kind of structural framework for the negotiation process. Mediation adds formality to negotiation in the form of some degree of process and control provided by the mediator.

Critics of mediation query the extent to which the involvement of a third party without decision-making powers makes mediation any different to unassisted negotiations. This question is based partly on the assumption that where a party intervenes in a conflict he or she should either act as the adviser of one of the parties or should fix the problem by making a binding decision. Particular criticism of mediation comes from lawyers who argue that they bring most of their clients' disputes to a negotiated conclusion, albeit sometimes on the steps of the court, and that a mediator could contribute little to an already effective system.[8] In the *settlement* model of mediation it is correct that the mediator chairs the process and does not contribute significantly to the nature and style of the negotiations. However, in the *facilitative* model there are a number of qualitative changes which mediators can bring to negotiations. The mediator can assist in the establishment and maintenance of negotiation guidelines, in providing structure and momentum, in improving the communication process, in imparting problem-solving techniques to the parties and in confronting the parties with the consequences of non-settlement. The mediation process and mediator techniques tend to moderate extreme behaviour, to facilitate creative option generation and to promote more efficient and productive problem-solving than is the case in unassisted negotiations. In these ways mediation differs qualitatively from other negotiations.[9]

Mediation and conciliation

Conciliation is a form of assisted negotiation between two or more parties in which an additional person, the conciliator, intervenes in various ways with the object of facilitating a settlement between the parties. However, there is as little agreement on the definition of conciliation as there is on that of mediation and there is an extensive

---

7   This is the expression of S Roberts 'Mediation in family disputes' (1983) 46 *Modern Law Review* 537 at 544. The 'support' can range from mere moral support to the supporter acting as the party's 'champion'.
8   See the section on Efficiency and Mediation at pages **54–66**.
9   This is not to deny that some lawyers may play a mediative role in unassisted negotiations; they may also act as quasi-mediators in a formal mediation.

debate on the differences and similarities between the two processes.[10] In all versions of this debate there are many areas of overlap between mediation and conciliation, for example in relation to their flexible procedures. However, some commentators maintain that there are also differences of definition, and that conciliation should be positioned on the mid-point of a spectrum, with mediation at one end and arbitration at the other.[11] The following points are made to substantiate this view:

(a) Conciliation is provided by public agencies and does not often take place in the private domain. It is therefore an 'institutionalised' dispute resolution system, and does not have mediation's 'alternative' character.

(b) Conciliation takes place in a statutory context which provides legal rules and standards. Conciliators are obliged to advocate these rules and standards, and therefore they are less 'neutral' than are mediators in some forms of mediation.[12] As the shadow of the law is strong in conciliation, there are limitations on the kinds of settlements to which the parties can agree.

(c) Conciliation is sometimes obligatory for the respondent or for both parties, and there are sanctions for non-participation in the process; it is less 'voluntary' than mediation.

(d) Conciliators have more 'interventionist' roles than mediators. They can intervene more actively on matters of content by referring to possible options, recommending various solutions, and otherwise influencing the parties and affecting the outcome.

(e) Conciliation systems are sometimes intended to have an educative dimension for one or more parties involved, with respondents sometimes committing themselves to specific improvements and to general programmes designed to avoid future problems.

(f) Where a conciliation is unsuccessful, there is usually provision for referring the matter to a board or administrative tribunal which resolves it through a binding decision based on the relevant rules and policies.

Other commentators point to the many variables in both mediation and conciliation, which make it impossible to distinguish between them in any meaningful sense. Each of the above assertions about conciliation could also be made, to some degree, about mediation, and definitional terms such as 'neutral', 'voluntary' and 'interventionist' are notoriously difficult to pin down. Thus the *evaluative* model of mediation is just as 'interventionist' and quasi-arbitral as conciliation. It is also interesting to note that in some writings, and in some countries, the terms are used in ways opposite to those presented earlier.[13]

---

10 J Riekert 'Alternative dispute resolution in Australian commercial disputes: quo vadis? (1990) 1 *ADRJ* 22; H Astor and C Chinkin *Dispute Resolution in Australia*, Butterworths, Sydney, 1992, at pp 61–4; N Mulcahy 'Conciliation and race complaints' (1992) 3 *ADRJ* 21; and J Wade 'Mediation – the terminological debate' (1994) 5 *ADRJ* 204.

11 J Riekert, ibid, at p 33.

12 D Bryson 'Mediator and advocate: conciliating human rights' (1990) 1 *ADRJ* 136. Bryson defines conciliation as 'mediation within a legal framework', with the conciliator acting as 'an advocate for the law while remaining impartial to the parties'.

13 See for example the definitions of P Condliffe *Conflict Management – a practical guide*, TAFE Publications, Abbotsford, Victoria, 1991, at p 24; L Susskind et al (eds) *The Consensus Building Handbook – a comprehensive guide to reaching agreement*, Sage Publications, California, 1999, at p 616, and further at p 629 wherein 'conciliation' is described as a 'process of building positive social relationships between disputing parties through site visits, casual conversations, facilitated workshops and so forth'.

Although the term 'conciliation' is gradually being disused in the UK, nevertheless a range of UK ADR organisations provide this process.[14] Two types of conciliation processes are evident:

- An informal procedure designed to facilitate communication between the parties, where the conciliator is not a decision-maker for the parties.[15]
- An evaluative process in which the conciliator recommends a solution to the dispute.[16]

Conciliation in the family context needs to be distinguished from reconciliation, which attempts to re-unite spouses.[17] Confidentiality and expeditiousness are common characteristics of all conciliation processes. The conciliation rules of a range of ADR organisations provide for degrees of formality.[18]

The preferable view is that there are insufficient differences between mediation and conciliation to justify distinct definitions. The terms can be used interchangeably. More important than definitional distinction is an appreciation of the breadth of both processes and an understanding of what is intended by the terms in particular contexts.[19] For reasons of convenience, only the word mediation is used in this book, unless conciliation is employed in a statute or other source.

Mediation and counselling

Counselling is a skilled process designed to deal with the emotional, behavioural or psychological problems of a client. There is a great deal of diversity in the practice of counselling but most forms have the objective of redressing a pathology or malfunction, or at least of bringing the client to terms with it.

---

14 For example, UK Employment Advisory Conciliation and Arbitration Service ('ACAS'), Arab-British Chamber of Commerce, Institute of Civil Engineers, Chartered Institute of Arbitrators and a wide-range of Ombudsman and Consumer Dispute Resolution Schemes (Banking, Building Societies, Pension and Insurance Ombudsmen); The National Consumer Credit Federation; Qualitas; The Personal Investment Authority; The Mail Order Traders' Association; and The Scottish Motor Trade Association.

15 For example, ACAS.

16 There are a number of examples of this type of conciliation in the UK. The Chartered Institute of Arbitrators' Consumer Dispute Resolution Scheme provides that a conciliator's report, together with the conciliator's suggestions for settlement, will form the basis of a possible agreement between the parties. The Institute of Civil Engineers' Conciliation Procedure provides that, if the parties cannot reach a negotiated solution, the conciliator will make a recommendation as to how the matter should be settled. For further information, see the section on Mediation Organisations in Chapter 7.

17 See the Glossary section in H Brown and A Marriott, *ADR Principles and Practice* (2nd edn), Sweet & Maxwell, London, 1999; and University of Newcastle upon Tyne Conciliation Project Unit, *Report to the Lord Chancellor's Department on the costs and effectiveness of conciliation in England and Wales*, March 1989, at p 11.

18 Compare International Chamber of Commerce (ICC) Rules of Optional Conciliation with the UNCITRAL Conciliation Rules and the ICSID Rules of Procedure for Conciliation, which, in terms of formality, are similar to arbitration rules.

19 As J Wade 'Mediation – the terminological debate' (1994) 5 *ADRJ* 204 at 207 points out, the distinction can be politically significant where public funds are allocated to 'mediation' or 'conciliation'. This tends to reinforce demarcation lines.

There are many differences between mediation and counselling. While the primary object of mediation is to make practical and efficient decisions about disputes, the primary object of counselling is to address long-term issues of behaviour, growth, or moral development.[20] Mediation does not offer long-term intervention therapy, nor is it concerned with psychological or behavioural problems, other than to the extent that these prevent the parties from making decisions. The focus in mediation is not on personal change, as it is in counselling, nor does it require a therapeutic relationship between professional and client. While mediation involves two or more parties with an interpersonal conflict, counselling sometimes involves only one party with an intra-personal problem. Counselling deals more with the past, in relation to the causal factors which lead to the problem, whereas mediation deals mainly with the present and future and gives less attention to past causes.

Nevertheless, there are similarities between mediation and counselling, both of which belong to the 'helping professions'. Egan depicts three stages in the practices of the helping professions:[21]

Stages in Helping		
Stage	**Scenario**	**Activities**
Stage 1	The present scenario	• Telling the story • Focusing • New perspectives
Stage 2	The preferred scenario	• New scenarios • Critique • Choice and commitment
Stage 3	Helping clients act	• Brainstorming strategies • Formulating a plan

There are clear parallels between these stages and the structure of mediation.[22] Moreover, in the *therapeutic* model, mediation does have counselling features.[23] It may, for example, deal initially with the need to empower one party in the same way in which this is dealt with in short-term counselling. Even where mediation does not

---

20 J Folberg and A Taylor *Mediation: a comprehensive guide to resolving conflicts without litigation*, Jossey-Bass, San Francisco, 1998, at pp 28–36; J Haynes 'Mediation and therapy: an alternative view' (1992) 10 *MQ* 21; and M Meltsner 'The jagged line between mediation and couples therapy' (1993) 9 *Negotiation Journal* 261.
21 G Egan *The skilled helper: a systematic approach to effective helping* (5th edn) Brooks/Cole Publishing, Pacific Grove, California, 1994, at p 7.
22 On the stages in a mediation, see Chapter 4.
23 Any dispute resolution process, including litigation, can have therapeutic benefits, particularly for the 'successful' party, but this would only be an incidental benefit and not a primary objective.

have a discrete therapeutic phase, it may serve to change the way in which parties perceive conflict, the way in which they relate to one another, and the way in which they act in resolving the matters in dispute.

Because of the overlaps between counselling and mediation in family disputes, some writers argue that it is possible and desirable to integrate therapy and mediation within the same system.[24] The balance, however, is a delicate one. If emotional issues are dealt with beyond a certain point, they may make it more difficult to negotiate on pressing practicalities, such as the need to pay the credit card bill within a few days. The difficulty of achieving this balance is revealed in the changing views of a prominent family mediator, John Haynes.[25] In his early writing, Haynes argued that mediation should first deal with the emotions involved in conflict, in order to provide the basis for coming to a practical resolution of that conflict. Here he depicted mediation in social work terms, involving a combination of social work problem-solving and therapy skills. More recently he has argued that combining the mediation and social work roles is confusing for both the parties and the mediator, and it might prevent the parties from negotiating an agreement on practical matters. While it is necessary for the mediator to acknowledge emotional issues, if the conflict is the product of serious psychological problems, mediation is inappropriate and the party should be referred to counselling.

Despite these views on the relationship between mediation and counselling, several working models of *therapeutic* family mediation have been developed.[26] These models begin with a therapeutic stage in which counselling is undertaken with the parties individually before the mediation. As the process unfolds:

- children are seen by therapists;
- professionals qualified in child and developmental psychology who understand the couple's and children's dynamics are used;
- disempowered parties are assisted with assertiveness skills;
- lawyers are consulted before any agreement is signed; and
- there is provision for structured monitoring of the mediated agreements.[27]

The advantages of these systems are that they can be used in circumstances where the non-therapeutic models of mediation might be inappropriate because of the emotional state of one or both of the parties. They avoid the necessity to choose between two potentially beneficial forms of skilled help. Co-mediation provides a convenient structure in which two professionals, one with counselling and the other with mediation skills, can combine their expertise for the benefit of the parties.[28]

---

24 E Renouf 'The uneasy sixth stage of mediation' (1992) 3 *ADRJ* 257 at 259. On the relationship between 'therapy' and 'structure', see G Meggs 'Issues in divorce mediation – methodology and ethics' (1993) 4 *ADRJ* 198.

25 J Haynes *Divorce Mediation: a practical guide for therapists and counsellors*, Springer Publishing, New York, 1981; and J Haynes *The fundamentals of family mediation*, New York Press, Albany, 1994. In the latter work, he refers to his own change of views, at pp 28–9.

26 E Renouf, op cit, at pp 259–62. These practical models do not necessarily coincide exactly with the paradigm model referred to above, in Chapter 1.

27 Ibid, at p 261.

28 T Gee and P Urban 'Co-mediation in the family court' (1994) 5 *ADRJ* 42 at 46. On co-mediation, see Chapter 4.

Mediation and private adjudicatory processes

Arbitration involves the submission of a dispute to an arbitrator who resolves it by making a decision, called an award.[29] The award is normally binding on the parties; it can be enforced through the courts, and it is not subject to appeal or review, except where the arbitrator has misconducted himself or herself or acted unfairly. The arbitrator is required to render a decision in the light of the facts of the case, and these facts are determined on the basis of evidence presented by the parties. The presentation of evidence can take place on an informal basis with few technical rules, or with all the evidential formality and procedural technicalities of court proceedings. After hearing the arguments of the parties or their lawyers, the arbitrator is required to base the decision on relevant legal rules and principles or, where the parties request it, on principles of equity and fairness. Arbitration can be triggered by an arbitration clause in an agreement, by the parties' mutual decision once a dispute has arisen, or through a court referral, on the application of the parties.

Adjudication is a process which leads to the resolution of a dispute, either on an interim or final basis, without requiring recourse to arbitration or litigation first.[30] Adjudication has been statutorily mandated in the case of certain construction disputes[31] by the Housing Grants, Construction and Regeneration Act 1996.[32] If a construction contract, which falls within the ambit of the Act, does not make provision for adjudication, the process will be deemed to be implied, together with the procedural requirements in the Act.[33] The aim of adjudication under the Act is to produce a temporary resolution of a dispute arising in the course of performance of a construction contract. This process provides, therefore, an interim binding assessment, which can be enforced by summary judgment.[34]

These processes share with mediation greater potential flexibility and greater party control than the formal court system. There are also usually private and confidential processes. Mediation differs from these processes in that the mediator is not intended, and does not have the authority, to use his or her expertise to render a decision which is binding on the parties. The difference is strongly evident in *facilitative mediation* where the process/content distinction is more evident; in *evaluative mediation*, by contrast, the mediator performs a quasi-adjudicatory function and the boundary with these other procedures is blurred. Because a mediator is not a formal decision-maker, mediation does not give the same attention to the making of arguments as do the other processes. Another structural difference between the two is that arbitration has a close interaction with the court system, in terms of the parties' ability to obtain court orders to secure direct court enforcement of adjudicatory decisions. This has contributed to these processes becoming legalised and operating within a strong shadow of the law.[35]

---

29 S Henderson *The Dispute Resolution Manual*, DataLegal Publications, Spring Hill, QLD, 1993, at pp 33–6. On arbitration, see Mustill and Boyd *Commercial Arbitration* (2nd edn) 1989.
30 Academy of Experts: *Resolving your Dispute by Mediation* and *The Language of ADR – An International Glossary*.
31 See the section on Construction Disputes in Chapter 8.
32 11 Halsbury's Statutes (4th edn).
33 Section 114.
34 See the section on Construction Disputes in Chapter 8.
35 Hence the quip that arbitration is 'judging without wigs'.

This tendency has caused arbitration, in particular, to fall short of some of the potential ideals of flexibility, informality and efficiency. It tends to be categorised together with litigation, with mediation constituting an alternative to all these forms of adjudication.[36]

Mediation and neutral evaluation/case appraisal

The terms 'neutral evaluation' and 'case appraisal' refer to processes in which a dispute is referred to an independent third party who is required, on the basis of his or her expertise, to furnish a view on the merits of the dispute.[37] Here the two processes are dealt with as one and the same. The aim of the process is to provide a realistic appraisal of the strengths and weaknesses of each party's case. The process is similar to briefing counsel to provide an opinion on the merits, with the distinction that all the parties in dispute commission the same neutral, agree that neutral's terms of reference and receive a copy of the same opinion. Neutral evaluation/case appraisal is a potential option where a dispute requires a determination on a technical, scientific or other specialist issue which the parties may not be able to decide. It overcomes the problem of having two or more partisan experts presenting conflicting opinions on the matter. The evaluator/appraiser has a discretion as to procedure, but the parties could agree on how they should be heard and whether the expert should furnish reasons for the opinion.

Once the parties agree on the evaluator, the preliminary steps involve agreeing on a time, date and place for the process. Terms of reference are usually agreed at a preliminary meeting with the evaluator. The evaluator will often be provided with core bundles of reading materials, including a written statement outlining factors which might help the evaluator to reduce the issues in dispute and to assess the strengths and weaknesses of each party's case. At the evaluation process itself, the evaluator will make an opening statement explaining his or her role and outlining the procedure. Each party then has a brief opportunity, usually between 15 and 30 minutes, to summarise their case. In simpler cases, the entire procedure would be in writing. The evaluation, which is usually made in writing, summarises the strengths and weaknesses of each party's case and indicates the likely litigation outcome.

The process can be merely advisory, or, at the parties' request, it can be binding (sometimes referred to as 'expert determination').[38] Where the evaluation or case appraisal is non-binding, it is intended to constitute the voice of experience which

---

36 But compare Lord Chancellor's Department *ADR Discussion Paper*, November 1999, which includes arbitration in the definition of ADR, and distinguishes it from litigation.

37 L Street 'Binding and non-binding expert appraisal' (1990) 1 *ADRJ* 133. Also see the Lord Chancellor's Department *ADR Discussion Paper*, November 1999, ibid; and Commercial Court, *ADR Guidance Notes*.

38 Expert determination provides parties in dispute with an expert's decision, which is binding on the parties, subject to limited exceptions. Usually, a contract specifies a time limit and method for challenging or appealing an expert's determination. The process has its origins in valuation and technical disputes and a common usage of the process is the determination of rent reviews. The rules of evidence do not apply and the process is not bound by the law of arbitration, although there is a growing body of independent case law on the process: for more detail, see J Kendall *Expert Determination* (2nd edn) FT Law & Tax, London 1996 (3rd edn due in 2001).

will influence the parties in negotiating on their dispute, or in determining what issues to submit to another dispute resolution process. The evaluation may form the basis of a settlement between the parties; provide an incentive for the parties to pursue further negotiations; or an opportunity to narrow the issues which should be tried.[39]

Parties can bind themselves contractually to use evaluation or case appraisal in specified circumstances, or can elect to use the system for all or part of their dispute when conflict arises. Evaluation and case appraisal can also be connected to the court system, where it is sometimes referred to as early neutral evaluation ('ENE').[40] The practice of the Commercial Court in relation to early neutral evaluations allows a judge of that court to offer to provide the evaluation or to arrange for another judge to do so. The judge who provides the evaluation can take no further part in the court proceedings, either for interim applications or at trial.[41] Although early neutral evaluation is used in a number of jurisdictions, like the US and Australia,[42] little use has been made of it at this stage in the UK. The Lord Chancellor's Department Summary of Responses to its ADR Discussion Paper indicates that, although the majority of respondents agreed that early neutral evaluation has a useful role to play in court case management, the following qualifications were made:

- disclosure may be required to make the process effective; and
- if it is conducted by a judge, the evaluation should not be confused with the court's power of summary judgment.[43]

Evaluation/case appraisal and mediation have similar rationales, namely to encourage settlement on a timely and cost-effective basis and to avoid a court hearing. In both systems the parties are provided assistance on a confidential basis with the objective of facilitating a negotiated outcome. They are both informal and flexible systems and allow the parties more potential control than do arbitration and litigation. The evaluator/case appraiser tends, as a matter of practice, to perform a range of mediative functions, such as assisting the parties to explore settlement options, but neither system can guarantee a binding outcome. The main point of difference between the two is that in evaluation/case appraisal the third party is expected to use his or her expertise to influence the outcome by advising on the

---

39 For more detail, see Commercial Court, *ADR Orders in the Commercial Court – Guidance Notes for Litigants an their Lawyers.*

40 Editorial (1993) 4 *ADRJ* 255 at 255–6.

41 *Practice Note Queen's Bench Division (Commercial Court),* 7 June 1996 [1996] 3 All ER 383.

42 A range of empirical studies are available in relation to the use of ENE in the US. For example, for an examination of ENE's ability to improve the prospects for settlement, consider R Oakes *An analysis of early neutral evaluation in the United States District Court for the Eastern District of California,* Spring 1991 (unpublished work, California State University, Sacramento 1991). For an examination of ENE's effect on settlement time, costs and party satisfaction, consider RAND Institute for Civil Justice *An evaluation of mediation and early neutral evaluation under the Civil Justice Reform Act,* RAND Santa Monica, 1996. In Australia, the take-up of ENE may be explained by the imposition in some States of costs sanctions, which apply when the result at trial is not better than that recommended in ENE. ENE is used in Australia in personal injury and family maintenance proceedings.

43 Lord Chancellor's Department *ADR Discussion Paper: Summary of Responses,* August 2000. Available at http://www.open.gov.uk/lcd/consult/civ-just/adr

merits of the case. This is a more 'interventionist' role than the mediator is expected to perform in some models of mediation. It is only *evaluative mediation* that comes close to this function and the distinction between this model and evaluation/case appraisal is more obscure.

Mediation and facilitation

In facilitations, an outsider becomes involved in a problem with the objective of providing assistance to the parties, but without making any binding decisions for them.[44] Facilitators assist the parties in a wide range of matters which might contribute to their decisions, such as information gathering, fact finding, round table conferencing, public meetings, establishing voting criteria and private consultations. Facilitators provide leadership in developing, with the parties, processes and structures suited to the parties' problem, and they assist the parties in communication, negotiation and creative problem-solving. Facilitation is suited to problems with multiple issues and many parties, such as those in planning, land-use and environmental matters.[45] It can also be used in the employment situation, in voluntary associations and in other groups which require organisational cohesion and relationship building. The facilitators can be disinterested outside parties, experts in the area of the dispute, or nominated representatives of the participants.

Facilitation overlaps considerably with mediation and there is no clear-cut distinction between the two. Mediators are often referred to as 'facilitators of negotiation'. Both facilitation and mediation are process-oriented and can be used for multiple purposes, including dispute resolution and problem defining. Both mediators and facilitators are expected to:

- act impartially;
- aid in improving communications between the parties;
- enhance the negotiation process; and
- act as the agents of reality, but without making final decisions.

The main point of difference is that facilitation is more flexible and open-ended than mediation in terms of its procedures and potential uses. The process of facilitation is less structured than some forms of mediation. It can be used to assist one side in a dispute to identify its concerns, prioritise its interests and plan for negotiations with the other side; it could therefore constitute a preliminary step before a mediation. A facilitation could also result in certain issues being referred to one of the forms of mediation.

Using mediation in the mini-trial

The mini-trial or executive tribunal is a dispute resolution system which combines aspects of case presentation with mediation.[46] It is used when large organisations

---

44 S Henderson *The Dispute Resolution Manual*, DataLegal Publications, Spring Hill, QLD, 1993, at pp 54–8; and H Astor and C Chinkin *Dispute Resolution in Australia*, Butterworths, Sydney, 1992, at pp 64–5.
45 See the section on Environmental Disputes in Chapter 8 for further information.
46 H Astor and C Chinkin, op cit, at pp 141–3; S Goldberg et al (eds) *Dispute resolution:*

are in dispute with each other, and it is designed to bypass middle or junior management whose interests in the dispute may have caused it to become intractable. During the first stage, each organisation makes a presentation of their side of the dispute. The presentations are made to senior management representatives from each side, who could be the chief executives. They include evidence, documentation, advocacy and oral arguments on fact and law. After the presentations, the representatives retire to consider settlement options, in the knowledge of the strengths and weaknesses of both sides. The system allows for the exchange of information, both written and oral; it allows each side to hear the 'best case' of the other side; it focuses the attention of both sides firmly on the dispute, and provides the occasion for its resolution.

Unlike mediation, the first phase of the mini-trial has a positional orientation in that the parties make their best case presentations in terms of proposed outcomes and not underlying interests. In this sense it is adversarial, competitive and similar to the early stages of a court hearing. However, this stage could be chaired by an independent neutral third party and, given the informality and flexibility of the system, it may devolve into a consideration of settlement options. In the second phase, moreover, the independent party or another mediator could be used to facilitate the negotiations, along the lines of any of the four models of mediation.

Mediation and litigation

Litigation is a dispute resolution system in which the official courts of the land impose a binding decision on disputing parties. In Chapter 2, litigation was used as a point of reference in evaluating the underlying principles of mediation. It was shown that there were major apparent differences in respect of many features of the two systems. Litigation is a formal system regulated by rules of evidence, rules of procedure and directions from the courts. It is an adversarial system which signifies that the parties themselves define the dispute and present the evidence; the court's role is essentially to decide on the basis of the evidence and arguments presented. Adversarialism also entails that the court must decide between the parties and not attempt to reconcile or accommodate their interests. Litigation usually produces binary outcomes, with clear winners and losers. Litigation is coercive in that parties can suffer penalties if they do not participate in the process or comply with orders of court on matters such as the production of documents.[47] It is, subject to any right of appeal, a binding system in that if a party does not comply with a court order, officials of the state can enforce it, for example by taking possession of property. Finally, litigation is norm based, in that courts decide cases in terms of established

---

negotiation, mediation and other processes (3rd edn) Aspen Law and Business, New York, 1999, at pp 281–3; A Bevan *ADR: a lawyer's guide to mediation and other forms of dispute resolution*, Sweet & Maxwell, London, 1992, at p 13; H Brown and A Marriott *ADR Principles and Practice* (2nd edn), Sweet & Maxwell, London, 1999, at pp 362–71; L Boulle 'Mini-trial' in *The Laws of Australia*, 1997, vol 13.

47 Historically, sanctions were often not actually imposed, in accordance with the 'dog does not eat dog' principle: parties gave each other, on a reciprocal basis, extensive latitude in complying with requests and deadlines. This is now changing as courts take a closer supervisory role in the conduct of proceedings.

legal standards and not in terms of their own discretion or the needs and interests of the parties.

At one level, mediation appears to differ from litigation in all major respects. It is informal and non-adversarial, with decisions made by the parties which are not binding in the same direct way as court orders. However, some of the contrasts between mediation and litigation are based on overstated features of litigation, in particular its formality, inflexibility and binary outcomes. In reality litigation is a complex process, involving negotiation, case management, disclosure of information, compromise and settlement, and only in rare cases does it involve a court hearing. In the common law tradition, judges often attempt to achieve a compromise between the parties, either by suggesting or intimating that they attempt to negotiate a settlement or by constructing orders which give something to each side. There is a modern trend for judges to take a more active role in the conduct of cases and in the process to be less 'umpireal' and more 'managerial'.[48] Managerial judges perform mediatory functions in some situations. Modern case management systems require or invite parties to participate in settlement and mediation proceedings and costs sanctions are used to deter parties from conducting their cases in an extreme adversarial manner.[49] These innovations have been influenced in part by ADR developments.[50] Litigation in practice is not as formal and adversarial as its traditional depiction implies. Conversely, mediation can be coercive, in that one or both parties are compelled to enter into the process, and for all its claimed flexibility, mediation in practice does have structure and process. Both *settlement* mediation and *evaluative* mediation operate under the shadow of the law, and in these models the anticipated judicial outcome can be highly influential in shaping the mediated agreements.

Nevertheless, the fact remains that litigation and mediation provide significant contrasts on many aspects.[51] It has been suggested that mediation is most effective in situations when the adversarial process is weakest, namely where there is a long-standing relationship between the parties and an intermeshing of interests.[52] Despite the increasing interconnections between the two, mediation and litigation reflect widely differing approaches to dispute resolution.

---

48 H Astor and C Chinkin *Dispute Resolution in Australia*, Butterworths, Sydney, 1992, at pp 157–61.

49 Australian courts have indicated that costs penalties may be awarded if the parties fail to negotiate in good faith during a mediation: see for example the Australian case of *Capolingua v Phylum Pty Ltd* (1991) 5 WAR 137 per Ipp J. Query if CPR 44 may have this effect: see the section on Cost Sanctions in Chapter 9.

50 J Smith 'Can the advantages of ADR procedures be transposed to a judicial forum?' (1993) 4 *ADRJ* 298.

51 R Field 'The use of litigation and mediation for the resolution of custody and access disputes: a survey of QLD family law solicitors' (1996) 7 *ADRJ* 5, for a discussion of the advantages and disadvantages of mediation and litigation in family law disputes.

52 M Fulton *Commercial Alternative Dispute Resolution*, The Law Book Company, Sydney, 1989, at p 80. It has been said that 'the mediation system is the best means of resolving disputes to the satisfaction of the parties, the inquisitorial system is the best means of finding the truth, and the adversary system gives the most impressive display of "Justice being seen to be done"': quoted in P D Connolly 'By good disputing shall the law be well known' (1975) 49 *ALJ* 685.

Combining mediation with arbitration

Med-arb is an abbreviation for 'mediation-arbitration', a process for resolving typically a commercial dispute by mediation, but in the case of failure of mediation to achieve a resolution, the process proceeds to arbitration.[53]

In some cases the parties decide whether to proceed to arbitration even before the med-arb process begins. In other cases, the neutral determines whether, and if so when, mediation has failed. As a further alternative, the parties may agree in the course of the mediation, when impasse has been reached, that arbitration is appropriate in order to determine the dispute.

Med-arb should be distinguished from the situation, when the parties agree that a mediator should be appointed an arbitrator, solely for the purpose of issuing a consent award, which would make a settlement agreement immediately enforceable.[54] It should also be distinguished from the process where, following impasse in mediation, the parties request the mediator to provide a non-binding opinion.[55]

Med-arb has created debate in the UK over whether the mediator and arbitrator should be the same person in the same case. The mediator will have received confidential information in the course of a mediation. Since a mediation is conducted without prejudice, the mediator cannot rely on this information in an arbitration. In those circumstances:

'. . . it is difficult, if not impossible, for a neutral to disregard the parties' confidential compromise positions for settlement expressed during the mediation phase and then turn around and make a non-compromising award based on legally-assessed rights . . .'[56]

The related problem is that, if the parties are conscious that the dispute may go to arbitration if a mediation fails, they will not be candid with the mediator and will be reluctant to make concessions in the mediation.[57] A further problem is that the mediator may adopt an interventionist or judgmental approach in the mediation itself[58] as it is difficult, where the parties agree to med-arb before the process begins, to know when the mediation phase should give way to the arbitral.[59] The

---

53 See T Oyre *Med-arb: The Interface between Mediation and Arbitration*, at http://www. arbitrators.org/materials/articles. The survey conducted by the authors, referred to in detail in later sections in Part I, highlighted examples of med-arb use in the UK, including one example of med-baseball arbitration, indicating the scope for creativity. CEDR's Summer 2000 *Resolutions* magazine refers to an example of med-ex (mediation followed by expert determination): J Fordham 'Med-ex: an interesting variation on the ADR theme', *Resolutions*, Issue no 26, Summer 2000.

54 See Institute of Chartered Engineers *Conciliation Procedure* and The Academy of Experts *Guidance Notes for Mediators*.

55 See J Brett and S Goldberg 'Mediator-advisers: a new third party role' in M Bazerman and R Lewicki (eds) *Negotiating in Organisations*, 1983.

56 P Newman 'Mediation-arbitration: can it work legally?' (1994) 60(3) *Arbitration* 173 at 175.

57 See D Elliott 'Med-arb: fraught with danger or ripe for opportunity' (1996) 62(3) *Arbitration* 175 at 176.

58 In the article on med-ex by J Fordham, op cit, he explains how the mediator in one example adopted a judgmental approach in the mediation itself, and on a number of occasions said: 'If I have to determine this issue, I will find against you on it'.

59 See P Newman 'Mediation-arbitration: can it work legally?', op cit at 174.

implications of Article 6 of the ECHR, adopted into UK law by the Human Rights Act 1998, are discussed in Chapters 9, 11 and 12.

The following safeguards are being used in an attempt to avoid or minimise these difficulties:

- The mediation rules of some ADR organisations provide that a mediator cannot act as an arbitrator in relation to the same dispute unless the parties first agree in writing.[60] If the mediator and arbitrator are different people, however, this is likely to increase costs.
- The rules of other organisations provide that, if a mediator acts as an arbitrator in relation to the same dispute, he or she should obtain the parties' agreement that information received in the course of the mediation can be taken into account in the arbitration.[61]
- Similarly, some standard form mediation agreements provide that, in case the mediation is unsuccessful and the adjudication process follows, the third party can take into account documents and arguments put forward prior to and during the mediation.[62]
- The codes of conduct for mediators issued by most ADR organisations require the mediator to explain, if the parties have agreed to arbitration following an unsuccessful mediation, the process and the consequences of revealing information during the mediation which may later be used by the arbitrator for decision-making purposes.[63]

'Advisory mediation', where the mediator provides non-binding recommendations, can also overcome some of the difficulties. A further suggestion for overcoming the problems inherent in a med-arb process is the arb-med process, whereby an arbitration takes place, at which point the arbitration award is written, but is not disclosed to the parties, to enable an attempt at mediation to be made.[64]

Notwithstanding the difficulties with the med-arb process, it has been used successfully, particularly in the US, and a number of countries have, through legislation, encouraged the use of med-arb.[65]

Combining mediation with litigation

Mediation is being increasingly used as an adjunct to the litigation system. This is being brought about through procedural changes and case management imperatives. Allocation, case management conferences and pre-trial reviews provide occasions and opportunities for case settlement. The court may also discuss with the parties the

60 For example, Commercial Mediation Centre *Mediation Rules and Procedure*.
61 For example, Centre for Business Arbitration *Mediation Rules*; and World Intellectual Property Organisation *Mediation Rules*.
62 For example, J Fordham 'Med-ex: an interesting variation on the ADR theme', *Resolutions*, Issue no 26, Summer 2000.
63 For example, Commercial Mediation Centre *Mediator's Code of Conduct*; and ADR Group *Professional Code of Conduct for Mediators*.
64 Suggestion by Hammond Suddards Edge in 'Winning Solutions' *The Law Society's Gazette*, 11 November 1998.
65 For example, Alberta Legislature, British Columbia Labour Relations Code, New South Wales Commercial Arbitration Act, Singapore International Commercial Arbitration Act.

possibility of referring their case for mediation at these stages. UK civil justice reforms and court-connected mediation is considered in Chapter 7.

When is Mediation Appropriate?

As indicated at the beginning of this chapter, one of the major issues in modern dispute resolution is the question of finding the most appropriate method of resolution for each dispute, taking into account the type of dispute and the needs of the disputants.[66] A dispute resolution system will be appropriate where its procedures, goals and values suit the requirements of the parties' situation. Mediation will be appropriate where it is likely to result in a settlement and to achieve some of the other goals of mediation, and where its underlying principles are relevant to the circumstances. Judgments on appropriateness require an assessment of the nature of the dispute, the characteristics of the disputing parties and broader societal interests. This assessment will not be an objective exercise. First, it will always be a relative assessment in that one system will become more appropriate in the absence of other feasible options. The more inaccessible litigation is, whether for reasons of cost, delay or geography, the more appropriate alternatives to litigation become. Second, parties in dispute often have conflicting interests in terms of the way in which the dispute is dealt with. On some occasions both parties might have the same need for a specific form of dispute resolution, for example spouses may benefit equally from mediation. In other situations, each disputant might be better served by a different process, for example a small trader might need to assert legal rights through the court system while a large supplier might wish to assert its power through confidential negotiations. These subjective realities would make it difficult for the parties themselves to agree on the most 'appropriate' dispute resolution system. Third, any decision on appropriateness will be value-based. All dispute resolution processes have underlying principles which will be regarded differently by different persons; some will regard interpersonal relations as more important than enforcing legal rights, but others will not.

The matter of appropriateness is another area in which there can be little precision in mediation. It is not possible to specify the sufficient conditions of mediation, that is, circumstances which would ensure its effectiveness; nor can it be said that there are necessary conditions for its use, in the sense that it would be ineffective when these factors were absent. Thus most commentators suggest that mediation is likely to be inappropriate where there is a power imbalance between the parties, where there is only a single issue in dispute, and where there is no continuing relationship between the disputants. However, personal injury claims for damages by individual claimants against large insurers have all these characteristics, yet there is a growing use of mediation in this area. Some mediator standards attempt to define circumstances in which it would be inappropriate to commence mediation, or in which a mediation once commenced should be terminated.[67] Some mediation services have sophisticated screening procedures which are designed to exclude disputes and disputants which

---

66 K Kressel and D Pruitt 'Conclusion' in K Kressel et al (eds) *Mediation Research: the process and effectiveness of third party intervention*, Jossey-Bass, San Francisco, 1989 at pp 395–402.

67 On mediator standards, see Chapter 11.

are diagnosed as unsuitable for mediation.[68] On the other hand, there are situations in which judges are required to make discretionary referrals to mediation, but there is no indication of the criteria in terms of which the discretion is to be exercised.

Despite these difficulties, the literature and mediation experience suggest that the following factors are relevant in relation to when mediation is an appropriate, or an inappropriate, dispute resolution system:[69]

Mediation Indicators	
Suitability	**Unsuitability**
Moderate conflict	Matters of policy
Party commitment	Pure legal questions
Lawyer commitment	Ulterior motives
Continuing relationship	Personal danger
Power equality	Fact-finding required
Party ability	Credibility determinations
Multiple issues	Emotional problems
Adequate resources	Responsibility avoidance
No clear guidelines	Value differences
Proportionality issues	Proportionality issues
Privacy accepted	Court remedy needed
External pressure	Great urgency
Discrimination potential	Direct negotiation appropriate
	Inequality

Indicators of suitability for mediation

(a) *The conflict between the parties is moderate:* Where there is intense hostility, mediation may be unable to provide the control, protection and

---

68 For example, see the ADR suitability screen comprising 30 questions used by the CPR Institute for Dispute Resolution, 'Questions to assess ADR suitability regarding consensual ADR'. It was adapted from the screen developed by Debevoise and Plimpton under the leadership of Robert L King to help lawyers and their clients to decide whether or not to opt for ADR. Screening problems and clients is also a concern for other disciplines, such as psychology. The literature identifies between 250 and 400 different types of counselling and psychological help, and the matching of individuals with those processes is no simple matter: G Egan *The skilled helper: a systematic approach to effective helping* (5th edn) Brooks/Cole Publishing, Pacific Grove, California, 1994, at p 13.

69 J Stulberg *Taking Charge/Managing Conflict*, Lexington Books, Lexington,

influence necessary to generate constructive decision-making. On the other hand, where the hostility can first be dealt with through counselling, mediation may be an option thereafter. Likewise, where intense conflict leads to poor communication between the parties,[70] or stalemate, exhaustion and a cessation of hostilities, mediation might become an appropriate option for parties strongly motivated to resolve the matters in dispute.[71] 'Saving face' may be important for a party and mediation may offer the opportunity to tackle this issue.[72]

(b) *Both parties are committed to achieving a negotiated settlement*, accept the responsibility of making their own decisions, and accept the legitimacy of mediation. The stronger these commitments and acceptances, the more likely it is that the parties will respond to the facilitation of a settlement through mediation. Where the parties are not committed to having the conflict resolved, it would need to be sent to an adjudicator or administrative body. The parties' advisers or representatives, in particular lawyers, should also be committed to a negotiated settlement through mediation as professional advisers can readily undermine the process. It is argued that commercial disputes are particularly appropriate for mediation as organisations act through agents, negotiators or lawyers, and as a result the same degree of emotional attachment to a dispute is not apparent in the context of most commercial disputes as in other contexts, like family or personal injury cases.[73]

(c) *There is a continuing relationship between the parties*, either through necessity, for example parents in a matrimonial dispute,[74] or through choice,

---

Massachusetts, 1987, at p 54; A Acland *A sudden outbreak of common sense*, Hutchinson, London, 1990, at p 24; M Fulton *Commercial Alternative Dispute Resolution*, The Law Book Company, Sydney, 1989, at pp 81–3; G Clarke and I Davies 'Mediation – when is it not an appropriate dispute resolution process?' (1992) 3 *ADRJ* 70; H Brown and A Marriott *ADR Principles and Practice* (2nd edn), Sweet & Maxwell, London, 1999, at Chapter 18; and S Henderson *The Dispute Resolution Manual*, DataLegal Publications, Spring Hill, QLD, 1993, at pp 48–51.

70 K Mackie 'Negotiation and Mediation: from Inelegant Haggling to Sleeping Giant' in K Mackie (ed) *A Handbook on Dispute Resolution*, Routledge, London, 1991, at pp 88–9.

71 E J Costello 'To mediate or not to mediate? (1997) *Arbitration and Dispute Resolution Law Journal* 25. The study of the Bristol Law Society Mediation Scheme indicated that some solicitors regarded that entrenchment was a reason why a matter was unlikely to mediate successfully, whereas other solicitors considered that entrenchment would encourage them to refer a matter to mediation: M Davies, G Davis and J Webb *Promoting Mediation: Report of a study of Bristol Law Society's Mediation Scheme in its preliminary phase*, 1996 Research & Policy Planning Unit Research Study no 21, The Law Society, at p 22.

72 Law Society of Northern Ireland *ADR: the crucial psychological point*, The Law Society of Northern Ireland, 1999.

73 R Walton and R McKersie *A Behavioural Theory of Labour Negotiation*, 1965, at pp 286–91.

74 Using Maslow's terminology, mediation is particularly appropriate in family disputes as it aims to meet the parties' 'basic needs'. Child issues, in particular, lend themselves to mediation. Bowen, Bradshaw and Pottinger *Research to monitor the Cleveland Family Conciliation Service*, Teeside Polytechnic Papers in Law & Society, 1986, No 1; University of Newcastle upon Tyne Conciliation Project Unit, *Report to the Lord Chancellor's Department on the cost and effectiveness of conciliation in England and Wales*, March 1989, at p 127; and, according to Maslow, the basic needs include food, housing, healthcare and emotional security: Maslow *Motivation and Personality*, 1954, Chapter 3.

for example commercial entities which wish to do future business with each other.[75] Integrative Fixed bargaining, taking into account future interests, is more feasible where there is a continuing relationship. In this situation parties will be concerned not only about an outcome but also about the way in which it is achieved. In turn, mediation may offer an opportunity to improve a relationship.[76]

(d) *There is a rough equality of bargaining power between the disputing parties*, or the disparity in power is not so severe as to reduce the chances of a fair process. As there will always be some differences in power resources, the point at which the differential makes the process unsuitable is difficult to determine.[77] However, where there is a gross disparity such that one party can dictate the outcome, or the other could be intimidated into agreeing to a settlement which is prejudicial to its rights and interests, mediation would not be an appropriate option.

(e) *The parties have the capacity and abilities to negotiate*, or where they lack these qualities by virtue of youth or mental condition, have representatives who can negotiate on their behalf. This flows from the mediation principle of self-determination in terms of which mediating parties are required to make their own informed decisions on settlement options. Legal capacity is often required to turn mediated decisions into formal agreements.

(f) *There is more than a single issue in dispute* and the issues are sufficiently tangible to allow the parties to commit to a settlement or future course of action. Multiple issues provide the basis for collaborative and integrative bargaining, involving trade-offs, compromise and linkages between issues. Most commercial and family disputes involve multiple issues.

(g) *There are adequate resources*, such as funds, time and information. As mediation does not have the mechanisms for enforcing disclosure, it is not suited to circumstances where one or more parties do not have available information, for example on technical or scientific matters. There also need to be resources to negotiate over; mediation is unsuited where one party has nothing of value to place on the negotiating table.

(h) *There are no clear legal principles or other standards to guide the parties' decision-making* or appropriate remedy in law. Thus mediation might be unsuited in a claim for illness caused by passive smoking, where there are limited legal precedents or community standards. On the other hand, in some circumstances the uncertainty of external standards or jurisdictional difficulties might make mediation more attractive to parties as it allows

---

75 Davet and Bogoch 'Fixed Fight or Free-For-All?' (1980) 7 *Brit J Law & Society* 36. Axelrod suggests that when parties are faced with the choice of adopting either a competitive or co-operative approach in negotiations, in circumstances where the parties will meet or bargain again, the parties and the lawyers will co-operate: R Axelrod *The evolution of co-operation*, Basic books, New York, 1984. Compare cases where there are significant conflicts of interests as when it is unlikely that there will be a basis for future relations, in which case adjudicatory procedures are more likely: for example V Aubert 'Competition and dissensus: two types of conflict resolution' (1963) 7 *Journal of Conflict Resolution* 26 at 63–4.

76 F E A Sander and S B Goldberg 'Fitting the forum to the Fuss: A user friendly guide to selecting an ADR procedure' (1994) *Negotiation Journal* 55.

77 The question of power is considered at pages **70–72** and **454–459**.

them to take control over the outcome.[78] Also, the preferred settlement may not be achievable in litigation. Community disputes, in particular, may not be amenable to a remedy.[79] For example, parties may need an apology or an explanation for behaviour. Dignan et al suggest that mediation is most appropriate in community disputes involving mildly anti-social behaviour or a personality or lifestyle clash, although they do not rule out cases involving a degree of harassment or minor criminal acts.[80] Other commentators suggest that it is difficult to put an upper limit on the seriousness of a community dispute suitable for mediation.[81] The work of community mediation centres shows that the range of cases suitable for mediation includes noise complaints, boundary disputes, petty crime and lifestyle clashes.[82]

(i) *Responses to the Lord Chancellor's ADR Discussion Paper highlighted the proportion of the cost* of formal dispute resolution to the value of the claim as a factor determining suitability.[83]

(j) *The parties can accept that the process is private and the outcome is confidential.* Examples are celebrities in a matrimonial dispute, business persons wishing to protect trade secrets or parties anxious to prevent any public disclosure of their sexual orientation.[84] Where parties wish to publicise the process and outcome among their members, supporters or the general public, as in disputes between government and organisations accountable to the community, mediation would be less appropriate.

(k) *There is some external encouragement for the parties to settle in mediation.* Despite its consensual principles, there is relatively little spontaneous demand for mediation and it is often used effectively where the larger

---

78 The Study of the Bristol Law Society Mediation Scheme indicated that some lawyers refused to refer cases to mediation on the grounds that the case was considered too complex, whereas others considered that mediation was appropriate in such cases due to the high cost of litigation. Both the Centre for Dispute Resolution and the ADR Group were surveyed as part of the study. The Centre for Dispute Resolution considered that, in complex cases, mediation can simplify issues, thereby improving the chances of settlement. The ADR Group noted that, in multi-party cases, mediation provided an early opportunity for all the parties to meet, which may not occur in the litigation process: M Davies, G Davis and J Webb *Promoting Mediation: Report of a study of Bristol Law Society's Mediation Scheme in its preliminary phase*, 1996 Research & Policy Planning Unit Research Study no 21, The Law Society, at p 26.

79 C J Dignan et al *Neighbour Disputes: comparing the cost and effectiveness of a mediation and alternative approaches*, Centre for Criminological and Legal Research, University of Sheffield, 1996.

80 Ibid, at p 87.

81 See, for example, Cameron 'Community Mediation in New Zealand: A pilot project' (1988) *Journal of Social Welfare Law* 284.

82 R E Mackay and A J Brown *Community Mediation in Scotland: a study of implementation*, The Scottish Office Central Research Unit, Edinburgh, 1999.

83 Lord Chancellor's Department *ADR Discussion Paper: Summary of Responses*, August 2000, at paras 16, 25 and 28. The English Civil Procedure Rules place considerable emphasis on proportionality: the financial costs of resolving a dispute should not be out of proportion to the amount at stake. See the section on Civil Justice Reforms in Chapter 7.

84 H Astor 'Mediation for intra-lesbian disputes' (1997) 20 *Melbourne University Law Review* 953.

community encourages its use.[85] Here the larger community could comprise government, insurers, employers or social organisations.

(l) *The parties feel that they may suffer discrimination at the hand of the litigation process.*[86]

Indicators of non-suitability

(a) *There are broad matters of policy at stake affecting many people or the whole society*, such as constitutional, national security, public policy issues or human rights; or the parties wish to establish an authoritative precedent for future disputes of a similar nature, for example to end a pattern of malpractice in an industry, or otherwise to establish a test case. A party may wish publicity or vindication.[87] Third parties' interests might not be capable of being adequately taken into account in the mediation.[88]

(b) *The dispute involves a pure legal question*, for example the interpretation of a statute or a contract, and this interpretation will determine all aspects of the outcome.[89]

(c) *The parties have ulterior motives for using mediation*, for example to cause delay beyond a limitation period, to gather further information, to punish the other party, or to achieve some illegal or immoral purpose on a confidential basis. Disputes over power and reputation may also fall into this category.[90]

(d) *The use of mediation could involve the risk of personal danger* for one or more parties, or where the dispute revolves around issues of child abuse[91] or family violence or criminal activity.[92]

(e) *The dispute cannot be resolved without making complicated findings* of fact or credibility,[93] for example where a party's liability for damages depends

---

85 C McEwan and T Milburn 'Explaining a paradox of mediation' (1993) 9 *Negotiation Journal* 23. The authors find that even reluctant parties use mediation successfully and evaluate it favourably.

86 For example, a homosexual parent in a child custody dispute may feel more comfortable with the mediation process: H Astor 'Mediation for intra-lesbian disputes' (1997) 20 *Melbourne University Law Review* 953.

87 For example, in personal injury cases, where public sympathy is sought; or where there are allegations of fraud, which a party wishes to disprove publicly, and defamation cases.

88 F Sander 'Varieties of dispute processing' (1976) 70 *Federal Rules Decisions* 11.

89 Commercial Court Working Party on ADR *Second Report on ADR*, at File://A:/Commercial Court 2nd ADR Report.htm

90 M Galanter 'Reading the Landscape of Disputes: What we know and don't know (and think we know) about our allegedly contentious society' (1983) 31 *UCLA Law Review* 4 at 26. *The Funding Code – Decision making guidance*, June 2000, also refers to ulterior motives as a factor which it will consider when determining whether a funding certificate should be limited to cover mediation. On funding of mediation, see Chapter 9.

91 R E Mackay and A J Brown *Community Mediation in Scotland: a study of implementation*, The Scottish Office Central Research Unit, Edinburgh, 1999; and J Dignan et al *Neighbour Disputes: comparing the cost and effectiveness of mediation and alternative approaches*, Centre for Criminological and Legal Research, University of Sheffield, 1996.

92 J Dignan et al, ibid. However, a range of victim-offender mediation schemes operate in the UK. See the section on Community Disputes in Chapter 8.

93 H Genn *Central London County Court Mediation Pilot: Evaluation Report*, LCD Research Series, No 5/98, at p 31.

on determining the accuracy of conflicting versions of an accident. If a party does not trust the other, mediation will be difficult. If there is a lack of information, a party may be reluctant to mediate.[94]

(f) *One or more of the parties is in a disturbed emotional or psychological state*, for example denial, anger or severe depression,[95] or where one or more of the disputants does not want to take responsibility for any ultimate decision and wants to deflect blame.[96]

(g) *The dispute involves an uncompromising difference over matters of value or fundamental principle* which are not susceptible to negotiation, for example a policy conflict over affirmative action or the question of whether a church should have women priests.

(h) *Where there is a need for a remedy which only a court could provide*, such as an injunction or a protection order, or where something has to be achieved with great urgency. A case where default or summary judgment is appropriate may fall into this category.

(i) *Mediation is too expensive*, given the amount in issue.[97] If a trial is imminent, parties may consider that they have invested too much time and money to mediate.[98]

(j) *Where there is relational distance* between the parties, or it is a 'one-off' transaction, mediation could be difficult.[99]

(k) *Where direct negotiation is likely to produce a result.*[100]

(l) *Inequality or a serious imbalance of power* might serve to reproduce that inequality in mediation.[101]

---

94 A factor identified in both the Central London County Court and NHS Mediation Pilots: see H Genn *Central London County Court Mediation Pilot: Evaluation Report*, ibid at p 32; and L Mulcahy et al *Mediating medical negligence claims: an option for the future?* NHS Executive, 2000, at p xv.

95 This may also be a factor in personal injury claims, where the plaintiff may be suffering from psychological injuries as well as physical ones. See D Alcorn 'Mediation and the psychologically injured plaintiff' (1996) 2 *Queensland University of Technology Law Journal* 162.

96 See the Brown Report, op cit

97 H Genn, op cit, at p 33, but compare L Mulcahy et al, op cit at p xv, where solicitors surveyed for the NHS Mediation Pilot considered that the small or medium cases were suitable for mediation, but that complex and larger claims were not, largely due to the volume of evidence involved in clinical negligence claims.

98 R E Mackay and A J Brown *Community Mediation in Scotland: a study of implementation*, The Scottish Office Central Research Unit, Edinburgh, 1999.

99 Where there is relational distance between the parties or it is a 'one-off' transaction, the law may be used to settle a dispute between those parties: J Auerbach *Justice without law*, Oxford University Press, New York, 1983, at p 119. Where there is no prospect of future dealings between the parties, some commentators argue that it could be irrational for the parties to act co-operatively: R J Condlin 'Bargaining in the Dark: the normative incoherence of lawyer dispute bargaining role' (1992) 51 *Maryland Law Review* 1 at 12.

100 Personal injury cases are often cited as examples of cases where settlement frequently occurs through direct negotiation, a typical reason for refusing mediation given by the solicitors surveyed as part of the Central London County Court Mediation Pilot: H Genn, op cit, at p 32. See also the section on Personal Injury Disputes in Chapter 8.

101 J Auerbach *Justice without Law*, op cit, at pp 120 and 136; Cross *The Economics of Bargaining*, 1969, at pp 16–17; Schelling *The Strategy of Conflict*, 1960, at p 22; and C McClintock (ed) *Experimental Social Psychology*, 1972, at p 325.

Timing as a factor in the suitability of mediation

Mediation can be used at any time during the existence of a dispute, from its first overt signs to the proverbial 'eleventh hour' before a court hearing.[102] There are divergent views on the most appropriate timing for mediation. On one hand are those who argue that the sooner the mediation is held the better, as it will then be effective in avoiding an escalation of the conflict beyond its original issues, in preventing a test of strength and the parties becoming entrenched in their positions, in preserving relationships, and in saving time and costs.[103] On the other hand are those who argue that mediation should occur later in the life of a dispute as there needs to be some adversarial conflict and party frustration before it will be 'ripe' for a mediated settlement. At that stage, the parties are likely to be more motivated to disentangle themselves from conflict.[104] Delaying mediation also provides time to identify the issues in dispute, to conduct investigations and fact-finding, to secure medical or other reports, and to exchange materials.

There can be no hard and fast rule about the most appropriate timing for mediation.[105] It will depend on the nature of the dispute, the personalities of the parties involved and the availability of other remedies:

Civil/commercial cases

The timing of a civil/commercial mediation may be determined by the terms of a mediation clause in a contract between the parties.[106] The timing of a civil/commercial mediation may be influenced by whether the parties have sufficient information to enable them to confidently negotiate a resolution of the dispute. It is important that each party has the means by which to assess the strengths and weaknesses of their case.[107] Respondents to the authors' 2000 survey of 700 UK law firms highlighted feelings of 'ambush' when mediations were conducted too early, before adequate disclosure had occurred.[108] It is not necessary for all the documents to have been exchanged, as the parties can, as part of the preparations for mediation, agree to exchange information if the mediation takes place before disclosure has

---

102 M Anstey *Practical peacemaking: a mediator's handbook*, Juta & Co, Kenwyn, South Africa, 1993, at pp 58–60; and H Brown and A Marriott *ADR Principles and Practice* (2nd edn), Sweet & Maxwell, London, 1999

103 There is much evidence to show that as disputes escalate there develops a dispute about a dispute, known as a meta-dispute, when the way in which the dispute has been handled assumes major significance.

104 For an interesting discussion on the 'sources of ripeness', see D Pruitt and P Olczak, 'Beyond hope – approaches to resolving seemingly intractable conflict' in B Bunker and J Rubin (eds) *Conflict Co-operation and Justice*, Jossey-Bass, San Francisco, 1995, at pp 68–71.

105 Law Society of Northern Ireland *ADR's Place in the Course of Litigation* explains that the timing of a mediation following issue of proceedings is determined by the 'crucial psychological point', which occurs after impasse has occurred and re-opening direct negotiations has proved unsatisfactory.

106 See the section on Mediation Clauses in Chapter 12.

107 B A Filipowski *The Response of Business to the Challenges of ADR*, unpublished paper, Sydney, 1992, at p 8.

108 The results of the survey, conducted between December 1998 and April 2000, of 700 UK law firms, selected at random, are referred to throughout this book, where relevant.

been completed. A study of US federal district courts revealed that mediation was taking place increasingly earlier in the litigation process, not uncommonly before disclosure had taken place,[109] which suggests that the impact of legal proceedings cannot be predicted with certainty. In some situations the delays, cost, formality and other 'heartbreak factors' of litigation may be a powerful inducement for the parties to attempt mediation. On the other hand the distress and bitterness caused by the litigation process and the costs incurred may make the parties more determined to pursue victory through non-mediation methods.

External factors, such as changes in economic conditions, or an extraordinary internal factor, like an imminent strike, may provide, in the context of a civil/ commercial dispute, a window of opportunity for mediation.[110] Court-imposed deadlines and the English Civil Procedure Rules ('CPR') are also particularly relevant in the context of the timing of a mediation. A fundamental aim of the CPR is the settlement of disputes and, accordingly, that aim is served by consideration of mediation, even before proceedings are issued. Given the ability under the CPR to serve a Part 36 offer even before proceedings are issued, service of such a notice before proceedings are issued may also encourage mediation at that time. The CPR provides other windows of opportunity for mediation, after proceedings are issued:

- At the allocation questionnaire stage: the first question in the allocation questionnaire is, 'do you wish there to be a one month stay to attempt to settle the case?'
- A judge may use the opportunity of a case management conference to suggest mediation.
- At a pre trial review, the judge may also encourage the parties to consider mediation.
- The court has a power to suspend proceedings if it considers that this is appropriate, and this power may be used by the court to actively promote mediation, as has been the practice of the Commercial Court.[111]

Responses to the Lord Chancellor's ADR Discussion Paper suggested that judges should also remind parties about mediation on interim applications.[112]

When a limitation period is imminent, proceedings may be issued to protect a party's position, although it may be hoped to resolve the dispute by mediation. Apart from such a case, the view gleaned from the experience in other jurisdictions is that, once litigation has commenced, mediation is most likely to be successful if a trial date has been set.[113] That a trial may ensue if agreement cannot be reached in

---

109 E Plapinger and D Stienstra *ADR and settlement in the Federal District Courts: a sourcebook for judges and lawyers*, Federal Judicial Centre and CPR Institute for Dispute Resolution, 1996.

110 R T and B P Castrey 'Timing: A mediator's best friend' (1987) *Mediation Quarterly* 16 at 17.

111 See the section on Courts and Mediation in Chapter 7.

112 Lord Chancellor's Department *ADR Discussion Paper: summary of responses*, August 2000, at para 62.

113 G Davies *Mediation and the Courts – Inspiration or Desperation: 9 Questions which must be Answered*, Paper presented at 29th Australian Legal Convention, September 1995, at p 4. Compare response to Lord Chancellor's *ADR Discussion Paper*, ibid, that it is then too late, and that mediation should be considered upon issue of proceedings.

a mediation is likely to provide parties with the impetus to negotiate 'in the shadow of the law'.[114]

The findings of the Central London County Court Mediation Pilot indicated that, in 41% of the civil claims mediated, mediation occurred between three to six months after entry of defence, 13% occurred between six and nine months after entry of defence, 11% occurred between nine months and one year after entry of defence and 12% occurred after two years from entry of defence.[115] Over two-thirds of the solicitors interviewed for the Pilot study considered that their mediation had been held at the most appropriate time, although 2% considered that the mediation had occurred too early and 28% considered that the mediation had occurred too late, at which time the parties were so entrenched and legal costs so high that settlement proved difficult.[116]

Family disputes

Family mediation frequently occurs in the context of divorce proceedings and is either court requested or recommended. Otherwise, mediation takes place as a result of self- or solicitor-referral or following a meeting in accordance with legal aid (now called CLS Funding) requirements.[117] There is a view that, although mediation can be helpful early in a separation, there is the potential difficulty that one partner may not have accepted that the marriage could be at an end.[118] In addition, if partners are still living in the same house, it may be too early for mediation and counselling might be more appropriate. It is also considered preferable to have parties referred to mediation before they are at the stage of requiring social work intervention.[119]

One Australian study found that in family mediations, couples with current court applications had a significantly reduced chance of a successful outcome. It suggested that the presence of 'litigation shadow' has a tendency to interfere with the couple's capacity to be reasonable and conciliatory and is not conducive to outcomes.[120]

By way of broad generalisation it can be said that mediation should take place sooner rather than later in the development of a dispute, but delay will never be a reason in itself not to attempt it. There are even situations in which mediation takes

---

114 R Mnookin and L Kornhauser 'Bargaining in the Shadow of the Law: The case of Divorce' (1979) 88 *Yale Law Journal* 950.
115 H Genn *Central London County Court Mediation Pilot: Evaluation Report*, LCD Research Series, No 5/98, at p 47.
116 Ibid, at pp 48 and 116.
117 See Chapter 9, for consideration of legal aid changes and other funding issues.
118 University of Newcastle upon Tyne Conciliation Project Unit, *Report to the Lord Chancellor's Department on the cost and effectiveness of conciliation in England and Wales*, March 1989, at p 335.
119 Family Mediation Scotland *Information Pack*.
120 S Bordow and J Gibson *Evaluation of the Family Court Mediation Service*, Family Court of Australia, Research and Evaluation Unit, 1994, at p 84.

place after a formal decision has been rendered, for example at the time when parties are waiting for their appeals to go before the appellate court.

Refusing mediation services

In some professions, such as counselling, it is recognised that under certain conditions the best option may be that of 'no treatment'.[121] Under the no-treatment category are included clients who have a history of treatment failure or who seem to get worse from treatment, clients with malingering or fictional illnesses, people who are chronic non-responders to treatment, clients likely to improve on their own, and reluctant and resistant clients who refuse treatment. It is felt that it would be a disservice to the individuals and society if there was too much willingness to treat problems for which no effective treatment was available. The no-treatment option has several advantages:

- it involves the termination of destructive helping sessions;
- it stops clients and professionals from wasting time and money;
- it can postpone help until conditions are more favourable for it;
- it can help prevent clients and professionals from playing games with each other and themselves; and
- it can motivate clients to find help through other methods, including their own devices.

For other professionals, such as lawyers, a no-treatment decision is counter-cultural and more difficult to make and justify. For the mediation movement a no-treatment option should always be considered for the following reasons:

(a) There is some evidence that mediation is regarded by other professionals, including certain lawyers, managers and counsellors, as a dumping-ground for difficult cases.

(b) Some governments, legislatures and courts are introducing mediation services not because of the inherent qualities of mediation, but because it is seen as a system for the mass-processing of conflicts through quick and cheap routine procedures.

(c) Some parties misunderstand the mediation process and perceive and use mediation primarily for therapeutic purposes, particularly where it is provided in community programmes.

(d) Mediators are being tempted to take all manner of cases to develop their individual practices, to gain mediation experience, to satisfy the requirements of referring agencies and to advance the profile of mediation, even though these cases may not always be suitable for mediation.

In the light of these factors, it would be of assistance to the mediation movement if there were standard criteria for mediators to use in deciding whether or not to take on a mediation. In some contexts, there are sophisticated screening protocols for identifying cases which are inappropriate for mediation. In others there is very little screening and the matching of mediation to inappropriate cases is likely to result in individual horror stories and reputational problems for the mediation movement.

---

121 G Egan *The skilled helper: a systematic approach to effective helping* (5th edn) Brooks/Cole Publishing, Pacific Grove, California, 1994, at pp 206–7.

The Role of Mediation in other Dispute Resolution Systems

Mediation is not only a stand-alone system of dispute resolution but can also be combined with other processes such as arbitration and litigation, as outlined above. It can also be used as one element in the development of custom-designed dispute resolution systems, as in the mini-trial, also outlined above. Another example, *partnering*, is a process which provides a framework for improving working relations, often between parties to a construction project, with the aim of preventing disputes and encouraging the use of ADR, usually mediation, if disputes occur in the course of the project.[122] The partnering process usually begins with a joint workshop which includes the key stakeholders in a project, in order to open lines of communication and develop trust, as well as identifying potential areas of future dispute. A Partnering Charter usually formalises this process and encapsulates the parties' agreed vision for the relationship.[123]

A mediation process may also be adapted to accommodate another dispute resolution system or systems for specific purposes. *Ombudsmen*, for example, deal with complaints about services in public and private sectors and have wide-ranging powers to investigate complaints, recommend payment of compensation and to publish findings. A number of Ombudsmen use conciliatory methods and mediation, usually following an investigation but before publication of findings.[124]

---

122 A Edelman, F Carr and C Lancaster *Partnering*, IWR ADR Series no 4, 1991. For an overview of the legal aspects of partnering, see P Newman 'Partnering: with particular reference to construction' *Arbitration*, February 2000, at 39.

123 F Carr *Partnering: Dispute Avoidance – The Army Corps of Engineers Way*, American Arbitration Association, 1993; and see the sections on Government/Public Sector and Construction Disputes in Chapter 8.

124 See the sections on Mediation Organisations and Consumer Disputes in Chapter 7.

Part II — Process

4

The Mediation Process

Introduction

In Chapter 1 reference was made to four paradigm models of mediation and their defining characteristics. In this chapter there is a description of the main stages in the mediation process and the rationale for each stage. This can be referred to as the *standard* mediation process, in that most of the stages feature in all the models of mediation. However, in so far as the stages referred to can be associated predominantly with one of the four models of mediation, it would be with *facilitative mediation*. This model is more process-driven than the other models, in the sense that it focuses primarily on how decisions are made, and not on what decisions are made.

The flexibility of mediation, however, allows for immense variety. Generally speaking, the mediation process is unregulated. The number of stages and other features of the mediation process depend not only on the model of mediation being used but also on:

- the background, training and style of the mediator;
- the nature of the dispute and dispositions of the disputants;
- the availability of funds and other resources; and
- external factors such as the existence of a statute regulating the mediation.

Thus extensive preparatory activities occur more often in well resourced private mediations. In fact, descriptions of the stages of mediation often display an unconscious bias towards private mediations and overlook the constraints operating on other forms with limited resources.

Here the standard mediation process is examined in terms of four sequential phases: initiating mediation, preparatory matters, the mediation meeting, and post-mediation activities. In the second part of the chapter, reference is made to some variations on the standard mediation process.

The Mediator's Entry

Initiating mediation

The way in which mediators enter into disputes is important in securing the parties' commitment to mediation. It also provides an opportunity for mediators to develop the trust and acceptability which can provide a solid foundation for their later facilitation of the parties' negotiations.[1] There are three ways in which mediation can be initiated:

(a) The parties may make a joint approach to a person whom they regard as appropriate to mediate their dispute. Where referral to family mediation is direct, family mediation organisations may provide parties with a list of possible mediators, leaving it to the parties to make contact with a mediator direct. This can be referred to as contractual mediation: the parties jointly contract with an outsider for the specific purpose of assisting them in decision-making.[2] This may arise through their ad hoc negotiated efforts, or in the carrying out of a dispute resolution clause in their contract. In these cases the parties jointly diagnose the dispute as being potentially suitable for mediation. The parties can be presumed to have some understanding of the process and its strengths and shortcomings. Although the mediator will still have to develop trust and educate the parties about the process, his or her entry into the dispute is not likely to be problematic. In the case of private civil/commercial mediation, where the mediator is appointed with the assistance of a mediation organisation, the parties will usually be required to complete a document called a request for mediation form,[3] a mediation referral form,[4] a case referral form,[5] an application for mediation,[6] a request for mediation[7] or an application for appointment of mediator.[8] Some organisations charge a fee for appointing a mediator.[9]

(b) One party may approach a mediation organisation or a private mediator with a request to invite the other party or parties to a mediation. This request may be based on a relatively poor understanding of the nature of the mediation process. Staff of the organisation, or the mediator personally, will be required to educate the initiating party on the nature of mediation before approaching the other side. The approach to the other side requires diplomacy and tact in that this party may be ignorant about the process, may view mediation with suspicion, may regard the initiative as a sign of weakness, or may simply not desire the involvement of a third party in the dispute. Here the mediator may use printed literature, videos, personal contacts and the contributions of respected outsiders to inform the party about a mediator's ability to assist in decision-making. If this is successful, the mediator will have gained entry into the dispute.

(c) The mediation may be initiated by someone other than the disputing parties. A board, council or other body may approach the parties, or request a

---

1   E J Radford and P F Glaser, 'The Psychology of Mediation' in P Pretorius (ed) *Dispute Resolution*, Juta & Co, Kenwyn, South Africa, 1993, at p 51. Acceptability is a major issue for mediators – see M Anstey *Practical Peacemaking – a Mediator's Handbook*, Juta & Co, Kenwyn, South Africa, 1993, at p 10.
2   See K Kressel and D Pruitt's distinction between contractual and emergent mediation in *Mediation Research: the process and effectiveness of third party intervention*, Jossey-Bass, San Francisco, 1989, at p 189.
3   Academy of Experts.
4   ADR Group.
5   Centre for Dispute Resolution.
6   Chartered Institute of Arbitrators.
7   London Court of International Arbitration.
8   Royal Institution of Chartered Surveyors.
9   See the section on Mediation Organisations in Chapter 7.

mediation service to do so, in an attempt to persuade them to use the process. In victim-offender mediations, mediators are often probation officers or social workers, appointed by the range of services involved. Here the same diplomacy will be required as where one party initiates mediation in order to persuade the parties to give their informed consent to using the process. Multi-party or public sector mediation may require a team approach to handle the work required to get all stakeholders to the negotiating table.[10] There will be no approach by the parties, where a mediator might be appointed by a court or agency, and there is less discretion for the mediator to manage the way in which entry is made into the dispute. Despite this lack of discretion, the mediator's style and attitude still has power to enhance or limit both his or her legitimacy as a third party intervener, and affect the prospects of a successful outcome. It is usual, in the context of a family mediation, for a court welfare officer to act as a mediator. Even outside the family context, however, the court may have an involvement in the appointment. In the Central London County Court Mediation Pilot, for example, a court administrator appointed the mediators.[11] In the case of the London Patents County Court ADR programme, mediators are chosen from a panel maintained by the Court Administrator.[12] These court schemes can be compared with the practice of the Commercial Court, which maintains a list of individuals and bodies that offer mediation and other ADR services, to enable the parties themselves to agree upon a mediator, although the parties may by consent refer to the court for assistance in reaching an agreement on the appointment.[13] The study of the Central London County Court Mediation Pilot indicated that selection of a mediator by the Court led parties to attribute judicial qualities of impartiality to those mediators.[14]

Intake and screening

Where mediation is not compulsory, a formal intake procedure is often used to assess the suitability of the dispute and the disputants for mediation.[15] Sophisticated protocols are used by some mediation services to screen for indicators of non-suitability, such as domestic violence and child abuse. Intake also allows for an assessment of factors such as the equality of power resources, motivation and commitment, the availability of information and other relevant factors. Agencies providing mediation services usually have a referral network for cases deemed not suitable for mediation. Private mediators on the other hand tend to have less elaborate systems of screening and referral.

---

10 T Lesnick and J Ehrmann 'Selected strategies for managing multi-party disputes' (1987) 16 *Mediation Quarterly* 21.
11 See the section on Courts and Mediation in Chapter 8 for further details about this court scheme.
12 Ibid.
13 Queens Bench Division (Commercial Court) *Practice Note* 7 June 1996 [1996] 3 All ER 383.
14 H Genn *Central London County Court Mediation Pilot: Evaluation Report*, LCD Research Series, No 5/98, at p 113.
15 On the indicators of suitability and non-suitability of mediation, see pages **92–97**.

In the case of family mediation in the UK, cases are screened for domestic violence and child abuse. Section 27 of the Family Law Act 1996 requires mediators to ensure that parties participate in mediation without fear of violence or harm, and the codes of conduct of family mediation organisations make provision for this.[16] Each party is interviewed and these issues are raised either directly or indirectly before the mediation begins. The 'safety-oriented' approach[17] involves continuing attention to these issues throughout the mediation.[18] The other approach considers that parties who come to family mediation have screened themselves as suitable for mediation and that the mediator should respect their desire to mediate.[19] Raitt argues that successful screening is dependent on a women's ability to both recognise and declare abuse. She argues that a woman, who has been subjected to abuse, may feel under pressure to co-operate in a mediation against her interests.[20] Where abuse, violence or harm is suspected, it needs to be ascertained whether the affected party wishes to take part in the mediation. They should also be provided with information about relevant support services.[21] If a mediation takes place in a case where there is a fear of harm, steps should be taken to ensure the safety of the parties to and from the mediation.[22] One of the aims of mediation in such a case is to gain commitment from the parties to end the abuse.

In other cases, like community mediation, intake is more informal. The first contact is usually by telephone, when a visit is arranged with the complainant, to assess suitability for mediation. If a mediation is considered suitable, a visit is then arranged with the other party in order to assess whether a face-to-face meeting is possible. A visit usually follows written information about mediation to the other party, inviting them to make contact with the community mediation service. In some cases, mere notification of the dispute to the other party may lead to its resolution. A common problem for community mediation organisations is obtaining the agreement of all relevant parties to mediate.[23] In the context of community mediation, Dignan's study revealed that mediation is rejected due to geographical restrictions, a history of threats or violence, or the presence of harassment, power imbalance or mental illness.[24] Unlike civil/commercial or family mediation,

---

16 Codes of mediator conduct of the Law Society of England & Wales, Law Wise, NFM, FMA, the UK College of Family Mediators and CALM in Scotland. Also see the Family Law Act 1996, s 12. It has been suggested that screening should be extended to cover illnesses that may affect capacity: N Winner 'Capacity to Mediate' *Family and Mediation* vol 7, no 2, p 17.

17 This approach is advocated by most family mediation organisations in the UK.

18 For example, Law Society of England & Wales *Code of Practice for Family Mediators.*

19 This approach is difficult to reconcile with family mediator codes of practice, requiring mediators to ensure that parties participate willingly and voluntarily, are not influenced by fear of violence or other harm, and to identify cases of fear of violence or other harm.

20 F Raitt 'Domestic Violence and Divorce Mediation' (1996) 18(1) *Journal of Social Welfare and Family Law* at 11–20.

21 UK College of Family Mediators *Code of Practice.*

22 Ibid.

23 For example, see the study by R E Mackay and A J Brown *Community Mediation in Scotland: a study of implementation*, The Scottish Office Central Research Unit, Edinburgh, 1999.

24 J Dignan et al *Neighbour Disputes: comparing the cost and effectiveness of mediation and alternative approaches*, Centre for Criminological and Legal Research, University of Sheffield, 1996.

community mediation services frequently work with one of the parties, in an attempt to deal with a dispute, where it is not possible to work with both parties.[25]

The intake procedure is used to educate and reassure the parties as to the nature of the mediation process. In the context of family disputes, an intake appointment, where the nature of mediation is explained and consideration is given to the appropriateness of mediation, can be particularly helpful. An intake appointment can provide an opportunity to discuss financial circumstances and eligibility for legal aid; whether the parties believe that their relationship has broken down; if legal proceedings are afoot, what stage has been reached; and whether the parties feel threatened by a mediation.[26] Even if the dispute does not proceed to mediation, an intake appointment could encourage a couple to negotiate on their own.[27] Where proceedings have commenced, it is considered most useful that the intake interview or information meeting takes place at an early stage.[28]

In community mediation, agencies may seek to overcome resistance by ensuring that the parties understand how mediation works. A difficulty at this stage is for community mediation agency personnel to retain neutrality, as parties may seek an acknowledgment from them of their grievance.

The intake also allows the service-provider to assess the kind of mediator or mediators required for the particular dispute and disputants. There are different views as to the extent to which mediators themselves should be involved in the intake procedures.[29] This work is regarded as involving specialist skills and is undertaken by trained intake personnel, and much of it is conducted over the telephone. Private mediators normally undertake the intake work themselves, using it to diagnose the dispute and to establish a working relationship with the disputants.[30]

Selection of mediator

As pointed out above, in some contexts, the parties have no choice as to the mediator's identity, for example, in some court-connected or community mediation schemes in which the mediator is appointed by the relevant authority. The parties could at most ask for his or her withdrawal on conflict of interest grounds.[31] This may be the case for some private mediation services as well although the parties generally have a free choice of mediators in private mediation. Some other private mediation services may

---

25 Recent Mediation UK statistics show that, in that case, partial or complete resolution is likely to be reached in 50% of cases, compared with 80% when both parties agree to participate: M Doyle *Advising on ADR: the essential guide to appropriate dispute resolution*, Advice Services Alliance, London, 2000, at p 99.

26 Legal Aid Board, *Family Mediation Quality Assurance Standard*, at paras B1.9–1.22.

27 C Archbold et al *Divorce in Northern Ireland: unravelling the system*, Report to the Office of Law Reform, HMSO, 1999.

28 Ibid.

29 H Brown and A Marriott *ADR Principles and Practice* (2nd edn), Sweet & Maxwell, London, 1999, at pp 160–3.

30 R Charlton and M Dewdney *The Mediator's Handbook – skills and strategies for practitioners*, The Law Book Company, Sydney, 1995, at pp 185–6 for guidelines for persons undertaking intake activities.

31 See Chapters 11 and 12 for a discussion of conflicts of interest.

provide a limited panel of several members for the parties to choose from but give the parties the opportunity to solicit additional names to those initially provided.[32]

In all cases the question arises as to the characteristics, qualifications and skills which would be appropriate in the appointment of a mediator. This is relevant to mediation users when they have full or partial choice of mediator, and to government agencies or mediation services where they have a full or partial ability to nominate a mediator as the parties' satisfaction with the person recommended is essential for the effectiveness of a mediation.[33] The parties must have confidence in the mediator, in order to place trust in the mediator.[34] The selection of a mediator can be based on both objective and subjective factors. Among the objective factors are:

- (a)   mediation training;
- (b)   mediation experience;
- (c)   expertise in the subject matter of the dispute;
- (d)   membership of a professional organisation;
- (e)   accountability to mediation standards and ethics; and
- (f)   fee scales.

Among the subjective criteria are:

- (a)   standing in the community;
- (b)   reputation as a mediator or professional;
- (c)   personal style; and
- (d)   credibility to the parties and their legal representatives.

The following specific factors might be considered relevant in selecting a mediator.[35]

Personal attributes

There is undoubtedly a range of personal attributes which would be of benefit to mediators.[36] Here attributes refer to innate qualities and characteristics, rather than

---

32   See the section on Mediation Organisations in Chapter 7.
33   C Moore *The Mediation Process*, CDR Associates, 1989, at p 3.
34   See, for example, M Davies et al *Promoting Mediation: Research and Policy Planning Unit Report of a study of the Bristol Law Society Mediation Scheme in its preliminary phase*, Research Study No 21, The Law Society. The study of the Bristol Law Society Mediation Scheme highlighted instances where solicitors lacked confidence in the mediator and their skill to handle specialist matters in issue.
35   See K Slaikeu and R Hasson *Controlling the costs of conflict – how to design a system for your organisation*, Jossey-Bass Publishers, San Francisco, 1998, at pp 116–20; and National Institute for Dispute Resolution *Performance Base Assessment: a methodology for use in selecting, training and evaluating mediators*, Washington DC, 1995. The following performance dimensions are identified, based on a list of tasks that a mediator should be capable of carrying out competently: background information gathering, facilitating communication, communicating information to others, analysing information, facilitating agreement, managing cases and documenting information. Certain knowledge, skills, abilities and other attributes required of a mediator are also identified. They include reasoning, analysing, problem-solving, reading comprehension, writing, oral and non-verbal communication, emotional stability and maturity, sensitivity, integrity, impartiality, and a commitment to assisting others.
36   H Brown and A Marriott *ADR Principles and Practice* (2nd edn), Sweet & Maxwell, London, 1999, at pp 329–36; and J Stulberg *Taking Charge/Managing Conflict*,

the skills and techniques which can be learned and developed by mediators.[37] The Center for Public Resources' Commentary on its Mediation Rules provides a list of desirable attributes, which includes:

- articulateness and persuasiveness;
- flexibility and patience;
- good listening;
- problem analysis and problem solving ability;
- creativity;
- good negotiation skills.[38]

The results from a recent Australian survey ranked the most desirable attributes of a mediator in the following order of priority:

- patience;
- friendliness;
- sense of humour;
- good organisation skills, and
- empathy.[39]

Desirable attributes for mediators include intelligence, common sense, persuasiveness, scepticism and optimism. Much the same qualities would be of benefit in many other professions and it is difficult to isolate any personal traits which are unique to mediators.[40] Most of the attributes of mediators are similar to those of other professionals and skilled helpers such as counsellors, lawyers, managers or specialist negotiators. Nevertheless, it is possible to list some attributes which, while not unique to mediators, would be regarded as indispensable in most forms of mediation:

(a) *Trustworthy:* The engendering of trust is important in mediation; mediators should be persons who inspire trust in others. Trust can be provided through a mediator's reputation and association with a reputable mediation service, but it also needs to be developed and maintained during the mediation through the appearance of objectivity, reliability and honesty.

(b) *Non-judgmental:* Mediators need to be able to demonstrate impartiality throughout the mediation, not only in treating the parties fairly but also in suspending their judgment of the parties and their evaluation of the matters in dispute.

(c) *Empathetic:* Empathy goes beyond being non-judgmental in that mediators need the ability to comprehend the thoughts, perceptions and feelings of each party and to be able to acknowledge and validate them.[41]

Lexington Books, Lexington, Massachusetts, 1987, at p 37, asks wryly: 'Is he [sic] the proverbial nice guy who finished last and decided to try peacekeeping for a living?'

37 On these skills, see Chapter 6.

38 Center for Public Resources *Commentary on the Mediation Rules.*

39 Bond Dispute Resolution Centre *Reflections on conflicts – lessens learned*, Survey results, October 1999.

40 Less reverent typologies suggest: the patience of Job, the sincerity and bulldog features of the English, the wit of the Irish, the guile of Machiavelli, the hide of a rhinoceros and the wisdom of Solomon. See W Maggiolo *Techniques of Mediation*, Oceana Publications, New York, 1985, at p 73.

41 J Stulberg *Taking Charge/Managing Conflict*, Lexington Books, Lexington, Massachusetts, 1987, at p 38.

(d) *Creative:* Although mediation operates within the shadow of the law, mediators need to have a broad concept of relevance, imagination, and creative approaches to problem-solving. Creativity can be a product of mediation experience.[42]

(e) *Patient and persistent:* Mediations can be lengthy, repetitive and at times tedious, which might suggest that they are unproductive and should be terminated. While there is a duty to terminate mediations under certain situations, mediators should do this on objective criteria and not on the basis of their own impatience or frustration. Persistence can become oppressive where one or more of the parties feel that they will not be let out without a settlement,[43] and an agreement reached under these conditions could be invalidated on grounds of coercion or undue influence. Nevertheless, the mediator's persistence is an important attribute where parties are discouraged and wish to give up but there are good grounds for continuing.[44] Most mediators can testify to remarkable turnarounds from seemingly impossible deadlocks to satisfactory settlements within short periods of time.[45]

(f) *Self-reflective:* Mediators should be self-reflective practitioners. Self-reflection requires, at the most basic level, an honest critique of what went well in a mediation and what could have been done differently.[46] Self-reflection provides the basis for individual development as a mediator, and for accumulated knowledge about mediation practice. While all professionals should be self-reflective, this is particularly important for mediators in the light of the novelty of mediation practice.

(g) *Tolerance:* As globalisation occurs, it is important that a mediator is tolerant of other cultures and aware that cultural differences may play a very important role in the dynamics of a dispute. A mediator needs to be able to determine ways in which the needs of different cultures can be accommodated into the process of mediation.[47]

---

42 Thus it would be inconceivable for a mediator, faced with an impasse over access to children on Christmas day, not to raise, through whatever appropriate means, the option of rotating Christmas days over the years or of 'expanding the pie' by defining Christmas from 12pm on Christmas Eve to 8pm on Christmas day and inviting the parties to divide up this period.

43 There are anecdotes in mediation circles of mediators who adopt a 'starve the jury' approach and keep parties together until a settlement is reached. There will be fewer concerns about undue influence where the parties are powerful and have advisers present.

44 W Pengilley 'Hidden agendas and other matters' (1993) 4 *ADRJ* 53 at 68: 'Mediation is only for the persistent and the strong'.

45 In one mediation, the mediation started at 10am and at 11.15am one of the lawyers insisted that it be terminated for lack of progress. The mediator persisted and an agreement was reached at 6pm which, in the parties' view, was satisfactory. The mediator's persistence was vindicated.

46 This requirement is grounded in systems theory: see G Tillet *The Myths of Mediation*, 1991; G Kurien 'Critique of Myths of Mediation' (1995) 6 *ADRJ* 43 at 51.

47 L Lin 'Impact of cultural differences on dispute resolution' (1996) 7 *ADRJ* 197; S Beattie 'Is mediation a real alternative to law? Pitfalls for Aboriginal participants' (1997) 8 *ADRJ* 57; and B Goh 'Culture: the silent negotiator' (1999) 2(2) *The ADR Bulletin* 19.

Mediation competence and experience

There is a school of thought that mediation is an art and not a science, and that mediation skills are inherent and cannot be learned and developed.[48] The better view is that a mediator should have established competence in at least three areas:[49] knowledge of the theory and process of negotiation and mediation; the mediation skills of planning, organisation, communication, intervention and analysis; and attitudes appropriate for mediation, including an acceptance of its philosophy and ethics. Competence in these three areas can be developed through training, education and reflection.[50] Experience assists mediators in designing and driving the mediation in a manner which is most likely to produce an effective outcome.[51]

US studies have shown that a mediator who has actual or perceived experience of mediation is more likely to have an influence on the negotiations in the mediation.[52] More recent American studies have confirmed the correlation between experience of mediation and effectiveness in reaching a settlement.[53] However, a study of the mediators in the Suffolk County Massachusetts Civil Mediation Programme indicates that prior experience of mediation cannot always be relied upon as a strong predictor of effective performance and that more intensely trained mediators can realise better outcomes irrespective of their experience as mediators.[54]

The *facilitative* model of mediation identifies mediation competence and experience as important mediator qualities.

Expertise in the subject matter of the dispute

There is debate over whether a mediator should have expertise in the subject matter of a dispute, for example engineering expertise for a construction mediation or clinical expertise for a medical negligence mediation.[55] The view that mediators do

---

48 Mediators are born, not made: New South Wales Law Reform Commission *Alternative dispute resolution – training and accreditation of mediators*, Discussion Paper 21, 1989, at p 21. As J Stulberg *Taking Charge/Managing Conflict*, Lexington Books, Lexington, Massachusetts, 1987, at p 27, notes: 'A mediator does more than just "stay loose" or "use common sense"'.

49 D Cruickshank, 'Training mediators: moving towards competency-based training' in K Mackie (ed) *A Handbook of Dispute Resolution*, 1991, at p 248.

50 On mediator training and accreditation, see Chapter 11.

51 C Nupen 'Mediation' in P Pretorius (ed) *Dispute Resolution*, Juta & Co, Kenwyn, South Africa, 1993, at pp 39–40.

52 J Pearson et al 'The decision to mediate: profiles of individuals who accept and reject the opportunity to mediate contested child custody and visitation issues' (1982) 6 *J Divorce* 1.

53 J Pearson and M Thoennes, 'Divorce Mediation Research Results' in Folberg and Milne (eds) *Divorce Mediation: Theory and Practice*, Guildford Press, New York, 1988, at p 436; and R L Wissler 'A close look at settlement week' (1998) 4 *Dispute Resolution Magazine* 28.

54 J Pearson 'Family Mediation' in Ohio State University College of Law (eds) *Court Reform Implications of Dispute Resolution*, Ohio State University College of Law, 1995, at p 160.

55 David Shapiro, an international mediator, when asked by parties whether he knew anything about the subject matter of the dispute, pizza crust technology, replied 'what do you want, an expert pizza maker or an expert mediator?': *Law Society Gazette*, 15 July 1998.

not have to be experts in the subject matter of the dispute is consistent with the process/content distinction, the assumed neutrality of the mediator and the philosophical assumptions of the mediation system. The danger with expert mediators is that they may wish 'to supplant their own judgment of what is appropriate for that of the parties'.[56] This may not only frustrate the parties in the achievement of their goals, but may also diminish the acceptability of the mediator. Moreover, there is a danger that skilled experts may find it difficult to distinguish between their roles as professional accountants or architects, as the case may be, and mediators, or that they might disguise, say, their advising or counselling functions, in order to push the parties to a position which they as experts regard as appropriate.

There is, however, a market demand for mediators who are experts in the substantive areas of disputes.[57] This is particularly the case in respect of senior legal practitioners who, given the 'shadow of the law' reality, are seen to provide some kind of insurance against adverse legal repercussions in mediated settlements. Settling under the supervision of a legal expert also provides apparent security, in terms of shared responsibility, for lawyers referring clients to mediation. While these may be unconvincing reasons for the choice of senior lawyers, there are clearly strengths which such experts can bring to mediation, for example as 'agents of reality' in the mediation's separate meetings.[58]

In addition, in commercial mediation, if parties require a mediator to give a non-binding recommendation if parties reach impasse in the mediation, a specialist in the subject matter of the dispute is likely to be preferred. In that case, as well as in those cases where the parties believe that an expert in the subject matter is desirable, it is also possible to use co-mediation or a pupil mediator to obtain a blend of experience, with both mediation and subject matter experience.[59]

Desirable expertise is not limited to legal expertise, for example an engineer may be sought for a construction dispute, a practising doctor mediator in a professional negligence dispute and a mediator with environmental knowledge in an international environmental dispute.[60] In environmental and other large public interest mediations, some US commentators argue that mediators with relevant technical and scientific knowledge and public sector experience are desirable.[61]

The background qualifications and experience can enhance the value of mediation, provided the professionals are able to distinguish between their normal roles and

---

56   C Nupen 'Mediation' in P Pretorius (ed) *Dispute Resolution*, Juta & Co, Kenwyn, South Africa, 1993, at p 41. See also D Shapiro 'Expert mediators – not experts as mediators' *Resolutions*, Issue no 16, at p 4.

57   J Wade 'My mediator must be a QC' (1994) 5 *ADJR* 161 at 161–2. The market demand may be a product of misunderstanding about the nature of mediation and faulty assumptions about the functions of a mediator.

58   On separate meetings, see further below.

59   See, for example, Commercial Court Working Party on ADR *Second Report*; Centre for Dispute Resolution *Model Mediation Procedure and Guidance Notes*; Center for Public Resources *Model Procedure for Business Disputes in Europe*; and Commercial Court *ADR Orders Guidance Notes*.

60   H Gregorczuk 'The appropriateness of mediation in international environmental disputes' (1996) 7 *ADRJ* 47 at 52–4.

61   L Susskind 'Multi-party public policy mediation: a separate breed' *American Bar Association Dispute Resolution Magazine*, Autumn 1997 edition.

those of mediators. Even where non-expert mediators are used, they should at least be able to grasp what the issues are and to comprehend basic terminology in the area, as it would be inefficient to have to educate them about every element of the dispute. The *settlement* and *evaluative* models of mediation place this higher priority on substantive expertise than on process skills as desirable qualifications for mediators. David Shapiro explains:

'Insistence upon . . . subject matter expertise reflects most litigants' preoccupation with finding a legal or factual answer to a specific question where, under the guise of mediation, the mediator is expected to give a view on the merits of the case . . .' [62]

A study by Wheeler showed that specialists and non-specialists are treated differently by disputants.[63] American studies have also shed light on this debate. One US study found that a mediation is more likely to be successful if a mediator shares at least the social or cultural experiences of the parties or brings to the dispute a detailed knowledge of the parties' perspectives.[64] A more recent US study found that parties or their lawyers perceived that a mediator's lack of subject matter expertise was a factor in continued impasse in the mediation.[65] English studies of family mediation have shown that clients who believed that the mediator was not confident or familiar in handling the dispute, over for example children's issues, dismissed the possibility of a successful outcome.[66] The predominant school of thought in the UK, for much of the 1990s, has been that mediation expertise, rather than subject matter expertise, can translate to any context.[67] That school of thought also considers that subject matter expertise may tempt a mediator to take an evaluative or adjudicative approach.[68] Karl Mackie concludes:

'. . . if you have someone who specialises in [the] sector and is a good mediator, this will often be more effective – specialists will tend to have a quicker grasp of the various negotiating options that already exist in a field . . . there is a danger that their expertise may get in the way of their mediation role, but if they allow that to happen they are by definition unlikely to be excellent mediators in the first place . . .' [69]

---

62 D Shapiro 'Expert mediators – not experts as mediators' *Resolutions*, Issue no 16, p 4.

63 S Wheeler 'Lawyer involvement in commercial disputes' (1991) 18 *Journal of Law and Society* 241 at 244: although the study considered lawyers rather than mediators, the findings are relevant to mediators.

64 W Felstiner, R Abel and A Sarat 'The emergence and transformation of disputes: naming, blaming and claiming' (1980–1) 15 *Law & Society Review* 631.

65 S R Marsh *Materials from 5th Annual ADR Institute of the State Bar of Texas*, 1993 (available at http://www.adrr.com/adr4/statistics.htm).

66 See, for example, University of Newcastle upon Tyne Conciliation Project Unit, *Report to the Lord Chancellor's Department on the cost and effectiveness of conciliation in England and Wales*, March 1989, at p 306 where a solicitor reported about a mediator, following a family mediation: 'if you got somebody doing a lecture and he's lost, the audience knows he's lost. We were aware that he was lost so he couldn't do anything really except waffle about'.

67 M Davies, G Davis and J Webb *Promoting Mediation: Report of a study of Bristol Law Society's Mediation Scheme in its preliminary phase*, 1996 Research & Policy Planning Unit Research Study no 21, The Law Society.

68 Centre for Dispute Resolution *Court Referred ADR: a guide for the judiciary*, CEDR, London, 1999.

69 K Mackie 'Expert mediators – not experts as mediators: CEDR replies' *Resolutions*, Issue no 16, at p 5.

Professional background

An issue, which has generated debate, is whether a mediator should be a lawyer or have some other background. One US study has indicated that lawyers do not necessarily perform better than non-lawyers in civil mediation programmes.[70] If a mediation occurs after proceedings have been issued, legal knowledge would be helpful to put to the parties the legal consequences or cost implications of failing to settle the case at the mediation. Even in the case of community and family mediation, it is suggested that legal knowledge is important to aid the mediator in redressing power and information imbalances.[71] In family mediation, legal knowledge is considered to be necessary if financial and property issues are involved,[72] although codes of conduct for solicitor family mediators remind them that the function of a mediator is to be neutral and impartial and not to advise or represent a party in the mediation.[73] Respondents to the authors' 2000 survey of UK law firms provided a number of family mediation examples, involving non-lawyer mediators, where the type of settlement drafted in the mediation was inappropriate to the cases in question.[74]

Few generalisations are possible about the preferred professional backgrounds of mediators. Some consider that the primary role of barristers as advocates makes them unsuitable for the role of mediator. Others consider that solicitors themselves should not act as mediators since their training and partisan relationship with clients is incompatible with the role of mediator.[75] Others consider that, in the family context, where solicitors may act as consultants to mediators, solicitors may expose themselves to a raft of ethical dilemmas.[76] Yet others consider that solicitors are particularly well-suited to the role of mediator, with their knowledge of law and procedure and their experience in negotiation. Some social workers are insufficiently task-oriented to assist the parties to reach an outcome. Some former judges acknowledge the difficulty of moving from their elevated position of umpire at the bench of the courtroom to the modest position of facilitator at the veneer of the mediation table. But there are also exceptions to these patterns. Much will depend on the model of mediation which is required. In *settlement mediation* lawyers will be well-suited, social workers are well-trained for *therapeutic mediation*, and in

---

70 Finding relates to the Suffolk County Massachusetts Civil Mediation Programme, as reported by J Pearson 'Family Mediation' in *Court Reform Implications of Dispute Resolution*, Ohio State University College of Law, 1995, at p 160.

71 See, for example, L Webley *A review of the literature on family mediation: prepared for the Lord Chancellor's Advisory Committee on Legal Education and Conduct*, Institute of Advanced Legal Studies, 1998, at p 87.

72 University of Newcastle upon Tyne Conciliation Project Unit, *Report to the Lord Chancellor's Department on the costs and effectiveness of conciliation in England and Wales*, March 1989, at p 127.

73 For example, Law Society of England & Wales *Code of Practice for Family Mediation*.

74 The lawyers surveyed indicated frustration that these mediations had proceeded on entirely inappropriate bases for the types of case in issue, and that re-adjusting clients' expectations was difficult and took considerable time.

75 University of Newcastle upon Tyne Conciliation Project Unit, *Report to the Lord Chancellor's Department on the costs and effectiveness of conciliation in England and Wales*, March 1989, at p 54.

76 H Brown and A Marriott *ADR Principles and Practice* (2nd edn), Sweet & Maxwell, London, 1999, at p 237.

evaluative mediation, former judges are a possible choice. In the case of *facilitative mediation*, all professionals will be required to subordinate some of their traditional professional skills and attitudes and replace them with the process skills of this model. The layperson with no professional background but with a high degree of skill in the mediation process would also be a suitable mediator for this model.

Insider/outsider

In many cases, parties will select as mediators outsiders to the dispute in order to provide independence and neutrality. This is particularly the case with *facilitative mediation*. For instance, in international disputes, it has been suggested that the mediator should come from a country other than that of any party to the dispute, unless the parties agree otherwise.[77] In that context, the mediator is usually a person of prestige, a recognised leader.[78] However, in *evaluative mediation* use may be made of an 'insider' to act as mediator. An example of insider mediators would be supervisors in organisations. Insider mediators will have to gain acceptance from all parties in order to be able to use their position to full advantage.

Power to reward agreements

In some circumstances mediators may be regarded as appropriate because of their power to reward agreements. This is most evident in international conflicts where a major power which acts as mediator can promise and confer benefits on both sides of a conflict between nation-states, or groupings within a state. This capacity could also be a factor in the use of mediation in large organisations, in which a manager or supervisor could 'reward' the mediation behaviour of employees or managers.

Other factors

Among the other factors which might be considered in appointing a mediator are:

- the terms of the mediator's Agreement to Mediate;[79]
- membership of a professional association;
- accountability under a set of mediator guidelines and ethical standards;[80]
- the availability of professional indemnity insurance;
- the gender of the mediator;[81]

---

77 For example, Center for Public Resources *Model Procedure for Business Disputes in Europe.*
78 P Gulliver *Disputes and negotiations: a cross-cultural perspective*, Academic Press, New York, 1979, at p 216.
79 On Agreements to Mediate, see Chapter 12.
80 On which, see Chapter 11.
81 Compare US studies that show that the gender of a mediator does not appear to affect the outcome and nor does there appear to be a relationship between the gender of a mediator and disputants' satisfaction with the process or assessment of a mediator's effectiveness: see, for example, R Lim and P Carnevale 'Contingencies in the Mediation of Disputes' (1990) *Journal of Personality and Social Psychology* 259; and V Wall and M Dewhurst 'Mediator Gender: Communication differences in resolved and unresolved mediations' (1991) 9(1) *Mediation Quarterly* 63.

the level of fees charged by a mediator. A range of fee structures is used, for example, a flat rate and an hourly rate, which varies depending either upon the amount at stake in the dispute or the seniority of the mediator.[82]

A number of mediator codes of conduct set out three occasions when a mediator should not take up an appointment. The first is when a mediator does not have adequate time to conduct the mediation promptly.[83] Secondly, mediators should only accept appointments in cases where they regard themselves as competent.[84] Finally, conflicts of interest may prevent a mediator from either taking up an appointment or continuing a mediation.[85]

Preparation for the Mediation Meeting

Importance of preparation

There is considerable variation in the extent to which preparatory work is undertaken prior to the mediation meeting. In some situations relatively little preparation is done, and there is no prior contact between the mediator and the disputants. In other situations there are extensive preliminary contacts and preparation, including the *intake procedure*. The policy guidelines of some mediation services regulate the extent and nature of the preparatory work and emphasise the necessity of screening potential cases for suitability. In private mediations the intake procedure depends on the availability of time and other resources, the nature of the conflict and the parties, and the personal style of the mediator. In the case of a commercial mediation, mediation organisations provide the services of case managers to assist with preparations for a mediation. The conventional wisdom is that the more preparatory work is undertaken, the more likely the mediation meeting is to produce a settlement; preparation lays the groundwork for effective mediation.[86] In some cases the preparatory work will result in a settlement before the mediation meeting, the equivalent of settling 'on the steps of the courthouse'.

Information gathering and exchange

The gathering, exchange and analysis of information are important parts of the preparatory stages of mediation, although mediation does not provide the procedures found in the court system to ensure the discovery and disclosure of relevant

---

82 See the section on Mediation Organisations in Chapter 7 for further information on mediation fees.
83 See, for example, Academy of Expert's *Code of Conduct and Guidance Notes for Mediators*; ADR Group's *Professional Code of Conduct*; Commercial Mediation Centre's *Mediator Code of Conduct*; Centre for Dispute Resolution's *Code of Conduct*; and Center for Public Resources' *Model Mediation Agreement*.
84 See, for example, Mediation UK *Standards*; Commercial Mediation Centre *Mediator Code of Conduct*; and ADR Group *Professional Code of Conduct*.
85 See sections on Conflicts of Interest in Chapters 11 and 12.
86 C Moore *The Mediation Process: practical strategies for resolving conflict* (2nd edn), Jossey-Bass, San Francisco, 1996, at pp 81–190 for a strong endorsement of systematic preparatory activities.

information by the respective parties. Full disclosure may be required by the Agreement to Mediate[87] and the mediator or mediation service may, in the preparatory stages, be able to assist in identifying data which needs to be obtained and disclosed and to encourage and supervise the exchange.

However, a mediator is not required to make independent enquiries for information or verify the information provided.[88] In the case of civil/commercial mediation, it is usual for the parties to exchange, a week before the mediation, a written summary, providing a chronology of events and outlining the issues, which are agreed between the parties; the issues in dispute between the parties; each party's main legal, commercial or technical arguments; and any previous without prejudice offers made. The summary should not resemble a formal pleading. If a mediation organisation is involved, the summary is normally sent to the organisation, which will forward a copy of the summary to each other party and the mediator. Summaries are concise summaries, usually six to eight pages in length.[89] A joint submission by the parties, setting out in tabulated form, to provide a comparison, the issues over which there is agreement and those still outstanding would provide mediators with an invaluable aid. However, it is unusual for parties to co-operate to that extent at this stage of a mediation, although as mediation practice develops, this may begin to occur. The summary will be accompanied by a joint bundle of the main supporting documents. Where the mediation takes place during the course of legal proceedings, the parties usually exchange all reports and documents associated with litigation. However, as mediation is not fact-obsessed there is sometimes, by agreement, a more limited exchange of information. The mediator will usually receive copies of documents exchanged between the parties and may also be given information on a confidential basis, which will assist him or her in diagnosing the conflict, in assessing its suitability for mediation, and in developing a specific strategy for the subsequent stages of the mediation process. However, most mediators do not themselves require access to all the documentation associated with the litigation process.[90] Information gathering and exchange can also assist the parties to narrow the areas in dispute, and help to educate them about each other's case.

In comparison, in community mediation, the parties would not prepare summaries of a case or produce a joint bundle of documents ahead of the mediation. Parties would simply bring to the mediation relevant documents. In the case of family mediation, the mediator usually receives preliminary information from each party about their personal circumstances, which allows the mediator to assess if there are any issues, like violence, requiring immediate consideration. A structured approach is taken to

---

87 The model agreements to mediate used in family mediation typically require the parties to make full, frank and true disclosure of finances and to provide supporting documentation: see, for example, NFM's *Model Agreement to Mediate*.

88 See, for example, Law Society of England & Wales *Code of Practice in both Family Mediation and Civil/Commercial Mediation*.

89 The mediation procedures of a number of mediation organisations set out the requirements in relation to written summaries, for instance: Centre for Dispute Resolution, *Model Mediation Procedure*; Academy of Experts *Guidelines for Mediation* and *Guidance Notes for Mediators*; Centre for Business Arbitration *Mediation Rules*; and Center for Public Resources *Model Mediation Procedure for Business Disputes in Europe*.

90 For example, most commercial mediation organisations in the UK encourage parties to submit a six to eight page summary of their case and to exchange and refer only to essential documents.

gathering information regarding finances, involving as a first step completion by each party of an extensive questionnaire on their financial affairs. Although attempts may be made to receive this information ahead of the mediation, it is usual for the issue of financial disclosure to be discussed and arranged in the course of the mediation, once parties understand the requirements. If it emerges that one party is not willing to disclose information to another, the mediator needs to consider whether or not to continue with the mediation. Although the mediator avoids an inquisitorial approach, the mediator will seek clarification where information is inadequate.[91] Verification of information is an issue for the parties' solicitors. The fact that the mediator does not verify information should be explained to the parties. The mediator should also explain to the parties that he or she cannot guarantee child support calculations.[92] The mediator checks that the parties understand the meaning of documents and refers the parties to outside experts if further clarification is required.[93]

Determining which party representative should attend the mediation

The effectiveness of a mediation will depend on having the appropriate party representatives involved in the process.

Authority

A mediator will confirm before the mediation that authority to settle will be available at the mediation. The authority should also extend to executing the settlement agreement. Most mediation organisations, if these organisations are administering a mediation, will require written confirmation by each party that their representatives have the requisite authority.[94]

The authority issue can raise a number of difficulties. In community mediation it is not uncommon for a relative of the person in dispute to attend the mediation in place of that party. Even if that third party has authority to attend, it can be futile, since the aim of community mediation is usually to control behaviour, which is difficult if the party in dispute later claims that, as they have not agreed to the terms of any agreement reached in the mediation, they cannot be held to it.[95] In all kinds of

---

91 Law Society of England and Wales *Family Mediation Training Standards*.
92 Common provision in family mediator codes of conduct, for example: UK College of Family Mediators, the NFM and FMA.
93 UK College of Family Mediators *1999/2000 Directory and Handbook*, Sweet & Maxwell, London, 1999, at p A90.
94 For example, Academy of Expert's *Guidance Notes for Mediators*; Center for Public Resources *Mediation Procedure for Business Disputes in Europe*; London Court of International Arbitration *Mediation Procedure*.
95 Examples are given by R E Mackay and A J Brown *Community Mediation in Scotland: a study of implementation*, The Scottish Office Central Research Unit, Edinburgh, 1999. For example, the male partners of female neighbours in dispute met and agreed to regulate their respective partners' behaviour, but the agreement broke down. In another example, a mother agreed in a mediation that she would control her son, which led to serious tensions within her family. In a further example residents did not accept an agreement which had been reached in mediation by one of their neighbours.

mediation, any pre-determined limit on authority can reduce the prospect of reaching a successful outcome.[96] In civil/commercial mediations, if legal representatives appear in substitution for the parties, it will be more difficult for the lawyers themselves to negotiate a settlement.[97] In commercial and public sector mediations, in particular, the internal representatives of the parties are unlikely to have unlimited authority. The internal representative may have to contact a principal in the course of the mediation to receive approval for proposals. The mediation might need to be adjourned to allow the relevant approval to be obtained, typically in cases where Board or Committee ratification is required. Any agreement reached in the mediation would need to be made contingent upon that ratification, although a mediator may insist that the relevant party should have authority 'effectively to recommend' the outcome of the mediation to the Board or Committee.[98] The UK mediation pilot for planning appeals indicated that a reason for the failure to reach agreement included lack of delegated authority. The pilot highlighted that officers acting as representatives for an authority need to be 'stakeholders', in the sense of having authority to act or the appropriate status in the authority.[99] Any limitation on authority should be notified to the mediator, who may insist that the other parties be made aware of the issue, in case they wish to decline to proceed on that basis.[100]

Problems of authority may also arise if an insurer is involved in a dispute.[101] A representative from the insurance company or the insurer's solicitors will have the authority to settle, albeit frequently up to a pre-determined limit, at which point reference back to the principal at the insurance company would be required.[102] Where an insurance company attends a mediation without the insured party, for example the defendant in a personal injury case, experience indicates that the injured party may not be satisfied with the process as the anger and hurt is not directed to the appropriate person.[103]

---

96 L Street 'Representation in commercial mediation' (1994) *Australian Dispute Resolution Journal* 256.
97 See H Genn *Central London County Court Mediation Pilot: Evaluation Report*, LCD Research Series, No 5/98, at p 54.
98 D Shapiro 'Pushing the envelope – selective techniques for tough mediations' (2000) *ADRLJ* 117.
99 See section on Property-related Disputes in Chapter 8 and M Welbank *Mediation in the Planning System*, DETR, London, May 2000.
100 D Shapiro 'Pushing the envelope', op cit.
101 See D Foskett *The Law and Practice of Compromise* (4th edn), Sweet & Maxwell, London, 1996.
102 Occasionally, an insurance company may agree to abide by the terms of the settlement reached by the insured in a mediation. The Agreement to Mediate, issued by the Northern Ireland Law Society Dispute Resolution Service, contains the clause: 'in the event of any party to the mediation being insured in relation to the subject matter or issue the subject of the mediation such party shall be assumed to have advised the insurer/s and to have obtained consent to proceed with the mediation. The mediators shall not be under any obligation to have regard to the interest of any such insurer or other third party.'
103 In addition, insurance company representatives have, in those circumstances, expressed considerable discomfort in having to provide explanations sought by the injured party: M Dewdney, B Sordo and C Chinkin *Continuing development in mediation within the legal system and evaluation of the 1992–3 Settlement Week in New South Wales*, Law Society of NSW, 1993, at p 162.

Other requirements

It is preferable that the representative in a commercial mediation should not have a personal stake in the outcome of the mediation.[104] Although this may not be possible to achieve in each case, it is desirable that the internal representative of a corporate or institutional party in a commercial mediation is at one level higher in the structure of the organisation than that of the person who created the dispute.[105] The representative of a party in all types of mediation should also have the appropriate attributes, like empathy and good listening skills, to make the most of the attempt at mediation.[106] The representative should also have the requisite knowledge or technical skills to cover all the issues in the mediation. Alternatively, contact should be possible with the person with the relevant skills. The pilot mediation scheme in the UK for planning appeals, for example, revealed a number of cases, where the planner required input from an engineer, but could not make contact with an engineer, and was left in the position of either having to second guess the engineer or refusing to discuss the issue in the mediation, with the result that those mediations failed to achieve resolution.[107] Public sector/interest mediations, as in the case of environmental disputes, have shown that it is also important to involve persons who will be responsible for implementation of any agreement reached.[108]

Third parties

The issue of whether, and if so which, third parties should attend arises in the context of commercial disputes, where accountants and experts may be involved, and in relation to public interest/sector mediations, where there may be a need to include persons and organisations, beyond those parties in dispute. Interviews with groups of people may identify stakeholders in public interest/sector disputes. Although not parties to any court action or relevant agreement, there may be a large number of interested parties, who have a moral entitlement to be involved in the process. Indentifying these parties can be difficult as these kinds of disputes can have far-reaching implications. As an experienced US public sector mediator explains, it is necessary 'to go slow in order to go fast' during this phase of the process.[109] Determining who should be at the mediation table requires a shift in focus away

---

104 R Mnookin 'Why negotiations fail: An examination of barriers to the resolution of conflict' (1993) 8 *Ohio State Journal on Dispute Resolution* 235 at 238.

105 See, for example, E Green 'Corporate Alternative Dispute Resolution' (1986) 1 *Ohio State Journal on Dispute Resolution* 203 at 240; and B Blegvad 'Commercial Relations, Contract and Litigation in Denmark: A discussion of Macaulay's Theories' (1990) 24 *Ohio State Journal on Dispute Resolution* 390 at 402. It is suggested that, in some industries, like construction, however, politics are so bad that senior people are afraid to override decisions made by people at lower levels in the organisation: F Carr et al 'The Untapped Potential of ADR in the Construction Industry' (1995) *Federal Lawyer* 32 at 36.

106 L Mulcahy et al *Mediating medical negligence claims: an option for the future?* NHS Executive, 2000, at p xv.

107 M Welbank *Mediation in the Planning System*, DETR, London, March 2000, at p 50.

108 For example, G Bingham *Resolving environmental disputes: a decade of experience*, The Conservation Foundation, 1986.

109 L Susskind 'Multi-party public policy mediation: a separate breed' *American Bar Association Dispute Resolution Magazine*, Autumn 1997 edition.

from the number of interested parties to the categories of interests that should be represented. Careful consideration needs to be given to how the diversity of interests involved in the dispute can be adequately represented. Considerable effort may also be involved in persuading stakeholders to participate in the mediation. Susskind refers to a commonly-occurring problem in this context, of public agencies confusing mediation with arbitration, which in turn may lead them to resist the efforts to convene the process.[110]

In family mediation, as mediators have regard to children's wishes in the mediation, the issue arises whether this should be done by consulting directly with the children or by questioning the parents. There is no unanimity in approach on this issue. Some mediators prefer children to attend the mediation sessions, largely to control the sessions and prevent parents from becoming entrenched.[111] The conciliation scheme in the London Family Division requires children to be brought to the conciliation appointment. Although the aim of involving children is to ensure that their wishes are established, children are not asked to make decisions on issues.[112]

In all cases, it is necessary to consider whether there is some other person who is crucial to a resolution, even if that person is not a party. For example, in a neighbour dispute, a family business dispute, a mortgage case or a clinical negligence case, the spouse of a party may be critical to the resolution. Parties to a dispute can also confer rights on a third party, notwithstanding their non-involvement in a mediation, by virtue of the Contracts (Rights of Third Parties) Act 1999, discussed further in the context of enforcement of mediated agreements.

Contact with the parties

Where time, resources and relevant policies allow, mediators may decide to have personal contact with each party (and their lawyers) before the mediation. This is more likely to occur in private mediations, and some experienced mediators always attempt to interview each of the parties in person before the mediation meeting. This contact serves several purposes:

- Information and data can be more freely provided in a confidential setting without the confrontational atmosphere of a joint meeting.[113]

---

110 L Susskind 'Multi-party public policy mediation: a separate breed' *American Bar Association Dispute Resolution Magazine*, Autumn 1997 edition, where the author recommends that 'it is better to walk away from a possible mediation than to get involved when the parties are confused about what the process entails, or when a key party does not accept the premise that mediation is voluntary, and remains so right up until the agreement is signed'.

111 University of Newcastle upon Tyne Conciliation Project Unit, *Report to the Lord Chancellor's Department on the costs and effectiveness of conciliation in England and Wales*, March 1989, at p 330. In a recent study of family mediators in Scotland the differences in approach to this issue were apparent: F Myers and F Wasoff *A meeting in the middle—a study of solicitors' and mediators' divorce practice*, Scottish Executive, 2000, Chapter 5.

112 For detailed consideration of the issues relating to children, see D Saposnek 'The value of children in mediation: a cross-culture perspective' (1991) 8(4) *Mediation Quarterly*.

113 J Haynes *Divorce mediation: a practical guide for therapists and counsellors*, Springer Publishing, New York, 1981, at pp 10–17.

- Parties can be educated about the mediation generally and about the specific procedures which will be followed at the mediation meeting, without any embarrassment or loss of face. An outline of the role of the mediator and lawyers may also be provided.
- The mediator can establish a close working relationship with the parties and develop trust and acceptability.
- Where the contact takes place at the same venue at which the mediation will be held, it serves to familiarise the parties with the physical environment and amenities.
- A less empowered party can be reassured by the mediator and even have a 'rehearsal' for parts of the mediation meeting such as their party presentation (see below).
- Where each party to the dispute has more than one member, the contact sessions can be used to discuss how decisions will be made within each team.

Where there is prior personal contact, mediators and agencies are careful to ensure an approximate equality in the kind and amount of contact with the various parties so as to preclude any suspicion of favouritism or bias. In the mediator's opening (see below), reference is made to the prior contacts so that a subsequent allusion to them does not cause surprise and suspicion.

Preliminary meeting

In some mediations a preliminary meeting is held to consolidate the preparatory activities. Such a meeting provides an important opportunity to remove as many obstacles to an agreed outcome as is possible before the intensive discussions and negotiations at the mediation.[114] The preliminary meeting is convened and chaired by the mediator and is used to:

- assess the parameters of the dispute;
- specify what issues will be dealt with at the mediation meeting;
- arrange for the disclosure and exchange of information;
- establish that the parties at the mediation meeting will have authority to settle;
- identify the participants in the mediation meeting;
- settle the Agreement to Mediate; and
- make organisational arrangements.

InterMediation[115] has developed the *START ADR Protocol*,[116] which provides parties to a civil/commercial or multi-party mediation with protocols to assist them in the pre-mediation phase, with the following objectives in mind:

- to clarify issues;
- to check authority issues;
- to identify possible groupings of interests in multi-party cases; and
- to 'ring-fence' any issues, which the parties may wish to resolve prior to the mediation or by other ADR means.

---

114 G Charlton 'Preliminary conferences: a quality control tool for mediators' (1997) 8 ADRJ 114.
115 For further details on Mediation Organisations, see Chapter 7.
116 InterMediation *START ADR Protocol*, InterMediation, August 2000.

In some situations only legal advisers attend preliminary meetings but there is no restriction on the presence of the parties and other participants. Preliminary meetings have been evaluated in Australia as important contributors to effective mediation. It is not unknown for disputants to resolve their disputes at the preliminary meeting. Shapiro refers to pre-mediation issue identification as a possible catalyst for settlement, by sharpening the issues and casting doubt in the minds of the lawyers on the outcome, creating the opportunities for a negotiated resolution.[117]

Settling the agreement to mediate

Where there is a written Agreement to Mediate, this is normally settled before the mediation meeting, sometimes at the preliminary meeting. It is common in commercial disputes, and in other matters brought to mediation by lawyers, for the parties to sign an Agreement to Mediate.

It is usually signed by the mediator and any pupil mediator.[118] Even in the cases of community and family mediation, entry into a mediation agreement is practical and indicates commitment to the process and to resolution of the dispute.[119] In the case of community mediation, the agreement is usually informal, referring to the date of and place for the mediation.

In the context of commercial mediation, mediation organisations have standard mediation agreements, although the parties can, usually with the help of their lawyers and the mediator, draft their own agreement.[120] A mediator will usually contact the parties ahead of the mediation to ensure their understanding of the mediation process and the ground rules for the mediation. A mediation agreement will deal with the following issues:

- organisational and procedural matters;
- confidentiality and privilege;
- extent of disclosure of information;
- whether the mediation will be binding unless and until an agreement is reduced to writing and signed;
- whether, and if so how, the mediation can be terminated;
- the status of any litigation which is on foot;
- the parties' responsibilities for the costs of the mediation; and
- commitment to the process.

In community mediation a discussion about the costs of the mediation rarely occurs as mediation is usually free. Family mediation services may be free or

---

117 D Shapiro 'Pushing the envelope – selective techniques for tough mediations' (2000) *ADRLJ* 117 at 118. Shapiro's aim is risk avoidance, which is achieved by focusing the parties' minds on the issues and any doubts about their perceived strengths.
118 In some cases the agreements are also signed by the organisation administering the mediation. For example, the Law Society of Northern Ireland Dispute Resolution Service Agreement to Mediate is signed by the Law Society, the parties and the mediator and any pupil mediator.
119 Law Society of England and Wales *Family Mediation Training Standards*.
120 Unless Codes of Practice provide otherwise, the agreement to mediate need not be in writing, although it is good practice that it should be.

charged at a small fee or at private hourly rates. In the case of civil/commercial mediation, apart from some court mediation schemes, which involve either no or fixed fees, the costs of the mediation include the administration costs of any mediation organisation which is used; the costs of the venue, if applicable; and the mediator's fee, together with the mediator's personal expenses, such as travel and accommodation.[121]

Standard agreements stipulate that the parties bear their own legal costs, if any, of the mediation and share both the costs of the mediation and the fees of the mediator, which provides a further reassurance as to the mediator's impartiality. However, the parties may agree to share the mediation fee in some other proportion and one party may even agree to pay the entire mediation fee, for instance, to encourage the other party to attempt mediation.[122] In the settlement reached at the mediation, the parties may adjust their share of the mediation fees. In addition, the settlement may deal with the issue of the legal costs of both the mediation and any litigation which is on foot.[123] A consideration of the costs of a mediation may also require consideration to be given to the legal aid position, if relevant, of the parties.[124]

The Agreement to Mediate has the advantage of creating certainty on matters of law and procedure, it has an educative role for the parties, and it symbolically emphasises that mediation is more than 'just an ordinary discussion or negotiation'.[125]

---

121 In relation to costs:
- The Central London County Court mediation fee (£50) is split between the parties, unless they agree otherwise.
- The Law Society of Northern Ireland Dispute Resolution Service Agreement to Mediate provides that the cost of the first day of the mediation, as estimated by the Society, is payable in advance.
- The Centre for Dispute Resolution Fee Schedule sets out a sliding fee scale, depending upon the value of the claim, together with the mediator's preparation time and personal expenses.
- The London Court of International Arbitration Schedule of Mediation Fees and Expenses provides that a registration fee is payable for processing a Request for Mediation; an administration fee for time spent by the Secretariat in the administration of the mediation; expenses incurred by the Court in connection with the mediation, such as postage, telephone and room hire; and the mediator's fees and expenses. The mediator's fees are normally calculated in two ways, either by a fixed daily rate or an hourly rate. The mediator is also entitled to charge for time reserved, but not used, in certain circumstances.
122 For example, in the authors' experience, insurers, banks, local authorities, school boards and employers have all covered the full mediation costs.
123 In commercial mediations parties may agree that legal costs should be 'costs in the cause' in case the mediation is unsuccessful, and if a settlement is reached in the mediation, the costs will form part of that settlement. The Commercial Court's *Guidance Notes for Litigants and Lawyers* provides a form of ADR order, which stipulates that costs are in the cause: Commercial Court Working Party on ADR *Second Report*. See also the sections on Courts and Mediation and on Funding and Mediation in Chapters 7 and 9, for further information.
124 See the section on Funding and Mediation in Chapter 9.
125 A Acland *A sudden outbreak of common sense: managing conflict through mediation*, Hutchinson, London, 1990, at p 124.

Other preparatory matters

Whether or not there is a preliminary meeting or Agreement to Mediate, the mediator or mediation agency will have to attend to a range of organisational matters, often in consultation with the parties. These include the time and venue for the mediation meeting, the seating arrangements, access to facilities, and the duration of the mediation sessions. In some court programmes, use has been made of courtroom facilities (other than the bench) for the mediation meetings. While this is done for reasons of convenience, it had disadvantages in terms of the formal and legalistic aura of the environment. Because of the inherent flexibility of mediation, care and consideration should be given to the practicalities of the environment in which it occurs. Thus the venue should be accessible, have sufficient parking, and contain at least two rooms, one for joint meetings and the other for separate meetings. The confidentiality principle will be illusory if the rooms are not soundproof. Mediation at the premises of one of the parties may create a feeling of lack of neutrality.

In the light of the information gleaned during these early phases of the mediation, mediators are able to develop a hypothesis on what the dispute is really about, design a detailed plan for the mediation meeting, and prepare tactics and strategies for dealing with likely problems.[126] Where the co-mediation model is used, the mediators can prepare by discussing and defining their roles, functions and styles, and arranging ways of dealing with any communication or negotiation problems which arise between themselves. Good preparation is the key to effective mediation.

The Stages of the Mediation Meeting

Commentators identify different numbers of stages in the standard mediation process, ranging from seven stages to 12. The differences depend on methods of categorisation, and on whether preparatory activities are included within the stages.[127] Here attention is given to the mediation meeting only, which is depicted as having ten stages, each with its own objectives and rationale. Stages 1–5, together with the preparatory activities, can be characterised as the 'problem-defining' phase of mediation, and stages 6–10 as the 'problem-solving' phase.[128] The mediation movement has emphasised the importance of systematically identifying and defining conflicts before selecting options for their resolution.

---

126 C Moore *The Mediation Process: practical strategies for resolving conflict* (2nd edn), Jossey-Bass, San Francisco, 1996, at Chapters 5 and 6.

127 J Folberg and A Taylor *Mediation – a comprehensive guide to resolving conflicts without litigation*, Jossey-Bass, San Francisco, 1988, at pp 63–4 and 66–7; C Moore, ibid. See also H Astor and C Chinkin *Dispute Resolution in Australia*, Butterworths, Sydney, 1992, at pp 99–102; S Henderson *The Dispute Resolution Manual: a practical handbook for lawyers and other advisers*, DataLegal Publications, Spring Hill, QLD, 1993, at pp 104–14; and R Charlton and M Dewdney *The Mediator's Handbook – skills and strategies for practitioners*, The Law Book Company, Sydney, 1995, at pp 3–7, and generally for a step-by-step description of the various stages of mediation and recommended 'dos' and 'don'ts' for each stage.

128 S Henderson, ibid, at pp 104–5.

In some mediation training the two phases are symbolised by two triangles.[129] The upper triangle, on its base, represents the problem-defining phase in which the dispute, which may have been presented in narrow terms, is defined comprehensively in all its dimensions, without considering possible solutions. The lower triangle, on its apex, represents the problem-solving phase in which the dispute is narrowed down to specific outcomes. The transition from the problem-defining stages to the problem-solving stages is represented as 'crossing the triangles' (see diagram). The main variations are considered later in this chapter.

The Mediation Triangles

Preparatory Matters

Preliminaries

Mediator's Opening

Party Presentations

Identifying Areas of Agreement

Defining and Ordering Issues

Negotiation and Decision-making

Separate Meetings

Final Decisions

Recording Decisions

Closing Statement

Termination

Post Mediation Activities

Preliminaries

The mediator begins by taking the initiative in a short routine of meeting, greeting and seating for each party. This may involve some small talk and pleasantries. Where the mediator has not had prior contact with some of the parties, or their advisers, or where some of the parties have not met one another, the mediator will oversee the necessary introductions. Mediators should be alert to the fact that one or more parties may not have met the lawyers for the other side. In commercial mediations there may be a formal agenda which includes the names of those who will be present, and business cards might be exchanged. In all cases, mediators will

---

129 See above, in Chapter 2. The derivation of the triangles is not known. R Charlton and M Dewdney use an oval, and I Davies and G Clarke two rectangles. The geometry of mediation is still developing.

ascertain what names or titles will be used during the meeting. Usually first names only are used. Other preliminary matters which may be dealt with at this stage are time restrictions for the parties and the mediator, parking constraints, availability of amenities, and restraints on the use of mobile phones and other potential intrusions. The introductions and preliminaries may take no longer than two or three minutes. These serve to break the ice with the parties and settle them in, to reassure the parties and establish a good rapport with them. They also allow the mediator to assess the comfort levels of the parties.

Mediator's opening

The next stage of the mediation meeting is a 'formal' opening statement from the mediator, referred to here as the 'mediator's opening'. This is a very important feature of the process, regardless of how much prior contact has occurred between the mediator and the parties. It allows the mediator to explain both the nature of mediation generally and what will happen in the mediation meeting specifically. This is done in plain English, and without jargon, so as to demystify the process.[130] It allows the mediator to establish trust and credibility as a specialist in dispute resolution. It is crucial in establishing a positive and optimistic tone to the proceedings. This is done by expounding the credentials of mediation as a dispute resolution method (sometimes by referring to its success rates) and by affirming the parties' ability to resolve the dispute by making their own decisions. The mediator's opening also allows anxious parties to 'settle in' without having to speak, and to seek clarification or information. It can vary in length from a few to ten minutes, depending on the amount of preparatory contact which has taken place and the familiarity of the parties with mediation. The mediator's opening is usually presented orally, but some mediators distribute written copies of the main points or use overhead projectors. Where mediators omit an important ingredient from their opening they can refer to it later during the process.

Most mediators will do the following in their openings:

    (a)   Commend the parties on selecting mediation as their preferred dispute resolution method, or otherwise endorse their presence at the meeting.

    (b)   Establish that the parties are participating on a voluntary basis (in cases where mediation is not mandatory).

    (c)   Explain the nature and objectives of mediation, in terms of making decisions to resolve the parties' problem, and also in terms of the need to define the issues, to seek common ground and to engage in collaborative problem-solving.

    (d)   Clarify the roles of the mediator and the parties. This is particularly important in view of the common assumption, even when there has been a thorough intake procedure, that where a third party is involved in a dispute he or she will make a decision for the parties.[131] The mediator will also distinguish the role of legal representatives in mediation from their role in

---

130 N Rogers and R Salem *A Student's Guide to Mediation and the Law*, Matthew Bender, New York, 1987, at p 63.

131 H Astor and C Chinkin *Dispute Resolution in Australia*, Butterworths, Sydney, 1992, at p 100.

litigation, namely to assist clients in defining the problem and devising potential solutions for it, as opposed to acting as their zealous advocates.[132]

(e) Emphasise the impartial role of the mediator and his or her responsibility to conduct a fair and equitable process.

(f) Explain the order of proceedings during the mediation meeting, including the joint and separate sessions, and refer to the informality of and flexibilities in the process.

(g) Verify that the parties have authority to settle the matters in dispute, or that the necessary authority is attainable. Where the participants are present in representative capacities, authority will seldom be unlimited, and each should explain to the other the scope of their authority.

(h) Propose some basic guidelines for the conduct of the mediation meeting.[133] Mediators usually refer to the need for parties not to interrupt others (including the mediator) and not to denigrate or otherwise abuse each other. Some mediators refer also to the fact that the optimum conditions for mediation are co-operative and problem-solving attitudes from all parties.

(i) Advise the parties that the mediation meeting is confidential and without prejudice, where this is the case. As discussed below,[134] these are not straightforward aspects of the mediation process.

(j) Clarify any special conditions for the mediation, for example that any agreement will only be binding once it has been reduced to writing, that the mediator will terminate the meeting under certain circumstances or that the mediator is required to make a report on the mediation to an external body.

(k) Invite the parties to commit, or recommit, to the process on the terms which the mediator has outlined. This serves to reinforce the voluntary nature of mediation where the process is not mandated by court or law. Where the mediation is compulsory, this joint commitment provides the mediator with some leverage if either of the parties breaches the basic guidelines.[135]

The party presentations

During the next stage of the mediation meeting, each party is invited to make a short presentation.[136] While it is normal for the claimant to commence, this is not an

---

132 Further attention is given to the roles of the respective parties in Chapter 5.

133 Some mediators refer to the guidelines as 'ground rules'. For an extensive list of suggestions regarding the formulation of ground rules for agreement regarding the processes in general, see Recommendation 5 and Appendix 3 of the Report and Recommendations of the Society for Professionals in Dispute Resolution (SPIDR) Environment/Public Disputes Sector Critical Issues Committee, USA. The report and recommendations were adopted by the SPIDR Board in January 1997.

134 See Chapter 12.

135 R Charlton and M Dewdney *The Mediator's Handbook – skills and strategies for practitioners*, The Law Book Company, Sydney, 1995, at pp 8–14. See also pp 14–15, 202 and 204–5 for suggestions on how the opening statement may be delivered if co-mediation is applied. See further Chapter 6.

136 Unlikely in family or community mediations: see the variations in the process at the end of this chapter. Experienced mediators in commercial cases may use pre-mediation meetings in place of opening presentations. Shapiro supports this, but suggests that opening presentations are essential in cross-cultural cases or where there is a significant

invariable rule; in some mediations there may be no clear distinction between claimant and defendant. Normally no interaction between the parties is allowed at this stage, the speaker presents an uninterrupted narrative, and the presentation is directed to the mediator.[137] Where the parties are legally represented, the parties make their presentations, after which the mediator invites the lawyers to add anything which they regard as appropriate; this system is more consistent with the assumptions of mediation, but the converse procedure is also followed in practice.

If the parties' solicitors make the opening statements, the mediator will ask the parties themselves if they wish to add anything.[138] Mediators attempt to limit the time taken for the party presentations[139] in order to prevent feelings of exclusion and alienation in the non-speaking party.[140] Parties are reassured that there will be occasion for a full airing and detailed discussion of all matters at later stages of the mediation.

As regards the focus of the party presentations, this will depend on the nature of the dispute, the type of disputants, and the request made by the mediator. If the mediator invites the parties to talk about their concerns, they are likely to refer to needs and interests of subjective relevance to them. If the mediator asks what they would like to achieve in the mediation, they are likely to make positional claims. If the mediator asks the parties what the issues are, they are likely to refer to legal rights and obligations. If the mediator asks the parties to describe the facts of the dispute, they are likely to narrate a self-justifying story. In *facilitative mediation* mediators attempt to focus the parties on their underlying needs and interests and to prevent detailed legal propositions or positional claims being presented at this stage. In this model, the parties are invited to focus on their concerns.

There is an inevitable phase in every mediation when the parties make attribution statements about the other.[141] Ventilating emotion, hostility, anger, regret or sadness may occur at the beginning of the mediation process.[142] This phase requires attentive listening by the mediator and validation by the mediator of each party's feelings

---

factual dispute, in which case it is important for each party to hear the others' views: D Shapiro 'Pushing the envelope – selective techniques for tough mediations' (2000) *ADRLJ* 117 at 122.

137 H Brown and A Marriott *ADR Principles and Practice* (2nd edn), Sweet & Maxwell, London, 1999, at pp 167–77. This is notwithstanding that the mediator will not make determinations on the merits, as would a judge.

138 H Genn *Central London County Court Mediation Pilot: Evaluation Report*, LCD Research Series, No 5/98, at p 116 gives examples of how solicitors could improve on their opening statements: for example, to make the presentation more 'slick'; and by providing a more practical, less legal, view of a case.

139 '. . . begin by explaining that you are unhappy about the bother, the trouble and the expense that their litigation is causing them . . . Listen patiently to all their complaints . . . They will not be short, particularly the first time around': Lord Irvine Lecture to the Academy of Expert's Faculty of Mediation and ADR, January 1999, citing the *Charitable Arbitrator* written in 1688.

140 The duration of the presentations normally falls within the range of 10 and 20 minutes.

141 J M Gottman *Marital Intervention: Experimental Investigations*, Academic Press, New York, 1979.

142 M Dewdney, B Sordo and C Chinkin *Continuing development in mediation within the legal system and evaluation of the 1992–3 Settlement Week in New South Wales*, Law Society of NSW, 1993.

about the situation.[143] Mediators may warn parties that antagonistic behaviour is not helpful in reaching a resolution.[144]

During the party presentations mediators will ask open questions, and an occasional clarifying question, but will refrain from questioning the speaker too intrusively.[145] In co-mediation one mediator will maintain contact with the speaker while the other keeps notes of what is said. In some mediation services, mediators summarise each party presentation, both to check the factual accuracy of what they have heard and to acknowledge the emotions behind the factual content. This can be of particular value where a mediating party feels that professionals involved in the conflict have not appreciated the true nature of their concerns. There are also systems of mediation in which each party is requested to summarise the other party's opening presentation.

The party presentations have three major functions in the mediation process. First, they serve to inform mediators about the nature of the dispute where they have had no prior information or to provide mediators with a broad picture; this information is used to construct a list of issues on which decisions are needed. Second, they allow each side to state their concerns in a safe environment in which the other side is compelled to listen; this ensures that each side can hear directly the real, as opposed to imagined, concerns of the other. Third, they constitute a relatively unthreatening introduction to the mediation in terms of uninterrupted time, an opportunity to be heard by an attentive third party, and an opportunity for some venting of emotion. They also serve to encourage and initiate the parties' active participation in the mediation process.[146]

Some mediators begin a discussion of the issues in dispute between the parties in the joint meeting following the presentations and more experienced mediators will attempt to encourage discussion for as long as usefully possible. They will usually end the initial joint session by establishing an agenda for the mediation, in collaboration with the parties.

Identifying areas of agreement

From the information provided in the party presentations, and from other material at their disposal, mediators attempt to identify existing areas of agreement between the parties. These may be agreements on substantive matters, for example that a business partnership has been highly successful in the past, or on procedural matters, for example that both parties wish to avoid litigation and undue expense. These are sometimes referred to as 'easy agreements'.

The purposes of this stage of the mediation are to establish an affirmative mood and to provide a productive basis for the negotiations ahead. It reminds highly-conflicted parties that there is some common ground between them, which may have been

---

143 Quine et al *Community Mediation of Disputes between Neighbours*, The Grubb Institute, London, 1990.
144 W E Simkin *Mediation and the dynamics of collective bargaining*, Bureau of National Affairs, Washington DC, 1971.
145 On appropriate kinds of questions in mediation, see Chapter 6.
146 R Charlton and M Dewdney *The Mediator's Handbook – skills and strategies for practitioners*, The Law Book Company, Sydney, 1995, at pp 18–36.

overlooked because of mutual antagonism and poor communication. It also fosters a climate of consent. The areas of agreement can be visually presented on a board or paper, and can be used subsequently to provide a sense of achievement and to maintain the momentum. In some cases it may only be possible to identify areas of agreement at a high level of abstraction, for example that the 'best interests of the children' should prevail in a family dispute. This remains, however, an important stage in the mediation process, which is sometimes overlooked by mediators.

Defining and ordering the issues

After identifying areas of agreement, mediators develop, in consultation with the parties, a list of those issues which are in dispute and require decisions. The issues are preferably defined in terms of interests and not in terms of positions, facts or legal rights.[147] One of the mediator's functions is to present the issues neutrally, in plain language, and, as far as possible, in mutualised terms.[148] Some mediators couch the list of issues as a series of problem-solving questions. The list of issues will often be visually presented on a board or flip chart, which can provide a source of reference during the remainder of the mediation. Mediators request the parties to prioritise the matters for discussion and show the priorities on a board or on the flip chart.

The purpose of the issue identification phase is to provide clarity and structure to a problem which may have been presented in cluttered disarray. The list of issues divides the overall dispute into discrete parts and serves as an agenda for the remainder of the mediation meeting. It presents a sense of finiteness to the dispute, although issues can, if necessary, be added at a later stage. It reassures each party that their issues have been noted and will be dealt with as the agenda is addressed. The visual depiction of the issues allows for completed matters to be checked off, thereby contributing a sense of progress to the discussions.[149]

Negotiating and decision-making

Once a prioritised list of issues is available, the mediation moves into the problem-solving phase. This is symbolised by the cross-over into the lower triangle.[150] The negotiation and decision-making stage is the core part of the process and will normally occupy most of the time in a mediation. Its purpose is to involve the parties in constructive negotiation as a basis for quality decision-making. Other purposes include: identifying and exploring in detail the major elements of the dispute; encouraging direct communication between the parties; providing the opportunity for the venting of feelings; promoting mutual understanding of past events and perspectives; shifting from positions to identifying needs and interests; noting

---

147 Compare Henderson *The Dispute Resolution Manual: a practical handbook for lawyers and other advisers*, DataLegal Publications, Spring Hill, QLD, 1993, at p 107.

148 On the mediator's function of converting concerns into issues, see Chapter 6.

149 For more on this stage of the mediation process and its management, see R Charlton and M Dewdney *The Mediator's Handbook – skills and strategies for practitioners*, The Law Book Company, Sydney, 1995, at pp 44–61. See also Chapter 6.

150 On this symbolism, see triangles diagram above.

options, emerging common grounds, concessions and agreements in principle; and enabling the mediator to understand the parties' perspectives in order to set the scene for any subsequent reality testing.[151] There is no set sequence for this stage and the negotiation dynamics may take it in many different directions.

A variety of styles are used by mediators during this stage. In the *facilitative* model, the mediator uses strategies to encourage the parties and their advisers to communicate directly with one another 'across' the negotiation table. Here the mediator's role is to make only those interventions which assist the communication process and render the negotiations productive. In *evaluative* and *settlement* mediation, mediators are more likely to direct the communications through themselves, to engage in questioning of the parties and their representatives, and to intervene by, for example, suggesting options. Some mediators may begin this stage in a non-interventionist mode and become more interventionist as it progresses.

This stage could include some or all of the following aspects:[152]

Exchange of information and views

This stage may commence with an exchange of information and views on past events. While mediation is not suited to resolving disputes of fact, the exchange of perceptions on the past may clear the air and assist the parties to focus subsequently on the negotiable issues. Shapiro provides an example, where each party had a number of executives at the mediation, and were each asked to describe their version of the events, with the result that they had changed their perceptions, from believing that the other party was lying to accepting that the party could have different recollections. They could also see how a judge would have difficulty in determining the truth.[153] This stage, therefore, enables parties to explain their motivations for past conduct and the significance of particular events to them. Where emotions are high, there may be considerable venting of feelings as parties communicate with one another about the past.

Development and exploration of options

After the exchange of views, mediators encourage the parties to develop and explore a wide range of possible options for settling the dispute. Part of the mediator's function is to establish a climate in which each party feels able to suggest options which they regard as feasible, regardless of the other's expected reaction, and in which each refrains from reactive judgment or criticism of other options. This can be facilitated through brainstorming, hypothetical questions and the encouragement of creative thinking. Shapiro suggests another mechanism, 'challenge mediation',

---

151 R Charlton and M Dewdney *The Mediator's Handbook – skills and strategies for practitioners*, The Law Book Company, Sydney, 1995, at p 63.

152 R Charlton and M Dewdney, ibid at pp 76–82, also suggest that mediators make effective use of this stage by assisting the parties to gain a sense of progress, giving the parties undivided attention, fostering a sense of realism in the parties' expectations and performing a consistent facilitating role in the parties' negotiation and communication.

153 D Shapiro 'Pushing the envelope – selective techniques for tough mediations' (2000) *ADRLJ* 117 at 119.

whereby the mediator challenges each party to come up with a solution that will satisfy all the parties.[154] Where agreements fall into place they are noted by the mediator, but there is usually an attempt to consider a broad range of options before narrowing them down into specific agreements. Where there is no creativity from the parties in the development of options, the mediator has to decide on process options that will assist the parties to develop alternatives in an objective and non-judgmental way.

Evaluation and selection of options

One of the mediator's functions in this part of the mediation is to facilitate collaborative problem-solving. He or she should encourage the parties initially to evaluate options in terms of their mutual needs and interests and to select those which satisfy both their interests and external standards of fairness and reasonableness. The mediator should invite the parties to consider the possible consequences, in terms of practicality and viability, of various options. The mediator may also encourage the parties to consider *in principle* agreements and move subsequently to matters of detail. The evaluation and selection of appropriate options may also require external advice on matters of law, taxation, financing, and the like. During this phase, the mediator can practise a number of strategic interventions to make the negotiations more productive and to avoid predictable problems. He or she attempts to involve the parties in problem-solving negotiation.[155]

Bargaining

Where the parties' needs and interests cannot be met by problem-solving negotiation, they will have to engage in distributive bargaining. This refers to the final transactional part of the negotiations when the parties attempt to use trade-offs, packaging and compromises to reach an agreement. It may also include incremental bargaining on the last issue, where the parties attempt to close the final gap between them by making reciprocal concessions or splitting the difference. The final bargaining may produce a pragmatic outcome, or it may result in a stalemate and the failure of the mediation to produce a settlement.

The separate meetings

In this stage of the mediation, the mediator meets separately with the individual parties.[156] The mediator will normally remain in the joint meeting room with one party and direct the other party to another venue. Where there are legal representatives or other advisers present, they will normally attend the separate meetings with their clients, but the mediator may meet separately with each party alone. Many commentators regard the separate meetings as the most important feature of mediation and

---

154 D Shapiro 'Pushing the envelope – selective techniques for tough mediations', ibid at 122.

155 See Chapters 2 and 5.

156 The American term 'caucus' is sometimes used for separate meetings but is avoided in this text. 'Private meetings' is also avoided because of its conspiratorial overtones.

one of its defining characteristics as a dispute resolution system. Sometimes these claims are overstated, as the separate meetings by no means lead to dramatic breakthroughs in all cases. There are also a number of concerns about mediators speaking separately and confidentially with each of the parties.

Functions of separate meetings

Separate meetings can perform many functions in a mediation. They can:

- allow the parties to refer to additional concerns which they are unable or unwilling to raise in the joint meetings;
- allow mediators to seek further information, to discover BATNAs or Best Alternative to Negotiated Agreements,[157] WATNAs or Worst Alternative to Negotiated Agreements, MLATNAs or Most Likely Alternative to Negotiated Agreements, and to probe for hidden agendas;
- assist mediators in understanding the motivations of the parties and their priorities and in developing empathy and trust with them individually;
- give the parties time and space to vent pent-up emotions with the mediator, without jeopardising the progress of the negotiations;
- allow the mediator to test how realistic proposed options are and, where appropriate, to disenchant parties with their positions;
- allow mediators to coach the parties in constructive communication and to rehearse negotiation tactics and techniques;
- allow mediators and parties to develop and consider new alternatives and ways of presenting them; and
- allow mediators to impose more pressure for settlement than is possible in the joint sessions.

Timing and circumstances of separate meetings

Mediators are required to make strategic judgments as to when and why separate meetings are held. There are many circumstances in which mediators may decide that separate meetings are appropriate, including the following:[158]

- early in the mediation (after the party presentations), in order to establish whether there are any concerns which have not yet been raised but need to be addressed for the resolution of the dispute, or to gather information which has not been disclosed;
- if a breakdown or deadlock has developed in the negotiations, in order to change the dynamics of the negotiation process, to analyse the problem with each party separately, and to engage in 'reality testing';[159]
- if destructive and antagonistic tendencies are developing in joint sessions, so as to give each side private space, to allow the expression of emotions, and to discuss options with them in a more clear-headed way;

---

157 See Chapter 2.
158 S Henderson *The Dispute Resolution Manual: a practical handbook for lawyers and other advisers*, DataLegal Publications, Spring Hill, QLD, 1993, at pp 108–9; and G Meggs 'Issues in divorce mediation – methodology and ethics' (1993) 4 *ADRJ* 198 at 203.
159 On reality testing, see Chapter 5.

- where a party is disempowered and unable to cope adequately with the negotiations, in order to provide some recovery time and space and to assist the party to function satisfactorily in the process;
- if the parties are deviating from the mediation guidelines, in order to re-educate them on the nature of the mediation process and to invite them to recommit to it;
- where the parties are unable to provide feasible settlement options in each other's presence, in order to provide a risk-free environment for generating settlement options;
- where there are shortcomings in the parties' negotiating skills, in order to coach them in, and allow them to rehearse, constructive negotiation techniques;
- where the mediation has broken down or become unproductive, in order to assess party objectives and decide whether the mediation should continue or be terminated; and
- if it is requested by the parties themselves, or by their advisers.

Potential concerns about separate meetings

There are several potential sources of concern about this aspect of the mediation process. The main concern revolves around the fact that separate meetings afford mediators considerable power and leverage over the parties and their decisions. While mediators do not have formal decision-making authority, they do have potential influence in respect of the parties' decisions. The separate meetings enhance this potential influence by virtue of their privacy, the additional information they reveal, the alliance-building which takes place with the mediator, and the strategic control which the mediator has in respect of the duration, number and nature of the meetings.[160] Where mediators transmit offers between the parties in separate meetings, they have an additional source of leverage in terms of how the offers are packaged and presented. If this strategic position is used to pressure the parties unduly into settlement it deprives the parties of their responsibility for decision-making, contrary to the self-determination assumptions of the mediation process.

There are other concerns about separate meetings. The first is that the very notion of mediators speaking privately with each side, to the exclusion of the other, could engender suspicion and undermine the trust required in the mediation process. The second is that mediators may be influenced or manipulated by communications made in the separate sessions. The third is that there might be an inadvertent breach of confidentiality by mediators in respect of matters disclosed to them in the separate meetings. The fourth is that if too much of the mediation is conducted through separate sessions, it will reinforce the detachment and division between the parties and preclude the mutual education of the parties by one another.[161] The fifth is that the separate meetings can result in miscommunications and errors if mediators shuttle messages back and forth between the parties. There is a danger that the

---

160 J Haynes *The fundamentals of family mediation*, New York Press, Albany, 1994, at p 62 argues that in family mediation, separate meetings give mediators too much power and undermine their credibility. The same might be said for some other mediations.
161 See H Brown and A Marriott *ADR Principles and Practice* (2nd edn), Sweet & Maxwell, London, 1999, at pp 206–10.

mediator becomes merely a messenger for the parties. These potential problems require mediators to develop safeguards in relation to the separate meetings.

Safeguards in relation to separate meetings

In relation to some potential problems, for example the inadvertent disclosure of confidential matters, mediators need to be mindful and diligent; some, for example, keep careful notes on matters which must not be divulged. In respect of others, for example in relation to the suspicion and undermining of trust, there needs to be sufficient explanation, education and reassurance by mediators. One device for allaying suspicion is to focus on the withdrawing party, and to present the separate meeting as an opportunity for that party to consider issues raised, reconsider their interests and offers, have some rest and refreshment, and plan the rest of the mediation. Where the mediation has been conducted predominantly through separate meetings, it is advisable for closure or termination to take place in joint session.[162] This allows for a joint reappraisal of progress and consideration of future options. This also ensures a common understanding of the status of the negotiations and obviates future misunderstandings or blame for the mediator. The most far-reaching safeguard is to avoid separate meetings altogether.[163] By way of less drastic safeguards, mediators will do the following:[164]

(a) where there is a separate meeting with one party, always meet with the other party or parties – this tends to be a rigid rule of practice;

(b) ensure that the separate meetings do not take too long in order to maintain momentum, and advise the absent party of any delays beyond the announced time for the meeting;

(c) ensure that each party's separate meetings take equal time, as far as this is possible;

(d) reassure the parties about the confidential nature of the separate meetings, if this is the principle under which they are operating;

(e) give the withdrawing party a task to perform while they are alone, for example checking figures or contacting advisers (alternatively a pupil or co-mediator may conduct separate sessions simultaneously with the mediator);

(f) commence the separate meetings with open-ended questions and invite the disclosure of additional concerns from the parties;

(g) prepare the parties at the end of the separate meetings for the continuation of negotiations when the joint meetings are resumed;

(h) avoid any hint, when the parties come back into joint session, about concessions, offers or other developments which occurred in the separate meetings; and

(i) avoid adding to the confidentiality problem by convening the separate meetings too early in the mediation process, which results in most of the disclosures being cloaked with confidentiality.

---

162 See M Anstey *Practical Peacemaking – a Mediator's Handbook*, Juta & Co, Kenwyn, South Africa, 1993, at p 96.

163 See No separate meetings at page **152**.

164 S Henderson *The Dispute Resolution Manual: a practical handbook for lawyers and other advisers*, DataLegal Publications, Spring Hill, QLD, 1993, at p 108; and for a list of 'dos' and 'don'ts' for separate meetings, see R Charlton and M Dewdney *The Mediator's Handbook – skills and strategies for practitioners*, The Law Book Company, Sydney, 1995, at pp 101–3.

Returning to joint meetings

Where the separate meetings have served their purpose, mediators reconvene a joint session of all participants, although in some cases they may wish to maintain the momentum by keeping the parties in separate meetings. There are, however, some kinds of communication which mediators are wary of conveying between the parties because of the potential risks involved.[165] These include threats and 'final offers or demands', which may signal the rejection of the mediation process by one or other party, and significant new information which could fundamentally change the direction of the negotiations. In these cases mediators are advised to convene a joint session, which returns direct responsibility for the negotiations to the parties themselves and reduces the risk of misunderstandings. It is consistent with the assumptions of mediation for the parties to accept direct responsibility for manipulative negotiation tactics and for the assessment of additional information. Even where most of the mediation is conducted through separate meetings, it is advisable for mediators to close or terminate the process in a joint session.

Final decision-making

In most mediations the parties are brought together again after the separate meetings. The purposes of this stage are to conduct further discussions, to engage in final bargaining, and to settle the finer details of the agreement. To make this stage productive, mediators often insist that the parties focus only on present and future issues, and not reopen the past. The mediator's function is to ensure that all issues in dispute have been dealt with, that no points of agreement have been overlooked, that the parties are satisfied with the final product,[166] and that they have considered all possible eventualities, and that the potential for future disputes is minimised. Mediators may suggest that the parties consider contingency plans to deal with uncertain future developments. They may invite them to consider including a dispute resolution clause in the agreement, a monitoring arrangement for specified actions which have to be taken, and even continued mediator assistance in the implementation of the agreement. Where the parties have not reached agreement, the mediator will invite them to make decisions on other ways of dealing with the dispute.[167]

Recording the decisions

In most mediations the final agreement is reduced to writing, and the Agreement to Mediate may make this a condition of the process. It is rare in commercial matters for the agreement not to be reduced to writing. In some cases heads of agreement are

---

165 M Anstey *Practical Peacemaking – a Mediator's Handbook*, Juta & Co, Kenwyn, South Africa, 1993, at pp 94–5.

166 Mediators are advised in training courses to establish from the parties that they can 'live with' the proposed agreement, instead of inviting difficulties by asking whether they are 'happy' with it.

167 For more on the management of the resumed joint meetings and final decision making, see R Charlton and M Dewdney *The Mediator's Handbook – skills and strategies for practitioners*, The Law Book Company, Sydney, 1995, at pp 104–15 and 118–20.

drafted and signed at the mediation meeting, to be subsequently refined by lawyers into a comprehensive contract. In cases in which the agreement is not complex, a full contract may be drafted at the mediation meeting. Where legal advisers are present they will usually draft the agreement, and where there are no lawyers some mediators will perform this role. Some suggested drafting guidelines include:

(1) The agreement should be drafted in a positive tone.
(2) The agreement should be clear and sufficiently detailed to avoid future interpretation problems.
(3) The agreement should clarify respective responsibilities and commitments of the parties.
(4) The agreement should state that it has been reached as a result of mediation.[168]

Mediators should ensure that the parties are satisfied with the accuracy of the written agreement. The final agreement may include goodwill statements on future behaviour and dispute resolution clauses for future conflicts. Where legal and other relevant advisers are not present, the parties may wish to, or may be advised by the mediators to, consult external advisers before the agreement is signed. As there is always the risk that the parties will feel pressured to reach a settlement, especially after a long and gruelling mediation session, the agreement may include a 'cooling off' period.[169] If part of the agreement is to be made public, it will be necessary for the parties to waive the confidentiality principle in respect of those clauses.

Closing statement and termination

Mediators formally terminate the mediation process so that it is clear when their responsibilities are complete and when the confidentiality principle comes to an end. Mediators terminate the mediation on a positive note, regardless of how successful it has been. This they do in a closing statement in which they compliment the parties on their endeavours and acknowledge that any outcome is a product of their own efforts. Where agreement has been reached, mediators encourage the parties to ensure that there is compliance with it. Where no agreement has been reached, mediators encourage the parties to agree to have a cooling off period before they decide to pursue other dispute resolution processes such as litigation, and to consider reverting to mediation at a later stage or not to re-open issues on which they have achieved consensus. Mediators also highlight the achievements of the parties, for example, the narrowing of the issues in dispute, in order to encourage the parties to continue to attempt to settle their dispute amicably and so that they do not leave the mediation with a sense of failure. Mediators also clarify the areas of agreement and list unresolved issues if that would assist the parties' subsequent efforts at settling the dispute. Parties are reassured as to the confidentiality of the proceedings. Mediators may mention possible post-mediation procedures, such as consultation with lawyers or disclosure of the outcome to a court or other institution. The parties are bid farewell and, where it is necessary, a party who feels vulnerable is allowed to leave the mediation venue first.

---

168 R Charlton and M Dewdney *The Mediator's Handbook – skills and strategies for practitioners*, The Law Book Company, Sydney, 1995, at p 116. See also Chapter 6.
169 P Davenport 'What is wrong with mediation' (1997) 8 *ADRJ* 133.

How long it takes to get to this stage of the process will vary in each case, although some generalisations can be made for each mediation type, civil/commercial, family and community. The Academy of Experts' *Guidance Notes* indicate that a commercial mediation can take between four and six weeks from the first discussion between the parties about mediation to finalising settlement terms.[170] The Commercial Court's *Guidance Notes* provide the following timeframe:

- Day 5:   discussion between the parties about choice of mediator;
- Day 6:   parties choose the mediator;
- Day 10:   preliminary meeting takes place;
- Day 15:   parties exchange case summaries;
- Day 20:   mediation starts; and
- Day 22:   Court is informed of the result.[171]

The Commercial Mediation Centre's *Mediation Rules and Procedures* set out a more generous timetable:

- 14 days to appoint a mediator;
- another 14 days to exchange information;
- another 28 days to the first mediation session; and
- the entire process should be completed within 90 days at most.[172]

Centre for Dispute Resolution statistics show that the average length of the mediation meeting itself was 1.3 days in 1998 and 1.1 days in 1999.[173] In comparison, Central London County Court mediations are limited to three hours. Family mediations take place over a number of sessions, usually between 1 and 1.5 hours long, and typically about six sessions are required. Community mediations frequently take a few hours in the case of disputes between individuals or, in cases involving community-wide disputes, may take place over a number of sessions, each a few hours long.

A mediation may fail to achieve a resolution for a number of reasons. A different dispute resolution process may be more appropriate to resolve a particular dispute. The dispute might not be ripe for mediation, either because the parties are too hostile or cannot accept the realities of the situation, or further investigations and information might be required. The parties might hold genuinely different views about the merits of the dispute. Inadequate information or preparation can doom a mediation to failure.[174] Insufficient time or other time pressures, for instance if a party needs to leave the mediation by a certain time, can also lead to failure, particularly if there has not been adequate diagnosis of the dispute. Emotional and other barriers might prevent settlement. If there is a particularly bad feeling between the parties or they can't or won't listen to each other, settlement will be difficult. Cultural and language difficulties can also provide stumbling blocks in a mediation. The parties may have hidden agendas, which were not identified or tackled adequately in the mediation. Parties may have misunderstood what the mediation involves. Lack of negotiation skills on the part of the parties and their lawyers can

---

170 Academy of Experts *Answers to frequently asked questions about mediation*.
171 Commercial Court *ADR Orders: guidance notes for litigators and their lawyers*.
172 Commercial Mediation Centre *Mediation Rules and Procedures*.
173 Centre for Dispute Resolution *Press Release*, 26 April 1999; and in *Resolutions*, Issue no 24.
174 S Marsh *Summary of 5th Annual ADR Institute of the State Bar of Texas*, which refers to US statistics which support the proposition.

lead to poor results. Antagonistic or emotionally involved lawyers, or lawyers who have provided clients with optimistic advice or who have focused solely on the legal issues, can create major difficulties in achieving settlement at a mediation. The possible settlement range might be small and settlement might only occur after reflection following the mediation. If costs have escalated, parties may feel that they have invested too much time and money in the conflict to settle at the mediation. If the parties lose confidence in or cannot trust the mediator, settlement is unlikely.[175]

Post-Mediation Activities

Ratification and review

Some mediated agreements require ratification from external bodies to whom the negotiating parties are accountable, such as boards, committees or councils. In other situations it may be understood that agreements will be reviewed by lawyers, accountants or other professional advisers after the mediation. Ratification and review provide safeguards for the mediating parties. They also provide an opportunity for persons not privy to the mediation dynamics and the efforts of the negotiating parties to destabilise significant decisions made in mediation. In the case of public sector/ interest mediation, this stage of the process is likely to involve transforming a number of informally negotiated understandings into an agreement and ensuring that all the parties commit to the agreement. Parties who, although not involved in the mediation process, are stakeholders may need to be persuaded into accepting the negotiated agreement. Usually, the agreement will require re-negotiation at this stage, and during implementation of it. The time involved in reaching a final agreement should not be underestimated.

Official sanction

In some cases the sanction of a court or other external authority is required to validate a mediation agreement. Thus if a parent of an infant involved in an accident concluded a settlement on behalf of his or her child, the terms of the settlement will have to be approved by the court.[176] Where mediation has been incorporated in the procedure of a court or statutory tribunal, the mediated agreement may have to be placed before the court or tribunal for an order to be made in those terms. Parties to private mediations may sometimes wish to apply to the court for an order giving effect to their mediated agreement. This is especially common when the case has already been commenced in court. Where the court enters a judgment or makes an order in accordance with the terms of a settlement agreement, the party in whose favour the judgment is entered or the order is made may then enforce the settlement agreement as a judgment or order of the court. Where court sanction is not obtained, mediated agreements have the same status as any other agreement.[177]

---

175 H Genn *Central London County Court Mediation Pilot: Evaluation Report*, LCD Research Series, No 5/98, at p 112 where among the litigants who did not settle at mediation, 40% stated that they either never had any confidence in the mediator or had lost that confidence during the mediation.
176 For example, Civil Procedure Rules, r 21.10.
177 See the section on Enforceability of Mediated Settlements in Chapter 12.

Referrals and reporting

Mediators may, in their discretion, refer one or more parties to psychologists, lawyers or social workers for professional assistance. No referral can be made compulsory, unless there is legal authority for it. Some referral agencies need to be informed about the outcome of a mediation, although not the content of any agreement. There may also be reporting duties on matters of sexual or child abuse, as required by statute, professional codes or contractual provisions.[178] No referral or report can be made in a way which breaches the confidentiality principle, except where the principle is suspended for that purpose.[179] The *Commercial Court Guide* provides that, if a dispute is not finally settled in a mediation, the parties should inform the Court by letter of the steps which have been taken towards settlement and, without prejudice, why those steps have failed.[180]

Mediator debriefing

In some situations an extensive post-mediation debriefing and feedback session is conducted between co-mediators or between mediators and supervisors. This involves a critical analysis and evaluation of the mediation session and the completion of a written report. Debriefing serves several functions. It allows mediators to deal with their own emotional circumstances resulting from the mediation. It encourages mediators to develop self-awareness as a basis for improvement and development. It assists with quality control by providing information to supervisors within the mediation service. It constitutes a structured form of mediator accountability and provides a basis for responding to complaints from consumers. Finally, it provides, subject to confidentiality constraints, a store of information on mediation for use in relation to matters such as success rates, research, funding and continuing training requirements.

The co-mediation model makes debriefing more immediate and concrete. Ideally the process should resort to specifics and not be too generalised. A co-mediator is likely to be more receptive to debriefing criticism if he or she has in advance solicited feedback on specific issues. Solo mediators can debrief alone, or with the assistance of an experienced external mediator, again subject to confidentiality constraints. To be effective, debriefing needs to be constructive and honest, which requires skills, confidence and some expertise in the art.

Other follow-up activities

Some mediators assume the responsibility of monitoring the mediated agreement and supervising its implementation.[181] This is intended to maintain the momentum achieved by the parties and to prevent non-compliance, whether through neglect or

---

178 See Chapter 11 on standards.
179 See Chapter 12 for legal issues.
180 Commercial Court *Commercial Court Guide*, August 1999, Appendix 7.
181 J Folberg and A Taylor *Mediation – a comprehensive guide to resolving conflicts without litigation*, Jossey-Bass, San Francisco, 1988, at pp 65–72.

subsequent doubts or hesitancies. Certain issues, like arrangements for the children and financial issues following family mediation may require revision. In some situations mediators will 'shepherd' the settlement through all subsequent stages up to the making of a consent order by the relevant court.[182] Mediation organisations are able to conduct follow-up activities through their own staff to ensure the faithful execution of the contract and to offer remedial services should there be any problems. Mediators or organisations may also hold funds or documents for release once there has been due compliance with an obligation in the mediated agreement.[183]

Variations in the Mediation Process

Variations in relation to the number of mediators

In many situations more than one mediator is used in the same mediation. In most of these cases there will be two mediators, but occasionally there will be three or more. The term *co-mediation* is used in this book for any situation in which there is more than one mediator. The use of a single mediator is referred to as *solo mediation*. Typically, community and family mediators work in pairs. A form of co-mediation in family mediation, called *anchor mediation*, involves a sole mediator throughout the process, with an additional mediator joining, if required, typically when financial or property issues arise.[184] Solo mediation is the main model used in civil/commercial mediation, although a mediator may work with a pupil mediator. The tasks of the pupil will vary, depending on his or her expertise. In some cases, the pupil will observe the parties' reactions and be able to relay the detail of the discussions, which the mediator may miss in the course of questioning a party in private session.

The co-mediation process

Essentially co-mediation comprises the same stages as solo mediation, with a higher degree of preparation and structure and some differentiation of functions in the early parts of the process. Some mediation organisations use the designations Mediator 1 (M1) and Mediator 2 (M2) to depict the two roles, but without suggesting primacy for one mediator. While the designations are by no means universal, they are useful in the present context.[185]

As regards preparation, co-mediators need to discuss how they will communicate in the mediation meeting and how to deal with differences between themselves.

---

182 Forrest Mosten, attorney and mediator from the United States, Bond University, 1993.
183 H Brown and A Marriott *ADR Principles and Practice* (2nd edn), Sweet & Maxwell, London, 1999, at p 351.
184 Brown and Marriott consider that the use of consultants raises difficult issues of whether the consultant is responsible to the parties, the mediator or the mediation service and recommend that lawyer consultants should be guided by the Law Society: H Brown and A Marriott *ADR principles and practice*, ibid, at p 234.
185 M Dewdney *Stages in mediation and underlying rationale: basic model*, unpublished, May 1994. See also R Charlton and M Dewdney *The Mediator's Handbook – skills and strategies for practitioners*, The Law Book Company, Sydney, 1995, at pp 197–205 for another discussion of issues relating to co-mediation.

Teamwork is an essential requirement for successful co-mediation and this is made easier where the co-mediators have attended the same training programme. At the mediation meeting, it is customary for the mediators to introduce themselves, and the mediators' opening is shared more or less equally between them with a structured division of labour. During the party presentations M1 engages with the speaking party through eye contact, open body language and reflective listening,[186] while M2 takes notes of what is being said. At this stage M1 is in charge of the process and must be attentive to the rate of delivery, the clarity and the length of the speaking party's presentation, to the reactions of the non-speaking party, and to the ability of M2 to take notes. Either mediator may ask clarifying questions at the end of each party presentation. The note-taker (M2) will usually summarise back to each party the factual substance and some of the emotional content of their presentation. During this process, M1 has the opportunity to transform concerns into issues.[187] M1's proposed list of issues is discussed initially between the mediators, and then with the parties. M1 transcribes the list of issues to a whiteboard or flip chart. He or she also assists the parties to prioritise the issues.

The negotiation and decision-making stage is initiated by M1. During this stage there is no differentiation of functions between the mediators but good modelling requires that each should intervene more or less equally in the process. It might sometimes be appropriate, with regard to the qualifications and expertise which each mediator brings to the process, for one mediator to be more active than another, particularly in relation to a specific topic of discussion. This may also occur where one mediator feels unable to make any constructive contribution to the process. However, the non-intervening mediator can still perform a useful function by observing the behaviour of the parties, taking occasional notes, identifying recurring themes in the dialogue or subtleties in the negotiations, and accumulating matters of value (such as an apology, a concession or a creative option) which might otherwise 'fall off' the negotiation table. These activities can provide the basis for an appropriate contribution at some subsequent stage of the process.

During the separate meeting stage, the mediators remain together when meeting with each party. It would threaten the impartiality of the process and the acceptability of the mediators for them to separate and for a different mediator to meet with each party. In the separate meetings it is not unusual for mediators to make unequal contributions. The mediator who was inactive in joint session may assume a more dominant role, or a mediator may have particular strengths, by reason of professional background, personal style or mediation experience, in this facet of the process. The gender of the mediators may dictate differential roles in the separate meetings, particularly where emotions have been high or where one party needs to be reassured and empowered. Likewise, factors of technical expertise, seniority or legal knowledge may result in differing roles for the co-mediators in relation to reality-testing, empowerment and empathy.

In co-mediation the mediators may also decide to have a separate meeting between themselves. The separate mediators' meeting allows the co-mediators to resolve difficulties between them, to assess strategies, to identify options and to support each other. Such a meeting would be imperative where one mediator was of the view that

---

186 On these skills and techniques, see Chapter 6.
187 On this technique, see Chapter 6.

the mediation should be terminated. The decision to have a meeting between the co-mediators should be announced to the parties, the reasons for the meeting should be made clear to the parties and the meeting should not last for longer than is reasonable in the circumstances.

The division of labour may resume in the closing stages of co-mediation when one mediator undertakes the drafting of the agreement, and the other maintains contact with the parties, checks the agreement against the agenda, and is attentive to matters of detail. The final variation which co-mediation involves is a structured debriefing between the mediators.[188] Debriefing has the advantage of directness and immediacy where both parties have participated in the same process. Despite training in the art of constructive feedback, however, co-mediators are not always honest or forthright with each other in this exercise.

Potential advantages of co-mediation

There are a number of potential advantages of co-mediation, some of which relate to the parties, some to the mediators and some to the mediation movement as a whole:[189]

(a)   *Additional resources:* co-mediation involves a doubling of available mediator resources in all facets of the mediation. It allows the co-mediators to complement each other's strengths, to consult with each other and to avoid mediation fatigue.

(b)   *Division of labour:* co-mediation allows for a division of labour, particularly during the early stages of the mediation when the mediators need to perform a wide range of essential functions in a short period of time.

(c)   *Matching of mediators with parties:* the co-mediation model allows for the matching of the gender, race, age or class attributes of the parties with those of the co-mediators in order to promote the acceptability of, and the parties' comfort with, the process. The most obvious example of matching is in family mediations where it is common to have male and female co-mediators.

(d)   *Selection of professional backgrounds:* co-mediation allows for the selection of more than one professional background where this might con-tribute to the success of the mediation. It is common in family mediations to draw on the resources of one mediator trained in law and another trained in the social sciences. Similar arrangements are possible where the matters in dispute involve questions of law, science, technology, the environment or construction. Another variation is where one co-mediator is highly skilled in the mediation process and the other is experienced in the subject-matter of the dispute.

(e)   *Positive modelling:* co-mediation allows the mediators to model constructive communication, cooperative problem-solving and mutual respect. The way in which differences between the mediators are handled can have a healthy demonstration effect in the process.

---

188   On debriefing, see above.
189   J Folberg and A Taylor *Mediation – a comprehensive guide to resolving conflicts without litigation*, Jossey-Bass, San Francisco, 1988, at pp 140–6.

(f) *More stable dynamics:* two disputants and a single mediator can constitute an unstable system where the mediator directly or indirectly favours, or is perceived to favour, one party, or where a party tries to manipulate the mediator into supporting him or her.[190] Co-mediation, which involves the participation of at least four persons, is less susceptible to these dynamics.

(g) *Mutual debriefing:* co-mediation allows for immediate and direct supervision and mutual debriefing. The significance of debriefing has been dealt with above.

(h) *Training:* co-mediation allows for a form of apprenticeship training and mediator assessment. Beginner or inexperienced mediators can gain experience and confidence in the protective environment of co-mediation. Co-mediation also allows for continuing training; even experienced mediators can benefit from exposure to the skills and techniques of other colleagues.

(i) *Mediator accountability:* while mediators do not have any formal decision-making authority, they have considerable power by virtue of their intimate involvement in the negotiation process and their access to information disclosed by one party only. In these situations co-mediators can help to keep each other honest.

(j) *Additional work for mediators:* co-mediation has the advantage of providing more work for those interested in mediating. This is a benefit for the mediation movement as a whole in that it produces more collective experience and expertise than would otherwise be the case.

Potential disadvantages of co-mediation

(a) *Negative modelling:* co-mediation introduces differences in mediator personality and style, and if the co-mediators do not model equality of status and teamwork, and are unable to resolve their own differences constructively, they may have a negative effect on the behaviour of the parties.

(b) *Additional expense and time:* the use of co-mediators is likely to make mediation more expensive, either for the parties, who are required to pay two mediators' fees, or for the mediation service which bears the costs. In some cases, the mediators share one set of fees. While this arrangement has no impact on the costs of mediation to the parties, it adversely affects the income of the mediators involved. The presence of an additional mediator could also lengthen the process, though the time factor is difficult to calculate accurately.

(c) *The patron syndrome:* where co-mediators have been selected to match the attributes of the disputants, this model could cause one or more party to view the matching mediator as his or her patron or champion and attempt to form an alliance with that mediator during joint or separate meetings.

(d) *Inability to match mediators:* where it is not possible to match the gender, race, age or class attributes of the co-mediators with those of the parties, and there are not one but two mediators from one party's affinity group, there might be perceptions of partiality and problems in maintaining trust.

---

190 This phenomenon is sometimes referred to as triangulation: see, for example, H Brown and A Marriott *ADR Principles and Practice* (2nd edn), Sweet & Maxwell, London, 1999, at pp 413–14.

(e) *Manipulation:* the intended or unintended use by the co-mediators of contrasting styles (good guy/bad guy routine) could manipulate parties into making concessions, revelations or settlements which would not otherwise have been forthcoming.

Variations in relation to scope of mediation

In family mediation there is a distinction between mediation on all issues and mediation on some issues only, for instance, property and finance or children. Traditionally, children issues have been the domain of the social professions, whereas property and financial issues have been the domain of lawyers. In some countries, mediation on child issues remains a separate area of mediation practice.[191] 'All issues' family mediation is now common practice in England and Wales.[192] Between 1995 and 1998 Family Mediation Scotland undertook a pilot project on all issues mediation, with the aim of developing competence in all issues mediation in Family Mediation Scotland affiliated services. All issues mediation is now available in seven of the Family Mediation Scotland services.[193] In Northern Ireland at this stage, child-focused mediation is the only type of family mediation practised.[194]

The distinction is considered artificial as resolution of an issue frequently depends upon the resolution of other issues, for instance, the resolution of financial issues often assists resolution of child issues. The UK College of Family Mediators' *Code of Practice* describes the scope of family mediation widely, encompassing all issues mediations, as follows:

- options for maintaining the relationship between the couple;
- parental responsibility towards the children;
- the fate of the family property;
- any other matters which it would be helpful to resolve.[195]

Variations in relation to the joint meetings

Multiple meetings

Many mediations are not finalised at a single sitting and adjournments are necessary. In some mediation contexts there is a routine adjournment in certain disputes, such as family matters.[196] Adjournments can play a number of functions in the mediation

---

191 For example, in France and America: M Roberts *Access to Agreement: a Consumer Study of Mediation in Family Disputes*, Open University Press, Milton Keynes, 1988 at p 7.

192 All issues family mediation developed out of a pilot scheme, which led to the establishment in 1988 of the Family Mediators' Association (FMA), as to which see the section on Mediation Organisations in Chapter 7.

193 Family Mediation Scotland *Information Pack.*

194 Office of Law Reform *Divorce in Northern Ireland: a better way forward*, Consultation Paper, Office of Law Review, December 1999.

195 UK College of Family Mediators *Code of Practice.*

196 Family mediation involves a number of joint sessions, usually two sessions in the case of mediation on child issues and six sessions in the case of all-issues mediation. Sessions are usually between one and two hours' duration.

process. They allow the parties to gather further information, such as valuations, to seek professional or other advice, to reassess their situation, to manage emotion and to plan offers and responses. They also allow the mediator(s), subject to the limits of confidentiality, to assess the progress thus far and to plan strategies for the subsequent sessions.

One of the problems with mediation adjournments is that there may be some regression in regard to points of agreement already reached. There is often a change in the interpersonal dynamics after an adjournment, with one party having become more assertive, or more intransigent. There may also be some inefficiencies, in that the parties have to revisit ground already covered earlier. These are not necessarily negative phenomena. Nevertheless in commercial mediations they are often averted by avoiding adjournments and persisting with the mediation until agreement is reached at a single session. This can lead to other dangers where one or both parties feel unfairly pressured into settling.[197]

Different venues

Mediation meetings are normally held at a single venue, a neutral location away from the original site of the dispute. Mediations conducted over a series of sessions may take place at different venues for reasons of space or logistics. The premises of each side may be used in rotation to show even-handedness to the parties. In some mediations all participants in the mediation travel to the site of the dispute to view a significant feature, such as the factory floor in an industrial matter or the building site in a construction dispute. For example, a site inspection in an environmental dispute can ensure that stakeholders are constructive participants in the process, giving it legitimacy from the point of view of the stakeholders.

Telephone conferences

Mediations can be conducted telephonically, because of geographical distance, limited resources, safety requirements or legal necessity.[198] A conference line is arranged with multiple connections to accommodate the parties, their advisers and the mediators. A number of basic guidelines need to be followed in these cases. Where only one party is geographically remote from the mediator and the second party is at the same venue as the mediator, the latter will be located at a telephone in a different room to uphold the appearance of impartiality; the mediator should also avoid making contact with the local party after the mediation. Where there are advisers or multiple parties participating, they need to identify themselves each time they speak in order to avoid confusion about who is talking. Particular diligence is required in maintaining confidentiality. The safest procedure is for the mediator to disconnect all parties on the conference line and to make separate calls to each party individually, before resuming the conference line for a further joint meeting. Finalising of the agreement can be problematic, and errors and misunderstandings can be avoided through the use of faxed copies of the draft agreements.

---

197 See Chapter 12 on legal issues.
198 For example where there is a protection order in place against one party in a family dispute which prevents both parties from being together.

While there may be logistical and financial reasons for conducting mediations through telephone conferences, there are also potential disadvantages. One of the most significant is that mediators are unable to observe and react to the non-verbal messages of the parties. There is also no possibility of mediators establishing the same rapport through interpersonal skills as they can when the parties are in their presence, nor of using visual aids for structuring and facilitating the negotiations. Nevertheless, modern practice encourages the conduct of mediations by telephone, closed-circuit television or other technologically-advanced means of communication, and it is sometimes the only way of making mediation services available. The Advisory Conciliation and Arbitration Service ('ACAS') conciliation process, which most closely resembles facilitative mediation, can be conducted entirely via telephone, although meetings can take place.

The internet and emails

Melamed makes an interesting observation that the internet is changing the way mediators work. The benefits of using the internet in mediation work include 'increased participant involvement, enhanced quality of consideration and cost savings'. Melamed singles out as a special quality the 'asynchronous' nature of the internet. For example, in comparison to 'real time' discussions, participants in email discussions do not need to respond immediately. They therefore have time to consider and develop options, and to fashion their response. He argues that most mediators are already using the internet to some extent to assist in their business promotion and mediation practice. So in a typical mediation, mediators may use face-to-face meetings and online communication on the internet, combined with phone calls, voice mail, faxes and ordinary mail. He suggests that mediators may find the baseline in mediation on the internet and use face-to-face meetings to further develop relationships, mark progress, and interactively engage in dialogue. Further, private sessions can be done online. While the internet suffers many drawbacks similar to those associated with telephone conferences, mediators may consider how face-to-face meetings and online strategies can be integrated for best effect. Some mediations are in fact being done completely online now.[199]

Press releases

In a public interest/sector mediation an important issue is how to ensure that communication is maintained between stakeholder representatives in the process and their constituents. Public seminars and press releases can facilitate information flow. Reframing in literal terms is also important in this context, in order to tackle deeply-held views. In a mediation over a dumping site, for example:

> '. . . rather than reframe: "so what you're saying is there is an odour from the landfill"; it would be preferable to say: "so what you're saying is that the air around [here] stinks . . . like rotten eggs".'[200]

No joint meetings

This is the implication of 'shuttle mediation', dealt with in the next section.

---

199   See the section on On-line Mediation in Chapter 9.
200   S Frisby 'Mediating an environmental dispute' (1999) 1 *Proctor* 23.

Variations in relation to the separate meetings

Held prior to the joint meeting for information gathering

In some situations the mediation commences with separate meetings for the purposes of gathering information and discovering the parties' concerns. The rationale for this is that parties might feel inhibited from disclosing important information in the early stages of the joint meeting. Where it is disclosed in preliminary separate meetings the mediator is able to assess its relevance, and if appropriate incorporate it into a more comprehensive agenda. A potential danger of using separate meetings to elicit information is that the parties may be tempted to manipulate an uninformed mediator by exaggerating or misleading in ways which would be challenged by the other side if presented in joint session.

Shuttle mediation

In some cases the whole mediation is conducted through separate meetings without the parties convening jointly at any stage. The mediator moves repeatedly between the parties, and is the sole vehicle of communication and negotiation. This is referred to as *shuttle mediation*, after the style of the shuttle diplomacy used in the settlement of disputes involving international relations. In interpersonal disputes this variation is warranted where the level of antagonism between the parties would render joint meetings counterproductive. It is also the only practical way of conducting mediations, other than through tele-conferencing, where one party fears violence or where there are protection orders preventing the parties from coming together. While shuttle mediation may sometimes be a practical necessity, it is not conducive to the preservation of relations between the parties. Another concern is that each party may be apprehensive about who is assisting the other.[201] It also gives more potential influence and power to mediators through their active role in the communications and in transmitting offers and counter-offers.

In civil/commercial mediation, it is common for a mediator to shuttle between the parties or to have private meetings with each party, after an initial joint meeting, in an attempt to identify each party's underlying interests. An essential pre-condition for the separate meetings is confidentiality. In the context of labour conciliation, the private session or 'caucus' has a slightly different meaning, as the caucus meeting is used purely to negotiate an outcome.[202] In family mediation, it is uncommon for shuttling to occur,[203] as in the context of community mediation, although shuttle mediation might be used if the parties are uncomfortable about meeting face-to-face.[204] In contrast, international or diplomatic mediation is usually conducted in

---

201 In a family mediation conducted on a shuttle basis, the mediator discovered, halfway through the process, that the wife's new partner had entered the wife's room, without the husband being aware of it. The mediator elected not to disclose this fact to the husband for fear of jeopardising the process and he was not specifically asked about this possibility. The matter settled.

202 See the section on Employment Disputes in Chapter 8.

203 UK College of Family Mediators *1999/2000 Directory and Handbook*, Sweet & Maxwell, London, 1999, at p A83.

204 The study of community mediation in R E Mackay and A J Brown *Community Mediation in Scotland: a study of implementation*, The Scottish Office Central Research

private or separate meetings between the mediator and each party. Mediation UK's 1995 survey of community mediation schemes revealed that face-to-face mediation occurred in 27% of cases and that the most common mediation model was shuttle mediation.[205] The shuttle mediation model is believed, in the community mediation context, to help the parties to save face, balance power and reduce threats to relationships.[206]

Separate meetings with advisers and parties

The flexibility of the mediation process allows the mediator to convene separate meetings with the lawyers or other advisers of the parties. This may be necessary to educate the advisers about their proper role in mediation, without their losing face before the clients. Where the mediator is a lawyer, he or she may wish to discuss legal issues with the parties' legal advisers. However, these meetings are used cautiously as they might raise concerns among the parties about a professional conspiracy. Conversely, the mediator may request all advisers to withdraw so that the mediator can confer with the parties alone. This may assist them to focus on their real needs and interests without any pressure from advisers.[207]

No separate meetings

In some training courses the separate meetings are presented as a routine and indispensable feature of the mediation process. Even where problem-identification and problem-solving have proceeded quickly and smoothly, separate meetings are called to establish how the participants are feeling about the process, whether there are any undisclosed concerns, and whether the proposed agreement satisfies the respective parties' interests. In other training systems, in particular for family and community mediation, separate meetings are presented as an optional variable which are called only in the discretion of the mediator or at the request of a party.[208] Some experienced mediators have resorted to a blanket policy of no separate meetings.[209] This is done mainly to avoid the potential suspicion and loss of trust which separate meetings might generate and to increase the prospect of co-operation between the parties. In such cases it is a condition of the mediation that it will be conducted with all parties jointly present throughout. This arrangement is not encountered frequently in practice.

Unit, Edinburgh, 1999 found that community mediators frequently explained their dislike of shuttling on the basis that they wished to avoid being used by the parties to merely pass messages between them.

205 Mediation UK *Community Mediation Service General Survey*, Mediation UK, 1995.

206 D Augsburger *Conflict Mediation across Cultures*, Westminster/John Knocks Press, Kentucky, 1992.

207 In the Spedley mediation when there were 50 people in the room and the mediator asked the lawyers to leave, only six people remained behind: see M Slattery 'The Spedley mediation from the inside' (1993) *Bar News* 23 at 28.

208 Shuttling, or private meetings, may provide a family mediator with a strategy to break impasse. If it is used, mediators need to ensure that confidences are maintained, although financial disclosure in a private session is open: see also Chapter 12.

209 Experienced mediators at the Annual Convention of the Society of Professionals in Dispute Resolution (SPIDR), Pittsburgh, Pennsylvania, USA, July 1992.

Variations in relation to the conclusion of a mediation

A mediator in a civil/commercial mediation may, if the parties have requested, make a non-binding recommendation as to the settlement terms,[210] which may encourage further negotiations between the parties, even a settlement, of the dispute. Whether or not a civil/commercial mediation involves a non-binding recommendation, a considerable amount of time may be required to reduce an agreement to writing. It is preferable that this occurs in the course of mediation itself, although if an agreement is complex, it is usual to agree heads of terms, signed by all the parties, and for the settlement agreement to be drafted by the lawyers subsequent to the mediation. It is important for all the parties to agree whether what is agreed at the mediation is intended to be legally binding. If it is intended to be legally binding, it should also be clear whether the agreement is immediately binding or whether it will become binding at some future date. The terms of the agreement must be clear, for instance, it needs to provide, if there is to be a payment of money, how much is to be paid, by whom, to whom and when. The agreement should specify what is to happen to any litigation between the parties and to the parties' costs of the action.[211] The agreement should also set out the consequences of non-compliance and, in the case of international parties, the choice of law and jurisdiction clauses. Alternatively, the parties may wish to include mediation or other alternative dispute resolution clauses to cover future disputes. Although it is for the parties' lawyers to advise them on the agreement, its legality and durability, most codes of conduct for mediators in civil/commercial cases remind them that they should withdraw from a mediation where there is any fraud or other offence of dishonesty in relation to the proposed agreement.[212]

In family mediation, it is frequently necessary to adjourn the mediation in order to allow the parties an opportunity to reflect and obtain legal advice. The parties may also decide to take up counselling or therapy. The conclusion of a family mediation usually results in a memorandum of understanding or summary.[213] There are different types of memoranda: a draft; an interim agreement; arrangements for the children; and a final without prejudice memorandum. A mediator does not draft a memorandum on the basis that it constitutes a binding agreement, except in limited circumstances, where independent legal advice is not required.[214] This affords parties the opportunity to obtain legal advice,[215] after which the non-binding memorandum can be converted into a binding form,[216] either as an agreement or court order. In

---

210 See, for example, Intermediation *Mediation Rules and Rules of Conduct*; Law Society of Northern Ireland Dispute Resolution Service *Agreement to Mediate*.

211 Central London County Court Form MD8A sets out the points for consideration when drafting a mediation settlement agreement.

212 For example, Law Society of Scotland *Code of Conduct and Guidance for Accredited Mediators*.

213 In Scotland, a written summary will be prepared if requested by the parties, as mediators feel that it may undermine the mediation and the 'good faith' arrangements made in the mediation: J Lewis *The Role of Family Mediation in Scotland: report of a research study*, The Scottish Office Central Research Unit, 1999.

214 Law Society of England & Wales *Family Mediation Training Standards*.

215 Law Society of England & Wales *Code of Practice for Family Mediation*.

216 Compare Marlow's view that the parties in family mediation need not consult with

Scotland agreements may be formalised through a Minute or Joint Minute of Agreement. Child support agreements finalised by the parties may, nevertheless, be varied or cancelled by the Child Support Agency.[217] The memorandum of understanding drafted by a mediator typically deals with the following issues:

- arrangements for the children or parenting plan;
- separation or divorce;
- division of assets;
- financial support and pensions;
- inheritance issues; and
- tax positions.[218]

It is not common for parties in community mediation to record or sign their agreements, except where an authority or agency is involved, as in victim-offender mediation. If the parties record their agreement, it will contain the names of the parties and the mediators and set out the terms agreed, usually in the parties' own words. It will also state that the agreement is not a legal document, although the agreement may have legal consequences, and accordingly the status of agreements reached in community mediations should be carefully considered.[219]

Contingent agreements are common in the context of multi-party public sector mediations. Agreements typically contain a schedule of commitments, the fulfilment of which will depend on the occurrence of specified events. Accordingly, such agreements require monitoring to ensure that the commitments are met. Such agreements may also need to be reviewed in light of any new information. In the context of public sector mediation, where intransigent third parties may be involved, an agreed outcome may have been reached, although third parties dissented to it, and those dissenting views can be recorded, without the agreement being affected.

---

separate lawyers, as would be the case if legal rules and principles were viewed as rights, but a single lawyer is preferable as the mediator requires an answer to particular points, not a range of legal opinions: L Marlow 'The rule of law in divorce mediation' (1985) 9 *Mediation Quarterly* 5 at 10–13.

217 UK College of Family Mediators *1999/2000 Directory and Handbook*, Sweet & Maxwell, London, 1999, at p A94.

218 Ibid, at pp A14–16.

219 See the elements which may determine whether or not a binding contract has been reached, discussed in Chapter 12, in the context of enforcement of mediated agreements.

5

Roles and Functions in Mediation

Roles, Functions and Skills

In this chapter attention is given to the roles and functions of those who are involved in the mediation process. The main focus is on mediators, and there is also reference to the parties, their advisers, and other potential participants. These roles and functions are related to the stages of mediation, referred to in Chapter 4.

For the purposes of this chapter, distinctions are made between the terms *roles*, *functions* and *skills*, although the three concepts overlap significantly and the distinctions are somewhat arbitrary. Here the term *roles* is used to refer to the overall aims and objectives of mediators. Thus the roles of mediators can be represented as being to create the optimal conditions for the parties to make effective decisions and to assist the parties to negotiate an agreement. These role descriptions operate at a high level of generality and do not disclose much about what mediators actually do. The term *functions* is used to refer to the more specific tasks and behaviours of mediators which contribute to the achievement of their overall roles, for example the function of improving the communication endeavours of the parties. At a still more specific level are the *skills* of mediators, which refer to concrete acts and interventions, such as arranging the seating or reframing the parties' statements. This chapter focuses mainly on the functions of mediators and others, and mediator skills are dealt with in the following chapter.

The Functions of Mediators
Categorising mediators' functions

The functions of mediators can be classified in different ways. Moore refers to contingent and non-contingent functions.[1] The non-contingent functions are the general moves which mediators make in all mediations, such as chairing the mediation meeting and involving themselves in the communication process. The contingent functions are the specific moves which mediators make in response to special problems in some mediations, such as calling separate meetings or brainstorming with

---

1   C Moore *The Mediation Process: practical strategies for resolving conflict* (2nd edn), Jossey-Bass, San Francisco, 1996, at pp 57–8.

the parties. Kressel and Pruitt[2] refer to three types of mediator behaviour: reflexive (those moves which orient mediators to the dispute and create the foundation for their future moves), substantive (those interventions which impact on the content of the dispute), and contextual (those moves which improve the process of decision-making). Henderson categorises the functions of mediators according to whether they relate to matters of procedure, communication or substance.[3] Some writers add an assertive-passive dimension to their categorisation of mediator functions.

These categorisations provide some assistance in understanding the different functions of mediators. However, categories always involve difficulties of classification, boundaries and terminology. They also suggest that the inventory of functions for mediators is a closed list of categories, which is not correct – there is an almost limitless number of actions which mediators can take. Mediators' functions should not, however, be seen as magical, or even mystical, as some mediators imply when asked about what they actually do. Their functions can be described, but always in a tentative and open-ended way.

Following is an undifferentiated list of 11 mediator functions. This includes both principal functions which mediators perform in their own capacity, for example developing trust and confidence, and supportive functions which they perform in a facilitative capacity, for example assisting the parties to negotiate constructively.

The diversity of mediator functions

It is clear that mediators, unlike judges, arbitrators and other umpires, cannot make formally binding decisions for the parties. As to what they can do, it is not easy to be so explicit. There is an almost unlimited array of interventions of great diversity which can be made, short of making a decision. Some are easy to describe and explain, others are subtle and less easily explicable. This is partly a function of the intricate communication and negotiation dynamic in which the mediator becomes involved. Between the disputing parties there are complex sequences of moves and counter-moves, acts and responses, causes and effects. The mediator interacts intimately with this complicated set of manoeuvres.[4] He or she initiates, reacts, adapts and retreats. This intricate mediator interaction influences and changes directions and outcomes.

The exact nature of a mediator's functions depends on the kind of dispute, the characteristics of the parties involved, the agency providing the mediation service, the terms of the Agreement to Mediate and whether there are mediator guidelines which attempt to define and describe the role and functions of the mediator.[5] They depend on which of the four models of mediation is being used, and on what stage of the mediation has been reached. They also depend on whether, as a matter of style, the mediator is directive or non-interventionist. Thus in the early stages of a

---

2   K Kressel and D Pruitt 'Themes in the mediation of social conflict' (1985) 41 *Journal of Social Issues* 179.

3   S Henderson *The Dispute Resolution Manual*, DataLegal Publishers, Spring Hill, 1993, at p 102. See also H Astor and C Chinkin *Dispute Resolution in Australia*, Butterworths, Sydney, 1993, at p 104.

4   C Moore *The Mediation Process: practical strategies for resolving conflict* (2nd edn) Jossey-Bass, San Francisco, 1996, at p 57.

5   On mediator guidelines, see Chapter 11.

private *facilitative mediation* conducted by a non-interventionist mediator the functions are likely to be limited to establishing and maintaining contact between the parties, providing a physical forum in which they can meet, being a neutral form of support for the parties' negotiations, and stimulating a two-way flow of information.[6]

The mediator creates an environment, which encourages the parties to express their feelings.[7] The mediator is non-directive and focuses on listening, which frequently has the result that the process is slow.[8] In the later stages of an *evaluative mediation* conducted by a directive mediator, they are likely to include, as well as the above, more robust procedural moves and intervention on substance.

Typical techniques include encouraging the parties to consider the strengths and weaknesses of their case[9] and stressing the consequences, particularly the costs, of failure to reach settlement in the mediation. Genn's study of the Central London County Court mediation pilot identified two types of approach: the 'cool authority' and the 'head-banging' styles. The cool authoritative mediator uses charm and sympathy to gain the confidence of the parties and may indirectly provide the parties with a view on the merits.[10] The head-bangers force consideration of the merits of the case and to the parties' bottom lines.[11] The study indicated that some parties found the head-banging approach appropriate, in particular for commercial disputes,[12] whereas other parties considered that the approach put undue pressure on them to settle.[13]

Whatever style the mediator prefers, however, the mediator, as with the parties and their lawyers, needs to be flexible in approach, so as not to pre-judge what will work in each case.[14] In the face of this diversity, mediators must be adaptive. They are

---

6 See S Roberts 'Toward a minimal form of alternative intervention' (1986) 11 *MQ* 25.
7 S Silbey and S Merry 'Mediator Settlement Strategies' (1986) 8 *Law & Policy* 7 at 19.
8 H Genn *Central London County Court Mediation Pilot: Evaluation Report*, LCD Research Series, No 5/98, at p 115, refers to a defendant's reaction to the therapeutic approach:
  '. . . it felt like going to the Samaritans . . . there was a lot of listening . . . I think it would be just all a bit too subtle.'
9 L Mulcahy et al *Mediating medical negligence claims: an option for the future?* NHS Executive, 2000, at p 38 where there is an example of a mediator using the technique:
  '. . . what I said to them was, "well, you are absolutely right if you say you are absolutely right. You must be going to win on that point. So, why do you think they are not conceding it? They are represented by a lawyer. Why do you think they are fighting that point?" '.
10 H Genn, Central London County Court Mediation Pilot Evaluation, op cit, at p 141.
11 Ibid, at p 142.
12 Ibid, at p 140 where a businessman's view of the head-banging approach is explained:
  '. . . when you are dealing with commercial dealings . . . you can grab it by the throat . . . businessmen just want to reach some sort of a compromise . . . and for a mediator to take the bull by the horns and give his opinion.'
13 L Mulcahy et al, op cit, at p 67 in the case of clinical negligence mediations.
14 Bond Dispute Resolution Centre 'What skills and attributes do experienced mediators possess?' (1999) 3 *Bond Dispute Resolution News*. The survey of experienced Australian mediators reported in that article revealed that many renowned mediators had admitted that they should not work so hard, but hand more of the process over to the parties. This is also reflected in the views of some of the mediators surveyed as part of the NHS Mediation Pilot: see L Mulcahy et al, op cit, at p 37:
  '. . . it's very powerful as a mediator to tell the parties that they have to make the decisions . . . you have to put the onus on them . . .'

required to make tactical judgments on what action is appropriate for each particular problem.[15] Experienced mediators develop an understanding of the role and functions which the dispute and disputants require them to play.[16] For instance, educated clients with experienced advisers may require no more than some basic structure and rules of communication, while complex cases or parties with limited negotiating skills may require a wider range of functions from mediators. Any list of mediator functions indicates not what mediators invariably do, but what they might do in the appropriate circumstances. How a mediator decides what to do is a matter of professional judgment, intuition, trial and error, and knowledge of the science of mediation.

Mediator Functions

In the performance of their overall roles, mediators can undertake the functions of:[17]

- developing trust and confidence;
- establishing a framework for co-operative decision-making;
- analysing the conflict and designing appropriate interventions;
- promoting constructive communication;
- facilitating negotiation and problem-solving;
- educating the parties;
- empowering the parties;
- imposing pressure to settle;
- promoting reality;
- advising and evaluating;
- terminating the mediation.

Developing trust and confidence

It is regarded as an essential requisite for successful mediation that the parties have trust and confidence in the mediator.[18] Surveys of practising mediators have found that they

---

15 P Carnevale, R Lim and M McLaughlin 'Contingent mediator behaviour and its effectiveness' in K Kressel et al (eds) *Mediation Research: the process and effectiveness of third party intervention*, 1989, at p 213.

16 C Nupen 'Mediation' in P Pretorius (ed) *Dispute Resolution*, Juta & Co, Kenwyn, South Africa, 1993, at pp 42–8.

17 C Moore *The Mediation Process: practical strategies for resolving conflict* (2nd edn), Jossey-Bass, San Francisco, 1996, at pp 18–19; H Brown and A Marriott *ADR Principles and Practice* (2nd edn), Sweet & Maxwell, London, 1999, at pp 248–65; S Henderson *The Dispute Resolution Manual*, DataLegal Publications, Spring Hill, QLD, 1993, at p 102; J Stulberg *Taking Charge/Managing Conflict*, Lexington Books, Lexington, Massachusetts, 1987, at pp 31–7; D Paratz *Mediation – a user's guide*, Australian Commercial Disputes Centre, 1992, at pp 25–9; J Wade 'Strategic interventions used by mediators, facilitators and conciliators' (1994) 5 *ADRJ* 292.

18 M Anstey *Practical Peacemaking – a mediator's handbook*, Juta & Co, Kenwyn, South Africa, 1993, at p 10; P Carnevale and R Pegnetter 'The selection of mediation tactics in public sector disputes: a contingency analysis' (1985) 41 *Journal of Social Issues* 41 at 65; and E Radford and P Glaser 'The psychology of mediation' in P Pretorius (ed) *Dispute Resolution*, Juta & Co, Kenwyn, South Africa, at pp 51 and 57.

regard the building of this trust relationship as their most important task. Here trust denotes an acceptance among the parties that the mediator is reliable, will remain impartial and will not allow personal views or values to influence the discussions. Trust in the mediator serves to secure and maintain the parties' commitment to the process. It is the basis on which the mediator establishes a working association with the parties. Where parties in dispute are distrustful of each other, they might still be prepared to take risks with a third party on whom they feel they can rely.[19] This trust can be used by the mediator in carrying out other functions. Thus where trust has been established, a party may use the mediator as a 'sounding board' to test privately whether a particular proposal is useful or viable before it is presented to the other party in joint session.[20]

Trust must be first developed in the preparatory stages and must be preserved throughout the mediation process. It can be acquired and enhanced in a variety of ways:

- through showing concern and respect;
- through affirming the mediator's experience and credentials;
- by explaining and validating the mediation process;
- through good listening skills and understanding of the parties;
- through sound interpersonal skills, impartiality and even-handed conduct of the process; and
- through empathy and bonding during the separate meetings.

Some mediators refer to their contacts with influential others outside the mediation process to reinforce levels of trust.[21] Mediators also need to acknowledge and address the specific needs of particular participants: the status needs of chief executives, the reputational needs of lawyers, the security needs of support persons. By establishing rapport with all participants, mediators develop a sound platform for performing other necessary functions.

Other steps that may be taken to promote trust and confidence include ensuring the representation and effective participation of stakeholders, refraining from advocating a one-sided perspective on substantive matters, safeguarding the confidentiality of private communications with the parties, developing and enforcing guidelines that are jointly formulated and acceptable, and addressing situations where it appears that any party is not acting in good faith.[22]

While the early development of trust is imperative, mediators might have to recover from a partial loss of trust and confidence where they have appeared to be biased

---

19 See S Henderson *The Dispute Resolution Manual*, DataLegal Publications, Spring Hill, QLD, 1993, at p 98.
20 H Brown and A Marriott *ADR Principles and Practice* (2nd edn), Sweet & Maxwell, London, 1999.
21 D Kolb 'To be a mediator: expressive tactics in mediation' (1985) 41 *Journal of Social Issues* 11–26.
22 M Elliott 'The role of facilitators, mediators and other consensus building practitioners' in L Susskind et al (eds) *The consensus building handbook – a comprehensive guide to reaching agreement*, Sage Publications, California, 1999, at pp 218–19. For a list of guidelines to establish and maintain the credibility of agreement seeking processes, see Appendix 4 of the Report and Recommendations of the Society of Professionals in Dispute Resolution (SPIDR) Environment/Public Sector Critical Issues Committee. The report and recommendations were adopted by the SPIDR Board in January 1997.

towards one party or where the process has become impacted. This can be achieved through further explanation as to the mediator's roles and functions, and reassurances as to the mediator's impartiality. Trust and confidence are easier to gain in the early stages of mediation than they are to recover in the later stages.

The other side of the trust coin is the 'scapegoat' concept. Stulberg suggests that the mediator can be a 'lightning rod for the parties' frustrations and concerns'.[23] This suggests that where parties are not altogether satisfied with the outcome of the mediation, but are prepared to accept it, they may be able to attribute some blame for the result to the mediator.[24] This could be particularly important where they have difficult constituents with whom to deal. This, however, is a subsidiary function of the mediator which requires delicate execution. The role of scapegoat should not be assumed too readily by mediators.

Establishing a framework for co-operative decision-making

The mediator establishes a framework, or favourable climate, for co-operation between the parties. There are at least three aspects to this function: the physical, the emotional and the procedural. Examples of these follow.

(a)   *Physical:* The mediator takes the initiative in convening a physical meeting of the parties. This is done at an accessible and comfortable venue with the appropriate amenities. This is a practical function, which could extend to the mediator manipulating the environment to make it as conducive as possible to co-operative interaction. The mediator may also be required to persuade one of the parties that mediation is appropriate, in other words to get them to the negotiating table. The convening function provides the first dimension of the framework and takes place during the early stages of the process.

(b)   *Emotional:* The mediator also creates an emotional climate which is conducive to co-operative decision-making.[25] This entails factors such as a positive tone, a mood of confidence, reassurances as to confidentiality, reduction of tension through humour, and the provision of a safe environment for the venting of emotions. Some mediators take time to normalise and validate the concerns of parties as they express them, and to preserve face for everyone at the mediation meeting.[26] Much of the emotional climate is developed through good communication, for example by easing tense dialogue between disputants through tact, palatable wording and a 'sympathetic presentation of each side's position to the other'.[27] The emotional dimension of the framework is developed during all stages of the mediation.

---

23 J Stulberg *Taking Charge/Managing Conflict*, Lexington Books, Lexington, Massachusetts, 1987, at p 35.
24 C Moore *The Mediation Process: practical strategies for resolving conflict* (2nd edn), Jossey-Bass, San Francisco, 1996, at p 19.
25 K Kressel and D Pruitt 'Themes in the Mediation of Social Conflict' (1985) 41(2) *Journal of Social Issues* 179.
26 J Haynes *The fundamentals of family mediation*, State University of New York Press, Albany, 1994, at p 9.
27 S Touval and I Zartman 'Mediation in international conflicts' in K Kressel et al (eds)

(c)　*Procedural:* The third dimension of the framework for co-operation is a structural and procedural one. In exercising this function, mediators assist in providing a defined order of proceedings, the development and use of an agenda, the maintenance of order and sequence, the management of procedural conflicts, and space and timing arrangements. Where there are multiple mediation meetings, the structure extends to a clear and convenient timetable for the future. The mediator 'chairs' the mediation meetings, which is an authoritative role, though it need not be carried out in an authoritarian way.[28] In these matters of process and structure the mediator assumes a leadership role, subject to appropriate consultations with the parties. This can also be seen as a management function for the mediator,[29] the mediator becoming a 'process controller'.[30] Mediation is not an 'unstructured bull session'.[31]

The mediator's opening statement[32] provides an opportunity to establish the structural aspects of the process, including the mediation guidelines on which the meeting will be based. Mediators have a range of intervention strategies with which to oversee the guidelines where they are breached by one or more parties. These include:

- ignoring the breach as inconsequential or otherwise not requiring intervention;
- distracting the parties from the breach with an innocuous question;
- neutrally restating the guidelines and requesting a fresh commitment to them;
- reprimanding the offending party or parties;
- breaking into separate meetings; and
- using shaming techniques to bring the parties back to business.

Which of these strategies is tactically appropriate will be a matter for the mediator's judgment. Structure is also provided during the mediation meeting by the mediator visually displaying information and lists of issues on boards or paper. This serves to reassure parties that their concerns will be addressed, it allows priorities to be established and progress to be monitored, and it provides a point of visual reference if the discussions become confrontational.

One of the mediator's roles is to assist the parties in prioritising the agenda issues and moving systematically through them. Thus in a matrimonial dispute they may elect to deal first with short-term needs, such as the payment of overdue accounts, before less urgent matters, such as the final division of property. The mediator might also provide leadership in relation to sequence by encouraging easier matters to be dealt with first, on the grounds that success in these matters will provide encouragement and a positive climate for more difficult issues.

Mediation Research: the process and effectiveness of third party intervention, Jossey-Bass, San Francisco, 1989 at p 115.

28　J Stulberg *Taking Charge/Managing Conflict*, Lexington Books, Lexington, Massachusetts, 1987, at p 31.

29　H Brown and A Marriott *ADR Principles and Practice* (2nd edn), Sweet & Maxwell, London, 1999; and J Haynes and G Haynes *Mediating Divorce: casebook of strategies for successful family negotiations*, Jossey-Bass, San Francisco, 1989, at pp 16–17.

30　S Henderson *The Dispute Resolution Manual*, DataLegal Publications, Spring Hill, QLD, 1993, at p 101.

31　No pun intended. The source of this quotation cannot be located.

32　See Chapter 4.

A certain amount of custom design may have to go into both structure and sequence. Moore refers to the importance of the mediator designing a detailed plan, in the sense of a 'sequence of procedural steps initiated by the intervener', for the mediation.[33] This will be particularly important during the early stages of the mediation, but the function will continue throughout. The initial planning covers questions of who should participate in the mediation, the best location or venue, appropriate procedures for the meeting, and ways of dealing with deadlocks. Some of the planning may be done in co-operation with the parties, where the circumstances and the parties' capacities allow. Thus where one or more of the negotiating parties represents a constituency, the process will need to be structured so as to provide information to constituents, or even to the media via press statements. Likewise, where one party is inarticulate or anxious, the normal sequence of events might have to be altered to allow them to settle in and develop confidence. Finally, the procedure may need to be adapted to involve experts, advisers and other outside resources. In all these matters, mediators can contribute process and structure which would be difficult for the parties to attain on their own.

Analysing the conflict and designing appropriate interventions

Moore emphasises the importance of mediators continually analysing and assessing conflict situations in order to develop the most appropriate forms of intervention.[34] By diagnosing the central causes of the conflict, mediators can determine their choice of tactics and assist the parties to take appropriate action. The analysis may be complicated by the intricate nature of the dispute and the possibility that it has multiple causes, so the mediator is required to develop and test a hypothesis to support a particular intervention. If the intervention is inappropriate, the hypothesis will have to be revised, and the mediator will 'shift to another theory and begin the trial-and-error testing again'.[35] The role of conflict analyst and hypothesis tester will commence at the earliest stages of the mediation and continue throughout its duration.

To assist the diagnosis and intervention the mediator needs to undertake three related tasks:

Supervise the gathering and exchange of information

In cases in which litigation is anticipated, most of the relevant information will be available. In other cases mediators must supervise the gathering of information and, subject to requirements of confidentiality, manage the exchange of information between the parties. They may also organise an exchange of position statements between the parties to distil information and simplify the picture. They should encourage agreements on facts, or at least a narrowing of fact differences between the parties. The information gathering and exchange of information precedes the

---

33 C Moore *The Mediation Process: practical strategies for resolving conflict* (2nd edn) Jossey-Bass, San Francisco, 1996, at pp 141–3.

34 Ibid, at pp 58–63; and also M Anstey *Practical Peacemaking – a mediator's handbook*, Juta & Co, Kenwyn, South Africa, 1993, at pp 16–33. And see Chapter 2.

35 C Moore, ibid, at p 62–3.

mediation meeting, but may continue throughout the process. The object of this function is to provide a foundation for the accurate definition of the dispute.[36]

Facilitate the disclosure and acknowledgment of party needs

It is not infrequent that parties in dispute conceal their real needs from both the other side and their own professional advisers, not as a deliberate strategy but as part of the way in which humans respond to problems.[37] One of the functions of mediators is to go beyond the parties' presenting problems and assist them to articulate their underlying needs. These can include substantive, emotional and procedural needs. In so far as these needs can be dealt with in mediation, mediators assist the parties in defining them as issues for discussion.[38] Needs can be elicited and clarified through a range of interventions, including questioning, active listening and reframing.[39] The separate meetings may elicit further needs. The full disclosure of party needs contributes to a more comprehensive picture of the dispute. Once the needs have been elicited, the mediator's function is to ensure some acknowledgment by each side of the other's needs. The expectation is that this acknowledgment will reorientate the parties towards each other and develop a new and shared perception of the problem and their relationship.[40]

It is not only the parties' needs that are relevant. Family mediators in England and Wales are required to have regard to the general principles set out in s 1 of the Family Law Act 1996 when exercising functions in relation to the Act. Scottish family mediators must have regard to the principles contained in Part 1 of the Children (Scotland) Act 1995. The fundamental requirement imposes an obligation on family mediators to consider the welfare of children. Family mediator conduct rules elaborate on that requirement:

- the mediator should consider the needs and interests of the children;
- measures to satisfy the needs and interests of the children should be discussed; and
- the mediator is required to contact outside agencies or take other action if a child is suffering or is likely to suffer harm.[41]

---

36 Some mediator standards require mediators to oversee the information gathering and exchange. On problems and ambiguities in this area, see Chapter 11.

37 D Campbell and P Summerfield (eds) *Effective Dispute Resolution for the International Commercial Lawyer*, Kluwer, Boston, 1989, at p 116.

38 For an example of concerns and needs being changed into issues, see the section on this in Chapter 6.

39 On the skills associated with these interventions, see Chapter 6.

40 Fuller describes this 'reorientation' as the central quality of mediation: see L Fuller 'Mediation – its forms and functions' (1970–71) 44 *Southern California Law Review* 305 at 327. See also E Radford and P Glaser 'The psychology of mediation' in P Pretorius (ed) *Dispute Resolution*, Juta & Co, Kenwyn, South Africa, at p 56.

41 For example, the codes of conduct issued by the Law Society of England & Wales, Law Wise, NFM, FMA, the UK College of Family Mediators, CALM and FMS. The UK college of Family Mediators *Code of Conduct* provides, in order to ensure that the mediator can decide whether the parties' suggested proposals will satisfy the needs and interests of the child, the mediator should be trained to involve children in the mediation for this purpose.

Although it is the parents' responsibility to protect the interests of their children, a mediator's task is to assist the parents to do so, but does not amount to representing the interests of the children. The UK College of Family Mediators provides the following guidance:

- a mediator should encourage the parties to consider the needs of the children;
- the needs of the children should be explored from the child's point of view: accordingly, a mediator should encourage the parties to consider the children's wishes and should discuss with the parties whether and to what extent the children should be involved in the mediation in order for their wishes to be ascertained;
- if children are involved in the mediation for this purpose, the mediator should be trained for that purpose, provide appropriate facilities and obtain the child's consent.[42]

In the case of family mediation, mediators will also keep the possibility of reconciliation under review in the mediation.[43]

Clarify and define the issues in dispute

The negative effects of conflict may prevent the parties from having a clear perception of exactly which areas are (or are not) in dispute. Parties in conflict tend to define the problem unilaterally, which implies a solution which will benefit only that party, the 'more for you will mean less for me' mentality. Poor communication may distort perceptions of what the other side wants or what they are prepared to concede. An important contribution from the mediator is to assist the parties to achieve clarity on what is and what is not in dispute, and thereby define the conflict.[44] The issues can be wide-ranging, including emotional, personal, technical, commercial, cultural, factual and legal.[45] Before a dispute can be resolved, there needs to be clarity on what it is about.[46] Once the problem has been defined, the mediator can assist the parties to prioritise the individual issues in terms of those which require urgent treatment and those which can be dealt with subsequently.[47] Mediation can provide a major contribution to the resolution of the problem by first developing a joint and mutual definition of it.[48] Where the problem is neutrally defined, it will imply solutions which benefit both parties. Experienced mediators

---

42 UK College of Family Mediators *Code of Practice*.
43 Ibid.
44 C Nupen 'Mediation' in P Pretorius (ed) *Dispute Resolution*, Juta & Co, Kenwyn, South Africa, 1993, at pp 39 and 44.
45 M Dewdney, B Sordo and C Chinkin *Continuing developments in mediation within the legal system: evaluation of the 1992/93 Settlement Week Programme*, the Law Society, New South Wales, 1994 where at p 154 the authors outline the wide range of issues discovered in the cases surveyed.
46 M Thoennes and J Pearson 'Predicting outcomes in divorce mediation: the influence of people in process' (1985) 41(2) *Journal of Social Issues* 115.
47 P J Carnevale et al 'Mediator Behaviour and Effectiveness in Community Mediation' in Duffy, Grosch and Olczak (eds) *Community Mediation: A Handbook for Practitioners and Researchers*, Guildford, New York, 1991 who identified this behaviour with a successful outcome in mediation.
48 J Haynes and G Haynes *Mediating Divorce: casebook of strategies for successful family negotiations*, Jossey-Bass, San Francisco, 1989, at pp 20–1.

can anticipate the likely issues in self-contained fields, and can assist the parties to restate the concerns they present in terms of these standard issues.[49]

Promoting constructive communication

Parties in conflict tend to display poor communication skills, and ineffective communication can cause a dispute to escalate. Mediators have the function of opening up the channels of communication and assisting the parties to hear and understand each other. This function is important in all stages of the mediation and it has three dimensions. First, mediators must themselves be effective communicators, for example in practising good listening and questioning skills and in being attentive to non-verbal messages. This enables them to come to terms with the true nature of the dispute and it can provide a good example to the parties. Where there are two or more mediators, they can model, for the parties' benefit, effective communication techniques between themselves. Second, mediators intervene directly in the face of poor communication exchanges between the parties. Where the parties are not listening to or understanding one another, mediators may 'interpret' the communications to make them effective, summarise, reframe and otherwise assist the parties in hearing and understanding what each means and feels. When there is a series of separate meetings, mediators actually transmit messages between the parties. Here there is scope for even more direct communication intervention in that mediators can present offers and counter-offers in the most favourable way by adding 'noise' to the parties' own words.[50] Third, mediators can, in the privacy of separate meetings, advise and coach the parties on effective communication techniques, for example on how to respond to offers which they anticipate coming from the other side in ways which do not inflame the other party.

These communication functions of mediators involve a range of specific skills which are dealt with in Chapter 6.

Facilitating negotiation and problem-solving

While a mediator is not a party to the negotiations, he or she manages and influences the negotiation process in many important ways. In fact all the mediator's functions, in particular those relating to process and communication, have a general bearing on the style and tone of the negotiations and the attitude and behaviour of the negotiators. In addition the mediator has specific assignments relating to negotiation and problem-solving. These mediator functions are exercised mainly after the problem-defining stage of the mediation.

---

49 For example, John Wade, an Australian mediator, has developed from his family law experience a closed list of six issues in matrimonial property disputes and 16 issues in custody/access disputes: see further Chapter 13.
50 Thus a party's rejection of an offer can be made more palatable by the mediator referring to their continued commitment to the mediation, explaining their underlying concerns, pointing out their perceived disadvantage, and re-emphasising agreements already reached. The 'noise' added by the mediator is likely to make the rejection less damaging than the party's raw words.

The parties may adopt different approaches to negotiation,[51] and in all cases mediators can contribute towards making it more constructive and efficient.[52] The mediator will need to guide the parties and their lawyers in the techniques of negotiation, and may need to point out counterproductive behaviour or proposals.[53] If the parties adopt a positional bargaining approach, mediators operating within the *facilitative mediation* model will attempt to divert them into problem-solving negotiation. This requires interventions which shift the attention of the disputants away from positional claims towards their underlying needs and interests. Mediators can encourage them to separate the interpersonal aspects of the dispute from the substantive aspects, to seek common ground, to develop options, and to use objective criteria to evaluate possible settlement alternatives. They stimulate them to take into account future interests, in respect of both substantive benefits and the ways in which the parties will relate to each other.[54] Mediators can act as catalysts for creative problem-solving,[55] for example by brainstorming with the parties or referring to settlement options derived from their experience.

Where the parties persist in distributive bargaining, mediators have a particular responsibility in relation to predictable situations, such as 'crossing the last gap'.[56] The mediator might pre-empt this problem by securing the parties' commitment in advance to a method of crossing the gap, or he or she may shift the focus to procedural ways of dealing with it, such as referring the matter to an arbitrator or tossing a coin. The mediator may assist the parties in linking issues together, making conditional offers, or trading-off some losses for other gains. Some of the mediator's negotiation function is performed by educating the parties about the realities of negotiation. Thus he or she may apprise them in advance that negotiators often resist making the final concession for fear of losing face, or he or she may coach them during the separate meetings in how to make and respond to offers.

This mediator function implies a thorough understanding of the theories and practices of distributional and integrative negotiation. Mediators should preferably be sound negotiators themselves. They must at least be able to impart sound negotiation techniques to the parties. Some of the skills relating to these interventions are referred to in Chapter 6.

Educating the parties

Mediation is not primarily a didactic system, but mediators have both explicit and implicit educative functions. Most mediators explicitly educate the parties about the

---

51 On approaches to negotiation, see Chapter 2.
52 See M Anstey *Practical Peacemaking – a mediator's handbook*, Juta & Co, Kenwyn, South Africa, 1993, at p 79.
53 Law Society of England & Wales *Civil/Commercial Mediation Training Standards*.
54 John Haynes observes that the mediator's focus on the future has a 'serendipitous benefit' in that clients rarely complain about the future. It has the additional benefit of making the parties less likely to expect the mediator to act as a judge, as judges evaluate past conduct: J Haynes *The fundamentals of family mediation*, State University of New York Press, Albany, 1994, at p 12.
55 S Henderson *The Dispute Resolution Manual*, DataLegal Publications, Spring Hill, QLD, 1993, at p 100.
56 On possible techniques for crossing the last gap, see Chapter 6.

mediation process generally and about its strengths and limitations. All mediators educate the parties about the procedure which will be followed at the mediation meeting, and instruct them specifically on unusual features such as the separate meetings, and their objectives, logistics and duration.[57] Some mediators also educate the parties about aspects of conflict and its settlement. They provide 'mini-lectures' on the causes of conflict, possible interventions for different causes, the ordinary inclination of people in conflict not to make decisions, and the normality of doubt and indecision surrounding the final decisions.

Negotiation is sometimes talked about as a system in which the parties inform and educate each other about their needs and interests; as the manager of a negotiation process, the mediator is directly involved in this education dynamic. Mediators may achieve this in a variety of ways: through mini-lectures and explanations during the preparatory stages, through modelling sound negotiation behaviour in joint sessions, and through coaching and rehearsing in separate meetings. Thus in multi-party negotiations the mediator might advise each team in advance on the importance of internal decision-making procedures. He or she would then explain to them jointly how negotiation dynamics operate not only between the negotiation parties, but within negotiating teams, between the teams and constituents, and even within the ranks of constituents.[58] In separate meetings, the mediator might then practise with them ways of resisting threats or responding to apologies from the other team.

Mediation also has an implicit educative function for the participants.[59] In resorting to mediation rather than an umpireal model of dispute resolution, they are developing experience in direct decision-making and problem-solving which can be applied subsequently in other contexts. This more subtle educative dimension of the mediator's functions is often overlooked.

Empowering the parties

Some commentators suggest that one of the most important functions of the mediation process is its empowerment of the participants.[60] Here empowerment refers to all those ways in which the strengths of the mediation process increase the parties' ability to perform well and to feel good about their performance. It includes interventions which assist the parties to understand their situations, to communicate

---

57 Many mediator standards impose obligations that include advising on the elements of the process and the functions of the mediator, the importance of having necessary information available, the parties' right to legal representation or legal advice, the right to withdraw from the process and the mediator's right to terminate, the advisability of an executed agreement containing the terms of settlement and the probable costs to the parties of the mediation. On mediator standards, see Chapter 11.

58 See M Anstey *Practical Peacemaking – a mediator's handbook*, Juta & Co, Kenwyn, South Africa, 1993, at p 72; and T Colosi and A Berkeley *Collective bargaining: how it works and why*, American Arbitration Association, 1986, at pp 57–71, and their references to horizontal, internal, vertical and shadow bargaining.

59 M Power 'Educating mediators metacognitively' (1992) 3 *ADRJ* 214 at 214–15.

60 G Tillet *Resolving conflict – a practical approach*, Sydney University Press, Sydney, 1991, at p 56. See also W Faulkes 'Pursuing the best ends by the best means' (1985) 59 *ALJ* 457; and J Mowatt 'Some thoughts on mediation' (1998) 105 *South African Law Journal* 727.

effectively, to negotiate assertively, to make decisions confidently, and to feel satisfied with the mediation process and its outcome. It may also require a mediator to take a disruptive third party out of the mediation, where that third party undermines the empowerment process.[61] These are benefits which both parties can derive through a wide range of neutral and objective interventions from mediators. *Facilitative* and *therapeutic mediation* are likely to be the most empowering of the four paradigm models, with their focus on process and party self-determination. *Settlement* and *evaluative mediation* could have a minimal empowerment aspect, particularly where the parties' advisers dominate the process and the main focus is on the outcome. However, the fact that mediators cannot make binding decisions entails that the empowerment aspect will exist to some extent in all mediations.[62]

Empowerment is also relevant where there is a significant imbalance of power between the parties. This is a major issue in mediation theory and practice, requiring more extensive treatment than is possible here.[63] The issue is potentially relevant in many situations, for example where single citizens are mediating with the state, small unions with powerful managements, or abused spouses with their former partners. Here the question arises as to whether mediators should take steps to redress this imbalance of power, by increasing the power of the weaker party or reducing that of the stronger. Empowerment in these situations would go beyond even-handed assistance to both parties, and would mainly involve mediators in promoting and helping the causes of the weaker parties. In unassisted negotiations a power imbalance could have a direct impact on both the process of negotiation and its outcome, with the stronger party prevailing over the weaker in all respects. If this inequity and injustice are to be avoided when mediators assist in negotiations, it would suggest that their function should involve some empowerment of the weaker party so that the mediation decisions do not crudely reflect power disparities. On the other hand, mediators are not primarily protectors of the disadvantaged: this is the role of professional advisers, government agencies, support groups, and in some situations the courts through the due process of law and the enforcement of rights. There is therefore a grey zone in which mediators have some role in redressing power imbalances, without acting as the advocates or saviours of the weak. If they treat unequal parties evenly they will preside over unequal bargaining; if they intervene too strongly they will undermine their impartiality.

There are a number of considerations for mediators in trying to achieve this balance. They need to realise that power is a very complex issue with many dimensions. There are multiple sources of power[64] and the parties' perceptions of their own and the other

---

61 For an example of a domineering expert witness, see CEDR *Bulletin*, November 2000.
62 H Brown and A Marriott *ADR Principles and Practice* (2nd edn), Sweet & Maxwell, London, 1999, at p 130.
63 H Astor and C Chinkin *Dispute Resolution in Australia*, Butterworths, Sydney, 1993, at pp 105–9; C Moore *The Mediation Process: practical strategies for resolving conflict* (2nd edn), Jossey-Bass, San Francisco, 1996, at pp 333–7; J Folberg and A Taylor *Mediation: a comprehensive guide to resolving conflict without litigation*, Jossey-Bass, San Francisco, 1984, at pp 184–6; A Davis and R Salem 'Dealing with power imbalances in the mediation of inter-personal disputes' (1984) 6 *MQ* 17.
64 R Fisher 'Negotiating power – getting and using influence' 27(2) *American Behavioural Scientist*, November/December 1983, at pp 149–66, identifies the following categories of negotiating power: the power of skill and knowledge, of a good relationship, of a good alternative to negotiating, of an elegant solution, of legitimacy and commitment. B Mayer

side's power are as important as the actual power realities. Mediators can redress imbalances by creating doubts about the powers of the stronger parties, and assisting the weaker parties to use power of which they were unaware. Where there are potential power problems mediators should be assiduous in those parts of the mediation process which contribute towards an equalisation of power. These could include:

- intake and screening;
- exchange of information;
- equality of speaking time;
- conducting dialogue through the mediator rather than directly;
- using option of cooling off period;
- enforcement of the mediation guidelines on matters such as no interruptions or intimidation; and
- use of separate meetings.

Ultimately mediators can terminate or threaten to terminate a process where there is such a gross discrepancy of power that all the assumptions of mediation are being undermined. These interventions can be justified (with varying degrees of conviction) as process interventions.

In dealing with party empowerment, mediators themselves have many potential sources of power. In coming to mediation the parties have relinquished part of the control over their decision-making to the mediators, which is a source of both formal authority and real power for them. Other sources of mediator power are their status and prestige, their expertise as dispute resolvers, their real or perceived ability to inflict harm or withhold benefits and, in most cases, their personal attributes. As Wade observes: 'Virtually every step taken by a mediator involves the exercise of power.' [65]

At the end of the day mediators do have a role in empowering weaker parties, but they cannot be expected to redress all power imbalances. No dispute resolution process, including litigation, can neutralise power imbalances completely. The real issue for mediators is where to draw the line between a legitimate empowering function, on one hand, and illegitimate manipulation or partisanship, on the other. Wherever this line is drawn, one of the implications of the mediator's empowering function, however limited it might be, is that mediation cannot be seen as a value-free, neutral process.[66]

Imposing pressure to settle

Mediators are in a unique position to impose pressure on the parties with the object of pushing them into a settlement.[67] However, whether or not this is a legitimate mediator function is controversial. Some argue that a mediator's pushing and pressing for settlement undermines many of the assumptions and values of mediation, such as participation and self-determination for the parties, the process/content distinction, and

---

'Dynamics of power in mediation and negotiation' (1987) 16 *MQ* 75 identifies ten sources of power: formal authority, expertise, association, resources, procedure, sanctions, nuisance, habits, morality and personality. See also J Wade 'Forms of power in family mediation and negotiation' (1994) 6 *Australian Journal of Family Law* 40.

65 J Wade, ibid, at 54.

66 H Astor and C Chinkin *Dispute Resolution in Australia*, Butterworths, Sydney, 1993, at p 102.

67 D Shapiro, R Drieghe and J Brett 'Mediator Behaviour and the outcome of Mediation' (1985) 41(2) *Journal of Social Issues* 101 at 112.

the neutrality of the mediator. Others point to the reality that both in traditional societies and in modern industrial societies, mediators do, as a matter of fact, use pressure tactics, ranging from threats of divine retribution to predictions of disastrous court outcomes.[68] Kressel and Pruitt assert, in the light of survey studies, that in very intense conflicts the ability to produce settlements is associated with highly aggressive mediator behaviour, including threats to quit or suggesting that the dispute be decided by arbitrators.[69]

This topic is best managed by referring to the various ways in which mediators can exert pressure and the compatibility of each with different models of mediation, different disputants and different stages of the process. In all models of mediation it would be regarded as an appropriate function for the mediator to invite the parties to reflect on the consequences of their not settling the dispute themselves. In *settlement mediation* it would be regarded as appropriate to encourage them to move to a point of compromise. In *evaluative mediation* it would be regarded as appropriate for the mediator to provide his or her own view as to how the parties should settle. In separate meetings it would be regarded as appropriate for the mediator to reduce parties' unrealistic expectations and to emphasise the non-substantive benefits of settling. In no model or stage of mediation would it be appropriate for the mediator to threaten or intimidate one party into settling, or to use false deadlines to pressure them both. However, these variations do not involve clear boundaries and guidelines: the mere presence of a mediator may, in the subjective perceptions of some disputants, constitute a source of pressure to settle, while others may feel no threat from aggressive mediator behaviour.

A major concern about any pressure is that it may be induced by the mediator's own interests in a settlement. A related concern is that it will be applied more consistently to the weaker party, who is less likely to resist it. In the light of these concerns many mediator standards expressly prohibit such pressure.[70] There are also concerns that mediator pressure may affect the disputants' long-term relationships, that it may affect the future acceptability of that mediator, and that it may jeopardise the reputation of mediation as a whole. The reality is that mediators do impose settlement pressure, in many senses of this term, but how they should and should not do it, and the long-term effects of improper pressure, require further investigation and analysis.

Promoting reality

Mediators are often referred to as 'agents of reality' in so far as one of their functions is to encourage the parties to face the realities of their situations. The purpose of reality-testing is to make the relevant party reflect more systematically and practically on a position, behaviour or attitude, and to think beyond the present situation to future consequences. Reality-testing can apply to subjective factors which are particular to

---

68   K Kressel and D Pruitt 'A research perspective on the mediation of social conflict' in K Kressel and D Pruitt (eds) *Mediation Research: the process and effectiveness of third party intervention*, Jossey-Bass, San Francisco, 1989 at pp 394 and 418–20. See also F Myers and F Wasoff, 2000, whose survey of family mediators in Scotland identified the range of techniques used by mediators, including identifying and prioritising issues, which enabled them to steer parties towards preferred outcomes.

69   K Kressel 'Clinical implications of existing research on divorce mediation' (1987) 1 *American Journal of Family Therapy* 69. J Stulberg *Taking Charge/Managing Conflict*, Lexington Books, Lexington, Massachusetts, 1987, at p 36, notes that mediators are not in a popularity contest, and that parties must live with the agreement, not with the mediator.

70   On mediator standards, see Chapter 11.

the dispute, and to objective factors which are part of the wider picture. Thus it could relate to:

- the parties' substantive, procedural and emotional interests;
- resources such as time and funds;
- all aspects of a proposed settlement, including its degree of specificity, its durability and its fairness to all parties; and
- the possibilities which exist should the matter not settle.

In these matters the mediator can assist the parties to better understand and appreciate their interests, limitations and feasible options. Mediation is about what is 'do-able'[71] and if a party is holding out for something which is objectively unattainable then the mediator's function is to bring about more realistic expectations.

There are many ways in which mediators can serve as agents of reality: by providing information (for example about the costs of litigation), by advising (for example on the unlikelihood of an agreement being legally valid), and by asking reflective, hypothetical or critical questions:

- 'have you considered . . . ?'
- 'what if . . . ?'
- 'how do you think the other side would react to that suggestion?'
- 'how do you think a court would rule on that point?'
- 'what are the risks if you proceed to trial?'
- 'if they accept "x", would you accept "y"?'

It is again difficult to draw the line between legitimate and illegitimate reality-testing. The separate meetings allow the mediator more latitude in confronting the parties and disenchanting them with their unrealistic views. In order to avoid the perception of partiality, the mediator should give the assurance that the other party will be taken through a similar exercise. Some reality-testing is consistent with the process/content distinction in that the mediator asks generalised questions without implying any substantive knowledge of the topic. In other forms of reality-testing the mediator may use substantive knowledge, for example in querying whether a particular head of damage is viable in a personal injury claim. A common form of reality testing in civil/commercial cases requires the best and worst alternatives to be discounted by reference to the percentage chance of success, and by deducting irrecoverable costs.[72] This analysis involves substantive knowledge of litigation as well.[73] In the latter cases reality-testing comes close to advising or evaluating, and it may be experienced as a pressure tactic by a party.

Advising and evaluating

The educative role of mediators, referred to above, comes close to what is commonly understood as advising. However, most mediators, in deference to the process/content

---

71 J Stulberg *Taking Charge/Managing Conflict*, Lexington Books, Lexington, Massachusetts, 1987, at p 34.
72 R Fisher and W Ury *Getting to yes: negotiating agreement without giving in* (rev edn) Hutchinson Books, Boston, 1992.
73 For an example, see H Brown and A Marriott *ADR Principles and Practice* (2nd edn), Sweet & Maxwell, London, 1999, at p 216.

distinction, will not admit to offering legal or other professional advice to the parties, even when it is requested by them.[74] A restriction along these lines is found in some Agreements to Mediate and in mediator standards, and mediators will routinely recommend to parties that they bring their advisers to the mediation or request adjournments to take advice. Family mediators distinguish between 'legal advice' and 'legal information', which includes:

- the general legal principles which apply to a case;
- an indication of the type of solutions courts have reached in the past on particular issues and an indication if proposals are unlikely to be approved by a court; and
- assisting the parties to receive legal advice by formulating the issues requiring consideration by the parties' legal advisers.

Thus whereas a family mediator would be prepared to inform parties in a matrimonial dispute on the different methods of evaluating pension benefits, they would refrain from recommending one method over others. The same approach could be adopted by experts in other substantive areas, such as accountant mediators or engineer mediators, who might provide, on the basis of their expertise, information on the 'normal range' or 'standard quality', without expressly recommending an appropriate outcome. However, the distinction between information and advice will not always be easy to sustain and disputing parties might be forgiven for mistaking the former for the latter. As with many other mediation features, the legitimacy of a mediator's intervention on matters of information and advice will depend more on the way he or she intervenes, and the context of the intervention, than on abstract definitions. Thus general advice to the parties on constructive ways of negotiating would tend to be regarded as appropriate, while specific advice on the capital gains tax implications of a proposed settlement would be regarded as inappropriate.

The difference between a mediator advising and a mediator evaluating is a question of degree. Here evaluation refers to the mediator expressing his or her considered view on the merits of an issue in dispute, that is, assuming an umpireal role. In some situations there may be an expectation that the mediator will play some kind of evaluative function, for example where the parties select *evaluative mediation* on the assumption that the mediator will provide a considered view. The view may be based on the mediator's substantive knowledge, the expertise of another party in the mediation, or on simple common sense. The advantage of the mediator evaluating some aspects of the dispute is that it may provide a reliable foundation on which the parties can build a comprehensive settlement. Thus an experienced lawyer's evaluation is likely to be based on an expert assessment of what might happen if the dispute went to court, and this assessment may cause the parties to reassess their positions and reach a settlement. The mediator's considered opinion is an extreme form of reality-testing.

There are several arguments against mediators performing any evaluative function.[75] Some objections are ideologically based, for example that the mediator's role ought

---

74 J Wade 'Forever bargaining in the shadow of the law – who sells solid shadows? Who advises what, where, when?' (1998) 12 *Australian Journal of Family Law* 256.

75 H Brown and A Marriott *ADR Principles and Practice* (2nd edn), Sweet & Maxwell, London, 1999, at p 130.

to be restricted to process facilitation and the parties should be allowed to make their own decisions, for better or worse. Where mediators provide an evaluation, it will tend to be rights-based and will undermine the participatory, interest-based, norm-creating and consensual features of mediation. Even though the evaluation cannot be binding, it may have the same effect in practice. Other objections are pragmatic. An evaluation by the mediator might be based on insufficient information, it might result in a loss of neutrality and trust, it might make the dissatisfied party more intransigent, it might be in breach of a code of ethics, and it might result in a liability action against the mediator. There can also be marketing repercussions if some mediators resort to evaluation in a process which does not generally offer this service.

One way out of the evaluation predicament is to adapt the mediation process to accommodate another third party who can provide a neutral evaluation.[76] The evaluation could be non-binding, in which case it would be a factor in the continuing mediation, or it could be binding on the issues in question. This provides a clearer division of functions and precludes many of the problems listed above. However, it has obvious disadvantages in term of time and expense.

Terminating the mediation

Where the mediation has produced a settlement, mediators formally terminate the process. There are also situations in which the mediation is terminated before it has run its course. This is usually a discretionary function for mediators, but in some circumstances they may have an obligation to terminate.[77] The function of terminating before there is full agreement may be exercised in the following situations, where:

(a) one or both parties are in persistent breach of the mediation guidelines or refuse to co-operate in the process;

(b) it is apparent that one or both parties are no longer committed to mediation and are only using it for ulterior purposes;

(c) a hidden agenda surfaces which has negative ramifications for any agreement, for example where one party discloses that they will leave the country in the near future;

(d) one or both parties are incapable of negotiating or communicating effectively or are otherwise inhibited from making decisions;

(e) there is extreme antagonism towards, and a loss of trust in, the mediator;

(f) there is evidence of danger to life or property or that a child is suffering or is likely to suffer harm[78] or the agreement which the parties want to conclude is illegal in some respects;

---

76 On neutral evaluation, see Chapter 3.

77 In terms of applicable mediation standards or an Agreement to Mediate.

78 If a mediator considers that a child is suffering or is likely to suffer harm, the mediator will need to consider this issue with the parties in order to determine what steps should be taken to remedy the situation. Where it is necessary to protect a child in those circumstances, the mediator should contact an outside agency or take other appropriate steps. In such circumstances, it is important for the mediator to get the facts correct if those facts

    (g)   the threat of physical violence or some other form of power imbalance precludes free consent to a settlement arrangement;

    (h)   the relationship between the parties is so destructive that no meaningful negotiations can take place; and

    (i)   it is clearly apparent that agreement is impossible on any of the issues in dispute.

There are different justifications for the mediator's termination function. Policy considerations require that mediation should not serve to conceal illegality, nor to violate the rights of one of the parties against their wishes. Requirements of efficiency dictate that mediation should not be pursued to the point where it is an exercise in futility. Termination also entails recognition of the fact that mediation must justify its existence: if it is no longer appropriate, other methods of dispute resolution should be attempted. In practice, however, mediators do not often exercise the early termination function.[79] Where there are grounds to terminate, the mediator should canvass the possibility with each party in separate meetings. The method of termination should ensure that there is no inadvertent breach of the confidentiality of the separate meetings, although it may be difficult to prevent an 'innocent' party from inferring the real reason for termination. Nor should the method of termination further jeopardise the physical or psychological well-being of a vulnerable party. In cases of co-mediation, the decision to discontinue the process should be taken by both mediators after they have conferred privately on the matter. Where mediators terminate in the face of deadlock, they should discuss with the parties the feasibility of other dispute resolution options, such as arbitration or case appraisal.

The Functions of the Parties

One of the claims of mediation is that it allows the parties themselves to be present and participate directly and fully in the resolution of their dispute.[80] The term 'parties' usually denotes those most directly affected by the dispute and its settlement, in litigation terms the claimant and defendant. In some situations the participants in the mediation will be representatives or spokespersons of corporate entities or interest groups. The functions of the parties will vary according to the voluntariness of the process, the motivation of the parties, the model of mediation, the style of the mediator, and the existence or otherwise of legal requirements.

---

    are to be provided to third parties. If the parties act in a manner likely to be detrimental to the welfare of the child, the mediator should withdraw from the mediation: see The Law Society of England & Wales *Code of Conduct in Family Mediation*; the UK College of Family Mediators *Code of Practice*; and Legal Aid Board *Family Mediation Quality Assurance Standard*.

79 At the 1992 Convention of the Society of Professionals in Dispute Resolution in Pittsburgh, Pennsylvania, USA, there was a panel discussion in which six experienced mediators were asked, in the context of increasingly problematic hypotheticals, when they would terminate a mediation, and none found that any of the situations warranted termination.

80 See Chapter 2.

Preparation

Parties should prepare for a mediation in the same way in which they would prepare for a negotiation. This will involve consideration of matters of process, substance and organisation: time, venue, gathering of information, legal research, reading and preparation of documents, identifying and prioritising of interests, instructing of professional advisers, determination of bottom lines and existence of authority to settle, and assessment of alternatives to negotiated agreements. Parties should also prepare on strategic issues, such as appropriate styles of negotiation, division of roles in team negotiations, patterns of disclosure and concession-making, ways of dealing with internal conflicts during the process, and what tactics to adopt and how to respond to the other side's tactics. Good negotiation preparation also requires the parties to identify the other side's interests, consider the other's negotiation styles and consider options for collaborative problem-solving.[81]

Consenting to the Agreement to Mediate

Most private mediators, and some mediation organisations, have standard-form Agreements to Mediate.[82] The parties are usually required to sign the agreement before mediators commence their preparatory activities. Where there is also a costs agreement it may require advance payment to the mediator. Consenting to the agreement implies a good faith commitment to the mediation process, acceptance of the mediator's role and functions, and ordinarily also an intention to settle the dispute through mediation. However, the formality of consent will not always involve a full appreciation of the nature of mediation, in particular as far as the expected functions and behaviour of the parties are concerned.

Disclosure of information

Most Agreements to Mediate oblige the parties to make full disclosure of relevant information and documentation to each other. It is usual for parties to make available all materials which would be available through the relevant discovery or disclosure rules were the matter to proceed to litigation. This would include experts' reports, valuations, and taxation and financial statements. The mediator might request copies of this information, as well as the statement of case, reply and other court documents. In some contexts the mediator will request a summary of the dispute, or a history of the marriage, as the case may be. While the Agreement to Mediate might require these disclosures, the mediator has no authority to compel disclosure and has no formal control over the exchange of information. This can be a weakness where there is an information requirement and one party is reluctant to disclose.

---

81 R Fisher and D Ertel *Getting ready to negotiate: the Getting to Yes Workbook*, Penguin Books, New York, 1995, for a guide on preparing for negotiation using the interest-based approach.

82 See the section on Agreements to Mediate in Chapter 12. Also see the section on Mediation Organisations in Chapter 7.

Direct involvement

There is ordinarily an expectation that the parties will themselves be present at and participate in the mediation meeting.[83] In some cases this will not be possible, for reasons of ill-health or unanticipated absence. In other cases there may be an attempt to avoid the involvement of a party for tactical reasons, for example where it would expose a plaintiff to the observation, questioning and appraisal of the insurer. In these cases representatives participate on behalf of the parties. However, the assumptions of mediation are that, however active or inactive they might be, the parties should be personally present at and participate in the mediation meeting.

Good faith participation

Parties in a mediation are expected to participate in good faith. This entails making an honest attempt at resolving the dispute and abiding by the mediation guidelines. There is also a less well-defined duty to comply with the underlying assumptions of mediation, by attempting to communicate constructively and negotiate in a collaborative, problem-solving way.

Accordingly, parties should have authority to negotiate and settle the dispute at the mediation. Being prepared to give and take is a particularly helpful attitude in mediation.[84] To aid settlement, it is also helpful that each party is courteous to the other parties and to the mediator, or at least to avoid antagonistic behaviour. In the opening presentation, however, the parties are usually encouraged, either by their lawyer or the mediator, to 'get things off their chest'. Venting should be distinguished from a confrontational or aggressive stance, which could be harmful to progress in the mediation. Where a party is a company or other type of organisation, it is helpful that the representative does not attempt to defend past actions.[85] Chornenki provides the following check-list for party participation in mediation:[86]

- Focus on the problem.
- Commit to solving the problem.
- Be respectful in the sense of not engaging in behaviour which detracts from the energy or purpose of the meeting.
- Recognise other points of view.
- Be flexible enough to be responsive to the situation.
- Engage in honest and authentic communication.

The good faith requirement is becoming increasingly common in mediation clauses and Agreements to Mediate. The requirements for good faith participation in

---

83 See, for example, Centre for Dispute Resolution *Model Mediation Procedure Guidance Notes*.

84 The Law Society of New South Wales has set out these requirements in a *Charter for mediation practice – A guideline to the rights and responsibilities of participants*, 1997.

85 See, for example, the guidance provided the Centre for Dispute Resolution in its *Model Mediation Procedure Guidance Notes*; and the Center for Public Resources *Commentary on its Mediation Rules*.

86 R Chornenki 'Mediating commercial disputes: exchanging "power over" with "power with"' in J Macfarlane (ed) *Rethinking disputes: the mediation alternative*, Cavendish Publishing, London, 1997, at pp 165–8 .

mediation are difficult to determine and will have to be defined over time, in part by the courts. In many cases there will be no sanctions where a party does not participate in good faith. In others there could be sanctions imposed, for example, in the form of costs penalties.[87]

The Functions of Legal Representatives

Preventive action

Other than being consulted after a dispute has arisen, lawyers are becoming increasingly involved in conflict management. For example, lawyers are advising on the use of alternative dispute resolution clauses in contracts and assisting to set up dispute resolution procedures. It is more important now than ever for lawyers to know the alternative forms of dispute resolution in order to advise their clients effectively on appropriate options.[88] At the present time, mediation is often chosen on the advice of lawyers, either before or after legal proceedings have been instituted. In other situations parties consult lawyers for assistance in their self-selected mediation. In these cases lawyers will have some degree of involvement in the mediation process. While conventional litigation entails a relatively predictable role for lawyers, there are many variables in relation to legal representation in mediation. In overall terms, the role of the legal representatives is to support all aspects of the mediation process.[89] However, actual practice on this matter depends on the inclinations of lawyers, the wishes of the parties, the nature of the dispute and the extent to which there are complex legal or factual issues involved.[90]

Pre-mediation assistance

In some circumstances lawyers have to advise clients on whether and how to initiate or accept proposals for mediation. This involves an assessment of the appropriateness of mediation for the dispute and for the clients, a subject dealt with elsewhere.[91]

---

87 See Chapters 9 and 12.

88 B Sordo 'The lawyer's role in mediation' (1996) 7 *ADRJ* 20 at 27. See also D Spencer 'Liability of lawyers to advise on alternative dispute resolution options' (1998) 9 *ADRJ* 292.

89 *Mediation – A guide for Victorian solicitors*, prepared by the ADR Committee of the Litigation Lawyers Section of the Law Institute of Victoria, 1995, at p 33; and G Robertson 'The lawyer's role in commercial ADR' (1987) 61 *LIJ* 1148. See further J Wade 'Forever bargaining in the shadow of the law – who sells solid shadows? Who advises what, where, when?' (1998) 12 *Australian Journal of Family Law* 256; and B Sordo, ibid, at 20. For the role of lawyers from the mediator's perspective, see R Charlton and M Dewdney *The Mediator's Handbook – skills and strategies for practitioners*, The Law Book Company, Sydney, 1995, at pp 206–15, and for the role of lawyers as advisers to their clients at mediation, and how and where they could assist, see pp 215–18.

90 A Ardagh and G Cumes 'Lawyers and mediation: beyond the adversarial system?' (1998) 9 *ADRJ* 72.

91 See the section on When is mediation appropriate, in Chapter 3.

Lawyers should be mindful of the trap of expecting a mediation to cure a bad case on the merits.[92] If a case is appropriate for mediation, the lawyer may need to persuade the other parties and their lawyers to participate in mediation. The client will have questions about the process, which they will need to tackle. A common question is whether suggesting mediation will be perceived as a sign of weakness. Given the encouragement given by the Civil Procedure Rules to attempt ADR, clients should be less concerned about there being such a perception. Traditionally, the concern was tackled by either using a mediation organisation to liaise with the other parties about the process of mediation, or by having one party's principal contact the other party's principal to discuss the option direct. Educating the client about the process is an important phase in the preparation for a mediation. Showing the client a video of a mock mediation or conducting a mock mediation for the client can be particularly helpful as clients may have misconceptions about what the process involves. It is important to bear in mind that a client's first experience with mediation should be a good experience otherwise the client is unlikely to want to use the process again. The lawyer will also need to explain the fundamental characteristics of mediation, for instance, its without prejudice nature,[93] whilst warning that each party will know more about each other's interests, aims and motivations as a result of the mediation. Parties should be encouraged in the early stages of a mediation to be flexible in terms of their expectations of the mediation and settlement.

Once all the parties have agreed to attempt mediation, the lawyer's initial role will be to agree on the appointment of a mediator and the costs, together with the range of administrative issues, such as agreeing a date and venue for the mediation. The lawyer will then consider the terms of the mediation agreement, and ensure that those terms are appropriate. The lawyer will then turn his or her mind to preparation for the mediation. A lawyer needs to ensure that he or she has a good grasp of the facts and has identified the issues. Experts may be necessary to fully explain and clarify issues, which should be prioritised. Information will need to be collated and summaries prepared. Preparation will also involve considering each other party in the dispute and, in particular, their personalities and interests. Consideration of each other party's case may lead to debate on the strengths and weaknesses of a party's own case. Identifying weaknesses is particularly important as it provides a party with more realistic expectations about the outcome of a mediation. The worst case scenario or what is likely to happen if a settlement is not reached at the mediation allows a party to consider how to enlist a mediator's help to work around the problem. It is also important to prepare a negotiation plan for the mediation. This will involve identifying the client's needs and considering all the options which might meet those needs. It also involves evaluating the benefits and risks, together with the costs, of reaching a settlement and of failing to reach a settlement at the mediation. A consideration of the initial proposals to be made in the mediation is useful. For instance, it is a powerful gesture to make an apology, even without an admission of liability, as early as possible in a mediation. A negotiation plan has the benefit of managing each party's expectations. The plan should be fluid enough, however, to react to information which comes out in the mediation and proposals made by the parties at the

---

92 D Golann *Seminar Notes: Lawyer's Role in Mediation*, CEDR, May 2000.
93 See Chapter 12.

mediation. On occasions, parties have used the mediation process to persuade another party why they should not be making a contribution to any settlement.[94]

Care should be taken when preparing the opening statement for the mediation. It should not resemble opening submissions to a judge. The aim of the opening statement is not to persuade the mediator of the merits of a party's case, but to inform the other parties of the relevant facts and positions. It provides an opportunity to persuade other parties of a particular point of view. Sir Laurence Street, an international mediator, explains the value of the opening statement by using the analogy of holding a coin up to the parties: 'one side sees tails and the other heads, but the aim is to turn the coin so that each party sees the other side of the coin'. The opening statement need not be solely an oral presentation, but photographs, charts and other visual aids can be used. It is also important to consider who should take the lead in the opening statement, the lawyer or the client, and if the client, who from the client. Frequently, the lawyer will outline the position from a legal point of view, and the client will add to the opening statement, by way of providing the other parties with a better understanding of his or her commercial or personal concerns. What role the client will play will depend upon his or her articulateness, knowledge of the matters in issue and emotional state.

Poor organisation for mediation is a major factor inhibiting the potential for successful resolution. The lawyer's traditional role of providing the client with advice, assimilation of facts and negotiation assistance continue to be the lawyer's main responsibilities throughout a mediation.[95]

In the context of family mediation, it is usual for the parties to meet with the mediator unrepresented, but to receive initial advice on the process, and to take independent legal advice outside the mediation on issues arising in the mediation, from a lawyer. A lawyer may also assist the parties in family mediation to provide financial disclosure.[96] In community mediation also, lawyers frequently are not present in mediation.

---

94 For example, if party (A) is involved in a mediation for a formal reason, for instance it seeks to rely on an indemnity given to it by another party (B), if there is no dispute about the scope of that indemnity and party (A) does not anticipate having to make a contribution to the claimant in the dispute, party (A) may wish to clarify its position at the start of the mediation so that the mediation does not proceed on a false premise, for instance that party (A) will 'bridge any gap' in the mediation between party (B) and the claimant. Another example is where legally-aided parties are in dispute over property, if the settlement pie is limited to the value of that property, the position should be clarified at the start of the mediation. See also the later discussion in this Part on negotiation in mediation.

95 H Saunders 'We need a larger theory of negotiation: the importance of pre-negotiating phases' (1985) *Negotiation Journal* 249 at 254. See also A Blair 'Mediation: preparing and presenting' (2000) 22 *Corporate Counsel* 60.

96 On the role of lawyers in family mediation, see P McCarthy et al *Lawyers in family mediation*, Report to the Law Society, 1996; P McCarthy and J Walker *The role of lawyers in family mediation*, Family Studies Report No 2, September 1996; P McCarthy and J Walker 'Mediation and divorce law reform: the lawyers' view' (1995) 25 *Family Law* at 361–8; P McCarthy and J Walker 'Involvement of lawyers in the mediation process' (1996) 26 *Family Law* at 154–8; and P McCarthy *Mediation in divorce: are lawyers needed?* Annual Research Conference, The Law Society, London, 1996.

Assistance at the mediation meeting

There is no general obligation on lawyers to be present at the mediation meeting and they can instead be consulted by clients during adjournments or after the meeting has terminated. In most commercial mediations there is an expectation that lawyers will be present at both the preliminary meeting and for the duration of the mediation meeting. Where a legal opinion has been provided by counsel, it is preferable that the relevant lawyer also be present, particularly where the opinion has created an expectation in the client as to his or her entitlement to damages; if the lawyer is not present to sanction a reduction in the quantum of damages it may be difficult to settle the matter. Most mediators welcome and encourage the participation of lawyers.[97] If one party has a lawyer in attendance the other will normally follow suit, but in each case the presence or absence of a lawyer will be dependent on the client's instructions.

Lawyers who attend mediation meetings have a number of functions. They act throughout as advisers and consultants. They may have a direct role in the negotiation stages of the mediation, to the extent that they are surrogate negotiators. An important function for lawyers is to provide legal advice, for example on the meaning of a contractual provision, on quantum issues, or on the likely outcome if a matter were litigated. They may also give strategic advice on process and tactics. Their function is not to be formal, technical or legalistic. They are not expected to be rhetorical, to cross-examine or to display other facets of advocacy.[98] In some mediations the lawyers resort to negotiating with their own clients in a 'mediational' capacity, particularly in the separate meetings. Above all, lawyers are required to allow their clients to participate directly in the proceedings, this involvement being one of the important benefits which parties derive from the mediation process.[99]

How lawyers participate depends on the stage reached in a mediation. Where a lawyer makes the opening presentation, he or she needs to bear in mind that the presentation is not aimed at the mediator, but at the other parties and their lawyers, in order to clarify for them the issues and the party's position. The presentation affords an opportunity not only to state the party's case, but also for the parties to vent emotion. It provides the opportunity to express sympathy or regret and to make an apology, even without an admission of liability. The presentation is intended as an opportunity for exchange of information. If a party makes valid points in the presentation, it is useful to acknowledge them, which will also narrow issues in dispute. The importance of proper preparation for the presentation should not be underestimated. A lawyer who is put on the back foot by a better presentation by an opponent may create unnecessary anxiety for both him or herself and the client.

In relation to private sessions, the lawyer should have already considered with the client, ahead of a mediation, the prospects of success, the strengths and weaknesses

---

97 For example, Singapore survey studies have shown that lawyers play an important role both in preparing their clients for mediation and in taking part in the process with their clients: L Boulle and T Hwee Hwee *Mediation: principles, process, practice*, Butterworths, Singapore, 2000, at Chapter 11 and Annex A.

98 H Phillips 'Advocacy in Mediation' (1994) 64 *ALJ* 384.

99 For example, L Boulle 'Testing the Mettle: Queensland's First Settlement Week' (1992) 3 *ADRJ* 1.

of the case and the broader negotiating strategy. It is important that the lawyer has explained to the client, as discussed above, that the strategy is tentative and flexible. The client should also have been coached on principled or interest-based negotiation. In the private sessions, the mediator may rely heavily on the lawyer to answer questions about legal claims and to assist the mediator to brainstorm options. In between private sessions, the lawyer will need to work with the client to consider whether their strategy should change in light of the information gleaned in private sessions, from verbal and non-verbal signals from the mediator. These breaks provide an opportunity for the lawyer to consider with the client what trade-offs or concessions should be made. Frequently, the mediator will also rely on the lawyer to help manage the client's expectations or to encourage the client to take a more realistic or pragmatic or commercial view about their prospects. As part of the process of reality testing, the mediator will rely on the solicitor to accurately evaluate the client's best and worse alternatives to reaching a resolution in the mediation. Throughout this stage of the process, the mediator will focus on moving the client and the lawyer, if necessary, away from their initial fixed positions. Flexibility is the key, as revision of expectations and previous assessments of strengths and weaknesses of the case may be required. The mediator will encourage the client to be involved in this stage of the process, as it is particularly important that the client feels ownership of any solution, which is ultimately proposed. It is at this stage of the process that a lawyer, who has adopted an adversarial approach to the mediation, may allow a mediation to fail, by either mis-stating or failing to disclose the client's bottom line to the mediator. A lawyer may fail to take account of the value of non-monetary solutions, or may have taken an inflexible approach to the best and worst case scenarios.

The involvement of a lawyer in mediation is particularly important during the latter stages of the mediation, in order to consider whether, and to what extent, any legal constraints pertain to any settlement proposed.[100] The lawyer will need to consider, for example, whether all the relevant people are parties to the agreement; whether the agreement is legally and commercially viable; whether the agreement will otherwise be durable; and whether the proposed settlement will reduce the likelihood of future disputes. The lawyer should start drafting the settlement agreement as soon as heads of terms begin to emerge. A lawyer should not underestimate the length of time that may be required to draft the agreement. Input from specialists may be required, for instance a tax specialist. The lawyer must take care in drafting the settlement agreement, to ensure that it is legally binding, if that is what the parties intend.[101]

Lawyers can have less direct forms of involvement in the mediation meetings than that described above: they can be present but have the limited role of only speaking with their client when advice is sought; or they can be present throughout, but with speaking rights only after an initial period of an hour or two; they can be in attendance outside the mediation room for consultations during adjournments; or they can be accessible only by phone or fax.

---

100 H Erlanger et al 'Participation and flexibility in informal processes: Cautions from the divorce context' (1987) 21 *Law and Society Review* 585 at 598; and R Mnookin and L Kornhauser 'Bargaining in the Shadow of the Law: The case of Divorce' (1979) 88 *Yale Law Journal* 950 at 968–9.

101 See the section on Enforcement Issues in Chapter 12.

Protocols and ethical responsibilities for lawyers

Sir Laurence Street, an international mediator, includes a clause in his Standard Agreement to Mediate which provides that the legal advisers will observe the spirit of a mediation protocol which applies when he mediates.[102] This protocol emphasises the informal and non-legal context of mediation, the need for clients to take as direct a role as they wish to, and the non-advocatory role expected of lawyers. It describes the role of legal advisers as being to:[103]

- advise and assist clients;
- discuss with each other, and with their respective clients, legal, evidentiary, or practical matters suggested by the mediator or requested by their clients;
- prepare the terms of settlement or heads of agreement at the end of the mediation for the parties' signature.

As regards lawyers' ethical duties in mediation, solicitors and barristers are bound by the conduct rules for solicitors and barristers and are subject to the supervision of the Law Society and the General Council of the Bar, respectively. As Sammon points out, there is no general duty akin to that owed by the lawyer to the court, although this duty might operate in court-attached mediation.[104] There would be a duty not to participate in mediation for ulterior purposes, or to present a case which the lawyer knows to be false. The preservation of confidentiality is another ethical requirement, but this is really an extension of the existing fiduciary duties. Some mediator standards in Australia require mediators to report unprofessional behaviour by lawyers to the relevant Law Society.

Genn's study of the Central London County Court Mediation Pilot indicated that the settlement rate of mediation was highest when neither party had legal representation at the mediation.[105] She found that the success rate was lower, at 55%, when both parties were legally represented at the mediation, although the lowest settlement rate occurred when only the claimant was legally represented.[106] Inadequate preparation is frequently perceived as the most common impediment to settlement in mediation.[107] Lawyers frequently adopt a formal and adversarial approach, particularly in the early stages of the mediation.[108] Dispute resolution lawyers traditionally view disputants as

---

102 L Street 'Representation at Commercial Mediations' (1992) 2 *ADRJ* 255. In his mediator's opening Street urges lawyers to be at 'your clients' elbows' and not 'in front of them'. See also S Williamson 'The silent revolution in dispute resolution' (1994) 68 *Law Institute Journal* 10–11.

103 L Street, ibid. The protocol also provides a role statement for the parties.

104 G Sammon 'The ethical duties of lawyers who act for parties to a mediation' (1993) 4 *ADRJ* 190 at 191.

105 Settlement rate was 72% in that case: H Genn *Central London County Court Mediation Pilot: Evaluation Report*, LCD Research Series, No 5/98, at p vi.

106 Ibid, at p 53.

107 Ibid, at p 16 where it was reported that some lawyers admitted that they could have been better prepared for the mediation. Lack of preparation was also highlighted as the most common impediment to settlement in the New South Wales survey conducted by M Dewdney, B Sordo and C Chinkin *Continuing developments in mediation within the legal system: evaluation of the 1992/93 Settlement Week Programme*, the Law Society, New South Wales, 1994.

108 L Mulcahy et al *Mediating medical negligence claims: an option for the future?* NHS Executive, 2000, at p 65 where one lawyer explained:

adversaries, in the sense that if one wins the other must lose. Lawyers are also trained to think in terms of rights and, in turn, may underestimate the importance of other issues, like emotional issues or reduce such issues to amounts of money.[109] Lawyers are also frequently disparaged for lacking ordinary commonsense.[110] In mediation, domination by the lawyers can deprive the parties of the 'day in court' benefit of mediation and prevent the party from developing a rapport with the mediator. Inflexibility by parties and lawyers is also a common problem in mediation. As developments in a mediation unfold, lawyers may be required to moderate or change their strategy or the advice previously given to the client.[111] Criticism has also been levelled at barristers' involvement in mediation. Advocacy skills used at trial do not transfer well in the mediation context:

'. . . on the occasion I have used a barrister at mediation . . . he added little . . . this is no reflection on the barrister involved but as the process was not adversarial and as we had worked out our case in advance, he could add little on the day . . .'[112]

In addition, it has been argued that barristers have a limited relationship with the client and are too remote to allow them to adopt a conciliatory approach.[113] The most common issue with lawyer representation in mediation is the use by lawyers of the same rules of manipulation and intimidation they may use in litigation:[114]

'. . . solicitors approach mediation with the wrong mindset and make the mediation confrontational . . . they complicate the issues and focus on technical legal points . . . which precludes the possibility of settlement . . .'[115]

'I had drafted the opening speech in quite a formal way and I realise now that was a mistake because basically I started by denying liability . . . the plaintiff sat in tears all the way through it . . .'

109 Redmont 'The transactional emphasis in legal education' 26 *Journal of Legal Education* 253 at 255; and Kennedy 'How the law school fails' 1 *Yale Law & Society Review* 71.
110 Ayer 'Isn't there enough reality to go around? An essay on the unspoken promises of our law' 53 *NYU L Rev* 457 at 489–90. An example by Professor Kenney Hegland in 'Why teach trial advocacy? An essay on never ask why' in *Humanistic Education in Law*, Monograph III, 1982, at pp 68–9 relates to a question being posed to a first year contracts law class and the response received:
    '. . . in a long term instalment contract, seller promises buyer to deliver widgets at the rate of 1000 per month . . . in the third month seller delivers only 999 widgets. Buyer . . . rejects the delivery . . . if you were seller what would you say? . . . the 8 year old son of one of my students [responded]: "I'd say I'm sorry".'
111 See T and H Allen *Draft competencies for lawyers in mediation*, CEDR, 2000. For an overview in the context of Australian mediation, see J Wade 'In search of new conflict management processes: the lawyer as macro and micro diagnostic problem solver' (1995) 10(2) *Australian Family Lawyer* 23; J Wade 'In search of new conflict management processes: Part II' (1995) 10(3) *Australian Family Lawyer* 16; and J Wade 'Lawyers and mediators: what each needs to learn from and about the other' (1991) 2 *Australian Journal of Dispute Resolution* 159. In the context of US mediation, see 'Digging deeper: Mediation issues grow more complex as the rewards from better solutions continue to increase' (1998) 16(11) *CPR Alternatives* 184.
112 View of one respondent to authors' 2000 survey of UK law firms.
113 University of Newcastle upon Tyne Conciliation Project Unit, *Report to the Lord Chancellor's Department on the cost and effectiveness of conciliation in England and Wales*, March 1989, at p 125.
114 C Menkel-Meadow 'Pursuing settlement in an adversary culture: A tale of innovation co-opted or "the law of ADR"' (1991) 19 *Florida State University Law Review* 1 at 17.
115 View of one respondent to authors' 2000 survey of 700 UK law firms.

Some commentators regard the issue of lack of co-operation by lawyers in mediation as a wider issue, encouraged by hourly charge rates.[116] A number of US authors have, over the years, addressed the issue of whether increased use of mediation would lead to a reduction in lawyer fees. Arguments against this proposition include that lawyers can apply the time saved by mediation to other fee-earning matters and that it is also possible for lawyers' practices to develop so that virtually all their billable time is spent on mediation.[117]

Notwithstanding the potential difficulties identified above, a lawyer can be a valuable asset in a mediation provided that he or she appreciates the role of a representative in mediation, as outlined above, negotiation theory and the ability to manage the client's expectations. A skilful lawyer can make creative use of the mediation process to influence and persuade an adversary as to the appropriate settlement range in a particular case.[118]

There is wide agreement that lawyers have an indispensable role to perform in mediation where the complexity of the dispute, the legal issues, or the requirements of the client necessitate their expertise, and where they understand and are committed to the process.

The involvement of lawyers creates an additional challenge for mediators. The mediator's responsibility to assist the parties to preserve face extends to lawyers and other advisers. This can become difficult where a lawyer is threatened with losing face in front of his or her own client, and in front of the other lawyer and party. Loss of face can occur through lack of familiarity with the process, lack of preparation or unanticipated developments.[119] Mediators have to resort to one or more techniques, such as reframing, generalising, or separate meetings, to mitigate damage to legal and other professional advisers.[120]

Post-mediation activities

Lawyers may be involved in a variety of ways after the mediation has concluded. They may have to convert heads of agreement into a detailed contract or make use of a cooling-off period to advise clients before the agreement becomes operative. In some cases they will draft consent orders for the relevant court and pursue all matters necessary to obtain a court order.

---

116 R J Gilson and R H Mnookin 'Disputing through Agents: Co-operation and conflict between lawyers in litigation' (1994) 94 *Columbia Law Review* 504 at 547; and A A S Zuckerman 'Quality and Economy in Civil Procedure – the case for commuting correct judgments for timely judgments' (1994) 14(3) *Oxford Journal of Legal Studies* 535.
117 For example, L Riskin 'Mediation and Lawyers' (1982) 42 *Ohio State Law Journal* 29 at 53.
118 See samples of skilled lawyers in mediation in L C Mann 'Mediation of Civil Cases' 67 *Detroit Law Review* 531.
119 For example, in one mediation, a solicitor could not say whether or not the valuation of a business included a component for goodwill. A major face-saving strategy was required.
120 On mediator skills and techniques, see Chapter 6.

The Functions of other Participants in Mediation

(a) *Professional advisers:* accountants, psychologists, engineers and other professionals can participate as advisers in the mediation process along similar lines to legal advisers. Litigators could be involved but they would be required to adapt their role to the collaborative, interest-based nature of mediation.

(b) *Lay assistants or supporters:* it is not unusual for parties to bring friends, family members or work colleagues to the mediation to assist them in the process, through advice, reassurance or merely making up the numbers. In some cases it may be necessary for supporters to remain outside the mediation meeting, for reasons of space or where the other party objects to their presence, and agreed procedures are required to keep them informed of developments. If supporters are present they might be observers only or, by arrangement, might participate in all or parts of the process. The presence of supporters has potential implications for the confidentiality principle.

(c) *Witnesses:* witnesses may be present at the mediation meeting and may provide information at their disposal, but this is usually done in an informal way and not through evidence-in-chief, cross-examination and re-examination as in a court hearing. However, the involvement of witnesses in mediation could provide the other side with some strategic advantages in preparing for trial.

(d) *Experts:* experts may participate in mediation in the same way as witnesses. Where there are opposing experts, the mediation process may be conducive to achieving some level of joint agreement among them. Some mediators meet in separate sessions with the various experts, to ascertain what agreement can be reached between them. Others ask the experts to meet on their own and report back to the mediation meeting with a single report which identifies points of agreement and areas of disagreement.

(e) *Constituents:* constituents are those people, such as ratepayers or residents, who are represented by spokespersons at mediation meetings. It may be possible for them to observe the proceedings or to obtain agreed reports on developments.

(f) *Interpreters:* in court, use may be made of interpreters. Given the emphasis in mediation on constructive communication, the role of interpreter, if one is required, is critical. Those involved should be conversant with the mediation process and its values.

(g) *Children:* this issue has been considered earlier in this chapter. There are different views as to whether children should participate in divorce. Some writers argue that the potential disadvantages far outweigh the advantages, for example, that children should not be forced to make choices between parents.[121] Others argue from a children's rights perspective that the children, as rational beings, can participate in mediation, subject to various safeguards: the parents should agree to their involvement, all parties should be

---

121 See, for example, M Roberts *Mediation in Family Disputes* (2nd edn) Arena, Aldershot, Northhamton, 1997, at Chapter 9. See also G Meggs 'Issues in Divorce Mediation – methodology and ethics' (1993) 4 *ADRJ* 198 at 206–7.

adequately prepared for the process, and children should not be forced to make decisions.[122] The mediation process can be adapted, for example to allow the children to see the mediator(s) only in a separate meeting. As far as possible, children are protected from witnessing any further hostilities between their parents. They are sometimes interviewed by the mediators in order for the mediators to assess their relationship with each parent and their perspective on the situation. This is done to facilitate the mediators' discussions with the adult disputants. For the children's social and psychological needs, behavioural scientists may be required to assist in mediation.[123] Haynes recommends that where the parties are genuinely open to changes in their parenting scheme, children may be invited to a mediation meeting to review the agreement.[124] This also provides the opportunity for the mediator to explain aspects of the parents' separation which the husband and wife have been unable to do, and to answer children's questions, for example on the possibility of changing the parenting plan in the future.

(h) *Defendants:* it is not usual for drivers or employers to participate in personal injury mediations in motor vehicle or industrial accident mediations respectively. Normally only the insurer and its legal representative are present. However, there might be some procedural and psychological value for the claimant to have the defendant present. It might also be more even-handed where liability is disputed, in that where the claimants are present the insurer can assess their strengths and weaknesses as witnesses, and the claimant would have the same benefit in relation to the driver or employer.

There are no set rules or protocols for the participation of the above parties. The informality and flexibility of the mediation process allow for whatever involvement the circumstances may require. The nature of their participation should be negotiated by the disputing parties with the assistance of the mediator, preferably in advance of the mediation meeting. Where there is no agreement the mediator may have to make a decision, with the potential risk that one or both parties will reject the decision and abandon the mediation. Mediators should also remember that the above participants are not signatories to the Agreement to Mediate and their commitment to confidentiality should be secured through a separate undertaking. Another potential difficulty for mediators is that, unlike the situation in a court or tribunal hearing, they have no authority and only limited control in respect of these parties' involvement and manner of participation.

The Functions of Non-participants

In many mediations parties not present at the meetings may have significant roles in the overall effectiveness of the process. These parties are known as 'external

---

122 H Brown and A Marriott *ADR Principles and Practice* (2nd edn), Sweet & Maxwell, London, 1999, at pp 237–8. See also D Saposnek 'The value of children in mediation: a cross-cultural perspective' (1991) 8 *MQ* 325.
123 G Meggs 'Issues in Divorce Mediation – methodology and ethics' (1993) 4 *ADRJ* 198 at 207.
124 J Haynes *The fundamentals of family mediation*, State University of New York Press, Albany, 1994, at pp 135–6.

ratifiers'. In some cases they might have a formal ratifying role, as in the case of a company board in a commercial matter. In other cases the external party's ratification is of an informal nature in that they have influence over the party to the agreement and might destabilise their decisions if they do not approve of them, for example a conservation group in a planning dispute or a new partner in a matrimonial dispute. In these circumstances the mediator's first responsibility on becoming aware of the ratification problem is to establish, together with the relevant party or both parties, whether the outside group can be involved at the negotiating table. Where this is not feasible, the mediator should assist the relevant party to prepare for and deal with the external ratifier. The other party might be activated to assist in this process through the fear of otherwise losing the deal. Clearly a non-existent ratifier could be invoked by one party to provide leverage in the negotiations.[125]

---

125 W Ury *Getting past no – negotiating with difficult people*, Business Books, London, 1991, at p 23.

6

Skills and Techniques of Mediators

Mediator Proficiencies

Mediators need to be proficient in a wide range of skills and techniques. This chapter describes some of those skills and techniques which form the practical acts and interventions adopted by mediators. None of these skills and techniques is unique to the practice of mediation. They are used in different forms and styles by social workers, lawyers, psychologists, counsellors and managers. For example, a skill often closely associated with mediation is 'reframing', but this is widely used by professionals in the social sciences. Mediators are just one group of skilled helpers whose competencies have much in common with those of other skilled helpers.[1]

Some lists of mediator proficiencies imply that only divine beings could qualify for the role. In reality, each mediator can have only a limited 'tool-box' of skills and techniques. The kind of tools possessed by each mediator will depend on their training, experience and personal attributes. Professional background is also important: counsellor mediators tend to have good listening skills and lawyer mediators tend to have good drafting skills. Each mediator has a wide discretion in selecting a particular tool from the tool-box of skills which they possess. Each skill or technique should further one or other of the *functions* of mediators.[2] Sometimes a single skill or technique can contribute to more than one mediator function. When and how a technique or skill is exercised will be a matter for the discretion of each mediator in the particular circumstances. Each will fall somewhere along a continuum of appropriate and inappropriate interventions; for example summarising or not interrupting may be highly appropriate in some cases but very inappropriate in others. Ultimately a particular skill or technique is only relevant if it serves the objective of assisting the mediating parties in making sound decisions.

Certain mediator skills, such as active listening or empathising, are sometimes regarded as 'soft' skills which are innate in some people and cannot be learned. In reality, all mediator skills and techniques can be learned, practised and developed to some extent. They can also, with varying degrees of objectivity, be measured and assessed.

---

1 H Brown and A Marriott *ADR Principles and Practice* (2nd edn), Sweet & Maxwell, London, 1999: see Chapter 15; and G Egan *The skilled helper – a problem-solving approach to helping* (5th edn), Brooks/Cole Publishing, Pacific Grove, California, 1994.
2 On the functions of mediators, see Chapter 5.

As this book is not a mediator's practice manual, there is no attempt to describe and explain mediator skills and techniques exhaustively. Reference is made to a selection of skills and techniques and to their relevance in mediation.

Organisational Skills and Techniques

In creating a framework for co-operative decision-making,[3] mediators must exercise a range of organisational skills and techniques. These can be categorised as 'macro skills' in that they are general overall plans and interventions which contribute to the effectiveness of mediation.

Supervising arrivals and departures

Mediators must plan and supervise the arrivals, waiting and departures of all parties.[4] They should follow basic courtesies in relation to arrivals: be on time, meet parties as they arrive or have them met, introduce themselves in a professional but cordial fashion, and indicate how they should be addressed. They should escort each arrival to a waiting area and avoid any appearance of having spent significant time with one party before the other arrived. It might be necessary to provide separate waiting areas for parties where there is history of hostility, destructive interaction or violence.

In some circumstances mediators will have to supervise the departure of the parties from the mediation venue. This will be necessary where there has been high emotion and tension in the mediation session or where the mediation has taken place despite a past history of violence between the parties. The best arrangement is to allow the 'victim' or threatened party to leave the mediation venue first, and to allow sufficient time for them to depart before allowing the other party to leave.

Arranging seating

Studies show that seating arrangements have important implications for the negotiating behaviour of parties in conflict.[5] Where parties are seated opposite each other across rectangular tables, it tends to produce polarised and competitive behaviour, whereas if round tables with no physical boundaries are used, it tends to dilute differences and make parties more collaborative. Mediators can arrange seating in terms of several variables: the use or non-use of a table, the shape of the table, the placement of chairs, the individual space provided for each party, and the physical features of the room.

---

3   See the section on Establishing a framework for co-operative decision-making in Chapter 5.
4   J Folberg and A Taylor *Mediation: a comprehensive guide to resolving conflicts without litigation*, Jossey-Bass, San Francisco, 1984, at pp 100–2.
5   C Moore *The mediation process: practical strategies for resolving conflict*, Jossey-Bass, San Francisco, 1996, at pp 150–2.

Stulberg suggests two basic principles in relation to seating.[6] First, each distinct party (in the sense of interest group) should have a separate and equal space. Thus where a manager is mediating among the sales, marketing and research departments of a company, the representatives of each department should have their own physical space. This arrangement indicates that it is acceptable to have separate and sometimes competing interests; to intersperse the parties among one another is to make naive assumptions about 'working together'. Second, the mediator should be between the parties, equidistant from each, and closest to the door. This position symbolises the mediator's leadership role and neutrality. It also allows him or her to intercept a party who decides to leave and appropriately suggest other options without the party disappearing from the nearest exit before any intervention is possible.

As regards tables and chairs, mediators have to assess what is culturally appropriate for the parties and the dispute. A rectangular table with formal seating, in the style of a traditional boardroom, tends to be used for commercial disputes. However, boardroom styles are themselves changing towards the use of round or oval tables, which can be more appropriate for business mediations. Neighbourhood and community mediation services tend to use less formal tables and chairs, arranged in rectangular, circular or triangular fashion. In some mediations there are no tables and the mediation has the style of a lounge room discussion. In most cases parties will sit in identical chairs, equidistant from the door, but where one party is fearful of the other he or she should be placed closer to the door. Where resources allow, a set of modular tables is effective in that it allows mediators to re-arrange seating to suit disputes of different natures and sizes. Some mediators also make minor adjustments to seating during adjournments in the mediation. They may set the chairs so that the disputants face and talk to the mediator during the early stages, but rearrange them later so that the parties face one another with the intention of making them communicate directly, rather than indirectly through the mediator. In the separate meetings, some mediators ask the parties to sit in different places which are not associated with the stress or positional demands experienced in the joint meeting.

In all aspects of seating, mediators need to make practical choices based on their best judgment. However, in some situations the choices are too significant for mediators to make alone, and in others, resources allow no real choice. Thus in large-scale mediations involving international relations and diplomacy, seating and room arrangements may have to be negotiated extensively with the parties before the mediation. Conversely in some community mediations, held in draughty neighbourhood halls, there is little choice of furniture and mediators make do with whatever is available.

The diagram opposite shows possible seating arrangements for different kinds of mediation.

Improving the emotional climate

Mediators have many potential techniques for improving the emotional climate between the parties.[7] They must reassure anxious parties about the stages and

---

6 J Stulberg *Taking Charge/Managing Conflict*, Lexington Books, Lexington, Massachusetts, 1987, at pp 61–3.
7 See the section on Establishing a framework for co-operative decision-making in Chapter 5.

Forms of Mediation Seating

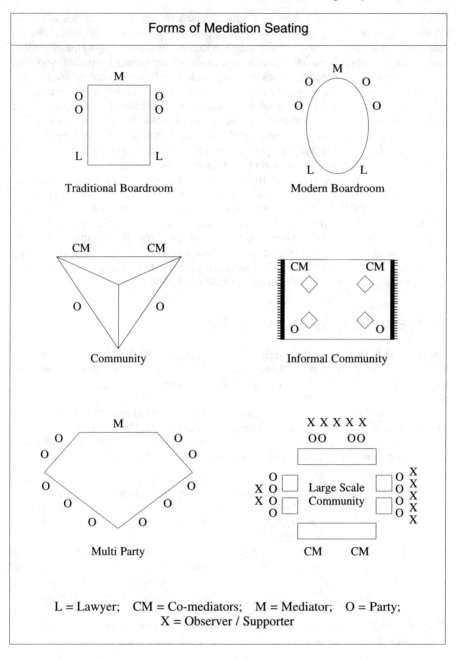

L = Lawyer;   CM = Co-mediators;   M = Mediator;   O = Party;
X = Observer / Supporter

procedures of mediation, encourage them as to their ability to reach appropriate decisions and refer to examples of successful mediations in similar circumstances to their own. These interventions require interpersonal skills, sensitivity, warmth and some psychological 'stroking' of the parties. They are particularly important in the early meeting and greeting routines and in the mediator's opening statement, both of which can provide an important sense of 'ritual' in the mediation process.

Court systems have well-established rituals based on traditional modes of dress, address, style and hierarchy. Generally, mediation in western societies has no established tradition of rituals. In communal societies, by contrast, systems of conflict management – some of which resemble mediation – have numerous rituals involving the exchange of gifts, eating, drinking and smoking, signs of respect, singing and movement. Ritual lends a sanctity and mystique to the proceedings, suggesting that the business at hand has a social importance greater than the interests of the individuals. It also lends a sense of purpose and even-handedness to the proceedings. In the absence of equivalent rituals, mediators need to consider spending time on preliminary courtesies among all present, on exchanging pleasantries on incidental matters, on initiating a formal round of introductions, on attending to how the parties should address one another, and on making some acknowledgment and affirmation of all parties present. Mediators may also provide food, drink and other refreshments,[8] which can be 'ritually' served in a way which shows respect for, and the equality of, all parties present. Consumption becomes a common activity, participated in equally by all participants, which temporarily distracts attention from the negative features of the dispute during the settling-in phase. Imaginative mediators might develop additional rituals appropriate to the mediation process. For example, coffee, tea or snacks could be made available throughout the mediation.

Presenting material visually

There is a slogan in mediation circles: 'The Visual is Vital'. Mediators require skills in using whiteboards, flip charts, overhead projectors and other visual aids effectively, to assist the parties to systematise, organise, understand and recall what is being said. The visuals also help to 'separate the people from the problem',[9] in that mediators can direct the parties' gaze to a visually-presented agenda item in order to avert a destructive interpersonal exchange between them. Points of agreement can also be recorded on whiteboards or butcher's paper, and these can be occasionally highlighted to maintain a mood of optimism and sense of progress.

Most of the skills in presenting things visually involve basic common sense. Mediators should locate the whiteboard or flip-chart where they are equally visible to all parties. They should write legibly and in sufficiently large writing to avoid embarrassment to poor-sighted parties. Prior screening can determine whether one or more parties is illiterate; for such people written agendas are not a good thing.[10] Mediators should attempt to spell accurately, should not erase important written material (which makes flip-charts more useful than whiteboards), should not use permanent markers on whiteboards, and should keep away from electronic whiteboards if they find basic technology a challenge. They should be careful about what is written prominently as inflammatory words may distract or distress a party for as long as they are visible. They should also be sensitive to a 'playschool' resistance from those who regard themselves as too seasoned to be inflicted with whiteboard presentations.

---

8 Serving and drinking cups of tea has ritualistic overtones in many societies and takes place in some mediations.
9 See section on Interest-based Bargaining in Chapter 2.
10 In one mediation, extensive use was made of flip charts to develop an agenda, prioritise the agenda items, and record areas of agreement. When the parties were asked to sign the final agreement, it was discovered that one of the parties was illiterate.

Facilitation Skills and Techniques

Converting concerns to issues

Parties in conflict tend to make their presentations in terms of positions, that is, proposed solutions to the problem, and not in terms of interests, that is, underlying needs which they want satisfied.[11] One of the important skills for mediators is to redirect the negotiations away from positional claims towards underlying interests. There are a number of skills involved in this transition. Mediators often invite parties to talk about their 'concerns', which may elicit from them presentations on needs, interests and positions. Mediators then convert the concerns into 'issues', that is, generalised versions of the parties' concerns which, as far as possible, mutualise the problems. In this process mediators attempt to replace an egocentric view, or views, with one which reflects both sides of the problem. Thus, if parents both claim exclusive custody of the children, the mediator might suggest that they see the problem as one of meeting each parent's need for appropriate involvement in the children's lives and a good relationship with them. Mediators also move from a specific definition of the problem to one which is more generalised and acceptable to both sides. Thus a claim by one spouse for 60% of the matrimonial property might be presented as a need for a fair and equitable division of property which takes into account past contributions and future needs. By ignoring the specific figure, the mediator opens up the negotiating process to more options. Mediators will also include the interests of both sides in the definition of the problem. Thus in a dispute between a school board and the principal over their respective functions, the mediator might define the problem in terms of the need for an arrangement which allows the board to have overall supervision of policy-making in the school while at the same time allowing the principal to have the final say on matters of administration.

These principles can be illustrated by reference to a hypothetical dispute between two professional partners, Sarah and Jonathan. Sarah, the older and more traditional partner, is concerned about the new class of clients Jonathan is bringing into the firm, the length of time these clients take in paying their bills, Jonathan's continual complaints about Sarah's use of secretarial resources, and Jonathan's possible goal of easing Sarah out of the firm and taking over the partnership. Jonathan, the younger and more progressive partner, is concerned about the small share of the profits he is receiving, the firm's conservative approach towards its client base, Sarah's use of secretaries for charity works, and the amount of time Sarah spends out of the office on the golf course. The mediator might convert these concerns into the following issues, presented as problem-solving questions:

- How should profits be distributed between Sarah and Jonathan?
- What mix of client categories is most appropriate for the partnership?
- How can the partners balance work and outside commitments?
- How can the payment of bills be speeded up?
- How can secretarial time be allocated appropriately?
- How can future relations in the partnership and office be improved?

Here the mediator has converted the parties' concerns into a set of questions which are generalised, interest-based, open-ended, mutualised and future oriented. If the parties accept this definition of the problem, the questions will provide a foundation

---

11 On the significance of these terms in 'interest-based' negotiation, see Chapter 2.

for problem-solving negotiations between them. The mediator will assist the parties to prioritise the questions and use them to structure the problem-solving stages of the mediation.

Dealing with emotion

Mediators usually encounter people in stressful circumstances in which highly negative emotions are displayed.[12] In mediation high emotions should be controlled, but not forbidden. This requires that mediators have specific skills and techniques.

Dealing with the mediator's own responses to high emotion

Mediators must not allow their individual reactions to the parties' emotions, for example anger or sadness, to determine the way such emotions are dealt with. Mediators should be attuned to their own responses to emotional outbursts and develop mechanisms to manage these without affecting the mediation. Thus mediators should not move parties into separate meetings merely because of their own discomfort at high levels of anger. They are, however, able to call an adjournment to obtain some release from the intensity of high emotions for themselves.

Recognising and diagnosing emotion

Mediators must recognise emotion, diagnose it and select an appropriate intervention for dealing with it.[13] Parties in mediation have normally suffered loss of some sort and they will be moving through different stages in the grieving process, which include shock, denial, bargaining, anger, depression, and acceptance.[14] If this phenomenon is not recognised and dealt with in an appropriate way, it may block any chances of reaching substantive agreement. Another emotion which may play an important role in a mediation and which is often overlooked is shame.[15] Intense feelings are usually forcefully expressed, but mediators must also be aware of outward signs of internal distress, such as taut facial muscles or heavy perspiration. Mediators must then tentatively diagnose the emotion in order to determine an appropriate intervention strategy. In some cases mediation may be premature and the mediator will recommend professional help for dealing with denial or depression. In other cases the mediator's humour may be sufficient to defuse an emotion and get the negotiations back on track. However, while mediators need to recognise and diagnose emotional problems, they do not need to resolve them.

Acknowledging and allowing venting of emotions

Mediators should normally acknowledge the parties' strong feelings on the grounds that acknowledgment alone might lessen their intensity. To make the

---

12 See J Folberg and A Taylor *Mediation: a comprehensive guide to resolving conflicts without litigation*, Jossey-Bass, San Francisco, 1984, at p 91; and C Moore *The mediation process: practical strategies for resolving conflict*, Jossey-Bass, San Francisco, 1996, at pp 162–9.
13 C Moore, op cit, at p 165.
14 See generally E Kubler-Ross *On death and dying*, Macmillan, New York, 1969.
15 N Serventy 'Understanding shame in mediation and dispute resolution' (1998) 9 *ADRJ* 150.

acknowledgment more accurate, mediators must engage in active listening[16] which will help both them and the parties to pinpoint and understand the emotions before acknowledging them. Mediators may also decide to allow one or both parties to vent their negative feelings, on the assumption that this cathartic release is a necessary prerequisite for rational discussions.[17] A strong venting of emotion by one party may be necessary to allow the other side to realise the extent of the speaker's distress. In some contexts there may be an expectation of 'ritualised venting', for example in management/ union mediations.[18] However, where one side needs control and protection, venting by the other will have to be closely monitored by the mediator. Venting must be considered a means to an end. Rather than allowing parties to engage in their normal destructive patterns of conduct, mediators need to assist them discuss matters in a more constructive way.[19]

Limiting or suppressing emotion

There are several situations in which mediators need to limit or suppress the parties' emotions. They must do so where it may escalate out of control or into destructive conduct which might seriously threaten or injure the other party. They must also do so where the expression of emotion is not genuine but is a negotiation tactic designed to intimidate the other side into making concessions. Where mediators decide to limit emotion, there are different degrees of intervention from which they can choose:

Degrees of Intervention to Limit Emotion	
Moderate	• Attempt to distract parties • Ask deflective questions • Refer to list of issues
Authoritative	• Identify unacceptable expressions of emotion • Remind parties of the guiding principles of mediation • Ask parties to recommit to the process
Forceful	• Chastise the parties • Break into separate meetings • Threaten to terminate the mediation unless the emotion is controlled

These interventions require fine judgment in balancing the need for allowing a constructive venting of intense emotions with the need for avoiding destructive, intimidating or disempowering tactics. Mediators can use the mediation process creatively to achieve the balance by:

- suggesting adjournments for tissues and tea;

---

16 See section below on Listening actively.
17 See the references to the 'controlled burn', in the section on Conflict is not necessarily a negative phenomenon in Chapter 2.
18 C Moore *The mediation process: practical strategies for resolving conflict*, Jossey-Bass, San Francisco, 1996, at p 167.
19 J Stulberg *Taking Charge/Managing Conflict*, Lexington Books, Lexington, Massachusetts, 1987, at p 63.

- calling separate meetings for safer emoting; or
- inviting the parties themselves to suggest ways of dealing with destructive emotions.

Ultimately mediators should be providing a secure environment, and this security may actually encourage the expressing of emotions in the knowledge that it will not lead to violence.

Managing the process

As managers of a process, mediators require chairing and managerial skills to make the process effective and efficient. The mediator will need to call on these skills throughout the process. The mediator should ascertain that the parties at the mediation have authority to settle. He or she should give sufficient explanation of the process, repeated if necessary, to ensure that there are no procedural surprises for the parties, particularly in the use of separate meetings. The parties should be kept to the agenda, and the mediator must ensure that discussions are not repetitive or irrelevant. As managers of the process, mediators must also take the initiative on who should speak first, when to break into separate meetings, when to adjourn and when to terminate. They must use mediation's procedural flexibility to ensure that they adapt and modify the system to meet the needs of the parties. In all cases they need to be assertive, that is, neither aggressive nor submissive, in performing their management functions.[20] They must exercise these skills and techniques to ensure that the parties feel that they 'have their day' in mediation.[21]

Negotiation Skills and Techniques

Mediators facilitate negotiations between the parties and do not negotiate directly with them. This implies that while they do not practise negotiation skills directly, they should transfer some of their negotiation expertise to the parties. Mediators can effect this transfer before and during the mediation meeting by educating, coaching, advising and informing the parties on the best negotiation practices. As to what is transferred, some mediation guidelines[22] require mediators to promote 'interest-based bargaining', a term derived from the negotiation principles of Fisher and Ury.[23] These principles were developed in relation to unassisted negotiations and do not furnish a clear set of techniques for a third party in facilitated negotiations. Some mediation guidelines attempt to provide further guidance in relation to the negotiation responsibilities of mediators, for example in stipulating that they must ensure 'a balanced dialogue and must attempt to diffuse any manipulative or intimidating negotiation techniques utilised by either of the participants'.[24] In reality,

---

20 For more on assertiveness, see R Bolton *People skills: how to assert yourself, listen to others and resolve conflicts*, Simon and Schuster, Brookvale, New South Wales, 1987, in particular pp 115–76.
21 An analogy to 'having your day' in court.
22 On mediator guidelines and standards, see Chapter 11.
23 R Fisher and W Ury *Getting to yes: negotiating an agreement without giving in* (rev edn), Hutchinson, Boston, 1987; and see section on Interest-based Bargaining in Chapter 2.
24 American Bar Association *Standards of Practice for Lawyer Mediators in Family*

however, mediators can only deal with some of the parties' negotiation tactics and others have to be met with 'benign neglect'.[25]

What follows is a discussion of some of the ways in which mediators can intervene in the negotiation process.

Emphasise common ground

Mediators should accentuate the fact that there is some common ground between the parties. This should be done early in the negotiations, preferably after the parties' presentations.[26] In the case of the partners Sarah and Jonathan referred to above, the mediator might refer to the fact that the partnership has been successful in the past, that each partner needs to balance work and outside interests, and that both agree that a new arrangement should be negotiated rather than dissolving the partnership. This technique might require the mediator to present the areas of agreement at a high level of generality, for example in a matrimonial mediation that both parties are committed to the best interests of the children. Nevertheless, even at this level the mediator's intervention serves to show common ground which might not have been appreciated previously because of the intensity of the conflict and the fact that the parties had not communicated directly for some time. The common ground provides a platform on which to negotiate other agreements and generates an air of optimism, mutuality and confidence. This is a technique not practised frequently enough by mediators.

Increase the issues

In many negotiations there appears to be only a single issue at stake, often the question of how much money should be paid. In these situations, mediators require techniques to get the parties to acknowledge and deal with other issues, both substantive and non-substantive. Multiple issues are easier to bargain on than single issues. They provide more scope for trade-offs, reciprocal concessions and packaging, and are less likely to result in the dreaded last gap which is difficult to bridge. In the case of a dispute over an amount of money, the mediator needs to get the parties to consider a number of issues besides the main issue of the amount. These could include:

- timing of payment;
- form of payment (bank cheque, cash);
- method of payment (lump sum, instalments);
- security for deferred payment; and
- interest on default of payment.

The parties can also bring into the equation legal costs, other professional costs, and the mediator's fee.[27] Other matters which might be considered are the reputational value of publicity or confidentiality for the terms of agreement, and future business arrangements between the parties. While these matters will tend to be subordinate to

---

Disputes, 1984, Washington DC.

25 J Haynes and G Haynes *Mediating Divorce: casebook of strategies for successful family negotiations*, 1989, at p 46.
26 See also the section on Party Presentations in Chapter 5.
27 In a mediation involving a 'single issue' of money, the parties reached an impasse over

the central issue of the amount of money, they may constitute sufficient value to one or both parties to be helpful in reaching an agreement on money matters. They also allow the party making the final monetary concession to save face through being able to prevail on a lesser issue. All disputes can be converted into multiple issue disputes to some degree.[28]

Making and responding to offers

Mediators require techniques for imparting to the parties their knowledge about making and responding to offers. Both the timing of offers and acceptances, and the extent of concessions made, are crucial in negotiations. There is a slogan that 'The right offer at the wrong time is the wrong offer', which indicates that some parties require a sense of struggle before they will be satisfied with an outcome. If an offer is accepted too quickly, the offerer will devalue the acceptance and attempt to gain further value from the negotiations.[29] Sometimes a series of small concessions is tactically more suitable than a single large concession. Some of this information can be imparted to the parties in the separate meetings, and mediators can coach them on appropriate ways of responding to offers, acceptances and rejections.

Linked bargaining

Linked bargaining involves the conditional coupling of one negotiation issue with another. It is best illustrated by an example based on the partnership dispute referred to above. The mediator might say to partner Jonathan, 'If you were to get a fair arrangement on the sharing of profits, what sort of absences from the office by Sarah could you live with?' Similarly he or she might say to Sarah, 'Let's assume that you come to a reasonable deal on your absences from the office, what then could you offer Jonathan on the use of secretarial resources?' The object of conditional linked bargaining is to open up the negotiation process to a consideration of options under conditions of safety for the parties. If Jonathan makes constructive concessions on the absence of Sarah from the office, they are conditional on a deal being reached on the profit issue and do not constitute a unilateral concession. Likewise if Sarah concedes the need for some limit on secretarial resources being used for charity works, it is conditional on agreement being reached on her absences and can later be withdrawn without any appearance of inconsistency. This approach forces the parties to concentrate on a single issue, without slipping into other issues. In getting the parties into the mode of conditional linked bargaining, mediators use terms such as 'reasonable', 'fair' and 'appropriate' in the conditional terms.[30] It can become a pattern for constructive deal-making throughout the bargaining stages of the mediation.

---

the last gap. When one side offered to pay the mediator's (modest) fee, the other side crossed the whole gap, although it was considerably larger than the fee.

28 On the need for mediators to be trained in issue enlargement, see R Whiting 'The single-issue, multiple-issue debate and the effect of issue number on mediated outcomes' (1992) 10 *MQ* 57.

29 This phenomenon is known as reactive devaluation: see R Mnookin 'Why negotiations fail: An examination of barriers to the resolution of conflicts' (1993) 8 *Ohio State Journal on Dispute Resolution* 235. See fns 51 and 52 below.

30 Referred to by John Wade as 'weasel words'.

Brainstorming

Brainstorming is designed to generate creative and lateral thinking among the parties.[31] In mediation it can be suggested by mediators as a way of moving forward when the negotiations have bogged down. It involves each of the parties being encouraged to propose settlement options, however unrealistic they might be, without any evaluation allowed from the others. The brainstorming dynamic is designed to reduce inhibitions based on the fear of negative evaluations, to provide a risk-free generation of ideas without any party being committed to specific proposals, to encourage the parties to stimulate each other's creative imagination, and to illustrate the wide number of conceivable ways of dealing with the problem. After the brainstorming activity, the mediator assists the parties to evaluate the various options in terms of their desirability, practicality and cost. Even where this brings the parties back to the unpalatable option first thought of before the matter came to mediation (for example, having to sell the family home), this option is now perceived to be the only realistic one in the circumstances,[32] and therefore acquires more legitimacy.

Dealing with deadlocks

Deadlocks are situations in which both negotiating parties refuse to move and it appears that the mediation will not achieve a settlement. The best techniques for dealing with deadlocks in negotiations are to prevent or prepare for them. In some negotiations one party, after settlement has been reached on all declared issues, makes a last-minute additional claim, known as an 'add-on'. In the partnership example referred to above, Sarah might insist that Jonathan procure five new 'traditional' clients in the following year, or Jonathan might demand a new computer system not previously mentioned. The add-ons might be genuine afterthoughts, or deliberate strategies to force the hand of the other party, or an indicator that the relevant party does not wish to settle the matter.[33] In some negotiations there can be a deadlock towards the end caused by the loss of face problem; each party feels that it has conceded too much and there would be a loss of face in any further compromise. Mediators can inform the parties in advance about these predictable impasses and they can openly discuss ways of pre-empting or dealing with them. In the case of the add-on problem, mediators can continually ask the parties whether all relevant issues have been disclosed, thereby making it less easy to sabotage the process at the end. In the case of the loss of face problem, mediators might suggest that the parties plan in advance how to deal with the last issue or assist them in preventing a single issue being left outstanding.

---

31 The term lateral thinking derives from E de Bono *Lateral thinking: a textbook of creativity*, Penguin Books, Sydney, 1970.

32 In a dispute between a local authority and a council tax payer, the mediator invited the parties to consider all logical options for the taxpayer's land affected by a buffer zone. The options included donating it for the public benefit, using it in a council-owner joint venture, selling it to a third party, dividing the land, developing a park named after the owner, and granting the owner compensation. The brainstorming revealed a wide range of conceivable options, but only a single feasible one – the last one.

33 See I Ricci's reference to 'negative intimacy' in *Mom's House, Dad's House: making shared custody work*, Collier Macmillan Publishers, London, 1982, at pp 83–6.

Mediators might also resort to the following strategies to deal with deadlocks:

- suggest an adjournment, with relevant homework for each party;
- recommend that the parties obtain legal or other professional advice;
- change one or more of the negotiators for each team;
- seek, from the parties, further background information about the dispute;
- request a single expert to give a binding/non-binding view on part of the dispute; and
- move from the substantive deadlock to discussing procedural ways of moving forward.

On occasions, lawyers could be responsible for impasse. Lawyers can become entangled in a dispute, play the 'litigation game' or engage in strategic behaviour to the point that they lose sight of the client's interests.[34] The mediator may direct questions, in that case, to the lawyers:

- 'what are your costs to date?'
- 'what would be the cost of trial in this case?'
- 'even if your client won, could they recover all their costs?'
- 'how long would it take to have this matter resolved by trial?'
- 'can you guarantee that the client will be successful at trial?'

In family mediation, where the parties are frequently unrepresented, a mediator may tackle the problem of conflicting legal advice by helping the parties to formulate questions to take back to their legal advisers for consideration.[35]

Apart from impasse created by conflicting legal advice, the parties may have different perceptions about the fairness of settlement proposals. Having the parties indicate what to them would make the proposed settlement fairer would be an appropriate approach. A party may reach impasse due to personal or emotional factors, which may be explored with that party in a private session or, in the case of family mediation, by counselling.

Crossing the last gap

The last gap is a special type of deadlock. It occurs where the parties have made decisions on all issues except one and have reached an impasse on this one. It often involves an amount of money. The mediators' knowledge of negotiation may have to be used to educate the parties on possible ways of bridging the last gap.[36] Thus mediators might refer to the following logical options and invite the parties to select the most appropriate:

- split the difference (classical compromise);
- spin a coin or draw straws (or other random chance variations);
- re-open decided issues and engage in linked bargaining;

---

34 J Rubin and F Sander 'When should we use Agents? Direct vs Representative Negotiation' (1988) 4(4) *Negotiation Journal* 395 at 397.
35 See, for example, Law Society of England & Wales *Family Mediation Training Standards*.
36 J Wade 'The last gap in negotiations – why is it important? How can it be crossed?' (1995) 6 *ADRJ* 93.

- give the disputed amount to a third party[37] (for example children or charity) or spend on a lottery ticket;
- divide the last gap into sub-issues (increasing the issues);
- leave best offers on the table and allow a specific time within which either party can accept the other's offer; and
- put the disputed amount 'in storage' and agree to deal with it after a lapse of time, during which the rest of the agreement comes into effect.

More selfless is the 'shaming' tactic, in which mediators offer to pay the difference themselves in the hope that it will embarrass the parties into bridging the gap. The main weakness of this tactic is that the mediator's offer may be accepted.[38]

Communication Skills and Techniques

Much conflict is based on poor communication, and poor communication can obstruct conflict resolution.[39] Communication is a problem when it is ambiguous, uncertain, destructive or over-emotional. Mediators require skills and techniques in many facets of communication, both as communicators themselves and as facilitators of the parties' communications. Mediators need to make themselves understood, to understand the parties, and to assist the parties to understand themselves and each other.[40] This is a complex issue as communication is affected by many factors including culture, class, gender, education and emotional state.

While there are many forms of communication, in most mediations the focus is on interpersonal, face-to-face communication, which is not didactic but interactive and dynamic. Good communication skills should be practised by mediators at all stages of the mediation but they will be of particular significance during the following three phases:

(a) the introductory stages, including the mediator's opening, the party presentations, and the development of the agenda, where it is important to understand the parties and define the dispute in appropriate terms;

(b) in the separate meetings, when the functions of mediators change and they both develop an alliance with each party and act as devil's advocate in the

---

37 In a construction mediation, the parties crossed the last gap by giving the disputed amount to charity.

38 David Shapiro, an experienced international mediator, refers to a case, where the mediator offered to waive his fee to enable the parties to cross the gap. The parties considered that it demonstrated partiality, and the mediation failed.

39 See Promoting constructive communication in Chapter 5.

40 H Brown and A Marriott *ADR Principles and Practice* (2nd edn), Sweet & Maxwell, London, 1999, at p 254. Mediators often have to facilitate or even conduct difficult conversations. For a 'how to' book on managing difficult conversations, see D Stone et al *Difficult conversations – how to discuss what matters most*, 1999. According to the authors, each difficult conversation is made up of three conversations – the 'what happened?' conversation, which involves disagreement about what has happened or what should happen; the feelings conversation, which asks and answers questions about feelings; and the identity conversation, which is the conversation that one has with oneself about what the situation means. The book discusses approaches, strategies and skills to manage each of these conversations constructively and avoid common pitfalls.

face of intransigence; and

(c) in the closing stages of the mediation, when it is important to avoid last-minute slippages and loss of face problems and to end on a positive and congratulatory note, without the mediator appearing patronising or self-interested in the settlement.

Appropriate verbal communication

Mediators need to develop an appropriate communication style and use of language. Generally they need to speak in a quiet, confident manner and to give complete and specific messages. They should use plain and intelligible words, and avoid legal and technical terms where these would not be understood by particular parties. Mediators should avoid negative language which is redolent of conflict, or is threatening to the parties. Where the parties themselves use inappropriate words, mediators should replace them with more suitable terms. Some examples of replacement terms are:

Positive Replacement	
Parties' Term	Mediator's Replacement
• Conflict, dispute	• Problem, situation
• Relate the facts	• Give your understanding/perceptions
• Reach agreement	• Make decisions
• Negotiations	• Discussions
• Positions, claims	• Viewpoints, how you see things
• Compromise, concessions	• Suggestions, ways of dealing with
• Custody and access	• Parenting arrangements
• Foreclosure	• Financial arrangements

Positive language can extend beyond single terms to the ways in which parties conceptualise issues. Thus where a party persists in mentioning what he or she does not want, the mediator must insist on an indication of what he or she does want. Or where a neighbour in dispute protests about not being able to play loud music for limited periods each day, the mediator should focus on the majority of time when the music can be played. Through the use of appropriate positive language, mediators can restructure the parties' perceptions of the problem and open the way for constructive problem-solving. In many cases the modelling of appropriate language will be followed by the parties.

Effective listening

A large part of the mediator's time is spent on listening to the parties. This is particularly the case in *facilitative mediation* but, because mediation is designed to open up the discussions to matters which might not be accommodated in pleadings and litigation, effective listening skills are a basic requirement for the mediator in all models of mediation.[41] Effective listening involves more than hearing spoken words: it involves properly understanding the meaning of messages.[42] A number of lessons may be drawn from the Chinese character that represents 'listening', pronounced as 'ting':[43]

(耳) **Ear**
Physiologically, we need ears to listen. Listening involves bending our ears to people.

(盁) **Eyes**
We listen with our eyes too. We know someone is listening to us when there is eye contact.

聽

(一) **One or Undivided attention**
Active listeners focus their attention on the person who is talking.

(王) **King**
True listening treats the other person as royalty. We honour the person when we listen. We acknowledge that what he or she says is important.

(心) **Heart**
Effective listening involves paying attention not just to facts but also to feelings being communicated.

Communication theorists refer to the ability of the listening brain to cope with almost twice as much communication as is provided by social speech. The listener's 'excess capacity' can be used both negatively, for example to plan a response or think of other issues, or positively, for example to identify the emotional content of the speech or distinguish broad patterns and themes.

While many professionals have developed listening skills, they may have developed in the context of a profession's narrow conception of what is relevant. By way of broad generalisation, lawyers tend to focus more on facts and information when listening, and then mainly on the 'material facts' which are relevant to a legal resolution. Social workers tend to focus more on feelings and emotions when listening to parties in conflict. Each tendency has its strengths and weaknesses in mediation. Lawyer mediators could improve their listening skills by being attentive to non-substantive matters which are important to the parties, while social workers could improve by picking up on substantive matters relevant to practical decision-making.

---

41 P Condliffe *Conflict management – a practical guide*, TAFE Publications, Abbotsford, Victoria, 1991, at p 45; and G Tillet *Resolving conflict – a practical approach*, Sydney University Press, Sydney, 1991, at pp 21–31.

42 M Anstey *Negotiating Conflict: insights and skills for negotiators and peacemakers*, Juta & Co, Kenwyn, South Africa, 1991, at p 228.

43 From the training materials of Meta HR & Communication and reproduced with their kind permission.

Causes of ineffective listening

The many factors potentially hindering effective listening can be categorised as follows:[44]

(a) Causes relating to the speaker: inaudibility, annoying mannerisms, physical appearance, tone of voice, speed of delivery, incoherence of presentation, boring content.

(b) Causes relating to the listener: inattention, discomfort, fatigue, attention to responding or questioning the speaker, ignorance of the subject-matter, psychological deafness,[45] emotional involvement, lack of comprehension skills, inability to absorb, judgmental attitude.

(c) Causes relating to environmental factors: external noise, bad lighting, poor acoustics, uncomfortable seating.

Mediators have to avoid creating barriers to effective listening. Charlton and Dewdney identified the following situations:

(a) Where the mediator finishes the sentence for the speaker.

(b) Where the mediator is talking at the same time as the parties or allows the parties to talk at the same time.

(c) Where the mediator tunes out the speaker and allows his or her own mind to move on.

(d) Where the mediator is playing with an object or doodling.

(e) Where the mediator is faking attention.

(f) Where the mediator is taking excessive notes and has his head down all the time.[46]

Listening actively

The concept of active listening denotes that good listening is not just a passive exercise.[47] Active listening involves hard work. The listener must be physically attentive, concentrate on and encourage the speaker, display an attitude of interest and concern, be non-judgmental, not be preoccupied with responding, and not be distracted by non-relevant matters. There are several goals of active listening. The first is to clarify uncertainties and avoid misunderstandings in the communication process; it enables the listener to put together a full picture of facts, content and feeling. The second is acknowledgment, that is, to indicate to a speaker that their

---

44 R Bolton *People skills: how to assert yourself, listen to others and resolve conflicts*, Simon and Schuster, Brookvale, New South Wales, 1987, at pp 15–16; and see P Condliffe *Conflict management – a practical guide*, TAFE Publications, Abbotsford, Victoria, 1991, at p 45.

45 For example, where a listener is unable to conceive the effect which domestic violence might have on a victim's behaviour.

46 R Charlton and M Dewdney *The Mediator's Handbook – skills and strategies for practitioners*, The Law Book Company, Sydney, 1995, at pp 169–70.

47 As Tillet points out, effective listening is not a passive activity like sunbathing but an active process: G Tillet *Resolving conflict – a practical approach*, Sydney University Press, Sydney, 1991, at p 27. See also G Egan *The skilled helper – a problem-solving approach to helping* (5th edn), Brooks/Cole Publishing, Pacific Grove, California, 1994, at pp 94–100.

message has been heard. The third is to help the speaker to understand better their own feelings and emotions. There are three broad categories of skills in active listening, each with a number of elements:

(a) *Attending skills:* These involve a sense of being with the client, both physically and psychologically. They include physical attention, a display of interest, appropriate body movements, encouraging noises and congenial seating. Egan refers to the **SOLER** micro-skills of attending: **S**quarely face the client, adopt an **O**pen posture, **L**ean towards the client at times, **E**ye contact, **R**elax.[48]

(b) *Following skills:* These involve indicators that the listener is comprehending the speaker. They include providing cues, not interrupting, giving minimal encouragement, taking notes, asking relevant questions, summarising and refraining from giving advice.

(c) *Reflecting skills:* These involve feeding back to the speaker the listener's understanding of their meaning, with reference to feeling as well as content. They include identification and acknowledgment of content and feeling, summarising content and feeling, clarifying questions and synthesis.

Other elements of active listening include:

- being physically and mentally prepared;
- trying to comprehend the speaker's frame of reference;
- looking for patterns, organisation and themes in the speaker's messages;
- avoiding emotional responses and moralising; and
- being aware of one's own frame of reference.[49]

Reframing

Reframing is one aspect of active listening and is regarded as an important skill for mediators.[50] Reframing involves the mediator responding to a communication from one party, or an exchange of communications between parties and, without repeating what they have said, reworking their words, terms and phrases. The mediator's response uses different words, emphasis and intonation to reflect part of what the previous speaker has said, but to change the frame of reference around it. The underlying theory is that the mediator's reframing intervention can change a party's perceptions about the dispute, or one aspect of it, and the change of perception can

---

48 G Egan *The skilled helper – a problem-solving approach to helping* (5th edn) Brooks/Cole Publishing, Pacific Grove, California, 1994, at p 91; see also D Hawkins et al *The Legal Negotiator: a handbook for managing legal negotiations more effectively*, Longman Professional, Melbourne, 1991, at p 120, for their variation, 'SOLVER'. See also P Condliffe *Conflict management – a practical guide*, TAFE Publications, Abbotsford, Victoria, 1991, at p 47.

49 See further R Charlton and M Dewdney *The Mediator's Handbook – skills and strategies for practitioners*, The Law Book Company, Sydney, 1995, at pp 168–73 for active and passive listening.

50 See R Bandler and J Grinder *Reframing: neuro-linguistic programming and the transformatting of meaning*, Real People Press, Moab Utah, 1982; H Brown and A Marriott *ADR Principles and Practice* (2nd edn), Sweet & Maxwell, London, 1999, at p 257; C Moore *The mediation process: practical strategies for resolving conflict*, Jossey-Bass, San Francisco, 1996, at pp 217–23. See also R Charlton and M Dewdney, ibid, at pp 173–6.

affect that person's attitude and behaviour in the negotiations. People in conflict tend to have a rigid version of reality, and reframing attempts to get them to see things in a different light. Successful reframing changes parties' perspectives and perceptions, which might open the door to changed conduct. For example, commentators point to 'reactive devaluation' by parties at this stage of the process: when a concession or proposal is made by one party, the opponent devalues it simply because it has originated from the other side. Reactive devaluation can be avoided by having the mediator announce the concessions or proposals.[51] In addition, the mediator can reframe concessions or proposals, in order to make them attractive to the party receiving them.[52] In Fuller's words, mediators can strip messages of their 'vituperative' content and can focus the parties' attention on the benefits of co-operation.[53]

One way of conceptualising reframing is in terms of the design of jokes.[54] A joke-teller encourages a certain point of view, but when the punchline is delivered the listener is able to see the preceding story in a different light. On the face of it, the punchline is incongruous, but when the listener catches the joke by seeing the previous narrative in a different light, then the incongruous becomes congruous. The humour is caused by the surprise, relief or delight which occurs when the punchline is delivered and the listener has to change his or her erroneous expectation. In other words, a scene is first described from one viewpoint, and then rearranged, sometimes by a single word. Likewise, mediators, through reframing, have the capacity to restructure the parties' perceptions of a dispute situation. In joke-telling the switch-over is temporary and gives rise to humour, whereas in mediation it can be permanent and give rise to insight.[55] While the joke-teller reframes to achieve laughter, the mediator reframes to contribute to problem-solving. Ury,[56] who uses the term reframing in a slightly different way, points out that every message is subject to interpretation and that reframing can be used to direct attention back to the problem of satisfying both sides' needs and to promote a mutual and therefore positive perception of the problem.[57]

This theoretical outline can be illustrated as follows. In the stock joke about sheep theft, the accused party is told by the magistrate that the evidence against him is inadequate and that he is accordingly acquitted. The accused replies, 'Thank you your worship, does that mean that I can keep the sheep?' The punchline causes the listener to think about the previous information in a different light: the accused was not innocent and had not only stolen the sheep but also beaten the court system. In the mediation context, both parties in a partnership dispute may initially perceive things in terms of past contributions, frustrated expectations, legal rights, and possible dissolution. By reframing their language, a mediator may cause them to perceive

---

51 F Sander and J Rubin 'The Janus Quality of Negotiation: Deal making and dispute settlement' (1988) 4 *Negotiation Journal* 109.
52 R Mnookin 'Why negotiations fail: an exhibition of barriers to the resolution of conflicts' (1993) 8 *Ohio State Journal on Dispute Resolution* 235 at 246 and 249.
53 L Fuller 'Mediation: its forms and functions' (1971) 44 *Southern California Law Review* 305.
54 See J Cooley 'Mediation and joke design: resolving the incongruities' (1992) 2 *Journal of Dispute Resolution* 250.
55 E de Bono *Conflicts: a better way to resolve them*, Penguin Books, Sydney, 1985, at p 25.
56 W Ury's *Getting past no: negotiating with difficult people*, Business Books, London, 1991, at pp 59–86.
57 To shift the perception, by way of analogy, from the 'half empty bottle' to the 'half full bottle'.

things in terms of present financial interests, new management and communication practices, future profitability and new business opportunities.

Functions of reframing

Reframing can serve one or more of the following purposes, although a single reframing intervention cannot serve all six. It can serve to:

- remove an accusation, hostility or verbal sting (the detoxifying function) and substitute neutral language;
- reorientate the parties from a negative to a positive perception of an issue;
- shift the focus from a positional claim to underlying interests;
- remove a personal judgment and shift the focus from the people to the problem;
- focus the parties' attention on the present and future and away from the past; and
- mutualise concerns and issues, suggesting that the parties combine against the problem.

Examples of reframing

The table on page **208** sets out possible mediator reframes for various party statements. It also indicates the objectives of each reframe, and the relevant party's hypothetical response. The responses show that the reframes achieved differing levels of success.

Problems with reframing

There are a number of potential difficulties with reframing, particularly when performed by neophyte mediators:

- it is a difficult art and if practised badly may be experienced by the speaker as nothing more than annoying parroting;[58]
- it might be seen as patronising;
- it could be perceived as the mediator favouring one party and losing his or her non-partisan role; and
- it is essentially a micro-technique which might not succeed in changing the broader narrative.[59]

Non-verbal communication

Much has been written about the importance of non-verbal communication in all spheres of human interaction.[60] Non-verbal communication comprises all those ways

---

58 Parties may think, 'Why does he keep repeating everything I say?'.
59 On this interesting debate, see J Rifkin et al 'Toward a new discourse for mediation: a critique of neutrality' (1991) 9 *MQ* 151; and M Feer 'On "toward a new discourse for mediation: a critique of neutrality"' (1992) 10 *MQ* 173.
60 See, for example, G Nierenberg and H Calero *How to read a person like a book*, Thorsons Publishers, Wellingborough, Northamptonshire, 1980; A Pease *Body language: how to read others' thoughts by their gestures*, Sheldon Press, London, 1981; G Tillet *Resolving*

Forms of Reframing			
Party statement	Mediator's Reframe	Objectives of Reframe	Possible Party Response
He has always been a hopeless business person, never delivers on time . . .	So, Rick, if deliveries were on time you could plan the production process better . . . ?	Remove judgment Shift focus from people to problem Shift focus from past to future	Well, I suppose that would help . . .
All I've had since she became a tenant is lies, nothing but bloody lies . . .	So, Shanna, you see things differently to Leigh . . . ?	Remove verbal sting, accusation Introduce neutral language	Yes, very differently . . .
We need to get rid of this fascist management style, they'll close the factory before they give the wage increase we want . . .	So, Ian, you want to negotiate an appropriate level of benefits for this industry and this enterprise . . . ?	Shift focus from position to interests Reorient from negative to positive perception	Yes, we want fair wages, an appropriate deal . . .
Well how do you operate with a senior partner who takes for ever to decide on even the smallest matters . . . ?	So Mieka is careful about making decisions which affect your partnership . . . ?	Reorient from negative to positive perception Mutualise concerns	Well, she is careful, but she takes a long time about it . . .
I refuse to settle unless Greg gives the car to me . . .	So, Margaret, we need to talk about transportation in the future . . . ?	Shift focus from position to interest Mutualise concerns	That's right, how am I going to get the children to day care without transport?
I have to get out of this mediation now . . .	So, Bill, you're anxious about whether you can negotiate successfully . . . ?	Shift from position to interest	No, I have to pick up the children . . .

of communicating other than through the spoken or written word. In some situations it can be the most important feature of communication, with greater significance than verbal messages. It can convey status, contempt, power, superiority, anxiety or lack of confidence. It can serve to threaten, intimidate, encourage or reassure. Mediators need to read and understand the non-verbal communications of the other parties. They also need to be aware of their own non-verbal communication throughout the process; the control and manipulation of their own non-verbal messages can be an effective tool for mediators.[61] Some aspects of non-verbal communication follow.

Physical environment

The physical environment includes the locality, appearance and connotation of the building in which the mediation is held (for example courthouse, community centre), the style and affluence of the entrance and general premises, the size and degree of formality of the mediation room, the seating arrangements, the location of the parties in relation to walls, exits, clocks and windows, and all other physical features of the mediation environment. These factors all convey messages to the parties, and have the potential to be planned and arranged by mediators in advance of the meetings.

Paralanguage

Paralanguage comprises those additions to the spoken word which add to the meaning of the words themselves. Examples of paralanguage are tone, inflection, volume, pitch, emphasis, sighs and yawns. The tone of spoken language is a particularly important clue to the speaker's state of mind and meaning. Mediators need to attend to all forms of paralanguage and to diagnose their significance.

Body language

Body language refers to all aspects of bodily appearance and movement which convey messages to observers.[62] It includes clothing, physique, posture, body movements, hand gestures, facial expressions and eye motions. Body language can convey a wide range of attitudes and emotions, and needs to be recognised and diagnosed by mediators. The parties can fake or mask body language to some degree, but this is less easy to do than is the case with verbal communications. Sometimes it is extremely difficult to disguise body language, for example tone of voice or physiological reactions such as blushing and shortness of breath.

There are many divergences in the use and significance of body language among cultures, classes, genders and occupations. There is probably no single bodily gesture which would have a uniform meaning across all these categories of people. Thus in western culture, eye contact is a signal of openness, trustworthiness and respect,

---

conflict – *a practical approach*, Sydney University Press, Sydney, 1991, at pp 24–7; and C Moore *The Mediation Process: practical strategies for resolving conflict* (2nd edn), Jossey-Bass, San Francisco, 1996, at pp 186–90.

61 J Folberg and A Taylor *Mediation: a comprehensive guide to resolving conflicts without litigation*, Jossey-Bass, San Francisco, 1984, at p 117.

62 A Pease *Body language: how to read others' thoughts by their gestures*, Sheldon Press, London, 1981; and J Folberg and A Taylor, ibid, at pp 117–24.

whereas averted eyes are a sign of evasiveness or lack of confidence. In many non-western cultures, eye contact is a sign of rudeness and disrespect, particularly with a higher status person, and averted eyes convey respect and esteem. Some generalised features of body language in western societies include the following: open limb positions imply receptivity to what is being said, crossed or folded limbs suggest defensiveness; forward-leaning body posture suggests attentiveness, a backward stance suggests indifference; open hands suggest plain dealing, closed fists or pointed fingers suggest aggression.

The skills of reading and interpreting body language involve a combination of intuition, awareness, training and experience. The mediator's first function is to observe non-verbal messages, though much micro-language in the face and eyes is not easy to detect. The mediator then needs to make an inference, for example that blushing or dilation of the pupils represents increased anxiety or fear, and intervene appropriately. A mediator should not, however, read too much into a single cue. A sudden bodily movement may be caused as much by discomfort, habit or a medical condition as it is by increased anger or boredom. Where behavioural signals occur in clusters, for example dilation of the pupils, heavier breathing and hand movements together, they are easier to diagnose. Body language is highly relevant where there is incongruence between the verbal and non-verbal messages, for example where the words signify assent but the crossed legs or nervous eyes suggest the opposite. Close eye contact is necessary to detect incongruities between the spoken word and body language. Mediators can use separate meetings to raise and deal with body language issues. They can check out the meaning of one party's gestures, which may be well-understood by the other party. They can advise a party on annoying habits of which they were unaware, such as fidgeting or nervous tapping. They can also inform each party about strong signals from the other to which they might have previously been oblivious.

Mediators also need to be attentive to their own body language, which can reveal bias, impatience or boredom. Some actions will be generally appropriate in mediation, for example open body positions, direct eye contact and congruent facial expressions. Others will usually be inappropriate: for example frowning when a party is making their opening presentation or folding the arms when a party is proclaiming the veracity of their view. Yet others require the mediator to make judgments and adaptations for particular circumstances, for example choice of clothing,[63] handshake, gaze[64] and facial expressions. Some long-held habits, which could disconcert or mislead the parties, may be difficult for mediators to adapt.[65] Experienced mediators use body language as a significant resource: for example they can guide the conversation between the parties with simple hand directions to ensure that they speak directly to each other.

Questioning

Mediators can use questions for many different purposes: to seek and give information, to gain attention, to maintain control, to check the accuracy of

---

63 The clothing of the parties is also significant. In a mediation between a police officer and an elderly female, the police officer arrived in uniform. The other party experienced this as threatening, and with proper planning it could have been avoided.

64 One of the definitions of a mediator is someone who can sleep with his or her eyes open.

65 Videos go a long way towards developing self-awareness of unconscious tics and twitches.

communications, to help the parties to start thinking, and to suggest options for settlement.[66] The amount of questioning undertaken by mediators depends in part on the model of mediation being used. In the *facilitative* model of mediation very few direct questions are asked of the parties, but the mediator does request them to explain matters to each other. In the *settlement* and *evaluative* models, more questioning takes place. The stage of the mediation is also an important consideration. In the early parts of the joint meetings many mediators will tend to ask few questions and restrict those to open questions, whereas in the separate meetings they will use more questions and switch to probing or reflective questions. The amount of questioning will also depend on professional background and personal style. Haynes and Haynes[67] suggest that mediators accomplish most of their work through questions, but this is not a universal view. There is no doubt that some mediators over-rely on questions, and the communication lapses into interrogation and cross-examination.[68]

Rather than adopting a quantitative approach to questions, it is better to appreciate the many categories of questions which mediators might ask and to assess the appropriateness of each category for the particular dispute, disputants and stage of mediation. The following are some categories and examples of questions which mediators might ask, and an indication of when each might be appropriate. They are based on a fictional workers' compensation claim.

Open questions

Open questions are general and indeterminate and give the parties wide latitude in answering. They are appropriate at most stages of the mediation process. They are unthreatening, do not disclose partiality and are a practical way of getting the parties to disclose and exchange information. An open question, allowing for a wide range of responses, is 'Julie, would you like to describe in your own words how the accident at work has affected your life?' A more focused open question gives the speaker less time to ramble: for example, 'Could you tell us more about how the accident has affected your work performance in the last 12 months?'[69]

Closed questions

A closed question usually invites an affirmative or negative response, or some other very specific answer: for example, 'Could you tell me, Bill, whether your method of working contributed to the accident in any way?' Because of the narrower range of

---

66 H Brown and A Marriott *ADR Principles and Practice* (2nd edn), Sweet & Maxwell, London, 1999, at pp 338–9; D Hawkins et al *The Legal Negotiator*, Longman Professional, Melbourne, 1991, at pp 123–6.

67 J Haynes and G Haynes *Mediating Divorce: casebook of strategies for successful family negotiations*, 1989, at pp 32–4.

68 P Condliffe *Conflict management – a practical guide*, TAFE Publications, Abbotsford, Victoria, 1991, at p 47; J Folberg and A Taylor *Mediation: a comprehensive guide to resolving conflicts without litigation*, Jossey-Bass, San Francisco, 1984, at p 109, refer to questions as the 'most overused tool' in the novice mediator's repertoire. Unfortunately, the overuse is not restricted to novices.

69 J Stulberg *Taking Charge/Managing Conflict*, Lexington Books, Lexington, Massachusetts, 1987, at p 78.

answers they allow, closed questions give greater control to the mediator than open questions. They are generally less suitable than open questions. They are definitely not appropriate in the early stages of mediation, nor where they invoke a defensive response from the party being questioned.

Clarifying questions

Clarifying questions are used to illuminate the mediator's understanding of a communication, whether on matters of fact or emotion: for example, 'Is it correct, Mr Jolsen, that you were under the impression that the machine had been serviced shortly before the accident?' Clarifying questions enable the party to verify, modify or refute the mediator's understanding of the situation. They are appropriate where parties are not being sufficiently specific on important issues, particularly in separate meetings.

Reflective questions

Reflective questions involve the mediator picking up a key word or phrase used by one of the parties and reframing it into a question which causes the party to think about the issue in a qualified and possibly more positive way. Thus an employee who indicates that he feels disempowered in the mediation might be asked, 'So at the present time you feel that you have little power?' Reflective questions are appropriate throughout the mediation where the mediator needs to intervene through active listening or reframing. They might comprise a single word used by a party and repeated as a question: for example, 'Disempowered?'

Probing questions

Probing questions solicit further information, specificity or justification. Thus a mediator might ask probingly, 'John, if you are retrained for another position by your employer, how will you deal with the new technology which has been a problem in the past?' Probing questions may demand a justification: for example, 'Why do you want that particular form of rehabilitation?' As probing questions might make the parties defensive, they are more appropriate in the separate meetings.

Leading questions

Leading questions imply their own answer: for example, 'Now Bernadette, you have been the production manager of this company since 1993, is that correct?' In the court context, leading questions can only be used for limited purposes, for example to elicit uncontroversial information. In mediation they could also be used for this limited purpose but are generally considered to be inappropriate because they involve the questioner eliciting information which he or she considers relevant. They also tend to be fact-centred and not person-centred.

Cross-examining questions

Cross-examining questions are designed to test the accuracy or reliability of the person questioned. In court hearings, cross-examining questions are also used to discredit a witness, often by contrasting one statement with another in an accusatory manner: for example 'Mr O'Moore, you are now saying that there were adequate safety precautions, but did you not earlier concede that the machine had a notorious reputation in the factory?' Generally this type of questioning is not appropriate for mediators, and lawyers are not permitted to cross-examine parties or witnesses in mediation.

Hypothetical questions

Hypothetical questions raise a general possibility, without any commitment being made. They are regarded as highly suitable for mediation, particularly in the negotiation stages. Thus a mediator may ask, 'As we are stuck on the amount to be paid, would it be useful to consider the timing and terms of payment?' While this may amount to the mediator 'suggesting' one aspect of the solution, the hypothetical way in which it is raised allows the parties either to reject it or to explore it further. Parties can also use hypothetical questions to raise possible options without being committed to them: for example 'If we were to agree on the compensation in this matter, what would you be able to do on the issue of safety training?'

Disarming/distracting questions

Mediators sometimes use questions with the sole purpose of leading the parties away from a destructive interchange and refocusing them on the issues. An example of a distracting question by the mediator, in the context of an angry exchange over safety conditions, is, 'How many employees were there in the company?' A disarming question is, 'Would it be correct that you have both acted in good faith throughout this difficult time?' These kinds of question are appropriate where the mediator decides that they are the best tactical intervention in the face of destructive tendencies.

Rhetorical questions

A rhetorical question is asked not to obtain information but to make a point or produce an effect. Thus a mediator may ask, 'Which of you wants to go through a torturous trial?' to imply that no reasonable person would contemplate such an option. Rhetorical questions in mediation might be an appropriate way of confronting the parties with reality, as in the above example. They would be inappropriate where they disclosed the mediator's view on the merits.

Suggestive questions

Where mediators are reluctant to make statements which impinge on the merits of the dispute, they may resort to a suggestive question: for example, 'Would it be possible to consider ways of using the company's resources to help the employee with alterations to his house?' However, these questions could also draw the mediator into matters of content and are usually used when the parties are making no headway in creating settlement options on their own.

Directed and undirected questions

A directed question is asked of a particular party in the mediation, whereas an undirected question is asked generally and can be responded to by any party. The directed question is appropriate where the mediator wishes to control the disclosure of information. The undirected question is appropriate where the mediator not only wants the disclosure of information but also wants to find out about the respective roles of the parties and their relationship with each other. Thus the undirected question, 'How did employees feel about safety before the accident?' may reveal not only which party has a good understanding of this issue, but also the nature of manager-worker relationships.

Reiterating

Mediators need to prevent anything of value 'falling off' the negotiation table. In the heat of the moment it is possible for an apology, a concession or a significant offer not to be heard by the non-speaking party. Here the mediator might either ask the speaker to repeat the statement, or personally reiterate what was said. Reiteration can be used to step up a weak signal coming from one party and not being heard by the other. Helping the parties to hear one another when they are not listening adequately and are talking past each other is part of the mediator's general role as a communicator.

Paraphrasing

Paraphrasing is an intervention which picks up on an aspect of one party's statement, usually its emotional content, and seeks a response to this aspect from the other party. It is a technique used by mediators to keep the dialogue moving between the parties in a way which deals with important issues and feelings. Paraphrasing is a significant feature of *facilitative mediation* where it is regarded as more in keeping with the objectives of mediation than a series of questions by the mediator. The following interchange illustrates the mediator's use of paraphrasing:

Mediator:	'Mr Wade, Mr Cavanagh is saying that although the bank was legally justified in its actions, they have caused him considerable stress and embarrassment in his community, can you respond to him on that?'
Mr Wade:	'Look, we regret the embarrassment very much. Mr Cavanagh, you were always a good customer and we acknowledge that the collapse of your business was not altogether your fault. But at the end of the day, a bank is a business not a charity.'
Mediator:	'Mr Cavanagh, Mr Wade has expressed his regret at the inconvenience to you and has emphasised that you were a good customer. How do you feel now that you have heard that?'
Mr Cavanagh:	'Well, it's the first time I've ever heard that language from a bank, but I'd still like to keep the business . . .'

Paraphrasing should be done evenhandedly so that the mediator does not only paraphrase the communications of one party. It can become strained where it is the only intervention which keeps the parties communicating with each other.

Summarising

Summarising involves the mediator briefly restating the important features of the preceding discussion and also identifying the dominant feelings of the parties. Summarising serves several purposes:

- it provides a neutral and organised version of a line of discussion;
- it simplifies convoluted exchanges, and it reminds parties about progress made;
- it allows the mediator to test his or her understanding;
- it provides acknowledgment to the parties that they have been understood;
- it establishes a platform for the next round of discussions; and
- it assists mediators to develop trust by using key words spoken by the parties and similar word associations.

Summarising requires mediators to retain, recall and condense information and to identify and acknowledge emotions.

As regards timing, summarising can take place at different stages of the mediation, for example:

- after the party presentations;
- after each item on the list of issues has been dealt with;
- at the end of the separate meetings;
- at the resumption of a mediation after it has been adjourned;
- when the parties reach an impasse; and
- before the agreement is finalised.

In the early stages of a mediation the summarising will tend to identify the contrasting positions of the parties, whereas later in the mediation it will emphasise points of agreement.

Note-taking and drafting

It is rare for mediation proceedings to be recorded and for a transcript to be produced. Nevertheless, mediators normally take only very limited notes and seldom act as scribes in any comprehensive sense.[70] Brief notes are taken in the early stages to record names correctly and to assist in identifying the issues, establishing common ground, and constructing an agenda. In the negotiation stages, mediators need to record offers, the sequence of offers and counter-offers, important settlement options and details of points of agreement. Mediators should also record concessions, acknowledgments and apologies made by the parties but lost in the heat of the moment, and refer to them as soon as it is tactically appropriate to do so. In addition to this, mediators should keep notes of issues raised but not dealt with. In the separate meetings notes are taken to record important confidential information as a way of avoiding its inadvertent disclosure.

Mediators require techniques to balance note-taking with the 'following' and 'attentive' skills referred to above. This requires mediators to be selective in what is taken down. A common technique is for mediators to draw a line down the centre of a page and to use a different side to record each party's phrases or key words during the party presentations. Common ground between the parties can be identified with connecting lines across the page. Co-mediation allows one mediator to perform

---

70 But see H Brown and A Marriott *ADR Principles and Practice* (2nd edn), Sweet & Maxwell, London, 1999, at pp 350–1. Lap-top computers and electronic whiteboards assist with note-taking but can be distracting and raise confidentiality problems. See also the section on Defining and ordering issues in Chapter 4.

these functions, while the other follows and attends to the speaking party. Mediators need to be sensitive to any sudden changes, for example when they stop taking notes or start taking them, as this may concern the parties. Notes are normally destroyed after the mediation, often in the presence of the parties.

In some situations mediators will require drafting skills. They may be responsible for drafting a written record of the agreement or issues on which no agreement was reached. Here the mediator requires the techniques of a good wordsmith – the ability to use plain English, to reflect the parties' intentions, to use the parties' own words where appropriate, to record sufficient detail, to avoid ambiguity and lack of clarity,[71] and to use appropriate grammar and syntax. In commercial disputes, where parties are usually legally represented, the lawyers tend to draft the agreement. Even here mediators may have an editorial or advisory role in the drafting.[72]

Other communication skills

Empathising

Empathising has been referred to as an 'essential skill' in dispute resolution.[73] Empathising involves mediators understanding and accepting without judgment what the parties are saying. It requires mediators to suspend their own biases and any evaluative function. It does not involve mediators becoming sympathetic with one of the parties' positions, or agreeing with them, or indicating that they are justified in their viewpoints. It is the skill of getting inside the dispute, of understanding it from each party's point of view, and of communicating that understanding to the parties. This involves moving beyond factual data and acknowledging the parties' anger, anxiety, confusion, fear and the like. Acceptance of these emotions is shown by acknowledging, reflecting and clarifying the parties' feelings.

Empathising is not an inherent quality which mediators either have or do not have. As with other mediator skills, it is possible to be trained in empathy, particularly in communicating understanding to the parties. While it is a useful technique, it should not be overused as some parties may not expect that their deep-seated feelings will be acknowledged and aired in mediation.

Using humour

The appropriate use of humour is an important technique for mediators.[74] Laughter serves to relieve tension and relax the parties and can even be used to make a point in a subtle way. Humour will be appropriate where it is not at the expense of the

---

71 In some cases parties may only be able to agree on a draft where there is sufficient ambiguity to allow each of them to portray it as a victory to their followers. This requires a different drafting skill. Planned ambiguity can, of course, have long-term disadvantages.

72 See Chapter 4 for guiding principles for drafting settlements.

73 G Tillet *Resolving conflict – a practical approach*, Sydney University Press, Sydney, 1991, at p 83. See also C Moore *The mediation process: practical strategies for resolving conflict*, Jossey-Bass, San Francisco, 1996, at p 210 and G Egan *The skilled helper – a problem-solving approach to helping* (5th edn) Brooks/Cole Publishing, Pacific Grove, California, 1994, at pp 106–8.

74 A M Wimmer 'The jolly mediator: some serious thoughts about humour in mediation'

parties and does not reflect on sensitive matters. Self-directed humour is the safest for mediators, and sarcasm is seldom proper. The timing of any attempts at humour is also important. If used too early in the process, humour may be taken as a sign of flippancy or as an evasion of the real issues. If used when emotions are very high, it may be seen as insensitive. Humour should not be used too frequently and mediators should leave their full comic routines at the door of the mediation room.

Using silence

Mediators can use silence strategically to induce one or both parties to make an offer or proposal which might otherwise not be forthcoming. This can be a manipulative strategy where a party is embarrassed by silence and volunteers information which might otherwise have remained confidential. Mediators themselves should not be afraid of silence and should use it where they judge it to be an appropriate method of furthering the negotiations without it being intimidating.[75]

Avoiding Mediator Traps

Mediators require skills and techniques to avoid several 'traps'[76] into which they can readily fall. The traps include:

Being inadequately prepared

There are two levels at which mediators could find themselves unprepared. The first relates to the specific case which they are mediating. Here they need to be prepared on the nature of the dispute and disputants, the possible causes of the conflict, potential interventions and organisational matters. The second relates to the general features of all mediations. Here they need to be prepared on theories of conflict, negotiation strategies, communication dynamics, dealing with impasses and emotions, and the other skills and techniques required in mediation. In some cases there will be no occasion for specific preparation as the mediator receives no prior knowledge of the case, and only generic preparation is possible.

Losing control of the process

One of the primary functions of mediators, as outsiders to the dispute, is to provide structure and control for the parties. While mediators may share their control with

---

(1994) 10 *Negotiation Journal* 193; K King 'But I'm not a funny person – the use of humour in dispute resolution' (1988) 4 *Negotiation Journal* 119; and J Stulberg *Taking Charge/Managing Conflict*, Lexington Books, Lexington, Massachusetts, 1987, at p 100.

75 J Stulberg *Taking Charge/Managing Conflict*, ibid at pp 100–1, advises, 'let silence ring'.

76 See J Haynes 'Avoiding traps mediators set for themselves' (1986) 2 *Negotiation Journal* 187–94; see also M Dewdney *Common problems for mediators*, 1994, unpublished; and I Hanger 'Eight practical pitfalls observed in mediation' (1995) 6 *Queensland ADR Review* 8.

the parties, for example on whether there should be an adjournment or whether advisers should be present, they should also retain ultimate control over the process, particularly regarding the mediation guidelines. While mediators may on occasions overlook minor breaches of the guidelines, for example where the parties interrupt one another, they should intervene where the breaches amount to their losing control. Mediators should also not lose control to lawyers or other advisers to the parties, who should be there in a supportive and not a principal or controlling role.

Losing impartiality

Impartiality is both an ethical requirement for mediators and a pragmatic condition for retaining the parties' confidence. There are many ways in which mediators may forfeit the appearance of impartiality: by being judgmental, by arguing with or acting as the advocate of one of the parties, by giving advice, by questioning too directly, or by disclosing their feelings through body language. Impartiality is difficult to maintain where the mediator is an expert in the substantive area of the dispute or where there are strong value issues at stake, for example allegations of victimisation in the workplace, environmental degradation or domestic violence at home. However, while impartiality is hard to establish, it is easily lost, and mediators should be assiduous about avoiding the partiality trap.

Ignoring emotions

Mediation aspires to acknowledge the emotional and psychological dimensions of conflict more than some forms of conflict management. Whereas emotional factors have very limited relevance in the litigation process, mediation allows them to be expressed, acknowledged and validated. Thus in a personal injury claim against a large organisation, the plaintiff, spouse and relations can all be allowed to vent their feelings of anger, frustration and despair before an attempt is made to negotiate on issues of liability and damages. Some mediators fall into the trap of forcing the parties into a cool, rational and objective approach towards reaching a settlement. Where mediators ignore overt or underlying emotions, there is a danger that the parties might not be ready to move to a resolution, that they will find the process alienating and ungratifying, or that a settlement may later come unstuck.

Moving too quickly into solutions

Mediation places a high premium on defining the dispute in terms of underlying needs and interests before moving into solutions. Where mediators allow parties to move too quickly into solutions there is a danger that they will focus only on monetary or material factors and ignore matters of emotional significance or process value. There is also a danger that the parties will move into incremental bargaining and fail to close the final gap, or reach a financial settlement which does not exploit all potential sources of value at the negotiation table. A quick solution may also fail to address the underlying issue, in which case the settlement may not be durable. Mediators should also recognise that their own interests in achieving settlements could induce them to fall into the solution trap.

Being too directive

It has been shown that one of the most debated issues in the theory and practice of mediation is the appropriate degree of directiveness of mediators.[77] There are several dangers in mediators being too directive. They may lose the trust of the parties, the parties may feel coerced into settlement, mediators may pursue their personal agendas, the settlement may not reflect the parties' interests, and the market image of mediation may be damaged. While the directiveness trap is a question of degree, mediators should recognise the underlying premise that mediation allows for party self-determination on matters of content.

Failing to recognise futility

Where an impasse cannot be broken, a mediator may be able to help the parties most by recognising that it is futile to continue. Shapiro refers to one such case, where the mediator terminated the mediation, whereupon the dispute settled within a few hours thereafter. He cites another case, where the parties were surprised by the mediator's refusal to continue, and changed their intransigent positions.[78]

---

77 See Chapter 1.
78 D Shapiro 'Pushing the envelope – selective techniques for tough mediations' (2000) *ADRLJ* 117 at 124.

Part III — Practice

7

The Mediation Movement in the UK

Introduction

Part III of this book deals with mediation practice in the UK. Here mediation practice is understood in a broad sense to include all activities carried out in the name of mediation and conciliation, and closely related Alternative Dispute Resolution ('ADR') systems. The impact on mediation practice by the civil justice reforms in England and Wales, courts in the UK, a wide range of mediation organisations, lawyers, other professionals, industry and government is examined in the next chapter. The breadth of mediation practice in the UK is described in Chapter 8. The policy issues, which are likely to have far-reaching implications for mediation practice in the UK are considered in Chapter 9, whilst some of the practical issues, which may change the face of mediation practice in the UK are considered in Chapter 10. The important issues of mediation quality, training and standards are discussed in Chapter 11. In Chapter 12 the legal issues associated with mediation practice are explored. Chapter 13 provides an overview of likely future trends and themes in mediation practice in the UK. It is hoped that this Part of the book will provide a starting point for further inquiry into how the practice of mediation in the UK should develop. The next chapter traces the evolution of mediation practice and sets the context in which mediation is practised in the UK.

Evolution of Mediation in the UK

Traditional mediation is believed to have its roots in Confucianism. The peaceful organisation of society, according to Confucius, starts from proper inquiry and understanding. Inquiry and understanding lead to compassion and empathy, the core of Confucianism. The principle of harmony is another basic tenet of Confucianism that aspires toward a conflict free, group-based system of social interaction.[1] The concepts of inquiry, understanding, empathy and forging harmonious relationships are the essence of mediation.

In distributing justice, Confucianism requires that the needs of each party are taken into account. There is an emphasis in Chinese culture, therefore, on achieving

---

1   O Shenkar and S Ronen 'The cultural context of negotiations: the implications of Chinese interpersonal norms' (1987) 23(2) *The Journal of Applied Behavioural Science* 266.

collective good, so that the merits of each party in a dispute are secondary.[2] The objective is the restoration of social order and the integrity of the collective whole.[3] Finally, according to Confucianism, a person defines his or her identity, rights and obligations according to the perceived relationship between the parties. As such, his or her sense of procedural and distributive justice varies according to that perception. Right and wrong are not determined by the merits of each case regardless of the relative position or relationships between the parties. Mediation emphasises preservation of harmony and relationships, and de-emphasises the rights or wrongs of the matter in dispute.

There is an absence of study on how the traditional form of mediation was conducted. However, it is clear that it was not institutionalised, but was highly informal and unstructured. For example, mediation rules and procedures and mediators' codes of conduct did not exist. Mediation training was also non-existent. It is said that generally one or more disputants would initiate the mediation by approaching an authority figure, often a respected leader or elder with standing in the community, to act as an intermediary. The intermediary derives his or her authority from the parties' deference to him or her and their trust in his or her capabilities, knowledge, experience and sense of fairness. Disputes are resolved through moral persuasion and a strong emphasis on the importance of maintaining harmonious relationships.[4] A mediator in a traditional mediation plays an active role. He or she intervenes with the primary objective of restoring the ties of the parties. He or she may be described as an educator of good social conduct and may chide the parties for their roles in the dispute, hence reinforcing standards of behaviour expected of upstanding members of the community. The mediator may also be described as a guardian of community interests who reflects the collectivist, as opposed to an individualist culture.[5]

With industrialisation in the UK and globalisation of the economy, highly formal business practices and relationships underpin commerce, and transactions are complex and documented with great precision. The pace of work is demanding, and working environments in large organisations are impersonal. With urbanisation, people no longer live in communities that they closely identify with.[6] The culture

---

2   W Felstiner, R Abel and A Sarat 'The Emergence and Transformation of Disputes: Naming, Blaming and Claiming' (1980–1) 15 *Law & Society Review* 631.

3   M Galanter 'Reading the Landscape of Disputes: What We Know and Don't Know (and Think We Know) About Our Allegedly Contentious Society' (1983) 31 *UCLA Law Review* 4 at 58.

4   V Taylor and M Pryles 'The cultures of dispute resolution in Asia' in M Pryles (ed) *Dispute Resolution in Asia*, 1997, at pp 1–23. Other core values include the importance of family, emphasis on saving and planning, and a yearning for progress. However, it is noted that the similarities existed only at a superficial level and a more in depth analysis would reveal considerable divergence between the different countries and ethnic groups in Asia.

5   H Chia and S Chu 'Mediating across cultures – are we supplementing our cultural values through mediation?' *The Alumnus*, July 1999, at p 20.

6   N Tan and K Lim 'Community mediation – models for practice' Paper delivered on 27 March 1999 at the Second Conference on ADR: Mediation – yesterday's ideas, today's techniques, National University of Singapore, Singapore. *Conference Proceedings*, at p 47. See also L Lim and C Liew 'Community mediation – cultural roots and legal heritage', Conference Proceedings, ibid, at p 34.

emphasises individualism and personal liberty, privacy and personal space. These characteristics affect how differences are resolved in the UK. With increasing affluence, a 'fault-based' culture has developed. Litigation has been the 'usual' mode of formal dispute resolution in the UK. Litigation emphasises rights and entitlements. Other than turning to the courts, other impersonal means are employed to resolve disputes, including complaints to Members of Parliament, the police and other authorities.

Modern mediation has its roots in America, when in 1913 a small claims mediation scheme was introduced in the Municipal Court in Cleveland Ohio.[7] The development of mediation followed a period of significant growth in arbitration, which was considered at the time to be a strong indication by business of its aversion to courts.[8] In turn in the 1930s US judges urged lawyers to consider conciliatory methods of dispute resolution.[9] By the late 1960s, mediation was considered a means of increasing access to justice in the US.[10] By the mid to late 1970s mediation's potential for reducing court caseloads led to 'quantitative – efficiency' arguments in favour of mediation.[11] Mediation became part of a larger reform movement directed towards resolving the internal problems of courts.[12] The impetus for mediation in the US came from a conception of crisis in the US judicial system.[13] American judges' pre-occupation with mediation led to a plethora of court-sponsored schemes. By the 1990s, mediation in America was considered part of a trend towards private justice and, in particular, the use by organisations with economic power of private dispute resolution processes.[14]

In the UK in the early 1970s, the Finer Report[15] recommended mediation for the resolution of family disputes. It is believed that the failure to implement the Report proposals provided the impetus for the development of independent family mediation services in Bristol in 1978, which was followed by the establishment of the South East London Family Mediation Bureau at Bromley in 1979 and the National Family Conciliation Council in 1981. There were parallel developments in court-annexed family mediation, conducted by district judges or welfare officers. The first developments were in the Western Circuit in 1977. The endorsement provided by the

---

7 J S Auerbach *Justice Without Law?* Oxford University Press, New York, 1983, at p 97.

8 C Harrington 'De-legalisation Reform Movements' in R Abel (ed) *The Politics of Informal Justice, vol 1*, Academic Press, New York, 1982, at p 40.

9 J Resnik 'Failing Faith: Adjudicatory Procedure in Decline' (1986) 53 *University of Chicago Law Review* 494 at 535.

10 C Menkel-Meadow 'Pursuing Settlement in an Adversary Culture: A Tale of Innovation Co-opted or "The Law of ADR"' (1991) 19 *Florida State University Law Review* 6; and M Cappelletti 'Alternative Dispute Resolution Processes within the Framework of the World-wide Access to Justice Movement' (1993) 56(3) *Modern Law Review* 288.

11 W Landes and R Posner 'Adjudication as a Private Good' (1978) 12 *Journal of Legal Studies* 235.

12 C Harrington 'The Politics of Participation and Non-participation in Dispute Processes' (1984) 6(2) *Law & Policy* 203 at 204.

13 S Roberts 'ADR and Civil Justice: an Unresolved Relationship' (1993) 56(3) *Modern Law Review* 452.

14 G Bryant 'Privatisation and the New Market for Disputes: a Framework for Analysis and Preliminary Assessment' (1992) 12 *Studies in Law Politics and Society* 367.

15 Finer Report *Report of the Committee on One Parent Families*, Cmnd 5629, HMSO, London, 1974.

Booth Committee in 1995 to court-annexed family mediation[16] led to more widespread use of mediation by family courts. By 1993, for example, there had been approximately 6,500 independent family mediations and 19,000 court-annexed family mediations.[17]

Following closely on the heels of development in family mediation was the growth in community mediation from the mid-1980s. During a period of just over a decade, the number of community mediation services has rapidly increased. In 1985, for example, there were six community mediation schemes in England and Wales, and by 1995 there were 36 established schemes. The number increased to 65 in 1996.[18] One of the earliest schemes, the Bolton Neighbour Dispute Service, has been a model for the start-up of similar schemes throughout the UK. Following the appointment in 1991 of a co-ordinator, the Service trained 25 volunteers and had mediated about 50 cases in the first six months. Growth in other areas, in particular commercial mediation, began in the early 1990s, although in some areas, like personal injury and clinical negligence, take-up of mediation has occurred only more recently. Court-based mediation programmes were until the mid-1990s confined to family courts, but are now flourishing. The other characteristic of mediation growth in the UK has been the slower development in Northern Ireland and Scotland. Much of the activity there is still confined to family cases.[19]

The mediation movement in the UK has been motivated by a number of factors, including calls to preserve family, to reduce the costs of conflict and to make more responsible use of public resources for dispute resolution. By the mid-1990s, mediation in the UK was beginning to incorporate the typology identified by Harrington and Merry,[20] Auerbach[21] and Bush and Folger:[22]

- the 'satisfaction' rationale, particularly in the case of family mediation, where mediation is used as a tool for satisfying human needs;
- the 'social justice' rationale, especially in the context of community mediation, where mediation is used to help build communities;
- the 'social transformation' rationale for community and public sector dispute resolution, where mediation is used as a vehicle for transforming individuals and society;[23] and

---

16 Booth Committee *Report of the Committee on Matrimonial Causes*, HMSO, London, 1985.
17 Lord Chancellor's Department *Looking to the Future: mediation and the grounds for divorce*, London, HMSO, 1993.
18 T Marshall and M Walpole *Bringing people together: mediation and the reparation projects in Great Britain*, Research & Planning Unit, Paper 33, London HMSO, 1985; G Davis et al *A preliminary study of victim-offender mediation and reparation schemes in England and Wales*, Research Planning Unit, Paper 42, London HMSO, 1987; Mediation UK *Mediation Digest*, No 3, 1996; and J Dignan et al *Neighbour Disputes: comparing the cost and effectiveness of a mediation and alternative approaches*, Centre for Criminological and Legal Research, University of Sheffield, 1996.
19 R E Mackay and A J Brown *Community Mediation in Scotland: a study of implementation*, The Scottish Office Central Research Unit, Edinburgh, 1999.
20 C Harrington and S Merry 'Ideological Production: the Making of Community Mediation' (1988) 22(4) *Law & Society Review* 709.
21 J Auerbach *Justice without law*, Oxford University Press, New York, 1983, at p 57.
22 R A Bush and J P Folger *The Promise of Mediation: Responding to Conflict through Empowerment and Recognition*, Jossey-Bass, San Francisco, 1994.
23 In Northern Ireland, in particular, the use of mediation has sought to achieve

- the 'oppression' rationale, apparent in some commercial contexts, where mediation is used as an instrument of social control, a tool for the strong to use against the weak.

The mediation movement in the UK has been influenced by modern ADR movements and practices from overseas. Countries like the US and Australia, and to a lesser extent Canada, Hong Kong, South Africa and New Zealand, have influenced the direction and practice of mediation in the UK. The UK has looked to these countries and systems for ideas and to learn from their experience. Although it is unwise to adopt foreign practices in toto without scrutiny and review, it is too sweeping to reject the adoption of relevant and useful practices, without studying the implications of any differences in culture, demographics, economics, and legal developments.

The last 18 months has seen a spurt in mediation growth, across a range of sectors, in the UK. Civil justice reforms in England and Wales and access to funding for legally-assisted mediation parties have provided catalysts. It is an important time for the development of mediation in the UK, as a number of policy issues require debate and resolution, including public awareness of mediation, the extent to which mediation participation should be encouraged or compelled, whether and if so what kind of court-based mediation should be set up, and mediation training and standards. Although debate has been generated, critical questions remain unanswered. Despite the uncertainty in the future direction of mediation practice, there exists enormous interest in mediation across different fields and sectors, and mediation-related events and activities are increasing both in number and popularity. The recent past has seen more cases being submitted to mediation and the steady expansion of the scope of its application. Mediation organisations are proliferating, lawyers and other professionals are being trained in mediation, industry is piloting mediation schemes, government is both promoting and using mediation, and technical developments are encouraging innovative dispute resolution applications. Furthermore, the study of mediation, as well as research and development efforts, are on the rise.

More research is required and studies need to be conducted. Developments in the European Union need to be monitored, as these will also shape the future direction of mediation practice in the UK. The Lord Chancellor's Discussion Paper on ADR[24] has confirmed the Lord Chancellor's interest in the development of ADR is consistent with the government's aims, particularly following the appointment of the Lord Chancellor's Department Minister with responsibility for development of ADR. The Lord Chancellor has also announced an intention to launch an ADR awareness campaign and to set up a working party to develop ideas for increasing awareness. He will consider further mediation pilot schemes to explore the compatibility of different kinds of ADR with different types of dispute.[25]

This chapter describes how different institutions and groups have contributed to the mediation movement in the UK. The significant progress of the movement within the last 18 months can be attributed in part to the support it receives from the

---

reconciliation of divided communities: see the section on Mediation Organisations in this chapter, and to the section on Parades and Public Order, in Chapter 8.

24 Lord Chancellor's Department *ADR Discussion Paper*, November 1999.
25 Announced at the Centre for Dispute Resolution, Civil Justice Audit Conference, in April 2000.

judiciary and government. In the sphere of private, non-court-based mediation, mediation organisations, lawyers and other professionals, and industry have been prime contributors. Community mediation centres have spread the use of mediation throughout the community. Trade and professional bodies, public agencies and academics have also provided the necessary impetus for the development of mediation in the UK.

The Role of Civil Justice Reform
Lord Woolf's Report

That a lawsuit has been described as 'a machine which you go into as a pig and come out as a sausage',[26] captures some of the frustrations with the civil justice system. Those frustrations may explain in part why in over 90% of civil cases settlement occurs prior to trial and a substantial portion of the cases that do reach trial settle prior to judgment.

The Beldam Report, prepared for the General Council for the Bar, concluded that mediation should be offered to litigants at an early stage in the English court process.[27] The fact that litigation is not the only means of achieving appropriate and effective dispute resolution was the reason cited by Lord Woolf for including mediation and other forms of alternative dispute resolution in his inquiry on improving access to justice to English courts. Lord Woolf also wished to consider whether ADR could offer courts lessons in terms of their procedures.[28] Lord Woolf's Interim Report included the following recommendations:

- that courts should encourage the use of ADR;
- that parties should acknowledge at case management conferences and pre-trial reviews whether or not the parties had discussed the issue of ADR;
- that judges should take into account a litigant's unreasonable refusal to attempt ADR when considering the future conduct of a case.[29]

Lord Woolf made reference in his Interim Report to ADR developments in other jurisdictions. In the US, court reform has led to the multi-door courthouse concept, which allows parties to a dispute to submit details about the dispute and receive advice on the most appropriate forum for resolution, together with details of its cost and timeframe. The forums range from arbitration, mediation, expert determination, adjudication and ombudsmen. The concept has been piloted in a number of US courts since the 1980s.[30] In the United States, three-lawyer panels have also been

---

26 A Pierce *The Devil's Dictionary*, 1911. Pierce also defines a litigant as a 'person about to give up his skin for the hope of retaining his bones.'
27 Bar Council Committee on ADR (Chaired by Lord Justice Beldam), *Bar Council Report*, 1991.
28 Lord Woolf *Access to Justice: Interim Report*, June 1995, at p 136.
29 Ibid, at p 147.
30 For example, Columbia, Houston and Tulsa. See L Ray and P Kestner *The multi-door experience: dispute resolution and the courthouse of the future*, Standing Committee of Dispute Resolution, American Bar Association, Washington DC, 1988; and L Ray 'The multi-door court house idea: building the court house of the future' (1985) *Ohio State Journal on Dispute Resolution* 7.

piloted. The panels attempt to mediate a resolution of a dispute, but if unsuccessful, will provide the parties with a non-binding recommendation.[31]

The Civil Justice Reform Act 1990 changed the procedures in America's Federal District Courts with the aim of reducing the costs and delay of civil litigation, using a range of methods, including ADR.[32] Most recently, by the Alternative Dispute Resolution Act 1998, the US Congress has indicated that ADR should be a major part of court policy. The Act contemplates that each District Court should set up an ADR programme and encourage and promote the use of ADR.[33]

In Australia, issues of court reform gained pace in the early 1990s. The view there can be summed up by an abstract in *The Age* on 3 June 1922: 'British justice is an inspiring phrase, but inexpensive justice would be better'. Apart from cost concerns, a significant concern in Australia was that 'justice delayed is justice denied'. Delay, it was argued, implied court congestion and, in turn, that the quality of justice diminished due to time constraints on judges.[34] The economic model for court delay, developed by Posner, suggested that the standard solution of expanding courts and appointing additional judges does not work, as in the long run the increased capacity only serves to induce people to use the courts.[35] The early Australian reforms did not expand court facilities but introduced case flow management, specialist lists and the appointment of judges to monitor interim applications. In addition, an important goal was recognised to be the earlier settlement of cases.[36] The broad framework within which these developments occurred was provided by American case flow management.[37] Since those initial reforms, a combination of approaches have operated in the different Australian jurisdictions.[38]

Continental developments have also provided a basis for comparison. 19th century Codes of Civil Procedure[39] emphasised procedural informalism and control by the parties over every aspect of the proceedings.[40] In the late 1800s in Continental

---

31 For example, in Michigan. See *CPR Alternatives*, Special Issue: ADR in the Courts, vol 9, No 7, July 1991.

32 One judge commented, in relation to the changes, as follows:
   '. . . what I have seen . . . is movement from very little mediation . . . to a situation where not a single civil case is tried . . . without having some form of ADR . . . a real cultural revolution': *CPR Alternatives*, Winter Meeting; Mediating among Judges, vol 16, No 2, March 1998.

33 *CPR Alternatives*, ADR and the Courts: Now and in the Future, vol 17, No 5, May 1999.

34 Gordon J Samuels ACJ 'The Economics of Justice' (1991) 1 *JJA* 114 at 115.

35 R Posner *Economic Analysis of Law*, Little Brown, Boston, 1986; and R Posner *The Federal Courts: Crisis and Reform*, Harvard University Press, Cambridge, 1985.

36 J R T Wood J 'Case Management in the Common Law Division of the Supreme Court of New South Wales' (1991) 1 *JJA* 71.

37 P A Sallmann 'Managing the business of Australian High Courts' (1992) 2 *JJA* 80.

38 For example, the Family Court of Australia piloted a referral model with many of Sander's multi-door courthouse features. The model, called the 'Integrated Client Service', involves a central screening 'one stop shop' and a multi-disciplinary team in diagnosing the dispute and recommending the most appropriate dispute resolution process. The Portals Programme in Victorian courts was also based on Sander's multi-door courthouse idea. A number of jurisdictions have court-annexed mediation and early neutral evaluation has also been adopted through legislation and new court rules.

39 For example, French Code 1806, Italian Code 1865 and German Code 1877.

40 G Bryant 'The movement towards procedural informalism in North America and Western

countries, judges gained more control over the pace of proceedings and attempted to bring parties to an amicable settlement in litigation. This active role of judges is well established in European civil law countries. German jurisprudence, for example, emphasises that law is a product of compromise.[41] Danish judges offer parties possible solutions to their problems.[42] Dispute settlement, focusing on the maintenance of the relationships between commercial parties has become the central focus of the Danish Commercial Court, displacing to a degree dispute settlement based on laws.[43] In the Netherlands, informal mediation by judges is customary:

> '. . . the judges . . . will go to great efforts to try [to] settle the dispute between the parties rather than come to a final and formal decision.'[44]

Notwithstanding the proactive approach of Continental judges, the Council of Europe has called for further reform of Continental courts, in particular to reduce delay, although the response from the Continental countries has blamed delays on a shortage of judges.[45] Nevertheless, such informal court procedures have provided the foundation for the expansion of conciliation throughout Europe. An 18th century Norwegian Royal Edict, for example, promoted conciliation as an alternative to litigation. 'Good men' served as conciliators in private and lawyers were excluded from the process. Courts dismissed cases in which conciliation had not been attempted.[46] In Scandinavia, conciliation has become part of its cultural heritage.[47] Prussia created the institution of the 'Schiedsmann', or mediator, in 1808. Mediators were landed gentry who tried to resolve disputes amicably. Schiedsmänner still survive in some German states where they are chosen by local government and mediate minor criminal and civil matters.[48] In 1977 in France, local conciliateurs appointed by the Presidents of the relevant Courts of Appeal, where instructed to bring proceedings to an amicable settlement. In 1978, parties could voluntarily seek their services to resolve civil and minor criminal matters, but not disputes involving the Government.

A number of the issues relating to civil justice reform, which arose for consideration in other jurisdictions, also arose for consideration in England and Wales as part of Lord Woolf's Access to Justice Inquiry, in particular, the length of time it takes to bring cases to a conclusion and the proportion of costs to the value of the claim. In connection with the Inquiry, a number of surveys were carried out. In terms of the costs of litigation, the Inquiry found that, for example, small value commercial cases cost an average 174% of claim value. In terms of delay, building disputes, for example, take an average 34 months to conclude.[49] A fundamental recommendation

---

Europe: A critical study' in R Abel (ed) *The Politics of Informal Justice, vol 1*, Academic Press, New York, 1982, at p 186.

41 A H Herman *Law v Business: business articles from the Financial Times 1983–1988*, Butterworths, London, 1989, at p 18.

42 See B Blegvad 'Commercial Relations, Contract and Litigation in Denmark: A discussion of Macaulay's Theories' (1990) 24 *Ohio State Journal on Dispute Resolution* 390 at 408.

43 B Blegvad, ibid at 410.

44 *Alternatives*, Special Supplement, vol 17, No 4, April 1999, at p 72.

45 A Mizzi 'Euro law reform call' *The Law Society Gazette*, 15 June 2000.

46 J Auerbach *Justice without Law*, Oxford University Press, New York, 1983, at p 72.

47 Ibid.

48 G Bryant 'The movement towards procedural informalism in North America and Western Europe: A critical study' in R Abel (ed) *The Politics of Informal Justice, vol 1*, Academic Press, New York, 1982, at p 194.

49 Lord Woolf *Access to Justice: Final Report*, July 1996.

in Lord Woolf's Final Report was case management and, in particular, the use of a case management conference to explore the possibility of settlement and ADR.[50] Apart from the Commercial Court, case management had played a limited role for judges in the courts of England and Wales.[51] Yet, Lord Roskill in *Ashmore v Corpn of Lloyd's* [1992] 2 All ER 486 had stated:[52]

'... it is the trial judge who has control of the proceedings. It is part of his duty to identify the crucial issues and to see they are tried as expeditiously and as inexpensively as possible. It is the duty of the advisers of the parties to assist the trial judge in carrying out his duty. Litigants are not entitled to the uncontrolled use of a trial judge's time. Other litigants await their turn. Litigants are only entitled to so much of the trial judge's time as is necessary for the proper determination of the relevant issues.'

In addition, Lord Templeman had said:[53]

'... an expectation that the trial would proceed to a conclusion upon the evidence to be produced is not a legitimate expectation. The only legitimate expectation of any plaintiff is to receive justice. Justice can only be achieved by assisting the judge ...'

In 1973 Maureen Solomon put forward case management principles in a study carried out in America for the Commission on Standards of Judicial Administration. Many of the aims of case management identified by Solomon are mirrored in the aims of Lord Woolf's reforms:

- that litigants should be treated equally;
- that there should be timely disposition of cases;
- that there should be public confidence in courts; and
- that the quality of the litigation process should be enhanced.[54]

At the time of Solomon's study, there were concerns about lack of parity amongst disputants, particularly as pre-trial processes were extensive and burdensome, fuelled by wealthy clients. These difficulties prompted the case management and settlement focus.[55] Commentators also point to the need for case management to change the culture of lawyers in the way they handle their cases:

'... there is always a scheduled next date by which certain specified tasks are to be completed, and that next date is always quite short in relation to what the lawyers think is desirable or possible ...'[56]

'... lawyers look at their files about every two weeks since that period is about their maximum sense of urgency ...'[57]

---

50 Lord Woolf *Access to Justice: Final Report*, July 1996, at pp 62–3.
51 Compare the US, where the doctrine of separation of powers is constitutionally entrenched, and judges are responsible for court management, which, being non-adjudicative, has been delegated to court executive officers: R E McGarvie J 'Judicial responsibility for the operation of the court system' (1989) 63 *ALJ* 79.
52 At p 488.
53 At p 493.
54 M Solomon *Case Flow Management in the Trial Court*, Commission on Standards of Judicial Administration, 1973; and M Solomon *Case Flow Management in the Trial Court Now and for the future*, American Bar Association, 1987.
55 J Resnik 'Failing Faith: Adjudicatory Procedure in Decline' (1986) 53 *University of Chicago Law Review* 494 at 517, 521 and 524.
56 Flanders 'Modelling Court Delay' (1980) 2 *Law and Policy* 305 at 315.
57 L C Mann 'Mediation of Civil Cases' (1990) 67 *Detroit Law Review* 531.

Lord Woolf's aim in recommending ADR was avoidance of cost and time involved in litigation, and is an aim shared by users of mediation in England.[58] The National Consumer Council in the United Kingdom also surveyed over 1,000 people who had experienced a civil dispute and more than half the people surveyed indicated their displeasure with courts and their preference for assistance from a neutral who could help them to sort out problems rather than tell them what to do.[59]

The Civil Procedure Rules

In Lord Woolf's Final Report, he envisaged a new civil justice landscape with the following features:

- avoidance of litigation where possible;
- less adversarial and more co-operative litigation;
- less complex litigation;
- shorter and more certain timescales for litigation;
- more affordable litigation;
- equality between disputants;
- a court structure which meets the needs of litigants; and
- case management by judges.[60]

The overriding principles, identified by Lord Woolf, for the civil justice system were:

- fair treatment;
- just outcomes;
- reasonable costs;
- reasonable speed;
- an understandable civil justice system;
- certainty; and
- effectiveness.[61]

American commentators have highlighted that fundamental civil justice reform can be obtained by appropriate changes in civil procedure.[62] The Lord Chancellor addressed this issue in October 1997 when he announced the introduction of the following programme of reforms:

- a unified code of procedural rules;
- pre-action protocols, requiring information exchange and full investigation of

---

58 See, for example, H Genn *Central London County Court Mediation Pilot: Evaluation Report*, LCD Research Series, No 5/98, at p 102 where the view of one mediation user was given:

'I am trying to avoid legal costs because they could exceed the cost of the claim. I have got no respect for the legal system . . . you end up paying 3 or 4 times the value of the claim . . . I would rather write off bad debts than get involved in the legal system . . .'

59 M Winfield *Far from wanting their day in court: Civil disputants in England and Wales*, National Consumer Council, London, 1996, p 6; and National Consumer Council *Seeking Civil Justice*, National Consumer Council, London, 1995.

60 Lord Woolf *Access to Justice: Final Report*, July 1996, at pp 4–9.

61 Ibid, at p 2.

62 For example, J Resnik 'Managerial Judges' (1982) 96 *Harvard Law Review* 76.

cases prior to issue of proceedings and an attempt at compromise before issue of proceedings; and

- three case tracks, including a small claims procedure, with a limit of £5,000,[63] a fast track for claims up to £15,000 and a multi-track for claims over £15,000 and also complex, but low value, claims.[64]

The aim of achieving a unified procedural code for the civil courts in England and Wales was achieved by the Civil Procedure Rules ('CPR'), which came into effect on 26 April 1999, and apply to High Court and county court proceedings in England and Wales. The overriding objective of the Rules, set out in Part I, mirrors Lord Woolf's guiding principles in his Access to Justice Reports. The overriding objective is to deal with cases justly, which includes:

- ensuring that the parties are on a equal footing;
- saving expense;
- ensuring that a case is dealt with in a way which is proportionate to its value and complexity;
- ensuring that a case is dealt with expeditiously and fairly; and
- making efficient use of the court's resources.[65]

The CPR place a duty on courts to further that overriding objective through active case management, although the parties are required to help the court to do so.[66] CPR, r 1.4(2) sets out the activities which constitute active case management:

- encouraging the parties to co-operate;
- encouraging the parties to use ADR; and
- encouraging settlement.

Part 26 of the CPR provides the basis for encouraging ADR. In particular, CPR, r 26.4(1) provides:

'A party may, when filing the completed allocation questionnaire, make a written request for the proceedings to be stayed or the parties to try to settle the case by alternative dispute resolution or other means.'[67]

David Shapiro, an experienced international mediator, who trains judges in the role of mediation in the CPR, explains the operation of the CPR in this way:

- If all the parties want a stay, the judge will enter an order to that effect.[68]
- If the parties disagree on the type of ADR to be used, the judge has a

---

63 £1,000 for personal injury cases.
64 Lord Chancellor's Department *Modernising Justice*, December 1998.
65 CPR, r 1.1(1) and (2).
66 CPR, rr 1.3 and 1.4.
67 The case management questionnaire, in the first section on 'settlement', requests the parties whether they wish a stay to attempt to settle the case by negotiation or any other form of alternative dispute resolution and, if so, at what stage of the proceedings and for how long. The questionnaire also requires parties to give reasons if they do not wish to stay the case to attempt settlement. Compare New Zealand High Court Case Management Pilot Practice Note, at para 3, when it defines the aim of case management as identifying 'the issues in dispute and to encourage settlement by negotiation or the use of ADR techniques'.
68 A study of Federal Court practitioners in Australia revealed that practitioners agreed to a stay so as not to appear obstructionist before the judge: Federal Court, *Practitioner Consultations*, Sydney, 2/4/10, June 1999.

discretion to direct the parties to a particular ADR forum.
- If a party opposes a stay, the judge may on his own initiative grant a stay.[69]

In an Australian case, *Barrett v Queensland Newspapers Pty Ltd*,[70] the court outlined the factors which might persuade a court, in the face of opposition by one of the parties to ADR, to grant a stay on its own initiative:

- It could not be concluded that the mediation would not be successful.
- At least one party agrees to mediation.
- The application is made early in the life of the case and mediation could save substantial costs of preparing for trial.
- A trial of the matter is likely to take up significant court time (in that case, it was estimated at 10 days).
- There is a risk in litigating and, although a party may wish to litigate notwithstanding those risks, other parties ought not to be put at risk.
- A suitable mediator with the necessary skills can be found.

Although the pre-trial review questionnaire does not specifically refer to ADR, it seeks the parties' acknowledgement that they have complied with previous directions given by the court, which may include an ADR direction, and also gives the parties the opportunity to ask for further directions, which may include an attempt at ADR.[71] The CPR has introduced the possibility of cost sanctions if parties do not comply with the court's directions. In particular, under r 44.5(3), a court can have regard, when assessing costs, to a range of factors, including the efforts made before and during proceedings in order to try to resolve the dispute. In *Dyson and Field (Twohey Executors) v Leeds CC* (22 November 1999), the Court of Appeal reminded the parties that indemnity costs or a higher rate of interest on damages could be ordered for unreasonably rejecting ADR.

The experience in Scotland and Northern Ireland

A report prepared by Lord Cullen in December 1995 was limited to a review of the business in the Outer House of the Court of Session, the main first instance court. Although Lord Cullen recommended case management, his recommendations have not yet been implemented. Commentators in Scotland believe that a more comprehensive review of the Sheriff's Court and the Court of Session is required. With the advent of the Scottish Parliament, it is likely that a civil justice review will occur and that there will be pressure to adopt at least some of Lord Woolf's reforms.

In Northern Ireland on 19 May 1995, the Lord Chancellor at the time, Lord Mackay, delivered the MacDermott lecture, where he said:

'I doubt whether . . . the civil justice debate in England and Wales can have no relevance for Northern Ireland . . . there are sufficiently distinctive features of practice in Northern Ireland which suggests that it might be unwise to proceed on the uncritical assumption that in this instance either the diagnosis or the remedy will be apt for the Northern Ireland patient. Reform in England and Wales . . . is unlikely to provide a ready-made template for adjustment to the court process in Northern Ireland . . . It would be naïve to assume that the majority of Lord Woolf's suggestions and conclusions about the English system could

---

69 D Shapiro 'Alternative Dispute Resolution under the new Civil Rules: some guidelines for lawyers and judges' (1999) 18(7) *Litigation – the Journal of Contentious Business* 1 at 3.
70 District Court of Queensland, Samios DCJ (3 June 1999, unreported).
71 Pre-trial review questionnaire, part 'A', in relation to 'directions complied with'.

be applied in Northern Ireland without any modification . . . but we would be equally foolish to reject them as of no value to this jurisdiction.'[72]

The Government announced on 21 February 1998 that it would investigate civil justice reform in Northern Ireland and accordingly established the Civil Justice Reform Group. The Group has examined the accessibility and effectiveness of the civil justice system against the measures implemented in England and Wales as a result of Lord Woolf's Reports. One of the Group's aims was to identify the extent to which Lord Woolf's proposals should be applied in Northern Ireland.[73] The Group did not consider the civil appellate jurisdiction of the Court of Appeal or the House of Lords, or the family jurisdiction of the High Court, the county courts and the magistrates' courts. In the Group's Interim and Final Reports, the role of ADR in Northern Ireland's civil justice system was considered.[74] The Group acknowledged that Northern Ireland does not have a wide range of professional ADR providers, as in England and Wales. In turn, the number of trained mediators is low and both the legal profession and the public are not familiar with ADR.[75] Nevertheless, the Group was persuaded by arguments in favour of ADR and research on ADR to recommend a mediation pilot scheme in Northern Ireland.[76] Although the Group considers that mediation should be voluntary, for the purpose of the pilot the Group has recommended that judges should have the power to order a stay to allow the parties an opportunity to attempt mediation.[77] The Commercial and Medical Negligence lists of the Queen's Bench Division have been selected for the pilot. The evaluation of the scheme and ADR generally is proposed to be a long term project of a proposed Civil Justice Council.[78]

Issues for mediation arising out of civil justice reform in the UK

The Centre for Dispute Resolution[79] undertook, as part of its 10th anniversary, a MORI poll of 100 solicitors, half in private practice and the other half in-house, to track the performance of the CPR a year after implementation. It is useful to consider some of the results against Lord Woolf's principal aims, as stated in his reports:

- In terms of the aim of achieving equality between litigants, 37% of the poll considered that the CPR benefits claimants.[80]
- With regard to the aim of achieving just outcomes, 17% of the poll considered that the CPR has resulted in fairer outcomes.[81]
- 47% of the poll considered that the CPR has resulted in speedier resolution of

---

72 Reported by the Civil Justice Reform Group *Review of the Civil Justice System in Northern Ireland: Interim Report*, April 1999, at paras 4.3 and 4.6.
73 Ibid, at para 4.7.
74 Ibid, at section 7; and Civil Justice Reform Group *Review of the Civil Justice System in Northern Ireland: Final Report*, June 2000, at paras 137 and 138.
75 *Interim Report*, op cit, at para 10.73.
76 *Interim Report*, op cit, at para 10.75; and *Final Report*, op cit, at para 137.
77 *Interim Report*, op cit, at para 10.76; and *Final Report*, op cit.
78 *Interim Report*, op cit, at para 10.77; and *Final Report*, op cit, at para 138.
79 See the later section in this chapter on Mediation Organisations for further information about the Centre.
80 Centre for Dispute Resolution *Civil Justice Audit*, April 2000.
81 Ibid.

disputes, although that appears to have been at increased cost, as 35% of the poll considered that the CPR has actually increased the costs of litigation.[82]

- 36% of the poll considered that there has been a decrease in litigation since the CPR.[83]
- Overall, 80% of the poll indicated satisfaction with the CPR.[84]

Although the poll confirmed that settlements are occurring earlier under the CPR, the poll results also appear to indicate that this is largely attributable to Part 36 Offers.[85]

Notwithstanding the civil justice reforms and the CPR, a number of issues remain, insofar as mediation is concerned. An issue of particular concern is whether judges have embraced mediation.[86] Although Centre for Dispute Resolution statistics for 2000 show that 19% of their mediations over the preceding year were referred by judges, compared with 8% in the previous year, court referrals accounted for only 38% of the Centre's 141% increase in the number of mediations.[87] The MORI poll revealed dissatisfaction with the level of pro-activity by judges:[88]

- 'the judges are not raising mediation as an option unless one of the parties suggests it';
- 'there are few courts that take the bull by the horns themselves'; and
- 'the judge required a great deal of convincing that she should grant a stay to enable mediation to take place'.

The poll also revealed inconsistency in approach to mediation by judges.[89] It indicated that only a minority of respondents, 13%, considered that judges were prepared to order mediation.[90] Anecdotal evidence suggests that, even in cases where the majority of parties agree to mediate, judges are not making ADR orders.[91] Yet, the MORI poll revealed that 60% of interviewees considered that judges should even

---

82 Centre for Dispute Resolution *Civil Justice Audit*, April 2000.
83 Ibid. Figures released for the year ended June 2000 by the Lord Chancellor's Department confirmed the drop in litigation by 37% in the case of the Queen's Bench Division and 11% in the county court, although the Chancery Division saw a drop by 1% only and Family Court applications increased by 14%: M Mullaly 'Queen's Bench suffers one-third drop in claims' *Legal Week*, 20 July 2000, p 4; and S Allen 'County court claims fall' *The Law Society Gazette*, 20 July 2000, p 4.
84 Centre for Dispute Resolution *Civil Justice Audit*, April 2000.
85 'Woolf Reforms encourage settlements' *Solicitors Journal*, 14 April 2000. Part 36 of the CPR deals with offers to settle and payments into court. A Part 36 offer can be made under the CPR before proceedings are issued. A Part 36 offer of payment has a range of cost consequences, as set out in CPR, rr 36.13 and 36.14.
86 See the section on Courts in this chapter, for more information on court-based mediation and the courts' approach to mediation.
87 CEDR *Resolutions*, Issue no 26, Summer 2000, p 1.
88 Centre for Dispute Resolution *Civil Justice Audit*, April 2000, sections on 'Judges should initiate settlement discussions', 'Role of mediation' and 'Cases should not be stayed whilst settlement discussions are underway'.
89 CEDR *Civil Justice Audit*, April 2000, which reported that some lawyers considered that there was hostility to ADR in the Technology and Construction Court, and support in the Commercial Court.
90 Ibid. Compare, for example, the encouragement given to the parties by the QBD to attempt mediation in *GKR Karate (UK) Ltd v Sclanders* (15 September 2000, unreported).
91 'Practice: Mediation' *The Law Society Gazette*, 30 March 2000.

take the additional step, and initiate settlement discussions.[92] Even in cases which are stayed for an attempt at mediation to take place, few efforts are being made to monitor whether mediation is taking place in this period. Although some judges and masters have received mediation training, it is acknowledged that there needs to be greater knowledge of mediation and other forms of ADR within the judiciary.[93]

A further issue is that the only reference to ADR in the CPR is at the allocation stage.[94] In small claims cases, allocation provides the only opportunity for consideration of whether a mediation might be appropriate. In other cases, Lord Woolf envisaged that, apart from allocation, the case management conference and pre-trial review would also provide opportunities for consideration of mediation. However, there is no specific requirement for the parties to consider mediation at those other stages. Accordingly, if judges are not pro-active, as the MORI poll might suggest, some amendment may be required to the CPR in order to give effect to what Lord Woolf had envisaged.[95]

Another issue surrounds the operation of r 44 and the circumstances which a judge may take into account for the purposes of costs. 41% of the MORI poll considered that courts should at least award costs against a party who refuses mediation.[96] The authors' 2000 survey of 700 UK law firms[97] provided examples of circumstances where English judges were prepared to award costs in relation to mediation:

- where a party agreed to mediate, but failed to attend the mediation;
- where a party, who had persuaded another party to mediate on the basis that it said it wished to make an offer in the mediation to settle the case, failed to do so at the mediation.[98]

These and other issues have been raised[99] in a Discussion Paper on ADR towards the end of 1999.[100] The next section provides an overview of the response by UK courts to mediation developments. When viewed against, for example, the Australian 'access to justice' movement, a difference is apparent. The push for 'access to justice' in the UK has focused primarily on improving access to the courts, whereas 'access to justice' in Australia has focused primarily on improving access to alternatives to the courts.

---

92 Centre for Dispute Resolution *Civil Justice Audit*, April 2000; and 'Centre for Dispute Resolution, Civil Justice Audit' *New Law Journal*, 14 April 2000.

93 Lord Woolf reported in 'Focus: Civil Justice Reforms' *The Law Society Gazette*, 21 April 1999.

94 CPR, r 26.4.

95 Supported by responses to the Lord Chancellor's ADR Discussion Paper – Lord Chancellor's Department *ADR Discussion Paper: Summary of responses*, August 2000, at para 60.

96 Ibid. The focus groups interviewed objected to judges making enquiries about what happened in a mediation.

97 Other results from the survey have been reported, where relevant, in Parts I and II, and further results will appear, where relevant, in this Part.

98 Consider the section on Compulsion or Encouragement to Mediate in Chapter 9, for indicators of what constitutes good faith participation in mediation. The issue also arises whether according significance to events in a mediation on the issue of costs falls foul of privilege: as to which consider further the sections on privilege in Parts I and III, and *BM Armstrong v Meander Valley Council* (2000) TASRMPAT 3 for an Australian example.

99 The issues raised are explored further in this Part.

100 Lord Chancellor's Department *ADR Discussion Paper*, November 1999.

The Role of Courts

Courts in England and Wales

Overview

English courts are showing increased interest in mediation through a variety of methods, including Practice Directions, which draw parties' attention to ADR; allocation questionnaires, requiring parties to confirm that consideration has been given to ADR; and pilot mediation schemes. Some of these developments have taken place following Lord Woolf's review of the civil justice system, whereas other developments commenced even before his review. The mediation initiatives of the following courts will be outlined in this section:

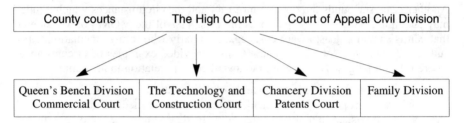

County courts

The largest county court in England and Wales is the Central London County Court. It deals with civil cases, except family disputes. A mediation pilot scheme commenced at the Central London County Court in May 1996. Mediation was offered in all defended cases above the small claims limit. Mediation took place only if all parties agreed. The mediations took place at the court and were limited to three hours in duration. The mediators were provided from five mediation organisations. The cost of each mediation was £50, shared equally by the parties. The objective of the scheme was to offer virtually cost-free court-annexed mediation. Originally, it was intended for the scheme to run for one year but was extended for a further 12 months. The impetus for the scheme was the disproportion between costs and claim value and the increase in number of litigants in person in county courts.[101]

In terms of administration of the Pilot, in cases falling within the ambit of the scheme, the court's Mediation Service sent an offer letter to the parties' solicitors, or to the parties direct if they were not represented, explaining the scheme, providing information about mediation and requesting that the court be informed within 14 days whether or not the offer to mediate was accepted.[102] If any party rejected the mediation, the court would then write to all parties, advising that mediation would not take place. If mediation was agreed by all parties, the fee was payable within seven days. The mediator received notification of the appointment, together with a

---

101   H Genn *Central London County Court Mediation Pilot: Evaluation Report*, LCD Research Series, No 5/98, at p 3.

102   The offer letter is 'MD4' and the information leaflet is 'MD5'.

copy of the documents sent to the parties, an introductory leaflet, check list and record of mediation form.[103] Mediations took place at 4.30 pm in the conference rooms of the court building. Before the mediation began, the parties would sign an Agreement to Mediate.[104] At the end of the session, the mediator and the parties completed a form,[105] outlining whether or not an agreement was reached and, if so, whether or not the parties would like a court consent order.

By March 1998, mediation offers had been sent in about 4,500 cases. The first mediation was held in July 1996 and between then and March 1998, 160 cases had been mediated as part of the Pilot.[106] Genn's study of the Pilot indicated that the rate at which both parties accepted mediation offers was about 5% throughout the life of the Pilot.[107] In order to improve take-up, special provisions were introduced, following discussions between the Lord Chancellor's Department and the Legal Aid Board, as it was then called, allowing solicitors, who acted for assisted parties, to recover the costs of preparation for mediation and a flat fee for attendance at mediation irrespective of the outcome.[108]

The Pilot has been evaluated by Genn and, following publication of her Evaluation,[109] the Lord Chancellor indicated his intention that the scheme should continue to operate.[110] Judge Butter has noticed that county court judges are encouraging parties to consider mediation following the introduction in April 1999 of the CPR and that there has been an interest in mediation from solicitors and parties.[111] The Lord Chancellor's ADR Discussion Paper[112] noted, however, that it may be too early to determine whether the increase in mediations and interest in the county court is temporary or a reflection of a genuine change in attitudes embracing mediation.

It has not been considered practical, at this stage, to implement the Central London County Court Mediation Pilot in the other county courts, although some of the respondents to the Lord Chancellor's ADR Discussion Paper suggested that the scheme should be extended to more, if not all, county courts.[113]

Further responses to the ADR Discussion Paper suggested the following improvements to the county court scheme:[114]

---

103 The introductory leaflet is document 'MD6'; the checklist is 'MD8' and the record of mediation form is 'MD8A'.

104 The Agreement to Mediation is form 'MD6'.

105 Form 'MD9'.

106 H Genn *Central London County Court Mediation Pilot: Evaluation Report*, LCD Research Series, No 5/98, at p 5.

107 Ibid, at p v.

108 The flat fee was £230 + VAT which was intended to cover attendance, travel and waiting time and the mediator's fee: R Halliburton 'London Mediation Scheme wins legal aid funds worth £20,000' *The Law Society Gazette*, 13 August 1997, at p 5.

109 The results of the research are referred to throughout this book, where relevant.

110 Lord Chancellor's Department *Quicker Settlement through Mediation*, 28 July 1998.

111 HHJ Butter QC speaking at The Centre for Dispute Resolution *Forum* on 29 September 1999. Judge Butter QC won a Centre for Dispute Resolution Award in 1998 for personal achievement in ADR for his work on the Central London County Court Mediation Pilot.

112 Lord Chancellor's Department *ADR Discussion Paper*, November 1999.

113 Lord Chancellor's Department *ADR Discussion Paper: Summary of responses*, August 2000, at paragraph 52.

114 Ibid.

- extension of the three-hour time limit;
- extension of its operation to 'in-court hours'; and
- extension of the scheme to small claims.

Commercial Court

The Commercial Court deals with commercial claims, which include any case arising out of trade and commerce or relating to a business contract, export and import of goods, carriage of goods, insurance, banking and finance or the operation of markets and exchanges.[115]

The Commercial Court has been at the forefront of case management efforts by courts in England and Wales. In the 1980s the court took steps to improve the efficiency of its procedures and, in turn, to reduce the cost of litigation.[116] One of the main problems identified by the court was a tendency for lawyers to leave preparations for trial until the last possible moment 'or even later'.[117] The court identified the methods by which preparation for trial could be advanced by many months, encouraging also early consideration of settlement in proceedings.[118] The court determined that most of its recommendations for change could be adopted voluntarily within the framework of its Rules at the time. Its recommendations sought to encourage judges, solicitors and barristers to co-operate in resolving disputes sensibly and economically.[119]

The new approach was reflected in Commercial Court Guides, with up-dates and progress reported in the court's end of year statements. An abstract from the court's 1992–1993 end of year statement encapsulates the approach of the court:

'... the Court plays a much more pro-active role ... and is increasingly prepared to take the initiative in suggesting ways in which litigation might be shortened and thus money and time saved ... There is considerable scope in many cases for dividing up the issues where the resolution of one or more might well enable [the parties] to settle their remaining differences without incurring the enormous financial burden of a trial ... The Court should not confine itself to looking for issues that ... would be legally determinative of the parties' rights and obligations but should also look for issues which, if resolved, would be likely to be commercially determinative.'

The Commercial Court introduced an ADR scheme, by issuing a Practice Statement on 10 December 1993.[120] The Statement advised that the court wished to encourage parties to consider the use of ADR and, accordingly, would invite parties, in appropriate cases, to consider whether ADR should be attempted. Amendments were also made to the standard questions to be answered by the parties in preparation for a Summons for Directions and to the standard questions to be answered as part of the Pre-trial Check List. Those questions ensured that lawyers considered with their clients the possibility of attempting resolution by mediation, conciliation or otherwise. The Clerk to the Court kept a list of the individuals and bodies that

---

115 See Commercial Court *Commercial Court Guide*, October 1999.
116 Commercial Court Committee *Report of the practitioner members of the Commercial Court Committee approved and adopted by the Commercial Court Committee*, 1985.
117 Ibid, at p 37.
118 Ibid, at p 38.
119 Ibid, at p 49.
120 [1994] 1 WLR 14.

offered ADR services, although the court did not recommend any individual or organisation.[121] The Lord Chief Justice extended the Practice Statement in 1995 by way of a Practice Direction to other Queen's Bench Division cases, by requiring parties to lodge with the court, not later than two months before the date of trial, a Pre-trial Check List which included questions as to whether ADR had been considered.[122]

The first Report of the Commercial Court ADR Working Party on 12 June 1996 made recommendations on Commercial Court ADR Orders and included a draft Practice Direction which was intended to give effect to the recommendations.[123] This Practice Direction was formally issued by Waller J on 7 June 1996.[124] The Practice Direction allowed judges to invite the parties to take positive steps to attempt ADR and, to that end, could adjourn the proceedings for a specified period of time to enable the parties to take such steps. In addition, the Practice Direction allowed judges, if they considered that an early neutral evaluation was appropriate, to offer to provide that evaluation or to arrange for another judge to do so. The parties could restore the Summons for Direction or other Summons in order to report back to the court the progress made by way of ADR or to obtain further directions for the proceedings.[125] The view of some of the Commercial Court judges was that, in order to allay concern by any party that suggesting ADR is a sign of weakness on the part of that party, the court could order ADR.[126] There have been occasions when mediation has been ordered by the court, even when all the parties opposed it.[127] The court's experience, however, has been that parties themselves frequently ask for consent orders to be made referring disputes to ADR.[128]

The Commercial Court's ADR Working Party reconvened in 1998 in order to review the operation of its ADR scheme between June 1996 and July 1998. Although the Committee discovered that a large number of ADR orders had been made, it noticed that the judges had conducted early neutral evaluation in only three cases. Not only did early neutral evaluation appear to be unpopular with parties and their lawyers, but it was also considered that many Commercial Court judges were uncomfortable with the process.[129] The Working Party concluded that early neutral evaluation could

---

121 The Commercial Court *End of Year Statement 1993–1994*.
122 Relevant questions were:
> '10. Have you or counsel discussed with your client(s) the possibility of attempting to resolve this dispute (or particular issues) by alternative dispute resolution?
> 11. Might some form of ADR procedure assist to resolve or narrow the issues in this case?
> 12. Have you or your client(s) explored with the other parties the possibility of resolving this dispute (or particular issues) by ADR?'
123 Commercial Court Working Party on ADR *First Report*, 1996.
124 [1996] 1 WLR 1024.
125 Ibid.
126 Rix J *Woolf Reforms*, Seminar at Simmons and Simmons, 30 June 1999.
127 For example, the *De Lorean* case where Colman J directed mediation, and the case settled three weeks later, ending almost a decade of litigation in America and England: see D Shapiro 'Alternative Dispute Resolution under the new Civil Rules: some guidelines for lawyers and judges' (1999) 18(7) *Litigation – the Journal of Contentious Business* 1 at 4.
128 Commercial Court Committee *Meeting Note*, 14 July 1997.
129 Rix J *Woolf Reforms*, Seminar at Simmons and Simmons, 30 June 1999.

assist parties in cases where there are some distinct issues on which preliminary views could be readily expressed without the need for substantial presentation of the merits, but that the court's Rules allowed speedy final determination of such issues in any event and that this may provide a more effective and economical method for disposing of a whole action rather than a non-binding early neutral evaluation.[130] The second difficulty highlighted by the Working Party in 1998 was that a suspension of the pre-trial timetable to allow an attempt at ADR could have substantial disadvantages. The court's experience was that parties could take many months to select a mediator and agree on the procedural steps for mediation. Although the court had attempted to minimise delay by making ADR orders in parallel with a timetable, which allowed certain steps to be taken to progress trials, such as exchange of witness statements, those orders had not always avoided delay, as parties frequently agreed to extend time at the next stage in the timetable.[131] The Working Party made the following recommendations to combat this difficulty:

- insertion in ADR orders of a date by which ADR must be completed;
- insertion in ADR orders of a date by which parties should exchange lists of neutrals and by which, if they are unable to agree on the appointment, the matter should be returned to the court; and
- by fixing a trial date.[132]

A third difficulty highlighted by the Working Party was that the court did not have a system for on-going contact with the parties in order to obtain information about cases that had been stayed for ADR. In order to discourage the parties ignoring an ADR order, the Working Party recommended that the parties should report back to the court their progress and reasons why ADR had not been attempted or was unsuccessful, without invading matters of privilege.[133] Accordingly, the court's form of ADR order was amended to reflect that the parties should provide written details of the ADR steps undertaken and, if applicable, the reasons for the failure of ADR.[134] Many cases, however, have come back to the court for trial without notice in advance explaining why ADR was not undertaken or had failed.[135]

A review of the Commercial Court's ADR statistics between June 1996 and December 1999 indicated that 118 ADR orders had been made, with an additional 17 cases then being considered for appropriateness for ADR.[136] The list below

---

130 Commercial Court ADR Working Party *Second Report*, 1998.
131 Ibid.
132 Ibid. See also the view of Australian commentators that, once litigation has been initiated, the main impetus towards settlement in mediation is the trial date: see the section on timing of mediation in Part I.
133 Commercial Court ADR Working Party *Second Report*, 1998.
134 Paragraph 5 of the form of ADR order provided:
  'if the matters in issue are not finally settled, the parties shall inform the Court by letter prior to [exchange of list of documents or of witness statements or exchange of expert's reports or setting down for trial] what steps towards ADR have been taken and (without prejudice to matters of privilege) why such steps have failed. If the parties have failed to initiate ADR procedures, they are to appear before [...] for further consideration of the Order'.
135 H Genn *University of London ADR Lecture* 10 December 1999.
136 The authors gratefully acknowledge the court's administration for allowing statistics to be reviewed and used for the purpose of this work.

indicates the breadth of ADR orders made by the court and the number of cases in which those orders were made up to that time:

Type of ADR Order	No of cases
Not to be set down for trial without an attempt at ADR	61
Adjourned for six weeks to attempt ADR	11
ADR settlement by [date] or else set down for trial	6
ADR to be attempted after exchange of witness statements	5
Adjourned for eight weeks to attempt ADR	5
ADR attempt to be made during six weeks after meeting with experts	4
No exchange of witness statements without an attempt at ADR	3
ADR to be attempted after discovery, but before exchange of witness statements	3
Parties to inform the judge at pre-trial review that ADR has been considered	2
ADR attempt not before meeting of experts	2
ADR to be attempted before exchange of lists of documents	2
ADR to be attempted before exchange of expert reports	1
ADR to be attempted after exchange of factual witness statements but before expert reports are exchanged	1
ADR to be attempted after inspection of documents	2
Time for discovery suspended for three months to allow ADR attempt	1
ADR attempt after service of reply	1
Adjourned for 11 weeks	1
Adjourned for three months	1
ADR within 28 days after exchange of expert reports	1
ADR within four weeks after inspection of documents	1
Adjourned four weeks to attempt ADR	1
Adjourned for four months to attempt ADR	1
ADR to be attempted after Court of Appeal judgment in a connected matter	1
ADR attempt two weeks after exchange of list of mediators	1

The ADR statistics also show a wide range of type of case referred to mediation:

Type of case	No of cases
Insurance	3
Professional negligence	5
Marine	6
Reinsurance	28
Maritime	32
Contractual – other	39

In terms of an analysis of the success or otherwise of the attempts made at mediation following Commercial Court orders, this is more problematic. First, feedback was not received in all cases where an ADR order had been made. Secondly, in those cases where the records show that the attempt at ADR was unsuccessful, it is not clear whether the parties were unsuccessful in agreeing to attempt ADR or were unsuccessful in reaching a resolution during ADR. In the cases where the parties provided feedback and could not even agree on ADR, the reasons cited included:

• parties did not consider ADR to be appropriate;
• one or more of the parties did not want to use ADR; and
• there was disagreement between the parties during pre-mediation meetings.

Finally, the statistics do not show, in those cases where ADR was unsuccessful, whether the parties reached a resolution after the attempt at ADR, and before trial. Bearing in mind those limitations, the statistics record the following results for the cases where ADR orders had been made between June 1996 and December 1999:

Result	No of cases	Percentage
No feedback	51	43
Unsuccessful	41	35
Successful	15	13
Pending	10	9

The latest Commercial Court Guide [137] provides:

• parties may apply for ADR directions at any stage;
• at the case management conference, the judge may invite the parties to use ADR, where the case appears appropriate for an attempt at ADR;
• the judge may, if appropriate, adjourn the case for a specified period of time to encourage the parties to use ADR. [138]

The Appendix to the Guide sets out the questions in relation to ADR that the parties need to consider in Commercial Court proceedings:

• Might some form of ADR assist?
• Has ADR been considered between the client and lawyers?
• Has ADR been explored with the other parties?
• Is an adjournment requested to attempt ADR?
• Would an ADR order in the standard form be appropriate?
• Are any other directions needed to allow ADR? [139]

The court's standard ADR order is in Appendix 7 of the Guide. [140] According to judges of the court, in the six months from April 1999 there had been a dramatic

---

137 Commercial Court *Commercial Court Guide*, October 1999.
138 Ibid, paras G1.5 – 1.7.
139 Ibid, Appendix 6.
140 The Order requires the parties to exchange lists of three neutrals by a certain date; to agree on the appointment of a neutral by a certain date; failing agreement on appointment of the neutral, the case management conference will be restored to enable the court to facilitate agreement on a neutral; the parties should take such serious steps

drop in the number of cases coming to the court, although waiting periods at the court have increased as judges are busier and as case management conferences are taking more time.[141]

Technology and Construction Court

Although the Official Referees Court has been renamed, as the Technology and Construction Court, its jurisdiction has remained unchanged. It deals with heavily documented cases, such as those involving construction contracts; information technology; claims against architects, engineers, surveyors and accountants; and environmental issues.[142]

Throughout the 1990s, the court suffered from serious delays, partly due to the proliferation of disputes in the construction industry, fuelled by the adversarial nature of sub-contracting relationships in the industry.[143] In an attempt to overcome this problem, the Official Referees Court, as it was then called, adopted a policy of referring cases to mediation or expert determination, where appropriate and possible. In those cases, Directions were suspended for four weeks, save for pre-trial review and trial dates. With the introduction of the CPR, the court will consider, at allocation, whether there should be a stay to attempt ADR.[144] The case management conference and pre-trail review also provide an opportunity for the court to provide ADR directions. A mediation initiative and ADR protocol have been introduced by the Court.[145]

---

as they are advised to resolve their dispute by ADR by a certain date; the parties should report back to the court the results; and there is also a provision for costs to be addressed in the Order. See also 'Precedent Mediation Order' included in the Centre for Dispute Resolution *Court-referred ADR: A guide for the judiciary*, Centre for Dispute Resolution, September 1999.

141 Rix J, speech given to the British Insurance Law Association, reported in 'Woolf sees court cases fall by a third' *The Lawyer*, 8 November 1999, at p 7. In 1998 Colman J received from the Centre for Dispute Resolution an award for personal achievement in ADR and his leadership in testing ADR in the Commercial Court.

142 CPR, Part 49C.

143 J Flood and A Caiger 'Lawyers and Arbitration: the Juridification of Construction Disputes' (1993) 56 *Modern Law Review* 412.

144 For an overview of the practice of the court, generally, together with some lessons from the past and indications of future development, see P Bowsher 'The Technology and Construction Court before and after the Woolf Civil Procedure Reforms' (2000) 1 *Int ALR* 19.

145 See further the section on Construction Disputes in Chapter 8. Reference to the Court's Registry confirmed that the judges of the court were encouraging mediation. The authors thank the Technology and Construction Court Registry for their comments. The Centre for Dispute Resolution's MORI poll (see the section on Civil Justice Reform for further details) referred to concerns by solicitors that some of the judges of the court are not supportive of mediation:

'I have found judges in the Technology and Construction Court to be anti-ADR . . . I have seen open hostility to it . . .' [CEDR *Civil Justice Audit*, April 2000, at the section on 'Judges – training in case management'].

However, the poll also highlighted that other lawyers had had a different experience:

'In the Technology and Construction Court, they have a very positive attitude for settlement . . . [some of the judges] will tell the parties, "go away and mediate", whether you like it or not . . .' [CEDR *Civil Justice Audit*, April 2000, ibid].

Chancery Division

The Chancery Guide deals with alternative dispute resolution in Chapter 17. The court recognises that ADR can reduce litigation costs and delay; preserve relationships and reputation; provide a wider range of possible solutions to disputes; and make more efficient use of limited judicial resources.[146] The Guide urges lawyers to consider the possibility of ADR and to ensure that clients are informed about the most cost-effective means of resolving disputes.[147]

Patents Court

An ADR programme in the Patents Court was set up on 2 October 1996, following developments in intellectual property dispute resolution, particularly by the establishment of the World Intellectual Property Organisation ('WIPO') Arbitration and Mediation Centre in Geneva in 1994.[148] The court's ADR programme is administered by the court,[149] is voluntary and can be used by parties in an intellectual property dispute, even if litigation is not on foot. No administrative fees are payable to the court and the venue, if available, is provided free of charge at the Central London Court House. Mediators are supplied by the Centre for Dispute Resolution and the Academy of Experts. Unless the mediators agree to act for free, a minimum fee of £50 is payable, which covers the mediator's preliminary work and up to three hours of mediation time. Unlike the Central London County Court mediations, the Patents Court mediations are not time-limited. The court has developed its own Rules for mediations conducted as part of its Programme.[150] The Rules allow a party who is reluctant to approach any other party to suggest mediation, to ask the Administrator to attempt to obtain the parties' agreement to mediation. The parties then choose a mediator from a panel of mediators, information about which is provided by the Administrator. If the parties cannot agree on the appointment, the Administrator will make the appointment. The Rules provide that a mediator may make proposals for, but not impose, settlement in the course of the mediation.

The aim of the Programme is to promote ADR and Ford J's view is that it should lead to the development of an integrated multi-door range of services by the court.[151] Genn's study of the Central London County Court Mediation Pilot briefly touched on the Patents Court scheme, commenting that, at that stage, it had suffered from a lack of take-up.[152]

Leeds Combined Court

In November 1998 the Northern Eastern Circuit Office and Taylor J, the Designated Civil Judge for Leeds approved, subject to formal approval by the Lord Chancellor's

---

146   Chancery Division *Chancery Guide*, 1999, at para 17.2. See *Guinle v Kirreh* (3 August 1999, unreported) for an example where the court encouraged ADR.
147   Chancery Division *Chancery Guide*, 1999, at para 17.4.
148   See the section on Intellectual Property Disputes in Chapter 8.
149   The Administrator is the Deputy District Judge of the Court.
150   Ford J *The Patents Court ADR Programme*, 1996.
151   Ford J, speaking at the CBI/CEDR conference, 28 October 1996, reported in Centre for Dispute Resolution, *Resolutions*, Issue No 15, at p 4.
152   H Genn *Central London County Court Mediation Pilot: Evaluation Report*, LCD Research Series, No 5/98, at p 2.

Department, a mediation scheme for the Leeds Combined Court Centre. It was proposed that the members of the Association of Northern Mediators[153] would provide the mediation services for the Scheme, which would include all cases at the Leeds Combined Court Centre. A leaflet describing mediation, setting out advantages and explaining its availability, would be produced either by the Court Service in Leeds or the Association of Northern Mediators. The leaflet would be sent by the court with the allocation questionnaire or, in sections of the court where no such questionnaire is used, with the first application for directions. If the parties agreed to mediate, a form would be sent to the Regional Law Society, who would maintain a list of mediators, accredited by CEDR, ADR Group or Academy of Experts. Mediations would be referred to mediators on a rota basis and other members, not being used as mediators for a particular case, would be encouraged to provide the venue, if the chosen mediator's premises are not available. It was proposed that, for smaller value claims, the cost would be fixed for the first four hours, with an hourly charge applying thereafter. For larger cases it was proposed to have a fixed fee per party for an initial 4–6 hour period, followed by an hourly rate.[154]

The Lord Chancellor announced at the Centre for Dispute Resolution Civil Justice Audit Conference[155] his Department's approval of the Scheme, which is now being run on a pilot basis. The Scheme will be evaluated by the Department of Law at Leeds Metropolitan University, using mediation report forms completed by both the mediator and the parties.[156] It is anticipated that similar schemes will be run in other combined court centres.[157]

Mercantile courts

Mercantile courts are in effect regional commercial courts, established in Leeds, Manchester, Birmingham, Liverpool, Bristol, Newcastle upon Tyne and Cardiff. Part 49H of the CPR contains practice directions for the courts. The Mercantile Courts' Guide includes a case management information sheet, which is required to be lodged seven days before the case management conference, and asks the following questions:

- Might some form of ADR assist to resolve the dispute?
- Has ADR been considered with the client?
- Has it been considered with the other parties?
- Should the case be stayed pending ADR?
- Are any other directions relating to ADR required?

The Guide also contains a Pre-trial Review Check List and asks some further questions on ADR:

- Would some form of ADR assist?
- Has ADR been considered with the client?

---

153 See the later section on Mediation Organisations.
154 The Association of Northern Mediators *Leeds Court Mediation* and *Notes of meeting to discuss court-approved mediation scheme*, 1999.
155 On 7 April 2000.
156 The Court Administration will need to assess the costs implications of operating the scheme, although that is to be limited to the circulation of information about mediation.
157 For example, in Manchester and Birmingham.

- Has it been explored with the other parties?[158]

The Leeds Combined Court Mediation Scheme will include the Leeds Mercantile Court.

Court of Appeal

The Court of Appeal's 1995 Practice Note[159] expressed the court's hope that some appeals may be found capable of resolution by mediation. Parties were encouraged to consider ADR by the personal recommendation of judges at the stage of seeking leave to appeal, even before the Woolf Reforms. For example, in a 1997 application, the court added the following postscript to its judgment in *Re H (A Minor)*:

'It seems to be that there are deep-seated anxieties held by both parties in this case, which are better fitted for some prolonged period of mediation . . . the Court Welfare Officer should be encouraged to explore what facilities . . . are available for such mediation to take place . . .'[160]

In *Chalmers v Johns* the court added the following postscript:

'. . . it does seem . . . that it would be very sad if the parents did not at least contemplate a reference to mediation . . . there are highly specialist and expert mediation services available to the parties . . . I would urge the parties and their advisers to at least give consideration to the availability of these facilities . . .'[161]

Parties to appeals were asked to indicate in confidence to the Registrar of Civil Appeals if the case was considered suitable for mediation. The court also introduced a pilot mediation scheme. A panel of senior lawyers was set up to mediate pending appeals on a pro-bono basis. The Master of the Rolls wrote to both parties, urging them to consider ADR and, if they did not wish to consider ADR, they were invited to discuss the reason. The offer to participate in the scheme was not sent in cases relating to family, immigration or judicial review cases. Between November 1998 and March 1999, parties in 250 cases had been invited to participate in the mediation scheme. In 12 cases both parties agreed to mediate.[162] In those cases, the mediations were organised by the Civil Appeals Office; were held in most cases at the Royal Courts of Justice outside office hours; and have not been limited in duration. Despite the slow take-up of the scheme, the Civil Appeals Office has confirmed that the Lords Justices continue to persuade parties to mediate.[163] For example, Ward LJ in *Dyson and Field (Twohey Executors) v Leeds CC* (22 November 1999) said, 'this is . . . the category of case in which . . . we should encourage the parties to use an ADR procedure . . . sooner rather than later'.

Family courts

Mediation, or conciliation as it was referred to in the context of family disputes, was widely practised in magistrates' courts before the Second World War, with the

---

158 See CPR, Part 49H and *Mercantile Courts' Guide,* 1999.
159 [1995] 1 WLR 1188.
160 [1997] EWCA 1424, per Ward LJ.
161 [1998] EWCA 3577, per Thorpe LJ.
162 H Genn *Central London County Court Mediation Pilot: Evaluation Report,* LCD Research Series, No 5/98, at p 2.
163 The authors thank the Civil Appeals Office for their assistance.

primary aim at that time of preserving marriage.[164] In 1971 a Practice Direction on matrimonial conciliation allowed the development of court-based conciliation for family disputes. The first attempt to institute a formal court-annexed family mediation service took place at Bristol County Court in 1976. Initially, its remit was limited to defended divorce cases, but in 1978 the scheme was extended to disputes over custody and access.[165] Growth in court-annexed family mediation was rapid, although the procedure for referral varied between courts. In some courts, the parties were invited to an appointment with the Court Welfare Officer, whereas in others, the process was initiated by a Registrar, who would encourage the parties to meet with a conciliator.[166]

The Booth Committee recommended[167] that mediation should be available at an initial hearing, which should take place as soon as possible after the filing of the petition, but that, in order to avoid pressure on the parties to reach agreement, the hearing could be adjourned for mediation to take place at another time.[168] A Practice Direction, issued on 28 July 1986, stipulated that before an inquiry and report by a Court Welfare Officer could be ordered, the judge or registrar should consider, where local mediation facilities exist, whether the case is suitable for conciliation and, if so, to make a direction to this effect in the Order. A conciliation scheme, which focuses on children's issues, was set up in 1983 in the London Family Division, governed by a Practice Direction of 18 October 1991. It provides that the parties, with their legal advisers, should attend a conciliation appointment, which allows the issues to be outlined to a district judge and court welfare officer. The court welfare officer attempts to conciliate an outcome, in a separate meeting which is privileged. If the conciliation is unsuccessful, the district judge provides directions for the further conduct of the matter, at which point neither the district judge nor welfare officer will have any further involvement in the application.[169]

Following recommendations by the Law Commission in 1990[170] that family courts should be given the power to recommend mediation either on their own or on either spouse's motion, the Family Law Act 1996 was drafted to include provisions, giving effect to the recommendations, although those provisions are not yet in force. The provisions would allow family courts to direct, at any stage in proceedings on the application of either party or on the court's own initiative, that the parties should attend a meeting to discuss the mediation option.[171] The provisions would also allow the court to adjourn proceedings to enable a meeting to occur and, if appropriate, for a mediation to take place. At the end of the adjournment, the court would be able to

---

164 University of Newcastle upon Tyne Conciliation Project Unit, *Report to the Lord Chancellor's Department on the costs and effectiveness of conciliation in England and Wales*, March 1989, at p 10.
165 Ibid, at p 12.
166 Ibid.
167 Booth Committee *Report of the Committee on Matrimonial Causes*, HMSO, London, 1985.
168 Ibid, at paras 4.54–4.57.
169 Compare New Zealand, where the parties to separation proceedings may ask that the matter be referred to mediation, which is carried out by family court judges.
170 The Law Commission *The Grounds for Divorce*, Law Commission No 192, HMSO, London.
171 Family Law Act 1996, s 13, the implementation of which has been put on hold, at this stage until some time in 2001.

require a report as to whether the parties attempted mediation; whether any part of the dispute had been resolved by mediation; whether any agreement had been reached in mediation; and whether there is a need for further mediation and, if so, whether any further mediation is likely to be successful.[172] Most recently, an Ancillary Relief Scheme in divorce cases, which had been piloted in 29 courts in England and Wales, makes provision for a Financial Dispute Resolution hearing to be conducted by a judge who will attempt to facilitate an agreement between the parties and may adjourn the case to allow for mediation.[173]

The framework in the Family Law Act 1996 is consistent with the 1998 Council of Europe Recommendation No R(98) 1 on Family Mediation, placing an obligation on Member States to:

- introduce or promote family mediation, where necessary, to strengthen existing family mediation; and
- take or reinforce all measures considered necessary, with a view to implementing a number of agreed principles for the promotion and use of family mediation as an appropriate means of resolving family disputes.

The Recommendation provides that mediation should not in principle be compulsory, although it supports court-referred mediation and recommends that States should set up mechanisms which would enable legal proceedings to be interrupted for mediation to take place.[174]

Courts in Scotland

The development of court-annexed mediation has been inhibited in Scotland as there is no divorce court welfare service[175] and, in the Sheriff Courts, where most applications for divorce are made, there is no equivalent to the Registrar. However, since 1990, as a result of changes to court rules, both the Sheriff Court and the Court of Session have been able to refer family disputes to mediation.[176] The fundamental difference between the courts is the need for parties' consent to mediation in Court of Session actions. In the case of the Sheriff Courts, although referral is mandatory, the parties are not compelled to mediate, but to find out more about mediation.[177] Anecdotal evidence suggests that Sheriffs have been reluctant to mandate referral to

---

172 Family Law Act 1996, s 14, the implementation of which has been put on hold, at this stage until some time in 2001.
173 See the section on Family Disputes in Chapter 8 for more information on the Scheme.
174 Funding changes, which provide a further impetus to the development of family mediation, are considered in Chapter 9.
175 Reports are normally prepared by social workers.
176 Ordinary Cause Rule 33.22 states, in relation to the Sheriff Court, that in any family action where parental responsibilities or parental rights are an issue, the Sheriff may, at any stage of the action, where he considers it appropriate, refer an issue to a mediator accredited to a specific family mediation organisation. In relation to the Court of Session, Rule of Court 49.23 states that, in any family action, where the custody of or access to a child is in dispute, the Court may at any stage of the action, if it considers it appropriate, with the consent of the parties, refer that dispute to a specified family mediation conciliation service.
177 F Garwood *The Scottish Scene*, UK College of Family Mediators, Issue 1, Summer 1997.

mediation in any event.[178] In addition, lawyers are sceptical about the benefits of mediation for dealing with financial issues.[179]

There is increasing support for a scheme of court-referred mediation in non-matrimonial matters in Scotland.[180] The Scottish Courts Administration, now part of the Justice Department of the Scottish Executive, has shown interest in mediation, for instance, through sponsorship of a mediation scheme linked with the Edinburgh Citizens Advice Bureau and the Edinburgh Sheriff Court.[181] Cases are referred to the scheme by an in-court adviser, a Sheriff or the Citizens Advice Bureaux. The scheme is primarily for small claims and summary cause cases, and family and neighbour disputes are excluded from the scheme's remit. Mediators from the Centre for Dispute Resolution and ACCORD provide the scheme with free mediation services.[182] The Royal Faculty of Procurators in Glasgow has formed a dispute resolution forum, and one of its early aims was to assist the formulation of more effective Sheriff Court rules in Glasgow, with the view to more efficient commercial dispute resolution.[183] The Law Society of Scotland has suggested that in certain prescribed actions or in a pilot area, parties should be asked to consider whether a dispute could be referred to mediation and, if not, to explain their reasons. The Law Society has recommended that, if parties agree to attempt mediation, the matter can be automatically referred to a court-appointed mediator. Courts should also have, the Law Society has argued, the power to order a case to mediation, although the court timetable should not be interfered with.[184]

Northern Ireland Courts

Case management techniques have been developed in a number of County Court Divisions, as well as in the High Court, in Northern Ireland. The listing arrangements for cases in the Chancery Division of the Northern Ireland High Court encourages a party to pursue settlement. A four week period is allowed prior to the fixing of a trial date to give parties an opportunity to explore settlement.[185] In relation to family matters, it appears that magistrates have not shown much interest in mediation, notwithstanding the requirement in the Children Order 1995 that courts should only make orders relating to children if that would be better than making no order at all. Northern Ireland commentators support the development of mediation as a means for providing parents with the opportunity to take control of decision-making about their children.[186] It appears that the main problem for the development

---

178 R Mays and B Clark *ADR in Scotland*, The Scottish Office, 1999, at p 77 referring to interviews with CALM mediators.

179 J Lewis *The role of mediation in family disputes in Scotland: report of a research study*, The Scottish Office Central Research Unit, Edinburgh, 1999.

180 R Mays and B Clark *ADR in Scotland*, op cit.

181 See the section on Mediation Organisations and consumers.

182 For an evaluation of the scheme, see N Loughran and L Cameron *Edinburgh Mediation Project: final report*, Edinburgh, May 1998.

183 D Semple 'When it really does pay to talk' *The Herald (Glasgow)*, 17 November 1999, at p 16.

184 Law Society of Scotland *Response to 'Access to Justice beyond 2000'*, 1998.

185 Civil Justice Reform Group *Review of the Civil Justice System in Northern Ireland: Interim Report*, April 1999 at para 10.66.

186 For example, C Archbold et al *Divorce in Northern Ireland: unravelling the system*,

of family mediation in Northern Ireland is the absence of a 'gateway' for referral to mediation at any stage in the family law system. Referrals to family mediation come mainly from Relate and the public direct.[187]

Future issues

Court promotion of mediation and the extent of court-based mediation are issues which will influence the demand for and supply of mediation. These issues are currently under consideration by the Lord Chancellor's Department. Given the number of questions these issues raise, and the impact that answers to those questions will have in the UK, this topic is considered separately in Chapter 9.

The Role of Mediation Organisations
Overview

This section outlines UK mediation organisations, catalogued by subject area and, within each subject area, geographically, with some reference also to other juris-dictions. In response to requests for a national directory of mediators and mediation organisations, the Lord Chancellor's Department is giving consideration to developing such a resource.[188] Overwhelming support for this suggestion was received from the respondents to the Lord Chancellor's ADR Discussion Paper.[189] Contact details for the organisations referred to in this section are provided in the footnotes to this section and in the Appendices to this book. This section is aimed at providing both an overview of the breadth of mediation development in the UK, and of the role played by mediation organisations, and a resource for those who may wish to refer a matter to mediation.

General civil/commercial mediation organisations
England and Wales

The Academy of Experts[190]
The Academy of Experts was founded in 1987, with a view to promoting the cost efficient resolution of disputes in the UK.[191] The Academy's Mediation Advisory

---

Report to the Office of Law Reform, HMSO, 1999, at p 201. The jurisdiction relating to divorce and ancillary matters is under review by the Office of Law Reform.

187 C Archbold et al *Divorce in Northern Ireland: unravelling the system*, Report to the Office of Law Reform, HMSO, 1999, at p 22; and see the section in this chapter on Mediation Organisations.

188 Lord Chancellor's Department *ADR Discussion Paper*, November 1999.

189 Lord Chancellor's Department *ADR Discussion Paper: Summary of responses*, August 2000, at para 40.

190 2 South Square, Gray's Inn, London WC1R 5HP; phone: 020 7637 0333; fax: 020 7637 1893; email: admin@academy-experts.org; and website: http://www.academy-experts.org/.

191 Academy of Experts *Guidelines for Mediation*.

Service provides advice on mediation to barristers, solicitors, professional institutions and organisations, as well as to disputants.[192] The Academy offers a mediator enquiry service and appoints mediators. The Academy can provide a venue for mediations. It administers independent mediation schemes on behalf of professional bodies, government departments, public corporations, private companies and trade associations. Schemes have been custom-made for commercial, employment, family, community and shareholder disputes. A scheme can be incorporated into an organisation's standard terms of trading or constitute a one-off agreement between disputing parties. The Academy maintains a separate list of mediators for each scheme and mediation fees are either charged on a standard or fixed fee basis.

The Academy's Faculty of Mediation runs a mediator training programme.[193] The Academy also publishes a wide range of mediation literature.[194] Its website provides useful information on mediation.[195] The Academy's Register of Qualified Dispute Resolvers is available both online and in hard copy. The Academy's mediations are usually charged either on a standard fee or fixed fee basis. The standard fee basis includes a placement fee and an hourly mediator fee. A minimum fee is usually specified. Travelling time is charged at a percentage of the hourly fee. A mediator's expenses are charged at cost.[196] The fixed fee includes administration, mediator fees and expenses. Fee information can be obtained from the Academy Secretariat.[197] Problems are referred to the Chairman of the Academy or the Mediation Committee.[198]

ADR Chambers (UK) Limited [199]

ADR Chambers has set up barrister and solicitor panels of neutrals who offer facilitative, evaluative and appellate mediation. Appellate mediation is intended for those who wish to attempt a private resolution of issues under appeal. The organisation also offers ADR training.[200]

ADR Group [201]

The ADR Group, a Bristol-based mediation organisation, has over 80 member firms nationwide. It provides mediation advice, assesses the suitability of disputes for mediation and recommends mediators. Its 'ADR Net' Directory lists its solicitor members who offer mediation services. The Group provides pre-litigation review ('PLR') to help parties decide whether to proceed with mediation or litigation; mediation case management; and mediation consultancy. Its members also offer

---

192 Academy of Experts *Guidelines for Mediation.*
193 See Chapter 11 on training and standards.
194 'What is mediation?'; 'Answers to frequently asked questions about ADR and mediation'; 'Mediation Application Form'; 'The Academy Mediation Scheme'; 'Guidelines for Mediation'; 'Guidance Notes for Mediators'; 'Agreement to Mediation'; 'The Academy Fixed Fee Scheme'; 'Mediation Training Booklet'; 'Expert Training for Experts and Dispute Resolvers'; 'Membership Services Pamphlet'.
195 http://www.academy-experts.org/
196 Academy of Experts *Schedule to the Mediation Agreement.*
197 Academy of Experts *Guidance Notes for Mediators.*
198 Ibid.
199 1 Knightrider Court, London EC4V 5JP; phone: 0207 329 4909; fax: 0207 329 4903; and website: http://www.adrchambers.co.uk
200 ADR Chambers *Settling disputes the private way*, ADR Chambers pamphlet.
201 36–38 Baldwin St, Bristol BS1 1NR; phone: 0117 946 7180; email: adrgroup@adrnet.co.uk; website: http://www.adrnet.co.uk.

telephone mediation. The Group provides mediators for a range of mediation schemes.[202] It also provides an extensive range of mediation training courses and a mediation video;[203] and publishes a wide range of mediation literature.[204] The ADR Group's mediation fees[205] in a standard case, involving 5–7 hours of mediation, are charged on a per party, per hour basis,[206] although preparation time is charged at a lower rate.[207] Mediator expenses are charged differently, depending on the kind of expense.[208] Different fees may be charged in complex matters. Telephone mediation and mediation of low value claims, for example, are usually charged at lower rates. Consultancy and PLR fees are negotiated on a case-by-case basis. The Group has recently launched a 'West Country initiative',[209] which will initially offer mediations for a flat rate,[210] and promote mediation through seminars.

Arab-British Chamber of Commerce[211]

The Arab-British Chamber of Commerce aims to create parity between Arab and non-Arab parties in dispute. It has produced a set of Conciliation and Arbitration Rules. The Arbitration Rules require parties to attempt conciliation first. The Chamber also appoints mediators, but is not a mediator training organisation.

Association of Northern Mediators[212]

The Association of Northern Mediators seeks to promote mediation throughout the Midlands, Northumbria, Cleveland, the North West and Yorkshire. It provides a Mediation Advice Line and lists of mediators, free of charge, divided into local and professional groupings. Its mediators usually charge an hourly mediation fee. The Association administers the Leeds Combined Court Centre Mediation Scheme.[213] It is not a mediator training organisation.

---

202 For example, the Central London County Court Mediation Scheme; the Housing Ombudsman Mediation Scheme; and the Leeds Combined Court Centre Mediation Pilot.

203 See Chapter 11 on training and standards.

204 'Mediation Clause'; 'Mediation Agreement'; 'Mediation Procedure'; 'Mediation Fact Sheet'; 'Mediation User's Guide'; 'Mediation Referral Form'; 'Mediation Preparation Notes'; 'Mediation Briefing Notes'; 'Code of Conduct'; 'Assuring competency and quality in Mediation: a Policy Document'; 'Effective Dispute Resolution: Foundation Training Course Brochure'; 'Mediation: an explanatory booklet'; 'Information Pack'; and 'ADR Group Protocol'.

205 See ADR Group *Mediation Costs Schedule*.

206 Ibid, which states that the standard hourly rate is £125 + VAT per party.

207 Ibid, which states that the charge is £75 + VAT per party per hour, although the mediator's first hour preparation time is included.

208 Ibid, which sets out that travel time is charged at the rate of £33.75 per hour + VAT; travel expenses are charged at either 37p per mile or the standard train fare; and refreshments and other items are charged at cost.

209 With six Bristol law firms (Burges Salmon, Clarke Wilmott, Beachcroft Wansbroughs, Veale Wasborough, Bevan Ashford and Bevans), the South West Chamber of Commerce, the South West Regional Development Agency and the Bristol Law Society.

210 The initial flat rate is £500 per party: *The Law Society Gazette*, 20 April 2000.

211 6 Belgrave Square, London SW1X 8PH; phone: 020 7235 4363; fax: 020 7245 6688.

212 Goodbard House, Infirmary St, Leeds LS1 2JS; phone: 0113 2469129; fax: 0113 2467518. Also see its pamphlet, 'What is mediation?'

213 See the section on Mediation and Courts in this chapter.

Centre for Business Arbitration[214]

The Centre for Business Arbitration provides a case management service to help parties to define the issues in a dispute and the areas of agreement and disagreement. This is a stand-alone service and is a necessary first step if the parties wish to proceed to mediation administered by the Centre. In addition, the Centre assesses cases for suitability for mediation, provides mediation case management and appoints mediators. It has a panel of barrister mediators and the panel list is available either from the organisation or online. It is not a mediator training organisation, but has produced a range of literature on mediation.[215] Panel mediators usually charge mediation fees on a sliding scale, varying with the amount of the claim.

Centre for Dispute Resolution (CEDR)[216]

CEDR, which celebrates its 10th anniversary in 2000, provides a wide range of mediation services, including mediation advice, assessment of suitability for mediation, appointment of mediators, drawing up mediation agreements, mediation case management, arranging mediation venue, exchange of summaries and documents, pre-mediation meetings with the parties to discuss concerns and follow-up services after mediations. In addition, the Centre provides facilitation, meeting support, executive tribunals, early neutral evaluation, expert determination, adjudication, dispute audits and a range of dispute schemes. The Centre has established an international committee, chaired by Lord Griffiths, to promote mediation internationally. It is involved with a number of ADR working committees and projects. It offers an extensive mediation and mediator training programmes and courses[217] and a mediation video. It was winner of the National Training Awards for the London Region in 1995. It has published a wide range of mediation literature.[218] The Centre also has a directory of mediators available online for members.[219] Mediation fees are usually charged on a sliding scale, varying with the amount of the claim, together with preparation time and expenses.

Chartered Institute of Arbitrators ('CIA')[220]

The CIA appoints mediators and conciliators and maintains a panel of mediators. The Institute also offers training and education in mediation. In relation to its consumer mediation scheme, refer to the section on consumer mediation.

---

214 11 Old Square, Lincoln's Inn, London WC2A 3TS; phone: 020 7491 9697; email: arbitration@lincolns-inn.com; and website: http://www.arbitration.lincolns-inn.com

215 'Case Management Rules'; 'Mediation Rules'; 'Case Management Request Form'; 'Mediation Request Form'; 'What is Case Management, Arbitration and Mediation?'; 'Why Come To Us?'

216 Princes House, 95 Gresham St, London EC2V 7MA; phone: 020 7600 0500; fax: 020 7600 0501; email: mediate@cedr.co.uk; and website: http://www.cedr.co.uk

217 See Chapter 11 on training and standards.

218 'Mediation Clauses'; 'Mediation Agreement'; 'Model Mediation Procedure'; 'Model Mediation Procedure Guidance Notes'; 'Code of Conduct'; 'ADR Route Map'; 'Referring a Case'; 'Mediation – some Questions and Answers'; 'CEDR Mediation Record'; 'Cutting the cost of Conflict'; 'Continuing Professional Development Document'; quarterly *Resolutions* magazine; 'Who we are and what we do'; 'Membership Fact Sheet'; 'What are the clients saying'; 'Mediation Skills Training Programme'; 'International Summer School Mediator Skills Training'; 'Mediator Handbook'; and an 'Information Pack'.

219 Membership benefits include the *Resolution* magazine, quarterly forums and discounts on training.

220 24 Angel Gate, City Road, London EC1V 2RS; phone: 020 7837 4483; fax: 020 7837 4185; email: 71411.2735@compuserv.com; website: http://ourworld.compuserv.com/arbitrators

Commercial Mediation Centre[221]

The Commercial Mediation Centre provides mediation, co-mediation, mediation consultancy, and training.[222] It has published a range of mediation literature.[223] The Centre charges an initial registration fee, which covers four hours of mediation time, and an hourly or daily rate thereafter, together with an administration fee.

Consensus Mediation[224]

Consensus Mediation provides mediators for civil/commercial disputes. Mediators are categorised as consultants, lead mediators, mediators or assistant mediators, depending on experience. Fees vary according to the value of the claim and category of mediator. An e-mediator service is also available.

Dispute Resolution Ltd[225]

Dispute Resolution Ltd assesses cases for suitability, appoints mediators and provides mediation case management and a venue for mediation. The company also offers mediation consultancy. Its training offers one, two or three day options. It has published a 'Mediation Agreement', 'Mediation Procedure' and 'Information Pack'. Mediation fees are based on a fixed rate, which includes four hours of preparation time, three hours of travelling time and three hours of mediation time, after which an hourly rate applies, depending upon the amount of the claim.[226]

Dispute Mediation[227]

Dispute Mediation consists of a panel of commercial lawyers and barristers. Its panel mediators provide fixed fee mediation which includes the costs of administration, venue and mediator.[228] Its publication, 'Mediation: a more effective way to resolve disputes', provides further details about the organisation.

In Place of Strife[229]

In Place of Strife focuses primarily on providing mediation services to the insurance industry. Its panel of mediators are CEDR-accredited. It has produced a range of mediation literature.[230]

---

221 Chancery House, 53–64 Chancery Lane, London WC2A 1QU; phone: 020 7430 2222; fax: 020 7430 2022; email: mediation@btinternet.com
222 One day and three day mediation option.
223 'Mediation Clause'; 'Mediation Agreement'; 'Mediation Procedure'; 'Assessing cases for Mediation'; 'Code of Conduct'; 'Training in Mediation Services'.
224 York House, 89 York Street, Norwich NR2 2AP; phone: 01603 665 845; fax: 01603 633 996; email: mediate@consensus.uk.com; website: http://www.consensus.uk.com
225 5 Cheviot Drive, Thornbury, Bristol BS35 2YA; phone: 01454 281244; fax: 01454 281911; email: dan@dispute-resolution.ltd.uk; website: http://www.dispute-resolution.ltd.uk
226 Dispute Resolution Ltd *Information Pack*.
227 AMC House, 12 Cumberland Avenue, Park Royal, London NW10 7QL; phone: 020 8838 0022; fax: 020 8965 0229; email: enquiries@disputemediation.co.uk
228 For claims up to £15,000, the fee is £1,750; for claims up to £50,000, the fee is £4,000; for claims up to £250,000, the fee is £6,000; and for claims in excess of £250,000 or which do not have a monetary value, the fee is negotiable. Fees are borne equally by the parties.
229 58 High St, Harrington, Northampton NN6 9NU; phone: 01536 418205; email: stops@mediate.co.uk; website: http://www.mediate.co.uk
230 For example, 'Mediation'; 'Fee Guidelines'; 'Specimen Mediation Agreement'; 'Application form for mediation services'.

InterMediation[231]

InterMediation's panel of mediators, called IM 100, consists of mediators from the top 100 legal and accountancy firms. The organisation has a Mediation Support Team, which can provide parties with advice on the mediation process; initiate contact with other parties; conduct the mediation administration; and provide follow up services. In addition to a mediation fee arrangement, based on a sliding scale depending upon the amount in dispute, the organisation offers a 'no settlement, no fee' option, which allows the mediator to be paid his or her fee in any event, but an additional fee to the organisation if the case settles. The contingency agreement is confidential between the parties and the organisation and the success fee is not dependent on the terms of the outcome and is agreed in advance.[232] The organisation's 'Information Pack' includes its Mediation Rules, Code of Practice, Notes for Guidance and Standard Mediation Agreement.[233]

International Dispute Resolution Centre[234]

The Centre was launched in March 2000 to accommodate mediations, and also offers a reading room and restaurant. It has the support of the London Court of International Arbitration, the Chartered Institute of Arbitrators, the London Maritime Arbitrators Association, ARIAS (UK), the Society of Construction Arbitrators, the Worshipful Company of Arbitrators and the City Disputes Panel.

Littleton Mediation[235]

Littleton Mediation has a panel of barrister mediators who provide mediation services and a venue for mediation. It is not a mediator training organisation. Mediation fees are currently by negotiation, although over time, standard hourly rates will develop. It offers parties a standard 'Mediation Agreement'.

London Court of International Arbitration (LCIA)[236]

Traditionally, the LCIA has provided arbitration services, but now also appoints mediators, provides a venue for mediation, and offers mediation case management, although it is not a mediator training organisation. Its 'Information Pack' provides useful mediation literature.[237] The court charges a registration fee, an hourly administration fee, mediator expenses and the mediator fees, which are charged either on an hourly or daily rate. A deposit is payable by each party in equal shares before the appointment of a mediator and if the costs at the end of the mediation are greater than the deposit, the shortfall is invoiced in equal shares, otherwise the parties are reimbursed.[238]

---

231 128 Cheapside, London EC2V 6BT; phone: 020 7600 4909; fax: 020 7600 6396; email: support@intermediation.com; website: www.intermediation.com
232 See the section on Funding and Mediation in Chapter 10.
233 InterMediation *Information Pack: Negotiation, Dialogue and Resolution*.
234 See website: http://www.idrc.co.uk; and phone: 020 7405 6500.
235 Littleton Chambers, 3 King's Bench Walk North, Temple, London EC4Y 7HR; phone: 020 7797 8600; fax: 020 7797 8699; email: clerks@littletonchambers.co.uk
236 Houlton House, 161–166 Fleet St, London EC4A 2DY; phone: 020 7936 3530; fax: 020 7936 3533; email: lcia@lcia-arbitration.com; website: http://www.lcia-arbitration.com
237 'Mediation Clause'; 'Mediation Agreement'; 'Mediation Rules'.
238 London Court of International Arbitration *Mediation Procedure*.

London Mediation Service[239]

The London Mediation Service was founded by the law firm, Lee & Pembertons, and targets disputes up to £15,000. The service was set up initially as a service for Lee & Pembertons' clients.[240]

Panel of Independent Mediators (PIMS)[241]

PIMS comprises a panel of seven highly experienced mediators.[242] Each mediator provides mediation services and fees are, by negotiation, charged at a daily rate, generally by reference to the dispute's complexity. PIMS is not a mediator training organisation. It has produced a booklet, outlining the wide experience of its panellists.

Reading Dispute Resolution Centre[243]

The Reading Dispute Resolution Centre provides case evaluation, negotiation and mediation services, and is not a mediator training organisation.

Workitout Resolution Company[244]

Workitout is a joint venture between Stewarts Solicitors and Berrymans, and provides mediation services for personal injury and clinical negligence disputes.

Scotland and Northern Ireland

A number of the professional bodies, providing mediation services in England and Wales, like the Institute of Civil Engineers, the Royal Institute of Chartered Surveyors and Institute of Chartered Accountants, also have offices and accredited mediator members in Scotland. The ADR Group and the Centre for Dispute Resolution also train and accredit mediators in Scotland and Northern Ireland. The Mediation Bureau is a private mediation organisation, which provides mediation services for civil/commercial disputes in Scotland.[245] The Bureau appoints mediators; and provides mediation case management, consultancy and training.[246] It has a standard 'Mediation Agreement' and 'Mediation Procedure'.[247]

Continental comparisons

Arbitration organisations throughout Europe provide mediation appointment services. For example, the Netherlands Arbitration Institute appoints mediators; the

---

239 Lee & Pembertons, 45 Pont St, London SW1X 0BX; phone: 020 7589 1114; fax: 020 7589 0808; email: law@leepem.co.uk
240 'Practice: Mediation', *The Law Society Gazette*, 30 April 2000.
241 The Panel Administrator, Ocean House, 24 Great Tower St, London EC3R 5AQ; phone: 020 7917 1745; fax: 020 7917 1746.
242 Philip Howell-Richardson, Andrew Paton, David Shapiro, Tony Willis, Nicholas Pryor, David Miles and Philip Naughton QC.
243 1 London St, Reading, Berkshire RG1 4QW; phone: 01189 509609; fax: 01189 502704.
244 63 Lincoln's Inn Fields, London WC2A 3LW; phone: 020 7692 5502; fax: 020 7831 6843; website: http://www.workitout.co.uk
245 Alderstone House, Kirkton South, Livingston, EH54 7AW; phone: 01506 641 7818; fax: 01506 417843.
246 See Chapter 11 on training and standards.
247 For more information, see its literature: 'Mediation: the essential facts'; and 'ADR pamphlet'.

Association Luxembourgeoise Pour l'Arbitrage provides lists of mediators to interested parties; the Danish Institute of Arbitration appoints mediators; the Board of Arbitration of Finland appoints mediators; the Chamber of National and International Arbitration of Milan appoints mediators, as does the Italian Arbitration Association. Chambers of Commerce throughout Europe are also providing mediator appointment services for commercial disputes.[248] For example, the Court of Arbitration, Madrid Chamber of Commerce and Industry appoints mediators, as does the Danish Chamber of Commerce and the Waren-Verein der Hamburger Börse. The International Chamber of Commerce based in Paris appoints mediators and provides mediation services. The Chambers of Commerce in Belgium have shown a keen interest in mediation services, and a number of Chambers have organised schemes. Reform in Italy in 1993 redefined the role of their Chambers of Commerce, providing them with new powers, governing the organisation of ADR services.[249] In Spain, Greece and Austria the Chambers of Commerce are also legally entitled to organise ADR services.[250] Other European organisations have developed specifically to provide commercial mediation services. For example, the Stockholm Chamber of Commerce set up a Mediation Institute in April 1999 to promote and administer commercial mediations. The Netherlands Mediation Institute (NMI) can appoint mediators and administer mediations under its own Mediation Rules. The NMI was founded in 1993 as an umbrella organisation in order to promote the development of mediation in the Netherlands. It has a Register of Mediators; its Mediation Rules were published in 1995; and it has developed a Code of Conduct for its registered mediators, together with a Model Mediation Agreement and Mediation Contract Clauses. The Danish Mediation Board was set up in order to appoint mediators.

Banking/finance mediation organisations

The City Disputes Panel ('CDP')[251] consists of dispute resolution specialists covering 25 sectors of financial services. It assesses cases for suitability for mediation, appoints mediators, provides mediation case management and consultancy. It also provides case appraisal, expert determination and arbitration services. It has a range of Working Parties, but is not a mediator training organisation. It charges a registration fee, case management fee, mediator fees at hourly rates and mediator expenses. It has published Mediation Clauses, with commentary, and Mediation Rules.

Community mediation organisations
England and Wales

Cardiff Mediation[252]
Cardiff Mediation provides neighbourhood and community mediation services, group conferencing, open forums and multi-party mediation. It provides management

---

248 For a thorough overview of the role of Chambers of Commerce in the various EU countries in the provision of ADR services, see V Federici (ed) *Chambers of Commerce in the European Union and alternative resolution of commercial disputes*, Union- camerie, September 1999.
249 Law No 580.
250 V Federici (ed), op cit.
251 Phone: 020 7440 7373.
252 Unit 2, St Clair Court, 3–11 West Bute St, Cardiff CF10 5EN; phone: 02920 316800;

and other support services to volunteer mediators and mediation services. It offers a range of community mediation training courses. The professional profiles of its mediators are available on request, as is a range of mediation literature.[253]

Mediation UK[254]

Mediation UK is an umbrella organisation for community conflict resolution initiatives, with particular emphasis on neighbour, victim-offender and schools contexts.[255] Mediation UK provides an information and referral service to identify relevant community mediation services, training or practitioners. It provides accreditation for both community mediators and community mediation services and offers help to groups that wish to set up such a service.[256] The Group organises meetings and conferences, with the aim of linking individuals and programmes. It has over 500 members and 3,000 volunteers are connected with its work.[257] It has an extensive range of mediation training courses, a training manual and videos.[258] It is proposing a national register of community mediators. It publishes a quarterly

---

fax: 02920 316801; email: cardiff@mediation.freeserve.co.uk

253 'Annual Reports'; 'What is Mediation? Your Questions Answered'; and 'Dispute Settlement Services'.

254 Alexander House, Telephone Avenue, Bristol BS1 4BS; phone: 0117 9046661; fax: 0117 9043331; email: mediationuk@mediationuk.org.uk; and website: http://www.cix. co.uk/~mediationuk/

255 The organisations caught by the umbrella include: Ashford Neighbour Conciliation Service, Bolton Neighbour Dispute Service, Bracknell Forest Neighbourhood Mediation Service, Bradford Mediation Centre, Brighton & Hove Mediation Service, Cambridge & District Community Mediation Service, Mediation West Cornwall, Coventry Mediation Partnership, Derby Mediation Service, Mediation Dorset, Guildford Community Mediation Service, Herefordshire Neighbourhood Mediation Service, Leeds Community Mediation Service, Leicester Mediation Service, Liverpool Mediation Service, Luton Mediation, Maidstone Mediation Scheme, Mediation Manchester, Milton Keynes Neighbour Dispute Mediation Service, Resolve, Norwich & District Legal Services, Mediation Norwich, Oxford Community Mediation, Plymouth Mediation, Portsmouth Mediation Service, Preston Area Neighbour Dispute Action, Rochdale Mediation Service, Mediation Sheffield, Waveley Community Mediation Service, Wolverhampton Neighbourhood Mediation Service, Face to Face – Neighbourhood Mediation in York, UNITE, Bromley Neighbour Mediation Service, Camden Mediation Service, Ealing Neighbour Mediation Service, Greenwich Mediation, Hackney Mediation Service, Hounslow Mediation Service, Lewisham Action for Mediation Project (LAMP), Lambeth Mediation Service, Southwark Mediation Centre, Tower Hamlets Mediation Service, Waltham Forest Neighbour Mediation Service, Wandsworth Independent Mediation Service, Cardiff Mediation, Mediation Mid Wales and Monmouthshire Mediation.

256 The process can last up to two years and involves a number of stages: establishing the need for the service, forming a steering committee, determining its structure, raising funds and other resources, recruiting a co-ordinator and mediators, publicising its services and obtaining referrals. See M Liebmann (ed) *Community and Neighbour Mediation*, Cavendish Publishing Limited, London, 1998, at p 69.

257 Mediation UK has established the following networks: community, victim/offender, work place, education/young people, environment, training and international mediation. It has initiated the Restorative Justice Consortium, a grouping of voluntary agencies acting in the criminal justice field.

258 See Chapter 11 on training and standards.

magazine and newsletter, together with a wide range of other materials, promoting mediation in the community field.[259]

Scotland

Community Mediation Dundee[260]

Community Mediation Dundee has operated since 1995 and provides a free independent mediation service for community/neighbourhood disputes. The type of disputes include anti-social behaviour, problems with the behaviour of children, noise and harassment.

Edinburgh Community Mediation Project[261]

The Edinburgh Community Mediation Project was established in 1995 and is managed by SACRO, a registered charity, which has provided mediation and reparation services for victims and accused persons since 1987. It provides a free independent mediation service to resolve community/neighbourhood disputes. Its main referral agencies are the Police and the Housing and Environmental Health departments of local councils. Its members recently voted to make accreditation of services a future condition of membership and it is proposed to make all members of community mediation services accredited by 2002.

---

259 'Mediation UK Standards for Mediators'; 'Mediation UK Standards for Mediation Services'; 'The need for community mediation services'; 'Guide to starting a community mediation service'; 'Directory of mediation and conflict resolution services'; 'Training manual in community mediation skills'; 'Handbook for the UK training programme in mediation skills'; 'Accreditation Pack'; 'Accreditation Scheme Mediation UK'; 'The use of art in working with conflict'; 'Mediation UK and its member services'; 'Mediation takes a FIRM hold'; 'Dictionary of Terms'; 'Religious notions relating to conflict resolution'; 'Elder Mediation Project'; 'Alternative Dispute Resolution'; 'List of conference papers'; 'MEDNews'; 'Mediation Digest'; 'Peer Mediation'; 'Mediation in Schools'; 'What is Peer Mediation?'; 'Conflict Resolution and Schools'; 'Schools Mediation and Conflict Resolution Services List'; 'Schools mediation and conflict resolution reading list'; 'Victim-offender mediation guidelines for starting a service'; 'Victim-offender mediation handbook'; 'Resolving crime in the community – mediation in criminal justice'; 'Mediation of criminal conflict in England'; 'Family/community group conferencing in criminal justice resource list'; 'Mediation and reparation'; 'A new direction for victims'; 'Mediation UK policy on diversion of offenders from court'; 'Mediation and victim support'; 'Conflict resolution skills in the probation service'; 'Criminal Justice policy'; 'Conflict resolution and neighbourhood watch'; 'Victim-offender mediation services list'; 'Victim-offender mediation resources list'; 'Victim-offender mediation reading list'; 'Repairing the harm – friends and restorative justice'; 'Restorative measures'; 'Restorative Justice – for victims, communities and offenders'; 'Community disorders and policing'; 'Neighbour disputes – comparing the cost effectiveness of mediation and conventional approaches'; 'Community mediation service general survey 1995'; 'Boundary disputes'; 'Noise from Neighbours'; 'Dealing directly with your neighbours'; 'Neighbours quarrels'; 'Community mediation services list'; 'Community mediation resources list'; 'Community mediation reading list'.

260 49 Meadowside, Dundee, Scotland DD1 1EQ; phone: 01382 206406.

261 27 York Place, Edinburgh EH1 3HP; phone: 0131 5572101; fax: 0131 5572102.

Fife Community Mediation Scheme [262]

The Fife Community Mediation Scheme was established in Kirkcaldy, with the help of Scottish Office Urban Aid Funding. Its referrals come from the Consumer Advice Bureau, the Rights Office, Fife Constabulary and Fife Council.

Livingston and District Community Mediation Service [263]

This service was initially sponsored by a US company. Although seven local community members have been trained in mediation, the service is still in its early stages of development.

Northern Ireland

The Mediation Network for Northern Ireland [264] is a voluntary organisation with charitable status formed to encourage individuals, public bodies and institutions to improve strategies for dealing with conflict in Northern Ireland. It maintains a core of panel of practising community mediators and provides community mediation services and an extensive range of mediation training courses. [265] The Network co-operates with the Northern Ireland Community Relations Council.

Computer mediation organisations

The British Computer Society [266] appoints mediators free of charge, and provides consultants to help prevent disputes during computer projects. It also provides expert determination and arbitration services. The terms and conditions of engagement of mediators is a matter for agreement between the parties and the selected mediator. The Society publishes a Register of Expert Witnesses who are also accredited mediators. The Society is not a mediator training organisation.

Construction and property mediation organisations

The Association of Consulting Engineers [267] provides mediation services and mediator appointments can be made by the President of the Chartered Institute of Arbitrators (CIA). [268] The British Institute of Architectural Technologists [269] also offers mediation

---

262　24 Hill St, Kirkcaldy, Fife, Scotland KY1 1HX; phone: 01592 597063; fax: 01592 593133.

263　St Kenneth's Community Resource Centre, Ogilvie House, Sinclair Way, Livingston, Scotland EH54 8HL; phone: 01506 435118.

264　128a Great Victoria St, Belfast BT2 7BG; phone: 01232 438614; fax: 01232 314430; email: info@mediation-network.org.uk; website: http://www.mediation-network.org.uk

265　See Chapter 11 on training and standards; and see Mediation Network for Northern Ireland *Transforming Conflict Training*.

266　1 Sanford St, Swindon, Wiltshire SW1 1HJ; phone: 01793 417417; fax: 01793 480270: email: alewis@bcs.org.uk; website: http://www.bcs.org.uk/

267　Alliance House, 12 Caxton St, London SW1; phone: 020 7222 6557.

268　See the section on consumer mediation organisations.

269　397 City Road, London EC1; phone: 020 7278 2206.

services. The Institution of Civil Engineers[270] provides conciliation services and appoints conciliators. If the parties fail to reach an agreement in conciliation, the Conciliation Procedure allows the conciliator to make a recommendation as to how, in his or her opinion, the matter should be settled. The Institution provides a list of conciliators on request.[271] The Landscape Institute[272] offers mediation services and mediator appointments can be made by the President of the Institute. The National House-Building Council[273] offers conciliation services for members and clients. The Royal Institute of British Architects[274] provides conciliation services and its President can make conciliator appointments. The Institute's Conciliation Rules do not allow the conciliator to impose a decision on the parties. Fees are charged on a sliding scale.

The Royal Institution of Chartered Surveyors ('RICS')[275] offers a wide range of mediation services. It has a mediation helpline and appoints mediators for property, construction and agricultural disputes. The Institution also administers a mediation scheme for the appointment of mediators in compulsory purchase disputes, where the acquirer has signed up to the scheme. The Institution offers adjudication, expert determination and arbitration services.[276] A directory of members and mediators is available in hard copy and online. The Institution has published a range of mediation literature[277] and has produced a mediation training video. Although it charges an administration fee for making mediator appointments, mediation fees are agreed direct between the parties and mediator.

Consumer mediation organisations

The Chartered Institute of Arbitrators ('CIA')[278]

The CIA administers the Consumer Dispute Resolution Scheme.[279] The Scheme provides that the conciliation process should normally take no longer than six weeks, but parties can agree to refer the dispute to arbitration if conciliation is either

---

270 1 Great George St, London SW1P 3AA; phone: 020 7222 7722; fax: 020 7222 7500.
271 The Institution also has a 'Conciliation Agreement'; and 'Schedule to Conciliator's Agreement', which covers the issue of conciliator fees and expenses.
272 6–8 Barnard Mews, London SW11 1QU; phone: 020 7350 5200; fax: 020 7350 5201; email: mail@l-i.org.uk; and website: http://www.li.org.uk
273 Buildmark House, Boycott Avenue, Old Brook, Milton Keynes, Bucks MK6 2RN; phone: 01908 691888; fax: 01908 678575.
274 Construction House, 56–64 Leonard St, London EC2; phone: 020 7251 0791.
275 Surveyor Court, Westwood Way, Coventry CV4 8JE; phone: 0207 2227000; fax: 0207 3343800; email: info@rics.org.uk; website: www.rics.org.uk. The Institution's main Scottish address is 9 Manor Place, Edinburgh EH3 7DN; phone: 0131 2257078; fax: 0131 2263599.
276 RICS *Gateway Directory of Services & Contacts*.
277 'Mediation Agreement'; 'Mediation through the RICS Dispute Resolution Scheme'; 'Solving property problems: A guide to the RICS Dispute Resolution Service'; 'Questionnaire to monitor mediators appointed by the Institution'.
278 24 Angel Gate, City Road, London EC1V 2RS; phone: 020 7837 4483; fax: 020 7837 4185; email: 71411.2735@compuserv.com; website: http://ourworld.compuserv.com/arbitrators
279 For a list of the Consumer Schemes administered by the CIA, see http://www.arbitrators.org/Services/consumerDet.htm. Also see the section in Chapter 8 on Consumer Disputes.

unsuccessful or is not helpful. The CIA also offers mini-trials and arbitration services. The Institute has published a range of mediation documents.[280]

Ombudsmen

Use of mediation by Ombudsmen is considered in further detail later in this chapter, although basic details, in particular their use of mediation, are provided in the table below.[281]

Ombudsman	Use of Mediation
Banking Ombudsman South Quay Plaza 183 Marsh Wall London E14 9SR Phone: 020 7404 9944 Website: www.obo.org.uk	The Banking Ombudsman explores whether there is scope for resolution by conciliation.[282]
Building Societies Ombudsman Millbank Tower Millbank London SW1P 4XS Phone: 020 7931 0044 Fax: 0207 931 8485 Email: blgsocombudsman@easynet.co.uk	The Ombudsman's office will first try to conciliate a resolution on an informal basis.[283]
Personal Investment Authority Ombudsman Hertsmere House Hertsmere Road London E14 4AB Phone: 020 7216 0016 Fax: 020 7712 8742	Parties are invited to settle by agreement first.[284]
Pensions Ombudsman 6th floor 11 Belgrave Road London SW1V 1RB Phone: 020 7834 9144 Fax: 020 7821 0065	The possibility for conciliation is explored when a complaint is received.[285]

---

280 'Dispute Resolution Clauses'; 'Explanatory Pamphlet'; 'Rules of the Consumer Dispute Resolution Scheme'; 'Application Form'; 'Guidance Notes'.
281 Regulators also oversee complaints handling by privatised utilities, like Ofwat for water companies, Oftel for telecommunications and Ofgem for the gas and electricity industries. See the section on Telecommunications Disputes in Chapter 8.
282 The Banking Ombudsman *Annual Report 1997–98*.
283 Building Society Ombudsman *Guide for Applicants*, September 1999.
284 Referred to in http://europa.eu.int
285 Telephone interview with Ombudsman's Office, November 1999.

Financial Services Authority 25 The North Colonnade Canary Wharf London Phone: 020 7676 0824 Fax: 020 7676 9712 Email: clare.boyle@fsa.gov.uk	The aim of the Independent Investigator is to resolve complaints by conciliation.[286]
Insurance Ombudsman 135 Park Street London SE1 9EA Phone: 020 7902 8100 Fax: 020 7902 8197 Email: complaint@theiob.org.uk Website: http://www.theiob.org.uk	The possibility for conciliation is explored when a complaint is received.[287]
National Consumer Credit Federation 98/100 Holme Lane Sheffield SG4J 1W Phone: 0114 2348101 Fax: 0114 2348101	The Management Committee of the Federation provides a conciliation service, followed by arbitration if conciliation does not resolve the dispute.[288]
Qualitas Maxwell Road Stevenage SG1 2EW Phone: 01438 316100 Fax: 01438 315800 Email: qualitas@ttlchiltern.co.uk	Qualitas provides a conciliation service for disputes relating to the purchase of furniture and floor covering. Adjudication is used if conciliation is unsuccessful.[289]
Mail Order Traders' Association Phone: 01704 563787 Fax: 01704 55111247	The Secretary provides a conciliation service.[290]
Scottish Motor Trade Association 3 Palmerston Place Edinburgh EH12 5AF Phone: 0131 2253643 Fax: 0131 2200416	A Complaints Committee first attempts to conciliate and may provide a non-binding recommendation. Arbitration follows if there is no settlement through conciliation.[291]

Consumer advice organisations

Consumer advice organisations provide a useful point of contact for consumers who seek mediation advice and assistance. In England and Wales, the following organisations are useful contacts for that purpose:

- Advice Services Alliance.[292]

---

286 The FSA meets the principles of the European Commission's Recommendation on the out-of-court settlement of consumer disputes [see http://europa.eu.int].
287 Telephone interview with Ombudsman's Office, November 1999.
288 Referred to in http://europa.eu.int.
289 Ibid.
290 Ibid.
291 Ibid.
292 4 Deans Court, St Paul's Churchyard, London EC4V 5AA; phone: 020 7236 6022; fax: 020 7248 3367; email: asa@cwcom.neg

- Consumers' Association.[293]
- National Association of Citizens' Advice Bureaux.[294]
- National Consumer Council.[295]
- Central Cardiff Citizens' Advice Bureau.[296]

In Scotland, the following organisations are useful contacts:

- Citizens' Advice Bureau Scotland,[297] which has launched a free mediation service for parties involved in consumer or small business disputes.
- Scottish Consumer Council.[298]

In Northern Ireland, the Central Belfast Citizens' Advice Bureau is the consumer point of contact.[299]

Employment mediation organisations

The Advisory, Conciliation and Arbitration Service ('ACAS')[300] provides a range of mediation services. Its Advisory Mediation Service provides information on the following three options:

- Advisory mediation, a co-operative and joint problem-solving approach using joint workshops or joint working parties.
- Conciliation, which aims to help the parties to reach a mutually acceptable settlement, and most closely resembles *facilitative mediation*.
- Dispute Mediation, which in the context of the service provided by ACAS, allows the mediator to make recommendations as a basis for settlement and is used when a conciliated settlement (either through advisory mediation or conciliation) is not possible.[301]

The Service appoints mediators and maintains a panel of mediators, from which appointments can be made. It also assists the parties to agree terms of reference for a mediation. It provides a range of mediation training courses and has produced two mediation videos, 'Working Together' and 'Effective Joint Working'.

Employment Advisory Specialists[302] provide employment mediation services and train mediators. The Service can draft the mediation agreement and administer a mediation. It provides mediation training courses to industrial relations managers.

---

293 2 Marylebone Road, London NW1 7DF; phone: 020 7830 6000; fax: 020 7830 7600; email: which@which.net
294 Myddleton House, 115–123 Pentonville Road, London N1 9LZ; phone: 020 7833 2181; fax: 020 7833 4362; email: consultancy@nacab.org.uk
295 20 Grosvenor Gardens, London SW1W 0DH; phone: 020 7730 4369; Fax: 020 7770 0191; email: infor@ncc.org.uk
296 71 Bridge St, Cardiff CF1 2EE; phone: 02920 398676.
297 26 George Square, Edinburgh EH8 9LD; phone:0131 6670156; fax: 0131 6684359.
298 Royal Exchange House, 100 Queens St, Glasgow G1 3DN; phone: 0141 2265261; fax: 0141 2210731; website: http://www.scotconsumer.co.uk
299 6 Callender St, Belfast BT1 5BN; phone: 02890 243196; fax: 02890 312336.
300 27 Wilton St, London SW1X 7AZ; phone: 020 7210 3613; fax: 020 72103708.
301 Further details of ACAS mediation services are provided in the section in Chapter 8 on Employment Disputes.
302 Email: employment@eas-challis.co.uk

Environment mediation organisations

The Environment Council[303] provides managed stakeholder dialogue, a facilitation process, which brings together stakeholders in an environmental dispute, with a view to reaching agreement on the way forward.[304] The Council provides a range of one, three and six day dispute resolution courses.[305]

Family mediation organisations

Throughout the UK

The UK College of Family Mediators[306] is an umbrella organisation for family mediation services in the UK. It was launched by National Family Mediation ('NFM'), Family Mediators' Association ('FMA') and Family Mediation Scotland ('FMS') in 1997 to educate the public in family mediation, promote high standards of conduct and training for family mediators and to provide details of registered mediators.[307] The UK College's three point strategy plan includes quality assurance, providing different levels of membership and assisting in the implementation of the Family Law Act 1996.[308] The College also hopes to gain statutory recognition.[309]

The UK College can help parties to locate family mediators, utilising its members' register and database. It also has a supervisors' consultancy register. Consistent with its aims of promoting high standards of professional conduct and training for mediators throughout the UK, it grants approved body status to family mediation services and has an established complaints and disciplinary procedure. The College has a comprehensive range of precedents, documents, magazines, articles and books on mediation.[310]

---

303 212 High Holborn, London WC1V 7VW; phone: 020 7836 2626; fax: 020 7242 1180; email: info@envcouncil.org.uk; website: www.the-environment-council.org.uk

304 The Environment Council *Annual Review 1999.*

305 See Chapter 11 on Training and Standards and the section on Environmental Disputes in Chapter 8.

306 24–32 Stephenson Way, London NW1 2HX; phone: 020 7391 9162; fax: 020 7391 9165; email: liz.walsh@btinternet.com; website: http://www.ukcfm.co.uk

307 The UK College of Family Mediators *Policies and Standards of the UK College of Family Mediators – objects and functions of the College,* at p 3.

308 UK College of Family Mediators *1999/2000 Directory and Handbook,* Sweet & Maxwell, London, 1999, at p A8.

309 Ibid.

310 Apart from its annual *Directory and Handbook,* it produces a range of precedents: for example, 'Open Statements of Financial Information' and 'Memorandum of Understanding'. To compliment the precedents, it has produced 'Guidelines on Memorandum of Understanding and Conflict of Interest'. The 'Standards and Code of Practice' and 'Training Standards' are core materials. The pamphlets 'Family Mediation, working to cover the emotional and financial costs of separation and divorce' and 'Creating the firm foundation for a growing profession' provide a useful introduction. The College also publishes the 'Family Mediation Gazette'.

England and Wales

Academy of Experts[311]

Since 1988 the Academy of Experts has provided family mediation services. The Academy subscribes to the UK College of Family Mediators' Standards and Code of Practice. It also runs a family mediation course lasting six days.[312]

British Association of Lawyer Mediators (BALM)[313]

BALM membership is open to any solicitor, barrister, judge, advocate or legal executive who practises in the UK, is normally at least 35 years of age and has undergone recognised mediator training. The Association administers family mediations, and provides a venue for mediations. It maintains a register of approved supervisors who provide supervision and case consultation. The Association provides networking opportunities for members and a wide range of mediation training courses through its training arm, Law Wise, a body approved by the UK College of Family Mediators.[314]

Family Law Consortium[315]

The Consortium provides family mediation services and has produced a comprehensive family mediation fact sheet.

Family Mediators' Association (FMA)[316]

The FMA was set up in 1985 to offer all issues mediation,[317] and its mediators now also offer sole and anchor mediation.[318] The Association also offers co-mediation, combining legal and therapeutic professionals. The FMA tends to attract the privately-paying market. It provides supervisor consultants, recognised by the UK College of Family Mediators, who support practising family mediators.[319] The FMA can provide a venue for mediations and professional indemnity insurance as part of its membership fee. It provides a wide range of mediator training courses.[320] The FMA is a founder member of the UK College of Family Mediation and now has over 400 members and almost 40 regional groups.[321] The FMA provides precedent and

---

311 See contact details, in the civil/commercial mediation organisation section, above.
312 The eight day course option includes commercial mediation training.
313 The Shooting Lodge, Guildford Road, Sutton Green, Guildford GU4 7PZ; phone: 01483 235000; fax: 01483 237004; email: a.logan@cableon.co.uk
314 See 'Code of Practice for Law Wise Family Mediation'; 'Law Wise, Disciplinary & Grievance Procedures'; 'Law Wise Family Mediation Training Programme for Accreditation'.
315 2 Henrietta St, London WC2E 8PS; phone: 020 7420 5000; fax: 020 7420 5005; email: flc@tflc.co.uk; website: www.tflc.co.uk
316 46 Grosvenor Gardens, London SW1W 0EB; phone: 020 7881 9400; fax: 020 7881 9401; email: hmc@globalnet.co.uk; website: www.familymediators.co.uk
317 See Part II, on the family mediation process and the difference between all issues and other family mediation.
318 Ibid.
319 See Chapter 11 on training and standards.
320 Ibid.
321 UK College of Family Mediators *1999/2000 Directory and Handbook*, Sweet & Maxwell, London, 1999 at p A136.

model materials to members on disk. It has published a wide range of comprehensive mediation literature.[322]

Family Mediation Cardiff[323]

Family Mediation Cardiff is affiliated to National Family Mediation (NFM) and provides a mediation service for separating couples in dispute about arrangements for their children.

National Family Mediation (NFM)[324]

NFM consists of over 70 local family mediation services in the North East, North West, Midlands, East, West and London.[325] NFM subsidises clients who cannot pay

---

322 'Mediation Practice Manual'; 'Directory of FMA trained mediators listed by County'; 'Supervisor/consultant Directory'; 'Policy Document on selection, recruitment, training and professional practice supervision and consultancy'; 'Guidelines to training policy and entry requirements for courses'; 'Training Courses – guide and information'; 'Training to mediate on all issues in separation or divorce'; 'Your training questions answered'; 'Support for people facing separation or divorce'; 'Annual Report'.

323 4th floor, St David's House, Wood St, Cardiff CF1 1ES; phone: 02920 229692; website: http://members.aol.com/fmcardiff

324 9 Tavistock Place, London WC1H 9SN; phone: 020 7383 5993; fax: 020 7383 5994; email: general@nfm.org.uk; website: http://www.nfm.u-net.com

325 Africa Caribbean Mediation Service Brixton, Divorce Mediation and Counselling Service London, Eye to Eye Mediation London, The Family Mediation Service – Institute of Family Therapy London, Mediation for Families London City, Mediation in Divorce Twickenham, Central Middlesex Family Mediation, North London Family Mediation Service, South East London Family Mediation Bureau, Berkshire Family Mediation Service, Hampshire Family Mediation Service, Kent Family Mediation Service, Milton Keynes Family Mediation, Sussex Family Mediation Service, Surrey Family Mediation Service, Thames Valley Family Mediation Service, Chiltern Family Mediation Service, Hertfordshire Family Mediation Service, Jersey Family Mediation, Cambridge Family Mediation Service, Norfolk Family Mediation Service, Peterborough Family Mediation Service, South Essex Family Mediation Service, West Essex Family Mediation Service, Mid Essex Family Mediation Service, Birmingham Family Mediation Service, Coventry & Warwickshire Family Mediation Service, Herefordshire Family Mediation Service, Lincolnshire Family Mediation Service, Northamptonshire Family Mediation Service, North Staffordshire Family Mediation Service, Nottingham Children and Families Mediation Service (FAME), Oxfordshire Family Mediation Service, Shropshire Family Mediation, South Staffordshire Family Mediation Service, Worcestershire Family Mediation Service, Boys & Girls Welfare Society Mediation Services, Bradford Metropolitan Family Mediation Service, Cleveland Family Mediation Service, Cumbria Family Mediation Service, Derbyshire Family Mediation Service, Durham Family Mediation, The Family Mediation Service Greater Manchester, Family Mediation Service North-West Yorkshire, Lancashire Family Mediation Service, Merseyside Family Mediation Service, Northumberland Family Mediation Service, South Yorkshire Family Mediation Service, Sunderland Family Mediation Service, West Yorkshire Family Mediation Service, York Family Mediation Service, Family Mediation Hull, Scarborough Family Mediation Service, Bristol Family Mediation Service, Exeter Family Mediation Service, Family Mediation North Wiltshire, Gloucestershire Family Mediation, North Devon Family Mediation Service, Plymouth Mediation, Salisbury Family Mediation Service, Somerset Family Mediation Service, Family Mediation Cardiff, Gwent Mediation Service, North Wales Family Mediation Service, Northern Ireland Family Mediation Service.

for mediation services through grants. It offers co-mediation on all issues relating to children, property and finance and provides a wide range of mediator training courses.[326] Lawyers often act as legal consultants to local NFM branches.[327] Twelve NFM services offer counselling for children.[328] NFM, a founder member of the UK College of Family Mediators, also keeps national statistics and an up-to-date list of its affiliated services. It also publishes a range of other mediation documents and literature.[329]

Professional Development and Training (PDT)[330]

PDT provides mediation training programmes, approved by the UK College of Family Mediators and by the European Forum Committee on Standards of Training for Family Mediation. In addition, it provides a wide range of mediation services, including a contact line, referral to mediators, support services for members, family mediation documents on disk, supervision and consultancy, publicity materials and a family mediation video. It has a family mediator register, which lists family mediators who have completed training, assignments and assessment.[331]

Relate[332]

Relate works in partnership with NFM to develop mediation services.

Solicitors' Family Law Association (SFLA)[333]

The SFLA is a national association of family solicitors, comprising about 4,000 members nationwide, which encourages the use of family mediation. The Association offers a helpline which provides mediators with advice, help and support from consultants. It maintains a list of solicitor family mediators. The SFLA provides comprehensive mediator training.[334] It publishes a range of family mediation precedent agreements and consent orders and a number of other family mediation documents and literature.[335]

---

326 See Chapter 11 on training and standards.
327 L Webley *A review of the literature on family mediation: prepared for the Lord Chancellor's Advisory Committee on Legal Education and Conduct*, Institute of Advanced Legal Studies, 1998, at p 23.
328 UK College of Family Mediators *1999/2000 Directory and Handbook*, Sweet & Maxwell, London, 1999, at p A120.
329 'Agreement to Mediate'; 'National Core Training Programme ("CTP")'; 'What is mediation?'; 'Changing the picture for the better'; 'Annual Report'; 'Annual Statistics Returns'.
330 17 Whitefriars, Sevenoaks, Kent TN13 1QG; phone: 01732 453227; fax: 01732 464133.
331 UK College of Family Mediators *1999–2000 Directory and Handbook*, op cit.
332 Herbert Gray College, Little Church St, Rugby CV21 3AP; phone: 01788 573241; fax: 01788 535007.
333 PO Box 302, Orpington, Kent BR6 8QX; phone: 01689 850227; fax: 01689 855833; email: 106002.3040@compuserv.com
334 See Chapter 11 on training and standards.
335 'The new ancillary relief pilot scheme'; 'Divorce procedure'; 'Good practice regarding the service in the family law context'; 'Good practice note on procedure on domestic violence cases'; 'Mediation rules for consultants'; 'Mediation selection of applicants for training, practice and accreditation process'; 'Mediation training, accreditation and re-accreditation – appeals procedure'; 'Mediation training for lawyers'; 'Courses in all issues mediation'; 'Specialist accreditation scheme 1999'; 'Association Rules'; 'Family Mediation' magazine; and 'Review' magazine.

Scotland

Comprehensive Accredited Lawyer Mediators (CALM)[336]

CALM is the Scottish equivalent to BALM, being a lawyer mediation organisation. Its members are accredited by the Law Society of Scotland to provide mediation services. As CALM's links are with the Law Society of Scotland, it has remained outside the UK College of Family Mediators' framework. It provides a mediation information line and details on local CALM-qualified family mediators. It has a list of over 70 members who are qualified family mediators. A CALM mediator normally charges an hourly rate, although the first meeting is usually free.

Family Mediation Scotland (FMS)[337]

FMS was set up in 1984 with funding from the Scottish Office and it is approved by the Lord President of the Court of Session as a family mediation organisation. The purpose of FMS is to develop family mediation in Scotland by developing a network of affiliated services, supporting those services, maintaining high standards of practice and educating the public on mediation, in particular, through research.[338] The FMS was a founder member of the UK College of Family Mediators, along with the NFM and FMA. FMS is run in a similar way to NFM in that local mediation services are affiliated to it.[339] The affiliated services abide by the UK College of Family Mediators' Code of Practice; use mediators trained, accredited and registered by FMS who are members or associates of the UK College of Family Mediators; and have management committees which include lawyers, social workers and other local community representatives. All FMS mediation services are run on a voluntary basis, although local services may pay their mediators.[340]

FMS mediators offer mediation on children's issues and some locations also provide mediation for issues relating to property and finances, which were previously made available exclusively by CALM mediators. FMS develops and supports child contact centres in Scotland, where children can spend time with the parent they do not live with, and currently there are 25 such centres in Scotland.[341] The FMS 'Time to Talk' Service was set up in response to the Children (Scotland) Act 1995 to enable children's views to be heard. FMS provides comprehensive national mediation training, organises continuing professional development events, offers supervision

---

336 42 Carden Place, Aberdeen AB1 1UP; phone: 01224 621622; fax: 01224 621623.
337 127 Rose St, South Lane, Edinburgh EH2 4BB; phone: 0131 2201610; fax: 0131 2206895.
338 Family Mediation Scotland *Information Pack*, section on 'Purpose' of FMS, at p 1.
339 Affiliated services include: Family Mediation Borders, Family Mediation Central Scotland, NCH Action for Children Dumfries and Galloway, NCH Action for Children Family Mediation Fife, Family Mediation Grampian, Family Mediation Highland, Family Mediation Lothian, Family Mediation Orkney, Shetland Family Mediation, Family Mediation Tayside, Family Mediation Western Isles and Family Mediation West. The contact details for affiliated FMS services are in the Appendices to this book.
340 Funding is not available for FMS mediation since their services are currently provided free of charge.
341 Family Mediation Scotland *Information Pack*, at p 10.

and trains tutors. The UK College of Family Mediators has authorised FMS as an approved mediation training body. FMS has also appointed an Education Officer, who aims to raise awareness of mediation among professionals, especially teachers of young people. FMS also has a National Development Officer, who is piloting a quality assurance system and developing agreed standards for family mediation services.[342] FMS has produced a range of family mediation literature[343] and has an extensive library containing all the books listed in the national training course reading list, a stock of mediation and related videos and a wide range of mediation and related journals.[344]

Northern Ireland

The Northern Ireland Family Mediation Service, based in Belfast,[345] offers family mediators who are registered in accordance with National Family Mediation and UK College of Family Mediators' standards. Mediators are paid a small hourly fee for mediation sessions and a half-hour payment for case preparation and writing up case notes.[346]

Republic of Ireland by way of comparison

Family Mediation Service[347]

The Family Mediation Service in the Republic of Ireland is a state-sponsored mediation service, launched in 1986, under the auspices of the Department of Social, Community and Family Affairs.[348]

---

342 Family Mediation Scotland *Information Pack*, at p 11.
343 Apart from the 'Information Pack' each affiliated service produces an 'Annual Report'. The notes above have drawn on the following 1999 Annual Reports: 'Family Mediation Central Scotland Annual Report', 'Family Mediation Borders Annual Report', 'Family Mediation Lothian Annual Report', and 'Family Mediation Tayside Annual Report'. In addition, the FMS has produced 'Registration Procedures'; 'National Training Course Information Pack'; 'Procedures on evaluation and training of mediators'; 'Statistical returns'; 'Selection and contracting procedures'; and 'Making arrangements after separation or divorce'. The FMS Information Pack outlines the purpose of FMS, its history and structure, the nature of mediation, demand for mediation in Scotland, source of referrals, the work of FMS, FMS affiliated services, support for family mediation in Scotland, the future for family mediation in Scotland and funding of FMS. The National Training Course Information Pack sets out the course dates and venues, course aims, the syllabus, preparation, evaluation and training staff.
344 For example, 'Community Care'; 'Family and Conciliation Courts Review'; 'Mediation Quarterly'; 'Family Law'; and 'Mediation'.
345 76 Dublin Road, Belfast BT2 ZHP; phone: 02890 323454; fax: 02890 315292; email: gerald.clark@relate-n-ireland.com
346 Relate *Annual Review*, 1999.
347 5th floor, Irish Life Centre, Lower Abbey St, Dublin 1. There are further services in Limerick, Cork, Balloonagh, Tralee and Kerry. Additional services are proposed for Athlone, Dundalk, Galway, Tallaght and Wexford.
348 Family Mediation Service *What is the Family Mediation Service?*

Mediators' Institute Ireland (MII)[349]

The MII is an umbrella body for mediators in the Republic of Ireland. Details about its training, accreditation and standards are provided in the section on training and standards, later in Chapter 11, to provide a comparison with the UK.[350]

Foreign mediation organisations

This section deals briefly with those overseas mediation organisations whose rules are being applied in the UK. The organisations which deal with general civil/commercial disputes include the American Arbitration Association ('AAA'),[351] the Center for Public Resources ('CPR')[352] and the International Chamber of Commerce ('ICC').[353] The AAA has produced a set of Commercial Mediation Rules; the CPR has a Mediation Procedure for Business Disputes in Europe; and the ICC has published Rules of Optional Conciliation.[354] The World Intellectual Property Organisation ('WIPO') has an Arbitration and Mediation Centre dealing specifically with intellectual property disputes.[355] WIPO appoints mediators, administers mediations, provides a venue for mediations, organises mediation support services and negotiates mediation fees. It can also offer med-arb. It maintains a list of mediators with specialised knowledge and experience in the technical, business and legal subject matter of intellectual property. Its fees include a registration fee and mediation fees are usually calculated either on an hourly or a daily rate. The WIPO Arbitration and Mediation Centre provides a range of workshops for mediators relating to intellectual property disputes and has produced a range of mediation documentation.[356]

The Role of Lawyers

This section examines the role of solicitors and barristers, as well as Law Societies and Bar Councils, in the promotion and development of mediation in the UK.

---

349 13 Royal Terrace West, Dun Laoghaire, Dublin; phone: 00353 12845277; fax: 00353 12800259.

350 Mediators' Institute Ireland 'Code of Ethics and Professional Conduct for Family Mediators', 'Complaints Procedure' and 'Accreditation of Professional Mediators in Ireland'.

351 140 West 51st St, New York 10020; phone: 001 212 4844000; fax: 001 212 7657274; website: http://www.adr.org

352 366 Madison Avenue, New York 10017; phone: 001 212 9496490; fax 001 212 9498859.

353 38, Cours Albert 1er, 75008, Paris, France; phone: 00 331 49532828; website: www.iccwbo.org

354 Consider the definition of conciliation in Part I.

355 34, chemin des Colombettes, PO Box 18, Geneva 20, Switzerland; email: arbiter.mail @wipo.int; website: http://arbiter.wipo.int

356 'Mediation Clauses'; 'Agreement to mediate'; 'Mediation Rules'; and 'Guide to mediation'. See also the section on Intellectual Property Disputes in Chapter 8.

Solicitors and mediation

Solicitor mediation achievements

UK mediation organisations boast large numbers of solicitor members. Over 130 law firms, for example, were founder members of the Centre for Dispute Resolution, and many more have since joined as corporate members. ADR Net, administered by the ADR Group,[357] comprises a network of over 70 law firms in England, Wales and Scotland. The London branch of ADR Net was established in 1999.[358] The *Chambers Guide to the Legal Profession*[359] and *The Legal 500*[360] have an ADR and mediation practice category respectively.[361]

To recognise law firm achievement in ADR, the Centre for Dispute Resolution launched in 1996 biennial ADR awards for law firms.[362] The 1998 and 2000 awards were won by Hammond Suddards Edge in recognition of the wide diversity of fields in which it uses mediation, from construction and engineering through to finance, intellectual property, information technology, pensions, energy, insurance, reinsurance, commercial contracts and international disputes.[363] The firm has estimated that mediation has achieved for its clients cost savings of £250,000 per case.[364] Runners-up for the 1998 award were Dibb Lupton Alsop, as it was then called, and Pinsent Curtis. DLA was recognised for its policy of examining the potential for mediation in every case; and its staff and client mediation education programme.[365] Pinsents was recognised for the encouragement given to clients to use mediation; its assessment of cases for ADR suitability; and its training of all litigators in the firm in mediation use.[366] Bunkers received special mention at the 1998 awards for excellence in their work in the development of mediation for personal injury claims. The runner-up for the 2000 awards was CMS Cameron McKenna in recognition of its development of pre-action protocols for commercial disputes. The firm was instrumental in setting up the Market ADR Commitment ('MAC'), an initiative

---

357 See the section on Mediation Organisations for an outline of the ADR Group's activities.
358 The London branch includes Lovells, CMS Cameron McKenna, Hammond Suddards Edge, Beachcroft Wansboroughs, Nabarro Nathanson, Ince & Co, Fladgate Fielder, Irwin Mitchell, Geoffrey Green Russell, Bray Walker, Lewis Silkin, Morgan Cole and Russell-Cooke Potter & Chapman: 'Top City firms form ADR Group' *The Law Society Gazette,* 1 December 1999.
359 Chambers & Partners *Chambers Guide to the Legal Profession*, Chambers & Partners Publishing, London, 2000.
360 J Pritchard (ed) *The Legal 500: the clients' guide to UK law firms*, Bath Press, 2000.
361 Listing leading mediators – solicitors and barristers, rather than firms.
362 The first awards were won by Baker & McKenzie, for its firm-wide mediation culture, evidenced by lawyer use of ADR case evaluation criteria. Clifford Chance and Lovells were runners up for the 1996 awards, in recognition of their efforts in training their lawyers, including non-contentious lawyers, in mediation.
363 'Winning Solutions' *The Law Society Gazette*, 11 November 1998; and CEDR, Press Release, 30 November 2000.
364 Hammonds Suddards *Alternative Dispute Resolution*, Mondaq Business Briefing, 25 March 1999.
365 J Duckers 'Woolf at door over Mediation Reform: Lawyers in fear of losing fees' *Birmingham Post*, 17 September 1999.
366 'Winning Solutions' *The Law Society Gazette*, 11 November 1998.

promoting the use of ADR in the insurance markets.[367] The firm's commercial litigation partners have also been trained as mediators;[368] it has contributed to the formation of the London Branch of ADR Net and an on-line international project launched by the ADR Group; and has used mediation across a wide range of subject areas. For example, in 1999, it used mediation in the following types of dispute:[369]

Type of Dispute	Amount of Claim—£
Insurance coverage	200,000
Insurance	1,600,000
Reinsurance	5,000,000
Multi-party insurance dispute	150,000
Libel	100,000
Construction	7,500,000
Construction	120,000,000
Building dispute	45,000
Architects' dispute	111,000
Architects' negligence	25,000
Architects' negligence	25,000
Engineers' negligence	1,275,000
Structural engineers' negligence	140,000
Surveyors' negligence	150,000
Surveyors' negligence	120,000
Valuers' professional negligence	250,000
Valuers' negligence	250,000
Accountants' negligence	350,000
Accountants' negligence	180,000
Accountants' negligence	50,000
Accountants'/Auditors' dispute	380,000
Product liability	12,000,000
Product contamination	10,000,000
Environmental contamination	600,000
Information technology	9,000,000
Banking	200,000
Banking	45,000
Banking	265,000
Negligent financial advice	65,000
Claim against financial adviser	25,000
Brokers' dispute	400,000
Insolvency	1,000,000,000

367 CEDR, op cit. For more information on MAC, see Insurance Disputes, Chapter 8.
368 'Top City firms form ADR Group' *The Law Society Gazette,* 1 December 1999.
369 The authors thank CMS Cameron McKenna for their assistance.

There are a wealth of other examples of mediation initiatives by UK solicitors. Addleshaw Booth & Co sponsored the Centre for Dispute Resolution/MORI poll[370] and Pinsent Curtis sponsored a survey of the attitudes of business towards mediation.[371] A large number of individual solicitors work tirelessly to promote mediation. The *Chambers Directory*[372] and *Legal 500*[373] provide a list of recommended solicitor mediators. Law Societies also provide details of solicitor mediators.[374]

Survey results

Further survey results are reported in Chapter 9. The focus here is on the take-up by solicitors of mediation.

Large versus small law firms?

Genn's study of the Central London County Court Mediation Pilot suggested that 'the fact that the litigation departments of commercial mega firms are beginning to speak the language of [ADR] will not have an immediate effect on the approach to litigation in the High Street'.[375] Surveys conducted over the last few years, and more recently, support her suggestion. The Bristol Law Society Mediation Scheme revealed a widely-held view by the solicitors interviewed that mediation adds nothing to standard solicitor negotiations.[376] The Scheme also revealed that solicitors were concerned about the risk to their relationships with clients in pressing a course of action which might prove unsuccessful.[377]

Genn's study of the Central London County Court Mediation Pilot found that the demand for mediation was lowest, at only 5%, when both parties were legally

---

370 Centre for Dispute Resolution *Civil Justice Audit*, April 2000 contains the results, which are also referred to, where relevant, in the section on Civil Justice Reforms above.

371 CEDR/Pinsent Curtis *Dispute Resolution Survey: initial analysis paper*, CEDR, March 2000 contains a summary of results, which are also referred to, where relevant, throughout this book.

372 The 2000 *Directory* lists the leading mediators in London as Tony Willis, Henry Brown, David Miles, Nicholas Pryor, David Shapiro, Edward Sibley, Stephen York, Jane Andrewartha, John Bishop, Eileen Carroll, David Cornes, William Walsh, Charles Dodson, Anthony Finchman, Stephen Tester, Julian Holloway, Jonathan Lux and Chris Newmark. It also lists the leading mediators in the regions as Philip Howell-Richardson, Andrew Paton, Jonathan Lloyd-Jones, Euan Temple, Anthony Glaister, Robin Bloom, Ronald Bradbeer, Michael Davies, John Gatenby, William Goyder, John Winkworth-Smith, Paul Houghton, John Kendall, Quentin Smith and Robert Langley.

373 The *Legal 500* lists Tony Willis, Stephen York, David Shapiro, Jane Andrewartha, Chris Newmark and Andrew Paton.

374 For example, The Law Society of Scotland provides, on request, a list of civil/commercial solicitor-mediators accredited by the Law Society of Scotland (the list supplied by the Law Society contains about 70 solicitors) and a list of solicitors granted accreditation as family law mediators by the Law Society of Scotland (the list supplied by the Law Society contains over 100 solicitors). For accreditation plans of the Law Society of England and Wales, see the section on Training and Standards.

375 H Genn *Central London County Court Mediation Pilot: Evaluation Report*, LCD Research Series, No 5/98, at p 36.

376 M Davies, G Davis and J Webb *Promoting Mediation: Report of a study of Bristol Law Society's Mediation Scheme in its preliminary phase*, 1996 Research & Policy Planning Unit Research Study no 21, The Law Society, at p 21.

377 Ibid, at p 23.

represented, compared to 12% when neither party was legally represented. Since the court sent the mediation offers to lawyers, in those cases where parties were legally represented, the rejection of mediation in those cases reflects, Genn argues, solicitors' reluctance to recommend mediation. Some lawyers interviewed by Genn revealed that, even when they had sought to take up the mediation offer, the other sides' lawyers refused.[378] Other lawyers interviewed by Genn admitted that they considered mediation to be useful only when lawyers were not involved in the case.[379] There was also one personal injury claimant firm, which wrote to the court at the beginning of the Pilot to advise that it would not refer any cases to the Scheme.[380] Genn's study of the Central London County Court Mediation Pilot highlighted the important role that solicitors play in influencing the demand for mediation.[381] A study of family mediation in 1997 also emphasised the importance of the role of solicitors as 'gatekeepers' to mediation.[382] Those findings are entirely consistent with the findings of the NHS Mediation Pilot Scheme.

The authors conducted a survey, between December 1999 and April 2000, of 700 law firms throughout the UK.[383] On a positive note, the survey revealed that, of those with mediation experience, only 0.04% had experienced fewer mediations in 1999 than in 1998. However, the majority of respondents had not yet experienced a mediation, although the percentage has decreased from 87.8% in 1998 to 72% in 1999, tending to suggest that the civil justice reforms have had an impact. Of the respondents who have had mediation experience, the largest proportion, 25% in 1998 and 15% in 1999, have only had one mediation. The largest increase was seen in the proportion of firms who have had between one and five mediations, the figure rising from 8% in 1998 to 20.2% in 1999. All other categories, 6–10, 11–15 and over 15 mediations, had shown increases. The number of firms who have participated in 6–10 mediations increased from 1.8% in 1998 to 4% in 1999; and the number of firms who have been involved in 11–15 mediations increased slightly from 1.4% in 1998 to 1.7% in 1999. Although in 1998 none of the respondent firms had had over 15 mediations, in 1999 2.1% had reached this level of participation in mediation, and in the case of five respondents, they had each completed between 20 and 23 mediations in 1999.

Geographical disparity

A June 1999 survey, conducted by the law firm DLA, of 500 top companies in the West Midlands revealed that more than 60% had not received any advice from their

---

378 H Genn *Central London County Court Mediation Pilot: Evaluation Report*, LCD Research Series, No 5/98, at p 135.
379 Ibid, at p 36. At p 35, Genn cites the view of another solicitor:
   '... for litigants in person – that's one thing, but for firms of solicitors, I think [mediation] is ridiculous ...'
380 Ibid, at p 20.
381 Ibid, at p vii.
382 Social & Community Planning Research *Report of interim findings of research into the role of mediation in family law cases in Scotland*, 1997.
383 The survey was conducted by sending 'fax back' questionnaires to randomly selected law firms in England, Wales, Scotland and Northern Ireland, although there were only a small number of returns from Scotland and Northern Ireland. A 30% overall response rate was achieved. Further results from the survey are reported, where relevant, throughout this book.

solicitors on mediation. 46% had received some literature on mediation at some stage and 16% had been advised to consider mediation clauses in their standard terms and conditions. Only 8% had had discussions with their lawyers about resolving a dispute through mediation.[384]

In-house versus private practice solicitors

The Centre for Dispute Resolution's MORI poll[385] highlighted some differences in attitude towards mediation between in-house and external solicitors. The poll indicated that 78% of in-house solicitors surveyed felt mediation should be required at some stage if a business dispute is litigated, although only 40% of external solicitors agreed. In addition, 56% of in-house solicitors considered that courts should award costs against parties who refused to take part in mediation, whereas only 26% of external solicitors agreed. 32% of in-house solicitors had reported being advised by external solicitors to use mediation rather than litigation.[386]

Reasons for solicitor reluctance

Shapiro summarises the frequently-cited reasons given for solicitor reluctance to mediate:

- it adds nothing to direct negotiations;
- it's a sign of weakness;
- the case is too complex;
- the legal issues are contested; and
- 'I have a strong case'.[387]

Early surveys of UK family solicitors suggested that they did not place great emphasis on a conciliatory approach.[388] A recent Scottish study of family solicitors indicated an overwhelming preference for direct negotiation between solicitors.[389] Surveys of family mediation have consistently revealed misunderstanding about mediation by solicitors and recommended that solicitors should be trained in what mediation involves, and when and what cases can be mediated.[390] Surveys have revealed similar results in relation to other civil cases. The Bristol Law Society Mediation Scheme identified as the core of the problem a lack of knowledge and experience by solicitors of the mediation process, of when mediation might be

---

384 J Duckers 'Woolf at door over Mediation Reform: Lawyers in fear of losing fees' *Birmingham Post*, 17 September 1999; Centre for Dispute Resolution *Press Release: New survey warns clients want better mediation advice*, 9 June 1999; and 'Lawyers say mediation is weak' *The Lawyer*, 14 June 1999.

385 Conducted in March 2000 and the results were released at the CEDR Civil Justice Audit Conference on 7 April 2000.

386 Centre for Dispute Resolution *Civil Justice Audit*, April 2000.

387 D Shapiro 'Trained neutrals' *New Law Journal*, 21 March 1997, at p 426. See also D Shapiro 'Bridge building: examining recent developments in ADR in the UK' *Axiom*, June 1998, at pp 350–1.

388 University of Newcastle upon Tyne Conciliation Project Unit, *Report to the Lord Chancellor's Department on the cost and effectiveness of conciliation in England and Wales*, March 1989, at p 123.

389 J Lewis *The role of mediation in family disputes in Scotland, Legal Studies Research Findings No 23*, The Scottish Office, Edinburgh, 1999.

390 University of Newcastle upon Tyne Conciliation Project Unit, op cit, at p 31.

appropriate and of what mediation could achieve.[391] Although that Scheme was some years ago, the more recent findings from the study of the Central London County Court Mediation Pilot also reveal ignorance on the part of solicitors about mediation.[392] The NHS Mediation Pilot, another recent initiative, similarly revealed misunderstanding by lawyers about what mediation involved.[393] The authors' 2000 survey of UK law firms revealed that lawyers themselves admitted lack of knowledge about, and lack of experience of, mediation. The survey also highlighted problems lawyers have had in persuading their clients, in face of little public promotion and understanding of mediation, and their opponents to mediate.

There have been suggestions that, even if lawyers were keen on mediation, they may not 'want to look silly in front of their clients'.[394] Some commentators have pointed to the experience with arbitration, when lawyers remained both suspicious and frightened of the process until they were assured of an important place in it.[395] Other commentators point to the reason for solicitors' nervousness about ADR that their clients may consider, after participating in a mediation process, that they do not need lawyers to use mediation again.[396] The authors' 2000 survey of UK law firms received a number of responses, confirming that lawyers are concerned that their clients may consider, following experience of mediation, that lawyers are unnecessary in dispute resolution. It has been suggested that lawyers may prefer dispute resolution methods that maximise the potential for a successful result and defence of rights.[397] If lawyers view themselves as advocates, they are also less likely to be willing to operate in forums other than courts.[398] In such cases, solicitors prefer finely-tuned procedural rules and case-by-case decision-making.[399] Ultimately, commentators argue, lawyers prefer processes over which they do not lose too much control.[400]

---

391 M Davies, G Davis and J Webb *Promoting Mediation: Report of a study of Bristol Law Society's Mediation Scheme in its preliminary phase*, 1996 Research & Policy Planning Unit Research Study no 21, The Law Society, at p 20. The CEDR MORI 2000 poll revealed the need for training on what cases are appropriate for mediation. In one example, clients told lawyers that the case was not appropriate given the high level of personal animosity between the parties, but the lawyers insisted that mediation should occur, as they considered that it was expected of them. The mediation failed due to the animosity: see Compulsion or Encouragement to Mediate, Chapter 9.

392 H Genn *Central London County Court Mediation Pilot: Evaluation Report*, LCD Research Series, No 5/98, at p 35.

393 Clients expressed surprise at how mediations were conducted, suggesting that they had not been properly briefed by their lawyers: L Mulcahy et al *Mediating medical negligence claims: an option for the future?* NHS Executive, 2000, at p 109.

394 Ibid, at p 59, referring to the view of one of the solicitors interviewed as part of the study of the Pilot.

395 J Auerbach *Justice without law*, Oxford University Press, New York, 1983, at p 109.

396 S Macaulay 'Non-Contractual Relations in Business: a Preliminary Study' (1963) 28(1) *American Sociological Review* 55 at 61.

397 B Blegvad 'Commercial Relations, Contract and Litigation in Denmark: A discussion of Macaulay's Theories (1990) 24 *Ohio State Journal on Dispute Resolution* 390 at 401.

398 M Galanter 'Why the "haves" come out ahead: Speculation on the limits of legal change' (1974) 9 *Law & Society Review* 95 at 151.

399 Ibid, at 119.

400 J Wade *In search of new conflict management processes – The lawyer as macro and micro diagnostic problem-solver,* Bond University Dispute Resolution Centre 1995, at p 3.

US authors suggested that lawyers are reluctant to mediate as they have an incentive to increase their billable hours on resolving a dispute,[401] although the experience in America has shown that clients were eager to express gratitude following successful mediations by sending lawyers more work.[402] In none of the UK surveys to date have solicitors cited, as a reason for refusing to mediate, the fear that fee income may be reduced. In Australia, solicitors feared that a reduction in fee income would occur, not because of ADR, but because of the lack of it and the increasing delays in courts and high legal costs associated with litigation.[403] Accordingly, a number of Australian law firms have set up Austsolve, an ADR service, aimed at overcoming the frustrations of corporate clients caused by court delays and high litigation costs.[404]

Barristers and mediation

Barristers' chambers are also amongst the Centre for Dispute Resolution's founder members. The 2000 *Chambers Guide to the Legal Profession* also lists leading barrister mediators.[405] Dispute Resolution by Barristers, launched in 1998 as an independent non-profit organisation, consists of a panel of barristers, who will assist parties to facilitate a settlement and can also, with the consent of the parties, provide a binding result, by way of arbitration, if the parties cannot reach a settlement.[406] Littleton Dispute Resolution Services Ltd focuses on mediation, rather than arbitration. The company trades as Littleton Mediation and is owned and operated by twelve Littleton Chambers' barristers.[407] The Centre for Business Arbitration, another ADR organisation formed by barristers, aims to provide a joint arbitration and mediation service. It is based in Lincoln's Inn and draws on the services of 51 barristers. The rationale for the joint service is to provide an alternative in case mediation is inappropriate or fails in a particular case.[408] A group of employment law

---

401 For example, R J Gilson and R H Mnookin 'Disputing through Agents: Co-operation and conflict between lawyers in litigation' (1994) 94 *Columbia Law Review* 504 at 533.

402 D Shapiro 'Trained neutrals' *New Law Journal*, 21 March 1997 at p 426.

403 For further insight into the attitudes of Australian lawyers to mediation, see A Zariski 'Lawyers and dispute resolution: what do they think and know (and think they know)? Finding out through survey research' (1997) 4(2) *E Law – Murdoch University Electronic Journal of Law* (at http://www.murdoch.edu.au/elaw/issues/v4n2/zaris422.html).

404 Law firms that have launched Austsolve are Arnold Bloch Leibler, Blake Dawson Waldron, Clayton Utz, Corrs Chambers Westgarth, Deacons Graham & Jones, Dunhill Madden Butler, Ebsworth and Ebsworth, Freehill Hollingdale & Page, Middletons Moore & Bevins, Minter Ellison, Phillips Fox, and Strongman & Crouch.

405 The silks listed in the 2000 edition of the Chambers guide, referred to above, include Philip Naughton QC, Stephen Ruttle QC, Robert Gaitskell QC, Michael Kallipetis QC, Lawrence Kershen QC and John Tackaberry QC. Amongst the leading juniors are Peter Aeberli, Elizabeth Birch, Graham Cunningham, Bruce Brodie and Colin Manning.

406 Dispute Resolution by Barristers can be contacted at 104 New Walk, Leicester, LE1 7EA (phone: 0116 2492020).

407 T Watkin 'Set Launches Mediation Business' *The Lawyer*, 12 April 1999.

408 See further details provided in the section on Mediation Organisations above. The Centre's panel list groups barristers into bands: A, B, C and D. Hourly rates are the highest for band A and the lowest for band D. Hourly rates range from under £200 per hour to over £300 per hour.

barrister mediators have set up Workplace Mediation Services, which is aimed at resolving sexual harassment cases using mediation.[409] In October 2000, 2 Harcourt Buildings launched a mediation scheme targeting construction disputes.

Law Societies, bar councils and mediation

England and Wales

Both the Law Society and Bar Council have issued favourable reports on ADR.[410] The Reports have made a number of recommendations relating to court-annexed civil mediation schemes; legal aid for mediation; lawyer training in ADR; the regulation and accreditation of ADR professionals; a review of professional conduct rules to clarify the responsibilities of lawyer mediators; and practice rules relating to the enforceability of mediated settlement agreements as orders of the court.

The first Law Society mediation scheme commenced in Bristol as an initiative of the Bristol Law Society's Civil Courts Committee in 1992, although a revised scheme was launched in 1994.[411] The Scheme appointed an administrator, who received enquiries, made contact with the parties or their lawyers and, if agreed, referred cases to the ADR Group or the Centre for Dispute Resolution for mediation.[412] The Scheme had also made provision for quarterly 'settlement days', when mediators would be available to mediate disputes; however, take up had not been sufficient for the 'settlement days' to occur.[413] The concept of 'settlement days' has been successful in Australia. For example, the programme in New South Wales in 1991 involved the mediation of 235 Supreme Court cases by 66 mediators who achieved a 65% settlement rate, although that rate did not include partially-settled matters. In the next programme, in New South Wales in 1992, 415 cases were mediated by 120 mediators, with similar settlement rates.[414] From August 1995 steps were taken by the Bristol Law Society to increase the take up of mediation in the Scheme, by encouraging the use of mediation clauses via the Society's International and

---

409 The Service has been set up by John Bowers QC, Tess Gill, Daniel Stilitz, Ian Gatt and Jason Galbraith-Marten.
410 The Law Society ADR Working Party *ADR – Report prepared by Henry Brown for the Courts and Legal Services Committee*, The Law Society, London, 1991 ('The Brown Report'); The Beldam Committee *Report of the Committee on ADR*, General Council of the Bar, 1991 ('The Beldam Committee Report'); and The Heilbron/Hodge Committee *Report of the Committee on ADR*, General Council of the Bar, 1993 ('The Heilbron Report').
411 M Davies, G Davis and J Webb *Promoting Mediation: Report of a study of Bristol Law Society's Mediation Scheme in its preliminary phase*, 1996 Research & Policy Planning Unit Research Study no 21, The Law Society, at p 12.
412 Mediation fees were charged at a fixed hourly rate for claims under £50,000 and at individually negotiated rates for higher value claims.
413 M Davies, G Davis and J Webb *Promoting Mediation: Report of a study of Bristol Law Society's Mediation Scheme in its preliminary phase*, 1996 Research & Policy Planning Unit Research Study no 21, The Law Society, at p 13.
414 M Dewdney, B Sordo and C Chinkin *Continuing developments in mediation within the legal system: evaluation of the 1992/93 Settlement Week Programme*, the Law Society, New South Wales, 1994, at p 1.

Business Committee and by encouraging its members to use mediation.[415] Referrals remained low, with the majority of referrals being from one large legal expenses insurer.[416] The scheme was re-activated in 1998.

More recently, the Law Society has been involved in a range of ADR initiatives.[417] An ADR Working Party has been set up to consider ADR policy and practice. Codes of practice for civil/commercial and family mediation have been developed, together with training standards for both civil/commercial and family mediation. The Society has produced a 'Guide to ADR' for the purpose of one-day ADR roadshows. It has set up an accreditation scheme for family mediators and has recently approved an accreditation scheme for civil and commercial mediators, with a view to developing a two-tiered panel, involving general members, who have little practical experience of mediation, and more experienced practitioner members. Regulation would be through training and experience gained in mediation.[418] The Law Society has also taken steps towards promoting England and Wales as the international choice for dispute resolution, including mediation.[419] There is a sponsorship arrangement between the Commerce and Industry Group of the Law Society and Inter-Mediation.[420]

Scotland

In April 1994 the Faculty of Advocates introduced a mediation service, consisting of a panel of nine accredited barrister mediators. In July 1994 the Law Society of Scotland also commenced a mediation service, called ACCORD, whose panel consists of accredited solicitor mediators. ACCORD does not handle family mediations, although the Law Society of Scotland accredits family law mediators. The Service advises on the suitability of a dispute for ADR; the most appropriate type of ADR; the selection of a solicitor mediator; and can provide the venue for ADR. The parties are required to submit a Joint Application to the Service. The parties can then either choose a solicitor mediator from the list provided by ACCORD or, if they cannot agree, the Service will appoint a solicitor mediator for them. The mediator is bound by the Law Society's Code of Conduct for ADR, and is also given assistance via the Service's 'Guidance for Accredited Mediators'.[421]

---

415 M Davies, G Davis and J Webb *Promoting Mediation: Report of a study of Bristol Law Society's Mediation Scheme in its preliminary phase*, 1996 Research & Policy Planning Unit Research Study no 21, The Law Society, at p 15.

416 Ibid.

417 Coinciding with the appointment of Hilary Lloyd, who was responsible for ADR policy (now assisted by Simret Parmar).

418 'Mediation scheme gets go ahead' *The Law Society Gazette*, 20 April 2000.

419 For example, see Law Society booklet, *England and Wales – the international choice for dispute resolution*.

420 For more information on InterMediation, see the section on Mediation Organisations above.

421 ACCORD *An introduction to ACCORD*. At this stage, take up of the scheme has been poor, although it has been suggested that the reason for this is that the Society has not been actively promoting it: B Mays and R Clark *ADR in Scotland*, The Scottish Office, 1999. ACCORD can be contacted at 26 Drumheugh Gardens, Edinburgh EH3 7YR; phone: 0131 226 7411; fax: 0131 225 2934; email: lawscot@lawscot.org.uk

Northern Ireland

In 1993 the Law Society of Northern Ireland announced its mediation service aimed at the business community.[422] The service registers a matter on receipt of a registration form and on payment of a fee. The Service recommends a mediator and, if confirmed by the parties, a preliminary meeting is arranged by the Service.[423] To date, take up of the scheme has been poor, notwithstanding that a Law Society survey in 1995 revealed that 23% of respondents who had consulted a solicitor about a problem found ADR attractive; 27% of respondents who had actually attended court were attracted by ADR; and in the case of respondents who were involved with on-going litigation, about 30% welcomed ADR.[424]

The Role of other Professionals

The Courts and Legal Services Committee of the Law Society cited, as one reason for the Bristol Law Society Mediation Scheme, that it was necessary to 'get the profession moving' otherwise lawyers would lose out in the mediation services market to other professionals.[425] A perusal of the Centre for Dispute Resolution's membership list indicates that a large number and variety of other professionals are included, such as accountants, surveyors, computer experts, management consultants, advertisers, public relations executives, and architects. In addition, an increasing number of accredited mediators come from a wide range of non-legal backgrounds, including accounting, surveying and medical. For example, the Northern Association of Mediators includes accountants, architects, engineers, employment advisers, healthcare advisers, insurance practitioners, IT specialists, bankers and surveyors.

In the US, the main threat of lost mediation participation for lawyers is considered to come from the big accounting firms.[426] The Institute of Chartered Accountants for England and Wales recognises that ADR will form an essential part of the accounting profession's role over the next decade.[427] The Institute is developing mediation and expert determination guidelines, and promotes mediation through its general literature and by encouraging members to include ADR clauses in their appointment contracts.[428] The litigation departments of large accountancy firms also promote ADR to their clients.[429]

---

422 The Law Society of Northern Ireland *Press Release: coming to terms in business – Law Society offers new mediation service*, 13 January 1993.

423 The Law Society of Northern Ireland, *Dispute Resolution Service*.

424 Civil Justice Reform Group *Review of the Civil Justice System in Northern Ireland: Interim Report*, April 1999.

425 M Davies, G Davis and J Webb *Promoting Mediation: Report of a study of Bristol Law Society's Mediation Scheme in its preliminary phase*, 1996 Research & Policy Planning Unit Research Study no 21, The Law Society, at p 12.

426 Center for Public Resources 'ADR and the 21st Century Law Firm' *Alternatives*, vol 16, No 2 March 1998, at p 47.

427 Centre for Dispute Resolution 'Accountants must take note of ADR' *Resolutions*, Issue no 18, Winter 1997.

428 Ibid.

429 For example, Arthur Andersons' Claims and Disputes Practice; Morison Stoneham Dispute Resolution Team; and Levy Gee.

The Role of Commerce/Industry

The support given to mediation, and the wide range of mediation schemes set up, by commerce and industry will be considered under separate subject areas in Chapter 8. This section serves to highlight the growing enthusiasm for mediation shown by commerce and industry in the UK.[430]

The Centre for Dispute Resolution was set up with the assistance of the Confederation of British Industry. Perusal of the Centre's membership list shows the wide breadth of commerce and industry represented amongst the membership, including retail, banks and financial services, insurance, engineering and construction, manufacturing, foods, computers, gas and petroleum, railways, telecommunications, electricity, publishing, motor car manufacturers, freight companies, glass manufacturing, ship brokers, factoring companies, mobile phone companies, post offices, scientists, electronics and toy manufacturers. The Centre has also set up a wide range of mediation schemes for commerce and industry.[431] To recognise mediation efforts being made by commerce and industry, the Centre for Dispute Resolution awarded, in 1996, ADR awards to Barclays Bank[432] and British Telecom. The 1998 CEDR Commerce and Industry award winners were the Solicitors Indemnity Fund[433] and ITT London & Edinburgh. The 2000 award winner was BNFL in recognition of its application of mediation in a highly public and emotive arena.[434] The Corporation of London also supported the launch of the City Disputes Panel, which focuses on wholesale financial markets disputes.[435]

The mediation studies conducted in England and Wales confirm enthusiasm for mediation by commerce and industry. For example, Genn's study of the Central London County Court Mediation Pilot indicated that in 45% of the cases mediated, both parties were companies and in 39% of cases, at least one party was a company. In 22% of the latter cases a company was a defendant and in 17% of those cases, the company was the claimant.[436] In addition, Genn revealed that the rate at which both parties accepted mediation was highest when a company was a party.[437] A survey of 500 West Midland companies by DLA in 1999 indicated that 37% of respondents

---

430 For US comparisons, see D Lipsky and R Seeber *The use of ADR in US corporations*, Cornell University School of Industrial and Labor Relations, Foundation for the Prevention and Early Resolution of Conflict (PERC) and Price Waterhouse LLP, New York, 1997.

431 For example, for the Building Employers' Confederation; Heating and Ventilating Contractors; Glass and Glazing Federation; a range of insurance and financial services companies; the Institute of Grocery Distribution and the Electrical Contractors' Association: The Centre for Dispute Resolution, *1990–5: 5 years of achievement*, Centre for Dispute Resolution, 1995.

432 In recognition of the involvement of senior executives at the Bank in dispute management. In the 18 months between January 1999 and June 2000, the Corporate Bank mediated almost two dozen cases of between £80,000 and $10M in value.

433 SIF's use of mediation doubled in 1997/98.

434 CEDR, Press Release, 30 November 2000.

435 See the section on Mediation Organisations above for further details about the Panel.

436 H Genn *Central London County Court Mediation Pilot: Evaluation Report*, LCD Research Series, No 5/98, at p 29.

437 Ibid: 12% in cases where both parties were companies; 9% in cases where a company was a claimant and 7% in cases where a company was a defendant.

had considered using mediation clauses.[438] The CEDR MORI poll in 2000 also highlighted the observations of lawyers that their business clients are driving the impetus for mediation.[439] Centre for Dispute Resolution statistics provide an insight into the largest industry users of mediation. The Centre's 2000 statistics show that the construction industry is the largest single user of mediation, followed by banking, law firms, the IT industry and insurers.[440]

There have been examples of the use by industry in the UK of ADR pledges, non-binding expressions of commitment to ADR, in the insurance and IT industries.[441] InterMediation has developed an Endorsement of Principles, designed to encourage active ADR implementation in industry. By signing the document, organisations:

> '... express ... commitment to consider the range of ADR options available ... and confirm ... [an] intention, when ... ADR [is used], to do so in good faith and as a serious attempt to resolve the issues concerned.'[442]

A number of reasons have been advanced to explain the enthusiasm for mediation by commerce and industry. On the one hand, ADR provides a cheaper and more expedient dispute resolution mechanism and, on the other, it enables business clients to quickly recover monies from other parties.[443] Genn's research on the Central London County Court Mediation Pilot revealed that ADR allowed businesses to achieve control over the settlement of the dispute.[444] 56% of respondents to the West Midland survey conducted by DLA admitted that they lost control over a matter when litigation began, which was a source of considerable dissatisfaction for them.[445]

---

438 J Duckers 'Woolf at door over Mediation Reform: Lawyers in fear of losing fees' *Birmingham Post*, 17 September 1999. The Centre for Dispute Resolution has drafted ADR provisions in standard forms of contract for the Institution of Civil Engineers, the Electrical Contractors Association, the Institution of Chemical Engineers and the Steel Stockholders' Association: The Centre for Dispute Resolution, *1990–5: 5 years of achievement,* Centre for Dispute Resolution, 1995.

439 Centre for Dispute Resolution *Civil Justice Audit*, April 2000, where the following extracts provide an insight:
   - '... clients are coming to us now and pushing the settlement culture ...';
   - '[clients] ... are forcing themselves because they know the courts will force them ...';
   - 'it is the ... clients who are ... driving the impetus towards mediation and ... ADR ...'

   See the section 'In the majority of cases, who initiates mediation?' in the Civil Justice Audit results, op cit, for more information.

440 CEDR, Press Release *CEDR Commercial Mediation Statistics April 1999–March 2000*, CEDR, July 2000.

441 For example, the MAC initiative in the insurance industry and the Millennium Accord in the case of the IT industry. Further information on these initiatives is available in the sections on those subject areas in Chapter 8.

442 InterMediation *START ADR Protocol: Endorsement of Principles*, InterMediation. Further information on InterMediation is provided in the section on Mediation Organisations in this chapter.

443 See, for example, M Davies, G Davis and J Webb *Promoting Mediation: Report of a study of Bristol Law Society's Mediation Scheme in its preliminary phase*, 1996 Research & Policy Planning Unit Research Study no 21, The Law Society, at p 15.

444 H Genn *Central London County Court Mediation Pilot: Evaluation Report*, LCD Research Series, No 5/98, at p 101.

445 J Duckers 'Woolf at door over Mediation Reform: Lawyers in fear of losing fees' *Birmingham Post*, 17 September 1999.

The Role of Government

The impact of government on mediation has been far-reaching, from the impact of the civil justice reforms and court promotion of mediation, outlined earlier in this chapter, together with support of mediation through funding in a number of different areas, including consumer disputes, crime, family, education, noise complaints, health, employment and the IT industry. Guidelines have also been issued on the use of ADR provisions in government contracts. Further details about support in particular areas are given in Chapter 8. Chapter 9 outlines the changes made to funding, to encourage mediation take-up. The Lord Chancellor's ADR Discussion Paper has sparked the debate on a number of important issues for the future development of mediation, and these will also be examined in Chapters 9 and 11. Government is also a user of mediation across a wide area of dispute, for example:

- The Environment Council offers an ADR service for public interest/environmental disputes.
- Local councils promote mediation in neighbourhood dispute resolution.
- The Department of Health/NHS Mediation Pilot has involved three health regions.
- The Housing Ombudsman refers tenancy disputes to mediation.
- The Scottish Citizens Advice Bureaux have piloted a mediation service.
- The Planning Inspectorate has run a mediation pilot and is currently considering expanding its consideration of mediation beyond appeals cases.[446]

The 2000 CEDR Award for Excellence in ADR in the Public Sector was won by the Housing Ombudsman, and a special commendation was received by the Planning Inspectorate.[447]

---

446 For further examples, see the section on Government/public sector Disputes in Chapter 8.
447 CEDR, Press Release, 30 November 2000.

8

UK Mediation Practice

Introduction

The practice of mediation in the UK is taking on an increasingly systematic and co-ordinated form as a result of efforts by courts, mediation organisations and government agencies. Some of the mediation activity in the UK is purposive, some is reactive – caused by the urge to jump onto the mediation bandwagon, while others are confused and contradictory. New mediation practice is thus constantly emerging. The confidentiality of mediation, and its lack of public documentation, makes it difficult to gain access to relevant information, particularly in relation to private mediation. This chapter aims to provide an overview of the practice of mediation across different subject areas in the UK, and later chapters will consider the range of practical and policy issues that is likely to impact on the future development of mediation practice. This chapter also seeks to highlight any specific issues confronting mediation practice in particular areas.

An A-Z of Mediation Practice

Art disputes

The benefits of mediation for the resolution of art disputes are primarily confidentiality and the avoidance of high costs of litigation. A possible disadvantage of mediation may occur in cases where determination of a particular issue is required, for example, in relation to a valuation or authenticity. If mediation fails to resolve the issue, an option would be to refer the issue to expert determination.[1]

In an Australian case, papers belonging to a wealthy family, which had been entrusted to a library, had been re-delivered to the family on their request, but were not returned to the library. The library argued that the papers had only been loaned to the family, whereas the family claimed that the papers were originally deposited with the library for safekeeping only. The dispute was settled by mediation, on undisclosed terms, illustrating the benefits of avoidance of publicity and high litigation costs.[2] In Australia the Arts Law Centre has promoted the use of mediation for the resolution of art

---

1 In relation to expert determination, see J Kendall 'Expert determination: its use in resolving art and antiquity disputes' *Art Antiquity & Law*, vol 2, Issue 4, December 1997, p 325.
2 For a more comprehensive examination of the case and mediation of art disputes in Australia, consider Sir Anthony Mason 'Mediation and art disputes' *Art Antiquity & Law*,

disputes. A dispute can be referred to the Arts Law Centre, at which point a legal officer assesses its suitability for mediation. If a case is suitable for mediation, the legal officer will advise the parties to seek legal advice, both in relation to their legal rights and obligations and on how mediation works. Members of the Arts Law Centre can obtain advice free of charge from a lawyer on the Centre's panel of lawyers.[3]

The Institute of Art and Law, based in Leicester, a body similar to the Arts Law Centre of Australia, is planning a similar dispute resolution service for the resolution of art disputes in the UK, which will offer mediation, expert appraisal, expert determination and arbitration options.[4] There have been concerns, in the case of disputes arising in the few main art auction houses in the UK, of conflicts of interest given that the small pool of art experts, who are suitable arbitrators or experts, are drawn from those houses. Mediation is a possible solution, by providing a larger pool of qualified mediators, for cases where mediation expertise rather than art expertise is appropriate, and by focusing on the neutral's ability to assist parties to resolve the dispute themselves, rather than by imposing a solution on them.[5]

Banking and finance

The banking and finance industry has been a significant user of mediation in the UK for a number of years.[6] It is not surprising that a specialist ADR organisation, the City Disputes Panel ('CDP'), has been set up for the banking and finance industry.[7] CDP was set up as a result of concern that the expense and length of litigation could adversely affect the pre-eminence of London as a world financial centre.[8] CDP offers mediation, and for that purpose has developed a set of Mediation Rules, and conciliation, where the neutral seeks to bring about a settlement, although the recommendations of the conciliator are non-binding. CDP's panel of neutrals comprises solicitors, barristers and judges, who are experts in banking and finance matters.[9]

---

vol 3, Issue 1, March 1998, p 31.

3 Arts Law Centre of Australia *Mediation Service Information Sheet*, Arts Law Centre of Australia, 1999.

4 For further information on Art Resolve, refer to the Institute of Art and Law, Leicester (phone 0116 2555146).

5 See the debate over subject matter expertise vs mediation experience in Chapter 4, in relation to the selection of mediator.

6 See, for example, Centre for Dispute Resolution *Resolutions*, Issue No 22, at p 7, where statistics collated by CEDR show the banking and finance industry as the largest user of mediation. The Centre's 2000 statistics show that 6% of disputes referred to the Centre were banking disputes: CEDR '2000 statistics' *Resolutions*, No 26. The authors' 2000 survey of UK law firms also revealed that 6% of the disputes referred to mediation by respondents to the survey were banking disputes.

7 See the section on Mediation Organisations in Chapter 7.

8 Lord Woolf *Access to Justice: Interim Report*, Lord Chancellor's Department, London, June 1995.

9 CDP's panel expertise is in the following fields: actuarial, audit, accountancy, building societies, commercial banking, compliance, corporate finance, derivatives, information technology, insolvency, international capital markets, insurance, reinsurance, investment banking, investment management, leasing, pension fund management, project finance, property finance, stockbroking, treasury, venture capital and offshore financial services.

Retail banks in the UK use mediation across a range of disputes, from disputes with customers, inter-bank disputes and other third party disputes, including internal employment cases. A number of retail banks have piloted mediation schemes for debt recovery cases. Fifty recoveries staff were trained in mediation at Barclays Bank and their pilot mediation programme required recoveries staff to defend decisions taken not to mediate. The programme should be considered in the context of Barclays' legal risk management guidelines, which provide that:

'disputes should be resolved as cost effectively and quickly as feasible . . . negotiation, whether informal or in the context of ADR, is normally the preferred way of resolving a dispute . . .'

The Bank gives effect to that policy by including ADR clauses in contracts with customers and third parties. It has also issued guidelines to its external lawyers, encouraging them to consider ADR options.

Mediation in debt recovery work provides an example of mediation use to encourage creative solutions, by affording debtors an opportunity to work out repayment proposals.[10] Mediation also allows financial institutions an opportunity to avoid the publicity, which may accompany litigation and tarnish the institution's image and, in addition, may encourage other customers to sue the institution.[11] Mediation also offers an appropriate mechanism for resolving debt disputes, where although the debt is due, there is some fault on the part of the bank, as in the case of mismanagement of the relationship or when it has made administrative errors. Mediation may also be helpful to deal with the emotional issues, which are frequently present in such cases. The cost of mediation may, however, make its use prohibitive in small value debt cases.

The Banking Ombudsman attempts to conciliate disputes before making a determination.[12] Under the Financial Services and Markets Act, the Financial Ombudsman Service will replace the five existing Ombudsmen schemes for banking, building societies, personal investment, investment and pensions, although during transition the existing Ombudsmen schemes will continue to operate. It is expected that a substantial proportion of complaints will be resolved speedily by conciliation, 'an honest broker' approach.[13] The Act also provides scope for mediation before determination by the Financial Services Tribunal. Although it is not yet clear how it will operate, it is proposed that companies and individuals threatened with fines or naming by the Financial Services Authority will have the option of attempting to reach a settlement through mediation.[14] Internet Banks,

---

10 For a more detailed discussion about debtor/creditor relationships, refer to E A Morse 'Mediation in debtor/creditor relationships' 20 *University of Michigan Law Journal* 606.

11 See M E Budnitz 'Arbitration and disputes between consumers and financial institutions: a serious threat to consumer protection' (1995) 10(2) *Ohio State Journal on Dispute Resolution* 271.

12 See the section on Mediation Organisations in Chapter 7, and the section on Consumer Disputes in this chapter.

13 Financial Services Authority and Financial Services Ombudsman Scheme: a joint consultation paper, *Consumer Complaints and the new single ombudsman scheme*, FSA, November 1999, at pp 30–1.

14 J Mackintosh 'Mediator option for financial wrongdoers' *Financial Times*, 17 August 2000, at p 31. See also J Virgo and P Ryley 'Mediation, penalties and enforcement' (2000) 13(3) *Compliance Monitor* 269. The Financial Services Ombudsman is due to commence operation in 2001.

which do not fall within the current jurisdiction of the Banking Ombudsman, have sought to develop alternative mechanisms for resolving disputes with customers. For example, the internet Bank, First-e, refers cases to a law firm, for screening purposes, that may then refer cases to an external and independent mediation or adjudication option.[15]

The use of mediation has also extended to project financing. For example, the Channel Tunnel Rail Link project involved a technical panel of engineers who considered construction-related disputes and a finance panel of accountants and financiers who considered disputes in relation to the financial provisions of the relevant agreements. The Docklands Light Railway involved two similar panels. Although such panels can ultimately adjudicate on disputes referred to them, where possible, panel members attempt to conciliate disputes, and the panels may have a preventative effect, by focusing the minds of the disputing parties, who may reach a solution to the dispute, ahead of any determination by the panel. The Treasury Task Force Private Finance Guidance suggests that ADR may offer a more efficient and cost-effective method of resolving disputes under a PFI Contract, suggesting a three-stage dispute resolution process, involving negotiation or consultation between the parties, ADR and, finally, arbitration, adjudication or the courts if the earlier steps are unsuccessful. In terms of ADR, it is suggested that financial, rather than construction or operational, disputes should be referred to a panel of financial experts for conciliation, rather than referring those disputes direct to arbitration.[16]

Increasing use of mediation and other forms of ADR by the banking industry in the UK is consistent with developments in other jurisdictions. The Center for Public Resources in New York, for example, has set up a Banking Industry Program, which encourages the use of ADR for the resolution of both inter-bank disputes and disputes between bank and customers. A range of inter-bank disputes have been resolved by ADR, including derivative transactions, disputes between agent banks and syndicate members and letters of credit.[17] In Australia, an early mediation initiative in the banking industry was the Farm Debt Mediation Act, which gave farmers in debt the opportunity to use mediation to formulate repayment proposals. A creditor of a farmer issues the farmer with a notice under the Act and the farmer must choose whether to mediate with the creditor. If the farmer elects to mediate, the creditor is obliged to mediate. The mediator must be accredited by the Rural Assistance Authority. If a farmer fails to request mediation, the rights under the Farm Debt Mediation Act are lost. The Credit Union Dispute Reference Centre, opened in Australia in 1996, provides negotiation, mediation and expert determination services. Common areas of complaint referred to the Centre are over-charging, service failure, disputed debiting or crediting of accounts, account closures and handling of third party security.[18]

---

15 J Fleming 'Lawrence Graham is dispute resolver for Internet Bank' *The Law Society Gazette*, 3 August 2000, at p 8.

16 Treasury Task Force information is available at http://www.treasury-projects-taskforce.gov.uk

17 Center for Public Resources *Banking Industry Program*, Center for Public Resources, New York, 1997.

18 G Cork 'ADR brings high interest returns in financial disputes – the Credit Union Dispute Reference Centre' (1998) 1 *The ADR Bulletin* 35.

ADR in the context of banking and finance disputes has resulted in wide-ranging debate in the theoretical ADR literature, regarding the possible disadvantages of mediation, in particular for consumers. For example, there is a concern in the literature that mediation may circumvent the legal constraints intended to protect consumers and may not provide impetus to the bank or financial institution to resolve systemic or underlying problems.[19] These issues could be addressed through legal representation or, if necessary, by termination of the mediation if there is abuse. The concerns appear to assume that the solution to endemic or systemic problems can only be achieved by litigation. However, since most cases are settled prior to trial, through direct negotiation, it is difficult to support the assumption.[20] As the industry watchdog, the Ombudsman would seem to be better placed than litigation to tackle systemic issues.

Concerns about mediation, expressed on the other hand by banks and other financial institutions, include that mediation may involve an implicit acceptance of liability, and that the only issue perceived by complainants in mediation is the size of the cheque that will be written by the institution.[21]

Charities

The National Council for Voluntary Organisations ('NCVO') set up a mediation service in 1995, with the aim of providing the voluntary sector with access to mediators. In 1998 a joint panel of both NCVO and Centre for Dispute Resolution mediators was formed, with the aim of providing mediation services to the charities and voluntary sector. An NCVO Helpline provides a point of contact and reported a steep increase in enquiries and referrals to mediation under the scheme from 1999.[22] The Charity Commission has issued a Guide for charities entering into contracts to provide services on behalf of public bodies. The Guide recommends that contracts include appropriate dispute resolution provisions and, in particular, some form of ADR. The Guide informs charities that mediation is being increasingly used to settle disputes without recourse to litigation and it also expresses the view that a charity is justified in paying the reasonable fees of an ADR service if there is a chance that litigation expenses can be avoided.[23]

---

19 See E A Morse 'Mediation in debtor/creditor relationships' 20 *University of Michigan Law Journal* 606 at 696; and R Abel 'The Contradictions of Informal Justice' in R Abel (ed) *The Politics of Informal Justice, vol 1*, Academic Press, New York 1982.
20 These issues are discussed further below in the context of consumer, discrimination and employment disputes. See also Part I, on the issue of effectiveness of mediation; Part II, in relation to the role of the mediator; and Chapter 11 for an outline of mediator standards.
21 B A Filipowski *The response of business to the challenges of ADR*, Westpac Bank, Sydney, 28 August 1992.
22 See the Centre for Dispute Resolution *Charities Unit – Mediation*, CEDR 1999; and Centre for Dispute Resolution, *Resolutions*, Issue 24, at p 3.
23 Charity Commission *Charities and Contracts: a guide for smaller charities entering into contracts to provide services on behalf of public bodies*, Document CC37, October 1998, available at http://www.charity-commission.gov.uk

Clinical negligence claims

Overview of UK developments

Data collected for Lord Woolf's Inquiry indicated that the average time between instructing lawyers to court hearing for clinical negligence cases was 5.4 years compared to, for example, 3.4 years for other professional negligence cases.[24] In addition to delay, Lord Woolf found that clinical negligence cases involved disproportionate costs compared to damages, a lower success rate than other personal injury litigation and greater lack of co-operation between the parties than in other types of litigation.[25] Lord Woolf considered that some of his findings may be explained by the fact that his Inquiry coincided with two significant developments in the field, the introduction of a new complaints procedure for NHS staff and the extension of the Health Service Ombudsman's jurisdiction to cover clinical complaints against NHS staff.[26]

An NHS Mediation Pilot, discussed further below, identified other reasons for the delay inherent in clinical negligence dispute resolution. Delay in some cases is desirable to allow a medical condition to stabilise.[27] In other cases, lack of expertise amongst solicitors dealing with clinical negligence work results in delay.[28] The involvement of experts is also a factor contributing to delay. Defensiveness and difficulty in obtaining information from hospitals was cited by 55% of respondents in the pilot study as a factor contributing to delay in settling clinical negligence cases.[29] Defensiveness on the part of Health Authority solicitors was also frequently cited by respondents as the explanation for delay.[30] Some even confessed that this defensiveness provided them with an incentive to pursue compensation.[31] Apart from delay in resolving clinical negligence disputes, the NHS Mediation Pilot revealed that 70% of respondents were either totally or very dissatisfied with the outcome they achieved in litigation, in particular, as the outcome of litigation did not help respondents to put the matter behind them.[32]

One of Lord Woolf's suggestions for clinical negligence claims was an effective pre-action procedure, to encourage early communication between parties and to ensure that claimants are aware of dispute resolution options, including ADR.[33] In terms of ADR, Lord Woolf suggested the possibility of in-house dispute resolution with claims managers, in those cases involving hospitals. In support, he referred to a study conducted by the Medical Negligence Working Group, which indicated that clinical negligence claims could successfully be mediated, even before proceedings

---

24　L Mulcahy et al *Mediating medical negligence claims: an option for the future?* NHS Executive, 2000, at p 17.
25　Lord Woolf *Access to Justice: Interim Report*, Lord Chancellor's Department, London, June 1995, at p 170.
26　Ibid, at p 173.
27　L Mulcahy et al, op cit.
28　Ibid, at p 50.
29　Ibid, at p 8.
30　Ibid, at p xiii.
31　Ibid, at p 8.
32　Ibid, at p 11.
33　Ibid, at p 179.

are commenced.[34] Lord Woolf did, however, express caution about ADR in the context of clinical negligence claims, as frequently there will be an imbalance of knowledge or power between patients and hospitals, in which case it is important to ensure that claimants are not disadvantaged by using informal dispute resolution procedures.[35] Nevertheless, Lord Woolf concluded that solicitors should advise clients in clinical negligence cases of all available dispute resolution options and consider at all stages of each case whether ADR is appropriate.[36]

The problem of inexperienced solicitors handling clinical negligence claims, identified by the NHS Pilot, was sought to be addressed when the clinical negligence legal aid franchise was introduced on 1 February 1999. The franchise is limited to solicitors who have clinical negligence claims expertise and are members of specialist panels of the Law Society and Action for Victims of Medical Accidents ('AVMA').[37] It is hoped that this will have the effect that:

'. . . claimants will be presented with a more realistic, less speculative and less self-interested assessment of the chances of success than has previously been the case.'[38]

The Commons Health Select Committee conducted an Inquiry into clinical negligence procedures in 1999. It noted that resistance to change in the legal and medical professions had minimised the potential impact of the Civil Procedure Rules. The recommendation made by the Director of the Health Complaints and Mediation Service was for mandatory mediation, in part as it would overcome that resistance, and in part since conciliation is offered in any event in the General Practitioners' complaints system.[39] The Committee published its Report in December 1999, recommending that the Government should improve the funding arrangements relating to mediation of clinical negligence claims, citing the NHS mediation pilot in support.[40]

The Clinical Negligence Pre-action Protocol, finalised in early 2000, attempts to provide a code of good practice to be followed in clinical negligence litigation. Section 5 of the Protocol deals with alternative dispute resolution. Apart from negotiation, it lists a range of other alternative mechanisms for resolving clinical negligence disputes, including the NHS Complaints Procedure, which is aimed at providing patients with an explanation of relevant events and, if appropriate, an apology, but is not designed to provide compensation for negligence. The Protocol also refers to mediation, early neutral evaluation, expert determination and arbitration.[41] The NHS Litigation Authority has accordingly instructed its panel law

---

34 L Mulcahy et al *Mediating medical negligence claims: an option for the future?* NHS Executive, 2000, at p 183.
35 Ibid.
36 Ibid, at p 195.
37 Legal Aid Board *A new approach to funding civil cases: Report to the Lord Chancellor*, October 1999, at p 92.
38 House of Commons *Select Committee on Health Minutes of Evidence*, 12 July 1999.
39 House of Commons *Select Committee on Health Appendices to the Minutes of Evidence*, 23 November 1999. The difficulty with conciliation, offered as part of that system, has been that, since conciliators have been employed by the health authority, there is a perception that they may not be independent.
40 House of Commons Health Committee, 6th Report 1998–99 Session, *Procedures related to adverse clinical incidents and outcomes in medical care*, 23 November 1999, Recommendation 130.
41 *Civil Procedure Pre-Action Protocols – Clinical Negligence Protocol*, available at http://www.open.gov.uk/lcd/civil/procrules

firms to consider the appropriateness of mediation in every case and to monitor the outcomes of mediations.[42]

The Funding Code requires complainants, who are eligible for legal aid, to exhaust the NHS Complaints Procedure in clinical negligence claims involving under £10,000. There are some exceptions, including urgency, in cases involving an infant's death or where the relationship between the NHS and the complainant has irretrievably broken down.[43] In Northern Ireland, the cost of clinical negligence litigation and the difficulty of qualifying for legal aid has prompted the establishment of an Action on Medical Negligence Association and a mediation service for clinical negligence cases is being mooted.[44]

UK statistics

The Bristol Law Society Mediation Scheme revealed that some solicitors considered that clinical negligence cases were too complex to be referred to mediation.[45] The study of the Central London County Court Mediation Pilot indicated that the acceptance rate of mediation in clinical negligence claims was under 1%.[46] Respondents in clinical negligence claims identified protection of their professional reputation as the reason for rejecting mediation.[47] The Centre for Dispute Resolution's 1999 statistics revealed that 4% of their mediations related to clinical negligence and personal injury claims.[48] The NHS Mediation Pilot was launched in April 1995 in two regions, Anglia/Oxford and Northern/Yorkshire. By April 1998 twelve cases had been mediated, eleven successfully.[49] Half the mediated cases involved obstetrics and gynaecology.[50]

NHS mediation pilot

Some basic principles were established at the outset of the NHS Mediation Pilot, in particular, that participation in the pilot should be voluntary; that mediation was unlikely to be successful in every case; and that mediation could usefully be used in

---

42 Legal Week National News 'NHSLA announces mediation audit' *Legal Week*, 20 July 2000.
43 Criterion 5.4.3. of the General Funding Code applies to clinical negligence claims, and provides that, if mediation is offered but rejected by a claimant, the practitioner must be able to justify the refusal to mediate, otherwise funding may be refused or discontinued. See further the section on Funding and Mediation in Chapter 9.
44 'Complaints Group hits admin problem' Belfast Newsletter, 15 August 1998. As to developments, generally, see S Polywka 'Mediation: life after the NHS Pilot Scheme?' (2000) 6(1) *C Risk* 25.
45 M Davies, G Davis and J Webb *Promoting Mediation: Report of a study of Bristol Law Society's Mediation Scheme in its preliminary phase*, Research & Policy Planning Unit Research Study no 21, The Law Society, 1996, at p 23.
46 H Genn *Central London County Court Mediation Pilot: Evaluation Report*, LCD Research Series, No 5/98, at p 18.
47 Ibid, at p 35.
48 Centre for Dispute Resolution *Press Release*, 26 April 1999.
49 L Mulcahy et al *Mediating medical negligence claims: an option for the future?* NHS Executive, 2000, at p xiii.
50 Ibid, at p xiv .

clinical negligence cases to narrow issues in dispute.[51] Mulcahy's study of the Pilot revealed that high value and complex cases were considered unsuitable or much harder to mediate.[52]

Of the cases that were mediated as part of the Pilot, a range of problems were highlighted. Some interviewees expressed concerns about perceptions of partiality in cases of a medically qualified mediator. Others considered that the doctor in question should be present in the mediation so that the claimant can have his or her 'day in court'.[53] Claims managers and solicitors considered that whether the doctor should attend should depend upon whether the individual was able to add value to the process, by being able to adopt a constructive approach.[54] Most interviewees considered, however, that a senior representative of the relevant health authority should be present at mediation.[55] There was also a commonly held view that claimants' partners should be present at mediation as they have also had to bear the consequences of the negligence alleged.[56] Apart from issues of who should attend the mediation, the further problem highlighted by Mulcahy's study was solicitors' lack of experience of mediation. Lack of experience was illustrated in a number of ways, for example, clients who expressed confusion about the mediation process, indicating that they had not been properly prepared by their solicitors[57] and instances of litigation tactics, like late disclosure of information, being used in mediation.[58] In one case, a solicitor refused to participate in mediation unless the mediator agreed to make an order as to costs.[59]

In relation to those cases which settled at mediation, the Pilot identified a range of settlements, including financial terms, apologies, explanations of medical decisions and future treatments. In one case, for example, it was agreed that a tour of the health department in question would take place so that the claimant could be assured that improvements had been made as a result of the claim.[60] The study highlighted that, although claimants' solicitors considered that their clients achieved in mediation a more appropriate range of remedies, respondents and their solicitors failed to recognise the value of non-legal remedies.[61] For the doctors involved in the mediations, whether as respondents or experts, mediation was considered a distraction from their medical duties.[62]

---

51 L Mulcahy et al *Mediating medical negligence claims: an option for the future?* NHS Executive, 2000, at p 22. For a mediation case report, refer to T Hall 'Billington v North Staffordshire Hospital NHS Trust' (2000) 6(2) *C Risk* 71.
52 L Mulcahy et al, op cit, at p 51.
53 Ibid, at p 34.
54 Ibid, at p 63.
55 Ibid, at p 76.
56 Ibid, at p 33.
57 Ibid, at p 64.
58 Ibid.
59 Ibid, at p 56. More generally, concern has been expressed by claimants' lawyers that the expense of mediation in clinical negligence cases may act as a deterrent to the take-up of mediation in this field: see R Wicks 'Mediating clinical negligence claims' (2000) 3 *Med Lit* 8.
60 L Mulcahy et al, op cit, at p 31.
61 Ibid, at p 105.
62 Ibid, at p 106.

US comparisons

An interesting approach to the mediation of clinical negligence claims was developed in Wisconsin through a Mandatory Mediation Panel System ('MMPS'). MMPS comprises a lawyer, who is the chair of the panel, a doctor or other healthcare professional with experience in the subject matter of the claim, and a public member. Clinical negligence claimants could file a request for mediation before instituting proceedings or within 15 days of filing a claim. Mediations had to be completed within 90 days of the request for mediation and formal discovery for trial, if proceedings had been instituted, could not take place during this period. The mediation panel aimed to facilitate settlement, by identifying strengths or weaknesses in each party's position and by discussing settlement options. The Panel made no binding recommendations or decisions. A study of MMPS in the early 1990s found much lower settlement rates than other court-connected ADR programmes and determined that the prohibition against discovery during the mediation period was a significant factor, as parties lacked critical information relating to the extent of injuries.[63] A more recent ADR initiative in the clinical negligence field in the US has been the establishment of a Commission on Healthcare Dispute Resolution, with the aim of developing ADR procedures and standards for disputes relating to healthcare treatment and health insurance coverage.

Commercial contract disputes

Specific kinds of contract disputes, such as construction contract disputes, will be considered separately in this chapter. This section considers the general issues relevant to commercial contract disputes. Genn, in her study of the Central London County Court Mediation Pilot, identified that acceptance of mediation was highest in disputes between businesses.[64] She also found that the demand for mediation was highest in breach of contract disputes and disputes in relation to the delivery of goods or supply of services.[65] The Centre for Dispute Resolution's 1999 statistics showed that commercial contract disputes accounted for 15% of their mediation caseload.[66] The figure had increased to 31%, according to the Centre's 2000 statistics.[67] As the section in this part on Commercial Court referrals to mediation shows, a large proportion of the Commercial Court cases referred to mediation are general commercial contract disputes. In the US, as early as 1993, a Deloitte & Touche survey found that the bulk of mediations related to breach of commercial contract claims.[68] Businesses also report large average cost savings per case, using mediation to resolve general contract disputes.[69]

---

63 S Keilitz 'Civil dispute resolution processes' in Ohio State University College of Law (ed) *Court Reform Implications of Dispute Resolution*, Ohio State University, 1995, at p 21.
64 H Genn *Central London County Court Mediation Pilot: Evaluation Report*, LCD Research Series, No 5/98.
65 Ibid, at p 18.
66 Centre for Dispute Resolution *Press Release*, 26 April 1999.
67 Centre for Dispute Resolution '2000 statistics' *Resolutions*, No 26. Respondents to the authors' 2000 survey indicated that 17.5% of the cases they had referred to mediation were commercial contract disputes.
68 Deloitte and Touche *1993 Survey of general and outside counsel*, Deloitte and Touche, 1993, at p 4.
69 See, for example, Centre for Dispute Resolution *Resolutions*, Issue 13, at p 4.

A number of explanations have been proffered to explain why commercial contract disputes attract mediation. Some argue that mediation is a way of overcoming middle and senior managers' emotional investment in hanging on to contract disputes, either to avoid admitting that they have handled a matter badly or in order to impress the Board by not giving in easily.[70] Mediation also allows businesses to retain control over their disputes and and the timing of settlement. It also allows business people to play a central role in the process, as they can bring to the process an understanding of what their underlying business interests are and the range of possible settlement options.[71] Mediation also offers an opportunity for a business deal to be re-negotiated. Issues can arise in the course of a contract, which were not contemplated at the time the contract was entered into, and mediation can provide a useful way of taking into account such factors. It also provides an opportunity for continued, modified or enhanced business relationships.

There is a wide range of examples in the UK of mediation in the context of commercial contract disputes. These include disputes over contract performance through to warranty claims. A range of schemes has also been set up to promote mediation for the resolution of commercial contract disputes. For example, the Bristol Chamber of Commerce set up a mediation scheme targeting business debt cases, with a view to enabling a creditor to determine at an early stage the reason for non-payment and, in cases of inability to pay, to use mediation to agree repayment terms.[72] Business Link Partnerships seek to allow small and medium-sized businesses access to quality expertise to aid their growth and increase competitiveness. New Business Link 'Centres of Expertise' will enable Business Link Partnerships to provide local businesses with access to specialist services, including ADR.[73] The Center for Public Resources has attempted to encourage the use of mediation for the resolution of business contract disputes throughout Europe by formulating a Mediation Procedure for Business Disputes in Europe.

Mediation has been widely used for the resolution of joint venture and franchise disputes, where continuing business relationships are critically important. A mediation scheme which seeks to facilitate resolution of franchisee issues for ESSO has been launched by the Centre for Dispute Resolution. In the US the Center for Public Resources has set up a Franchise Industry Program, whose members include a wide range of household names.[74] Under the Program the franchisee or the franchisor may propose mediation. In one example, Pizza Hut was able to resolve in a single day, using mediation, a three-year-old dispute with a franchisee, with whom it had had a 30-year relationship.[75] In Australia, the Franchising Code of Conduct, which is mandatory under the Trade Practices Act, provides standards of conduct for

---

70 See, for example, J Wade *In search of new conflict management processes – The lawyer as macro and micro diagnostic problem-solver,* Bond University Dispute Resolution Centre 1995, at p 12; and Center for Public Resources *Alternatives,* Special Supplement, vol 17, No 4, April 1999, at p 69.
71 H Mintzberg *The nature of managerial work,* Harper & Row, New York, 1973.
72 A Bevan *ADR: a lawyer's guide to mediation and other forms of dispute resolution,* Sweet & Maxwell, London, 1992, at p 41.
73 For more information, refer to Department of Trade and Industry *White Paper on Competitiveness,* DTI 1999.
74 For example, Pizza Hut, Burger King, McDonalds, Dunkin' Doughnuts.
75 Center for Public Resources 'An ADR arena suits Davids and Goliaths' *Alternatives,* vol 12, No 2 February 1994, pp iv–8.

franchisors and franchisees and an escalating dispute resolution procedure, which involves negotiation at the first level, followed by mediation if negotiation does not lead to a resolution. Any party to a franchise agreement may refer a problem to a mediator of their choice or may ask the Office of the Mediation Adviser, established by the Federal Department of Employment, Workplace Relations and Small Business, to appoint a mediator. The Office of the Mediation Adviser maintains a panel of specialist franchise dispute mediators across Australia and the expectation is that mediations will cost about AU$1,000 per party.[76]

Another application of a mediation in the context of commercial contracts is the use of mediators to act as independent and neutral deal-brokers at the time a contract is being negotiated. The 'deal mediator' uses mediation principles, in particular, identification of underlying interests and brainstorming options, in order to help the parties resolve the terms of the contract. The mediator acts as a facilitator, by assisting all the parties, not just one party. The skills are particularly useful for complex agreements, such as mergers and acquisitions.[77] In a reported US example, deal mediation was used in the negotiations leading up to the formalisation of a joint venture between General Motors and Toyota to establish a motor vehicle manufacturing plant in California. Although the parties were agreed in principle on the joint venture, there were two main obstacles, being opposition from the Workers' Union and Toyota's requirement that it should have freedom to run the plant as it saw fit. A former United States Secretary of Labor was appointed as a deal mediator, and achieved a resolution of all the obstacles, following seven months of mediation. The co-operative nature of the imminent venture, the good faith expectation between the parties entering into the venture and the long term nature of the venture were powerful incentives to use a mediator in this capacity.[78] In a UK example, deal mediation was used to resolved environmental issues, which were providing the stumbling block to a deal. A similar use of mediation is in the context of strategic alliances, where a facilitator assists alliance members not only to formulate their initial agreements, but also to resolve differences, which arise in the course of the alliance's operation.

Community (neighbour, crime and schools) mediation

UK community mediation services

There are about 120 community mediation services in the UK.[79] Mediation UK has published a Directory of mediation and conflict resolution services, which provides a useful source of information on the range of community mediation services available.[80] According to Mediation UK, the number of community disputes is rising

---

76 Department of Employment, Workplace Relations and Small Business *Franchising Code of Conduct*, Sydney.
77 For a more detailed discussion of the role of mediators in this context, refer to M Hager and R Pritchard 'Hither the deal mediators' (1999) 10(10) *ICCLR* 291; and R P Buckley 'The applicability of mediation skills to the creation of contracts' (1992) *Australian Dispute Resolution Journal* 227.
78 J Riekert 'ADR in Australian Commercial Disputes: Quo Vadis?' (1990) *Australian Dispute Resolution Journal* 31.
79 Mediation UK *Annual Report*, 1998.
80 For an up-dated list of services, refer to Mediation UK *Community Mediation Services*

by up to 20% each year.[81] This section considers the main areas of activity for community mediation organisations, namely in the context of neighbour, victim-offender and schools mediation.

Neighbour mediation

Mediation organisations and schemes

Neighbour disputes constitute the largest category of work for community mediation services. The 1995 Community Mediation Service survey indicated that 95% of the

---

Pamphlet, as up-dated. The December 1999 version of the pamphlet included AIMS, Aberdeen Community Mediation Project, Ashford Mediation Service, Bath Area Mediation, Bexley Mediation Service, Birmingham Mediation Service, Blackpool Mediation Service, Bliss Mediation, Bolton Mediation, Borders Mediation, Bradford Mediation, Breckland Neighbour Mediation Service, Brighton and Hove Mediation Service, Bristol Mediation, Bromley Community Mediation Service, Broxtowe Borough Mediation Service, CALM, Cambridge and District Community Mediation Service, Camden Mediation Service, Cardiff Mediation, Castle Morpeth Mediation, Community Action Project, Community Mediation 2000, Community Mediation Service, Coventry Mediation Partnership, Croydon Community Mediation, Croydon Independent Mediation Service, Derby Mediation Services, Devon Mediation Service, Ealing Neighbour Mediation Service, East Lothian Community Mediation Project, East Surrey Community Mediation, Eastbourne Community Mediation Service, Edinburgh Community Mediation Project, Elmbridge Independent Mediation Service, Face To Face, Falkirk Council Mediation Service, Fife Community Mediation, Greenwich Mediation, Guildford Community Mediation Service, Hackney Mediation Service, Hastings and St Leonards Mediation Service, Hounslow Mediation Service, Kingston Friends Mediation, LAMP, Lambeth Mediation Service, Leeds Community Mediation Service, Leicestershire Mediation Service, Lin Cronin Mediation, Luton Mediation, MINT, Maidstone Mediation Service, Mansfield Mediation Service, Mediation and Parent Support Service, Mediation Cornwall, Mediation Dacorum, Mediation Dorset, Mediation Manchester, Mediation Network For Northern Ireland, Mediation North Staffs, Mediation Norwich, Mediation Service For Canterbury, Mediation Somerset, Mediation South and West Wales, Mediation South Worcestershire, Mediation In Burnley, Mediation In Fareham, Mediation In Havant, Mediation In Kirklees, Mediation In Sheffield, Medway Mediation, Mid Surrey Mediation Service, Milton Keynes Community Mediation Service, Monmouthshire Mediation, Moss Side and Hulme Independent Mediation Service, New Forest Mediation, Newark and Sherwood District Council, Newham Conflict and Change Project, Newport Mediation, Northern Devon Community Mediation, Norwich and District Legal Service, Nottingham Mediation Service, Nuneaton CAB Mediation Service, Oxford Community Mediation, Peterborough Mediation, Plymouth Mediation, Portsmouth Mediation Service, Powys Mediation, Preston Area Neighbour Dispute Action, Resolve, Rochdale Mediation Service, Rugby Community Mediation Service, Sandwell Mediation Service, Shepway Independent Mediation Service, Shropshire Mediation Services, South Hams Mediation, Southwark Mediation Centre, Spelthorne and Runnymede Community Mediation Service, St Helens Mediation Dispute Service, Suffolk and East Mediation Service, Sunderland Mediation, The Independent Mediation Service, Tower Hamlets Mediation Service, UNITE, United Neighbours Community Mediation Services, Vale Neighbour Mediation, Walsall Mediation, Waltham Forest Neighbour Mediation Scheme, Watford and Three Rivers Mediation Services, Waverley Community Mediation Service, Welwyn Hatfield Mediation, West Kent Independent Mediation Service, Woking Mediation Service, Wolverhampton Neighbourhood Mediation Service, Wycombe Mediation Service.

81 N Gardner 'Mediation helps to mend fences' *Sunday Times*, 25 January 1998.

work of 16 community mediation services comprised neighbour disputes. Neighbour disputes comprised 92% of the work of a further service, and for eight community mediation services, neighbour disputes formed the bulk of their work.[82] Dignan's 1995 study of community mediation services indicated that over one quarter of the services confined themselves to a specific geographical area.[83] Key development issues for community mediation services dealing with neighbour disputes are credibility and funding. Dignan's survey highlighted that common funding sources for services providing mediation for neighbour disputes include:

- government departments;
- local charities;
- councils;
- industry and commerce.[84]

Dignan's survey also revealed that the total funds received by services ranged from less than £1,000 to over £80,000.[85] Funding issues create concerns that mediation services could become directed by funding opportunities, rather than by needs, and that time expended on fund-raising could be better spent on delivering mediation services.[86] Funding issues also create difficulties in retention of staff. Dignan's survey indicated that the majority of services had either no paid staff or a part-time employee only, creating concerns that volunteers might have to be paid in order to retain them.[87]

Information from mediation services dealing with neighbour disputes indicates that the bulk of mediations are self-referred and that other major sources of referrals are the Police, Citizens Advice Bureaux, local authorities and the Housing and Environmental Health Departments.[88] In terms of the outcome of neighbour mediations, Dignan's study found that the largest number of mediations were terminated, usually by withdrawal from the mediation by a party or referral of the case to another agency. The next largest category of cases resulted in either complete agreement on all issues presented in the mediation or a better understanding between the parties of each other's positions, although falling short of agreement.[89] Dignan's survey

---

82 J Dignan *Community Mediation Service: General Survey 1995*, Interim Report, Mediation UK, 1995, at p 4.

83 J Dignan et al *Neighbour Disputes: comparing the cost and effectiveness of a mediation and alternative approaches*, Centre for Criminological and Legal Research, University of Sheffield, 1996, at p 26.

84 J Dignan *Community Mediation Service: General Survey 1995*, op cit, at p 8.

85 Ibid, at p 7.

86 J Dignan et al *Neighbour Disputes: comparing the cost and effectiveness of a mediation and alternative approaches*, op cit, at pp 30–1.

87 J Dignan *Community Mediation Service: General Survey 1995*, op cit, at p 11.

88 See, for example, Cardiff Mediation *Annual Report 1997–98*; and R E Mackay and A J Brown *Community Mediation in Scotland: a study of implementation*, The Scottish Office Central Research Unit, Edinburgh, 1999.

89 J Dignan *Community Mediation Service: General Survey 1995*, op cit, at p 18: in 76 of the cases surveyed, the problem had been resolved without ultimate intervention by the mediation service; in 118 of the cases the dispute remained unresolved following mediation; in 263 cases an agreement on some of the issues presented in the mediation was reached; in 303 cases a better understanding of each parties' position was achieved,

indicated that the average cost of a completed mediation of a neighbour dispute was £318,[90] suggesting that for routine noise disputes, in particular, referral to mediation would cost more than, for example, handling by housing officers.[91] In cases involving some form of legal intervention, however, considerable cost advantages are possible if referral to mediation takes place.[92] The relevant costs of dispute resolution include the emotional effects on the parties and authority staff who deal with disputes.[93]

Dignan's study indicated, in terms of the number of cases handled by the community mediation services surveyed, that the minimum was two and the maximum was 234.[94] Services have experienced a steady increase in referrals from 1995. The maximum optimal load, according to Dignan, is 500 cases per year.[95] A common problem cited by mediation services in this field is the inability, due to lack of resources, to handle too many cases, but the dilemma that, in order to grow, more cases are required.

Noise disputes

Disputes about noise are the predominant type of neighbour dispute referred to community mediation services. The Community Mediation Service Survey conducted by Dignan in 1995 confirmed that almost half of all neighbour disputes referred to mediation were noise-related.[96] Information from a range of community mediation services since that study suggests that the position has not changed. For example, Cardiff Mediation's 1998 Annual Report shows that the bulk of referrals were noise-related disputes.[97] Councils around the UK report an increase in complaints about noise. Newcastle Borough Council reported in 1998 that complaints about noise had almost doubled in four years.[98] Aberdeen City Council reported that between 1 April and 31 December 1998, neighbour noise accounted for 63% of complaints.[99]

The Department of the Environment, Transport and the Regions (DETR) has been actively involved in encouraging the use of mediation for the resolution of noise

---

albeit that no specific agreement was reached; in 374 cases agreement was reached on all the issues presented in the mediation; and 465 cases terminated for 'some other reason'.

90 J Dignan *Community Mediation Service: General Survey 1995*, Interim Report, Mediation UK, 1995, at p 17.

91 J Dignan et al *Neighbour Disputes: comparing the cost and effectiveness of a mediation and alternative approaches*, Centre for Criminological and Legal Research, University of Sheffield, 1996, at p 79.

92 Ibid, at p 80.

93 Ibid, at p 60.

94 J Dignan *Community Mediation Service: General Survey 1995*, op cit, at p 14.

95 Ibid, at p 16.

96 J Dignan et al *Neighbour Disputes: comparing the cost and effectiveness of a mediation and alternative approaches*, op cit, at p 23.

97 Cardiff Mediation *Annual Report 1997–98*, Cardiff Mediation, 1998.

98 T Yaqoob 'Peacemaker in a war of words: New mediation service launches to settle neighbour disputes' *The Sentinel*, 10 October 1998, at p 12.

99 Aberdeen City Council 'Noisy neighbours is top complaint' *Aberdeen Press and Journal*, 9 April 1999, at p 3.

disputes since 1994. The Department set up a working party in 1994 to investigate whether there were alternative remedies that might provide faster, more cost effective, relief in the case of disputes over noise. In its conclusions, the working party had recommended mediation, which led the Department to issue an information paper, 'Mediation: benefits and practice', to environmental health and housing officers in local authorities in England and Wales. The Department also included, in response to noise complaints, a leaflet that outlined mediation. In turn, the Chartered Institute of Environmental Health produced a 'Noise Management Guide' in 1997, which recommended that mediation should be considered an integral part of a local authority's response to noise complaints.

Councils throughout the UK now support mediation as strategy for tackling noise problems. Apart from tackling the number of noise-related problems, councils point to a number of other benefits of resolving noise disputes using alternatives. The traditional options for handling these problems, including police involvement, court action or eviction, are time-consuming, expensive and antagonistic courses of action.[100] A nine month study, commissioned by the Scottish Executive, has also revealed that neighbour disputes can lead to serious health problems. One third of the people surveyed as part of that study took medication to help them deal with a neighbour problem; more than one in ten indicated that they were smoking considerably more as a result of the problems; the majority had suffered a range of symptoms, from headaches, sleeplessness and depression; and one in twenty had suffered heart attacks, strokes or asthma.[101] Mediation provides an opportunity to resolve neighbour disputes quickly and in a less antagonist manner.

Apart from mediation, another recent initiative tackling neighbour disputes has been 'good neighbour agreements' which are signed by families when they move to new housing estates, and are designed to promote a sense of community and peace amongst neighbours. Although the document is not intended to be legally binding, the aim is to build peaceful relationships between neighbours.[102]

Suitability of mediation for neighbour disputes

Amongst the aims of mediation for the resolution of neighbour disputes are encouraging self help, promoting social cohesion and reducing stress amongst individuals.[103] The distinguishing features of mediation in this context include paired mediators, significant efforts at the in-take stage of persuading the parties to attempt mediation, and dealing with issues of power and other imbalances. Dignan's study of neighbour disputes revealed six broad categories of dispute:

- Disputes involving mildly anti-social behaviour.
- Disputes resulting from a life-style clash.
- Disputes involving minor harassment.
- Neighbour disputes are incidental to other problems, for example, drug abuse.

---

100 B Wilson 'Mediation scheme for nightmare neighbours: bid to solve residents' rows' *The Journal (Newcastle)*, 10 April 1998, p 23.
101 J O'Sullivan 'Neighbour disputes are damaging your health' *The Independent*, 6 September 1999, at p 6.
102 N Shaefer 'New tenants promise to be good neighbours' *The Northern Echo*, 18 March 1999, at p 6.
103 R E Mackay and A J Brown *Community Mediation in Scotland: a study of implementation*, The Scottish Office Central Research Unit, Edinburgh, 1999.

- Disputes involving serious harassment or criminal activity.
- Care in the community disputes.[104]

Using Dignan's categorisation of neighbour disputes, his study found that mediation offers the most effective way of dealing with the first type of dispute, although the scope for savings in cost through mediation is limited and mediation services may find it difficult to cope with demand if all such disputes were referred to mediation.[105] In relation to the second kind of dispute, Dignan's study suggested that these disputes are the most difficult to resolve, in particular, as legal remedies are least likely to be effective and, accordingly, mediation may offer the most appropriate approach, although it is important that mediation takes place in such cases before parties' positions crystallise.[106] In relation to the third kind of dispute, Dignan's study indicated that some community mediation services are reluctant to take on these cases and that, in relation to the fourth kind of dispute, mediation is likely to play only a subordinate role.[107] Although the fifth category of dispute was found by Dignan to be extremely time-consuming for authorities, these disputes are unlikely to be referred to mediation:[108]

'... because mediation is a non-judgmental process, it is not appropriate where society's disapproval needs to be registered ...'[109]

Additionally, the care in the community cases were found to be the most intractable of all the disputes and involved the highest social and economic costs, but most of the agencies and mediation services surveyed by Dignan expressed difficulty in knowing how to deal with these cases.[110]

Crime and victim-offender mediation

An overview of victim-offender mediation

Victim-offender mediation can take place before criminal proceedings, in the course of criminal proceedings ahead of sentencing, or following criminal proceedings.[111] Most usually, victim-offender mediation occurs at the post-conviction stage as a sentencing option.[112] The types of crime mediated are wide-ranging, including arson,

---

104 J Dignan et al *Neighbour Disputes: comparing the cost and effectiveness of a mediation and alternative approaches*, Centre for Criminological and Legal Research, University of Sheffield, 1996, at pp 88–90.
105 Ibid, at p 88.
106 Ibid.
107 Ibid, at p 89.
108 Ibid.
109 J Dignan and A Sorsby, *Resolving Neighbour Disputes through Mediation in Scotland*, Scottish Office, 1999. See also L Mulcahy 'The devil and the deep blue sea? A critique of the ability of community mediation to suppress and facilitate participation in civil life' (2000) 27(1) *J Law & Soc* 137.
110 Ibid.
111 For further information on the Criminal Justice System, see Mediation UK (ed) *Victim-Offender Mediation Conference*, Mediation UK, 1994.
112 For US comparisons, see S Clarke 'Community justice and victim-offender mediation' in Ohio State University College of Law (ed) *Court reform Implications of Dispute Resolution*, Ohio State University, 1995. In Australia, statutes provide that mediators are to provide the court with a report on the attitude of the offender to mediation, to the

assault, theft, breach of peace, deception and fraud, reckless driving, disorderly conduct, possession of drugs, sexual offences and even manslaughter.[113]

A number of benefits have been identified, for victims, offenders, the community and the criminal justice system arising from victim-offender mediation.[114] Mediation provides an opportunity for victims to confront their offender, to receive explanations or an apology, to persuade the offender not to re-offend and to receive reparation. Mediation offers offenders an opportunity to proffer an explanation or apology, to demonstrate remorse and to accept responsibility for their actions. For the community, mediation has the potential to reduce repeat crime. In terms of the criminal justice system, mediation can reduce court delays and the costs of incarceration.

Indicators of suitability for victim-offender mediation include admission of guilt by the offender and a desire on the part of the offender to meet with the victim. A victim who refuses to mediate or who is fearful of or intimidated by the prospect of meeting the offender or who seeks revenge is unlikely to be suitable for mediation.[115] Victim-offender mediation schemes are premised on the basis that a refusal by the offender to participate in mediation must not adversely affect the offender, for example, in sentencing.[116] Screening cases to ensure suitability for mediation is an important part of the victim-offender mediation process.

Power imbalance is inherent in most of these mediations by virtue of the fact that one party is a victim and the other is a wrongdoer. Power imbalance can lead to two different problems. The first is that the mediator may adopt the role of advocate for the offender or, secondly, the mediator may adopt a victim-champion role, by blaming the offender. Nevertheless, victim-offender mediation involves a different model of neutrality, as the parties, including the mediator, will acknowledge that a wrong has been committed and the process is aimed at reparation.

Direct or face-to-face mediation is infrequent in victim-offender mediation. For example, Umbreit's 1993 study of victim-offender mediation services in England revealed that only 16% of cases involved direct mediation.[117] In terms of process differences, the mediator will initially spend considerable time with each party, explaining the process and trying to understand the consequences of the events on each party. The bulk of the mediation is aimed at helping each party with their emotional needs. For example, victims who participate in victim-offender mediation

---

victim and to the effects on the victim of the commission of the offence and any agreement between the offender and the victim as to actions to be taken by the offender by way of reparation: see, for example, the Sentencing Act 1997, s 85 (TAS) and the Sentencing Act 1995, s 28 (WA).

113 Mediation UK *Restorative justice: Does it work? Digest of current research on victim-offender mediation and conferencing*, December 1997.

114 For a more detailed consideration, refer to G Robinson *Victim-offender mediation: limitations and potential*, Oxford Centre for Criminological Research, University of Oxford, 1996; and T Billinghurst 'Benefits of mediation' (1999) 55(9) *Magistrate* 264.

115 M Price 'Comparing victim-offender mediation program models' (1995) 6(1) *VOMA Quarterly*.

116 M S Umbreit and A W Roberts *Mediation of criminal conflict in England: An assessment of services in Coventry and Leeds*, Centre for Restorative Justice and Mediation, School of Social Work, University of Minnesota, 1996, p 42.

117 Ibid, at p 27.

need to hear: 'you were wronged . . . it's not your fault . . .' [118] Umbreit refers to this aspect of the victim-offender mediation process as 'humanistic mediation', as it is driven by:

> 'a journey of the heart through a process of dialogue . . . between people in conflict . . . the emphasis is upon . . . empowering each individual . . . to recognise each other's common humanity, despite the conflict.' [119]

Ultimately the aim of the mediation is to rehabilitate the offender, by at least having the offender take responsibility for his or her actions. Unlike court sentencing, which constitutes punishment, mediation can result in restitution in the form of money, replacement or repair of damaged property and a range of other solutions.

Victim-offender mediation statistics

Marshall and Merry, reporting on victim-offender mediation research between 1985 and 1987, found that in 79% of victim-offender mediations agreement was reached and, of those, 57% were resolved by the offender providing an apology only and in 26% the offender provided, in addition, compensation or other reparation.[120] In a later study by Dignan, 86% of cases mediated were found to have resulted in agreement, of which 38% involved in apology by the offender only, whereas 62% involved, in addition, some form of compensation or reparation.[121] Umbreit's study revealed that offenders who participated in mediation were more likely to consider it important to apologise to the victim, when compared to similar offenders who did not participate in mediation.[122]

The UK studies of victim-offender mediation have indicated that both victims and offenders have been satisfied with their experience of mediation. Marshall and Merry found that 82% of victims considered that mediation had been valuable, compared with 86% of offenders.[123] In a later study by the Northamptonshire Adult Reparation Bureau, 71% of corporate victims and 62% of individual victims were found to be satisfied with mediation.[124] Umbreit's study found that 75% of victims were satisfied with mediation, with direct mediations resulting in higher levels of satisfaction among victims than indirect mediation.[125] Studies show that satisfaction occurs when explanations can be proffered. Umbreit's study highlighted that 80% of victims considered it important to receive an explanation from the offender, compared with 36% of victims who did not participate in mediation.[126] Additionally, 90% of victims participating in mediation considered that it was important that they had an opportunity to explain to the offender the impact of the crime on them, compared with 64% of victims who did not participate in mediation.[127] 93% of

---

118 M Price 'A victim-offender mediation model of neutrality' (1995) 7(1) *VOMA Quarterly.*
119 M S Umbreit and A W Roberts *Mediation of criminal conflict in England: An assessment of services in Coventry and Leeds*, Centre for Restorative Justice and Mediation, School of Social Work, University of Minnesota, 1996.
120 T Marshall and S Merry *Crime and accountability*, London HMSO, 1990.
121 J Dignan *Repairing the damage*, University of Sheffield, 1992.
122 M S Umbreit and A W Roberts, op cit, at p 23.
123 T Marshall and S Merry *Crime and accountability*, op cit, at p 165.
124 Northamptonshire Adult Reparation Bureau *Annual Report 1992.*
125 M S Umbreit and A W Roberts *Mediation of criminal conflict in England*, op cit, at p 19.
126 Ibid.
127 Ibid, at p 20.

offenders who participated in mediation stated that they considered it important that they had an opportunity to provide an explanation, compared with 59% of offenders who did not participate in mediation.[128]

Evidence has also emerged, suggesting that offenders who mediate with their victims are less likely to return to crime. Marshall and Merry's study showed that, of the Coventry group of offenders who had participated in direct mediation, 55% showed a reduction in criminal behaviour. Of the Wolverhampton group, 74% of offenders who had participated in indirect mediation and 55% of offenders who had participated in direct mediation had reduced their criminal behaviour.[129] In a Leeds study, 75% of the offenders who had participated in mediation as part of the pilot had no further convictions 12 months later and 68% had no further convictions two years later.[130] A second Leeds study, in 1989, found that 78% of the offenders who had participated in that pilot had no further convictions after 12 months, and 58% had no further convictions after two years.[131] By way of comparison, Umbreit's 1994 US study of four victim-offender mediation programmes in four different US States indicated that 18% of offenders who had mediated had committed a new criminal offence within one year, compared to 27% of offenders who did not participate in mediation. Of those who did re-offend, 41% of those who had previously participated in mediation had committed less serious crimes than before.[132]

Victim-offender mediation schemes

There are over 500 victim-offender mediation programmes in Europe and the UK.[133] NACRO has called for government funding to set up further mediation services in the UK.[134] Mediation UK produces an updated list of victim-offender mediation services.[135]

---

128   M S Umbreit and A W Roberts *Mediation of criminal conflict in England: An assessment of services in Coventry and Leeds*, Centre for Restorative Justice and Mediation, School of Social Work, University of Minnesota, 1996, at p 21.
129   T Marshall and S Merry *Crime and accountability*, London HMSO, 1990.
130   Leeds Mediation and Reparation Service *Annual Report*, LMRS 1992.
131   See M S Umbreit and A W Roberts, op cit, at p 60.
132   M S Umbreit *Victim meets offender: The impact of restorative justice in mediation*, Criminal Justice Press, New York, 1994.
133   M Price 'Victim-offender mediation: The state of the art' (1996) 7(3) *VOMA Quarterly*.
134   NACRO *Reducing conflict: building communities*, NACRO, 1999
135   Mediation UK *Victim-offender Mediation Services*, pamphlet: the December 1999 version provides contact details for Aberdeen Community Mediation Project, Amends, Boughton Hall Youth Justice and Young Abusers Service, Bradford Victim-Offender Unit, Brighton and Hove Youth Offending Team, Calderdale Victim-Offender Unit, City Of York Council, Coventry Mediation Partnership, Doncaster Victim-Offender Mediation Project, Edinburgh Mediation Reparation Service, Family Group Conferencing – Youth Justice, Glasgow Monitoring Project, Gloucestershire Diversion Unit, Intensive Support and Supervision Programme, Ipswich Caution Plus Scheme, Kent 16 Plus, Leeds Victim-Offender Unit, London Borough Of Hackney Youth Offender Team, Luton Mediation, MARVEL Mediation and Reparation Service, Maidstone Mediation Service, Mediation and Reparation Course, Milton Keynes Youth Crime Reduction Project, NACRO, NCH Action For Children, Norwich and District Legal Services Mediation Service, Plymouth Mediation, RENEW, Restorative Cautioning, Retail Theft Initiative, SACRO, Sandwell Mediation Service, Service To Victims Of Armed Robbery, Sheffield Victim-Offender Mediation Service, Stokes Croft

The 1998 Crime and Disorder Act provides for reparation orders and victim-offender mediation.[136] A range of pilots relating to the youth justice provisions in the Act[137] commenced in September 1998. In particular, the Act places a duty on local authorities, probation committees, police authorities and health authorities to deliver youth justice services in partnership with Youth Offending Teams (YOTs). The pilots were intended to help determine the structure of YOTs and youth justice services and to identify good practice in establishing and operating YOTs. NACRO was commissioned to provide reparation and mediation work to support the YOTs piloted in Westminster, Kensington and Chelsea and in Hammersmith and Fulham. In Hampshire, Southampton, Portsmouth and Isle of Wight reparation and mediation work is provided by NACRO, Crime Concern and Society of Voluntary Associates. In Wolverhampton a probation service officer, specialising in victim-offender mediation work, supports the YOT. The Sheffield Victim Offender Mediation Project and Luton Mediation support the YOTs in Sheffield and Luton respectively.[138] The 1998 Act's provisions have been built on by the Youth Justice and Criminal Evidence Act 1999, which is piloting a sentencing mechanism for 10–17 year olds pleading guilty and convicted for the first time, with the view to attempting mediation as a means to achieving reparation.[139]

The VOICES Scheme is a pilot project, based on a New Zealand model and organised by Bristol Mediation. It liaises with the Youth Liaison Panel, assisting the police, social services and education authorities, with a view to identifying suitable cases for victim-offender mediation. The scheme is aimed at juvenile offenders aged 17 or under who have been cautioned by the police.[140] Bristol stores which have been targeted by shoplifters are being urged to participate in the scheme. 92% of the juveniles who have participated in the scheme were male and 62% were aged 14 or under.[141]

The number of recent examples of victim-offender mediation schemes abound. For example, the Culverdale Victim-Offender Unit, which is funded by the West Yorkshire Probation Service, held more than 100 victim-offender mediations within a year of operation.[142] The recent experience in England and Wales coincides with similar pilot victim-offender mediation programmes in Scotland and Ireland.[143]

Youth Justice Centre, The Youth Offending Team South and North, VOCS, VOICES, Wakefield Victim-Offender Unit, Walsall Victim-Offender Mediation Scheme, West Midlands Probation, Wiltshire County Council Juvenile Diversion Scheme and The Youth Offender Mediation Project.

136 For a consideration of the legal issues arising, see R E Mackay and A J Brown 'Legal issues in community mediation' (1999) 2 *Jur Rev* 87.

137 The Youth Justice and Criminal Evidence Act 1999 also provides, in s 8, that the terms of any programme relating to a youth offender may make provision for the attendance by the offender at mediation sessions with the victim. See P Davies 'Restorative Justice' (2000) 56(6) *Magistrate* 170.

138 See up-dates at http://www. homeoffice.gov.uk

139 Guidance on the scheme is provided by the Home Office and Youth Justice Board: *The Referral Order: Guidance to YOTs*, January 2000.

140 Z Borno 'Looking guilt in the face' *Bristol Evening Post*, 26 April 1999, at pp 8 and 9.

141 Bristol Evening Post Editorial 'Police chief backs funding a project to cut shoplifting' *Bristol Evening Post*, 16 April 1999, at p 8.

142 B Kemp 'The exorcism' *The Times*, 23 January 1999, feature.

143 For example, see P Flanagan 'Payback for victims of crime' *The Mirror*, 18 November 1999, at p 15.

Information from a Norwich pilot victim-offender mediation scheme highlights some of the common problems, in particular, low referrals from the probation service, due in part to high turnover of staff handling files. There is a desire on the part of pilot schemes to obtain the assistance of the police and magistrates to screen cases for suitability for mediation, recognising the knock-on benefit of schemes, by referring victims to appropriate support agencies.[144]

Some European illustrations

Norway passed a Mediation Act in March 1991, which paved the way for the establishment of Municipal Mediation Boards which handle victim-offender mediations. The first attempts to set up conflict resolution boards in Norway took place in 1983, as an initiative within Child Welfare of the Ministry of Social Affairs, in order to develop an alternative to traditional methods of dealing with misdemeanours amongst youth. If the accused held to the agreement determined by the Board, and did not become involved in any further breaches of the law for six months, all charges were dropped unconditionally.[145] The Council of Europe's Committee of Experts on Mediation in Penal Matters has drawn up draft recommendations on victim-offender mediation, focusing on restorative, as opposed to punitive, justice; participatory, as opposed to authoritarian, procedures; and informal, as opposed to formal, procedures for dispute resolution.[146]

Mediation and education

Peer mediation

Peer mediation involves trained students who guide fellow students through a voluntary and confidential process, with the aim of facilitating resolution of conflicts in schools. The process enables young people to mediate conflicts involving people of similar age and background. The aim of peer mediation is to recognise that conflict is a normal part of school life and that it is better to address conflict early. It also recognises that conflict resolution skills are an important part of a young person's education. It increases students' self esteem, by fostering respect for others and building relationships.[147] It can promote a more conducive climate within schools and communities, and equip young people with skills to tackle differences without resorting to violence or other forms of anti-social behaviour, which in turn, it is hoped, will lead to fewer instances where children and young people have to face charges in court and be subject to judicial process. Peer mediation can also provide a useful forum to discuss general school problems.[148]

---

144 The authors thank the volunteers who discussed their experience of the scheme and their knowledge of similar schemes.
145 T B Nergård 'Solving conflicts outside the court system' (1993) 33(1) *British Journal of Criminology* 81.
146 As to how French courts have adapted, see A Crawford 'Justice de proximité – the growth of "houses of justice" and victim-offender mediation in France' (2000) 9(1) *Social & Legal Studies* 29.
147 Mediation UK *Peer mediation: It's good to listen*, 1996.
148 S Grose and W Alford 'The dispute resolution project: peer mediation in schools' in D Bagshaw (ed) *Second international mediation conference: mediation and cultural diversity*, 18–20 January 1996, Group for Mediation Studies, University of South Australia outlines the results of an evaluation of peer mediation in Australia.

Commitment and support are critical to the success of peer mediation schemes. Administrative, teacher, student and community support is required, in particular that of the school head.[149] Training and facilities for mediation are also essential. It is also helpful if a school's principles or philosophy are consistent with mediation.[150]

Suitability for peer mediation

Peer mediations generally deal with the problem of bullying in schools.[151] A number of peer mediation programmes have been set up to deal specifically with this problem. For example, Pupil Power is a strategy aimed at comprehensive schools in six boroughs in England and utilises, in addition to peer mediation, peer counselling and peer mentoring.[152] Even an Anti-bullying Network Information Line has been set up, and operates seven days a week.[153] In an Aberdeen programme, bullies were used as mediators as it was considered a way for the offending youths to gain attention and respect.[154]

Peer mediation projects

A number of organisations in the UK provide training in peer mediation and assist schools to develop peer mediation schemes.[155]

LEAP Confronting Conflict, one of the oldest organisations in this field, has developed a peer mediation model, called 'playing with fire', which has the following six elements:

---

149 J Cameron and A Dupuis 'The introduction of school mediation to New Zealand' (1994) 24 *Journal of Research and Development in Education.*

150 See Mediation UK *Mediation Works! Conflict resolution and peer mediation, Manual For Secondary Schools and Colleges*, 1998; J Lampen *Conflict Busters: the young people's guide to mediation in schools*, Ulster Quaker Peace Education Project, 1997; Advisory Group On Citizenship *Education for citizenship and the teaching of democracy in schools*, Qualifications and Curriculum Authority, 1998; V Smith et al *Peer Mediation Scheme: how to use peer group mediation effectively in junior and middle schools*, Bristol Mediation 1995; Scottish Consultative Council On The Curriculum *Sharing Strategies: ideas for integrating a key aspect of the European dimension into the curriculum*, 1995; R Cohen *Students Resolving Conflict: peer mediation in schools*, Goodyear Books, USA, 1995; and Manchester Development Educational Project *The School Issue: a practical guide to successful whole school change*, Manchester Metropolitan University, 1993.

151 See A Skinner *Bullying: an annotated bibliography of literature and resources*, Youth Work Press, 1996; D Tattum and D Lane (eds) *Bullying in schools*, Trentham Books, 1989; Kingston Friends Workshop Group *Step by step: Towards resolving bullying in schools*, 1996, video; Headstart *Tackling bullying*, London 1996.

152 L Richards 'Pupil pioneers could banish bullies' *Evening Chronicle*, 11 March 1998, at p 22.

153 'Buddies are best to beat school bullies' *Evening Standard*, 11 November 1999.

154 'Talking it through' *Aberdeen Press and Journal*, 29 October 1999.

155 For example, AVP, Antidote, Birmingham Development Education Centre, Catalyst Consultancy, Conflict Resolution UK, Crime Concern, Education in Human Rights Network, Fellowship of Reconciliation (FOR), Heartstone, Human Scale Education, Interfaith Network, Kingston Friends Workshop Group, LEAP Confronting Conflict, Lucky Duck Publishing and Training, Mediation UK, NAPCE (National Association of Pastoral Care in Education), National Coalition Building Institute, Parent Network, Peace Pledge Union, Quaker Peace and Service, RELATE, Self Esteem Network, SEAL, The Citizenship Foundation, UK Centre of Non-Violent Communication. An updated list of organisations, with contact details, is available from Mediation UK.

- The fuel, represented by different opinions.
- The spark, resulting from the outstanding issues.
- Smouldering, represents the search for shared interests.
- Fanning the flames, occurs in mediation when there is a mutual search for a solution.
- Stoking the fire, occurs when options for resolution are considered.
- The blaze, when aims are achieved.[156]

Other early peer mediation services include Kingston Friends Workshop Group, Newham Conflict and Change and the Quaker Peace and Service. A more recent initiative has taken place in schools in Tower Hamlets, organised by LEAP Confronting Conflict over a three-year period, focusing first on low-level conflict, such as teasing, then tackling mid-level conflict, such as bullying, and ultimately attempting to resolve high-level conflict, such as gang fighting.[157] The CRISP project, which commenced in four schools, has more recently doubled in size.[158] The project has sought to use mediation to resolve a wide range of disputes, from fighting through to stealing.[159]

In Northern Ireland the EMU (Education for Mutual Understanding) Promoting School Projects has developed peer mediation programmes in primary schools throughout Northern Ireland and has sought to build on the work of the Ulster Quaker Peace Education Project. The aim of the EMU project is to encourage children to use and trust non-violent methods of resolving conflict. Responses have varied, and some children have expressed preference for a judgment from the principal, rather than protracted discussions in mediation.[160]

A Europe-wide initiative, ENCORE, aims to develop mediation skills in schools throughout Europe by encouraging education authorities and governments to implement the recommendations contained in the Council of Europe Report on Violence and Conflict Resolution in Schools.[161]

Exclusions

Exclusions and potential exclusions provide an area ripe for mediation. Some local authorities have trained education staff to offer mediation for these issues. A pilot project in two Manchester secondary schools, for example, aims to tackle issues arising from exclusions between youths, schools and the youths' families.[162]

---

156 N Fine and F Macbeth *Playing with fire: Training for the creative use of conflict*, Youth Work Press, 1992.
157 For more information, see Mediation UK *Peer mediation: It's good to listen*, 1996, at p 25.
158 Schools are Babbington Community College, Brockington Community College, Castlerock High School, City of Leicester, Crownhills Community College, Fullhurst Community College, Lutterworth High and Shepshed High.
159 'Mediation service schemes aim to resolve school conflict' *Leicester Mercury*, 11 November 1999, at p 5.
160 For more information on the project, see Mediation UK *Peer mediation: It's good to listen*, 1996, at pp 10–12.
161 J Walker *Violence and conflict resolution in schools*, Council for Cultural Co-operation, Council of Europe, Strasbourg, 1989. Also refer to Gulbenkian Foundation, *Children and violence: A report of the commission on children and violence*, 1995.
162 G Symonds 'Mediation: Contributing to socially inclusive schools' *Mediation*, Autumn 1999, Mediation UK publication, at p 5.

Special educational needs

Following research, which aimed to determine best practice in the resolution of disputes over special educational needs,[163] local education authorities in England have received guidance from the Department of Education on the use of conciliation for the resolution of special educational needs, with the view to authorities providing conciliation before parents appeal to the Special Educational Needs Tribunal.[164] The Department of Education is funding a pilot conciliation scheme for special educational needs disputes.[165] In Scotland ENQUIRE was set up in 1999, funded by the Scottish Executive, to improve the provision of mediation for special educational needs cases.

Some overseas comparisons

In Australia, 'community justice programmes' refer to statutory-based community mediation services established within the administrative branch of government, which provide mediation at no charge to users. In setting up the centres, the government was motivated by the need to find an alternative and effective way of dealing with backyard disputes 'which cause great aggravation and often lead to serious crimes'.[166] It anticipated benefits through the reduction of resources in the justice system, the freeing of police to concentrate on fighting serious crimes, greater public respect for the justice system, less temptation for persons to take the law into their own hands and lower costs for processing cases. The community justice schemes regulate several features of the mediation process, such as confidentiality, non-admissibility of evidence, and the protection and immunities of mediators.[167] They have some of the most rigorous levels of quality and accountability, in the form of initial requirements for mediators, continuing training, skills audits, and debriefing protocols.

Competition disputes

There are a number of incentives operating to encourage the use of mediation to resolve competition issues. First, courts are considered inappropriate arbiters of complex economic concepts. It is also considered undesirable for courts to set the prices or terms of supply of goods, issues which frequently occur in competition disputes. In addition, it is inappropriate for courts to oversee continuing obligations, another issue which arises in competition disputes. Mediation, in the context of competition issues, allows the relevant market to reach workable solutions to their disputes.

Alternative dispute resolution has been encouraged in this context by the increasing trend in Europe for risk management and dispute prevention as the level of fines

---

163 J Hall *Resolving disputes between parents, schools and LEAs: some examples of best practice*, Department of Education and Employment, London, October 1999.

164 The Department of Education and Employment *The Programme of Action for Meeting Special Educational Needs*, 1998.

165 Conciliation is being provided by the Shaftesbury Society and it is proposed that an evaluation of the pilot will be produced.

166 New South Wales Legislative Council *Parliamentary Debates*, 6 March 1980, 5250.

167 See Chapters 11 and 12 for detailed discussion on these topics.

imposed by the European Commission increased.[168] The White Paper on Competitiveness[169] supports ADR as a means of achieving competitiveness. The Paper encourages business to collaborate to achieve competitive advantage by using co-operative approaches. It is also feared that, with changes to the Competition Act, effective from 1 March 2000, there will be surge of competition litigation. A survey conducted by Clifford Chance in 2000 indicated that 62% of respondents did not consider that they, or the courts, were equipped to deal with the likely increase in litigation, suggesting that there are incentives for other forms of dispute resolution.[170]

The use of mediation in this context has also been highly publicised by the Microsoft anti-trust litigation in the United States, where a federal judge agreed to act as mediator between Microsoft and the US government in an attempt to reach resolution of the dispute. Apart from its use in anti-trust litigation in the United States, mediation was first used by the Federal Court in Australia in relation to competition disputes. In the case of matters involving the protection of consumers, the Court recognised the dilemmas. On the one hand, in cases where there is a disparity of bargaining power and resources between the parties, the stronger party may have little incentive to mediate, hopeful that the weaker party will not pursue the matter in the face of increasing legal costs, but on the other hand, the stronger party may prefer to mediate where there is a risk of a large award of damages. Ultimately, however, agreements reached in mediation are susceptible to review by competition authorities.[171]

Computer/IT disputes

Range of disputes

Computer-related disputes frequently occur as a result of incomplete or too general technical specifications, vague or incomplete design briefs or inadequate hardware specifications. The range of disputes in the IT sector is wide, including disputes over systems software, development, modification, performance, licensing and consultancy.

Suitability for mediation

Maintenance of business relationships is particularly important in the IT sector as the choice of vendors and distributors is limited. Customer/supplier relationships depend largely on commitment and trust. The risk of bad publicity provides an additional incentive to use mediation for the resolution of IT disputes. Judges may also lack the technical expertise desirable for the speedy resolution of IT disputes. Some consider that knowledge of the relevant technology and industry practices and an understanding of the importance and operation of particular IT contract provisions are important attributes for mediators of IT disputes.[172] Others consider

---

168 See B Hunt 'Legal Risk Management' (1999) vol 18, No 6 *Litigation* 15.
169 DTI *White Paper on Competitiveness*, 1999.
170 S Zaki 'Competition reforms could swamp courts' *Legal Week*, 15 June 2000.
171 For example, see case comment: 'ECJ reiterates earlier judgment' (2000) 58 *EU Focus* 7, for consideration of Article 82 and C-259/98 *Carra* (8 June 2000, unreported) ECJ.
172 For example, M Turner 'Mediation of computer contract disputes' (1997) 7(6) *Computers & Law*.

that, essentially, IT disputes are contract disputes, requiring good mediator, rather than specialist IT, skills.[173] This debate aside, generally, the high cost of computer-related litigation encourages the use of mediation in this field. Mediation can help to identify the real or underlying issues, which can be disguised by technical detail. Mediation can also result in a solution, which could not be obtained in a court, such as system re-design,[174] and offers parties the ability to apportion responsibility for the problem and the solution, the approach which characterises the commencement of any IT project.

Use of mediation

In Chapter 7 the mediation proposals of the Technology and Construction Court were outlined. Where a party to a computer contract dispute is a government department, a Government Best Practice Statement encourages the use of ADR.[175] The mediation scheme set up by the Computing Services and Software Association (CSSA), in conjunction with the Centre for Dispute Resolution, is available where a party to a computer-related dispute is a member of the CSSA. The British Computer Society provides a mediator nomination service free of charge.[176] The Society has a range of mediators on its panel, with experience of disputes over systems development, modification, supply, licensing, project management and consultancy. Similarly, the Academy of Experts has a range of IT experts on their panel of mediators.[177] The Society for Computers and the Law has set up a working party, which is developing alternative dispute resolution procedures. The Chartered Institute of Arbitrators has developed conciliation and arbitration rules for the resolution of computer software disputes.[178]

There have been a range of high profile IT disputes, which have been successfully resolved using ADR, and have encouraged use of mediation in the UK. In an example of a high profile US case, *IBM v Fujitsu*, the issue was whether Fujitsu used IBM programming material in the development of its systems software. Although arbitration resolved the dispute, the arbitrators used a range of processes in the course of the arbitration, including mediation techniques, to help the parties reach agreement on a range of issues, such as the method for quantifying damages.[179] The collapse of Atlantic Computers and the subsequent administration of British and Commonwealth Holdings culminated in a high profile UK mediation, although the main issues in that case were insolvency, rather than IT, related.[180]

The Centre for Dispute Resolution's 1999 statistics showed that IT-related disputes accounted for 6% of its mediations.[181] The Centre's 2000 statistics show a slightly

---

173 D Shapiro 'Expert mediators – not experts as mediators' *Resolutions*, Issue no 16, at p 4.
174 M Turner 'Computer contract disputes' (1997) 8(3) *Computers & Law*.
175 See the later section on Government public sector disputes and CUP No 50.
176 Contact is Mr A Lewis, Registrar, The British Computer Society, 1 Sanford St, Swindon, Wilts SN1 1HH; phone: 01793 417417; fax 01793 480270; and email: alewis@bcs.org.uk.
177 See the section on Mediation Organisations in Chapter 7.
178 For example, Chartered Institute of Arbitrators *The Rules of the Computer Software for Solicitors Arbitration Scheme*, 2000 edition.
179 See K Mackie 'ADR in Europe – lessons from a classic US case' (1992) 5 *EIPR* 183.
180 The case is discussed in more detail in the section below on Insolvency.
181 Centre for Dispute Resolution *Press Release*, 26 April 1999.

increased figure of 7%.[182] The Centre's case summaries show a wide range of IT-related contract disputes, settled following between one and four days of mediation; involving between several hundred thousand and several million pounds; and resulting in cost savings of between a couple of hundred thousand and a couple of million pounds, including management time.[183] In one reported mediation relating to an IT dispute, the benefit of a cooling off period between mediation sessions was highlighted, particularly in cases involving extensive documentation.[184]

Lessons learned from Y2K

Even before 2000, Y2K litigation had commenced and some cases had been settled using mediation.[185] In the few months prior to 2000, Lloyds received a large number of claims in respect of Y2K compliance issues.[186] A £40m Y2K compliance dispute in relation to the development of a computerised management system was settled in late 1999 after 2½ days of mediation and saving, it is claimed, £0.5m in costs and six months of management time.[187]

As the Y2K problem is the first in a potential series of computer time-related problems, it is relevant to consider the lessons learned from Y2K in the context of dispute prevention and resolution methods. Action 2000 was launched in 1997, as an initiative by the Government to reduce the impact on the economy of the Y2K problem. As part of that initiative, Pledge 2000 was developed, a document containing a number of commitments, which customers and suppliers were asked to support. The basic commitment was to work co-operatively to resolve Y2K problems, rather than to pursue legal action. The City Disputes Panel[188] also set up a panel of judges, solicitors and IT consultants, who could resolve disputes involving financial institutions arising from Y2K problems. The Millennium Accord was launched by the Centre for Dispute Resolution at the end of 1998, with the view to reducing the cost of Y2K disputes, and was sponsored by Cable & Wireless, BAT and Nortel. The Accord principles included the use of mediation to facilitate Y2K disputes.[189] The Accord extended its reach beyond the UK to the US, Canada, Hong Kong, Singapore and Australia. Four hundred organisations in the private and public sectors signed the Accord. A key issue for many signatories was the opportunity mediation would afford to protect commercial relationships in the case of Y2K disputes. The Accord also included a set of dispute resolution procedures, a contract clause incorporating that procedure and a mediation agreement.[190] As part of the

---

182 Centre for Dispute Resolution 2000 Statistics, *Resolutions* No 26. The authors' 2000 survey of UK law firms indicated that, of the cases referred to mediation by the respondents, 3.2% related to IT disputes.

183 Centre for Dispute Resolution *Mediation case summary sheets*.

184 D Crosse 'If at first you don't succeed' (1999) 24 *Resolutions*.

185 In the US several cases have been decided and over 40 cases are pending: for an overview, refer to S McGhie 'Battling over the bug: Y2K and US court cases' *Comp & Law*, December 1999/January 2000, at p 22.

186 See S Passow 'Y2K claims bugging you?' *The Times*, 30 November 1999.

187 Centre for Dispute Resolution *Press Release*, 24 February 1999.

188 See the section on Mediation Organisations in Chapter 7.

189 Centre for Dispute Resolution *Press Release*, 24 February 1999.

190 Centre for Dispute Resolution *The Millennium Accord*, 1999.

Accord, a series of industry-specific focus groups had been set up to encourage information sharing and dispute prevention in the IT industry.[191]

The UK Y2K developments were similar to developments in other countries. For example, the French Government encouraged mediation for the resolution of Y2K disputes, in particular, to assist small and medium sized companies. In the US the House of Representatives in the Senate sought to legislate against Y2K problems by delaying litigation for a period of 90 days, to provide a window of opportunity for other forms of dispute resolution.

Although Y2K disputes have not created the problems which were originally feared, nevertheless the approaches adopted to deal with those disputes provide lessons for the resolution of IT-related disputes generally, in particular, the emphasis on collaboration and information sharing, with a view to maintaining commercial relationships and resolving technical problems.

Construction and building disputes

Nature of disputation in the construction industry

The Centre for Dispute Resolution 1999 statistics showed that the construction industry was the third largest group of mediation users,[192] which is not surprising given that construction is one of the largest industries in the UK and has a long history of disputation. Historically, the reason for the disputation was blamed on the problem that various sections of the industry act independently and, accordingly, the industry has become extremely adversarial.[193] The same issues are evident within projects, with distinct management teams, each often making independent decisions. Disputes in the industry are exacerbated by pressures, like cash flow problems.

The Latham Report[194] identified the cost of construction disputes as a major factor retarding the industry's competitiveness in the international construction market. The high volume of high value claims and the fact and document intensive nature of construction litigation explains the high cost of disputation in the industry. The adversarial manner in which disputants have pursued claims is an additional factor. There is also a perception that arbitration no longer provides a cheap and efficient means of resolving construction disputes.[195]

---

191 Centre for Dispute Resolution 'Millennium Accord industry focus groups' (1999) 22 *Resolutions.*

192 Centre for Dispute Resolution, *Resolutions*, No 22 at p 7, which shows that 13% of their mediations in 1999 were construction industry disputes. The figure has increased to 17% in 2000: CEDR '2000 statistics' *Resolutions*, No 26. The authors' 2000 survey of UK law firms indicated that 11% of the disputes referred to mediation by the respondents related to construction matters.

193 See Banwell Report, HMSO, May 1967; and Latham Report, HMSO, July 1994.

194 Latham report, op cit.

195 See P Brooker 'Survey of construction lawyers' attitudes and practice and the use of ADR in contractors' disputes' (1999) 17(6) *Construction management and economics.*

Adjudication

In light of the nature of disputation in the construction industry in the UK, Latham concluded in his report[196] that adjudication should be the normal method of construction dispute resolution in the UK. In response, a statutory right to adjudication was introduced in Part II of the Housing Grants, Construction and Regeneration Act 1996.[197] Neither the Latham Report nor the Act defines adjudication, although it is clear from the Act that adjudication is not arbitration.[198] Its nature is more like expert determination. The adjudication scheme under the Act provides that an adjudicator has 28 days to reach a decision, although the adjudicator can take a 14 day extension or can have a longer period if agreed by both parties. An adjudicator's award is binding, enforceable by summary judgment, and remains payable despite an intention to challenge it.[199] Adjudicators are not protected from third party claims.[200] A number of organisations offer services as adjudicator-nominating bodies.[201] The Government commenced a review in 2000 of the operation of the Housing Grants, Construction and Regeneration Act 1996 in order to determine if any changes are necessary.[202]

Mediation

Statutory adjudication for the resolution of construction disputes has not excluded the use of mediation in the industry. Disputes arising from contracts not caught by the Housing Grants, Construction and Regeneration Act could be mediated. In addition, the right to adjudicate under the Act is not an obligation, so that disputing parties can bypass adjudication and mediate, litigate or arbitrate if they choose.[203] There have also been instances where parties in the course of adjudication under the Act suspended the adjudication in order to attempt mediation. There is also likely to

---

196 Latham Report, HMSO, July 1994.
197 See Housing Grants, Construction and Regeneration Act 1996, s 108.
198 This would appear consistent with previous case law: for example, in 1990 the Court of Appeal rejected the argument that 'adjudication' under the JCT form of sub-contract qualified as arbitration, in A *Cameron Ltd v John Mowlem & Company plc* (1990) 52 BLR 24.
199 For example, *Macob Civil Engineering Ltd v Morrison Construction Ltd* [1999] BLR 93.
200 See Housing Grants, Construction and Regeneration Act 1996, s 108.
201 In England and Wales: Academy of Construction Adjudicators, Centre for Dispute Resolution, Chartered Institute of Arbitrators, Chartered Institute of Building, Confederation of Construction Specialists, Construction Industry Council, Construction Confederation, Institution of Chemical Engineers, Institution of Electrical Engineers, Institution of Civil Engineers, Official Referees Bar Association, Official Referees Solicitors Association, Royal Institute of British Architects, Royal Institution of Chartered Surveyors, and Institution of Mechanical Engineers. A separate list of organisations that offer the service in Scotland is available from the Scottish Office website (www.scotland.gov.uk) or from the Scottish Office, Construction and Building Control Group, Division A, Area 2J, Victoria Quay, Edinburgh EH6 6QQ (phone: 0131 2447468; and fax 0131 2447454).
202 See D Cornes 'All change for adjudication' *Construction Law*, July 2000, p 6. For the Scottish experience, refer to L Patterson 'A Scottish perspective on adjudication' *Construction Law*, March 2000, p 6.
203 2 Harcourt Buildings has set up a contracted mediation scheme for construction disputes. Parties enter into a contract agreeing that all disputes will be resolved through mediation.

be increased use of mediation following the introduction by the Technology and Construction Court of the new pre-action protocol covering construction and engineering disputes, as it requires parties to meet to explore alternative means of dispute resolution before litigation. The TCC Solicitors' Association also has its own ADR protocol for its members.

In addition, perceived drawbacks of adjudication initially encouraged the use of mediation in the industry.[204] In particular, it is recognised that, ideally, disputes should be resolved by negotiated settlement. Cultural differences frequently occur in disputes arising out of major projects, for example, if the parties are from the private and public sectors; have different commercial expertise; or are from different industries, like banks and the construction industry. Mediation enables such cultural differences to be taken into consideration. That adjudicators can award costs against a losing party in adjudication may also provide incentive to negotiate or mediate.[205] In complicated matters, it is considered difficult for an adjudicator to make a reasoned decision within the time-frame available. The 'ambush' problem, where the applicant for adjudication may spend weeks or months preparing his case, but a response is due within 28 days, has also been cited as providing an incentive to negotiate or mediate. The contractual chain, often involved in construction projects, could also create a mismatch of contractual dispute resolution methods. For example, one contract in the chain might not be covered by the Housing Grants, Construction and Regeneration Act, whereas a dispute at the other end of the chain might be resolved by adjudication, and may take many months before it is finally resolved by the courts or arbitration.

The Official Referees Court, renamed the Technology and Construction Court, encourages mediation to be used in cases where adjudication either does not apply to the contract in question or the parties agree not to use it.[206] A number of organisations in the construction field also offer mediation services. For instance, the Guild of Master Craftsmen, has offered its members a mediation and arbitration service. The British Surface Coatings Organisation launched a mediation service for its members. The service includes site inspection, laboratory analysis, guidance on problem rectification and mediation. The Royal Institution of Chartered Surveyors provides a mediation service for construction-related disputes. The HM Treasury Unit on Procurement developed its practice guidelines on the resolution of contract disputes involving the Treasury, including recommendations on the use of negotiation and other forms of ADR. The Best Practice Guidelines[207] provide that dispute management is essential to achieve early and effective dispute resolution and that good dispute management requires that consideration be given to the effectiveness and speed of the dispute resolution process selected; and to the

---

But note *R G Carter v Edmund Nuttall Ltd* (21 June 2000, unreported) (HHJ Thornton QC) where the mediation clause in the contract between the parties was found to undermine the right to refer a dispute to adjudication 'at any time' (s 108). See the section on Mediation Clauses in Chapter 12. On the use of mediation, generally, see C Ennis 'Mediation, construction and Woolf' (2000) 5(1) *C & EL* 8; and E Lightburn 'Mediation in international construction disputes' (2000) 17(1) *ICL Rev* 207.

204 Although, initially, take-up of adjudication was slow, it has increased significantly. Compare the dissatisfaction with adjudicatory procedures which led to mandatory mediation provisions in Canadian Construction Documents Committee Contracts.

205 Judge Marshall Evans QC in *John Cothliff v Allenbuild* (2000, unreported).

206 See the section on Courts in Chapter 7.

207 HM Treasury Central Unit on Procurement *Disputes Resolution*, CUP No 50.

need to preserve the working relationship between the parties.[208]

The Department of the Environment, Transport and the Regions (DETR), in its Consultation Paper, 'Combating Cowboy Builders',[209] suggested that mediation provides a less costly dispute resolution mechanism and that it should be a necessary component of the complaints handling mechanisms of trade associations. However, the Consultation Paper also recognised that cowboy operators may have little incentive to reach a resolution by way of mediation, so that trade associations should provide a fallback, for instance, independent arbitration.

A Working Group was established and recommended a Quality Mark Scheme, requiring builders to have effective complaints handling schemes and involving the establishment of an independent dispute resolution scheme for Quality Mark builders. The Quality Mark Initiative commenced in 2000 by way of pilots.[210] A wide range of construction disputes have been mediated in the UK, ranging from disputes over negligent design and construction to contractual breaches and delay; involving claims between tens of thousands of pounds and many millions of pounds; and settlement after between one and three days of mediation. The pairing of mediators, with legal and engineering or construction industry knowledge, has been used widely in UK mediations of construction disputes. Apart from the benefits of a team approach, utilising the different kinds of expertise beneficial for the resolution of construction disputes, pairing can also help to deal with the usually large volume of documentation and number of parties usually involved.

Dispute review boards

Like adjudication, dispute review boards are aimed at resolving problems during a construction project. The board is established at the time the contract is entered into and comprises three members who are experts in the type of construction involved in the project. One member is selected by each party and those two members select a chairman. The cost of the board is shared equally by the parties. The board makes periodic site visits and, if a dispute arises, it aims to facilitate a resolution, but will make non-binding recommendations otherwise. The cost of the board makes its use appropriate for particularly large projects, although boards have also been used successfully for smaller projects.[211] The Hong Kong Airport project involved a disputes review group of six members plus a convener. A panel of either one or three members was selected when a dispute arose, depending upon its nature and complexity. The Channel Tunnel project involved a dispute review board of five members. Disputes were heard by all five members, but decisions made by a three member panel, comprising the chairman and two others members, selected depending upon their particular expertise.

---

208 HM Treasury Central Unit on Procurement *Disputes Resolution*, CUP No 50, p 5.
209 Available at http://www.construction.detr.gov.uk
210 Cowboy Builders Working Group *Final Report*, DETR, July 1999. See also DETR Quality Mark information website: http//www.construction.detr.gov.uk/qmscheme
211 See G L Jaynes 'Dispute Review Boards' (1993) *International Construction Law Review* 159; and A Pike 'Dispute Review Boards' (1993) *International Construction Law Review* 467; S Woodward 'Panels prevent damaging disputes' (1999) 10(10) *Construction Law* 28; and R A Shadbolt 'Resolution of construction disputes by dispute review boards' (1999) 16(1) *ICL Rev* 101.

Dispute review boards can have the incidental benefit of dispute prevention, as parties are reluctant to submit frivolous or unmeritorious claims to them. In addition, the prospect of a board recommendation provides an incentive for parties to reach a negotiated settlement themselves. Ultimately, the role of the board has similarities to mediation, by facilitating communication between the parties, identifying issues and helping the parties to consider solutions. The main criticisms of a dispute review board, cost and the absence of a binding determination, suggests that mediation may achieve the same results, whilst avoiding the problems associated with it.

Partnering

Partnering is not so much a dispute resolution process, as a dispute prevention process. The core element of partnering is a partnering workshop, which allows the key decision-makers for each party involved in a project to meet to get to understand each other's priorities, needs and interests in the project. Essentially, it aims to build a successful working relationship, by opening communication and developing trust. In the context of dispute resolution, the workshop seeks to identify efficient dispute resolution methods, in particular, ADR. Parties acknowledge that disputes will occur in the course of a project and consider the appropriate methods by which those disputes could be resolved, other than by litigation or arbitration. Use of negotiation and mediation is promoted as these processes are consistent with the philosophy, which underpins partnering, that 'prevention is better than cure'. It is hoped that the partnering process will foster co-operation between the parties at an early stage and, in that way, avoid adversarial confrontation during the life of the project.

The initial partnering workshop is aided by a facilitator, who uses mediation skills, in order to facilitate communication between the parties and elicit their respective goals and responsibilities during the project. The ultimate aim of the workshop is to reach agreement on a partnering charter, which is in addition to the agreement between the parties in respect of the project itself. Following the workshop, the parties should follow up, by revisiting the charter, review the partnering process and evaluate each other's performance.

It has been reported that BAA intends to use a partnering process in the construction of Heathrow Terminal Five, in order to minimise the adversarial relationships which are common in the industry.[212] Bovis and Marks & Spencer, for example, have also used partnering arrangements.

Consumer disputes

Overview of developments

Office of Fair Trading surveys have found that almost half of the UK adult population have complaints about goods or services supplied in any 12 month period; that the majority take their complaints up with suppliers; that over two-thirds of those people supplied with goods achieve satisfaction by doing so, although only about one-third of the people supplied with services achieve satisfaction; but that

---

212 J D Allen 'Teamwork at Terminal 5' (1997) *Construction News* 4.

only a small proportion of consumers resort to redress mechanisms. In particular, the surveys have indicated a very low awareness by the public of mediation or conciliation.[213] The OFT suggested as early as 1991 that a negotiated solution to consumer disputes, if it can be reached cheaply and quickly, is preferred to litigation and that, accordingly, research on mediation and what constitutes good practice in this field is desirable. The OFT also suggested experimenting with reference out by courts of consumer cases to ADR.[214]

A study by the National Consumer Council in 1996 suggested, in relation to mediation of consumer disputes, that legal aid should be available and that consumers should have access to legal advice before agreeing to a settlement in mediation.[215] In addition, the Council proposed that multi-door dispute resolution programmes might be considered, which would provide a centre at which people could seek guidance, and a decision could be made, on the most appropriate dispute resolution mechanism for the particular dispute. It was suggested that the centre could operate out of existing facilities, such as Citizens Advice Bureaux or community centres.[216] In turn, it was suggested that a multi-door facility would promote the development of local mediation services.[217]

The Government's White Paper on Modern Markets[218] encouraged the promotion of good business practices through voluntary Codes of Practice, which would offer consumers effective complaints handling systems run by businesses and low cost dispute resolution mechanisms, like ADR. Following a consultation exercise by the OFT, the results were published in 1998, and indicated that in about 40% of unsatisfactory transactions, consumers did not complain, and in those cases where a complaint was made, satisfaction was not achieved in more than a quarter of cases.[219] The Report attributed the failure by consumers to complain on the low visibility of and lengthy or complicated complaints handling mechanisms.[220] The Report also suggested that ADR systems offered by businesses may not be perceived as independent or neutral.[221] The OFT recommended that a new standards-based regime should replace Codes of Practice and that the standards should include reference to an independent dispute resolution scheme, which would offer, as a first step, mediation or conciliation.[222]

US authors have provided a range of warnings about the use of mediation in the context of consumer dispute resolution. The consumer may be unsophisticated and unrepresented, which may raise issues of power imbalances and make the case difficult to mediate. Businesses, which use mediation regularly and have a better understanding of how to achieve their aims, may be advantaged by the process.[223]

---

213 See, for example, Office of Fair Trading *Consumer Redress Mechanisms*, November 1991.
214 Ibid, at pp 68–69.
215 National Consumer Council *Settling consumer disputes*, 1996, at p 34.
216 Ibid, at p 38.
217 Ibid, at p 39.
218 Department of Trade and Industry *Modern Markets: confident consumers*, White Paper, DTI, London, 1999. Also available at http://www.oft.gov.uk
219 Office of Fair Trading *Raising standards of consumer care*, 1998, at pp 9–11.
220 Ibid, at p 15.
221 Ibid, at p 16.
222 Ibid, at pp 26–32.
223 M Galanter 'Why the "haves" come out ahead: Speculation on the limits of legal change'

Mediation could be used by business to concede a particular claim, in an attempt to divert attention to a wider or endemic problem, which may be having a far wider impact on consumers.[224]

Range of dispute resolution methods

The small claims jurisdiction deals with a significant volume of consumer disputes by arbitration. A number of trade dispute resolution schemes provide for mediation or conciliation and arbitration for consumer disputes. Most schemes are administered by the Chartered Institute of Arbitrators.[225] For example, the Consumer Credit Trade Association offers a free mediation service; the National Consumer Credit Federation provides a conciliation service and arbitration if conciliation fails; Qualitas offers a conciliation service for all disputes related to the purchase of furniture and floor covering, overseen by the Qualitas Advisory Panel, which includes organisations such as Trading Standards and Citizens Advice Bureaux; the Mail Order Traders' Association's Secretary provides conciliation if complaints are not satisfactorily resolved after reference to member companies; and the Scottish Motor Trade Association refers complaints to an independent conciliation service, although either party is free to request that the complaint is referred to arbitration. In the public utility sector also, conciliation is used to resolve customer complaints, for instance, by the Office of Telecommunications.[226] The Chartered Institute of Arbitrators has also set up its own consumer dispute resolution scheme. The scheme provides for conciliation followed by arbitration if conciliation is unsuccessful. The conciliation process normally takes no longer than six weeks. Conciliation is intended to provide the parties with recommendations for resolution.[227]

A number of Ombudsmen schemes also provide redress for consumer complaints,[228] and utilise mediation and conciliation in an attempt to resolve disputes informally. Complaints organisations in the financial services sector attempt to resolve complaints, initially, by conciliation and, if this is unsuccessful, by adjudication. For example, the Banking Ombudsman uses conciliation in an attempt to broker a fair settlement, acceptable to both parties, and it has had increasing success in resolving complaints in

---

(1974) 9 *Law & Society Review* 95; S Goldberg et al *Dispute Resolution: Negotiation, Mediation and other Processes* (2nd edn), Little Brown & Co, USA, 1992, at p 389; and W Harris 'Consumer disputes and ADR' (1993) 4 *ADRJ* 238 at 239.

224 R Abel 'The Contradictions of Informal Justice' in R Abel (ed) *The Politics of Informal Justice, vol 1*, Academic Press, New York 1982, at p 306.

225 A list of schemes is available at http://www.arbitrators.org/Services/consumerlistdet.htm, and these cover commercial, leisure/travel, insurance, financial services, glass and plastics, household, telecommunications and water industries.

226 See the section on Telecommunications Disputes in this chapter. Also see the changes being proposed by the Gas and Electricity Consumers' Council. The Council issued a consultation document in February 2000.

227 Chartered Institute of Arbitrators *The consumer dispute resolution scheme*; *The rules of the consumer dispute resolution scheme*; *Suggested clause for inclusion in consumer contracts*; *Arbitration and the consumer*; *General information handbook*; *Guide to arbitration*.

228 There are government proposals to combine schemes to create a 'Super Bureau' which will provide a single point of contact for consumers.

this way.[229] Similarly, the Building Societies Ombudsman first seeks to facilitate an agreed settlement between the parties.[230] The complaints handling system, which will be set up by the new Financial Services Authority, will bring together the existing financial services Ombudsman schemes and provide for mediation.[231] The Pensions, Investment and Housing Ombudsmen also use mediation to achieve settlements.[232] The Insurance Ombudsman acts as a conciliator in an attempt to facilitate settlement or withdrawal of a complaint[233] and has set up an Advice Centre, which aims to facilitate the early resolution of complaints.[234] In some Ombudsman schemes, mediation is used to provide complaints with more appropriate redress: for example, the Funeral Ombudsman considers complaints, frequently involving requests for apologies or acknowledgments that errors had been made, in addition to compensatory measures. There has been a suggestion that Ombudsman schemes may be forced to become more legalistic, by virtue of the human rights legislation requiring that disputes receive a fair hearing, in which case there may be less opportunity for informal dispute resolution, like mediation.[235] Nevertheless, there are an increasing number of private mediation providers,[236] which offer consumers the mediation alternative.

Some future issues

Cross-border consumer disputes

Due to the expanding opportunities for cross-border transactions, in particular via the internet, problems for consumers in seeking redress across borders have become apparent. The first problem is the choice of forum. Although the Brussels Convention gives consumers some freedom in choosing the court in which they wish to sue a supplier who is based in another country, the Convention does not apply to certain transactions: for example, it does not apply to purchases paid in cash, disputes over accommodation or car rental abroad, or to property rights abroad.[237] Secondly, the Rome Convention might negate the benefits of the Brussels Convention in relation to forum, as it aims to ensure that the same law applies to a transaction, irrespective of the forum, and frequently a suppliers' own laws will apply on the basis that those laws will have the closest connection with the contract.

These problems prompted the 1992 Green Paper.[238] This was followed by a study commissioned by the European Commission in 1995, which concluded that, in the case of simple cross-border disputes:

---

229 See the Banking Ombudsman *Annual Report 1998*, at pp 10–11; and P E Morris 'The Banking Ombudsman' (1992) 2 *Lloyds Maritime & Commercial Law Quarterly* 227.
230 See Building Societies Ombudsman *Annual Report 1999*, at pp 12 and 17; *Building Societies Ombudsman Scheme*, 1998; and *Guide for Applicants*, 1999.
231 See the section on Banking Disputes in this chapter.
232 See the section on Mediation Organisations in Chapter 7; and the Pensions Ombudsman *Pensions Ombudsman – what he can do*, 1998.
233 The Insurance Ombudsman Bureau *Annual Report 1999*, at p 26.
234 Ibid, at p 6.
235 See National Consumer Council *Annual Review*, 1999.
236 See the section on Mediation Organisations in Chapter 7.
237 See Articles 13–15 of the Brussels Convention, although note that amendments to the Convention are being debated.
238 Green Paper *Access of consumers to justice and the settlement of disputes in the Single Market*, 1992.

'a party who has suffered damage in the amount of 2,000 ECU must in order to have access to justice first pay an "entrance fee" of 2,500 ECU [being court costs and lawyer's fees exclusive of VAT] in the prospect of recovering their loss within 12 to 64 months [depending on the country] . . . on the assumption that the defendant will still be solvent when the court makes its decision.'[239]

Subsequent efforts to achieve access to justice for consumers cross-border did not, however, go far. For example, a Commission Communication in 1997, which put forward proposals to revise provisions in the Brussels Convention, focused on revisions to speed up the enforcement of judgments.[240] Directive 98/27/EC,[241] adopted in 1998, enabled qualified entities to bring injunctions against companies which are engaging in harmful acts cross-border, although it has limited application to package travel, distance selling and product safety.

The most recent efforts to achieve access to justice for consumers involved in cross-border transactions have focused on out of court dispute resolution procedures. The Commission has developed a set of minimum criteria for ADR:[242]

- the neutral should be independent, impartial and competent;
- ADR should be transparent, providing consumers with referral rules, the cost of the procedure, the rules governing the procedure and the legal status of the procedure;
- the parties should be allowed to participate in the process;
- the procedure should be either free of charge or be of moderate cost and parties should not require legal representation;
- the consumer cannot be deprived of the protection afforded by mandatory provisions in any law in the State in which he or she normally resides;
- the process and any decision can only be binding on the parties if they consent; and
- the parties have a right to be represented or assisted in the procedure.

The aim is to create a database which will list out of court dispute resolution procedures which satisfy these criteria. Bodies which satisfy the criteria are already listed for Belgium, Denmark, Finland, Greece, Italy, Portugal, Spain, Sweden and the Netherlands.[243] This idea is based on European Consumer Information Centres, which were established in 1992, essentially to provide advice to consumers on EU and national legislation.[244] Consumer organisations have also been developing a protocol on cross-border disputes, with a focus on co-operation and ADR.

---

239 European Commission *Cost of legal barriers to consumers in the Single Market*, Com (98) 13 Final (14 February 1996), at p 9.
240 European Commission *Towards greater efficiency in obtaining and enforcing judgments in the European Union*, Com. (97) 609 Final (26 November 1997).
241 OJ L166/51 (19 May 1998).
242 See European Commission *Recommendation on the principles applicable to the bodies responsible for out of court settlement of consumer disputes*, 28 December 1997.
243 European Commission *Out of court bodies responsible for the settlement of consumer disputes*. Also available at http://europa.eu.int/comm/dg24/policy/developments
244 There are European Information Centres in Lille, Luxembourg, Barcelona, Gronau, Vitoria, Bolzano, Dublin, Kiel, Vienna and London. The London European Information Consumer Centre is the National Association of Citizens Advice Bureaux (Myddelton House, 115–123 Pentonville Road, London N1 9LZ; phone: 020 7833 2181; fax: 020 7833 4371).

The EOCD has published guidelines for consumer protection in the context of e-commerce,[245] by encouraging businesses, consumer representatives and Governments to provide ADR mechanisms for the resolution of e-commerce consumer disputes.[246] In time, it is hoped that on-line ADR will be the natural progression,[247] although there are already a number of on-line dispute settlement systems tackling consumer disputes. For example, IRIS, a French initiative, provides on-line mediation for the resolution of disputes of a non-commercial nature. A range of consumer and trade organisations provide trust seals, combined with mediation, such as BBBOnline, Webtrader and TrustedShops. On-line ADR for the resolution of consumer complaints provides opportunities for the simplest, speediest and lowest cost dispute resolution mechanism, provided that certain safeguards are maintained, such as regard to the consumer protection laws in the country of the consumer's residence.[248]

Complaints against solicitors

Since 1998 complaints against solicitors have risen dramatically. The monthly average number of complaints received increased from 1,859 in 1997 to 2,586 in 1998.[249] Various options for reducing the backlog of complaints have been considered, including mediation, although ultimately the Law Society's strategy has been to place responsibility for complaints with law firms,[250] requiring them to set up complaints handling procedures and appoint a solicitor to deal with complaints.

Concerns in Scotland over the handling of complaints against solicitors led to a study by the Scottish Consumer Council. It concluded that the number of complaints against solicitors that were successfully mediated between 1994 and 1997 had increased by almost 80%, and the number of complaints had only risen by 4% in that period.

There have been suggestions that an independent body should deal with complaints against solicitors.[251] Although legal services ombudsman schemes already operate in the UK, they can only consider the handling of a complaint, rather than the original complaint, although the Lay Observer in Northern Ireland has a discretion to do so.[252]

In Australia, mediation has been introduced to resolve disputes between clients and solicitors over fees. In Queensland, for example, a complaint over solicitors' fees is lodged with the Solicitors' Complaints Tribunal, which appoints an assessor, who is obliged to advise the parties that they should attempt mediation.[253]

---

245 EOCD *Recommendation of the EOCD Council concerning guidelines for consumer protection in the context of electronic commerce*, 1999.
246 See the section on E-commerce Disputes in this chapter.
247 Ibid; and see the section on On-line Mediation in Chapter 10.
248 Ibid.
249 S Allen 'Complaints rocket 40% to record level' *Gazette*, 21 April 1999.
250 M Rose 'OSS backlog plans' *The Law Society Gazette*, 11 August 1999.
251 C Fracassini 'Independent watchdog for lawyers proposed' *The Scotsman*, January 1999.
252 The Office of the Legal Services Ombudsman for England and Wales, the Scottish Legal Services Ombudsman and the Lay Observer for Northern Ireland.
253 M Graham 'Solicitor and own-client costs disputes: the new regime' (1999) 4 *Proctor* 32.

Corporate issues

Mediation has been used effectively to resolve disputes over mergers and acquisitions. Merger and acquisition agreements are also increasingly referring disputes to mediation in the first instance, and to arbitration if mediation fails.[254]

Mediation's potential has also been recognised in the resolution of shareholder disputes,[255] which frequently involve complex investigations and litigation, notorious for length and cost.[256] The Consultation Paper on Shareholder Remedies suggested that courts should have the power to adjourn cases to encourage parties to use ADR.[257] The majority of respondents to the Consultation Paper agreed. Accordingly, the Law Commission recommended that the Lord Chancellor should make changes to the rules governing unfair prejudice proceedings so as to refer to the court's power to adjourn at any stage in the proceedings to enable parties to use ADR, together with a reporting back requirement, similar to the Commercial Court's Practice.[258] The wider recommendation was that shareholder proceedings should be dealt with primarily by active case management by courts.[259] In turn, this would encourage mediation to take place at an earlier stage in shareholder proceedings.[260]

Apart from addressing issues of expense and time involved in litigation, mediation allows the underlying human causes of shareholder and other corporate disputes to be tackled.[261]

Defamation and freedom of information

The draft pre-action protocol for defamation cases encourages parties to consider mediation[262] and suggests that failure to do so may be taken into account when costs are awarded at the end of a case.

---

254 See, for example, AstraZenca and Novartis merger agreement, reported in the Regulatory News Service, 2 December 1999.
255 The authors' 2000 survey of UK law firms indicated that, of the mediations with which respondents had been involved, 8% related to shareholder disputes.
256 Harman J in *Re Unisoft Group Ltd (No 3)* [1994] 1 BCLC 609.
257 See *Shareholder Remedies*, Consultation Paper, No 142.
258 Law Commission *Shareholder Remedies Report*, No 246 (also available at http://www.open.gov.uk/lawcomm). In relation to the Commercial Court Practice, see the section on Courts in Chapter 7.
259 Ibid.
260 For example, *Re Rotadata Ltd* [2000] 1 BCLC 122. The authors thank James Corbett QC, St Phillips Chambers, Birmingham, for information he provided about this case, and about his experience of mediation in the context of Section 459 Petitions.
261 In this context, see L D Solomon and J S Solomon 'Using alternative dispute resolution techniques to settle conflicts among shareholders of closely held corporations' (1987) 22 *Wake Forest Law Review* 105; and R D Greenfield and C O Burt 'ADR in shareholder suits: Old wine in a new bottle' (1993) 135(2) *New Jersey Law Journal* 17. For an example of French courts encouraging the use of mediation for the resolution of corporate disputes, see P J Omar 'ADR in French company law' (1999) 10(2) *ICCLR* 75.
262 See M Manley 'Mediation in libel cases?' *Solicitors' Journal*, 24 March 2000, p 268; R Shillito 'Mediation in libel actions' (2000) 150 *NLJ* 122; and Q Smith and A Monaghan 'Diplomatic Defamation' (2000) 2(15) *Legal Week* 119.

Scotland's Freedom of Information Bill, due to come into force in 2001, empowers the Scottish Information Commissioner to resolve disputes over freedom of information by mediation. Similarly, in Queensland Australia, the Freedom of Information Act 1992 allows the Commissioner to attempt settlement of disputes over information through mediation. In six years of operation the Commissioner's Office has resolved about 80% of appeals informally.[263] In New Zealand, investigators in the Privacy Commissioner's Office use mediation as one of a number of processes to pursue settlement when there is a complaint of invasion of privacy.[264]

Discrimination

Discrimination, specifically in the context of employment, is considered in the section below on employment. In England, Wales and Scotland, discrimination complaints are considered by the Equal Opportunities Commission in the case of sex discrimination, the Disability Rights Commission in the case of disability discrimination and the Commission for Racial Equality in the case of race discrimination. In Northern Ireland the Equality Commission, created in 1999, has responsibility for all types of discrimination complaints.

The Equal Opportunities Commission has examined the potential for mediation in the context of sex discrimination cases, but has expressed concerns over imbalance of power, the focus in mediation on interests rather than rights and mediation's inability to address systemic problems. It is proposing a model of mediation, which will ensure that mediated agreements reflect the parties' legal rights.[265] In New Zealand, the Human Rights Act 1993 provides compulsory and funded mediation for sex discrimination complaints. Discussions are without prejudice and the mediator may advise the parties of the kind of outcomes that are likely if the complaint were to be successful at the tribunal.[266]

The Disability Access Rights Service (DARAS) provides conciliation, conducted by the ADR Group, for claims under Part III of the Disability Discrimination Act 1995 relating to discrimination against, less favourable treatment of and failure to provide adequate access for a disabled person relating to goods, service and facilities or the disposal or management of premises or land. A new scheme is due to commence operation in November 2000, and will be overseen by the new Disability Rights Commission.

Although the Northern Ireland Equality Commission does not yet use mediation, the Labour Relations Agency in Northern Ireland is developing a mediation option for religious discrimination complaints.

---

263 G Sammon 'What to expect from an external review under the FOI Act' (1998) 8 *Proctor*, pp 16–18.
264 Privacy Act 1993, s 74.
265 R Hunter and A Leonard 'Sex discrimination and alternative dispute resolution: British proposals in light of international experience' *Public Law*, Summer 1997. See also the discussion on concerns in the section on Employment Disputes in this chapter.
266 M Roche and F Joychild *The Human Rights Act – Discrimination in focus*, Institute for International Research, 1994.

E-commerce disputes

E-commerce can create a wide range of disputes, from those related to goods and services, for example, late delivery or defective goods, through to disputed payment, intellectual property disputes and misleading advertising. The increasing use of e-commerce has focused attention on consumer protection, primarily as the bulk of e-commerce transactions are characterised by low transaction values and a disparity of bargaining power between sellers and purchasers. These factors, coupled with the fact that sellers and purchasers may be in different jurisdictions, provide incentives for faster and cheaper dispute resolution methods. As e-commerce grows, the number of e-commerce disputes is likely to increase, which will encourage the development of on-line dispute resolution services.

There are a number of US examples of on-line dispute resolution for e-commerce disputes.[267] For example, e-Bay provides on-line mediation for disputes arising out of on-line auction transactions, provided by a site, called Up4Sale. Initially, in early 1999, a link in the Up4Sale site was provided to the e-Bay complaint form and two to four disputes a week were received at that time. From mid-March 1999, a link was placed on the e-Bay customer service page and during a two week period, 225 users filed a complaint. Mediation was adopted as the method of dispute resolution as it was considered that it would be easier to secure the consent of the parties to this process. A single mediator was used in each case. Upon receipt of a complaint, the mediator would email the other party and, if agreement to participate was reached, each party would then present their views to the mediator and each other. About 46% of the mediations were resolved, with the remainder reaching impasse.[268]

A Canadian example, Cybertribunal, an initiative of the University of Montreal, was set up in 1996 and ended in December 1999, having handled over 100 e-commerce disputes through mediation. The Cybertribunal site consisted of a reception module, a secretariat module and a mediation module. Completion of electronic forms, available in the reception module, would start the mediation. The forms were encrypted and sent to the secretariat module, which assigned a mediator. The mediation module would be used if the parties agreed to submit to mediation.

There have been a number of recent EU policy initiatives, which encourage the use of ADR and on-line dispute resolution services for e-commerce disputes.[269] In

---

267 For further details, see the section on On-line Mediation in Chapter 10.

268 For a more comprehensive discussion of the initiative, see E Katsh, J Rifkin and A Gaitenby *E-commerce, e-disputes and e-dispute resolution*, 2000. Available at http://www.disputes.net/cyberweek2000

269 For example, Proposal for a European Parliament and Council Directive on *Certain legal aspects of electronic commerce in the internal market*, 1999; Proposal for a Council *Regulation on jurisdiction and the recognition of judgments in civil and commercial matters*, COM (1999) 348 Final; Commission Communication *Out of court settlement of consumer disputes*, COM (1998) 198 Final; Recommendation of the OECD Council concerning *Guidelines for consumer protection in the context of electronic commerce*, OECD 1999; and Commission Recommendation on the *Principles applicable to the bodies responsible for out of court settlement of consumer disputes* (98/257/EC). For further information, see the section on Consumer Disputes in this chapter. Also see the section on On-line Mediation in Chapter 10.

particular, the Proposal for a Directive on certain legal aspects of electronic commerce in the internal market[270] provides that:

- Member States should ensure that out of court schemes for dispute settlement, including by electronic means, is available for disagreements between service providers and recipients;
- out of court settlement mechanisms should comply with the Commission's Recommendations on the principles applicable to the bodies responsible for out of court settlement;[271] and
- Member States should encourage out of court dispute settlement bodies to keep the Commission informed of their decisions.[272]

E-commerce disputes, whether sought to be resolved by conventional or on-line methods, will raise issues of jurisdiction, the applicable law and the enforcement of settlements. The Second Draft Report on the Proposal for a Council Regulation on jurisdiction and the enforcement of judgments in civil and commercial matters aims to address these issues. It provides that e-commerce disputes involving parties domiciled in different member states should be referred to an ADR scheme, accredited by the European Commission.[273] The proposals are not intended to affect a party's right to bring court action to resolve 'a point of law' or to enforce any out-of-court settlement reached. It is also proposed that the Commission will draw up standard terms and conditions for consumer-to-business e-commerce, including standard jurisdiction clauses. A single contact point, a 'clearing house', will be established in each Member State, which together will operate as 'EEJ-Net', the European Extra-Judicial Network, essentially a support mechanism for consumers to access out-of-court bodies in other Member States.

European ADR initiatives in the context of e-commerce are already under way. Eurochambres is developing mediation services for cross-border e-commerce disputes across Member States on-line. Webtrader is a two year project, which commenced in early 2000, funded by the European Commission, and managed by a number of independent consumer organisations in the Netherlands, Belgium, Italy, France, Spain, Portugal and the UK.[274] Initially, a mediation programme will deal with national and cross-border disputes between enterprises, bearing the Webtrader logo, and their customers. If mediation is unsuccessful, arbitration will follow. Ultimately, the aim is to provide dispute resolution on-line.[275] Ford Motor Company has, in conjunction with the Chartered Institute of Arbitrators in London, launched an on-line arbitration scheme for Ford customers across Europe who buy a Ford car on-line.[276] Another approach to e-commerce dispute resolution is dispute prevention through codes of conduct for e-commerce, like BBBOnline and TrustedShops.[277] In

---

270 See draft EC Resolution, 13 April 2000.
271 See the section on Consumer Disputes in this chapter.
272 See Article 17.
273 Proposal for Regulation COM(1999) 348-C5-0169/1999-1999/0154 (CNS).
274 By the organisation *Which* in the UK.
275 For further European on-line dispute resolution initiatives, see the section on On-line Mediation in Chapter 10.
276 The Institute operates the scheme via its website at www.arbitrators.org with a link from the Ford on-line shopping site at www.fordjourney.com. The case registration fee is £100.
277 See Chapter 10.

the UK the Government, the Consumers' Association and the Alliance of Electronic Business are working on establishing a body which will accredit e-commerce codes of conduct.[278]

Following a comprehensive study on cyberspace law, the American Bar Association has suggested that a global on-line standards commission should be set up to develop common standards and principles for e-commerce across different jurisdictions and new on-line forms of dispute resolution.[279]

Employment disputes

Advisory, Conciliation and Arbitration Service (ACAS)

The 1896 Conciliation Act introduced state conciliation services for employment disputes. Criticism over Government involvement resulted in the establishment in 1974 of the Conciliation and Arbitration Service, which was given statutory powers under the Employment Protection Act 1975. It was renamed in 1976 as the Advisory, Conciliation and Arbitration Service ('ACAS'). Its current statutory powers are included in the 1992 Trade Union and Labour Relations Act, as amended by the Trade Union Reform and Employment Rights Act 1993 and the Employment Relations Act 1999. It operates in England, Wales and Scotland, whereas the Labour Relations Agency provides similar functions in Northern Ireland. Research in the 1970s, 1980s and 1990s has indicated high levels of satisfaction with ACAS procedures.[280] In comparison, the American system of labour conciliation and arbitration has been criticised for its legalism and formality.[281]

ACAS provides a range of ADR procedures. Conciliation, most commonly used to resolve employment disputes, is a voluntary process, involving a series of separate or joint meetings between the parties and a conciliator, who facilitates negotiations, but does not impose any particular outcome on the parties. It is the ACAS dispute resolution method which most closely resembles mediation in the traditional sense. Advisory mediation, on the other hand, seeks to prevent disputes, by identifying and resolving the underlying or systemic problems in the work place. It involves joint workshops, which provide a forum for parties to identify problems and brainstorm options, and joint working parties, which provide the parties with a structured problem-solving approach, facilitated by ACAS staff. ACAS statistics show that organisational change and employee consultation constitutes the largest category of work for advisory mediation, which in 1998 numbered 530 cases.[282] ACAS also provides arbitration and dispute mediation, although the number of such references

---

278 Department of Trade and Industry *Modern Markets: confident consumers*, White Paper, DTI, London, 1999.

279 ABA News 'Governments should create "cyber-tribunal" says report' *Legal Week*, 20 July 2000, p 9.

280 See, for example, L Dickens and D Cockburn 'Dispute settlement institutions and the courts' in R Lewis (ed) *Labour law in Britain*, Basil Blackwell, Oxford 1986. For the most recent evaluation, see J Lewis and R Legard *ACAS Individual Conciliation: a qualitative evaluation of the service provided in industrial tribunal cases*, ACAS, 1999.

281 See, for example, F E A Sander 'Alternative methods of dispute resolution: An overview' (1985) 4 *University of Florida Law Review* 1 at 4.

282 *ACAS's work in 1998*, ACAS 1998, at pp 53–6.

has fallen over the last couple of years.[283] Dispute mediation is not mediation in the traditional sense, since the neutral makes recommendations as a basis for settlement. Before dispute mediation is used, the parties are expected to have attempted to resolve the matter by conciliation.

Employment tribunals

Employment tribunals provide redress for individual employment disputes in England, Wales and Scotland. In Northern Ireland employment claims are handled by the Central Office of Industrial Tribunals. Tribunal claims are advised to ACAS and the parties are given an opportunity to attempt a conciliated settlement first. Tribunal hearings are also conducted by chairmen adopting a hands-on case management and interventionist approach, with a view to settling cases.[284]

The Employment Rights (Dispute Resolution) Act 1998 aims to reduce delay in tribunals and encourage settlement in the following ways:

- The Act promotes ADR for unfair dismissal cases, by making arbitration a voluntary alternative to an employment tribunal hearing throughout the UK.[285] ACAS has designed an arbitration scheme, in accordance with the Act, which was introduced on a pilot basis in April 1999.
- The Act encourages settlement through compromise agreements by allowing any authorised employment adviser to sign off on a negotiated settlement of a dispute that would have gone to the tribunal.

The Employment Relations Act 1999 provides that, in the case of employees who have been dismissed for taking industrial action in breach of their contracts of employment, the tribunal is to take into account, when assessing whether employers have taken reasonable steps to resolve the dispute, whether conciliation or mediation had been attempted.[286]

Scope for mediation use

The majority of ACAS conciliation cases involve the private sector and the largest share of cases is generated by education and health, food and drink, transport and mechanical and electrical engineering sectors. Pay, terms and conditions, dismissal and discipline, recognition, redundancy and changes in work practices are the most frequently-occurring issues in collective conciliation cases.[287]

---

283   *ACAS's work in 1998*, ACAS 1998, at pp 69–70.
284   See Lord Woolf *Access to Justice: Interim Report*, Lord Chancellor's Department, London, June 1995, at p 145.
285   See also Employment Rights (Dispute Resolution) (Northern Ireland) Order 1998.
286   The Act inserts new s 238A into the Trade Union and Labour Relations Act 1992. The Irish Industrial Relations Act 1946 provides, in s 69, that the Chairman of the Industrial Court may, before the Court undertakes the investigation of a trade dispute, appoint a conciliation officer to act as mediator in the dispute.
287   *ACAS's work in 1998*, ACAS 1998, at pp 40–2. The Centre for Dispute Resolution's 2000 statistics indicate that 4% of its referrals related to employment disputes: CEDR '2000 statistics' *Resolutions*, No 26.

The difficulty, in the case of individual claims, is that complainants may not have access to mediation if it is not included in the employer's grievance procedure. Persuading an employer in those circumstances to participate in mediation is likely to be difficult unless the employee is a union member, in which case the union may attempt to persuade the employer to participate. In addition, there are tight time limits for bringing certain kinds of claims, so that claims would need to be submitted within time, although mediation could be attempted subsequently.

Although the Employment Rights (Dispute Resolution) Act 1998 has been criticised for not promoting the use of mediation for the resolution of unfair dismissal disputes,[288] parties can agree to refer unfair dismissal claims to mediation and proceedings for breach of employment contract can be stayed under the Civil Procedure Rules so that the parties may attempt mediation.[289] Workplace Mediation has been set up to provide mediation for sexual harassment cases. Attempting mediation would not forego rights to pursue the claim formally, if mediation were unsuccessful, and the process is intended to involve the employer, employee and alleged harasser.[290] Sex discrimination and bullying cases have also been successfully mediated.[291] US authors suggest a number of reasons why harassment and discrimination cases, in particular, should not be mediated, although for each argument put forward against mediation, arguments in support can be found. For example:

- Unlike mediation, formal grievance proceedings provide authority and legitimacy, yet those procedures may also hinder access to justice.[292]
- Although matters of principle may require an adjudicated resolution, disputes over principle frequently disguise other issues.[293]
- Although justice is the responsibility of formal institutions, justice is served if solutions satisfy the parties, and the safest way to ensure that this occurs is to negotiate the outcome.[294]
- Although an adjudication may provide the employer with an incentive to deal with systemic problems, a negotiated settlement can also make an employer rethink change practices.[295]
- Although a tribunal can only award compensation, a negotiated settlement can include an apology, reinstatement, and an agreed reference.
- Although power imbalance is addressed through adjudication, ADR processes ensure that the complainant exercises control over the proceedings and outcome.[296]

---

288 'Consider mediation' *The Law Society Gazette*, 1 December 1999, at p 9.
289 See the section on Courts in Chapter 7.
290 For further information about this service, refer to J Bowers 'Taking the harass out of harassment' *The Times*, 18 January 2000, at p 29.
291 The NSW Law Society offers a telephone mediation service for discrimination and harassment issues: Law Society 'Telephone advice and mediation service for resolving discrimination/harassment problems' (1998) 36(1) *Law Society Journal* (NSW) 77.
292 See D Hoffman 'ADR: An opportunity to broaden the shadow of the law' (1994) 21 *Human Rights* 20.
293 V Aubert 'Competition and dissensus: two types of conflict in conflict resolution' (1963) 7 *Journal of Dispute Resolution* 26.
294 See C Smart *The problem of rights in feminism and the power of law*, Routledge, London 1989.
295 Equal Opportunities Commission *How to bring a claim*, pamphlet, at p 3.
296 See B Mayer 'The dynamics of power in mediation and negotiation' in J Macfarlane (ed)

Some commentators argue that employment disputes, generally, are not suitable for mediation. For example, Weigand criticises mediation in this context as it may not achieve an organisational benefit:

> '. . . the result reached may satisfy both mediating parties at the expense of others in the organisation . . . mediation also does little to attack an underlying problem which may be widespread . . .'[297]

Weigand recommends the ombudsman model for employment disputes,[298] as an ombudsman often attempts mediation, but if it fails the ombudsman assumes the role of industry watchdog.[299] In contrast, Hurley makes the point that an employment dispute is 'halfway between family and civil litigation because it is about the breakdown of personal relationships . . . invariably there are strong emotions on both sides of the table, but in mediation some quite remarkable outcomes are possible . . .'[300]

In-house mediation schemes

A range of mediation schemes has sought to tackle employment problems, and provide an opportunity for mediation to also tackle problems between employees, interpersonal and intra-organisational issues. The Department of Health set up a scheme in 1998, whereby employee grievances are referred to a conciliator who may suggest solutions, but does not impose solutions on the parties. The Benefits Agency has used mediation, which has helped resolve approximately 150 complaints in the course of 1998/9. A number of local authorities also have workplace mediation schemes: for example, London Borough of Tower Hamlets. The London Fire and Civil Defence Authority (LFCDA) found that its traditional internal procedures, grievance, harassment and discipline procedures, did not provide satisfactory results, primarily due to the culture of blame by colleagues when complaints were made. The authority has trained staff in mediation techniques to deal with those issues.[301] The Government Personnel Department offers a mediation service to staff with harassment complaints and a follow-up service to ensure that agreements reached in mediation are being adhered to.[302]

US companies have had a longer history of in-house ADR schemes for resolving employment conflicts, including internal 'ombuds people' who facilitate dispute resolution, peer dispute review boards, management-employee dispute review

---

Alternative Dispute Resolution, Windsor 1997.

297 S Weigand 'A just and lasting peace: supplanting mediation with the ombuds model' (1996) 12(1) *Ohio State Journal on Dispute Resolution* 95 at 121.

298 See the section on Mediation Organisations and an outline of Ombudsmen schemes in Chapter 7.

299 S Weigand, op cit, at p 122.

300 D Hurley *Paper to Arbitrators' Institute New Zealand*, 1994, at pp 7–8.

301 T Buchanan 'Fighting fire with mediation' *Resolutions*, Issue No 23, at p 7.

302 Feedback has indicated that a major problem for mediation referrals has been the failure by one party or both parties to agree to use mediation for the resolution of harassment issues. Of the cases mediated, however, there has been a high success rate. The feedback from participants has been positive, in particular, that mediation provided the parties with an opportunity to resolve in a short period of time a situation which had troubled them for many months. The authors thank the Personnel Department for their feedback on the scheme.

boards and employee hot lines.[303] In New Zealand also, prevention and containing employment grievances has become recognised as the most desirable option for employers, encouraged, it is believed, by the statutory framework for mediation in the industrial context in New Zealand provided by the Employment Contracts Act 1991. It is believed that the statutory framework first created increased awareness on the part of both employees and employers of mediation, which in turn created awareness of the value of early resolution of employment grievances. Some New Zealand companies also use internal 'ombuds people'.[304]

Environment disputes

There is a debate world-wide over whether environmental mediation is appropriate and over the rate of success of environmental mediation. At one end of the spectrum studies suggest a success rate of between 75%–80%, irrespective of whether mediations are related to site-specific disputes or environmental policy issues, although these studies also suggest that implementation of mediation agreements is likely to be more successful for site-specific cases, rather than policy issues.[305] At the other end of the spectrum, commentators suggest that 90% of environmental cases are inappropriate for mediation,[306] and that mediation may provide an incentive to breach statutory environmental standards, in the expectation that mediation will enable settlement to be reached at a level of compliance below that which is statutorily mandated.[307]

Apart from this debate, the types of mediation used in this sector do not all conform to the classic model of mediation. Mediation techniques may, for instance, be used in an attempt to head off a dispute. An example is where a facilitation process takes place before environmental regulations are passed. Another process is 'scoping', where a facilitator seeks to attain the parties' agreement on what is and is not in issue, without at that stage attempting to resolve the matters in issue. Resolution of matters in issue by way of mediation generally makes use of the classic model of mediation.

The Environment Council has paved the way for the use of mediation in the environmental sector in the UK. Given that frequently multiple parties are involved, the Council prefers to use the term 'facilitation', rather than mediation, to describe

---

303 For more information, see Center for Public Resources *Program to resolve employment disputes*, CPR, 1998.

304 R Harbridge 'Dispute Resolution Procedures in New Zealand Employment Contracts' *AMINZ Newsletter*, September 1996.

305 For example, G Bingham *Resolving environmental disputes: a decade of experience*, The Conservation Foundation, 1986. See also C Napier 'The resolution of commercial environmental disputes using mediation' (2000) 11(2) *ICCLR* 49. See also the section on Multi-party Disputes in this chapter. Shapiro considers that, generally, environmental mediations, involving pollution issues, turn on each party's volume of pollutants, each pollutant's toxicity level and ability to pay: D Shapiro 'Pushing the envelope – selective techniques for tough mediations' (2000) *ADRLJ* 114 at 121.

306 For example, D Amy *The politics of environmental mediation*, Columbia University Press 1987; and M Jeffery 'Accommodating negotiation in environmental impact assessment and project approval processes' (1987) 4 *EPLJ* 244 at 250.

307 National Consumer Council *Settling consumer disputes*, 1996, at p 16.

the process used. The Council has been involved in an increasing number of facilitations, with approximately 60 in 1998 alone. The Council rationalises the increasing interest in mediation in this sector on the following grounds:

- litigation of environmental disputes involves considerable cost and delay;
- mediation can be used to ensure participation in environmental decision-making; and
- there has been a shift in focus in the sector from raising awareness of environmental issues to a need to find mutually-acceptable solutions.

The facilitators used by the Council include architects, planners and lawyers.[308] The Council promotes the 'stakeholder dialogue' process, which identifies as many stakeholder groups as possible, and leads to facilitative meetings with stakeholders, to uncover the needs, concerns and interests behind their stated positions.[309] The most publicised example of stakeholder dialogue is the Brent Spar Dialogue Process, which arose out of government plans to dispose of Shell Expro's Brent Spar Floating Oil Storage Buoy. The dialogue process was designed in response to a Green Peace campaign, objecting to the proposal to dispose of it in the North East Atlantic. The process involved a series of dialogue sessions, facilitated by the Council, involving the wide range of stakeholders, from across North West Europe, including NGOs, consumer groups, scientists, industry and academics. The aim was to ensure that the different views of stakeholders were identified and understood. The process also involved media briefings, an internet site and information circulars. Ultimately, the process indicated that the preferred solution was to re-use the Spar as a quay in Norway, which was approved by the UK Government.[310]

The stakeholder dialogue process is widely used by the Council to resolve local issues as well. For example, at the end of 1998 the Council started a similar dialogue process in relation to the transport of used nuclear fuel in the Cricklewood area. As a first step, the Council sought to identify interested groups with concerns over these issues. The first round of meetings took place in January 1999 and in February 1999 the questions from interested groups, which came out of the first round of meetings, were presented by the Council to British Nuclear Fuels and Direct Rail Services. By June 1999, British Nuclear Fuels and Direct Rail Services had prepared proposed options, which addressed the various concerns raised with them, covering issues such as routing trains and contamination levels. A further series of workshops with stakeholders has taken place to investigate stakeholders' views on the various options proposed.[311]

Another use of facilitation in this field was illustrated through a consensus-building process by Bedfordshire County Council to help resolve problems occurring following a reduction in car parking spaces in the area. The council trained local people as facilitators, who worked with the community to resolve past and continuing problems. A similar project is being used in Stratford.[312] An example of

---

308 The authors thank the Council for the information provided for use in this section.
309 The Environment Council *Stakeholder Dialogue – the Environment Council Approach*, pamphlet.
310 The Environment Council *Stakeholder Dialogue in Action – case study: The Brent Spar Dialogue Process*, pamphlet.
311 The Environment Council *Press Releases*, 7 December 1998, 15 January 1999, 3 February 1999 and 1 June 1999.
312 The Environment Council *Background and case studies*, pamphlet.

'scoping' by the Council has arisen in the context of a national stakeholder dialogue process on issues surrounding genetically modified organisms. Scoping workshops have been used to determine if a stakeholder dialogue process is the best option to identify all the issues and possible solutions involved.[313]

In the US, the Environmental Protection Agency is working on establishing a large pool of neutrals to help mediate environmental disputes involving federal agencies, as part of a wider programme to streamline its dispute resolution processes with private companies and individuals.[314] The US Institute for Environmental Conflict Resolution is also developing a website, which will provide training programmes on the prevention, management and resolution of environmental disputes.[315]

Family disputes

England and Wales

The significant development in the context of family mediation in the 1990s was the Family Law Act 1996, although the Act has not yet been implemented in full. Section 1 of the Act sets out the fundamental principles, which are intended to govern the operation of the Act, including that family disputes should be resolved with minimum distress to the parties and the children, in a way which promotes continuing relationships between the parties and the children, and without unreasonable costs being incurred.[316] Mediation is the favoured dispute resolution method within the system envisaged by the Family Law Act. The Act requires the attendance of one or both parties at an information meeting at the beginning of the process, which is intended to explore the suitability of mediation.[317] The form of the meeting will be determined by pilots.[318] In addition, the Act gives courts the power to adjourn proceedings to enable the parties to take part in mediation.[319] Finally, s 29 of the Act requires, in certain cases as a pre-condition for legal aid, that parties attend a meeting to discuss suitability for mediation.[320]

---

313 The Environment Council *Press Release*, 16 November 1999.
314 Center for Public Resources 'ADR briefs' *Alternatives*, No 11, December 1998, at pp 175–6.
315 Center for Public Resources 'ADR briefs' *Alternatives*, No 6, June 1999, at p 117.
316 Family Law Act 1996, s 4.
317 Family Law Act 1996, s 8.
318 See the section on Courts in Chapter 7. The pilot has been evaluated for the Lord Chancellor's Department by Janet Walker at Newcastle Centre for Family Studies at Newcastle University. Although three interim reports have been published (J Walker (ed) *Information meetings and associated provisions of the Family Law Act 1996*: first, second and third interim reports to the LCD, 1998 and 1999), the final report, although submitted to the LCD in September 2000, has not been released by the LCD as at publication of this book. The main rationale for the pilot was to determine what level of mediation services would be required. It was estimated in 1996 that only 110 accredited mediators were able to undertake financial and child-related mediations, yet on average there were 160,000 divorces each year: House of Commons, *Hansard Debates*, 25 March 1996.
319 See Family Law Act 1996, ss 13 and 14.
320 Family Law Act 1996, s 29; and see the section on Funding and Mediation in Chapter 9.

The provisions setting out the Act's underlying principles and s 29 of the Act have come into force, but the remainder of the provisions outlined above have not. The provisions concerning the initial information meeting and possible referral to mediation during proceedings have been shelved at this stage, until some time in 2001, although possibly indefinitely. The reason for this has been the disappointing results from initial information meeting pilots, which were run between June 1997 and May 1999. The pilot involved more than 5,500 married people and the results indicated that 39% considered that the meeting had the effect of persuading them to go to a solicitor for legal advice, whereas only 7% considered that they would go to mediation,[321] defeating the Government's objectives of encouraging the mediated settlement of family disputes.

Although s 29 has been introduced, it does not mandate the use of mediation, but requires clients who wish to apply for legal aid for representation in family disputes to attend a meeting with a mediator, unless they or the proceedings are exempt, to discuss the suitability of mediation. If mediation is considered unsuitable or if either party refuses to mediate, then the mediation will not take place. If the parties agree to mediate, but the mediation breaks down or is unsuccessful, the parties' obligations, for the purposes of legal aid, have been satisfied.[322] The main problems with s 29 of the Act, as a means for promoting the use of mediation in family disputes, are believed to be that:

- about 60% of cases will be exempt from s 29;
- about 25% of those cases caught by s 29 will not be suitable for mediation;
- about 30% of the cases which are suitable for mediation will not result in a successful mediation.[323]

It is hoped that, with the introduction of the Ancillary Relief Scheme, co-operation will be promoted as a result of a more interventionist role being taken by district judges and lead to improved ways of resolving property and financial issues. The Scheme applies to Ancillary Relief applications in certain courts.[324] The parties are required to complete a financial statement and to attend a Financial Dispute Resolution ('FDR') appointment, unless the district judge considers that it is not appropriate to do so, in which case the matter may be referred to mediation or negotiation.[325] The FDR meeting is conducted on a without prejudice basis and is treated as a meeting for the purposes of conciliation, with the aim being for the parties to reach agreement on matters in issue between them.[326] The judge may make recommendations on settlement, and will not continue to hear the case if it does not settle as a result of the meeting.[327]

---

321 H Siddle 'Family upheaval' *The Law Society Gazette*, 7 July 1999, at p 14; and L Tsang 'Separating the issues' *The Law Society Gazette*, 21 July 1999, at p 22.

322 For further information, see the section on Funding and Mediation in Chapter 9.

323 H Siddle 'Family mediation pilot project' *The Law Society Gazette*, 21 July 1999, at p 31.

324 The courts are Barnsley, Bath, Blackwood, Bolton, Boston, Bow, Bristol, Bury, Crewe, Guildford, Harrogate, Hertford, Kingston, Maidstone, Northampton, Salford, Southampton, Southport, Stafford, Staines, Stoke-on-Trent, Taunton, Teeside, Trowbridge, Tunbridge Wells, Willesden and Wrexham: Family Proceedings (Amendment No 2) Rules 1997, r 2.71. See 'Comment: ancillary relief comes in' (1999) 29 *Fam Law* 516.

325 Family Proceedings (Amendment No 2) Rules 1997, r 2.74.

326 Family Proceedings (Amendment No 2) Rules 1997, r 2.75.

327 The Scheme was evaluated by KPMG, who concluded that settlement rates had

There has been a suggestion that a way to tackle the issue of promoting mediation in appropriate family disputes is to require solicitors to advise clients on the availability of mediation, a recommendation made by the Lord Chancellor's Advisory Committee on Legal Education and Conduct.

Scotland

The Family Law Act 1996 does not extend to Scotland. The Family Law Act 1985 and the Divorce Act 1976 govern divorce law in Scotland. Family mediation centres developed later in Scotland than in England. The first independent mediation service was established in 1984 in Lothian. In 1986 the Scottish Association of Family Conciliation Services was set up to provide family mediation training and to standardise family mediation services. The national family mediation co-ordinating body, Family Mediation Scotland, was set up in 1987, and services affiliated to it were first set up in 1992.[328]

The main sources of referral to family mediation in Scotland are courts, solicitors and parties direct. A recent study of family mediation in Scotland has revealed that in about 40% of family mediations, legal proceedings have been initiated, and that in about 80% of family mediations, both parties have received legal advice ahead of mediation.[329] That study also found that the timing of mediation, from the point of view of the psychological or emotional stage reached in the divorce process, rather than the chronological stage reached, influences the success of a family mediation.[330] In Scotland, family mediation cases predominantly involve children's issues, as the courts are preferred for the resolution of financial issues. As in England and Wales, where children are involved, mediation must take account of the relevant Act, in this case the Children (Scotland) Act 1995.[331]

The recent study of family mediation in Scotland concluded that awareness and understanding of family mediation in Scotland is poor, which may account for its under-exploitation in Scotland, although the study concluded that, of the cases mediated, about 75% resulted in agreement.[332]

Northern Ireland

The Matrimonial Causes Order (NI) 1984, Family Law Miscellaneous Provisions (NI) Order 1984 and the Matrimonial and Family Proceedings Order (NI) 1989 govern divorces in Northern Ireland.

The use of family mediation in Northern Ireland is underdeveloped. It is believed that the reason for this is the lack of knowledge by the public and solicitors about family mediation services. In addition, divorce in Northern Ireland requires two

---

improved: see H Brown and A Marriott *ADR: principles and practice* (2nd edn), Sweet & Maxwell, London, 1999, at p 35.
328 Family Mediation Scotland *Information Pack*, op cit.
329 J Lewis *The role of mediation in family disputes in Scotland*, The Scottish Office, Legal Studies Research Findings No 23, 1999.
330 Ibid.
331 See Part II, on the special issues involved in family mediation.
332 Ibid.

years of separation by consent, and it is believed that this slower pace of divorce enables the parties to resolve the main issues before a decree is made.[333]

There is, however, enthusiasm for family mediation amongst the social work profession in Northern Ireland. Health and Social Services Trusts provide independent and informal mediation services, assisted by social workers, for family court proceedings and a number of pilot projects are underway.[334]

Republic of Ireland by way of comparison

Family mediation developed in the 1980s in the Republic of Ireland out of marriage counselling services. The Mediators Institute Ireland was established in 1983 and the state-run Family Mediation Service, was set up in 1986 to provide a free mediation service to assist couples, who have decided to separate, to reach agreement on all issues relating to their separation. The Service has recently expanded, as a key objective in the Government's 'Action Programme for the Millennium' was aimed at maintaining a tradition of family in Ireland, by providing support for families to ensure that, if marital relationships end, this is done amicably and that agreements, in particular in relation to children, are durable.

Government/public sector disputes

The use of mediation by government agencies is explored throughout this chapter, in the context of separate subject areas. Local authorities provide substantial support and funding to a wide range of community mediation services. A number of local authorities have also set up their own mediation schemes, in particular, to deal with neighbour disputes. Research carried out by the National Society for Clean Air and Environmental Protection, for example, found that 94% of local authorities do not intend to implement the Noise Act 1996, preferring mediation instead for the long-term resolution of noise disputes.[335] There are potential difficulties when local authorities use mediation to resolve neighbour disputes as local authority offices usually assume the role of mediators and, accordingly, may not be seen as impartial.

Government departments have also embraced ADR clauses in their purchasing and supply contracts. For example, HM Treasury's Central Unit on Procurement[336] recommended, in the case of purchasing and supply contracts, that consideration be given to ADR, including mediation. The Department of Health's conditions of contracting recommend negotiation and other forms of ADR for dispute resolution.[337] Similar provision is made in the Inland Revenue's terms and conditions of goods and services contracts, as in the case of the Ministry of Defence.[338]

---

333 The Office of Law Reform *Divorce in Northern Ireland: a better way forward*, Consultation Paper, Office of Law Review, December 1999, at pp 27–8.
334 Ibid, at p 61.
335 National Society for Clean Air and Environmental Protection *National Noise Survey 1999*, NSCA,1999.
336 HM Treasury Central Unit on Procurement *Disputes Resolution*, CUP No 50; and see the section on Construction Disputes in this chapter.
337 Department of Health *Purchasing Information*, available at http://www.doh.gov.uk
338 Defcon 530 and in the case of Scotland, Defcon 530a.

Mediation within the social services complaints procedure is also increasing. Some authorities have built mediation into their procedures, whereas others consider it on an ad-hoc basis. Apart from the mediation schemes and contractual provisions, referred to above, the Government regularly considers mediation on a case-by-case basis. 1999 statistics issued by the Centre for Dispute Resolution showed that the Government/public sector comprised 5% of mediation users.[339] Examples of cases mediated by the Government include disputes over development plans, local authority waste proposals and local authority services.

Despite the range of cases which have been mediated, the public sector also frequently declines to mediate, claiming that it would be against the public interest to do so, preferring instead the visibility of court adjudication.[340] Concern over power imbalances is another frequently-cited reason for refusal by public authorities to mediate. Another is that compromise might be seen as weakening government's commitment to policies.[341] This problem raises many of the issues, discussed above, in relation to the appropriateness of mediating harassment and discrimination cases, in the employment context. Although court adjudication may be appropriate where the public sector refuses to acknowledge an issue or problem, mediation is likely to be more appropriate in those cases where the needs and interests of particular individuals are at the core of the dispute. In addition, there is a range of disputes involving the public sector which cannot be easily or cost effectively resolved by adjudication: for example, neighbour disputes. The interests of third parties can be preserved by ensuring that any mediated outcome is in the public domain and by ensuring that mediation does not bypass the normal decision-making process of government, but seeks to find acceptable proposals to put forward in that process.[342]

Even in the context of disputes involving major public interest issues, the process of stakeholder dialogue, as outlined above in the case of environmental disputes, could be the answer, by providing an informal dispute resolution mechanism, whilst at the same time ensuring accountability, by taking on board the concerns of a wide range of stakeholders. The potential cost savings afforded by mediation, by obviating or reducing the involvement of police, government authorities, industry groups and even lawyers, should be considered in each case. Some mediators report that public authorities have agreed to mediate on the proviso that the mediator will 'sign off' on any agreement reached by the parties themselves, as a way of receiving an independent acknowledgement that the agreement is fair or, at least, has not taken advantage of any power imbalance.

Insolvency

Criticism by judges of the costs of administration and a number of reported cases, where such costs exceeded the recovery, provide incentive for mediation in this

---

339 Centre for Dispute Resolution *Resolutions*, Issue No 22, at p 7.
340 M Stubbs and D Tow 'Australian tests for mediation benefits' *Planning* No 1123, 16 June 1995, p 10.
341 W Kumar 'Opportunities for mediation' *Chartered Surveyor Monthly*, vol 7, No 4, January 1998, p 59.
342 C Shepley 'Mediation in the Planning System' *Planning Inspectorate Journal*, Issue 7, Spring 1997. See also *Dyson v Secretary of State for the Environment and Chiltern District Council* (1998) 75 P&CR 506, where the court found that, although the Planning Inspector could proceed by way of informal hearing, he should have taken an inquisitorial role.

area.[343] There have already been high-profile examples of mediation in this context. For example, the Barings case, which involved dozens of court applications, ultimately was resolved by the City Disputes Panel. More than 150 meetings were held as part of a lengthy conciliation process.[344] The other high profile example, the Atlantic Computers case, involved an £850m claim arising out of British and Commonwealth Holdings' insolvency following its acquisition of Atlantic Computers, which was riddled with liabilities. The mediation involved the administrator of British and Commonwealth Holdings, Ernst & Young, British and Commonwealth Holdings' bankers, BZW; Atlantic's bankers, Rothschilds; and the auditors, Spicers & Openheim and Coopers & Lybrand. Settlement occurred within four days, saving a trial which was scheduled to run for 20 months.[345] There is also scope for the use of mediation in a preventative role, by helping companies to formulate plans, long before the company finds itself in an administration or insolvency situation.

There are a number of court-annexed mediation programmes in US Bankruptcy Courts which may provide courts in the UK with some possible guidelines. For example, the programme of the Bankruptcy Court in the Southern District of New York has the following basic components:

- The court may direct a matter to mediation or the parties may choose to do so.
- The court maintains a register of mediators.
- If the parties cannot agree on the appointment, the court appoints a mediator.
- The mediator files a report with the court, confirming compliance or non-compliance with the requirements of the programme.[346]

Insurance disputes

Appropriateness of mediation

The typical way in which insurance litigation is run is perhaps best illustrated by a quote from an insurance litigator in Genn's study of the Central London County Court Mediation Pilot:

> 'I am acting for an insurance company. I have to use any tactic that I can, to pay as little as possible to the plaintiff. I intend to put the plaintiff to as much trouble as possible, in order to pay as little as possible . . .'[347]

---

343 Although the English Civil Procedure Rules, r 2.1(2) provides that the CPR does not apply to insolvency proceedings, a Statutory Instrument amended the Insolvency Rules 1986 with effect from 26 April 1999, and applies the new practice and philosophy of the Woolf Reforms to insolvency proceedings: see G Davis 'Insolvency proceedings in the age of Woolf, (2000) 1 *Insolvency Law* 33; and M Humphries 'Insolvency Mediation and ADR' (1999) 65 *Insolvency Bulletin* 7.

344 See the section on Mediation Organisations in Chapter 7, for more information on the City Disputes Panel.

345 C Timmis 'Litigation' *Legal Business*, March 1999; G Graham 'Former advisers settle B&C' *Financial Times*, 8 January 1999; and M Mullally 'Atlantic dispute sets ADR record' *Legal Week*, 21 January 1999.

346 United States Bankruptcy Court Southern District of New York *Court-annexed mediation program: Adoption of procedures governing mediation of matters in bankruptcy cases and adversary proceedings*. Also see the section on Compulsion or Encouragement to Mediate in Chapter 9.

347 H Genn *Central London County Court Mediation Pilot: Evaluation Report*, LCD

The rationale is that, by delaying payments, monies can remain invested, particularly when interest rates are high, and plaintiffs through frustration may settle for a lot less. On the other side of the coin, however, insurance companies are realising that pay-outs may have to be larger the later a case settles in litigation as the plaintiff has incurred additional costs. Insurance companies also have to place additional funds in reserve accounts to cover the cost of litigation and their own legal costs in keeping a file open can become excessive. Accordingly, the aims of insurance companies, to pay out as little as possible, and the aims of plaintiffs, to recover as quickly as possible, can be achieved through an early attempt at an ADR process, like mediation, before litigation expenses escalate and expectations increase.

Reinsurance cases are particularly suitable for mediation as these disputes provide opportunities for restructuring transactions, reconsidering the timing and categorisation of payments, and enhancing relationships. However, reinsurance may also provide insurers with a dilemma whether to settle in mediation, in case the reinsurer, that does not attend the mediation, later seeks to deny liability to indemnify the insurer for the settlement.[348]

Examples of mediation use

Insurance companies have embraced mediation in the UK. A legal expenses insurance company, which referred a number of cases to mediation under the Bristol Law Society's Mediation Scheme, provided the scheme with an important stimulus.[349] A large number of Commercial Court ADR referrals have been made in insurance and reinsurance cases.[350] The Centre for Dispute Resolution's 1999 statistics indicated that the UK insurance industry was the fourth largest group of mediation users, although the Centre believes that there are many more mediations conducted by the industry, which have not been picked up by its statistics.[351]

Notwithstanding the use made by the insurance industry of mediation, there is still widespread belief in the industry that, through information exchange, communication and direct negotiation, most insurance disputes should be capable of settlement and that mediation is likely to be used in those cases where the dispute cannot be settled by direct negotiation.[352] It is not surprising, therefore, that a survey

Research Series, No 5/98, at p 32.

348 A concern flowing from *Commercial Union Assurance Co plc v NRG Victory Reinsurance Ltd*, Commercial Court, 1 August 1997. For an overview of mediation in reinsurance cases, see J Lockey 'Providing a little reinsurance' (2000) 14(21) *The Lawyer* 33.

349 M Davies, G Davis and J Webb *Promoting Mediation: Report of a study of Bristol Law Society's Mediation Scheme in its preliminary phase*, 1996 Research & Policy Planning Unit Research Study no 21, The Law Society, at p 17.

350 See the section on Courts in Chapter 7.

351 Centre for Dispute Resolution *Resolutions*, No 22, at p 7. The Centre's 2000 statistics show that insurance disputes accounted for 4% of referrals, although professional negligence claims (with insurers involved) constituted 17% of referrals: CEDR '2000 statistics' *Resolutions*, No 26. The authors' 2000 survey of UK law firms indicated that insurance disputes accounted for 5.5% of referrals, although professional negligence claims accounted for a further 23.5% of referrals amongst the respondents to the survey.

352 A Broad 'Tackling the legal loopholes' *Post Magazine supplement*, 28 October 1999, p 5.

of claims managers in 1999 indicated that almost 70% preferred negotiation or other forms of dispute resolution to resolve insurance disputes, although 20% indicated a preference for mediation, and only about 6% for litigation.[353] These statistics show, in any event, that claims managers are more inclined towards early resolution of insurance disputes, rather than an adversarial approach.

Mediation has proved to be effective for the resolution of a wide range of insurance disputes, involving issues of both liability and quantum, in a wide range of subject areas, like products liability and professional negligence, and involving from a few thousand through to several million pounds. There is also scope for the use of mediation in a range of other insurance contexts, beyond disputes between insured and insurer, for instance claims by third parties over subrogation, between different insurers, and between insured and broker.

Dispute management efforts

Due to the volume of litigation, insurance companies strive to make litigation a controllable budget item. This requires a dispute management approach to litigation, developing early case review and budgeting.[354] ITT London and Edinburgh built, over a number of years, mediation into the management of its cases. It claimed to have saved more than £1m in professional fees in 1998 alone through the use of mediation.[355] Mediation also formed an integral part of the claims handling philosophy at the Solicitors' Indemnity Fund ('SIF'). During the 12 months to August 1999, 113 mediations took place, including one mediation which resolved over 180 claims, arising out of residential mortgage transactions in the early 1990s. Cost savings from that mortgage claim alone were estimated at up to £3m. In total, SIF's use of mediation is estimated to have saved the legal profession over £30m. SIF has enjoyed an 80% success rate using mediation.[356]

Dispute management efforts have extended beyond individual insurers to include industry-wide efforts. The International Underwriting Association of London (IUA) and Lloyd's Underwriter's Association (LUA) have formed a Working Party to promote mediation in the marine insurance market, in particular, third party claims, insurance coverage disputes and intra-market disputes. The Working Party will educate the insurance market about mediation and the long-term aim is to ensure that disruption to relationships in the industry does not occur due to disputation.[357] MAC (Market ADR Commitment) is another insurance industry initiative. It is a non-legally binding statement of intent by insurers to use ADR for the resolution of insurance disputes, initially focusing on professional indemnity claims. Signatories to this 'pledge' undertake to provide reasons why, in any particular case, ADR is considered inappropriate. If an insurer considers that the opposing insurer is being difficult about the ADR suggestion, reference can be made to a senior ADR representative, which has been appointed by each signatory.[358]

---

353   A Broad 'Tackling the legal loopholes' *Post Magazine supplement*, 28 October 1999, at p 5.
354   See the section on Dispute Management by Corporates/Industry in Chapter 10.
355   'Insurers join up' *Post Magazine*, 3 December 1998.
356   The authors thank SIF for this information. See also Solicitors Indemnity Fund *ADR settlement achieves major savings*, Press Release, 22 June 1999; and A Paton 'SIF's mediation support is vital' *The Lawyer*, 17 November 1998, at p 16.
357   D Taylor 'Press Release' *World Cargo News*, April 1999.
358   The authors thank the MAC signatories for information about the initiative. See also

Intellectual property disputes

The World Intellectual Property Organisation ('WIPO') has set up an Arbitration and Mediation Centre, which has the dual purpose, in relation to mediation, of a mediation administration and mediation resource centre. The Centre has developed a set of Mediation Rules, a Guide to mediation and a Standard mediation clause. The Centre's resource centre provides assistance in the drafting of ADR clauses; acts as intermediary between parties in dispute to discuss the suitability of the dispute for mediation; can appoint a mediator; arranges mediation conferences; and disseminates mediation publications. The Centre's services are open to all persons. Referrals of disputes to the Centre can occur either through a contract clause or by agreement between the parties. The Centre's Mediation Rules provide for the Centre to appoint a mediator. The Centre charges a registration fee, which is calculated by reference to the value of the mediation, and the mediator's fee is calculated either on an hourly or daily rate and there are minimum and maximum rates. Mediations administered by the Centre can take place anywhere in the world. The Centre can also, at the request of parties to a dispute, and for a fee, appoint a mediator, even in the case of mediations not administered by the Centre.[359] WIPO is collaborating with technology companies worldwide to establish an international mediation service for intellectual property disputes.[360] The other mediation scheme, established by WIPO, relates to domain names, and is discussed below.

Passing-off actions have provided a source of referrals to mediation. Mediation offers the opportunity to resolve such disputes in private, without additional exposure. To tackle 'look alike' disputes, household names in the grocery distribution industry launched a mediation service for members who became involved in these disputes.[361]

Cyber-squatting involves registration of a well known name, with which the registrant is not connected, in order to prevent the owner of the goodwill in that name from registering it. Litigation of disputes arising out of cyber-squatting,[362] such

---

MAC *Information Pack*, 1998. MAC signatories include A Grant Underwriting Agency, Aegon Insurance Company, AIG Europe (UK) Limited, Assitalia (UK) Limited, Chaucer Syndicates, Chartwell Underwriting Limited, Chiyoda Fire and Marine, Chubb Insurance Company of Europe, David Marshall & Others, Devonshire Claims Services Lloyd's Ltd, Equitas, Gan Insurance Company, HIH (UK) Limited, Hiscox Insurance Company Limited, Hiscox Syndicates Limited, Independent Insurance, ITT London and Edinburgh, Lombard General Insurance Co Ltd, PI Direct, RE Stone & Others, RJ Wallace & Others, Reliance National Insurance Ltd, Royal & Sun Alliance Ins Group PLC, Saturn Professional Risks Limited, SCOR (UK) Co Limited, Solicitors Indemnity Fund, Solicitors Indemnity Mutual Insurance, Standfast Insurance Services Limited, Swiss Re UK Limited and Trenwick International Limited.

359 WIPO Arbitration and Mediation Centre pamphlets: *The centre and its services*; *WIPO Mediation Rules*; *Guide to WIPO Mediation*; *Publications List*. See also F Gurry 'The Dispute Resolution Services of WIPO' (1999) 2(2) *Journal of International and Economic Law* 385.

360 J Fleming 'UN banking for mediation plans' *The Gazette*, 11 May 2000.

361 Household names like Birds Eye, Nestlé, Tesco, Proctor & Gamble, Safeways and United Biscuits signed up to the scheme: Centre for Dispute Resolution *Resolutions*, No 14, at p 2.

362 For example, *British Telecommunications plc v One in a Million* [1999] 1 WLR 903, CA.

as unfair competition, passing-off and trademark infringement, is costly.[363] Domain name registries run dispute resolution procedures, which may achieve cost savings. For example, the '.uk' domain is administered by Nominet UK Limited ('Nominet'). Nominet's dispute resolution procedure involves, as a first step, an attempt by senior executive staff of Nominet to facilitate a mutually acceptable resolution with the parties. If that intervention is not successful, Nominet may suspend a domain name. If the affected party is not satisfied with a suspension or a decision not to suspend, Nominet will, at that party's request, refer the matter to an independent expert for a recommendation. On the basis of that recommendation, Nominet will reconsider its earlier decision. If either party continues to be dissatisfied, the parties may agree to mediation, administered by the Centre for Dispute Resolution.

WIPO has developed an on-line dispute resolution system for disputes arising out of the registration of domain names. Their initial proposals distinguished between two systems of registration, gTLD-Mou and INternet ONE. The former creates seven new generic top level domains and the latter involves registration in a shared indexing system. WIPO proposed to resolve disputes in relation to the former system on-line using the following procedures, in turn:

- an Administrative Challenge Panel ('ACP') procedure, which would address the parties' rights in respect of a domain name, but would not provide monetary relief, other than the costs of the procedure;
- WIPO Mediation;
- in the case of an unsuccessful mediation, WIPO Expedited Arbitration.

In the case of disputes arising under the latter system, WIPO proposed on-line WIPO Expedited Arbitration. Following a consultation process, WIPO published its final report in 1999 on the management of internet names and addresses, which included a recommendation for mediation in the case of disputes over domain names, although not mandatory mediation.[364]

ICANN, the Internet Corporation for Assigned Names and Numbers, implemented its Uniform Domain Name Dispute Resolution Policy in 1999.[365] Its Policy has been adopted by all accredited domain-name registrars for domain names ending in .com, .net, and .org. It has also been adopted by certain managers of country-code top-level domains, like .nu, .tv and .ws. The Policy is between the registrar and its customer or domain-name holder. The Policy provides that most types of trademark-based domain-name disputes must be resolved by agreement, court action or arbitration before a registrar will cancel, suspend or transfer a domain name.[366] Its list of approved dispute resolution service providers[367] includes WIPO and e-Resolution.[368]

---

363 Apart from cost, the financial and psychological cost of enforcement frequently makes IP litigation 'a lottery'.

364 V Bindman 'IT body targets domain name abuse' *The Gazette*, 19 May 1999, at p 18.

365 Policy adopted on 26 August 1999 and implementation documents approved on 24 October 1999. For implementation schedule, refer to http://www.icann.org/udrp. For background, refer to Gilbert & Tobin solicitors 'Domain names: A view from the antipodes' *Mondaq Business Briefing*, 25 May 1999.

366 See M Weston 'Domain names – disputes and resolution: Part 1' (2000) 16(4) *CLSR* 224 for analysis of the new arrangements.

367 ICANN's principal documents include the Policy, Rules for the Policy, List of approved dispute resolution service provider and information concerning approval processes for dispute resolution service providers. ICANN also provides information on proceedings

It is likely that, as it becomes simpler to predict and obtain a quick resolution from courts, parties may opt for litigation, rather than ADR, for resolution of domain name disputes. Even if this were the case, intellectual property provides opportunities for creative use of mediation in a range of contexts.[369]

International issues

Mediation is a method of dispute settlement prescribed by the Charter of the United Nations.[370] The Security Council will assist in the settlement of disputes, which are likely to endanger international peace and security, but may call upon the relevant parties to attempt mediation.[371] Bush and Folger provide two rationales for mediation in international peace-keeping:

- the social justice rationale: mediation is used to organise individuals around common interests; and
- the transformation rationale: mediation transforms society through acknowledgment and empathy, and by providing people with a sense of their value and strength.[372]

Mediation Network Northern Ireland considers that the following assumptions also underpin international mediation:

- mediation serves justice, by seeking to uphold equity, diversity and independence;
- mediation transforms conflict, by enabling people to deal constructively with it; and
- not all conflicts are suitable for mediation.[373]

The selection of a mediator is critical to the success of an international mediation. It has been suggested that it is desirable that mediators in this context have a reputation for involvement in peace initiatives or charities without strategic interests.[374] The

---

commenced under the Policy, including a list of proceedings and statistical summary of proceedings: refer to http://www.icann.org/udrp

368 See http://www.disputes.org; and see the section on On-line Mediation in Chapter 10. In the US statutory enforcement under the US Anticybersquatting Consumer Protection Act 1999 provides an alternative for companies who seek to protect their on-line rights.

369 For example, a Mediation Board was developed within the Virtual Component Exchange to resolve disputes between supplier and buyer of silicon chips. The Exchange was designed to watermark silicon intellectual property blocks, allowing silicon intellectual property providers to know how many chips have been used in their blocks. Previously, silicon intellectual property providers sought one-off licensing fees because they could not track the number of chips manufactured using their blocks.

370 Charter of the United Nations, San Francisco, 26 June 1945, TF 67; Cnd 7015, art 33, para 1.

371 Ibid, at para 2.

372 R A Bush and J P Folger *The Promise of Mediation: Responding to Conflict through Empowerment and Recognition*, Jossey-Bass, San Francisco, 1994.

373 B McAllister, Paper presented at conference on 'Promoting justice and peace through reconciliation and co-existence', American University, Washington DC, 20 February 1999.

374 S Marsh *The lessons of Oslo*, 1998, available at http://adrr.com/adr4/oslo.htm. See also the section on selection of mediators in Chapter 4.

process used in international mediation does not normally mirror the classic model of mediation, as frequently mediation is conducted entirely in caucus, which is believed to focus the minds on the purpose of the process and avoids posturing. It is also common in the context of international mediation for agreements to be reached in stages, although this may also lead to the potential for escalation of disputes as the piecemeal approach may benefit one side over another.[375] The other distinguishing characteristic of international mediation is that the solution reached in mediation, even if it is final, is unlikely to lead to immediate peace as achieving peace is an organic long-term process. Mediation agreements frequently provide immediate conflict prevention measures, whereas longer-term measures, such as peace building, require the underlying causes of conflict to be tackled.[376]

A range of organisations in the UK provide conflict prevention and resolution services in the context of international disputes, including the Foreign and Common-wealth Office, the European Commission, Conciliation Resources, the Research Institute for the Study of Conflict and Terrorism, the Northern Ireland Community Relations Council and the Initiative on Conflict Resolution and Ethnicity (INCORE).[377]

Other than in relation to international peace-keeping efforts, mediation is also used in other international contexts. For example, the Antarctic Treaty Act 1967 seeks to ensure that the Antarctic is used for peaceful purposes only. The UK has agreed that if it is involved in a dispute with another contracting party in relation to the Antarctic Treaty, an attempt will be made to resolve the dispute by negotiation or mediation.[378] The Extradition (Drug Trafficking) Order 1997 provides in Schedule 1 that in the case of disputes over the interpretation or application of the Convention Against Illicit Traffic in Narcotic Drugs and Psychotropic Substances, the parties should attempt negotiation or mediation. The Social Security (United States of America) Order 1997 provides, in Schedule 1, a supplementary agreement amending the Agreement on Social Security between the governments of the UK and the US. The Schedule provides that, if disagreement cannot be resolved through negotiation, mediation or another mutually agreed procedure will be used.[379]

---

375 S Marsh *The lessons of Oslo*, 1998, available at http://adrr.com/adr4/oslo.htm. See also the section on selection of mediators in Chapter 4.

376 D Fatchett *Creating and expanding opportunities for preventing conflict*, Launch of Carnegie Commission's Report on preventing deadly conflict, 8 January 1998.

377 Foreign and Commonwealth Office, Conflict Prevention Section, K149, London SW1A 2AH; phone: 020 7270 5987; fax: 020 7270 3910; email: docs.und.fco@gtnet.gov.uk; website: http://www.fco.gov.uk. European Commission, Policy Planning Unit, 1A Rue de la Loi, 200 Brussels, D1049, Belgium; phone: 32-229-4091; fax: 32-229-8625; website: http://europa.eu.int. Conciliation Resources, Lancaster House, 32 Islington High Street, London N1 9LH; phone: 020 7278 2588; fax: 020 7837 0337; website: http://www.c-r.org. Research Institute of the Study of Conflict and Terrorism, PO Box 1179, Leamington Spa, CV32 6ZY; phone: 01926 833307. Northern Ireland Community Relations Council, 6 Murray St, Belfast, BT1 6DN; phone: 01232 311881; fax: 01232 235208; website: http://www.community-relations.org.uk. INCORE, Aberfoyle House, Northland Rd, Londonderry, BT48 7JA, Northern Ireland; phone: 01504 375500; website: http://www.incore.ulst.ac.uk.

378 Antarctic Treaty, art XI, Sch 1, the Antarctic Treaty Act 1967.

379 Amending art 21 of the Agreement.

Multi-party actions

Mediation can be a particularly effective means of resolving multi-party actions given the range of competing interests which may need to be reconciled. However, there are likely to be logistical difficulties in obtaining the consent of all parties to participate in mediation. One way of addressing this problem is to start the mediation with the parties who agree to participate, in the expectation that other parties will join in the process, for fear of losing out on a good settlement. If the mediation does not encourage the additional parties to participate, the mediation can still proceed and a resolution can be reached with those who participate in the mediation, unless the parties left outside the process are critical either to the success of the mediation or to the workability of any agreement reached.[380]

Another logistical difficulty in a mediation involving multiple parties is that the mediator will need to take almost a project management approach to setting up the mediation as there may be disagreements between the parties in relation to the administration, for instance, over venue; substantive issues, like the issues in dispute; and even the type of mediation process, for instance, whether the mediator should take an evaluative or facilitative approach or whether the mediator would be assisted by a further mediator. It is common for a number of shorter meetings to take place between the mediator and the parties or each party ahead of the mediation in order to discuss these issues. It is also common, at the mediation itself, to determine an agenda for the mediation, which may require a degree of facilitation by the mediator to ensure that all parties involved in the mediation are satisfied with the proposals. Multi-party mediations also provide an ideal opportunity for working parties during the mediation, when discussion on a particular issue, involving a number of the parties might break impasse.[381] Internal conflicts within individual camps frequently lead to impasse on issues, like whether to settle, on what terms and how to apportion responsibility for any settlement.[382]

In his final *Access to Justice* Report, Lord Woolf expressed concern over a particular category of multi-party actions, product liability group actions.[383] A Lord Chancellor's Department Consultation Paper on multi-party actions was issued in 1997 and in June 1999 a Second Consultation Paper was issued, which took into account responses to the first Consultation Paper and included draft Civil Procedure Rules and Practice Directions, the effect of which may be to dilute the use of mediation in this context. For example, the Rules suggest that a claim should be identified as a test claim, in which case it should not be settled without the court's permission, although the Lord Chancellor's Department is considering whether the court should have the power to prevent settlement altogether. The result in the test case should, it is argued, make it possible to negotiate other claims, although

---

380 For an example which involved opt-in and opt-out issues, consider the Agent Orange facilitated settlement: P H Schuck *Agent Orange on trial: mass toxic disasters in the courts*, The Belknap Press of Harvard University Press, Cambridge, 1986, at Chapter 8.
381 For further information see M Lesnick and J Ehrmann 'Selected strategies for managing multi-party disputes' (1987) 16 *Mediation Quarterly* 21 and see Part II for further discussion.
382 P H Schuck, op cit, at p 147. Shapiro considers that multi-party mediations generally turn on issues of market share, degree of fault and ability to pay: D Shapiro 'Pushing the envelope – selective techniques for tough mediations' (2000) *ADRLJ* 117, at p 121.
383 Lord Woolf *Access to Justice: Final Report*, July 1996, at Section IV.

mediation would be appropriate in those cases where there is a reason why direct negotiations are difficult or unsuccessful. For example, a party may argue that the facts are sufficiently different in one particular case to distinguish the result in the test case and may wish to use mediation to achieve a result better than that in the test case.

However, Lord Woolf recommended in his Final Report that there is a strong case for a court to approve all multi-party settlements involving lump sum payments to ensure that those settlements are fair. He suggested that, where the minority objected to a proposed settlement, the judge should hear those objections and resolve points of difficulty in borderline cases, which, once again, would dilute the use of mediation in this context.[384] Notwithstanding his concerns and recommendations:

- As a result of risk management procedures, like product recall and self-regulation, the level of product liability litigation has remained steady.[385]
- There are a number of reported mediations of product liability disputes, involving multi-party actions.[386]

In comparison, in the US, multi-party actions have frequently been resolved through elaborate judicial mediation efforts. Perhaps the most high profile was the litigation over Agent Orange, which settled through mediation by three Special Masters appointed by the District Court for the Eastern District of New York.[387] One of those mediators, David Shapiro, is an international mediator, now based in London.

Parades and public order

Following the Drumcree Parade in Portadown Northern Ireland in 1996, the Government established the Independent Review of Parades and Marches. The body published The North Report in 1997, which provided the basis for the Public Processions (Northern Ireland) Act 1998. The Act set up a Parades Commission to promote understanding of the issues concerning public processions in Northern Ireland, and to reach conclusions in relation to disputed parades.

The Act requires all public processions, with some exceptions, to be notified to the Commission. As s 2 of the Act imposes a duty on the Commission to promote and facilitate mediation as a means of resolving disputes concerning public processions, it relies on a team of Authorised Officers, managed by the Mediation Network for Northern Ireland, to:[388]

- gather information about each parade and invite submissions; and
- attempt to facilitate local resolution of any differences by promoting discussion and exploring options.

---

384 Lord Woolf *Access to Justice: Final Report*, July 1996, at p 245.
385 B Hunt 'Legal risk management' 18(6) *Litigation*, at p 19.
386 See, for example, A Spooner 'Woolf offers solution for business disputes' *Birmingham Post*, 22 October 1999, at p 22.
387 See P H Schuck 'The role of judges in settling complex cases: The Agent Orange example' (1986) 53 *University of Chicago Law Review* 337; P H Schuck *Agent Orange on trial: mass toxic disasters in the courts*, The Belknap Press of Harvard University Press, Cambridge, 1986; and see generally D Provine *Settlement strategies for Federal District Court Judges*, Federal Judicial Center, Washington DC, 1986, at pp 50–1.
388 See the section on Mediation Organisations in Chapter 7.

If mediation is not successful, the Commission issues determinations, which place conditions on individual parades. Although there are concerns that the Commission has become an adjudicative, rather than a mediatory, body,[389] the Commission is giving consideration to the further development of mediation.[390]

Pensions disputes

The Goode Report suggested the establishment of internal disputes procedures for pension funds. Since then, a range of statutes have mandated, in the context of pension schemes, internal dispute resolution procedures.[391] A number of regulations provide detail about internal dispute resolution procedures,[392] which encourage the use of conciliatory dispute resolution techniques at an early stage in pension disputes.

Other developments have also encouraged the use of mediation for the resolution of pensions disputes. For example, law firm Hammond Suddards Edge has run a mediation programme for pensions disputes.[393] Other developments, however, may reduce the need for mediation for the resolution of pensions disputes. For instance, law firm Linklaters is offering a conditional fee arrangement to clients appealing decisions from the Pensions Ombudsman.[394]

In a reported case of mediation over a £7.3m shortfall in a pension scheme, the mediation successfully resolved three years of litigation after three days. The mediation in that case is significant as it provides an example of a project-management approach to mediation. There were a number of parties and co-mediators, who spent almost two days in pre-mediation planning. Due to the range of issues involved, including those against the pension fund trustees, legal advisers and bankers, there were effectively six simultaneous mediations.[395]

Personal injury actions

Overview of UK developments

One of the findings of Genn's study of the Central London County Court Mediation Pilot was that personal injury actions are suitable for mediation even when liability

---

389 'UUP draws up guidelines for Parades Commission' *Belfast Telegraph*, 25 November 1999.

390 The Peaceful Assembly Act 1992 QLD (Australia) provides, in s 13, that no refusal to authorise a public assembly can occur without a mediation having taken place first.

391 For example, Pensions Act 1995, ss 10, 50, 124 and 174.

392 For example, the Occupational Pension Schemes (Internal Dispute Resolution Procedures) Regulations 1996 (enabled by the Pensions Act 1995); and the Occupational Pension Schemes (Internal Dispute Resolution Procedures) Regulations (Northern Ireland) 1996 (enabled by SI 1995/3213) NI 22.

393 'Winning solutions' *The Law Society Gazette*, 11 November 1998.

394 S Allen 'City firm turns to conditional fees' *The Law Society Gazette*, 25 August 1999, at p 4.

395 Centre for Dispute Resolution 'The value and use of time in mediation' *Resolutions*, Spring 1999. See also R Ellison 'The pensions seer' (1999) 28(10) *Pensions World* 58.

and quantum are in issue.[396] Opposing views were expressed in the Bristol Law Society Mediation Scheme, for instance:

'. . . a maximum of 5 out of every 100 cases . . . could be mediated because in most there was no scope for compromise – either the plaintiff had a broken leg or he didn't . . .'[397]

Judgments also provide examples of personal injury cases, crying out for mediation, but where the lawyers did not consider the option:

'. . . [this] was a classic case for mediation by a mediator with experience in this field of litigation. If this dispute had been referred to mediation, with the defendant's insurers present, it would almost certainly have settled six years ago . . .'[398]

1999 and 2000 statistics from the Centre for Dispute Resolution indicate that personal injury cases account for the smallest share of mediations.[399] Notwithstanding Genn's findings that mediation is suitable for personal injury cases, in the Central London County Court Mediation Pilot there was a very low take-up of mediation in personal injury cases, in less than 1% of cases.[400] Genn's interviews revealed that mediation was frequently rejected[401] on account that a case was considered too serious or complex.[402] In some cases, Genn found that mediation was not rejected, but postponed until a medical condition had settled. As one respondent to Genn's study explained, continuing symptoms could open solicitors to negligence claims if settlement occurred too early.[403]

Genn highlighted that mediation, in particular early in the proceedings, appears to be incompatible with the traditional personal injury defence strategy of making the plaintiff wait before any offers are made.[404] At a conference of the Association of Personal Injury Lawyers at the end of 1998, reluctance was explained by personal

---

396 H Genn *Central London County Court Mediation Pilot: Evaluation Report*, LCD Research Series, No 5/98, at p vii.
397 View of one personal injury lawyer interviewed for the study: see M Davies, G Davis and J Webb *Promoting Mediation: Report of a study of Bristol Law Society's Mediation Scheme in its preliminary phase*, 1996 Research & Policy Planning Unit Research Study no 21, The Law Society, at p 22.
398 *Walsh v Misseldine* [2000] EWCA 10, CA. A further example is *Gale v Superdrug Stores plc* [1996] 1 WLR 1089, CA. There are similar examples world-wide. For an Australian example, in the 'Voyager claims', *Commonwealth v Clark* (1993) Aust Torts Reporter 62 at 127, Beach J expressed displeasure at the delays in the litigation and advised the parties and their lawyers that mediation was suitable. The parties agreed to mediate, saving the courts, it was estimated, between 3.5 and six years of sitting time. In Canada also, in *Godi and O'Connor v Toronto Transit Commission*, Ontario Court of Justice (General Division) Court no 95-CU-89529, the court took exception to the delays, and in that case ordered the parties to mediate.
399 Centre for Dispute Resolution *Press Release*, 26 April 1999 and CEDR '2000 statistics' *Resolutions*, No 26. The 2000 statistics indicated that 3% of the Centre's referrals were personal injury cases. The respondents to the authors' 2000 survey of UK law firms indicated a smaller percentage, 1.2%, of mediated cases relating to personal injury claims.
400 H Genn *Central London County Court Mediation Pilot: Evaluation Report*, op cit, at pp 18–19.
401 Ibid, at p 33.
402 Ibid, at p 34.
403 Ibid, at p 130.
404 Ibid, at p 32.

injury lawyers to participate in mediation, citing in support that mediation could be expensive and might not be appropriate in complex cases. It was recognised, however, that there is considerable prejudice and ignorance about mediation amongst lawyers and insurance companies who deal with personal injury litigation.[405]

Despite the disappointing results of various mediation schemes and the attitudes of personal injury practitioners, there have been a number of developments, which provide more optimism for the application of mediation in this field. Bunkers, a Brighton law firm, won a Centre for Dispute Resolution award for its mediation pilot scheme for its personal injury clients. The scheme involved the training of staff and clients in ADR and ADR case review systems. Although the pre-action protocol for personal injury claims does not include ADR, the guidance notes provide a reminder that litigation should be used as a last resort.

The Centre for Dispute Resolution has also launched a personal injury mediation scheme, with the following features:

- 'strategic' mediation for catastrophic personal injury cases, like serious head or spinal injury cases, with the aim of facilitating early communication between claimant and insurer and encouraging creative solutions;[406] and
- 'time-limited' mediation for personal injury claims under £15,000, providing fixed-cost three-hour mediations.

Rationales

Commentators worldwide have sought to explain the behaviour of parties in personal injury litigation and settlement negotiations. A UK commentator has suggested that if personal injury litigation could yield a valuable precedent, this provides a justifiable rationale for rejection of mediation.[407] An American study of personal injury cases indicated that plaintiffs considered trial procedures fairer than settlement discussions as trials gave their cases more respectful treatment.[408] An Australian study of personal injury cases has explained the reason why settlements occur late in personal injury litigation by 'motivational mismatch'. The motivation of claimants and defendants is negatively correlated in the early stages of litigation, caused by claimants' reluctance to accept less and defendants' willingness to offer less at an early stage in litigation.[409] The study sought to explain why defendants, usually insurers, are unwilling to settle in the early stage of proceedings when they would be able to achieve more favourable terms, and concluded that:

---

405 'Personal injury groups slam forced mediation' *The Lawyer*, 20 October 1998.
406 S Allen 'Mediation plan' *The Gazette*, 8 December 1999, at p 4; and T Allen 'CEDR unveils strategic PI initiative' *Resolutions*, Issue No 25, at p 4.
407 For a wider discussion of public interest and personal injury litigation, see M Armstrong 'ADR and the public interest in personal injury' [1994] *Journal of personal injury litigation* 178.
408 E A Lind et al 'In the eye of the beholder: tort litigants' evaluations of their experience in the civil justice system' (1990) 24(4) *Law & Society Review* 953. See also P Randolph 'Scepticism about mediation' (2000) 150 *NLJ* 565.
409 R Davies 'Negotiating personal injury cases: A survey of the attitudes and beliefs of personal injury lawyers' (1994) 68 *The Australian Law Journal* 734.

- complex psychological factors are at play in personal injury negotiations;
- claimants are risk averse and, accordingly, may accept less as the case approaches trial.[410]

The study concluded that, although early mediation might provide a solution to 'motivational mismatch', the promotion of earlier settlement, through mediation or other means, might not necessarily modify the negotiation tactics of defendants, who derive benefit from exploiting the risk averse nature of claimants.[411] In the UK the Part 36 offer could tackle the issue of 'motivational mismatch' by providing an incentive for early settlement of personal injury cases.[412]

Comparisons with other jurisdictions

In Queensland Australia early neutral evaluation, instead of mediation, has been the ADR process utilised, to considerable success, for the early resolution of personal injury cases. It has been effective as it is backed up with potential cost consequences, as in the case of Part 36 offers in the UK. If a court's decision is no more favourable overall to a party who challenged the early neutral evaluation, the costs of the entire action, including the appraisal, is awarded against the challenger. The neutral provides a determination, which will be binding on the parties if neither party files with the court an election to proceed to trial, which, if is done, has to be done within 28 days from the neutral's evaluation.[413] In New South Wales, conciliation has been used to resolve personal injury claims occurring at the workplace, with high success rates.[414] A mandatory mediation scheme has operated in Ontario since 1990 for disputes involving personal injury motor vehicle claims.[415]

In the US the 'McDonalds coffee case' has provided encouragement to use mediation for the resolution of personal injury claims. In that case the claimants had been scalded by a cup of McDonalds' coffee, the temperature of which was about 180–190 degrees celsius. The plaintiff had spent over a week in hospital, received skin grafts and requested $20,000 to cover her medical bills. McDonalds refused to pay and later refused mediation, insisting on a trial instead. A jury awarded the plaintiff $160,000 in actual damages and punished McDonalds with a $2.7m punitive damages award. The case settled after post-verdict mediation.[416]

Planning disputes

In a number of jurisdictions, mediation is used widely for the resolution of planning disputes, such as zoning, building and development applications and traffic manage-

---

410 R Davies 'Negotiating personal injury cases: A survey of the attitudes and beliefs of personal injury lawyers' (1994) 68 *The Australian Law Journal* 734 at 748–9.
411 Ibid, at 741 and 749.
412 See the section on Civil Justice Reforms in Chapter 7.
413 Moynihan J *Case Appraisal*, QLD Supreme Court Report, Spring Quarter 1997.
414 T Beed et al *The role of conciliation*, Civil Justice Research Centre and Law Foundation of NSW, Sydney, 1990.
415 E Fleischmann and N Bussin *The institutionalisation of ADR: a case study of the Ontario Insurance Commission*, Toronto, 1996.
416 Butterworths personal injury litigation service *Personal injury litigation outside the United Kingdom*, at para [1095].

ment proposals.[417] Apart from avoiding litigation, mediation allows stakeholder involvement, encouraging improved communication and problem solving in the general community. It can also lead to narrowing of objections and creative solutions.[418]

In a 1998 Consultation Paper, examining the protection and management of sites of special scientific interest in the UK, ADR was suggested in relation to disputes over financial provisions in an offer of management agreement. Mediation was also considered to have scope for mediation in cases of refusal to give consent to undertake operations on sites of special or scientific interest.[419]

A UK pilot study has been carried out by the Planning Inspectorate to assess mediation as a possible alternative to the appeal process in view of the appeal system's costly and time-consuming nature. The pilot arose from DETR's statement, 'Modernising Planning', which included mediation as one of a number of proposals aimed at improving planning procedures. In September 1998 a brochure was produced, in order to publicise the mediation pilot. The Planning Inspectorate wrote to local planning authorities in November 1998 and April 1999, inviting them to participate in the pilot. 51 cases were mediated as part of the pilot. The majority of cases related to 'householder' applications, mostly involving design issues, although a number of cases involved policy issues. The main findings of the pilot were:

- planning disputes involving design issues are best suited to mediation, whereas disputes involving policy issues alone are least suitable;
- mediation is likely to result in only a modest reduction in appeals; and
- delay is likely to occur in the decision-making process if mediation were incorporated into the planning system.[420]

The report made the following recommendations:

- voluntary mediation should be encouraged;
- a permanent mediation service for planning disputes would be beneficial;
- a best practice guide on the use of mediation for planning disputes should be developed; and
- study is needed on the use of mediation in other planning contexts.[421]

If mediation is to have a wider role in the resolution of planning disputes, a number of issues will need to be addressed. At which stage, for instance, in the planning process from pre-application to post-appeal stage should mediation take place? Is there any reason why mediation would be inappropriate at any particular stage? Mediation before determination would, for example, require the period for determination of a planning application to be suspended or extended. The UK pilot study referred to Australian research,[422] and concluded that the most productive points of intervention in the planning system are likely to be:

---

417 Mediation in this context is used widely in the US and Australia.
418 E Munoz 'ADR in local government – using dispute resolution to resolve planning disputes' (1998) 1(2) *The ADR Bulletin* 24.
419 DETR *Sites of special scientific interest: Better management and protection,* Consultation Paper, 10 September 1998. See also DETR *Outcome of Consultation Exercise,* August 1999.
420 M Welbank et al *Mediation in the Planning System,* DETR, London, May 2000, at p 11.
421 Ibid, at p 12. The need for this may have been highlighted by *Dyson v Secretary of State for the Environment, Transport and the Regions* (1998) 75 P&CR 506.
422 Ibid, at pp 18 and 19.

- during the planning application processing stage, after the Development Control officer has visited the site, but before a formal recommendation has been made by him, since mediation may effect scheme modifications desired by the officer;
- after the Development Control Committee has met, as mediation may afford the Committee an opportunity to accept a revised scheme; and
- after the Committee has determined and refused an application, as mediation may allow the applicant to determine if there is a way forward, before appeal.[423]

Another issue is whether external or internal mediators should be used. In Australia, one local authority employed an in-house mediator, who was separated from council decision-making processes.[424] Further options would be to create a mediation panel, using a combination of internal and external mediators. In New Zealand mediation is provided for planning disputes under the Resource Management Act 1991. The Act allows the Planning Tribunal, of its own motion, to direct mediation before or at any time during the course of a hearing.[425] In Ontario planning mediation is conducted by the Provincial Facilitators Office or the Board of Negotiation, which is part of the Ontario Municipal Board.

Probate and trusts disputes

Probate and trust disputes can create extreme difficulties for resolution due to potentially complex family dynamics, strained relationships, fixed expectations and emotional issues. Mediation can achieve timely resolution, which could be important if a family business, for instance, requires certainty and continuation. It can help to repair or enhance relations between trustees and beneficiaries, which is particularly important if trust administration will take some time. Hidden interests are rarely easily disclosed by one family member to another or to trustees and executives, and mediation provides an opportunity for important interests to be taken into account. Mediation may also increase the probability of reconciliation between family members.[426]

The Administration of Justice Act 1985, s 49 permits a probate claim to be compromised without a trial if every 'relevant beneficiary' has consented. There will be occasions when a mediated agreement will need court sanction, for instance, if the rights of the unborn are affected.

Professional negligence claims

As the respondents to the Bristol Law Society Mediation Pilot indicated, mediation for the resolution of professional negligence claims has the advantage of providing

---

423 M Welbank et al *Mediation in the Planning System*, DETR, London, May 2000, at p 67.
424 E Munoz 'ADR in local government – using dispute resolution to resolve planning disputes' (1998) 1(2) *The ADR Bulletin* 24 at 25.
425 R Somerville 'Mediation and the planning tribunal' (1996) *Lawtalk*, Issue 486.
426 See P Hodson 'Mediation: an alternative to trust litigation' (2000) 6(10) *Trusts and Trustees* 11.

a private method of dispute resolution. The recognition that mediation provides advantages in the resolution of these disputes is reflected in the statistics currently available and the take-up of mediation for the resolution of professional negligence claims. For example, the Centre for Dispute Resolution's statistics for 1998 indicated that professional negligence claims constituted 19% of the Centre's mediations, and in 1999 the figure had risen to 22%.[427] The figure had fallen to 17% in 2000.[428] Those statistics also indicate that mediation is being used to resolve negligence claims by a wide range of professionals, including solicitors, architects, surveyors, insurance brokers and estate agents. The Centre's statistics show that three out of four professional negligence cases mediated by the Centre between 1997 and 1998 involved solicitors and that solicitors enjoy a higher success rate, when compared to the Centre's overall average success rate, and that this pattern has continued.[429] Genn's study of the Central London County Court Mediation Pilot indicated that in about 5% of professional negligence cases both parties agreed to mediate; in about 4% of cases the plaintiff alone wished to mediate; and that in one-fifth of professional negligence cases the defendant alone sought to mediate. Accordingly, although 5% of professional negligence cases were mediated, in about 29% of the cases at least one party had sought to mediate.[430]

The use of mediation for the resolution of professional negligence claims received public attention following reports of resolution through mediation of the De Lorean case. The mediation related to a 12-year litigation brought by the Government against an accountancy firm for alleged negligence in auditing the De Lorean sports car company. The mediation is significant, in part as it achieved a resolution of a long-standing dispute involving many millions of pounds in legal fees alone, and in part as the mediation occurred after the Commercial Court ordered the parties to mediate despite their protests.[431]

The pre-action protocol for professional negligence claims envisages the use of mediation. It provides that parties can agree at any stage to attempt mediation. If a party is approached with a suggestion to mediate, the protocol sets out the options available to the responding party:

- to agree; or
- if the suggestion is premature, to explain what the appropriate timing should be; or
- if some other form of ADR is considered appropriate, to give reasons for that belief; or

---

427 R Verkaik 'Survey finds city firms turn to mediation for negligence cases' *The Law Society Gazette*, 15 July 1998, at p 8.
428 Centre for Dispute Resolution '2000 statistics' *Resolutions*, No 26. The authors' 2000 survey of UK law firms revealed that, of the mediations, with which the respondents to that survey had been involved, 23.5% were professional negligence claims.
429 Ibid; and see M Rose 'More law firms turn to mediation as a way to settle negligence claims' *The Law Society Gazette*, 6 May 1999. The authors' survey of UK law firms indicated that, of the professional negligence cases mediated, 58% related to lawyers, 12% to accountants, 12% to architects, 5% to brokers, 5% to valuers, 3.4% to engineers, 3.4% to surveyors and 1.7% to doctors.
430 H Genn *Central London County Court Mediation Pilot: Evaluation Report*, LCD Research Series, No 5/98, at p 19.
431 See R Verkaik 'Commercial Court imposes ADR order to end De Lorean battle' *The Law Society Gazette*, 19 November 1997, at p 10.

- if they disagree that ADR is appropriate, to give reasons.

The protocol also provides that, if any alternative method of dispute resolution, whether or not under some other pre-action procedure, is considered appropriate by the parties, the protocol can be suspended for that other method of dispute resolution to be used. However, if these other methods fail to achieve a resolution of the dispute, the protocol for professional negligence claims should be used before litigation is commenced.[432]

Property-related disputes

An overview

The Centre for Dispute Resolution's 1999 statistics showed that 28% of the Centre's mediations for that year related to construction or property disputes.[433] A 1997 poll by the Royal Institution of Chartered Surveyors ('RICS') of 200 property lawyers in England and Wales indicated that 70% considered that mediation is an effective means of resolving a wide range of property disputes.[434] Mediation in the context of property disputes offers an opportunity to re-structure, usually longer-term, arrangements, for instance, in relation to service charge disputes, rent reviews and tenancy renewals. Even in the context of unpaid rent disputes, mediation can provide an opportunity, especially where there are trading or other reasons why the rent is unpaid, to make alternative arrangements, which perhaps over time will result in the rent being paid.

One disadvantage of mediation in property disputes, especially lease disputes, is the potential power imbalance between the parties, particularly where the landlord is a large corporate landlord. A mediator should be alert to the existence of any such power imbalance. In addition, power imbalances between landlords and tenants vary with economic conditions, so that power imbalance is likely to favour a tenant in an economic recession. In Australia, mediation has been statutorily mandated in the case of disputes over retail leases,[435] as a means of creating a balance of power between the parties. The rationale appears to be that, by forcing landlords to mediate, it is possible to avoid the 'take it or leave it' philosophy, tying tenants into onerous leases, where the landlord is a large company, and the tenant's only contact with that landlord is through on-site managers, whose aim is to protect the landlord's interests.[436] Mediation has also been statutorily mandated in Australia in relation to the management of strata schemes[437] and retirement villages[438] and in the case of native title disputes.[439]

---

432 Professional negligence draft pre-action protocol, July 1999.
433 Centre for Dispute Resolution *Press Release*, 26 April 1999.
434 Reported in RICS News on their website at http://www.rics.org.uk/csm/archives/nov97
435 For example, Retail Shop Leases Act 1984 (QLD) and Retail Leases Act 1994 (NSW).
436 See P Prindable 'Is mediation an alternative in commercial lease dispute resolution?' (1994) 5 *Australian Dispute Resolution Journal* 99.
437 For example, Strata Schemes Management Act 1996 (NSW).
438 For example, Retirement Villages Act 1999 (QLD).
439 Native Title Act 1993 (Cth).

The Royal Institution of Chartered Surveyors dispute resolution service

RICS offers a mediation service for property-related disputes. RICS will then contact the other party to the dispute free of charge, in order to attempt to achieve an agreement to mediate. If the parties agree to mediate, the President of RICS can appoint a mediator. The Service has a standard form of Mediation Agreement, and the fees and costs of the mediation are agreed with the parties before the mediation begins. There are a wide range of disputes which have been handled by the Service, including:

- rent reviews;
- lease renewals;
- land boundary disputes;
- land valuation disputes;
- landlord and tenant disputes; and
- local authority housing disputes.[440]

RICS has also designed a Mediation Scheme, in conjunction with the Country Landowners Association ('CLA'), which aims to resolve compulsory purchase disputes. The Scheme was devised in response to expensive, wieldy and time-consuming litigation in the Lands Tribunal. The Scheme provides a fixed cost, one day mediation. These costs are shared by the parties. The Scheme provides that the parties should endeavour to conduct the mediation within the following timetable:

- application for appointment of mediator, within one week of date of formal claim;
- four weeks for mediation preparation;
- one week for exchange of statements of case;
- two weeks until mediation;
- one day for the mediation.

It is hoped that mediation, even if unsuccessful, will clarify the issues and help claimants to decide whether to seek a Lands Tribunal decision.[441]

Housing and tenancy disputes

Lord Woolf in his final *Access to Justice* Report recommended the use of mediation to resolve housing disputes and that information about mediation schemes should be provided via county courts, solicitors, law centres and other agencies.[442] In 1996 the Independent Housing Ombudsman set up a mediation scheme, under the Housing Act 1996, to which housing disputes in England could be referred, either by tenants living in housing association properties or by landlords of certain private properties.[443] The scheme has been used to mediate a wide range of housing disputes, including transfers and allocations, disrepair, harassment and determination of rent

---

440 The Royal Institution of Chartered Surveyors booklets *Mediation* and *Solving property problems*.
441 'Commercial property' *The Journal (Newcastle)*, 18 November 1998, at p 40.
442 Lord Woolf *Access to Justice: Final Report*, July 1996, at Chapter 16.
443 It does not include local authority landlords, who are covered by the Local Government Ombudsmen.

and service charges.[444] In Scotland the Housing Association Ombudsman investigates complaints about housing associations and co-operatives registered with Scottish Homes, and offers a mediation service. The availability of mediation via the Ombudsman should be considered by a funded client and could be a factor for refusal to fund full representation.[445]

The National Approved Letting Scheme (NALS) has a mediation scheme, which can be used by tenants if they are dissatisfied with a letting agent. The Advice, Information and Mediation Service (AIMS) offers mediation for disputes in relation to sheltered housing in England and Wales. Community mediation organisations also provide mediation services for a wide range of landlord/tenants and leasehold disputes. In Scotland the mediation scheme run by the Edinburgh Citizens Advice Bureau can be used in the case of disputes over rent deposits.

In Australia, tenancy disputes are mediated in accordance with statute, which requires the mediator to provide a record of whether the parties participated in mediation and whether they reached agreement in mediation. Provided that the consent of the parties is obtained, the record can also refer to the terms of the agreement.[446] In New Zealand also, the Residential Tenancies Act 1986 established mediation as a dispute resolution option for tenancy disputes.

Hedge disputes

There have been a number of hedge disputes in the UK, resulting in years of litigation and legal costs, requiring in some cases that the properties bordering on the hedge in question be sold to cover legal costs. In one example, a boundary dispute began in 1979, lasted 17 years and resulted in £100,000 in court costs.

In order to tackle these problems, the Government launched a consultation exercise, to identify not only the extent of the problem, but also possible solutions. The Consultation Paper identified mediation as a possible solution for resolving hedge disputes.[447] A difficulty in using mediation for the resolution of hedge disputes is that mediation requires the goodwill of the parties to be effective. Responses to the Paper suggested that mediation could be incorporated into a new statutory complaint procedure.[448]

A particular advantage of mediation in this context is that frequently hedge disputes are part of a wider problem or involve other issues, which may not be uncovered using adversarial dispute resolution. Mediation also has the potential advantage of

---

444 Enquiries at the Ombudsman's indicated the Scheme's procedures may be changed.
445 *The Funding Code – decision making guidance*, June 2000. For more detail, see the section on Funding in Chapter 9.
446 For example, Residential Tenancies Act 1995 (SA) and Residential Tenancies Regulations (ACT). See the section on Compulsion or Encouragement to Mediate in Chapter 9 for a discussion of mediator reporting issues.
447 Department of the Environment, Transport and the Regions (DETR) *High hedges: Possible solutions*, Consultation Paper, September 1999, which covered England and Wales. For Scotland, see Scottish Executive *High Hedges: the extent of problems and possible solutions in Scotland*, 1999.
448 DETR *High hedges: Possible Solutions, Summary of Responses*, August 2000.

ensuring that these kinds of disputes are resolved, whilst maintaining civility between neighbours.[449]

Railway industry disputes

The rail industry has set up two dispute resolution procedures, the Railway Industry Dispute Resolution Procedure and the Access Dispute Resolution Procedure. The industry procedure relates to contractual or liability claims following a disruption or an accident. The procedure provides ADR as a dispute resolution option. Reference under the procedure is made, in the first instance, to a committee which adjudicates on the issues. If either party is dissatisfied, referral to mediation or arbitration is possible. The access procedure applies to disputes between Railtrack and Train Operators. Parties may seek adjudication by specialist committees. If either party is dissatisfied, they can appeal to the Regulator. In the absence of specific provisions for appeal to the Regulator, the parties may refer to mediation or arbitration, as in the case of the industry procedure.

Religious and church conflict

Churches face both internal and external disputes, and not uncommonly, a large number of disputes. For example, in the Church of England alone, each diocese usually has six disputes at any one time.[450] The disputes can be bitterly acrimonious, damaging relationships and, potentially, the purpose of the Church. Church conflict can also create instability in the general community. Mediation provides an opportunity to understand and address both personal and denominational issues. Mediation enables such disputes to be resolved without publicity and has the potential to save legal costs. In a high-profile Church dispute in 1998, relating to the dismissal of the organist at Westminster Abbey, the enquiry was reported to have cost an estimated £600,000.[451]

The Centre for Dispute Resolution is developing an interdenominational mediation faculty to mediate disputes within the Church context. Another approach is offered by the Christian Mediation and Arbitration Services ('CMAS'), which provides mediation services to Christians of any Church affiliation. It has dealt with a range of disputes, including commercial property, financial, trusts and personal injury disputes.[452] The Mediation Network for Northern Ireland also runs a Church Mediation Project.

Sport disputes

Mediation offers sports people the opportunity to resolve disputes quickly, in particular, if the dispute involves the issue of whether the sports person can return to

---

449 See also the section on Community Disputes in this chapter.
450 R Verkaik and R Lindsay 'Freemasons in an unbrotherly feud over old lodge' *The Independent*, London, 26 July 1999.
451 C Garner 'Churches go for training on how to stop disputes becoming unholy rows' *The Independent*, London, 5 October 1999, at p 3.
452 CMAS, PO Box 78, Greenford, Middlesex UB6 OJR; phone: 020 8993 6886; fax: 020 8992 1164.

sport. In the dispute between Richie Woodhall, then WBC Super Middleweight Champion, and boxing promoter, Frank Warren, an expeditious resolution of a contractual dispute between them was required as Woodhall had to fight again, within a few months, in order to retain his WBC belt. The dispute was settled by mediation within two days.[453] Apart from speed, mediation also provides the parties with a private and confidential dispute resolution process. Sports people are concerned not to be labelled as trouble-makers if they are involved in court disputes. This could, in turn, affect future sponsorship and other opportunities. The image of the relevant sport may also suffer as a result of high-profile litigation. Even if a dispute affects a particular sports person, the dispute can have ramifications on that person's club. Sports people can also use mediation to ensure that any agreements reached are confidential. For example, if a sports person seeks to end a sponsorship contract, the sponsor may agree but may not wish other sports people to have the impression that they may also break their contracts or for any suspicion to be raised over the quality of the sponsor's product.[454] Sports ultimately revolve around small communities and continuing relationships, which can be enhanced or maintained through mediation.

A wide range of sport disputes are suitable for mediation, including:

- wage disputes;
- disputes between governing bodies and sponsors; and
- disputes between clubs and managers.[455]

There is a debate over whether mediation is suitable for disciplinary matters, such as doping disputes. David Richbell, a mediator of sports disputes, considers that mediation has a place in doping disputes, by re-introducing into sport persons who have been suspended; facilitating reconciliation between a sports person cleared of doping charges with that person's club or sponsors; and by managing appropriate communications within and outside the sport. An example of an unsuccessful mediation in this context arose out of the £1.5m libel case brought by Vialli, a Turin footballer, against Roma's coach, Zeman, for allegations of doping.[456]

Sporting organisations generally have internal arbitration processes. The culture is, however, shifting from arbitration to mediation and early neutral evaluation. The Sports Disputes Resolution Panel ('SDRP') was set up in 1999 to promote the use of ADR for the resolution of sports disputes. Current members include the Athletes Commission, British Olympic Association, the Central Council of Physical Recreation, the Institute of Professional Sport, the Institute of Sports Sponsorship, the Northern Ireland Sports Forum, the Scottish Sports Association and the Welsh Sports Association. It handles all sports disputes, including disciplinary matters, and maintains a list of neutrals, who are experts in sport and the law. It has established a Mediation Procedure, together with a Model Mediation Agreement. It also has a set of Rules for an Advisory Opinion, whereby a neutral provides the parties with a non-binding opinion.[457]

---

453 Centre for Dispute Resolution *Mediation – boxing clever*, Press Release, 6 July 1999. The authors also thank McCormicks for the information they provided.
454 The authors thank David Richbell of CEDR for his comments.
455 The authors thank Mark Gay of Denton Wilde Sapte for his views. See also I Blackshaw 'Is mediation the answer?' (2000) 3(4) *Sports Law Bulletin* 2.
456 R Thomas 'Vialli starts £1.5m libel case in Rome' *The Guardian*, London, 14 April 1999.
457 Sports Dispute Resolution Panel *Rules for arbitration, mediation procedure and rules*

Tax disputes

The Adjudicator is an impartial referee of claims that Customs and Excise, the Contribution Agency or the Inland Revenue have handled a matter badly. The guiding principles for complaints handling by the Adjudicator's Office are impartiality, efficiency, accessibility and helpfulness. The Office will seek to mediate a settlement of a complaint, where that is possible. For example, in 1997 the Office settled by mediation about 40% of the complaints it had investigated. A formal recommendation is made by the Adjudicator if mediation is either unsuccessful or not possible.[458]

Mediation for the resolution of tax disputes became highly publicised after the successful mediation in the US of a multi-million dollar tax dispute between DuPont and the Internal Revenue Service. The mediation had been part of a pilot mediation programme by the Internal Revenue Service, aimed at corporate tax appeals, in an attempt to improve the examination and appeal processes and to achieve a more timely resolution.[459] In Australia, taxation objections concerning amounts in dispute of less than AU$5,000 and decisions by the Commissioner of Taxation refusing a request for an extension of time within which to make a taxation objection may be referred to mediation.[460]

Telecommunications

In September 1999 the Director General of Telecommunications issued a Consultation Document on procedures for resolving certain disputes between consumers and telecommunications operators and amongst telecommunications operators themselves.[461] The background to the Document is that the Government announced an intention to introduce legislation, under which Consumer Councils for utilities, including telecommunications, will be set up. These Councils will be responsible for handling consumer complaints against utility companies. The Document recognises that there may be some overlap between the remit of the proposed Consumer Councils and the proposed procedures in the Document. The Document proposes two sets of procedures.

The first set would apply to disputes over telephone bills and the terms and conditions under which telephone services are provided. In relation to these kinds of disputes, the Document proposes arbitration. The party in dispute with the provider would pay between £15 and £20 for the arbitration, but this sum would be returned if the arbitrator found in favour of that party. The rationale is that frivolous claims would be discouraged, without dissuading parties from seeking arbitration. The Document explains that arbitration is, in the context of these disputes, preferable to

---

for an advisory opinion, STRP, October 1999. See Chapters 1 and 3 for an overview of early neutral evaluation.

458 The Adjudicator's Office, *Annual Report 1997*, at pp 11–16.

459 R Gettlin 'IRS pilot mediation program helps resolve DuPont case' *SPIDR News*, vol 20, No 2, 1996, at pp 7 and 13.

460 B Thompson 'Small Taxation Claims Tribunal' (1997) 6 *Proctor* 16.

461 Office of Telecommunications *Proposed new dispute resolution procedures for fixed telecommunications*, Consultation Document, September 1999.

mediation as it offers finality. The Document also acknowledges that telecommunication service providers should be using a form of mediation or conciliation in order to attempt to resolve disputes by themselves in the first instance. The second set of procedures are proposed to apply to disputes between telecommunications operators about the availability of services, for instance, interruption, termination, variation or reduction. It is proposed that OFTEL should deal with this type of dispute as it does with other disputes. Initially, therefore, OFTEL would decide whether the case should proceed to investigation and, if so, to investigate the matter and, ultimately, make a determination.[462]

A Consultation Paper, on regulation of access services for digital television,[463] proposes obligations on operators of conditional access services for digital television, whether satellite, terrestrial or cable. Although the proposals are limited to digital television services provided by broadcasters, the Paper suggests that conditional access technology is likely to be used to control access to other digital services. The proposals include a dispute resolution procedure, which proposes mediation, although parties would be free to litigate if they desired.[464]

Trade disputes

The World Trade Organisation (WTO) has developed a Dispute Settlement Understanding for trade disputes. The aim of the procedures is to achieve a mutually acceptable solution to the parties to a trade dispute. The procedures apply to the agreements listed in Appendix 1 to the Understanding. The Dispute Settlement Body administers the rules and procedures. The Understanding provides, in Article 5, that mediation may be undertaken voluntarily by the parties, although the Director-General may offer mediation with a view to assisting the parties to settle a dispute. The Article specifies that mediation is confidential and without prejudice to the parties' rights.[465]

---

462 See *Director-General of Telecommunications Statement: resolving disputes between fixed telecommunications service operators*, September 2000.

463 Department of Trade and Industry *The regulation of conditional access services for digital television,* final consultation paper on detailed implementation proposals, 1999.

464 The Chartered Institute of Arbitrators has devised arbitration procedures for telecommunications disputes, for example, the Arbitration Procedure for disputes over television and telecommunication services supplied by NTL (available at http://www.arbitrators.org/Materials/Schemes).

465 Documents are available at http://www.wto.org. For consideration of mediation in the context of shipping disputes, generally, see S Starbuck 'Shipping can no longer afford to shun mediation' (2000) 10 *M Advocate* 26.

9

Demand and Supply Issues in Mediation

Introduction

Chapter 7 examined the main players in the development of mediation in the UK, and Chapter 8 outlined the extent of mediation practice in the UK. The take-up of mediation is still low in the UK, a factor which will be considered in the first part of this chapter. The Lord Chancellor's Department is giving consideration to a number of issues, and the future decisions taken in relation to those issues are likely to impact on the take-up of mediation. The first issue is whether there should be compulsion or, in the absence of compulsion, encouragement to use mediation and, in either case, what form it should take. Secondly, the issue arises whether courts should be doing more to make mediation available, even if its use is not compelled. The first issue is a 'demand-side' issue, as its focus is on creating demand for mediation, whereas the second issue is a 'supply-side' issue, in that its main aim to provide access to mediation.[1] An issue which straddles both sides of the equation is funding for mediation. Recent developments have made mediation accessible to legally-assisted persons, which in turn promotes the voluntary take-up of mediation. The aim of this chapter is to consider those three issues, to provide an overview of the arguments in favour of and against the particular course of action, providing also, where possible, an indication of how some of these issues have been resolved in other jurisdictions.

Take-up of Mediation in the UK

Civil/commercial cases

In England and Wales

In the period before the introduction of the Civil Procedure Rules ('CPR'),[2] the County Court Mediation Pilot was studied. The results indicated that in only 5% of

---

1 For more detailed consideration of the 'demand' and 'supply' issues in mediation, see P Edelman 'Institutionalising dispute resolution alternatives' (1984) 9(2) *Justice System Journal* 134.
2 As to which, see Chapter 7.

cases did both parties agree to mediate their dispute. In 9% of cases, only the plaintiff accepted the offer to mediate, and in 6% of cases, only the defendant accepted the offer.[3] Although 47% of the offers had been made in personal injury cases, only 4% of those cases went to mediation.[4] Genn cited lack of experience of mediation by lawyers, fear of showing weakness by accepting mediation and resistance to the idea of compromise as reasons for the low take-up of mediation in the Central London County Court.[5] There is also acknowledged to be low public awareness of ADR in the UK.[6]

Since the CPR, the ADR Group has reported a three-fold increase in its workload, with 123 mediations in the six months to March 2000.[7] 44% of those cases involved commercial contract, company and share disputes and 21% involved professional negligence cases.[8] The Centre for Dispute Resolution reported a 100% increase in mediations in 1999, with approximately 500 cases, compared to the 252 in 1998.[9] CEDR reports that the main area of increase has been in higher value commercial cases.[10] The Centre's statistics also show that an increasing proportion of cases are being referred from outside London.[11] In addition, at least one in five commercial mediations referred to the Centre is of an international nature, and an increasing number of mediations have no connection to the UK.[12] Notwithstanding the statistics from the ADR Group and CEDR, the overall take-up of civil/commercial mediation remains low, when compared with the number of cases issued in the courts.[13]

It appears to be acknowledged that following the introduction of the CPR, there has been a reduction in the number of cases being issued and a high rate of early

---

3 H Genn *Central London County Court Mediation Pilot: Evaluation Report*, LCD Research Series, No 5/98, at p 15. In the period covered by the study, 4,500 offers were made and in 160 cases both parties agreed to mediate.

4 Ibid, at p 20. The NHS Mediation Pilot (L Mulcahy et al *Mediating medical negligence claims: an option for the future?* NHS Executive, 2000) found that the most common response for the failure to refer clinical negligence cases to mediation was lack of suitability (at p 58).

5 H Genn, *Central London County Court Mediation Pilot Evaluation*, op cit, at p v.

6 The Lord Chancellor's Department *ADR Discussion Paper*, November 1999, at para 5.8 refers to surveys on public awareness of arbitration schemes and ombudsmen, concluding that a quarter of the population have not heard of any of the main schemes.

7 S Allen 'Unnecessary Caution' *The Law Society Gazette*, 30 March 2000, at p 30.

8 See the *Law Society Gazette*, 20 April 2000.

9 S Allen 'Unnecessary Caution' op cit; and Centre for Dispute Resolution *Press Release: A Mediation a Day*, 26 April 1999.

10 Especially in the brackets £500,000–£1m and £10m+: Centre for Dispute Resolution *Resolutions*, Issue No 22. The Centre's statistics for April 1998–May 1999 showed that the largest percentage of cases, 18%, fell into the bracket £1m–£5m: Centre for Dispute Resolution *Press Release: A Mediation a Day*. The Centre's statistics for 1999–2000 show that 44% of mediations fell in the £100,000–£1m bracket; 23% fell in the £1m–£10m category; and 3% fell in the over £10m grouping: Centre for Dispute Resolution *Resolutions*, Issue no 26, Summer 2000, p 1.

11 Centre for Dispute Resolution *Resolutions*, Issue no 22, at p 7; and CEDR *Press Release*, July 2000.

12 P Davidson 'No dispute over ADR success' *The Lawyer*, 25 October 1999, at p 12.

13 S Allen 'Unnecessary caution', op cit, who states that 2 million cases were issued in the county courts during 1999.

14 See, for example, P Sutton 'Woolf's reforms: a curate's egg?' *The Times*, 26 October 1999; Post Magazine, Legal Supplement 'Woolf overview – not so traditional now' *Post*

settlements.[14] The issue arises whether these results can be attributed to the increased take-up of mediation. Various commentators and survey results suggest that the results are attributable to mediation, in particular:

- a greater awareness generally of mediation; [15]
- court encouragement of parties to attempt mediation; [16]
- the mere threat of court encouragement of mediation; [17]
- clients are more enthusiastic or fearful of possible cost sanctions if they do not agree to mediate; [18]
- increasing occurrence of mediation even before issue of proceedings.[19]

Other commentators and survey results indicate other reasons for the results, including:

- the CPR have caused claimants and their lawyers, in particular, to re-think their approach to litigation; [20]
- a tightening of legal aid; [21]
- front-loading of costs; [22]
- Part 36 offers; [23]
- earlier trial dates.[24]

It is not clear, therefore, that the post-CPR results are attributable to mediation. However, it is likely that there will be a continued increase in the take-up of mediation in England and Wales, and statistics show that the breadth of application of mediation in civil/commercial disputes in the UK is wide. The authors' 2000 survey of UK law firms indicated, consistent also with the Centre for Dispute Resolution 2000 statistics, that the largest categories of mediation use relate to commercial contract, professional negligence and construction disputes. Those

---

Magazine, 28 October 1999; and the CEDR MORI poll, reported in Centre for Dispute Resolution *Civil Justice Audit*, April 2000.

15 Post Magazine, Legal Supplement: 'Woolf overview – not so traditional now' *Post Magazine*, 28 October 1999; and M Swallow 'London Courts lose out as litigants head for regions' *The Lawyer*, 24 May 1999.

16 Referrals to CEDR from the courts has risen from 4% at the time of introduction of CPR to 14% by June 1999: Centre for Dispute Resolution *Resolutions*, Issue No 24, at p 2.

17 Centre for Dispute Resolution Press Release *CEDR mediations double with introduction of Woolf Reforms*, 2 August 1999.

18 Evident from a number of the responses to the MORI poll: see Centre for Dispute Resolution *Civil Justice Audit*, April 2000; Centre for Dispute Resolution *Bulletin: the Woolf Reforms six months on*; and CEDR Members & Mediators Forum, 29 September 1999.

19 Ibid.; and potentially motivated by Part 36 offers made before issue of proceedings.

20 Post Magazine, Legal Supplement: 'Woolf overview – not so traditional now', op cit.

21 Ibid.

22 Supported by CEDR MORI 2000 poll results, reported by Centre for Dispute Resolution, *Civil Justice Audit*, op cit.

23 Ibid.

24 For example, when a trial date was brought forward a year from the one proposed by both parties at a case management conference under the CPR, the parties settled the case, which involved the administrator of the Maxwell companies and its auditors: see the report in 'First case management conference prompts Coopers settlement', *Legal Business*, July/August 1999.

statistics show that, at the other end of the spectrum, are personal injury and defamation cases. The points below show the results from the authors' survey, with the figures in brackets representing CEDR's statistics for 2000:[25]

- Professional negligence 23.5% (17%)
- Commercial contract 17.5% (31%)
- Construction 11% (17%)
- Shareholder/company 8%
- Banking 6% (6%)
- Insurance 5% (4%)
- Property 4.5%
- Employment (4%)
- IT 3.2% (7%)
- Probate 3.2%
- IP 2.4%
- Shipping (2%)
- Product liability 1.5%
- Environmental disputes 1.5%
- Personal injury 1.2% (3%)
- Defamation 1.2% (1%)
- Tax 1.2%
- Sports 0.8%
- Insolvency 0.8%
- Community 0.8%
- Aviation 0.4%

Two issues emerge from these statistics. The first is to consider whether the take-up, generally, of mediation should be increased. The second is to consider whether efforts should focus on those areas where demand for mediation appears lowest.

In Scotland and Northern Ireland

Studies of ADR in Scotland have uncovered limited evidence of ADR practice in civil/commercial cases.[26] For example, by the end of 1998:

- ACCORD had mediated 17 cases since its inception;[27]
- the Faculty of Advocates had mediated two cases;[28]
- the Advisory Conciliation and Arbitration Service ('ACAS') had received about 700 conciliation referrals during the year; and
- the Consumer Advice Bureaux had handled three mediations in total.[29]

In Northern Ireland, little mediation activity is taking place outside family and community cases. In the case of Scotland and Northern Ireland efforts at civil justice

---

25 The CEDR statistics appear in CEDR *Press Release*, July 2000. For further information see the sections on the separate subject areas in Chapter 8.
26 Except in family cases: R Mays and B Clark *ADR in Scotland*, The Scottish Office, 1999.
27 For further information on ACCORD, see the section on Law Societies, Bar Councils and Mediation in Chapter 7.
28 For further information on the Faculty of Advocates, see the section on Law Societies, Bar Councils and Mediation in Chapter 7.
29 For Scottish statistics, see R Mays and B Clark *ADR in Scotland*, op cit.

reform may bring their experience of ADR in line with that of England and Wales. It is also necessary to consider, in the context of Scotland and Northern Ireland, whether there are any specific factors, which have the effect of discouraging use of mediation. For instance, it has been suggested that the longer divorce period in Northern Ireland provides ample opportunity for consensual dispute resolution. Others point to the fact that there are no 'gatekeepers' to the mediation process in those jurisdictions, compared to the courts in England and Wales that exercise that function.

Family cases

In England and Wales

The University of Newcastle's research on family mediation resulted in the production of a number of reports in the 1980s and 1990s, which show that family mediation take-up remains low in England and Wales.[30] The reason appears to be ignorance about mediation.[31] The Annual Reports of the various family mediation organisations also provide useful statistics. For example, National Family Mediation ('NFM')[32] provides mediation services for over 7,000 couples per year and 20% of those cases are referred from courts.[33] The University of Bristol is in the process of collating the most up-to-date statistics on the use of mediation in family disputes in England and Wales.[34]

In Scotland

As in England and Wales, the available statistics appear to indicate that the number of family mediations is small in comparison to the number of family disputes and family mediators in Scotland. Between 1994 and 1995 Family Mediation Scotland ('FMS') handled 3,669 case referrals.[35] As at 1996, 21 CALM family mediators who had responded to a study by Mays and Clark confirmed that 170 cases in total had been mediated.[36] Recent statistics are also available via FMS Annual Reports, for example:

- the 1998/1999 Annual Report shows that 6,044 cases were referred to FMS;[37]
- the Family Mediation Central Scotland Annual Report for 1998/99 shows 154 mediation referrals and a total of 51 mediations started, 17 on all issues and 34 on child issues;[38]

---

30 L Webley *A review of the literature on family mediation: prepared for the Lord Chancellor's Advisory Committee on Legal Education and Conduct*, Institute of Advanced Legal Studies, 1998, at p 10.

31 Ibid, at p 26.

32 For further information about NFM, see the section on Mediation Organisations in Chapter 7.

33 UK College of Family Mediators *1999/2000 Directory and Handbook*, Sweet & Maxwell, London, 1999, at p A120.

34 The statistics are likely to be published in 2001.

35 R Mays and B Clark *ADR in Scotland*, The Scottish Office, 1999.

36 Ibid.

37 Family Mediation Scotland *Annual Report*, 1999.

38 Family Mediation Central Scotland *Annual Report*, 1999.

- Family Mediation Borders Annual Report 1998/99 refers to a 45% increase in referrals;[39]
- the Family Mediation Lothian Annual Report 1998/99 confirms 955 referrals and 417 mediation sessions.[40]

FMS statistics show that the majority of referrals to family mediation in Scotland are made direct by the public, with a small proportion being referred by courts, solicitors and other agencies.[41] A recent study by Lewis of family mediation in Scotland provides a useful insight into the characteristics of mediated family disputes:[42]

- 82% involved issues relating to children only, 3% involved financial issues only and 15% involved all issues;
- 57% were commenced either before or within a year of separation;
- 13% of cases involved couples who were still living together at the time of referral to mediation;
- 57% resulted in an agreement on all issues, 21% on some of the issues and 22% in no agreement;
- 66% of self-referred cases reached agreement on all the issues raised, whereas 43% of court-referred cases reached agreement; and
- 25% of cases involved some form of violence.

Those statistics can provide useful information, when considering demand and supply issues, such as possible time considerations, if mediation is mandated.

In Northern Ireland

The Family Mediation Service of Northern Ireland statistics for 1995/96 show that 43% of family mediations were self-referrals.[43] Relate Northern Ireland statistics show that there were 150 mediations in 1996/97.[44] The low rate of referrals to family mediation in Northern Ireland has been explained on the basis that there is widespread confusion about the nature of mediation. Surveys have shown that the awareness of mediation is lower than the awareness of reconciliation services.[45] However, it is also acknowledged that funding of and staffing levels in family mediation organisations in Northern Ireland are inadequate to meet any increased demand for family mediation services.[46]

This latter tension highlights the interaction of the 'demand' and 'supply' sides to the mediation equation: efforts made to increase demand need to be met by adequate supply, and vice versa. The position currently throughout the UK is that the supply side is not being matched by the demand side of the equation.

---

39 Family Mediation Borders *Annual Report*, 1999 which indicates that there were 148 referrals to the service during 1998/99.
40 Family Mediation Lothian *16th Annual Report*, 1999.
41 Family Mediation Scotland *Annual Report*, 1999, which shows that, of 2,916 referrals in 1999, 2,192 were self-referred, 141 were court-referred, 386 were referred by lawyers and 197 were referred by other agencies.
42 J Lewis *The role of mediation in family disputes in Scotland*, Legal Studies Research Findings No 23, The Scottish Office, 1999.
43 Family Mediation Service of Northern Ireland *Annual Report*, 1996.
44 Relate Northern Ireland *Annual Report*, 1997.
45 C Archbold et al *Divorce in Northern Ireland: unravelling the system*, Report to the Office of Law Reform, HMSO, 1999, at p 206.
46 See the section on Funding and Mediation in this chapter.

Community disputes

Mediation UK Annual Reports show an increase in the number of community mediation services, from 59 in 1991 to 135 in 1997.[47] The Community Mediation Service General Survey in 1995 indicated that 10 mediation services had received less than 50 referrals per year, whereas two London mediation services received over 300 referrals per year.[48] In Scotland, the Edinburgh Community Mediation Programme had mediated just over 100 disputes in total to 1996, and the Dundee Mediation Scheme had received 14 case referrals since its establishment.[49]

The main source of community mediation referrals is self-referral and, to a smaller extent, housing departments, environmental health departments, community advice bureaux and the police.[50] The most common dispute mediated by community mediation services relates to noise, followed by abusive, anti-social and children behavioural problems.[51] Mediation UK's 1998 statistics indicated that 25% of referrals resulted in termination because one of the parties withdrew from the mediation; that 20% resulted in an agreement being reached; and that in 12% no agreement had been reached.[52]

In the community context, although courts may not be used or even contemplated for the bulk of disputes handled, the potential benefits that could be derived through court-based mediation could be achieved through local authority or public agency-based mediation.

Compulsion or Encouragement to Mediate

UK versus other jurisdictions

In the case of family mediation, the Booth Committee considered that the decision whether to take part in mediation must rest with the parties because success in mediation depends upon the willing participation and co-operation of the parties.[53] The Family Law Bar Association maintained in the late 1980s that mandatory reference to family mediation was a waste of time and money and could even exacerbate disputes.[54] The 'Looking to the Future' White Paper emphasised that

---

47 Mediation UK *Annual Reports,* 1992–97.
48 M Liebmann (ed) *Community and Neighbour Mediation*, Cavendish Publishing Limited, London, 1998, at p 77.
49 R Mays and B Clark *ADR in Scotland*, The Scottish Office, 1999.
50 Mediation UK *Annual Report*, 1998.
51 Ibid.
52 Ibid.
53 Booth Committee *Report of the Committee on Matrimonial Causes*, HMSO, London, 1985, at para 4.59.
54 University of Newcastle upon Tyne Conciliation Project Unit, *Report to the Lord Chancellor's Department on the cost and effectiveness of conciliation in England and Wales*, March 1989, at p 41.

family mediation should be voluntary in order to be effective.[55] Changes in the funding of legal services,[56] however, have raised concerns about 'back door' compulsion into family mediation for those who receive funding. A pre-condition for funding in family cases is a meeting with a mediator in order to determine whether mediation is suitable.[57] The Family Mediation Service in Northern Ireland also supports compulsory intake appointments, to consider suitability for mediation, as long as that does not lead to compulsory mediation.[58] In the case of funded non-family cases also, a funding certificate may be limited to mediation where a client appears, for no good reason, to refuse to mediate or where a client is invited to take part in an established mediation scheme, like the Central London County Court Mediation Pilot.

The Housing Ombudsman has required that certain disputes between tenants and council landlords be mediated, and certain construction disputes are now subject to compulsory adjudication under the Housing Grants and Regeneration Act.[59] The Commercial Court has ordered parties to mediate, even in cases where the parties did not wish to do so.[60] However, feedback from judges and mediators in such cases has been that frequently parties attended the mediation, stating that they were attending solely for the purpose of obtaining a trial date. Different considerations are likely to come into play today, in light of CPR, r 44, the implications of which are discussed later in this chapter.

Apart from the cases mentioned above, mediation in the UK is essentially voluntary. Indeed, in Lord Woolf's Interim Report, he stated that ADR should not be compulsory.[61] In relation to dispute resolution options for consumers, the Director General of Fair Trading considered in 1996 that the choice of dispute resolution system must lie with disputants, even if a dispute would be better dealt with by ADR.[62] In his Final Report, although Lord Woolf remained of the view, he did so 'with less certainty than before', that the use of ADR should not be compelled.[63]

American commentators have long held the view that, if voluntary rates of mediation participation are high, compulsion is not necessary, so that the issue of compulsion should only arise if voluntary rates of mediation participation are low.[64] Since UK mediation surveys have shown low voluntary take-up of mediation,[65] mandating mediation may facilitate wider acceptance of mediation.[66] As American

---

55 *Looking to the Future,* Cmnd 2799, at paras 5.28–5.31.
56 See the section on Funding and Mediation in this chapter.
57 Ibid; and see Family Law Act 1996, s 29.
58 F Garwood *The Scottish Scene,* UK College of Family Mediators, Issue No 1, 1997.
59 For further details on mediation in property/tenancy and construction disputes, see the separate subject areas in Chapter 8.
60 See the section on Courts and Mediation in Chapter 7.
61 Lord Woolf *Access to Justice: Interim Report,* Lord Chancellor's Department, London, June 1995, at p 136.
62 National Consumer Council *Settling Consumer Disputes,* 1996, at p 25.
63 Lord Woolf *Access to Justice: Final Report,* 1996, at p 65.
64 L V Katz 'Compulsory ADR and Voluntarism: Two-headed monster or two sides of the coin?' (1993) *Journal of Dispute Resolution* 1.
65 See the section on Statistics in this chapter for further information.
66 K J Mackie *A handbook of dispute resolution: ADR in action,* Routledge, London 1991, at p 93.

reports point out, voluntary low take-up of mediation should not be presumed to indicate a lack of interest in mediation, but a range of possible factors, including fear of signalling to the other side a desire for compromise and, frequently, ignorance by the parties or their lawyers about alternative dispute resolution processes.[67] Compulsory ADR could therefore provide a way of overcoming these other problems as well.[68] The Lord Chancellor has been giving consideration to whether ADR should be made compulsory.[69] The majority of respondents to his ADR Discussion Paper indicated disapproval of attempts to make mediation compulsory.[70] The Lord Chancellor has mooted an 'opt out' of mediation approach, whereby the assumption would be that a case will be mediated, unless a party opts out of mediation.[71]

In comparison, legislative efforts to mandate mediation and settlement conferences allowing judges to facilitate settlements, are prevalent in the US.[72] US commentators have suggested that a more sophisticated understanding of negotiation and alternative dispute resolution has led to a willingness to mandate their use.[73] In Saskatchewan mediation was mandated in civil cases. In Australia, legislation promotes the use of mediation in a range of subject areas[74] and court rules allow judges to mandate mediation.[75] In Singapore compulsion applies to all personal injury cases and to other cases over a financial threshold.[76] Lord Woolf in his Interim Report explained the prevalence of compulsory ADR in the US and other jurisdictions on the basis of a lack of court resources.[77]

Ultimately, what is required is an evaluation of the costs and benefits of compulsion. As Sowerby writes, in relation to the position in New Zealand, the issue requires 'thought and careful judgment'.[78]

---

67 Society of Professionals in Dispute Resolution ('SPIDR') *Mandated participation and settlement coercion: Dispute resolution as it relates to the courts*, 1991.

68 The Lord Chancellor's Department *ADR Discussion Paper*, November 1999, at para 7.20.

69 P Rodgers 'ADR should be made compulsory says Irvine' *Legal Week*, 11 November 1999, at p 6.

70 Lord Chancellor's Department *ADR Discussion Paper: Summary of responses*, August 2000, at para 68. Northern companies also indicated, in response to an ADR Group/DLA survey, that they rejected mandatory mediation: 'Mediation confusion' *The Law Society Gazette*, 17 August 2000, at p 8.

71 The Lord Chancellor's Department *ADR Discussion Paper*, November 1999. The 'opt-out' option was adopted by courts in Ottawa and Toronto.

72 L V Katz 'Compulsory ADR and Voluntarism: Two-headed monster or two sides of the coin?' (1993) *Journal of Dispute Resolution* 1.

73 Ibid.

74 For example, in relation to farm debt and native title disputes.

75 For example, Supreme Court Act (SA) 1935, s 65 provides that the court may, with or without the consent of the parties, appoint a mediator and refer a civil proceeding or any issues arising in a civil proceeding for mediation.

76 Success in a mediation also results in a refund of mediation fees.

77 Lord Woolf *Access to Justice: Interim Report*, Lord Chancellor's Department, London, June 1995, at p 136.

78 W Sowerby 'The proposal that the court be empowered to order parties to mediation' [1996] *DRB* 16.

Arguments for and against compulsion

Arguments in favour of compulsion

Some of the potential advantages of mandatory mediation include the following:[79]

(a)   Mandatory programmes increase the number of cases coming to mediation and therefore reduce court backlogs and the ignorance and suspicion of mediation among users and their advisers.

(b)   Mandatory mediation provides a better basis for surveying the effectiveness of mediation services; there is self-serving bias in surveying the success of only those matters in which the parties have selected mediation as their preferred dispute resolution option.

(c)   There can be more adequate administration of mediation and supervision of its quality if it is provided on a large-scale basis and economies and scale can make it more cost-effective.

(d)   The timing of mediation can be controlled in mandatory programmes in order to save costs and time, to avoid destructive tendencies in the way the conflict is being managed, and to prevent a deterioration in the parties' relationship.

(e)   Mandatory programmes have an educative effect for lawyers and other professionals, which might increase their expertise and confidence in advising on the use of the system, in appropriate circumstances, within or outside the mandatory arrangements.[80]

(f)   Surveys show relatively high success rates in certain mandatory programmes and relatively high satisfaction ratings from those for whom it is mandatory. This is because even if parties are initially reluctant to participate in mediation, a skilled mediator may still be able to assist them to reach an agreement.[81]

Arguments against compulsion

Compulsory mediation is contrary to one of the basic tenets of mediation, that it relies upon the willingness of the parties to reach an agreed solution:

> '... mediation assumes that the parties have a commitment to achieving a workable outcome ... its value is low where a party uses it to appear [to a court] to be doing the "right thing" ...'[82]

In the US, the distinction is drawn between compulsion to enter into mediation and compulsion within the mediation and since compulsion to mediate is pressure of the former kind, there should be no objection.[83] The rationale, that even if parties are

---

79   M Dawson 'Non-consensual alternative dispute resolution: pros and cons' (1993) 4 *ADRJ* 173 at 175–6.

80   For a more detailed consideration of the issues, see A Limbury 'Compulsory ADR before commencing proceedings?' *The ADR Bulletin*, vol 1, No 2, June 1998.

81   F Clarke *Court-ordered mediation in NYC*, reported at http://www.adrr.com/adr4

82   J Fisher and M Blondel *Couples mediation: a forum and a framework*, NSW Marriage Guidance, 1993.

83   S Goldberg et al *Dispute Resolution: Negotiation, Mediation and other Processes* (2nd edn), Little Brown & Co, USA, 1992.

coerced to mediate, it is still up to them to participate in the process and to work out the terms of any settlement in the mediation,[84] was the fundamental basis of two decisions of the New South Wales Supreme Court. In *AWA Ltd v Daniels (t/a Deloitte Haskins and Sells)*, the court stated:[85]

> '. . . to say that ADR has failed because one party does not want to participate in the process, does not recognise that the process has been established precisely to deal with parties in dispute who believe that settlement of their problem is impossible. Further, where the participation of a third party is prescribed . . . this criticism fails to recognise any value in that third party's participation in the process.'

In *Hooper Bailie Associated Ltd v Natcon Group Proprietary Ltd*,[86] Giles J also distinguished between the consensual nature of mediation and the entry into that process, commenting:

> '. . . what is enforced is not co-operation . . . but participation in a process for which co-operation . . . might come.'

In the UK it may be difficult to reconcile these views with the right of access to a court, guaranteed by article 6(1) of the European Convention on Human Rights, which has been incorporated into UK law by the Human Rights Act 1998. Against this, it can be argued that:

- mediation complements access to courts,[87] and does not displace it,[88] so that if mediation fails, the parties could resume litigation;
- it is the reference to mediation that is compulsory, not participation in the process, so that further access to courts is not extinguished, but merely postponed;
- if mediation were built into the court process, in one of the ways outlined in the next section, then it would become a potential step in litigation, and could not be viewed as denying access to courts or denying access to courts at the time of a person's choice.

Arguments of this kind have successfully defeated objections to compulsory mediation in the US on the right to trial or right to access to courts grounds. US courts have balanced the benefits of mediation against the burdens of trial delay and cost.[89]

---

84 R Ingleby 'Court sponsored mediation: the case against mandatory participation' (1993) 56 *Modern Law Review* 441 at 446.

85 *AWA Ltd v Daniels (t/a Deloitte Haskins and Sells)* (1992) 7 ACSR 463.

86 (1992) 28 NSWLR 194.

87 C Harrington 'Delegalisation Reform Movements' in R Abel 'The Contradictions of Informal Justice' in R Abel (ed) *The Politics of Informal Justice, vol 1: The American Experience*, Academic Press, New York 1982, at p 37.

88 Compare a strike out application in certain circumstances: in *Arrow Nominees Inc v Blackledge* [2000] 1 BCLC 709 (Chancery Division), the court refused to strike out a case on the basis of contumacious contempt of court, on the ground that to do so in the circumstances might be a breach of Article 6.

89 See generally *Airey v Ireland* (1979) 2 EHRR 305 for a consideration of Article 6. In that case, the European Court of Human Rights held that Article 6 did not imply an automatic right to legal aid but imposed an obligation on States to make courts accessible and offer financial help in appropriate circumstances. This Article is also discussed in the context of Ethical Standards in Chapter 11 and Mediation Clauses in Chapter 12.

Lord Woolf, in his Interim Report, also pointed to US evidence that ADR may be less effective when parties have not chosen to participate in it, as a further reason why mediation should not be compulsory.[90] It is unclear whether mandatory mediation would reduce the expense and time involved in litigation.[91] Some US commentators argue that, even if mediation were to reduce the expense and time involved in litigation, this could encourage more litigation and, in turn, increase overall court costs.[92] Some US findings also suggest that compulsory mediation would give less satisfaction to participants than voluntary mediation.[93]

There is also concern that compulsory mediation will provide a hurdle to overcome on the way to trial,[94] with the result that parties will participate in a perfunctory fashion, in which case mediation would constitute an expensive exercise in futility. Compulsory mediation also requires a stock of competent and affordable mediators.[95] In addition, it is difficult to justify compulsory referral to mediation, in preference to another form of ADR, which may be better suited to a particular dispute.

There are further concerns that compulsory mediation benefits those who intend to abuse the process, for example, by seeking information to improve their court case. A related concern is mediation's inability to protect the weak from the powerful.[96] If accompanied by financial incentives to go to trial, it could force parties to compromise rights, with particular disadvantage for poorer litigants. Compulsory mediation might, it is argued, create a two-tiered justice system, with one tier reserved for the poor who cannot afford litigation and who do not qualify for legal aid. Commentators also criticise mandatory mediation on the basis that it reduces opportunities for judge-made law, although against that it can be argued that at least one party in every piece of litigation is drawn into the litigation involuntarily and without desiring to have the dispute adjudicated according to law:

'... the question should perhaps be whether mandating mediation ... is preferable to placing control in the hands of an opponent, who may be forcing [the other party] to spend thousand of [pounds] in litigation while refusing a face-to-face discussion.'[97]

---

90 Lord Woolf *Access to Justice: Interim Report*, Lord Chancellor's Department, London, June 1995 at p 143. This issue was also picked up by Lord Irvine in a speech given to the Faculty of Mediation and ADR at the Academy of Experts on 27 January 1999: see http://www.open.gov.uk/lcd/speeches/1999. Studies in Maine showed that 43% of compulsory cases and 42% of voluntary cases settled in mediation: S Kelitz 'Civil Dispute Resolution Processes' in Ohio State University College of Law (ed) *Court Reform Implications of Dispute Resolution*, 1995, at p 9.
91 L V Katz 'Compulsory ADR and Voluntarism: Two-headed monster or two sides of the coin?' (1993) *Journal of Dispute Resolution* 1.
92 R Posner 'The summary jury trial and other methods of ADR: Some cautionary observations' (1986) 53 *University of Chicago Law Review* 366.
93 J Alfini 'Summary jury trial in State and Federal Courts' (1989) 4 *Ohio State Journal on Dispute Resolution* 213, reporting findings from Florida research.
94 Anecdotal evidence from mediations in Commercial Court cases indicates a number of instances when parties have attended a mediation and advised the mediator that they had attended for the sole purpose of obtaining a trial date.
95 The concern voiced in the UK is that there are a large number of trained mediators, but a small number with any mediation experience.
96 T Grillo 'The Mediation Alternative: Process Dangers for Women' (1991) 100 *Yale Law Journal* 1545.
97 S Goldberg, F Sander and N Rogers *Dispute Resolution: Negotiation, mediation and other processes*, Little Brown & Company (2nd edn) 1992.

There are additional concerns where mandatory mediation is attached to the court system. Some argue that there can never be genuine mediation within the domain of the courts and that court officials and litigation-minded lawyers will pervert the system so that it becomes an alternative method of litigating rather than an alternative to litigation.[98] Conversely it is argued that attaching mediation to the courts discredits the judicial system by confusing the role and identity of the courts in the eyes of their users, who expect binding decisions on their legal rights when they select court processes, and not court-sponsored negotiations. Nevertheless, there is, in some countries, a long history of compulsion to mediate.

Some basic considerations in any case

What kind or degree of compulsion or encouragement?

Even if mediation were to be made compulsory, what form of compulsion should be used? Should it, for example, be automatic?[99] Arguably, another type of compulsion mechanism, albeit by the 'back door', is the compulsory meeting, for applicants in England and Wales in legally-aided divorce litigation. The meeting is used to assess suitability for mediation. However, a mediation will not proceed if either party does not agree to mediate and even if parties attend mediation following such a meeting, they can leave at any time if they are not happy with progress.[100] The compulsory meeting idea could have wider application in the UK, by requiring all cases to be screened for mediation suitability.

The compulsion mechanism being considered by the Lord Chancellor's Department[101] is 'opt out' mediation. There would be a presumption that mediation will occur, unless the parties show that the case is not suitable for mediation. The Lord Chancellor's Department considers that this option might strike the necessary balance between increasing the use of mediation in suitable cases and allowing access to courts.[102] The other option being considered by the Lord Chancellor's Department, and supported by respondents to the Department's ADR Discussion Paper, is for judges to use the powers in the CPR to put pressure on litigants in appropriate cases to attempt mediation.[103] Experience in complex litigation, both in

---

98 J Effron 'Alternatives to litigation: factors in choosing' (1989) 52 *Modern Law Review* 480.

99 Which may create difficulties in light of the European Convention on Human Rights, Article 6: see the earlier discussion of the Act in this section.

100 Equivalent to the Australian experience: see, for example, H Astor and C Chinkin *Dispute Resolution in Australia*, Butterworths, Sydney, 1992, at p 48.

101 The Lord Chancellor's Department *ADR Discussion Paper*, November 1999.

102 Ibid. The approach was adopted in New Jersey, where parties had to show cause why mediation was not appropriate: see, for example, P Tractenberg 'Court-appointed mediators or special masters: a commentary' (1988) 12 *Seton Hall Legislative Journal* 81 at 85. Of the respondents who commented on this issue in response to the Lord Chancellor's ADR Discussion Paper, they tended to feel that opt-out schemes verged on coercion to mediate: Lord Chancellor's Department *ADR Discussion Paper: Summary of responses*, August 2000, at para 70.

103 Lord Chancellor's Department *ADR Discussion Paper: Summary of responses*, August 2000, at paras 68 and 69.

the US and the Commercial Court in England, indicates that parties respond to alternatives when judges suggest participation in ADR.[104] Apart from concerns in relation to the Human Rights Act, discussed above, the suggestion also raises concerns over:

- the proper role of courts; and
- whether, technically, CPR allows this.[105]

Others argue that there is already a degree of compulsion in civil/commercial cases by virtue of the costs provisions in the CPR, allowing judges to take into account the behaviour of the parties, including attempts to settle the case, when making orders as to costs.[106] There is also evidence of support in Scotland for a negative incentive to mediate, whereby an unreasonable refusal to mediate may incur costs and the inability to secure legal aid.[107]

Cost sanctions for failing to mediate or for unreasonable conduct in mediation?

Even if an element of compulsion were introduced, compulsion does not extend to forcing parties to reach an agreement in mediation. The issue then is whether there is any mechanism, which could encourage parties to participate in the process, with a view to reaching agreement, if one is possible.[108] The issue is also relevant if mediation is not made compulsory.

In Lord Woolf's Interim Report, he recommended that judges should be able to take into account a litigant's unreasonable refusal to attempt ADR when deciding on the future conduct of the case. He also indicated in that Report that he would be taking advice on whether unreasonable refusal should be taken into account by judges in determining costs as well.[109] In his Final Report, Lord Woolf recommended that an unreasonable refusal to participate in ADR or unco-operation in the course of ADR should be taken into account by courts in deciding what order to make as to costs.[110]

---

104 Maatman 'The future of summary judgment in the Federal Court' (1988) 21 J *Marshall L Rev* 455. In relation to the Commercial Court, see Chapter 7 for further details.

105 The CEDR MORI 2000 poll of lawyers revealed their belief that challenges are likely against court orders requiring parties to mediate as the Rules do not, technically, allow the courts to do this. The Rules allow judges to stay proceedings, but not to require parties to mediate. See Centre for Dispute Resolution *Civil Justice Audit*, April 2000. However, the cost sanctions, possibly by virtue of CPR, r 44, indicate that the Rules may allow judges to order mediation practically, if not technically.

106 CPR, r 44. The ADR Group's *Mediation Procedure,* at para 10.2, warns parties in a mediation that a court may impose an adverse costs order where a party is deemed to have been unreasonable in refusing to mediate. The cost sanction issue is discussed in more detail further below in this section.

107 R Mays and B Clark *ADR in Scotland*, The Scottish Office, 1999.

108 See, on the sanctions issue generally, R Ingleby *In the ball park: alternative dispute resolution and the courts*, Australian Institute of Judicial Administration, Melbourne, 1991.

109 Lord Woolf *Access to Justice: Interim Report*, Lord Chancellor's Department, London, June 1995, at p 144.

110 Lord Woolf *Access to Justice: Final Report*, July 1996, at p 302.

Rule 44 of the CPR now gives civil courts[111] in England and Wales the power to award or deny costs in light of all the circumstances, including efforts made in an attempt to resolve the dispute.[112] In one Commercial Court case, where the parties refused to mediate, although the court allowed them a trial date, it considered that, whatever the outcome of the trial, neither side should have its costs for the action.[113] By comparison, when this costs issue was considered by the Commercial Court's ADR Working Party, it did not agree that a party, even if it refused mediation or was responsible for the failure of a mediation to achieve a settlement, should be penalised in costs.[114] The Rules of some mediation organisations have been drafted to reflect the CPR.[115]

Potential cost sanctions under CPR, r 44 raise the following issues:

- when is a refusal to participate in mediation and when is conduct in mediation unreasonable; and
- how does the court inform itself of the conduct of parties in mediation without trespassing on confidentiality and privilege.

Reasonableness of conduct

The issue of reasonableness arises in two contexts: whether a refusal to mediate is reasonable and, if a mediation takes place, whether the conduct of the parties in the mediation was reasonable. In relation to the first issue, respondents to the Lord Chancellor's ADR Discussion Paper considered that the following reasons for refusal to mediate should be considered reasonable:[116]

- if a party requires an injunction or other remedy only available from a court;
- where the costs of ADR would be disproportionate to the value of the claim;
- public interest or policy issues are involved;
- settlement through direct negotiation is imminent;
- summary judgment or strike out is appropriate;
- belief that one of the parties has no desire to attempt genuine settlement discussions.[117]

---

111 Does not include family courts.
112 34% of respondents to the Lord Chancellor's ADR Discussion Paper were in favour of sanctions for unreasonably refusing to try ADR: Lord Chancellor's Department *ADR Discussion Paper: Summary of responses*, August 2000, at para 71.
113 D Shapiro 'Alternative Dispute Resolution under the new Civil Rules: some guidelines for lawyers and judges' (1999) 18(7) *Litigation – the Journal of Contentious Business* 1 at 7.
114 Commercial Court ADR Working Party *Second Report*, 1998.
115 For example, the Commercial Mediation Centre's Agreement on Fees provides that, if the mediator finds that the mediation has been initiated or conducted frivolously or vexatiously by one of the parties, the mediator may order that party to pay the fees of the mediation in full.
116 Lord Chancellor's Department, *ADR Discussion Paper: Summary of responses*, op cit, at para 72.
117 In *M v H* [2000] 1 FLR 394, the court considered that a refusal to mediate was unreasonable and justified award of costs to the willing party; and in *Wade v George Little Sebire & Co* (29 September 1999, unreported) (QBD), a refusal to mediate (and a failure to respond to a Part 36 offer) resulted in indemnity costs being awarded against the unwilling party.

In relation to the second issue, of the reasonableness of conduct in mediation, some jurisdictions highlight the issue by requiring parties to participate in mediation in 'good faith'. The rules of some mediation organisations in the UK also specify that parties are required to participate in mediation in 'good faith'.[118] The attitude in those jurisdictions to what constitutes a lack of 'good faith' could provide an insight into what might be considered 'unreasonable' behaviour in the UK. US cases have found that a failure to appear at a mediation or failing to prepare for a mediation indicate that the 'good faith' requirement had not been met.[119] In one US case, the court found that a refusal to co-operate with the mediator; denying the other party an opportunity to put forward proposals for resolving the dispute; being agitated and belligerent; or being hostile about the process would indicate a failure to participate in 'good faith'.[120] Other factors which might indicate that a party has not acted in 'good faith' include failing to pay mediation fees and failing to help the mediator to start and finish the mediation within the time fixed for the mediation.[121]

The Supreme Court of Western Australia has given some indication of what might constitute unreasonable behaviour, and which may justify a cost sanction being imposed:

> '[where a party in mediation] adopts an obstructive or unco-operative attitude in regard to attempts to narrow the issues and where it is subsequently shown that, but for such conduct, issues may have been reduced, the extent to which the trial has been unnecessarily extended is a relevant factor when deciding the question of costs.'[122]

In a further Australian case, the Native Title Tribunal listed, in relation to a statutory duty to negotiate 'in good faith', the criteria which may indicate unreasonable conduct:[123]

* unreasonable delay in initiating communications;
* failure to make proposals;
* unexplained failure to communicate with other parties within a reasonable time;
* failure to contact one or more of the other parties;
* failure to follow up a lack of response from another party;
* failure to organise a meeting between the parties;
* failure to take reasonable steps to facilitate and engage in discussions between the parties;
* stalling negotiations with unexplained delays;
* making unnecessary postponement of meetings;
* sending negotiators without authority to settle the dispute;
* refusing to agree on trivial matters;
* shifting position when an agreement seems imminent;
* adopting an inflexible non-negotiable position;

---

118 For example, Commercial Mediation Centre's *Mediation Rules and Procedures*; and Centre for Business Arbitration *Mediation Rules*.
119 For example, *Barsoumian v Szozda* 108 FRD 426; and *Flaherty v Dayton Electric Manufacturing Co* 109 FRD 617.
120 *Graham v Baker* 447 NW 2d 397.
121 G Davies and J Lieboff 'Reforming the civil litigation system; streamlining the adversarial framework' (1994) 14(10) *Proctor* 10.
122 Ipp J in *Capolingua v Thylum Proprietary Ltd* (1991) 5 WALR 137.
123 *West Australia v Taylor* (1996) 134 FLR 211 at 224–5.

- failing to make any counter-proposals;
- unilateral conduct which harms the negotiating process, for example, issuing inappropriate press releases;
- refusing to sign a written agreement which governs the negotiation process;
- failing to do what a reasonable person would do in the circumstances.

Clearly, a number of those criteria could apply equally to the mediation context.

Respondents to the Lord Chancellor's ADR Discussion Paper considered that a failure to agree on a mediator or to provide information during the mediation and a failure to attend the mediation with appropriate authority should be regarded by a court in determining whether a cost sanction should be imposed. Respondents made the distinction between such behaviour and 'tough negotiation', which should not be penalised.[124]

Confidentiality, privilege, natural justice and neutrality issues[125]

The US and Australian cases show that the issue of what constitutes unreasonable behaviour or behaviour which is not 'in good faith' requires a case-by-case examination.[126] If a court is to investigate parties' conduct before and during a mediation, an additional three problems arise.

In order for a court to investigate the conduct of parties, the first problem is what mechanism would allow the court to be informed of that conduct. A report to the court could be provided either by the parties or the mediator. Such a report may need to provide the court with some understanding of the parties' attitudes in the mediation, the conduct of their lawyers in the mediation, whether there was any non-attendance at the mediation, the reasons for any adjournment of the mediation and whether and, if so, what kind of outcome was achieved in the mediation. Providing this information is contrary to the confidential and without prejudice nature of the mediation process. Some believe that inroads into confidentiality is 'a price which has to be paid to secure the genuine commitment on both sides to the mediation',[127] whereas others believe that that confidentiality cannot be impinged upon.[128] Invading confidentiality may also act as a deterrent to attempting mediation in the first place,[129] which creates a vicious circle. The mediator's role can also be rendered difficult by reporting requirements as parties are more likely to be guarded with their comments.

---

124 Lord Chancellor's Department *ADR Discussion Paper: Summary of responses*, August 2000, at para 74.
125 See Chapter 12 for a discussion of the legal issues which arise.
126 C McPheeters 'Leading horses to water: may courts which have the power to order attendance at mediation also require good faith negotiation?' (1992) *Journal of Dispute Resolution* 377; and E Sherman 'Court-mandated ADR: what form of participation should be required?' (1993) 46 *SMULR* 2079.
127 Lightman J, reported in D Shapiro 'Alternative Dispute Resolution under the New Civil Rules: some guidelines for lawyers and judges' (1999) 18(7) *Litigation – the Journal of Contentious Business* 1.
128 For a detailed analysis, see J Hamilton 'Protecting Confidentiality in Mandatory Mediation: lessons from Ontario and Saskatchewan' (1999) 24 *Queens' Law Journal* 561 at 567–72.
129 The CEDR MORI 2000 poll revealed a number of concerns from lawyers about judges enquiring into the conduct of parties in a mediation: Centre for Dispute Resolution *Civil Justice Audit*, April 2000.

The following options may address this problem:

- disclosure may be required in limited circumstances, for example, fraud or misleading conduct;
- reporting could be limited to advising the court if a party did not attend the mediation at all;
- advice on whether or not an agreement was reached in the mediation could be required, without disclosure of the contents of any agreement;[130]
- the issue of the parties' conduct in the mediation could be raised by the court with the parties or their lawyers direct, not with the mediator.[131]

By way of example, the Legal Services Commission is informed of a client's refusal to participate in mediation through a report made by the client's solicitor, the opponent or someone else on the client's behalf.

The second problem is the issue of natural justice to the parties. If, for example, a mediator is obliged to report to a court on the parties' conduct in a mediation, the mediator should inform the parties and they should be entitled to examine the mediator's report and to examine the mediator.

The third difficulty, in relation to a court's investigation of parties' conduct in a mediation, is the neutrality of the trial judge who may receive access to confidential or privileged information in the mediation report itself. In the Western Australian case of *Ruffles v Chilman and Hamilton*[132] an application was made for the trial judge to disqualify himself on the basis that, due to comments made by the mediator to the judge following an unsuccessful mediation, the judge was no longer neutral:

'. . . the integrity of [mediation] is of critical importance . . . this requires that there should be no communication between the mediator on the one hand and the judge who will either hear or is hearing the action . . . [otherwise,] confidence in the process of mediation is likely to be seriously compromised.'[133]

US commentators have suggested that these difficulties could be overcome by requiring parties to undertake certain preparations ahead of the mediation, for example, by requiring parties to exchange position papers; requiring the parties to

---

130 By way of example, the District Court Rules (QLD) 1968 provide, in s 399, that the mediator should ensure that the agreement is sealed, endorsed 'not to be opened without an order of a District Court or judge' and filed in the court. Compare Tenancy Tribunal Act (ACT), s 21 which requires the mediator to specify in a report the terms of any mediated agreement in relation to tenancy disputes.

131 In a Mercantile Court case in Leeds, the judge made such enquiries, for the purpose of exercising a discretion on costs, although ultimately the judge did not take into account the evidence about the parties' conduct in the mediation. Respondents to the Lord Chancellor's ADR Discussion Paper referred to the power given to the court in the CPR, r 18.1(1) to order a party to give additional information in relation to the matter in dispute at any time as providing justification for this approach: see Lord Chancellor's Department *ADR Discussion Paper: Summary of responses*, August 2000, at para 79. For more detail on issues of confidentiality and privilege, see Part I and also further sections on these issues in Chapter 12.

132 (1996–7) 17 WAR 1.

133 Per Kennedy J. This case and the issues it raises are considered in detail in D Spencer 'Communication between mediator and judge leads to finding of bias' (1997) 8(4) *Australian Dispute Resolution Journal* 308.

bring to the mediation all relevant documents; and requiring party representatives to have authority to settle at the mediation. These requirements could be set out in an ADR order or form part of the Agreement to Mediate.[134] It would then be a case for a court through basic questioning of the parties to consider whether the stipulated requirements had been met.[135] Shapiro suggests that the judge could ask the parties a range of direct questions, which would not disclose the content of the mediation itself, for example: 'Did you agree on a mediator? How many sessions did you have? How long did these last? Was someone there who had the authority to settle the case? Would you be prepared to try again with a different mediator?'[136]

Other sanctions?

In comparison to court rules in some of the Australian jurisdictions, the CPR do not go so far as to stay a claimant's case if the claimant refuses to mediate or is unco-operative in a mediation.[137] Although this form of sanction was suggested in responses to the Lord Chancellor's ADR Discussion Paper, the suggestion was limited to extreme cases. Further suggestions in response to the Discussion Paper included refusal by the court to allocate a trial date;[138] reduction in or refusal to award statutory interest; and publication of a 'name and shame' list.[139]

Protections

If mediation is mandated, consideration would also need to be given to what additional conditions should apply in order to protect the parties. For example, in relation to:

- the cost of mediation;
- the quality of the mediation process;
- the training and qualifications of mediators; and
- on-going evaluation.[140]

---

134 The Commercial Court's proposed ADR Order sets out a list of requirements: see See Commercial Court *Commercial Court Guide*, October 1999. The standard Mediation Agreement and Mediation Rules and Procedures of most UK mediation organisations set out similar requirements.

135 E Sherman 'Court-mandated ADR: what form of participation should be required?' (1993) 46 *SMULR* 2079.

136 D Shapiro 'Alternative Dispute Resolution under the new Civil Rules: some guidelines for lawyers and judges' (1999) 18(7) *Litigation – the Journal of Contentious Business* 1; and Lord Chancellor's Department *ADR Discussion Paper: Summary of responses*, August 2000, at para 7.31.

137 G Davies and J Lieboff 'Reforming the civil litigation system; streamlining the adversarial framework' (1994) 14(10) *Proctor* 10.

138 For the implications of this in the light of the Human Rights Act, see the discussion in the section above.

139 Lord Chancellor's Department *ADR Discussion Paper: Summary of responses*, op cit, at para 75.

140 See Chapter 11, on Training and Standards, for an overview of the approach, in those jurisdictions where mediation is mandated, which requires mediators to satisfy certain minimum qualification requirements.

Court-annexed Mediation

In the US, the issue of court-annexed mediation was considered a natural progression as adjudication and negotiation is viewed as a continuous process.[141] In the UK, where at this stage alternative dispute resolution is considered a distinct process from the courts, at least in cases other than family disputes, the debate is over whether, and to what extent, mediation should be court-annexed.

Arguments in favour of court-annexed schemes

Some of the arguments in favour of court-annexed mediation focus on the advantages for courts, in the form of reduction in delays, and by allowing limited judicial resources to be freed up to handle public interest and complex cases.[142] Problems can occur, however, if courts rely on court-annexed mediation with the unrealistic belief that it can resolve all access to justice problems.[143]

Other arguments in favour of court-connected mediation focus on the benefits for litigants, by providing them with more dispute resolution options and increased satisfaction with the court system.[144] In Singapore, by way of example, two surveys conducted by the courts suggest that court-annexed mediation has a positive impact on court users.[145] This factor may have prompted the extension of the use of mediation beyond civil cases to include other types of cases in the courts, including assessment of damages and disputes over costs of civil proceedings.[146] American studies show that litigants who have used court-annexed mediation report satisfaction with the process and consider that it provides a fairer and more personal process than court adjudication.[147] The comparison is difficult to make, however, in the absence of data relating to comparable procedures.[148] Although the Rand

---

141 American judges participate, at least to some extent, in attempting to settle cases that come before them: see, for example, M Galanter 'The emergence of the judge as a mediator in civil cases' (1996) 69(5) *Judicature* 257.

142 See M Fix and P J Harter *Hard cases, vulnerable people: an analysis of mediation programs at the multi-door courthouse of the Superior Court of the District of Columbia*, The Urban Institute and State Justice Institute Washington, 1992, for a study of the effects of one ADR programme on a US court. See also L Ray 'The multi-door courthouse idea: building the courthouse of the future . . . today' (1985) 1(17) *Ohio State Journal on Dispute Resolution* 7; and L Ray and P Kestner *The multi-door experience: dispute resolution and the courthouse of the future*, Standing Committee on Dispute Resolution American Bar Association, Washington DC, 1988, II-4.

143 See S Press 'Court-connected ADR: policies and issues' (1995) 28 *Forum* 5.

144 Ibid; and J Macfarlane *Ontario civil mediation pilot flagship*, available at http://acjnet. extn.ualberta.ca/docs/minagont.html, 19 March 1998, for an evaluation of the Ontario government's pilot court-annexed mediation service focusing on client satisfaction and the impact on settlement rates and timelines.

145 L Boulle and T Hwee Hwee *Mediation: principles, process, practice*, Butterworths, Singapore, 2000, at Chapters 5, 11 and Annex A.

146 The *1996 Judiciary Annual Report*, at p 53. See Chapter 7 for details of court-based mediation schemes.

147 J Pearson 'An evaluation of alternatives to court adjudication' (1982) 7 *Justice System Journal* 420.

148 R Ingleby *Why not toss a coin? Issues of quality and efficiency in Alternative Dispute*

Corporation concluded that court-annexed ADR offers litigants a more satisfying form of justice, its report of court-annexed ADR in US Federal District courts under the Civil Justice Reform Act 1990 was neutral.[149]

Arguments against court-annexed schemes

A fundamental objection to court-annexed ADR schemes is that ADR processes should be kept separate from courts, ensuring that courts limit their function to adjudication, and that ADR is an option provided by neutrals separate from the court.[150] There is also the fear that active promotion of settlement by judges, whether by mediation or other means, may lead to the risk that judges will form an impression of a case based on incomplete evidence.[151] There are also concerns that, if judges promote settlement, the fairness, independence and impartiality of the judicial system as a whole may be prejudiced.[152] These concerns are particularly appropriate, it is argued, in light of the Human Rights Act,[153] which will seek to ensure that the right to a fair trial is protected.[154] Even suggestions about mediation from a judge can weigh heavily with parties, and may exert undue pressure to mediate.[155] Studies in court-annexed family mediation in England and Wales suggest this concern, with parties admitting that the connection between the court and mediation provided a powerful incentive to attend mediation.[156] Some of the studies even revealed that the parties felt, if they did not participate in court-annexed mediation, this would be held against them later by a judge.[157]

Resolution, Paper presented at the AIJA 9th Annual Conference, 1991.

149 Rand Corporation *An evaluation of mediation and early neutral evaluation under the Civil Justice Reform Act*, Institute for Civil Justice, 1996.

150 Although only a small number of judges were interviewed as part of the CEDR MORI 2000 poll, those who responded considered that mediation should be kept separate from the court, even to the extent that they did not feel that they should be drawn into discussions over appointment of mediators: Centre for Dispute Resolution *Civil Justice Audit*, April 2000. The view of some family judges also, in the early 1980s, was that mediation should be kept separate from any element of court interference: see, for example, University of Newcastle upon Tyne Conciliation Project Unit, *Report to the Lord Chancellor's Department on the costs and effectiveness of conciliation in England and Wales*, March 1989, at p 49.

151 Sir Laurence Street 'The Courts and mediation – a warning' (1991) 2 *Australian Dispute Resolution Journal* 203; and Sir Laurence Street 'Mediation and the judicial institution' (1997) 71 *Australian Law Journal* 796.

152 Ibid.

153 Came into effect in October 2000.

154 F Maher 'All is fair in mediation' *The Lawyer*, 27 March 2000.

155 S Roberts 'ADR and Civil Justice: an Unresolved Relationship (1993) 56(3) *Modern Law Review* 452 at 468.

156 University of Newcastle upon Tyne Conciliation Project Unit, *Report to the Lord Chancellor's Department on the costs and effectiveness of conciliation in England and Wales*, March 1989, where, at p 286, the following views of participants in mediation were reported:
   • 'I just presumed that I'd got to attend . . . and that was it . . .'
   • 'I greeted it . . . as though it was a legal obligation . . .'

157 Ibid, at p 287.

Apart from the degree of connection to courts or judges, another fundamental objection to a court-annexed ADR scheme is the concern that ADR might not be as effective as when it is undertaken independently of the court process.[158] Also, the emphasis in mediation on parties themselves making decisions about the dispute may be extinguished if mediation is located within the framework of the courts.[159] If mediation is court-annexed, it may also lead to unnecessary formality and, in turn, anxiety and intimidation, which feelings may be carried into a mediation, rendering the mediator's role more difficult.[160] Time pressures are also more likely when mediation is court-annexed.[161] Depending on the degree of connection to the courts, the danger is that ADR becomes overly formal. In New Zealand, for example, where mediation is available within the Employment Tribunal, critics comment:

> '. . . mediation at the tribunal has become a legal forum where advocates with vested economic interests argue against each other from prepared mediation statements, acting out choreographed tactical exchanges, designed to assess the opposition's arguments rather than resolve the dispute.'[162]

On a more theoretical level, it is argued that private and court-annexed mediation are entirely different processes with different characteristics.[163] US commentators, in particular, have argued that court-annexed mediation should not be considered mediation at all, but as an additional litigation strategy, more aptly described as 'litigotiation'.[164] Court-annexed mediation extends state control to what, in essence, is private dispute resolution[165] and, in turn, regulation of mediation may become covert.[166] US studies also show that the private and public costs of court-annexed mediation programmes can lead to greater expense, congestion and delay in courts as more people are prepared to litigate, in the knowledge that an ADR process will provide a fallback position.[167]

---

158 G Davis and K Bader 'In-court mediation: The consumer view, Parts I and II' *Family Law*, vol 15, No 3; and University of Newcastle upon Tyne Conciliation Project Unit, *Report to the Lord Chancellor's Department on the costs and effectiveness of conciliation in England and Wales*, March 1989.

159 University of Newcastle upon Tyne Conciliation Project Unit, *Report to the Lord Chancellor's Department on the costs and effectiveness of conciliation in England and Wales*, op cit, at p 15.

160 Ibid, at p 300.

161 For example, time-limited mediations in the Central London County Court Mediation Pilot. Compare the approach of the Patents Court: see the section on Courts and Mediation in Chapter 7.

162 L Skiffington 'There must be a better way: alternative dispute resolution' [1997] *ELB* 24.

163 P L Whissler 'Mediation and adjudication in the small claims court: the effects of process and case characteristics' (1995) 29 *Law & Society Review* 323.

164 M Galanter 'Worlds of deals: using negotiation to teach legal process' (1984) 34 *Journal of Legal Education* 268.

165 R L Abel 'Conservative conflict and the reproduction of capitalism: The role of informal justice' (1981) *International Journal of the Psychology of Law* 9.

166 S Roberts 'ADR and Civil Justice: an Unresolved Relationship (1993) 56(3) *Modern Law Review* 452.

167 R J MacCoun, E A Lind and T R Tyler *ADR in Trial and Appellate Courts*, RAND, Santa Monica, 1992, at p 98.

The UK position

An overview of the UK position is considered from the point of view of civil cases.[168] In relation to family court-annexed mediation, the Booth Committee highlighted the incompatibility of the same court officer carrying out in the same case both mediation and welfare reporting.[169] Judges have expressed the same view in a number of decisions,[170] as have respondents to family mediation surveys.[171]

The Courts and Legal Services Committee of the Law Society of England and Wales recommended court-annexed mediation for other civil cases following publication in 1991 of a report by its ADR Working Party.[172] A mediation scheme launched shortly afterwards by the Bristol Law Society was intended to be court-annexed, but the Lord Chancellor's Department took the view in 1992 that it would not be appropriate for courts to assist mediation pilot schemes in this way.[173] The scheme was restructured as an out-of-court mediation scheme. Even an application for mediation form, designed by the Bristol Law Society and local district judges, and intended to be enclosed with automatic directions issued by district judges,[174] was dropped in case it was perceived as a referral to mediation by the court.[175]

The Central London County Court Mediation Pilot limited court involvement to administration of the Pilot, including distribution of information on mediation, sending mediation offers, arranging the mediators, and providing a venue for mediations.[176] The mediation pilot for the Leeds Combined Court Centre also involves the Court to the limited extent of administration, including distribution of information on mediation and the scheme.[177] The Court of Appeal writes to parties, requesting them to consider the mediation option.[178] The Patents Court ADR Programme[179] is administered by the Court through an Administrator who is the Deputy District Judge of the Court. The Court's involvement goes further than administration, as the Administrator can be asked to encourage parties to attempt mediation and, if parties are unable to agree on the mediator, the Administrator can

---

168 For an overview of mediation in criminal cases, see the section on victim-offender mediation in Chapter 8.

169 Booth Committee *Report of the Committee on Matrimonial Causes*, HMSO, London, 1985, at para 41.2.

170 For example, *Re H* [1986] 1 FLR 476; *Scott v Scott* [1986] 2 FLR 320; *Clarkson v Winkley* (1987) 151 JP Jo 526.

171 A number of those surveys are reported by the University of Newcastle upon Tyne Conciliation Project Unit, *Report to the Lord Chancellor's Department on the costs and effectiveness of conciliation in England and Wales*, March 1989, at p 51.

172 The Law Society ADR Working Party *ADR – Report prepared by Henry Brown for the Courts, and Legal Services Committee*, The Law Society, London, 1991 (The Brown Report).

173 M Davies, G Davis and J Webb *Promoting Mediation: Report of a study of Bristol Law Society's Mediation Scheme in its preliminary phase*, 1996 Research & Policy Planning Unit Research Study no 21, The Law Society, at p 12.

174 Ibid, at pp 13 and 14.

175 Ibid.

176 For further details, see the section on Courts and Mediation in Chapter 7.

177 Ibid.

178 Ibid.

179 Ibid.

make the appointment.[180] The Commercial Court has maintained a list of ADR providers throughout the life of its ADR scheme. Its involvement extends beyond mere distribution of information to making ADR orders, even in cases where all the parties refuse to mediate,[181] and if parties cannot agree on the appointment of the neutral, the issue can be referred back to the Court.[182]

The Lord Chancellor indicated in April 2000 that his Department will support court mediation pilots,[183] although it is not yet clear to what extent any schemes will provide for court-annexed mediation. It is easy to see how court-annexed mediation is the next logical step in the reforms, which have already taken place, following Lord Woolf's Report. The results of the CEDR MORI 2000 poll suggested that court users may welcome changes, even more fundamental than court-annexed mediation, since 60% of poll respondents expressed a desire for judges to initiate settlement discussions in the course of litigation.[184]

The Lord Chancellor's Department ADR Discussion Paper outlined the following options for the future:

- Mediation schemes, using court facilities, might be attached to every civil and high court trial centre, along the lines of the Central London County Court Mediation Pilot, although the issues of funding for administration and payment of the mediators need to be addressed.[185]
- For fast track or small claims, an 'off the peg' mediation scheme is more likely to keep costs proportionate to the value of the claim. Such a scheme may require court staff to administer the mediation and arrange mediators. Like the Central London County Court Mediation Pilot, it is likely that such a scheme would involve time-limited mediation and fixed fees.[186]
- For multi-track, and higher value cases, private mediation is likely to be more appropriate and the court's role, as with the Commercial Court ADR Scheme, might be confined to identifying appropriate cases for mediation and providing parties with lists of ADR organisations.[187]
- Mediation schemes might not be linked to courts at all, but instead to the Community Legal Service.[188]

None of the suggestions extended so far as to include, as an option, providing court officers to mediate cases. The Lord Chancellor's suggestions also focused on civil/commercial disputes only, and excluded family cases. The bulk of respondents to the Discussion Paper agreed that litigants in the fast track and small claims would benefit from ADR schemes offering a set service and fixed fees, and that parties in multi-track cases should make their own ADR arrangements.[189]

---

180 Ford J *The Patents Court ADR Programme*, 1996.
181 For further details, see the section on Courts and Mediation in Chapter 7.
182 Announced by the Lord Chancellor at the CEDR Civil Justice Audit in April 2000.
183 For further details about his Reports, and consequent reforms, see the section on Civil Justice Reforms in Chapter 7.
184 Centre for Dispute Resolution *Civil Justice Audit*, April 2000. In the small claims jurisdiction, for example, district judges already use a wide range of procedures aimed at achieving settlement in cases, including mediation, conciliation and arbitration.
185 Lord Chancellor's Department *ADR Discussion Paper*, November 1999, at para 6.14.
186 Ibid, at para 6.19.
187 Ibid, at para 6.18.
188 Ibid, at para 6.17.
189 Lord Chancellor's Department *ADR Discussion Paper: Summary of responses*, August

Basic considerations for court-annexed mediation

Assuming that court-based mediation schemes will develop in the UK, a number of considerations arise, particularly given the experience in other jurisdictions, like the US and Australia.[190]

The fundamental consideration is the degree of connection to the court. A mediation programme may reside in the court; or be directly responsible to the court; or be a private service, to which the court refers cases for mediation. Over time, court-annexed mediation programmes in the US, for example, have become more detached from the courts due to the large number of private mediation services, lack of funds for court-supported programmes and insufficient court facilities.[191] Experience in the US has also shown that the degree of connection issue may depend on whether uniformity is required and the degree of flexibility required to allow changes as lessons are learnt.[192] In Australia, the degree of connection varies between courts. For example, the Family Court of Australia provides a range of ADR services, even before proceedings are filed, including ADR information sessions, voluntary mediation counselling and mediation services. In comparison, 'Settlement Weeks' in Australia, Canada and New Zealand have provided a form of court-annexed mediation, albeit that the connection to courts has been limited to courts inviting litigants to participate in a 'mediation blitz'. Feedback from such attempts in each country has confirmed that the 'Weeks' have had a significant impact on public attitudes and perceptions of mediation.[193] Mediation Weeks help to raise the profile of mediation among lawyers, court users and the general public. Lawyers are also provided with an opportunity to practise their mediation advocacy skills. Such benefits would be invaluable to the relatively young mediation movement in the UK.

The next fundamental consideration is whether mediation services should be supplied by personnel employed or appointed by the court. This issue depends largely on the degree of connection of the programme to the court. For example, in the Federal Court of Australia, most mediations are conducted by court registrars. A related, albeit distinct issue, is whether judges themselves should use mediation techniques to attempt to resolve disputes.[194] The English courts have not yet sought to take control over settlement discussions.[195] The US experience indicates that judges are motivated to pro-actively settle small value cases in order to free up

---

2000, at paras 55 and 56.

190 For a detailed discussion, see E Plapinger and M Shaw *Court ADR – elements of program design*, CPR Institute for Dispute Resolution, New York, 1992.

191 S Press 'Court-connected ADR: policies and issues' (1995) 28 *Forum* 5.

192 Ibid.

193 For example, J Marshall 'Mediation Week 1996 reviewed' (1996) *Lawtalk*, Issue 486, at p 54. In the UK, the Bristol Law Society Mediation Scheme, outlined in Chapter 7, attempted 'Settlement Days'.

194 As in the US, where it is considered an atypical dispute that requires court resolution: D Provine 'Justice à la carte: on the privatisation of dispute resolution' (1992) 12 *Studies in Law, Politics & Society* 345.

195 Compare the apparent desire of lawyers for judges to do so, as identified by the CEDR MORI 2000 poll, reported in the Centre for Dispute Resolution *Civil Justice Audit*, April 2000; and see C Glasser 'Civil Procedure and the Lawyer – the adversary system and the decline of the orality principle' (1993) 56 *Modern Law Review* 307.

valuable court time for the most complex cases, as these are likely to take up substantial trial time.[196]

The next fundamental issue is funding.[197] The US experience shows that the temptation is to expend too little or no funds, particularly if the goal of court mediation programmes is to make more efficient use of limited court resources.[198] Included in the issue of budgeting is whether mediators should be paid and, if so, by whom and how much.[199] A study of Federal District courts in the US revealed that, although initially most schemes had been run on a pro-bono basis, by 1996 over two-thirds required parties to pay mediation fees.[200]

A further consideration is the method by which cases are to be selected for mediation. There are a range of possibilities, including:

- that all cases could be eligible;
- that a mandatory cap might apply;
- that certain cases could be exempted, for example on public policy grounds, such as cases involving fraud or domestic violence;
- that the selection could be done on a case-by-case basis, by reviewing the court documents, interviewing the parties or by requesting the parties to fill out a questionnaire.[201]

The latter option emerged from the US 'multi-door' courthouse model, developed by Professor Frank Sander and trialled in a number of US courts since the 1980s, involving a case intake and diagnosis mechanism and a diversity of dispute resolution processes to which referrals could be made. Professor Sander envisaged:

'. . . by the year 2000 not simply a courthouse but a dispute resolution centre, where the grievant would first be channelled through a screening clerk who would then direct him or her to the process, or sequence of processes, most appropriate to his or her dispute.'[202]

The US experience has indicated that, although classes of cases can be readily identified as eligible for court-annexed mediation programmes, determination of

---

196 J A Wall and D E Rude 'Judges' mediation of settlement negotiations' (1987) 72(2) *Journal of Applied Psychology* 234.
197 The Rand Report concluded that the administrative costs for courts ranged from US$130–$490 per case depending on the number of referrals: RAND Corporation *An evaluation of mediation and early neutral evaluation under the Civil Justice Reform Act*, Institute for Civil Justice, 1996.
198 S Press 'Court-connected ADR: policies and issues' (1995) 28 *Forum* 5.
199 Frank Sander, who invented the multi-door courthouse idea, is a strong proponent of state funding of mediators participating in court-connected mediation programmes, in the same manner as judges, but that, if this is not possible, volunteer neutrals should be used: F Sander *Emerging ADR issues in State and Federal Courts*, American Bar Association Litigation Section, Chicago, 1991.
200 E Plapinger and D Stienstra *ADR and settlement in the Federal District Courts: a sourcebook for judges and lawyers*, Federal Judicial Centre and CPR Institute for Dispute Resolution, 1996.
201 1998 survey by Kessler and Finkelstein in District Columbia confirmed that intake requires experienced ADR professionals: H Brown and A Marriott *ADR Principles and Practice* (2nd edn), Sweet & Maxwell, London, 1999, at p 93.
202 F Sander 'Varieties of dispute processing: Address to The Pound Conference' (1976) 70 *FRD* 79 at 130.

which case within the class should be mediated is more difficult.[203] A multi-door courthouse has been established in Singapore, and is considered the cornerstone[204] of the courts' ADR efforts. It seeks to increase public awareness of dispute resolution processes. It also acts as a one-stop service centre that assists the public in locating appropriate dispute resolution mechanisms by matching a dispute with an appropriate resolution forum. It further provides administrative assistance by directing disputants to appropriate dispute resolution programmes in the various divisions of the courts and outside the court system also.[205]

Related to the issue of screening or case selection are issues of when the selection should be made;[206] by whom;[207] and whether mediation should be compulsory for the selected cases, for specified categories of cases or within the court's discretion.[208] The US experience, in relation to the issue of who should make the selection, has identified four different approaches:

- parties assess their own cases for ADR suitability;
- professional consultants screen cases for suitability;
- court staff assess cases based on interviews, questionnaires or pleadings; and
- judges may make assessments, for example, on a case management conference.

On the issue of the extent of compulsion of the reference to mediation by courts, the following are possibilities:

- Court referral without formal authority: this type of court-annexed mediation takes place where the court, on its own initiative, suggests or recommends that the parties proceed to mediation, or encourages the parties to consider mediation.
- Referral in the court's discretion, with the parties' consent: this type of court-annexed mediation takes place where the statutes, rules of court or practice directions provide for the court to refer matters to mediation with the consent of the parties. This allows the parties to 'opt out', an option currently being considered by the Lord Chancellor's Department.
- Referral in the court's discretion, without the parties' consent: this category takes place where statutes, rules of court or practice directions allow the court to make a referral in its discretion, notwithstanding the objection of one or more parties. This is provided for extensively in Australia, for example, in Victoria, in the Supreme Court, in the County Court, and in the Building Cases lists of both courts.[209] It also operates in Queensland.[210] The statutes and

---

203 P Edelman 'Institutionalising dispute resolution alternatives' (1984) 9(2) *Justice System Journal* 134.
204 *Solutions*, a publication of the Ministry of Law, Issue 2, March 1999, at p 12.
205 *Singapore Academy of Law Newsletter*, November/December 1999, Issue no 63, at p 2.
206 For example, at issue of proceedings; close of pleadings; within a certain period of time after issue of proceedings; or before a hearing date.
207 For example, the court (and then the question is whether it should be a judge, master or other court staff); the parties; or private ADR organisations.
208 Macfarlane considers that it is indefensible to screen cases by reference to area of law: J Macfarlane *Court-based mediation for civil cases: an evaluation of the Ontario Court (General Division) ADR Centre*, Faculty of Law, University of Windsor, 1995.
209 Supreme Court Act 1986 (Vic), s 25; County Court Act 1958, s 47A; and 'Mediation in the County Court' (1988) 62 *LIJ* 11.
210 The amending Act amended the Supreme Court of QLD Act 1991, the District Courts

rules provide a high degree of regulation of court-connected mediation.[211]

- Mandatory referral: this type of court-connected mediation takes place where statutes, rules of court or practice directions make it compulsory for the court to refer the parties to mediation. For example, the Australian Federal Court Rules make provision for compulsory conciliation conferences in respect of property matters at which registrars perform some mediative functions.[212]

There is evidence in the UK of the operation of the first three types of referral mechanisms. The Commercial Court has stayed cases, in order for parties to attempt mediation, notwithstanding their objection, even if this were not the intended consequence of CPR, r 26.[213]

Consideration also needs to be given, in the case of court-annexed mediation programmes, to the mediation process itself. For instance, should the court protect confidentiality and, if so, how?[214] Should mediation be time-limited and, if so, for what duration? Should courts allow the option of more than one mediation session? Should courts address the issue of enforceability of agreements reached in the course of a mediation? Should courts have some obligation to ensure the quality of mediation services, for example, by ensuring that mediators have been trained or accredited or comply with a particular code of conduct? Alternatively, should courts certify or approve mediators?

Concerns about these issues in other jurisdictions have been greater where mediation is also compulsory,[215] in which case courts may also need to consider complaints procedures. The fear is that, once mediation becomes institutionalised to this extent, it will become unduly formal, hedged with rules and requirements. In the US, National Standards for Court-Connected Mediation,[216] developed in 1992, recommended that court-annexed mediation programmes should:

- provide information about mediation;
- establish criteria for referral;
- develop criteria for selection, training, accreditation and monitoring of mediators;
- establish ethical standards for mediators;
- have policies on confidentiality and on communications between mediators and the courts;
- provide protection from civil liability for court staff mediators.

Act 1967, the Magistrates Courts Act 1921 and the Judicial Review Act 1991.

211 See, for example, Uniform Civil Procedure Rules 1999, Part IV, Division 3.

212 Australian Family Law Act 1975 (Cth), s 79(9)(b) and (c).

213 See Chapter 7 for further discussion on the CPR.

214 For example, should confidentiality attach to the court's administrative arrangements, to the pre-mediation meetings, and to the mediation itself. The Alternative Disputes Resolution Act of 1998 requires US federal district courts to establish confidentiality and conflicts of interest rules which will apply to their ADR programmes: Public Law 105–315 at 28 USC.

215 See the section above on Compulsion or Encouragement to Mediate.

216 Center for Dispute Settlement, Institute of Judicial Administration and State Justice Institute *National Standards for Court-connected Mediation Programs*, Washington DC, 1992.

An additional issue is whether mediators should be required to report to the court about a mediation.[217] Finally, every court-related mediation scheme requires monitoring and evaluation, with a view to ascertaining whether the programme has been effective.

Although these issues raise more questions than they provide answers, they make the point clearly that considerable thought, care and judgment is required, in particular, to ensure that the court-annexed system serves its intended purpose.

Funding Issues in Mediation

Community Legal Service Funding

Developments in England

History of legal aid developments

Historically, there has been a concern that legally-aided parties have no incentive to achieve early settlement. However, information from family solicitors in the late 1980s indicated that mediation could obviate the need for legal aid or at least reduce the cost of the legal aid certificate.[218] In their Second Report on ADR[219] the Law Society also considered that legal aid or other state funding could be crucial to the development of ADR. The Lord Chancellor's White Paper on Legal Aid suggested that legal aid should be expanded to provide a broader range of services, including mediation.[220] A review of civil justice and legal aid by Sir Peter Middleton in 1997 identified three main problems with the legal aid scheme, including the cost of the scheme, its inability to target priority areas and, generally, poor value for money.[221] He suggested that the Government should extend funding to ADR.

---

217 See the section on Courts and Mediation in Chapter 7, and forms required in the case of county court and Patent Court mediations. By way of comparison, in Ottawa, the mediator was required to identify whether some or all issues had been settled in mediation, but not the content of any agreement reached: J Macfarlane *Court-based mediation for civil cases: an evaluation of the Ontario Court (General Division) ADR Centre*, University of Windsor, 1995. See the section above on Compulsion or Encouragement to Mediate for a discussion of the problems associated with mediator reporting requirements.

218 University of Newcastle upon Tyne Conciliation Project Unit, *Report to the Lord Chancellor's Department on the cost and effectiveness of conciliation in England and Wales*, March 1989, at p 29.

219 Law Society of England and Wales *Second Report on ADR*, 1992.

220 The Lord Chancellor's Department *White Paper on Legal Aid: striking the balance*, 1996. In addition, there was concern that negotiations could take place without legal advice and, accordingly, that legal advice should be made available for mediation. The authors' 2000 survey of UK law firms (results appear where relevant throughout this book) identified an example of a judge, frustrated by the futility of the parties fighting a legally-aided case (where there would be nothing left to distribute after the statutory charge was satisfied), wrote to the Legal Aid Board (as it was then called), requesting it to fund a mediation in that case.

221 Sir Peter Middleton *Report to the Lord Chancellor: Review of civil justice and legal aid*, Lord Chancellor's Department, September 1997.

In a 1998 Consultation Paper on Access to Justice With Conditional Fees, the Government confirmed its wish to modernise legal aid because the system was out of date and it was not flexible enough to allow the government to target priority areas.[222] The Lord Chancellor's White Paper *Modernising Justice*, published in December 1998, set out the proposed programme of reforms in legal services, including legal aid.[223] In particular, the White Paper explained that the Access to Justice Act 1999 would replace the Legal Aid Board with a Legal Services Commission, which would prepare a Funding Code setting out the criteria according to which it would fund legal services.[224] The Access to Justice Act 1999 stipulates that the criteria set out in that Code should reflect the principle that, in many family disputes, mediation would be more appropriate than court proceedings.[225]

Family Law Act 1996, s 29

Section 29 in Part III of the Family Law Act 1996 amended the Legal Aid Act 1988 and introduced legally-aided family mediation. It requires, for certain family cases, that suitability for mediation is considered before legal aid will be granted. The aim is to encourage individuals eligible for legal aid to have regard to mediation as an option. The requirement does not apply to certain procedures[226] or if an exemption applies.[227] Otherwise, the applicant will not be granted funding for legal representation unless he or she first attends a meeting with a mediator to determine whether mediation is suitable in the particular case and whether mediation could take place without either party being influenced by fear of violence or other harm. If mediation appears suitable, the mediator will help the party applying for legal representation to decide whether to apply for mediation instead.[228] In considering suitability for mediation, the mediator takes the following factors into account:

- the willingness of the parties to negotiate;
- whether the dispute cannot be mediated;
- whether there are any imbalances of power, for instance, mental or physical incapacity of a party; and
- whether child protection issues are involved.[229]

Even when a mediator considers that a case is suitable for mediation and the applicant agrees to proceed with mediation, an appointment is offered to the

---

222 The Lord Chancellor's Department *Consultation Paper: Access to justice with conditional fees*, 1998.
223 Lord Chancellor's Department White Paper: *Modernising Justice – the Government's plans for reforming Legal Services and the Courts*, December 1998.
224 See Access to Justice Act 1999, s 8.
225 Access to Justice Act 1999, s 8(3).
226 Emergency applications, existing proceedings, amendments Children Act 1989, Part IV or V proceedings, MCA 1973, s 37 or Family Law Act 1996, Pt IV proceedings: Family Law Act 1996, s 29(3G).
227 If the applicant has a disability or is unable to travel to the mediation; if the applicant's partner is unable to attend a mediation because he/she is abroad or is in detention; if the applicant has fear of violence or harm from their partner; where no mediator is available within 14 days after an appointment is sought; if no mediator who can deal with the subject matter of the mediation is available; and where, in the case of a mediation on financial issues, either party is bankrupt: see Family Law Act 1996, s 29(6).
228 Legal Aid Act 1988, s 15 inserted by Family Law Act 1996, s 29.
229 Legal Aid Board *Guidance for solicitors and mediators involved in the pilot implementation of Part III of the Family Law Act 1996*, 1999.

applicant's partner. If the partner does not respond within 14 days or does not wish to attend a meeting with a mediator or attends the meeting with a mediator, but refuses to attempt mediation or the mediator then considers that mediation will not be suitable, the mediator acknowledges this in writing, allowing the applicant to proceed with an application for funding. It is only if the applicant's partner attends the meeting with a mediator, the mediator considers that mediation would be suitable and the partner agrees to attempt mediation that the matter proceeds to mediation.

These mediation referral procedures contemplate that preliminary advice should be given to parties who proceed to a meeting with a mediator.[230] If a matter proceeds to mediation, the advice and assistance given in relation to the mediation, if the mediation is successful or partially successful, is exempt from the solicitor's charge. The statutory charge does not attach to the costs of a legally-aided mediation whether the mediation is successful, partially successful or unsuccessful.[231]

The Access to Justice Act 1999 repeals s 29 of the Family Law Act 1996, although its existence will continue until its operation is reviewed following introduction of the Funding Code.[232] The operation of s 29 of the Family Law Act 1996 is being reviewed by way of pilot, rather than national implementation. The aim of the pilot is to review the arrangements in place to meet the demand for family mediation services. Although s 29 is contained in Part III of the Family Law Act 1996, which was implemented in 1997, its implementation was made subject to satisfactory review. Section 29 has been piloted in a number of areas throughout England and Wales.[233] The Funding Code will incorporate Part III of the Family Law Act 1996, with improvements, following the experience of the s 29 pilots.[234]

Under the s 29 procedure, applicants can only be referred to a mediator who has been approved by the Legal Services Commission to undertake s 29 work.[235] In addition, mediation suppliers must adhere to a code of conduct in order to receive public funding for s 29 mediation.[236] These requirements were forged out of the Lord Chancellor's 1996 White Paper on Legal Aid,[237] which contemplated grants in the

---

230 See the section below on the Funding Code.
231 The Civil Legal Aid (General) (Amendment) (No 2) Regulations 1999 amended the Civil Legal Aid (General) Regulations 1989 to exempt the costs of giving advice and assistance relating to mediation in family matters from the statutory charge.
232 See the section below on the Funding Code.
233 Northamptonshire, Bristol, Cambridge, Manchester, Birmingham, Coventry, Brighton, Cardiff, Chester, Leeds, Liverpool, Newcastle, Nottingham, Reading and London. Janet Walker at Newcastle Centre for Family Studies at Newcastle University has been researching the pilots. She has issued three interim reports (J Walker (ed) *Information meetings and associated provisions within the Family Law Act 1996*: first, second and third evaluation reports to the LCD, 1998 and 1999) and a summary (J Walker (ed) *Summary of research in progress*, LCD, 1999). Her final report has been submitted to the LCD, but has not been released by them at time of publication of this work.
234 See D Hodson *The Family Law Act: Where now?* Paper present at UK College of Family Mediators' Annual Conference, 1 July 1999.
235 Funding was provided to assist national mediation bodies and local mediation services with the development of mediation services to meet the contract requirements in appropriate circumstances.
236 See the section on Training and Standards in Chapter 11.
237 Lord Chancellor's Department *White Paper on Legal Aid: striking the balance*, 1996.

form of franchises to mediation providers, who satisfy good professional practice standards and quality-assured standards of provision and delivery of mediation services. The information meeting pilots ended in May 1999. More than 5,500 people attended an individual meeting and more than 2,100 people attended a group meeting. 7% of attendees proceeded to mediation.[238] Respondents to the authors' survey of UK law firms in 2000 disclosed dissatisfaction with the information meetings as there was considerable delay in some cases before clients could receive legal advice.

Research has been commissioned on publicly-funded mediation services,[239] in particular, on mediation outcomes, client satisfaction, the well-being of children and the cost and speed of mediation.[240] The research will consider children and all-issues mediation.

The Funding Code

On 26 October 1999 the Funding Code was published, providing a draft set of rules relating to the funding of civil cases as part of the Community Legal Service. In addition, two further documents have been published, 'A new approach to funding Civil cases' and 'Testing the Code'. Comments on the proposal were invited by the end of November 1999, with a view to final amendments being made to the Code, although the basic structure of the Code would remain unchanged. The Code came into operation on 1 April 2000 when the Community Legal Service was formally established. The new Legal Services Commission took over from the Legal Aid Board and what was legal aid is now the Community Legal Service Fund. The concepts of advice, assistance and representation under the Legal Aid Act 1988 have been replaced by 'levels of service'. The two main levels of service are Legal Help and Legal Representation. Legal Help replaces advice and assistance and is delivered through general civil contracts. Legal Help does not include the provision of mediation or arbitration.[241] Legal Representation covers representation in court and tribunal proceedings and replaces civil legal aid and ABWOR. Legal Representation also does not include the provision of mediation or arbitration.[242]

The Funding Code and the Access to Justice Act 1999 have provided increased emphasis on ADR:

- by encouraging the expeditious resolution of disputes without unnecessary or protracted court proceedings (Access to Justice Act, s 4(4)(c));
- by ensuring that the most appropriate service is funded (Access to Justice Act, s 8(4)); and
- by seeking to obtain best value for money when funding legal services (Access to Justice Act, s 5(7)).

In relation to family cases, the Funding Code provides that General Family Help is available for those cases which do not need to be referred to mediation under the

---

238 L Tsang 'Separating the issues' *The Law Society Gazette*, 21 July 1999, at p 22.
239 The research has been conducted by a team from the University of Bristol, headed by Professor Davis. The results have been provided to the Legal Services Commission, but had not been released by the LSC at the time of publication of this work. See also M Winner 'Is the research on mediation providing the answer?' (2000) 30 *Fam Law* 138.
240 G Davis 'Monitoring publicly-funded mediation' [1997] *Fam Law* 591.
241 Funding Code, section 2.
242 Ibid.

Code or where a mediator has determined that the case is not suitable for mediation or where a family mediation has been unsuccessful.[243] The aim of General Family Help is to encourage partners to negotiate and to expedite disclosure of information from a partner, with a view to resolving the family dispute without the need for trial. The Funding Code preserves the s 29 procedure in the Family Law Act 1996, outlined above, requiring parties, in certain cases, to consider the suitability of mediation before receiving legal aid funding or legal representation at court.[244] That procedure applies to all applications for General Family Help, outlined above, and for Legal Representation, unless an exemption applies. As with the s 29 procedure, certain proceedings are exempted.[245] In addition, if certain circumstances exist, the dispute is exempt from the meeting with the mediator requirement:

- if the interests of justice require legal representation as a matter of urgency;
- where no mediator is available to hold the meeting;
- if the applicant is an extended family member who is involved in proceedings concerning a child;
- where the applicant is a respondent in family proceedings, in respect of which a court date has been notified; and
- the applicant has a fear of violence or other harm from the partner.

The Code also makes available Help with Mediation in order to ensure that mediation is supported by good quality legal advice. Help with Mediation is limited to:

'. . . advice to a client in support of family mediation, help in drawing up any agreement reached in mediation and, where appropriate, help in confirming such an agreement in a court order.'[246]

It is only available from solicitors with a contract with the LSC in family law. Help with Mediation does not extend to the costs of direct negotiation.[247] Help with Mediation can also be refused if it is more appropriate for the party to be assisted by way of Legal Help.[248] Initial advice in aid of a mediation is given by way of Legal Help and it is expected that the time limit applicable to Legal Help should be used up before Help with Mediation is granted.[249]

The Code defines family mediation as:

'. . . mediation of a family dispute, including assessing whether a mediation appears suitable to the dispute and the parties and all circumstances.'[250]

Accordingly, mediation beyond the initial meeting with a mediator, can only be provided if the mediator is satisfied that mediation is suitable for the dispute, the parties and in all the circumstances.

---

243 Funding Code, section 11.
244 Funding Code, section 7.
245 Proceedings under the MCA 1973, the Magistrate's Courts Act 1978 and Parts I–III of the Children Act 1989.
246 Funding Code, section 2.
247 The Legal Aid Board *A new approach to funding civil cases: Report to the Lord Chancellor following consultation*, October 1999.
248 Funding Code, section 11.
249 Ibid.
250 Funding Code, section 2.

The Code, however, extends funding of mediation beyond family disputes to non-family cases as well. Although family mediation is the only form of ADR which is currently funded directly, funding in other cases can be provided as disbursements under Legal Help or Legal Representation (and occasionally Support Funding) and may cover advice and assistance in preparing for mediation, the representative's attendance at mediation and the mediation fees. In addition, the Code allows for the funding of all forms of alternative dispute resolution, not only mediation, like arbitration and early neutral evaluation. Legal Representation can be refused if a complaints or ombudsman scheme can be pursued before litigation.[251] In addition, Legal Representation may be refused if the case appears suitable for mediation, the other party is prepared to attempt mediation and where there is a specific mediation scheme and the Legal Services Commission considers that the scheme's procedures are effective.[252]

The Legal Services Commission has issued guidance on the application of the funding criteria to ADR.[253] A person who is in receipt of funding will not require authority from the Commission to mediate, although authority can be obtained in relation to the mediator's fees. The Commission intends to provide further guidelines on fee levels for mediation, following discussions with a range of mediation providers.[254] At this stage, its guidance provides that mediator fees should not exceed basic prescribed rates for lawyers providing county court advocacy under certificates for Legal Representation, although the current guidance recognises that the costs of a commercial mediator in a complex case may be higher. The Commission also encourages parties in an unsuccessful mediation to put forward their best without prejudice offers, and further funding decisions will be made in light of those offers.[255] The Commission's guidance under the Code has been made with the benefit of a review of the Lord Chancellor's Department Discussion Paper on ADR.[256]

Apart from family and civil/commercial disputes, the Legal Services Commission intends to explore community mediation further, with a view to considering the potential for contracting with community mediators.[257]

Developments in Scotland

In Scotland eligible parties may obtain legal aid for mediation in relation to issues arising from divorce or separation. Legal advice and assistance may also be available in relation to preparation for a mediation. There is no legal aid franchising as in England.[258] Legal aid is not currently available for mediation in non-family

---

251 Funding Code, section 5.
252 The Legal Aid Board *A new approach to funding civil cases: Report to the Lord Chancellor following consultation*, October 1999, at p 64.
253 See *The Funding Code – decision making guidance*, June 2000. See also the CLS *Outline of Regulatory Framework*, available at http://www.legalservices.gov.uk/stat; and to its *Practical Guide to CLS Funding*, available at http://www.legalservices.gov.uk/leaflets
254 The Legal Aid Board *A new approach to funding in civil cases*, op cit, at p 63.
255 Ibid; and *The Funding Code – decision making guidance*, op cit, at s 7.8(6).
256 Lord Chancellor's Department *ADR Discussion Paper*, November 1999.
257 The Legal Aid Board *A new approach to funding in civil cases*, op cit.
258 On legal aid in Scotland, see the Legal Aid (Scotland) Act 1986.

disputes. The Scottish Office has indicated a willingness to explore ways in which encouragement to mediate in non-family disputes can be given through legal aid.[259]

The Scottish Office's 1998 Consultation Paper, 'Access to Justice: beyond the year 2000', focused primarily on the level of expenditure on civil legal aid in Scotland and the chapter dealing with mediation focused primarily on family mediation. Family disputes account for over half the civil legal aid budget in Scotland, which has led the Scottish Office to focus on whether more should be done to promote the use of mediation in these actions in particular.[260] The Access to Justice Consultation Paper made the following proposals in relation to legal aid:

- that a mediation intake interview should be a pre-requisite to any civil legal aid application;
- that direct legal aid for mediation should be available where a mediation organisation has assessed mediation to be suitable in a particular case and at least one of the parties is eligible for legal aid;
- that pilot studies should evaluate the effectiveness of mediation;
- that there should be Legal Aid Board contracts for mediation intake interview work.[261]

In its response to the Access to Justice Consultation Paper, the Law Society of Scotland considered that 'a gateway into mediation' via intake sessions is not appropriate because a person's entitlement to legal aid should not be dependent upon participation in mediation or postponed until after an attempted mediation.[262] The Law Society has proposed that solicitors should satisfy the Legal Aid Board that a case is not suitable for mediation or that the legally-aided party is not refusing to participate if mediation is suitable.[263]

Developments in Northern Ireland

In Northern Ireland eligible parties may obtain legal aid for family mediation. The Family Mediation Service in Northern Ireland receives £21 per client, although the Service cannot directly claim that sum and must rely on solicitors to claim it and reimburse them. The experience of the Family Mediation Service is that payment is rarely received and, in any event, is inadequate to cover the actual cost of a mediation.[264] Unlike England and like Scotland, there is no legal aid franchising in family mediation in Northern Ireland at this stage.

The Civil Justice Reform Group in Northern Ireland expressed the concern that legally-aided parties will not take up ADR unless legal aid extends to ADR and, accordingly, the Group has recommended the extension of legal aid to cover ADR in all civil cases in Northern Ireland.[265] The Government commissioned a review of

259 The Scottish Office News Release: *McLeish outlines proposed reforms to Scotland's Civil Legal Aid system*, 27 March 1998.
260 Ibid.
261 See Scottish Office Consultation paper: *Access to justice beyond the year 2000*, 1998.
262 Law Society of Scotland *Response to the Access to Justice Consultation Paper*, August 1998.
263 Ibid.
264 C Archbold et al *Divorce in Northern Ireland: unravelling the system*, Report to the Office of Law Reform, HMSO, 1999, at p 198.
265 Civil Justice Reform Group in *Review of the Civil Justice System in Northern Ireland:*

legal aid in Northern Ireland in 1999, to draw upon the consultation which resulted in England's White Paper, *Modernising Justice*.[266] One option suggested in Northern Ireland was to bring mediation organisations within the scope of bodies to whom public funds for legal services can be made available, which would allow these organisations to provide advice for and assistance in mediation in appropriate circumstances.[267] The Consultation determined that a Legal Services Commission would be established, and indicated general support for funding for ADR, but that participation in ADR should not be a precondition for legal aid.[268]

Effect on mediation

Genn's study of the Central London County Court Mediation Pilot revealed that, in cases where the plaintiff had legal aid, the settlement rate was lower than average.[269] In addition, Genn found that mediation was rejected by both parties in 85% of cases when the plaintiff was legally-aided.[270] Genn concluded that these statistics suggest that when a plaintiff is legally-aided the pressure to settle may not be as strong, as the cost implications for the plaintiff are reduced.[271]

Lord Woolf in his Interim Report suggested that a reason for the low take-up of ADR in civil cases could be the lack of availability of legal aid for mediation.[272] The study of the Bristol Law Society Mediation Scheme, however, suggested that legal aid was not a material factor when parties considered whether to mediate, although two solicitors claimed that the unavailability of legal aid at that time to cover mediation costs had prevented them from considering mediation in other cases.[273] In the case of the Central London County Court Mediation Pilot, following the introduction of legal aid for the purposes of the pilot in August 1997, Genn observed that the legal aid provisions had only been used in one case to March 1998. This led Genn to conclude that the absence of legal aid for mediation had been used by parties or their lawyers to rationalise their failure to take up mediation, albeit that they did so for other reasons.[274] Accordingly, the evidence available in England so far suggests that legal aid is not a significant factor determining whether or not parties will attempt mediation, and may dissuade settlement in mediation.

Interim Report, April 1999 and *Final Report*, June 2000.

266 Office of Law Reform *Public Benefit and the Public Purse: legal aid reform in Northern Ireland*, The Office of Law Reform, 1999; and see M C Davey (1999) The Writ *Journal of the Law Society of Northern Ireland* 102 at 103.

267 Office of Law Reform, ibid. For an overview of Eire, see S Connelly 'Looking to the future: family mediation in the Republic of Ireland' (1999) 17(7) *ILT* 106.

268 'The Future of Legal Aid in Northern Ireland', presented to Parliament by the Lord Chancellor, September 2000.

269 H Genn *Central London County Court Mediation Pilot: Evaluation Report*, LCD Research Series, No 5/98, at p vi.

270 Ibid, at p 31.

271 Ibid, at p 56.

272 Lord Woolf *Access to Justice: Interim Report*, Lord Chancellor's Department, London, June 1995, at p 144.

273 M Davies, G Davis and J Webb *Promoting Mediation: Report of a study of Bristol Law Society's Mediation Scheme in its preliminary phase*, 1996 Research & Policy Planning Unit Research Study no 21, The Law Society, at p 22.

274 H Genn *Central London County Court Mediation Pilot Evaluation*, op cit, at p 30.

Concerns have been expressed that, for legally-aided parties in family disputes, mediation is compulsory by 'the back door' of the legal aid provisions. These concerns do not distinguish between a requirement to mediate on the one hand, and a requirement to consider mediation as a possible dispute resolution mechanism on the other, which is the aim of mediation in-take sessions.

Conditional and contingency fees, and legal expenses insurance

Developments in England

The Courts and Legal Services Act 1990 introduced conditional fee agreements, whereby a lawyer receives in the event of success his or her usual fee, together with a percentage uplift on that fee, in all cases except family and criminal proceedings.[275] The Act empowered the Lord Chancellor to prescribe the types of cases in which such fee arrangements could be used and to determine the maximum percentage uplift allowed. The Conditional Fee Agreements Regulations 1995 determined that the maximum uplift was 100% and that conditional fee arrangements would be available in personal injury actions, insolvency cases and European Court of Human Rights cases. Although conditional fee arrangements are usually referred to as 'no win, no fee' arrangements, solicitors can charge a fee if they lose the case, provided that the client agrees.

The Law Society of England and Wales has produced guidance on conditional fees and a model conditional fee agreement. The Law Society has also suggested that the uplift applied should not exceed 25% of damages recovered. The Law Society has also arranged insurance for clients against having to meet the other parties' costs in personal injury cases. In 1997 a survey of 120 firms of solicitors and a study of 197 conditional fee cases in the personal injury field concluded that the average uplift charged by solicitors was 43%, although in 10% of cases it was close to the maximum 100%. The voluntary 25% cap recommended by the Law Society was found to be used by almost all solicitors.[276]

In Sir Peter Middleton's report to the Lord Chancellor, reviewing civil justice and legal aid, he recommended that conditional fees should take precedence over legal aid wherever practicable, and that the position of contingency fees should be reconsidered as such fees may create an incentive for lawyers to achieve the best possible result for the client.[277] In the case of contingency fee arrangements, the lawyer is paid depending on the amount of damages recovered, rather than the amount of work that has gone into recovering those damages. Although contingency fees have been used in England, these have been limited to non-contentious work, which includes most tribunal cases, and contentious work where proceedings have not been issued. Accordingly, a contingency fee arrangement can be used if a

---

275 Courts and Legal Services Act 1990, s 58.
276 See Policy Studies Institute *Conditional fees well established but questions about fairness remain*, Press Release, 1997.
277 Sir Peter Middleton *Review of civil justice and legal aid: Report to the Lord Chancellor*, Lord Chancellor's Department, September 1997, at paras 5.49 and 5.50.

settlement is reached in a case without proceedings being issued, but if proceedings are issued none of the work can be subject to a contingency arrangement, although a conditional fee arrangement can be used instead. Sir Peter Middleton also considered that legal expenses insurance could provide a way for increasing access to justice.[278]

Following that review, the Government indicated in the 1998 Consultation Paper, 'Access to Justice with Conditional Fees', its willingness to extend conditional fee arrangements to all proceedings, except in family and criminal cases.[279] In addition, the Consultation Paper indicated the Government's intention to remove legal aid funding once conditional fee arrangements develop.[280] Finally, the Consultation Paper suggested that the uplift payable to a solicitor in the event of a successful case, and legal insurance premiums, should be paid by the losing party so that the winning party would not have these items deducted from his or her recovery.[281]

In the summary of responses to its Consultation Paper, the Lord Chancellor's Department confirmed that there was general support for its proposal to extend conditional fee arrangements, except in defamation proceedings, where the responses expressed a concern that conditional fee arrangements would encourage litigation in the hope of achieving settlements, which in turn would deter the media from free reporting,[282] although some firms do provide conditional fee arrangements for defamation cases.[283] Responses to the Consultation Paper also supported the proposal that the success fee and insurance premium should be recoverable from the losing party.[284]

Following this consultation, the Conditional Fee Arrangement Order 1998 was passed, providing that conditional fee arrangements, with a maximum percentage uplift of 100%, are available in all proceedings in England and Wales, except for criminal proceedings (other than under Environmental Protection Act, s 82) and specified family proceedings. The White Paper *Modernising Justice* confirmed that the Access to Justice Act 1999 would allow a successful litigant to recover the success fee and related insurance premium from the losing party and would allow conditional fee arrangements in disputes relating to the division of matrimonial property.

The Access to Justice Act 1999, by s 27, replaced ss 58 and 58A of the Courts and Legal Services Act 1990, and provided that conditional fee arrangements must relate

---

278 Sir Peter Middleton *Review of civil justice and legal aid: Report to the Lord Chancellor*, Lord Chancellor's Department, September 1997, at paras 5.51–5.53.
279 Lord Chancellor's Department *Consultation Paper: Access to justice with conditional fees*, 1998 at para 2.7.
280 Ibid.
281 Ibid.
282 Lord Chancellor's Department *Conditional Fees Consultation: summary of responses to the Lord Chancellor's Department Consultation Paper*, July 1998, at section 1.
283 For example, Peter Carter-Ruck & Partners has provided a conditional fee defamation action scheme since December 1998, which includes the option of after-the-event insurance, and the firm claimed an unbroken run of success for the scheme: see the *Law Society Gazette*, September 1999, at p 22.
284 Lord Chancellor's Department *Conditional Fees Consultation: summary of responses to the Lord Chancellor's Department Consultation Paper*, July 1998, at section 4.

to the proceedings, and specify a percentage uplift not greater than that specified by order. The Conditional Fee Agreements Order 2000, which revoked the 1998 Order, provides that conditional fee agreements can relate to any proceedings, except family and criminal proceedings (including those under Environmental Protection Act, s 82), and specified the maximum uplift as 100%. Regulations are provided by the Conditional Fee Agreements Regulations 2000, which revoked the 1995 Regulations.

The Access to Justice Act also allowed a further arrangement, which although called a conditional fee, was previously referred to as the speculative fee. Under this arrangement, the lawyer charges the normal fee if he or she wins a case and no fee or a discounted fee if he or she loses a case. Success fees are not charged.[285] Housing disrepair cases brought under Environmental Protection Act, s 82 can only be subject to this kind of conditional fee arrangement.

The Access to Justice Act 1999 also introduced recoverability of the success fee and related insurance premium. The Lord Chancellor's Department Consultation Paper, 'Conditional Fees: sharing the risks of litigation', provided a number of suggested guidelines on the operation of the conditional fee provisions in the Access to Justice Act 1999. In relation to recovery of the success fee and insurance premium, in particular, the proposals were that:

- the opponent should receive notification of the conditional fee arrangement and whether a success fee is being claimed;
- both parties should be able to challenge the success fee through an assessment by the court; and
- the recoverability of the success fee and related insurance premium should not be retrospective.[286]

The Civil Procedure Costs (Amendment No 3) Rules 2000, effective on 3 July 2000, provide detailed provisions relating to recovery of the success fee and insurance premium, for example:

- confidentiality of the level of the success fee is preserved during proceedings;
- assessment of the reasonableness of the success fee is decided on the basis of what was reasonable at the time it was agreed and involves consideration of factors like what other funding options were available and the availability of pre-existing insurance cover.

---

285 Also referred to as 'Thai Trading' arrangements. The arrangements were ruled to be lawful by the Court of Appeal in February 1998 in *Thai Trading Co v Taylor* [1998] QB 781, although at the time Rule 8 of the Solicitors' Practice Rules prohibited such arrangements for solicitors in contentious proceedings. Those rules were amended in January 1999 to allow any arrangement permitted under statute or common law. In *Awwad v Geraghty & Co* [2000] 1 All ER 608, the Court of Appeal considered the effect of a Thai Trading arrangement entered into in 1993 and concluded that, since the Solicitors' Practice Rules had the effect of statute, such arrangements were unenforceable in 1993. Although such agreements entered into after the Conditional Fees Agreement Regulations 2000 (1 April 2000) are enforceable, uncertainty remains for agreements entered into between 1 January 1999 and 1 April 2000.
286 Lord Chancellor's Department *Consultation paper: Conditional Fees – Sharing the Risks of Litigation*, 1999.

A number of organisations have made innovative strides in relation to conditional fee arrangements. The law firm Linklaters, for example, has indicated its willingness to conduct all forms of litigation on a conditional fee basis. The firm is currently targeting appeals from decisions by the Pensions Ombudsman. Pursuit, an after-the-event insurance aimed at supporting conditional fees arrangements, is structured like a success fee in a conditional fee arrangement, in that the premium, which is agreed in advance, only becomes payable if the client wins the case.[287] The Law Society has proposed that a 'conditional legal aid fund' could provide legal aid funding to cover the initial costs of investigating a claim, and the solicitor could then complete the work on a conditional fee arrangement. If the solicitor is successful, a proportion of his success fee could be reimbursed to the legal aid fund to cover the initial start up costs. Unsuccessful parties' costs could be met by the fund. A similar proposal has been put forward by the Bar Council in the form of a 'contingency legal aid fund'.[288] Community Legal Service (Cost Protection) Regulations 2000, reg 6 provides that, where an insurance policy is inadequate to cover an opponent's costs, the Commission will be liable for the excess.

Developments in Scotland

Unlike England and Wales, there are no legal barriers in Scotland to speculative actions. The Scottish Office considers that speculative fee arrangements secure access to justice, by removing risk from clients and transferring that risk to solicitors. The Scottish Office is considering whether legal aid funding should be removed in certain actions in favour of speculative fees.[289]

Developments in Northern Ireland

At this stage there are no legislative provisions for conditional fees in Northern Ireland. The Government is giving consideration to the introduction of conditional fee arrangements as an alternative way of funding cases.[290] The Government recognises, however, that conditional fee arrangements will only develop in Northern Ireland once a range of competitive legal expenses insurance is available.

Effect on mediation

It has been suggested that conditional fee arrangements, by charging an uplift which is a proportion of fees, provides an incentive for lawyers to spend more time on cases in order to increase fees earned and, accordingly, a disincentive to achieve earlier

---

287 The UK insurer behind the scheme is Royal & Sun Alliance: see H Peto 'In Pursuit of truth and justice' (1999) 18(6) *Litigation: The Journal of Contentious Business* 2.

288 For an outline of these and other proposals, see Sir Peter Middleton *Report to the Lord Chancellor: Review of civil justice and legal aid*, Lord Chancellor's Department, September 1997.

289 The Scottish Office News Release: *McLeish outlines proposed reforms to Scotland's Civil Legal Aid system*, 27 March 1998.

290 Office of Law Reform *Public Benefit and the Public Purse: legal aid reform in Northern Ireland*, The Office of Law Reform, 1999.

settlement, for instance, by mediation.[291] Shapiro refers to United States experience in such cases, which confirms that settlements were delayed, with the consequence that work was performed which was unnecessary.[292] The rationale for excluding from the Access to Justice Act 1999 conditional fees arrangements in matrimonial property disputes was the concern that these arrangements would undermine government policy to promote amicable divorce settlements.

Contingency fees, on the other hand, which depend on the amount of damages obtained, provide an incentive for lawyers to increase the amount recovered, which may also provide a disincentive to settle, for instance by mediation, when the solicitor considers that the amount of recovery can be increased by holding out or going to trial. In addition, contingency fee arrangements do not lend themselves to creative solutions. US commentators have confirmed the tendency of lawyers on contingency fees arrangements to avoid outcomes that do not create a fund of cash out of which the lawyer can be paid.[293]

In relation to legal expenses insurance, the concern frequently voiced is that insurance provides an incentive for the insured party to play a waiting game. The incentive will be even greater when premiums can be recovered from the losing party. An additional concern is the definition of success in some legal expenses policies, which provide a financial threshold before a case is deemed to have been won, which would provide a disincentive to settle the case, for instance by mediation, unless and until that threshold is achieved.

Genn's study of the Central London County Court Mediation Pilot suggests that legal insurance cover may have an impact on mediation. For example, in one case, the plaintiff rejected mediation on the basis that, being covered by legal expenses insurance, the plaintiff intended to put as much pressure as possible on the defendant.[294] In another case, a solicitor for the defendant observed the effect of legal expenses insurance as follows:

> '. . . a lot of the time, because of . . . legal expenses insurance, the cost pressure is more on us than on the . . . plaintiff. If we had had a privately-funded plaintiff . . . it would have been very different . . . it would have settled . . . even prior to mediation and . . . then they would have had to take a more realistic view . . . we are really up against the wall with legal expenses insurance. At least with legal aid you can make an application to have costs offset against damages and that's . . . the lever . . .'[295]

The incentive to play a waiting game as a result of legal expenses insurance, may be outweighed by the interests of the lawyer and the insurer. In addition, after-the-event legal expenses insurers are likely to take on only those cases they expect to win and,

291 See N Rickman 'The impact of plaintiff finance on personal injury litigation: An empirical analysis' (1999) 5 *Litigation Funding*.

292 D Shapiro 'Alternative Dispute Resolution under the new Civil Rules: some guidelines for lawyers and judges' (1999) 18(7) *Litigation – the Journal of Contentious Business* 1.

293 See, for example, H Kritzer 'Adjudication to settlement: Shading in the gray' (1986) 70 *Judicature* 161; H Kritzer *Let's make a deal*, University of Wisconsin Press, Madison Wisconsin, 1991; and R Fisher 'He who pays the piper' (1987) 6(1) *Corporate Counsel Review* 75 at 81.

294 H Genn *Central London County Court Mediation Pilot: Evaluation Report*, LCD Research Series, No 5/98, at p 33.

295 Ibid, at p 132.

accordingly, it is suggested that in these cases insurers will not prefer to mediate.[296] Some legal expenses insurers have identified only certain classes of cases as suitable for mediation and, accordingly, other types of cases are not even considered for mediation.[297] Other legal expenses insurers leave decisions on how to run the case, including the decision whether to mediate, to their external lawyers.[298] Given the expectation under the Civil Procedure Rules to consider mediation, these approaches may alter. In addition, legal expenses insurers have been considering inserting clauses into policies that require parties to endeavour to resolve the dispute by mediation in the first instance.[299] A legal expenses insurer, which was responsible for the majority of the cases referred to the Bristol Law Society Mediation Scheme, had included a clause into some of its policies, which gave it the power to determine how a dispute would be resolved.[300]

Commentators have suggested a mediation contingency fee, where no party pays the mediator a fee unless the dispute is settled in the mediation.[301] A conditional fee arrangement was found to be valid by an English court in a case where solicitors agreed to pursue the claim by arbitration.[302] The interesting issue which arises is whether a similar arrangement entered into by a mediator or mediation organisation for the purpose of resolving a claim by mediation would create any difficulties.[303] Most mediator codes of conduct specify mediator neutrality. That neutrality may be impugned if a mediator receives a success fee for a successful mediation. The Academy of Experts' Code of Conduct prohibits mediators from entering into agreements to receive a contingency fee in respect of a mediation.[304] Even where a success fee is payable to a mediation organisation, rather than the mediator, this may also raise neutrality issues, as the mediator may be motivated to reach a resolution by the prospect of receiving additional mediations from the organisation, which in turn may encourage the mediator to put undue pressure on parties to settle in mediation.[305]

---

296 S Threadgold 'Legal Expenses: Meditating on mediation' *Post Magazine*, 7 October 1999, at p 26.

297 Ibid.

298 Ibid.

299 Lord Chancellor's Department *Conditional Fees Consultation: summary of responses to the Lord Chancellor's Department Consultation Paper*, July 1998, at section 14.

300 M Davies, G Davis and J Webb *Promoting Mediation: Report of a study of Bristol Law Society's Mediation Scheme in its preliminary phase*, 1996 Research & Policy Planning Unit Research Study no 21, The Law Society, at p 31.

301 For example, R Fisher 'Why not contingent fee mediation' (1986) *Negotiation Journal* 11 at 12.

302 *Bevan Ashford v Geoff Yeandle (Contractors) Ltd (In Liquidation)* [1999] Ch 239.

303 One of the fee options provided by InterMediation is 'no settlement no fee', whereby the mediation organisation, InterMediation is paid an uplift if a mediation is successful.

304 Academy of Experts *Code of Conduct*.

305 For example, the InterMediation 'no settlement no fee' scheme provides that mediators are paid a fee in any event and are not aware of the success fee arrangement in place between the mediation organisation and a party. The InterMediation Information Pack confirms that mediators are expected 'to achieve overall success in resolving cases in line with established market expectations', which raises the concerns above. On the other hand, settlement is an aim of every mediator.

Other funding issues in mediation

Funding issues are, on the one hand, significant to the parties in a mediation, but, on the other, equally an issue for mediation organisations. This issue is less important in the context of commercial mediations as commercial mediation organisations usually charge an administration fee, in addition to mediator fees. Some exceptions have occurred in pilot mediation schemes, where civil/commercial mediations have been subsidised: for example, the Central London County Court and Court of Appeal mediation schemes. In commercial mediation it is usual for the costs of the mediation to be shared between the parties, although some other proportion may be agreed between them. For example, an insurance company operating an ADR policy may meet the costs of a mediation in full in order to encourage the use of ADR. Scottish examples have shown no adverse effect on the parties' perceptions of neutrality of the mediator in such cases.[306]

Lack of funding, however, is a major concern in family, consumer and community mediation. The public considers that mediation services in these areas should be free. These mediation organisations rely on funding from the charitable sector, local councils and donations from users of the service.[307] Some community mediation services are considering sliding scale fees, depending on the wealth of clients, so that clients who are unable to pay will continue to receive mediation services free of charge.[308] A review of family mediation organisations in Scotland has shown the wide range of sources of funding, including charities and commercial firms. Family Mediation Central Scotland, for example, receives funding from banks, solicitors, charities and trusts.[309] Family Mediation Lothian receives funding from a range of local councils.[310] Family Mediation Tayside's funding comes primarily from a range of trusts and charities, including the National Lottery.[311] Sources of funding are similar in England and Wales and Northern Ireland.

---

306 R Mays and B Clark *ADR in Scotland*, The Scottish Office, 1999.
307 However, Relate Northern Ireland Financial Statement for the year ended 1997 indicates that under £2,000 was received in donations from clients.
308 M Liebmann (ed) *Community and Neighbour Mediation*, Cavendish Publishing Limited, London, 1998, at p 72.
309 Family Mediation Central Scotland *Annual Report 1998–9*, at p 14.
310 Family Mediation Lothian *16th Annual Report 1998–9*.
311 Family Mediation Tayside *Annual Report 1998–9*.

10

Evolving UK Mediation Practice Issues

Introduction

In this chapter some practical issues in mediation are considered, although these issues also affect the demand for and supply of mediation. Unlike the issues considered in the last chapter, the issues here are private issues, although there may be aspects in each case which already are or are likely to become regulated or monitored. The first issue considers the basic considerations in setting up a mediator practice, together with the particular considerations in the case of the practitioner who prefers, instead, to practise as advocate in mediation. Issues of quality, standards and accountability are explored in the next two chapters. Ultimately, the aim for both the mediator and the advocate is to create a viable practice, which in the context of mediation may well depend on creating demand for mediation. The lawyer who is trained to screen cases for mediation suitability and is knowledgeable about the mediation process not only provides clients with access to mediation, by virtue of his or her expertise, but can also help provide the demand for mediation, which will ensure that mediators' practices are viable. The second issue considers how organisations can put in place dispute management systems, which may incorporate mediation as a dispute resolution option or preference. This issue is linked to the first: by generating mediations, organisations, corporates and industry are in a unique position to drive the mediation movement in the UK. Finally, the issue of on-line dispute resolution is considered, which may provide an effective cross-border mediation supply device. In time, as mediation experience grows, these issues will require more attention than the overview provided here.

Establishing, Marketing and Managing a Mediation Practice

Objectives

Although each mediation practitioner's objectives will differ, the following objectives are likely to be important factors for any practitioner:

- to develop mediation skills and expertise;
- to create a demand for mediation services; and
- to develop a commercially viable mediation practice.

Incentives

The particular incentives may differ, depending on whether practice as a mediator or as a mediation advocate is being contemplated. As Chapter 7 shows, the number of mediation organisations and mediators in the UK is rapidly increasing. Accordingly, there is a high incentive for mediators to consider marketing and how to differentiate themselves. Although Chapter 7 also provided examples of lawyers taking a range of mediation initiatives, the surveys and studies in the UK to date show a low take-up of mediation and an indication that lawyers, as gatekeepers to the mediation process, may not yet have fully embraced mediation as part of the UK dispute resolution landscape and that there is still a widespread lack of knowledge about mediation. However, that a range of law firms, from small through to medium and large firms, have taken serious steps to integrate mediation into their practices provides an incentive for practitioners to be able to offer clients a comparable competitive service. Lawyers also have an incentive to mediate as a result of changes in attitude to mediation by the courts[1] and in legal aid.[2] Lawyers should at least be able to advise clients in dispute on the mediation option,[3] to avoid possible cost sanctions in case the client is found to have unreasonably refused to participate in mediation.[4]

Pressure on lawyers to consider mediation is also coming from clients and insurers, who are beginning to embrace mediation.[5] A number of insurance companies have signed an ADR pledge to signify their commitment to the process.[6] Some insurance companies are also considering, as a pre-condition of providing legal expenses cover, that insureds should mediate first. Pressure from clients, in particular business clients, also provides an incentive to consider the extent to which mediation should be incorporated into the practice.[7] Larger organisations are turning their minds to dispute management,[8] by applying to dispute resolution the basic management principles of controlling dispute resolution and settlement to problems; achieving efficiency through savings in time; and creating commercial solutions to problems. In addition, users of mediation experience high levels of satisfaction with mediation. This factor, coupled with generally high rates of success in mediation, make mediation an attractive dispute resolution service for clients. In turn, therefore:

> '. . . if [lawyers are] going to serve their clients well, [they] should be adept at representing them in ADR processes . . .'[9]

Although the UK surveys on mediation have not revealed any concern by lawyers that their take-up of mediation will reduce their fees, if that were a concern, the ability to resolve disputes, using mediation, in less time than by litigation or direct

---

1 See the section on Civil Justice Reform in Chapter 7.
2 See the section on Funding and Mediation in Chapter 9.
3 See the section on duty to advise on mediation in Chapter 12.
4 See the section on Compulsion or Encouragement to Mediate in Chapter 9.
5 See the section on Insurance Disputes in Chapter 8.
6 Called Market ADR commitment ('MAC'), which is discussed in more detail in the section in Chapter 8.
7 See the section on Lawyers and on Corporates/Industry and Mediation in Chapter 7.
8 See the section on Dispute Management in this chapter.
9 See the views of a range of US law firm representatives in Center for Public Resources 'ADR and the 21st Century Law Firm' *Alternatives*, vol 16, No 2 March 1998.

negotiation, would provide an opportunity for lawyers to deal with more cases or new business. It is perhaps unfortunate that most of the mediation schemes in the UK to date have been either pro-bono or involved payment by the parties of very low mediation fees, as this may give the false impression that advice, representation or advocacy in mediation on the one hand and mediator practice on the other should not be remunerative. A 1994 survey of US law firm practices by the Center for Public Resources reported that a number of firms were then billing $1m per year for mediation work.[10] There is no reason why the same result should not occur in the UK. As the Lord Chancellor has stated:

'. . . practitioners . . . who are able to offer competent and successful . . . mediation services will find that they are part of a burgeoning – and profitable – new profession . . .'[11]

There are also some less tangible incentives for law firms to embrace mediation, in particular, as a mechanism for increasing lawyer job satisfaction and encouraging recruitment.

Mediator practice on the one hand, and advocacy in mediation practice on the other, are considered separately below as they constitute different practices, with different start-up, marketing and management issues, although where there are similar considerations, these are indicated. The separate treatment is particularly important for lawyers, who may wish to provide neutral services and represent clients in mediation. Apart from the field of family disputes, where lawyers frequently provide the services of neutrals, the dual role may be confusing to clients and may also create conflict of interest dilemmas.[12] It is for this reason that the Law Society recommends, in the case of lawyer mediators, that a mediator practice is seen to be separate from other legal practice, which would include representation of clients in mediation.

A mediator practice

Initial steps

Development of credentials through training, accreditation, mediation experience, evaluation and networking is the necessary first step in developing a career as a mediator. The next chapter provides information and generates debate on these aspects. Alongside credentials development is the development of infrastructure and resources, in particular premises, equipment, documentation and referral networks. Relevant documents include codes of mediator conduct, precedent mediation agreements and mediation procedures. Establishing referral networks involves making contact with lawyers, accountants, other professionals, industry, government and other agencies which will need to be educated about the appropriateness of mediation as a referral option.

Marketing

Altobelli has made the point that the normal product cycle has four stages, being introduction, growth, maturity and decline, whereas from a mediation consumer's

---

10 Centre for Public Resources *Law Firm ADR: 1994 survey findings*, CPR, New York, 1994.
11 See full text at http://www.open.gov.uk/lcd/speeches/1999
12 See Part I.

perspective, he suggests that there are five, being awareness, interest, evaluation, trial and adoption.[13] Given that in the UK mediation is still in its introductory stage, and consumer awareness is low, educating the consumer should be an important aspect of a mediator's marketing plan.

How mediation is classified as a product has a bearing on appropriate marketing strategies. Mediation is a service, as opposed to goods, which creates different market realities. As an intangible, mediation is difficult to display, communicate and price. Being heterogeneous, consistency of service quality is a problem for mediators as horror stories about any one mediator can have market repercussions for all other mediators. As a product, which involves simultaneous production and consumption, it is difficult to achieve economies of scale through centralisation, so that mediation should be marketed on a relatively decentralised basis.

Adopting the basic concept of the 'four Ps' of marketing, of product, price, promotion and place, provides an insight to the appropriate marketing mix for a mediator:

- The product is mediation, which has unique claims in relation to client involvement, creative outcomes, cost and time effectiveness. Accordingly, although mediators provide an intangible service, the value that can be added by mediation can be referred to in tangible terms, and distinguished in this way from competitor services, like litigation and arbitration.
- Price depends on cost of production and the value which a client is prepared to pay for the service. Although discount prices may be used to stimulate short-term take-up of mediation, this cannot be sustained longer-term. Market mechanisms will determine pricing structures for mediators. Excess supply of mediation services over demand will put downward pressure on the mediator fees that can be charged.
- Promotion of a mediator's services can be achieved through brochures, publications, presentations at conferences, media features and educational activities, like training.
- In terms of place, as Folberg and Taylor point out, mediation does not require a special setting, in that the 'have process, will travel' philosophy applies.[14]

Other mediation marketing factors include competition, segmentation and specialisation:

The current lack of regulation of mediation in the UK allows a range of professions to move into the mediation market. At the same time, there is flux in the traditional professions, with blurring of boundaries, and consumer activism, creating more demanding external market forces, providing both opportunities and threats for mediators.

The mediation market can be divided into two broad segments, the conflict management area, generally, and the dispute resolution area, more specifically. Within the latter, there are further segments, for instance, different substantive areas of dispute, like personal injury or construction matters, and between repeat users, like insurers, and one-off users, like consumers, of mediation services. Segmentation allows the mediator to focus his or her marketing and to achieve a competitive edge.

---

13 T Altobelli 'Are you getting enough? Marketing mediation' (1999) *ADR Bulletin* 113.
14 J Folberg and A Taylor *Mediation: a comprehensive guide to resolving conflicts without litigation*, Jossey-Bass, San Francisco, 1984, at p 296.

Mediators can also market themselves as generalists, for example as ABC Mediation Service, or as specialists in certain kinds of disputes, as with ABC Employment Mediation Service.

Issues of concept, model and brand are also important for mediators. Individual satisfaction is the prevailing concept in the current promotion of mediation. The current models of mediation are facilitative or evaluative. Brand or individual mediator style will depend on each mediator's personality, background and life experience.

Securing referrals is both an aspect of marketing and the fruitful result of marketing. There is likely to be little scope for direct or self-referral to private mediators, except in the case of satisfied prior mediation clients. Mediators need to develop referral networks. Structured sources of referral are the ideal arrangement for mediators, whereby work is obtained, for example, from a mediation organisation or as a result of inclusion of the provider in a dispute resolution clause or scheme.

Management

Management of a mediator practice involves a range of practical issues, from receiving payment for work through to following up referrals and receiving client feedback.

Practice as an advocate in mediation

Initial steps

Initially, it is necessary to receive a commitment from the partnership to integrate mediation into the practice. Although mediation is not owned by dispute resolution lawyers,[15] the initial efforts should focus on the dispute resolution lawyers in any firm. Internal policy statements or guidelines can be used to identify relevant goals. A mediation point of contact indicates commitment to the practice.

Initial steps need to focus on in-house mediation training[16] and dissemination of information on mediation. A wide range of mediation training is available from mediation organisations.[17] Mediation representation training should include an overview of the mediation process;[18] interest-based and other types of negotiation;[19] techniques for representing clients in mediation;[20] and methods for encouraging clients and the representatives for the other parties in a dispute to attempt

---

15 Increasingly, commercial lawyers are drafting dispute resolution provisions and are applying mediation principles to transactional work ('deal mediation'), as well as being used as mediators in disputes, as previously discussed in Part I and also in Chapter 8.

16 Responses to the Lord Chancellor's ADR Discussion Paper considered that there should, in any event, be either some form of compulsory mediation training for lawyers or mediation training as part of the Continuous Professional Development Programme for solicitors: Lord Chancellor's Department *ADR Discussion Paper: Summary of responses*, August 2000, at para 33.

17 See Chapter 11 on Training Standards and Mediation.

18 See Part II.

19 See the section on Negotiation in Mediation in Chapter 2.

20 See the section on the Role of Lawyers in Mediation in Chapter 5.

mediation.[21] Training through role play and observation provides effective mediation representation teaching methods. Training also provides an opportunity to involve other practice areas in a firm,[22] as well as clients themselves. Whatever format is adopted, training needs to be regular, in order to ensure that all lawyers handling disputes have basic training and that, once the basic training has been received, the skills are practised. Apart from skills training, it is also useful to circulate mediation information and up-dates. A useful mediation information dissemination tool is email, as it can raise awareness of mediation internally, and provide accessible mediation advice within the firm and for clients.

Creating a stock of precedents is also a useful early exercise. Precedents should include mediation orders, agreements to mediate, mediation procedures, rules for the conduct of mediation, protocols of behaviour for lawyers and other professional advisers, and mediation clauses. Case assessment forms encourage lawyers to consider the appropriateness of mediation and other forms of ADR in every dispute. Tracking forms are aimed at compiling statistics in order to gauge results and, in particular, whether time and money has been saved and client satisfaction increased by way of ADR. A check list, outlining the steps in preparation for a mediation, which can be refined as mediation experience increases, is also a useful tool. Compiling a directory of neutrals can save time at the appointment of mediator stage. As with lawyers' directories of barristers, these are compiled either through word of mouth or previous mediation experiences. The stock of mediation forms and precedents should also include mediation text books, journals and a copy of the literature provided by mediation organisations. As the field grows, so too will the case law, which should be monitored.

Mediation practice requires case review and evaluation for ADR suitability. Doubts can be resolved by requesting assistance from a mediation organisation. Most organisations conduct meetings with prospective parties, in order to discuss the possible application of mediation to a particular dispute. Timing also needs to be considered, for example, whether a window of opportunity under the CPR can be taken advantage of. Case review also involves, potentially, persuading a client and the other parties to a dispute to attempt mediation. If mediation is then pursued, lawyers need to be adept at preparing themselves and their clients for mediation,[23] and be comfortable in representing clients in mediation. A record should be kept of all cases proceeding to mediation, in particular, the type of case; at what stage mediation was attempted; the duration and outcome of the mediation; an estimate of any cost and time savings achieved; and an indication of the client's thoughts on the process. It is also useful to keep a record of the mediator used and of their performance, including successful and unsuccessful techniques. In the US, mediation case management and tracking has led to the development of specialised software, for example, 'Mediation Manager'.[24]

Marketing

Many of the marketing concepts, outlined above in the context of a mediator practice, are equally relevant in this context, in particular:

---

21 See the section on the Enforceability of Mediation Clauses in Chapter 12.
22 Not least of all as non-litigation lawyers may be able to encourage clients to take up mediation in specific subject areas.
23 See Part II.
24 Trademark of Tek Data, Portland, 04112.

- The need for awareness raising, through firm mediation brochures or sections on mediation in brochures on specific subject areas, mediation seminars and newsletters for clients, mediation mail shots and featuring mediation experience in beauty parades.
- The 'four Ps', including consideration of alternative fee arrangements for repeat mediation users or for ancillary mediation services, such as audits or screening cases for suitability for mediation.
- Competition, segmentation and specialisation, where specialisation will largely be influenced by the firm's areas of practice and clients.
- Concept, model and brand, where brand will depend on the firm's wider ambitions.

Different referral issues arise. Self-referrals will be the norm, with prospective clients bringing their dispute directly to the firm. Firms may also seek to develop structured sources of referral, for example, through mediation clauses in contracts and referral by the Law Society.

Management

Although the firm's commitment is essential, the day-to-day management of a mediation practice should be the responsibility of a designated lawyer, who is the main mediation contact for the firm and its clients, and who can oversee the development of mediation training, the dissemination of mediation information and the collation and creation of mediation resources.[25] In larger firms, an ADR committee can also be a useful tool for gaining firm-wide and client support. A mediation practice group is not recommended as it gives the impression that mediation skills should be concentrated in a person or group of people in the firm, rather than encouraging all lawyers, particularly all the dispute resolution lawyers in a firm, to have at least a basic knowledge and understanding of mediation, in particular, from the point of view being able to advise the client on the option, its suitability and timing.

Dispute Management by Organisations and Industry

Dispute management is an attempt by organisations to make dispute resolution an integral part of their culture, rather than a phenomenon which is external to the organisation or the province of experts outside the organisation. It has emerged as a result of a realisation that successful business planning and management is not limited a to consideration of market position, developing products, budgeting and day-to-day operations, but extends to avoiding and managing conflicts.[26] In part, however, organisations also seek to create internal procedures for managing disputes

25 Centre for Public Resources *Law Firm ADR: 1994 survey findings*, CPR, New York, 1994 found that 22% in this position at the law firms surveyed spent 60%–100% of their time on ADR; 33% spent 20%–60% on ADR and 45% spent up to 20% on ADR.
26 See R Keefe and W Rheaume 'Pre-Dispute Planning for Business' (1993) 48 *Arbitration Journal* 39.

to insulate their activities from the legal environment and the costs, time and public relations consequences which may result from external dispute resolution, in particular, litigation.[27] Dispute management assumes that conflict is not detrimental to an organisation, but is the essence of the organisation.[28] It assumes that disputes are the by-product of an organisation and are capable of being managed, using the same tools the corporation uses to manage other aspects of its business.[29]

Dispute management involves setting up internal dispute resolution programmes or systems and, as ADR becomes more prevalent, those programmes or systems will incorporate ADR. A system may include a range of tools, including:

- internal policies on ADR;
- external expression of commitment to ADR;
- dispute resolution clauses in contracts;
- dispute handling policies and procedures;
- early intervention by a person not intimately involved with the dispute;
- screening processes to determine the most appropriate dispute resolution option;
- internal training on communication, negotiation, problem-solving and dispute resolution options;
- in-house dispute managers.

British Standard 8600 identifies visibility, accessibility and fairness as the key attributes of a good dispute resolution process.

Since ADR encourages a preventative approach to dispute resolution, the benefits of ADR, by way of achieving the aims of dispute management, become more obvious to organisations. In particular, ADR can raise awareness of endemic problems in an organisation; it enhances the range of dispute resolution skills available in an organisation; and can help prevent problems from escalating into disputes.[30] Ultimately, ADR helps an organisation to create a more comprehensive dispute management programme.

Various incentives can prompt an organisation to embrace dispute management. A large number of the same type of disputes, for instance employment disputes or debt collection cases, could trigger the approach. A crisis, like a strike, could provide the initial impetus. Organisations, which are about to enter into a long-term business venture, may also consider that a systematic approach to dispute resolution has benefits. Structural change in an organisation can also provide an opportunity for dispute management efforts. Privatisation, for example, may provide a basis for re-considering an industry's approach to dispute resolution.[31]

---

27 L Edelman, H Erlanger and J Lande 'Internal Dispute Resolution: The transformation of civil rights in the work place' (1993) 27(3) *Law & Society Review* 497 at 499.

28 D Kolb and S Silbey 'Enhancing the capacity of organisations to deal with disputes' (1990) *Negotiation Journal* 297 at 298.

29 E Green 'Corporate ADR' (1986) 1 *Ohio State Journal on Dispute Resolution* 203 at 229.

30 See J David and T Anderson *Grievance management in the New South Wales Public Sector*, 1995, at p 4.

31 In Australia, for example, industry codes of conduct such as the Franchising Industry Code, Oil Code, and National Electricity Code, provide a benchmark for dispute avoidance and resolution.

In developing an internal dispute resolution programme, commitment is required at executive level, although responsibility for implementation of the system would be in the hands of a manager who reports to the executive. The programme is usually designed by a dispute resolution consultant or adviser who understands the range of ADR processes and when to use them; has dispute resolution skills; and has an understanding of the relevant industry or is able to acquire that knowledge quickly. Ultimately, the system will need to be supported by an adequate budget and resources, for instance, staffing, facilities, equipment, training and manuals, key factors identified in British Standards 8600 for effective handling of complaints.

The adviser would normally start by diagnosing the existing dispute resolution systems and problems in the organisation: for instance, which disputes occur and why; and what procedures are available to resolve those disputes and whether, and if so how, those procedures are being used. Part of the analysis will also require an understanding of the current dispute resolution culture of the organisation. Having diagnosed the problems and culture, the adviser is better placed to design an appropriate programme. The focus of the programme will be on early resolution of disputes using the lowest cost method to achieve that outcome. This requires an escalation of procedures. It is for this reason that ADR frequently features significantly in any internal dispute management programme. The system should also provide for external review or determination where internal attempts become deadlocked. Finally, the system should also ensure that the organisation learns from past mistakes. Following the design phase is the implementation phase. Before a programme can be implemented, the appropriate training internally would need to occur. Clear and simple dispute handling policies and procedures would be disseminated. Apart from awareness, endorsement of and support for the programme are necessary.[32] Ideally, the programme should be piloted and evaluated before full implementation. Commentators suggest that a change in the dispute resolution culture of an organisation and the people working in it can take from between two and seven years.[33]

The experience in other jurisdictions has highlighted that having a system which handles disputes badly can lead to greater dissatisfaction than having no system at all. The most frequently cited example of this is poor complaint handling systems in organisations.[34] In the US, a breed of organisational ombudsman has emerged, who reports at or the near the top of an organisation, although outside ordinary management lines. The organisational ombudsman is a communications channel, complaint handler and dispute resolver, particularly for employment-rated disputes.[35]

Dispute management examples are wide-ranging. A very simple form of dispute management is the use of ADR clauses.[36] An example of more sophisticated dispute management efforts relates to internal employment grievance procedures within organisations. In the UK the Institute for Grocery Distribution, for example, set up a

---

32   ACCC *Benchmarks for dispute avoidance and resolution – A guide*, Sydney 1997.
33   J David 'Designing a dispute resolution system' (1994) 1(1) *Commercial Dispute Resolution Journal* 27.
34   American Express – SOCAP *Study of complaint handling in Australia*, Report No 2, 1995.
35   For more detail, see M Rowe 'Options, functions and skills: what an organisational ombudsman might want to know' (1995) 11 *Negotiation Journal* 103.
36   For a discussion of the dispute management benefits of ADR clauses, see G Akasen 'Legal considerations in using arbitration clauses to resolve future problems which may arise during long-term business agreements' (1972–3) 28 *Business Lawyer* 595; A Angel

system to tackle 'look alike' disputes, involving negotiation and referral to mediation.[37] British Telecommunications' Dispute Management Division has used mediation throughout the organisation for a number of years. It has slowly changed its culture by introducing targets into the annual bonus scheme for the number of mediations referred.[38] Barclays Bank introduced a policy, which provides guidance both internally and to the bank's external lawyers, that disputes should be resolved as cost effectively and quickly as feasible and, where appropriate, through negotiation or other forms of ADR. A mediation scheme has also been launched by the Bank to deal with recovery disputes. The Bank's IT procurement contracts, other contracts for the supply of goods or services and outsourcing agreements entered into by the Bank would normally include an escalating ADR clause. The Bank's corporate customer relationship contract also includes ADR provisions.

Dispute management and, to that end, the use of dispute resolution systems have developed into sophisticated structures in other jurisdictions, in particular the US and Australia. By way of example, in Australia privatised industries have developed entire codes regulating dispute management and referral to appropriate dispute resolution options, as in the case of the electricity industry. By way of a further Australian example, in order to deal with disputes between the Australian Medical Association and the Department of Health regarding the terms of engagement for certain medical officers, a structured mechanism for dealing with disputes was initiated. Stage 1 of the process involved direct negotiation between the visiting medical officer and health service. If these attempts were unsuccessful, mediation was attempted, but, if unsuccessful, arbitration provided a final decision.[39] In the US, Motorola, for example, organised an ADR team as part of its participant management programme, which encouraged employees to develop solutions to problems, as a means of developing a dispute management plan.[40]

On-line Mediation

Advantages versus disadvantages

Technology, like telephone and video conferencing[41] and on-line communication, enables meetings and hearings to take place without all the parties having to be

---

'The use of arbitration clauses as a means for the resolution of impasses in the negotiation of, or during the life of, long-term contractual relationships' (1972–3) 28 *Business Lawyer* 589; R Coulson 'Dispute management under modern construction systems' (1983) 46 *Law & Contemporary Problems* 127; D Harris and C Veljanovski 'Remedies under contract law: designing rules to facilitate out of court settlements (1983) 5 *Law & Policy Quarterly* 1997.

37 Centre for Dispute Resolution *Resolutions*, No 14, 1996, at p 2.
38 Centre for Dispute Resolution *Resolutions*, No 22, 1999, at p 8.
39 Sir Laurence Street 'Agreed structure for dispute resolution: AMA v Department of Health' (1994) *Australian Dispute Resolution Journal* 185.
40 See T Peters and R Waterman *In search of excellence: lessons from America's best run companies*, Harper Collins, New York, 1993; and M O'Reilly and M Mawdsley 'The management of disputes: a risk approach' (1994) *ADRLJ*, at pp 260–8.
41 There is a video-conferencing pilot scheme at the Royal Courts of Justice in London, Cardiff and Leeds. If it proves successful, video-conferencing will be implemented throughout the civil justice system.

physically present at the same location. This kind of technology may result in more efficient, cost effective and less damaging dispute resolution than hearings before a tribunal or judge.[42] In the context of international disputes, on-line mediation may avoid jurisdictional and conflict of law issues.[43] The Net, however, is not completely divorced from the laws of the jurisdictions within which it functions, although a body of law is likely to develop to govern jurisdictional issues arising from the use of the Net.[44] In the meantime, reference to the parties' choice of applicable law and jurisdiction will be important, unless the provisions are likely to be unenforceable in any event.[45]

On-line mediation is considered to be particularly useful in cases where the parties are unable to be in the same geographical location. The physical and psychological distance, which would result from on-line mediation, may also reduce the amount of hostility between the parties.[46] Some commentators suggest, however, that emotional hostility is not avoided or reduced by on-line mediation since the parties may become more entrenched in their positions and the intervention of the mediator might not be able to prevent this from occurring as the parties can choose when to allow that intervention.

There is also the problem of loss of momentum with on-line mediation. For example, in one mediation conducted via the internet in the US, the mediator did not hear from either party for two weeks. Ultimately he received an email from one party advising that the other party was on holiday, but that the other party could be contacted via a personal email address. Unbeknown to the parties, the mediator did not have their personal email addresses. Each had been frustrated by the lack of communication, as had been the mediator.[47] On-line mediation also makes it more difficult for the mediator to reality test each party's position as parties can, with the benefit of time and reflection, rebut points made by the mediator.

On-line mediation allows a mediator to reframe by paraphrasing or cutting and pasting the parties' sentences in order, where necessary, to modulate tone, filter angry or emotional emails and to prioritise issues. Although in a face-to-face mediation the mediator has an opportunity to do so following private sessions with each party, the mediator may not be able to do so in a joint session and may not have the benefit of a period of reflection, which on-line mediation may afford.[48] Without

---

42 See Lord Chancellor's Department *ADR Discussion Paper*, November 1999.
43 See, for example, H Perritt *Dispute resolution in cyberspace: Demand for new forms of ADR*, Paper presented at Cyberweek 2000. Copy is available at http://www.disputes. net/cyberweek2000/ohiostate/perritt/.htm
44 See, for example, R Gellman *A brief history of the Virtual Magistrates Project: the early months*, Paper presented at NCIAR Conference, 22 May 1996. Copy is available at http://mantle.sbs.umass.edu/vmag/GELLMAN.htm
45 E Katsh, J Rifkin and and A Gaitenby *E-commerce, E-disputes and E-dispute resolution: in the shadow of e-Bay*, Paper presented for Cyberweek 2000. Copy is available at http://www.disputes.net/cyberweek2000/ohiostate/katsh.htm. See the section on E-commerce Disputes in Chapter 8 for discussion of EU proposals in relation to jurisdiction and dispute resolution procedures in the context of e-commerce.
46 R Granat *Creating an environment for mediating disputes on the internet*, Paper presented at NCAIR Conference, 22 May 1996. Copy is available at http://mantle.sbs.umass. edu/vmag/granat.htm
47 J Krivis 'Mediating in Cyberspace' *CPR Alternatives*, vol 14, No 10.
48 E Katsh et al, op cit.

the benefit of body language or facial gestures, however, it may be difficult for a mediator to ascertain how a party feels about particular issues. In the context of family mediation, it may be difficult to screen cases for violence or other abuse. Face-to-face contact provides a mediator not only with information, but also with important signals. On-line mediation may also fail to provide the parties with a 'day in court' experience, which has been identified by studies as having a benefit to parties in dispute.[49] On-line mediation also does not have the symbolic closure, which a face-to-face mediation provides, when the parties reach an agreement, are congratulated by the mediator, sign an agreement and shake hands.

Costs might be reduced by using on-line mediation. For instance, mediation organisations will need to spend less time on the administration of mediation, arrangement of meetings between parties and mediators, and exchange of information between parties. The problem of finding a suitable venue for mediation is also reduced. Opportunity costs for lawyers may also be created, in cases where their attendance at a mediation is required for a short period of time only. A fundamental disadvantage of on-line mediation, however, is the need for access to the relevant technology. Many people are still uncomfortable with computers. Another disadvantage of on-line mediation is its reliance on text, which creates the time-consuming task of reading and responding to emails. This problem will be reduced in the future as the technology becomes more advanced and reliance on text decreases.[50]

Respondents to the Lord Chancellor's ADR Discussion Paper did not indicate a great deal of support for on-line mediation, fearing that the dynamics and psychology of mediation requires physical proximity, although on-line arbitration, adjudication, expert determination and early neutral evaluation did receive support.[51]

Some basic requirements

On-line dispute resolution needs to be accessible and trustworthy.[52] Accessibility requires that:

- the dispute resolution option is visible to the user;
- on-line tools can trace the status and history of a dispute;
- timely responses are possible;
- forms are in clear language; and
- affordability is guaranteed.

Trustworthiness involves authentication procedures, security measures and assurance of confidentiality and anonymity.

---

49 See Chapter 2, in particular the section on value claims of mediation.
50 E Katsh, J Rifkin and and A Gaitenby *E-commerce, E-disputes and E-dispute resolution: in the shadow of e-Bay*, Paper presented for Cyberweek 2000. Copy is available at http://www.disputes.net/cyberweek2000/ohiostate/katsh.htm
51 Lord Chancellor's Department *ADR Discussion Paper: Summary of responses*, August 2000, at para 58.
52 For detailed consideration of these criteria, see M Wilikens et al *Out-of-court dispute settlement systems for e-commerce: report of exploratory study*, Joint Research Centre, Italy, 2000 (also available at http://dsa-isis.jrc.it/ADR).

Examples of on-line dispute resolution

Although the number of examples in the UK at this stage is small, an indication of the developments which may occur in the UK can be gleaned from the examples in other jurisdictions, in particular the US. Although the examples relate to a range of dispute resolution methods, not limited to mediation, an overview of the examples may provide some useful guidance for on-line mediation. They may also offer parties an additional option in the course of a conventional mediation which reaches impasse.

Court determination

In the US the iCourthouse was designed to provide a streamlined version of the court system by allowing plaintiffs and defendants in certain cases to file a claim which, in turn, is considered by jurors, who register on-line and, ultimately, provide a verdict. The charge is US$200 per case.[53] A German example, Cybercourt, is a private initiative of the Association of IT Law, which uses email combined with chatbox technology to enable the adjudication procedure.[54]

Arbitration

The Virtual Magistrates Project is a US on-line arbitration service and fact-finding system for disputes involving users of on-line systems, where users claim to have been harmed by wrongful messages and system errors. The service considers complaints about messages, postings and files involving copyright or trademark infringement, misappropriation of trade secrets, defamation, fraud, anti-competitive practices, inappropriate material, invasion of privacy and other wrongful content. The scheme was implemented in 1996 and the procedural rules are posted on the VMAG website. Complaints are screened by the American Arbitration Association and, if a case is determined to be within the jurisdiction of the scheme, the American Arbitration Association would select a virtual magistrate from a list maintained by the Association. Upon selection, the magistrate would provide the respondent with the complaint. Respondents have a specified period of time within which to respond through the website. The magistrate then makes a decision within a specified period of time. Once a decision is made, the salient details about the complaint, the response and the decision are posted to part of the website, which is open to the public. A code of conduct has been developed to guide magistrates. A fee of $10 is payable by the complainant for the service in order to discourage frivolous cases. In the first two years of VMAG's existence, only one case had been determined by a magistrate.[55]

Another US website, Cyberarbitration, operates along similar lines to the Virtual Magistrates Project. It deals with two categories of dispute, domain names disputes[56] and other disputes. A standard form cyberarbitration agreement and procedures have

---

53 See http://www.i-courthouse.com
54 See http://www.cybercourt.de
55 See http://vmag.org
56 See the section on Intellectual Property Disputes in Chapter 8.

been designed. The procedures outline the appointment of the arbitrator. A statement of issues and evidence is presented and exchanged on-line by each party, although the parties may request a face-to-face meeting or hearing. The arbitrator provides a cyber award which is intended to be binding.

Across Europe, Ford Motor Company has launched an on-line arbitration scheme, in conjunction with the Chartered Institute of Arbitrators in London, to tackle disputes arising from on-line car purchases.[57] In the UK, Dispute Resolution by Barristers (DRB), an alliance of 50 barristers from Oxford and the Midlands, has set up an on-line arbitration service. A party may, on payment of a small fee, obtain the scale of fees and list of arbitrators. To set up a first meeting, the selected arbitrator is advised by email. A traditional face-to-face meeting or on-line arbitration can follow. In the case of on-line arbitration, the arbitrator will require documents and submissions to be sent electronically. Meetings can take place within a closed chat room, if required. An arbitrator's decision is posted electronically and usually within a specified period of time.

Automated settlement

A number of on-line 'arbitration' systems do not resemble traditional arbitration, but constitute blind-bidding automated settlement systems. For example, the US website, Cybersettle.com, involves the initiation of a case and the submission by the claimant of first, second, and third-round blind settlement offers. The site then informs the other party that the claim is on-line and available for settlement. The other party submits three rounds of blind settlement demands. For each round, Cybersettle compares the demand to the corresponding offer. If the offer and demand are within a certain range, usually 30% or $5,000, the case is settled for the median amount. If the range is wider in all three rounds, the claim does not settle, in which case the parties are notified and are free to continue with traditional dispute resolution methods. In that case, the settlement offers and demands are not revealed.[58] A similar US website, Clicknsettle, also allows parties to submit offers. The parties agree ahead of the process the range within which the offer and demand should fall before the dispute will be settled by splitting the difference.[59]

These kinds of blind-bidding systems have been useful in the context of insurance disputes. Cybersettle claims to have settled over 5,000 disputes involving more than $20m of claims.[60] SettleOnline, another US on-line arbitration site, which operates like Cybersettle.com and Clicknsettle.com, claims that its success lies in removing personality conflicts and posturing between the parties in dispute.[61] This site indicates that the cost is between $75 and $250 per claim, depending upon the value of the claim.[62]

---

57 See also the section on E-commerce Disputes in Chapter 8.
58 See http://www.cybersettle.com
59 See http://www.clicknsettle.com
60 E Katsh, J Rifkin and A Gaitenby *E-commerce, E-disputes and E-dispute resolution: in the shadow of e-Bay*, Paper presented for Cyberweek 2000. Copy is available at http://www.disputes.net/cyberweek2000/ohiostate/katsh.htm
61 See http://www.settleonline.com/
62 Ibid.

A number of blind-bidding systems have launched in the UK, including Cybersettle.com, eSettle.co.uk and WeCanSettle.com. Workitout's blind-bidding system is to launch in June 2001.

Mediation

The US On-line Ombuds Office is a pilot project of the National Center for Automated Information Research (NCAIR). The service provides on-line mediation.[63] It was established in 1996 and the disputes covered by the service include conflicts between members of news groups and discussion lists over domain names; between competitors; between internet access providers and subscribers; and relating to intellectual property.[64] In 1999 the service began to mediate disputes arising from e-Bay, an American on-line auction site. Approximately 150 disputes were filed in a pilot two-week period.[65]

Another American website, Internet Neutral, administers mediations in accordance with its Rules and the agreement of the parties; maintains a list and biographies of a range of mediators; can provide a range of technology, like video conferencing, facilitate virtual mediation; and also trains mediators in internet communication skills. The service was set up in 1998 and although dozens of cases have been submitted to the service for possible resolution, a case has not yet progressed to actual mediation using on-line facilities.[66] The half-day fee for each party is $250, which includes two hours' preparation time. Beyond that flat rate, the charge is $125 per hour, shared by the parties. The service's website provides a wide range of information and documents.[67]

A further American system, Online Mediators, allows a party to engage in on-line mediation by completing a disagreement information form. The system then makes contact with the respondent in order to determine if they wish to participate. If so, the respondent also completes a disagreement information form. The system then assigns a mediator to the case, who contacts each party on-line. There is a set fee for the mediation. If an agreement is reached in mediation, an agreement form is completed, although it is up to the parties to determine if that agreement should be legally enforceable. Following the process, the parties are asked to complete an evaluation form.[68]

'Time Out for Mediation' is an American organisation which aims to increase the use of mediation on-line. Its mediation process commences following completion of an on-line questionnaire. The organisation contacts the other party in the dispute and, if they agree to participate, the mediation process continues. Communications

---

63 See http://www.ombuds.org
64 See R Georges *Dispute settlement in Cyberspace*, 23 March 1998. Copy available at www.futurelawyer.com/display
65 A transcript of some of the cases is available at http://www.disputes.net/cyberweek2000/ebay
66 B Beal *On-line mediation: has its time come?* Paper presented at Cyberweek 2000 Conference. Copy is available at http://www.disputes.net/cyberweek2000/ohiostate/beal/htm
67 For example, 'Internet mediation in a nutshell'; 'Internet mediators'; 'The internet forum'; 'Fees'; 'Standards of conduct for mediators'; 'Rules'; 'Contract provisions'; 'Forms'; 'Disclaimers'; and 'Links to other mediation websites'. See http://www.internetneutral.com
68 Further information on the service is available at http://www.onlinemediators.com

are generally through email, although in some cases telephone or mail communication is used. The mediation fee is $50 per hour.[69]

Virtual Mediation, another US service, was launched, initially in conjunction with the University of Massachusetts, in order to resolve student complaints under the University Rules. Maryland's On-line Mediation Service, called Mediate-net, was initially set up to test the effectiveness of conducting mediation on the internet and focused on family disputes and health disputes between consumers and health organisations. The service uses real-time chat, electronic conferencing, email and video conferencing. An unusual aspect of the service is that it is supported by a website on Maryland Family Law and Health Law, accessible to parties to inform them about the law that might apply to their disputes.[70] SettlementNow is an on-line mediation service, which focuses on insurance disputes. A further American website, Resolution Forum, is engaged in a project with the State Bar of Texas to test on-line mediation and advanced communications technology.

In Singapore, e-CDR-I provides on-line co-mediation with foreign judges, and can be used in conjunction with video conferencing. There are also a number of Continental examples. The World Intellectual Property Organisation has an on-line mediation and arbitration service.[71] IRIS Mediation is a French initiative, founded in 1997, which provides on-line mediation for consumers in disputes arising over e-commerce transactions.[72] FSM is a German on-line mediation service organised on a self-regulatory basis by German internet service providers to deal with complaints by internet users related to internet content.[73] E-Mediation is a Dutch on-line mediation service.[74]

In the UK, Consensus Mediation was launched in 2000, providing on-line mediation, e-Mediator, primarily for smaller business disputes, consumer disputes and family disputes. The service also offers face-to-face mediations.[75] The process for setting up and running an on-line mediation is the same as for a traditional mediation, with the exception that the arrangements and interactions occur on-line. Another UK initiative has involved the ADR Group in launching a mediation network involving the foreign offices of some of its member firms to develop cross-border on-line mediation.

Negotiation

The US website, One Accord, is a negotiation support system. The site uses software, which assists parties to identify their interests and to assess their best and worst case positions. The software enables suggestions for settlement to be made based on calculations utilising the information provided by the parties. The first step requires the parties to establish a shared description of their dispute and to enter

---

69 For further information about this service, see http://www.fredey.com
70 See http://www.mediate/net.org
71 See the section on Intellectual Property Disputes and Mediation in Chapter 8.
72 See http://www.iris.sgdg.org/mediation
73 See http://www.fsm.de/bes/index.html
74 See http://www.e-mediation.nl/
75 J Fleming 'Former Eversheds lawyer claims a first in on-line mediation' *The Law Society's Gazette*, 20 April 2000, at p 20.

private information independently. The software is also able to graph each parties' priorities and preferences. With the range of possible best and worst case scenarios and individually-determined outcome preferences, the software can then suggest solutions to the problem. This occurs, however, after the parties attempt to resolve the dispute themselves, with the assistance of the software. A similar US site is 'the Mediator'.[76]

Case management

A UK service, Lynxlaw, provides, for larger cases requiring dispute resolution, a case management service. The service is aimed at both public and in-house lawyers. Clients are billed direct on a fixed-cost basis.[77]

Trust seals with ADR

Webtraders, who have received a trust seal from a third party organisation, indicating compliance with certain minimum quality standards for e-commerce, may offer on-line consumer complaints and mediation services as a service to member traders. Examples include BBBonline,[78] a US subsidiary of the Council of Better Business Bureaus, Which?Webtrader,[79] an initiative of the UK consumer organisation Which?, and Trusted Shops,[80] a German system launched in 1999.

Future challenges

It is likely that in the near future, greater use of electronic exchange of documents will be used in mediations. The challenge for the longer term will be to develop technology and software which will provide for enhanced communication and information management. It is also likely that on-line mediation will not be fully utilised until video conferencing becomes readily available. One commentator has postulated that 24 hour dispute resolution centres may emerge, allowing parties in dispute to receive advice on legal issues, as well as the most appropriate dispute resolution mechanism and a list of neutrals, and providing access to on-line facilities.[81]

---

76 For further information, see http://www.mcn.org
77 See A Mizzi 'Solve disputes on-line' *The Law Society's Gazette*, 12 February 2000, at p 5.
78 See http://www.bbbonline.org
79 See http://www.which.com/webtrader
80 See http://www.trustedshops.org
81 E Clark 'Arbitration, dispute resolution and the worldwide web' *The Arbitrator*, August 1997.

11

Quality and Standards in Mediation

Introduction

Issues of training and standards are becoming increasingly important in mediation. Individual mediators have a need to improve their levels of competence and ethical behaviour for the benefit of users of their services and for the reputation of their practices. The mediation movement as a whole needs to present the service in the best light, compared to competitive services; it also needs to be seen to respond to pressures from the consumer movement for protection and safeguards. There are also pressures on mediation, as a relatively new service, to establish its effectiveness and levels of user satisfaction, a burden not borne to the same extent by more established dispute resolution systems.

Quality and standards in any occupation can be promoted in different ways, such as training, accreditation and licensing, the setting of guidelines and standards, information and publicity, discipline and liability. They can be promoted through four broad structures:

  (a) informed consumer choice and forces of the market;
  (b) self-regulation by the occupation, with or without involvement by other interested parties;
  (c) indirect state regulation, with a statutory framework involving members of the occupation, government, consumers and other parties; and
  (d) direct state regulation, imposed through statute and government agencies.

This chapter begins by exploring current UK mediation training and standards. The chapter ends by examining standardisation and regulation of mediators. Liability of mediators is considered in the next chapter.

Mediation Training in the UK
Some concerns

The preliminary issue is whether there is a need for mediators to be trained.[1] The following arguments are made against such training: mediation skills are innate and

---

1   See H Astor and C Chinkin *Dispute Resolution in Australia*, Butterworths, Sydney, 1992, at pp 215–9 for a summary and critique of these arguments. The issue was canvassed in

cannot be taught and learned; the philosophy of mediation requires mediators to be ordinary people acting responsively, not another category of remote professionals; mediators' authority comes from the consent of the disputants whose acceptance of and trust in a particular mediator is more important than any imposed training requirements; and it is educationally too difficult to devise an adequate training system, particularly given the flexibility of the mediation process. There are powerful counter-arguments to all these contentions. Although the debate should be academic as there are extensive training facilities for mediators in the UK, the arguments still find some resonance in practice. For example, it is not uncommon for disputants to request 'senior members or persons' from any particular profession to act as their mediators. The amount of mediation training received by such 'senior members or persons' does not seem to be a source of concern to the disputants.

Genn's study of the Central London County Court Mediation Pilot highlighted that mediators require good training and experience.[2] Currently there is no formal requirement in the UK for training or qualifications and any person can hold themselves out to be a mediator. Mediation organisations have sought to address this problem by establishing their own training and accreditation schemes. The amount and type of training varies between organisations providing commercial, community and family mediation, as outlined below.[3]

Law Societies and training

Law Societies have developed training standards for mediators. The Law Society of England & Wales, by way of example, identified the need in 1992 for training, both in relation to representation of clients in mediation, as well as training solicitors to become mediators.[4] The Law Society has now developed training standards for solicitors who practise as mediators in civil/commercial and family cases respectively. These standards are not compulsory, but are recommended for solicitors wishing to offer ADR services.[5]

In the case of family mediation, the Law Society's Training Standards recommend certain minimum requirements, before training is undertaken, including qualification as solicitor, a level of maturity and life experience, and a commitment to mediation. In the case of both family and civil/commercial mediation training, the Society's Training Standards suggest that a range of teaching methods, including tutorials, discussion groups, videos, role plays, exercises, reading and feedback, should be incorporated. The basic aim of the training should be to enable trainees to under-stand the mediation process; the theory of mediation; the limitations of mediation; practical mediation skills; and practical issues, such as insurance, legal aid and marketing. In the case of family mediation, trainees are required to have knowledge

---

the New South Wales Law Reform Commission *Alternative dispute resolution – training and accreditation of mediators*, Discussion Paper 21, 1989 at pp 21–5. See also A Zilinskas 'The training of mediators: is it necessary?' (1995) 6 *ADRJ* 55.

2   H Genn *Central London County Court Mediation Pilot: Evaluation Report*, LCD Research Series, No 5/98, at p vii.

3   However, see the proposals of the Joint Mediation Forum in relation to the National Mediation Council, in this section.

4   Law Society of England and Wales *Second Report on ADR*, 1992.

5   Principle 22.01 of *Guide to the Professional Conduct of Solicitors* (8th edn) 1999.

of family law and the law relating to adoption and child abduction. There are also special issues in the case of family mediation training, including family dynamics, counselling or therapy, triangulation, fairness and power imbalances and the welfare of children.

In the case of both family and civil/commercial mediation, the Society's Training Standards provide the following basic training requirements:

- An understanding of the steps which should be taken before a mediation commences, for example, how to persuade parties to mediate. In the case of family mediation, the ability to screen for domestic violence and child abuse is recommended, together with the ability to help the parties identify relevant agencies for advice and other resources.
- Knowledge about how to conduct the mediation itself, from determining seating arrangements through to making the opening statement, gathering information, identifying interests, brainstorming and testing options, and recognising and overcoming impasse. In the case of family mediation, persuading the parties to make full and accurate financial disclosure is important.
- The skills required to mediate a case, for example to gain the parties' trust and confidence; to draw information from them through questioning, listening and reframing; and to deal with emotion and recognise power imbalances.
- Finally, in terms of bringing a mediation to a close, trainees should recognise when it is appropriate to end a mediation; to oversee drafting of understandings reached by the parties; and to assist with implementation of agreements reached.[6]

The Law Society of England & Wales provides accreditation of family mediators if certain training and other requirements are met. In terms of mediator training, the Law Society recommends that courses should last for at least 60 hours over eight days, using a wide range of teaching methods. Training should include family dynamics and child development issues; a theoretical understanding of mediation, including power imbalance and gender issues; the limitations of mediation; and the practical skills required to conduct a mediation. In addition, trainees require practical knowledge of insurance, legal aid and marketing.[7] In terms of its other recommended requirements, a solicitor family mediator should hold a practising certificate; have completed the initial training requirements; have at least 24 hours over two years of practical experience; at least 22 hours over two years of further training; and at least 11 hours of supervision. If there is a failure to achieve accreditation within five years, the applicant requires refresher training. Family mediator re-accreditation occurs every five years.[8]

The Law Society of Scotland accredits solicitor family mediators under the Civil Evidence (Family Mediation) (Scotland) Act 1995. The Law Society requires that an applicant has undertaken appropriate family mediation training[9] as the first step to

---

6   See Law Society of England & Wales: *Training Standards for civil/commercial mediation*; and *Training Standards for family mediation*.
7   See Law Society of England & Wales *Training standards for family mediation*.
8   The Law Society of England & Wales *Standards for accreditation and re-accreditation and supervision/consultancy in family mediation*.
9   Training provided by CALM is considered appropriate.

accreditation. A reference of suitability from a Sheriff or senior legal practitioner is required, in addition to relevant family law experience. The Law Society's accreditation panel may grant accreditation, reject an application or allow accreditation subject to conditions. Accredited mediators are required to mediate and undertake further training each year.[10]

Mediation organisations and training

Civil/commercial mediation organisations

The Academy of Experts' Faculty of Mediation provides mediator training, consisting of four modules. Module 1 is a two-day qualifying course. Module 2 is a one-day mediator's tutorial. The one-day Module 3 is continuing mediation training and Module 4, also one day, is an assessment day. The two-day foundation module provides an introduction to ADR and, in particular, mediation. Participants practise as mediators in mock mediations. The Academy also provides advance training, which builds on Module 3, by enlarging mediation skills and developing techniques to handle difficult situations. Familiarisation Training is a one-day workshop which aims to compare different types of ADR.[11]

The ADR Group has a two-day foundation mediation training course, outlining the range of dispute resolution options; negotiation theory; effective communication; risk analysis; breaking impasse; and generating settlement. The Group also runs a half-day awareness course, providing an intensive introduction to mediation. The Group provides a one-day course for lawyers on representation in ADR. The Group has also produced a mediation video.

The Centre for Dispute Resolution has a Training Faculty, which provides a wide range of training courses. Mediator training is a five-day course, which can be taken as a residential or non-residential course, either normal or fast track. The course potentially leads to accreditation following an assessment procedure. The Centre offers two-day conciliator training courses in a range of areas, including health, education and sports disputes. It offers a one-day ADR users workshop. Its 'Lawyers' Role in ADR, Parts I and II' courses are aimed at equipping lawyers with the skills to represent clients effectively in mediation. It offers a wide range of courses on other subjects including: avoiding business disputes, creative problem solving, effective business negotiations, communication skills and business and complaints handling. 'Negotiating your way out of conflict' can be taken as a half or one-day course and 'Mediation skills at work' is a two-day programme. For in-house lawyers, there are courses on how to succeed as an in-house lawyer; from lawyer to manager; managing corporate legal services; ADR for in-house legal advisers; and creative problem solving. There are also workshops on negotiation and techniques for representing clients in ADR through to expert determination and adjudication. The Centre has produced a Mediator Training Handbook and mediation video. It has a continuing professional development booklet and a 'cutting the cost of conflict'

---

10 See Law Society of Scotland *Code of Conduct for Solicitor Mediators*; and *Guidance for Accredited Mediators*.
11 Academy of Experts *Expert Training for Experts and Dispute Resolvers*, booklet.

training booklet. The Centre was winner of the London Region National Training Awards in 1995. The Centre, together with the Academy of Experts and the Chartered Institute of Arbitrators, have agreed a protocol, recognising each other's ADR training.

The Chartered Institute of Arbitrators offers a five-day mediation training course, with a focus on commercial and construction disputes. The Commercial Mediation Centre provides a one-day in-house mediation course for trainee solicitors and a three-day in-house mediation course for solicitors and barristers leading to a certificate in commercial mediation.

In Scotland, Mediation Bureau provides mediator training leading to accreditation in addition to training for lawyers who wish to represent clients in mediation, which is a two-day course. The Centre for Dispute Resolution and the ADR Group also provide commercial mediation training in Scotland. The Centre and ADR Group also provide commercial mediation training in Northern Ireland.

Various civil/commercial mediation organisations also accredit mediators. Accreditation requires mediators to substantiate mediation experience or continuing professional development. American research indicates that favourable outcomes in a mediation are associated with the experience level of the mediator.[12] The Academy of Experts and the ADR Group publish Registers of their accredited mediators. The Centre for Dispute Resolution, for example, accredits mediators through an assessment procedure over two days following the foundation mediator course outlined above. The Centre's continuing professional development requirements depend upon the date of accreditation, and include mediator practice, submission of written reports of mediations, personal debrief and supervision, skills training, group participation and promotion of ADR.[13] The Law Society is developing an accreditation scheme for civil/commercial solicitor mediators, and proposes a two-tier panel, involving general and practitioner membership, depending on training and mediator experience.

Community mediation organisations

Community mediation organisations operate selection procedures for mediator training. Those procedures include checks, aimed at determining whether a person has any prior convictions. Some organisations select by way of application form, references and interviews. Apart from ascertaining any prior convictions, the aim of the selection procedures is to gain an understanding of a person's skills, work history and traits.

Mediation UK's community mediation training programme has been endorsed by the National Open College Network (NOCN) and, since it is recognised as a national vocational training programme, successful accreditation via the training programme enables mediators to obtain a nationally-recognised vocational qualification. The training programme provides an introduction to mediation and deals with preparation for a mediation, managing a mediation and working as a community

---

12 J Pearson 'Family Mediation' in Ohio State University College of Law (eds) *Court Reform Implications of Dispute Resolution*, Ohio State University College of Law, 1995.
13 Centre for Dispute Resolution *Bulletin: Launch of continuing professional development for CEDR mediators*, January 1999.

mediator. The training involves group discussion, observation, feedback, peer assessment and trainer evaluation. Trainees are required to understand the principles of mediation, ethics and equal opportunities legislation. The training emphasises self-awareness and communication skills, and encourages a basic knowledge of the law and courts.[14] Training for victim-offender mediation includes knowledge on crime and the criminal justice system. Specialist training is required for community mediators who work with juveniles. Provided that a certain level of knowledge and skills is attained, trainees proceed to a probationary period, when their work is monitored. Support and supervision is provided to trainees during this period through meetings with a supervisor through to peer supervision and mentoring.[15] Apart from its Community Mediation Skills Training Manual, Mediation UK has produced a wide range of other training materials, including a Peer Mediation Manual; Conflict Resolution Skills Workshops; a comprehensive range of publications on neighbour, victim-offender and schools mediation; and community mediation training videos.

Family Mediation Scotland provides a range of community mediation training courses. In Northern Ireland the Mediation Network for Northern Ireland provides mediation and conflict resolution skills training, a range of programmes, lasting between one and six days. Their community awareness training is two days long. They provide a one-day peace building course, another one-day community relations course and a community relations and community development course. Restorative justice is a one-day course; organisational change is a six-day course; and transforming conflict is a two-day course.

Community mediator accreditation requires evidence of experience, references, a commitment to continuing professional development and evidence of competent mediation practice. There are two routes by which evidence of competent practice can be provided. The first is by Mediation UK's APL route and, secondly, by the Scottish/National Vocational Qualification (NVQ). The Scottish National Vocational Qualification is offered in Scotland and the National Vocational Qualification is offered in England, Wales and Northern Ireland. The separate qualifications recognise the different education system in Scotland. There are, however, reciprocal arrangements, providing recognition of each qualification across the UK. The development of S/NVQ has been part of the National Development Agenda for vocational education in training.[16] The APL route is equivalent to S/NVQ, except that it is assessed by Mediation UK's assessors. It is intended that the APL route will operate until S/NVQ is freely available. A number of organisations have been approved as providers of this qualification.[17]

Family mediation organisations

Special issues in family mediation training

Family mediation training needs to equip mediators with awareness of areas which may require specialist family mediation experience, for instance, in finance and

---

14 Mediation UK *Training Manual in Community Mediation Skills*.
15 M Liebmann (ed) *Community and Neighbour Mediation*, Cavendish Publishing Limited, London, 1998, at pp 125–7.
16 See Department of Employment *Prosperity through skills*, London 1993.
17 For example, City & Guilds.

child issues. All family mediators need to be trained to recognise and respond to domestic violence, child abuse and power imbalances. Mediators also need to be trained in gender and cultural issues in order to appreciate issues which may be important to different ethnic and religious backgrounds. The ability to provide legal information is also considered an important aspect of family mediation training.[18]

England and Wales

The UK College of Family Mediators and the Law Society of England & Wales have developed a set of family mediation training standards for adoption by family mediator trainers. Family mediation training is provided by a large number of organisations. The UK College of Family Mediators has approved the following training bodies: National Family Mediation (NFM), Family Mediators' Association (FMA), Solicitors' Family Law Association (SFLA), Professional Development & Training (PDT), Family Mediation Scotland (FMS), LawWise and the Academy of Experts.

The UK College has standards for training of family mediators, in addition to continuing professional development requirements, as a basis for accreditation. Its mediator training requirements are a training programme of 105 hours, which covers mediation knowledge, principles, values and skills. In addition, at least 10 hours of mediation practice with an approved trainer is required within 18 months of the taught course. Co-mediation with an experienced mediator, together with super-vision and consultancy, is required. Assessment is by written work and supervisor, trainer or peer evaluation.[19] In terms of its other accreditation requirements, there are different requirements for associates and full members. Associates need a minimum of 10 hours of mediation per year within three years of attaining associate statues; four hours of professional practice, supervision or consultancy, or 10% of mediation hours, whichever is higher; and seven hours of further training. Full members require 15 hours of mediation each year; two hours or 5% of mediation hours, whichever is higher, of professional practice, supervision or consultancy; seven hours of further training; and recommendation for continued membership.[20]

The SFLA follows the Law Society's recommended family mediation training standards. It trains experienced family solicitors in sole and co-mediation in all issues mediation. It also provides consultancy and other professional support services. Its courses are open to solicitors with three years' post-qualification experience or five years' experience as a member of ILEX. Trainees are also required to show that 25% of their work is devoted to family work. The SFLA runs a foundation course of eight days' duration. Following the course there are three days of written assessment, 40 hours of mediation, three days of continuing education, three days' sole and anchor mediation practice and one day of written assignments.[21] The accreditation requirements of the Solicitors' Family Law

---

18 Family mediators, responding to a survey, acknowledged that they felt 'out of their depth' in relation to financial and property issues and considered that they required more training to deal with these issues: University of Newcastle upon Tyne Conciliation Project Unit, *Report to the Lord Chancellor's Department on the cost and effectiveness of conciliation in England and Wales*, March 1989.
19 See UK College of Family Mediators *Standards and Code of Practice*, 1998; *Directory and Handbook 1999–2000*; and *Creating the firm foundation for a growing profession*.
20 Ibid.
21 See Solicitors' Family Law Association *Mediation rules for consultants*; *Mediation*

Association (SFLA) aim at a five-year cycle, during which time mediators, following completion of their basic training, are required to undertake mediation practice; continuing education and training; peer group discussions; consultancy; and have a practicing or ILEX certificate.[22]

The FMA trains and supports mediators from counselling and legal backgrounds to work in pairs or alone. The training leads to accreditation. The FMA also provides training to family lawyers and other professionals who wish to support clients through family mediation. There is a range of continuing professional development courses, and a professional practice supervisor two-day course. The FMA has produced a Mediation Practice Manual. The FMA's entry requirements to mediator training courses require the candidate to be a solicitor or barrister, with three years' post-qualification experience, and references. Other candidates require a degree and a professional qualification in social work or family therapy, with three years' post-qualification experience, and references. Candidates who meet the criteria attend a selection procedure, which allows the FMA to assess their appropriateness for training. The mediator training course is ten days' duration, providing an introduction, an overview of the theory of mediation, psychology, family law and dispute resolution. It also includes written assessment and 40 hours of co-mediation. Apart from the foundation training, FMA also provides three-day sole and anchor mediator training courses; a two-day professional practice supervisor course; and a wide range of one-day courses for continuing professional development.[23]

The Family Mediators' Association (FMA) accreditation requirements include mediation practice; further education and training; written work; and appraisal. The continuing education and training programme offered by the FMA covers a wide range of areas, including children and mediation, family law, domestic violence, drafting memoranda of understanding, finance and mediation, franchise and marketing, and supervision and consultancy.[24]

NFM provides training and continuing professional development for family mediators who wish to practise in an NFM-affiliated service. Training occurs over one year, combined with practice, and the programme complies with the European Charter for Training of Family Mediators. NFM has published the 'National Core Training Programme (CTP)'. NFM selection criteria include aptitude for mediation and at least five years' work experience, including responsibility for inter-personal relations or a relevant degree. Training consists of an induction course, formal training and co-mediation, following by one year of work experience, 75 hours of which must include supervised direct mediation.[25] National Family Mediation

---

selection of applicants for training, practice and accreditation process; *Mediation, training, accreditation and re-accreditation: Appeals procedure*; *Mediation training for lawyers*; and *Courses in all-issues mediation*.

22 See Solicitors' Family Law Association materials, op cit.

23 Family Mediators' Association *Policy document on selection, recruitment, training and professional practice supervision and consultancy*; *Guidelines to current policy: domestic violence, child protection and direct consultation*; *Assistance for those facing separation or divorce*; *Guidelines to training policy and entry requirements*; *Training Courses*; and *Training to mediate on all issues in separation or divorce*.

24 See Family Mediators' Association materials, op cit.

25 National Family Mediation *Steps towards competent service practice in all issues mediation*.

(NFM) selects mediators when there is a vacancy and in this way guarantees that mediators will receive practical experience and supervision. Accreditation is received upon completion of face-to-face mediation and following an independent assessment of competence.[26]

Law Wise requirements for accreditation are that mediators demonstrate knowledge of mediation procedure, conduct mediations and undertake further education and training, of at least three days each year.[27]

Law Wise provides mediator training for solicitors and barristers, who have at least three years' post-qualification experience including a substantial amount of family work, and references. It provides foundation mediator training over five days. There is an advanced course of three days' duration. For accreditation, 40 hours of supervised mediation practice is required.[28] Law Wise also provides support for its trained mediators.

PDT's selection procedure considers qualifications and experience, and an applicant's suitability for mediation. Assessment is done by written application and references. Maturity is valued. Family lawyer candidates are required to have three years' post-qualification experience in family law. The foundation mediator training involves 49 hours' training.

The Legal Aid Board's Quality Assurance Standard provides that supervisors should have at least three years' experience as a mediator; have conducted 45 hours of mediation; and are required to continue to conduct at least 15 hours of mediation annually.[29]

Scotland

Family Mediation Scotland (FMS) training complies with UK College of Family Mediators requirements. On the other hand, CALM's requirements enable its members to attain Law Society accreditation. In Scotland the Civil Evidence (Family Mediation) (Scotland) Act 1995 sets out family mediation training requirements and also allows the Lord President of the Court of Sessions to approve organisations offering family mediation training. The Act stipulates that family mediation training should cover, at least, the mediation process; Scottish law on divorce, property, finance, domestic violence and financial support for children; Scottish court rules and procedures; the emotional aspects of separation; child development; and resource and referral agencies. Family Mediation Scotland (FMS) has a pre-registration period, which lasts for at least six months, and needs to include at least ten mediations, in which the parties have at least had a joint meeting. If an assessment panel determines that an applicant has adequate competence as a mediator, an application for registration is made to FMS. The panel may determine that an applicant needs to develop further skills before registration is given or that a person is not suitable for mediation.[30] FMS has a continuing professional

---

26 See National Family Mediation *National Core Training Programme*; *What is Mediation? Annual Report*, 1998.
27 See Law Wise *Code of Practice for Law Wise family mediation*; *Disciplinary and Grievance Procedures*; and *Law Wise family mediation training programme for accreditation*.
28 Law Wise *Family mediation training programme for accreditation*.
29 Legal Aid Board *Family Mediation Quality Assurance Standard*, November 1998.
30 See Family Mediation Scotland *Information Pack*.

development programme on a range of topics, from conflict management, mentoring and children's interests.[31]

The selection process by FMS is done by application form, interview and a selection exercise. Candidates are required to have professional experience in law, social work or counselling and/or a strong educational background, together with appropriate personal attributes. The foundation mediator training course has ten modules from introduction, through to mediation theory, children's needs and mediation practice. Written work and supervision follow the training.[32]

CALM's selection criteria include a significant proportion of time spent on family law work, and references. The core mediator training programme consists of three residential weekend courses and three practice skills days. The weekend courses cover a wide range of issues, including ethics, the mediation process, psychology, children's issues, financial issues and property issues. Trainees are also required to undertake six months of supervision at a local mediation service.[33]

Northern Ireland

Training and accreditation requirements are those of the organisation, with whom the mediator is affiliated with, for example, NFM, FMA or the UK College of Family Mediators.

Republic of Ireland by way of comparison

The Mediators Institute Ireland's selection interview is followed by a training course of 120 hours, divided into two modules. The first module focuses on knowledge and mediation skills development. The second module focuses on ethics and specialist training through co-mediation and supervised mediation.[34] The Institute provides two mechanisms for accreditation. The first method is via a formal degree, together with professional experience and training. The second route is by practical work experience, together with supporting references and training. Re-accreditation occurs every two years. Accredited training courses involve a core module of 60 hours, followed by a further 60 hours of practical experience under a training contract. The core training module covers conflict analysis, negotiation, the mediation process, psychology and mediation skills, professionalism and codes of conduct. The practical experience component involves co-mediation, further education and training and written agreements from mediations.[35]

Specialist mediation organisations and training

In relation to environmental disputes, the Environment Council offers a range of stakeholder dialogue training. The foundation course in facilitation and mediation is a six-day course. There are additional courses, for instance, on working with stakeholders, which is a three-day management development course in process

---

31 Family Mediation Scotland *Annual Report 1999*.
32 Family Mediation Scotland *Registration procedures*; *National Training Course Information Pack*; and *Procedures and evaluation of training mediators*.
33 CALM *Central Statistical Information*.
34 Mediators Institute Ireland *The accreditation of professional mediators in Ireland*.
35 Mediators' Institute Ireland *The accreditation of professional mediators in Ireland*; and B Wood 'Mediators' Institute Ireland' *Fam Med* vol 4, No 3, at p 10.

design and facilitation skills. An introduction to stakeholder dialogue is a half-day briefing course. The World Intellectual Property Organisation (WIPO) provides a range of mediator workshops for intellectual property specialists. The Royal Institute of Chartered Surveyors has produced a mediation training video.

Universities and training

Universities and other academic institutions have also begun to offer mediation courses in the UK. Most law schools now provide some introductory courses on negotiation, mediation and other forms of ADR. The College of Law provides courses for trainee solicitors to equip them with the basic skills to represent clients in mediation. Nottingham Law School provides a similar course for qualified solicitors, called 'Mediation Advocacy'. The Oxford Institute of Legal Practice offers Certificate and Diploma courses in mediation. The Certificate course takes at least 18 months and the Diploma course is a further year's duration. The course covers mediation skills, family law and ethics. Supervised practice occurs over the course. A dissertation and mediation theory practice is required in order to obtain the Diploma.[36] The London School of Economics offers a Certificate course on dispute resolution, which is taught over twelve successive weeks. In addition, it offers courses, which provide credit for the European Masters Degree in Mediation. The Masters Degree involves post-graduate training through a partnership of European universities.

ADR training is also offered in Scottish law schools. For example, the University of Dundee and the University of Strathclyde provide mediation training as part of the Diploma in legal practice. University of Aberdeen offers negotiation skills training in its Legal Practice Course.[37] A Diploma in Mediation Studies can be obtained from the University College, Dublin. It is a one-year part-time course covering commercial, community, marital and victim-offender mediation, and multi-party disputes involving peacemaking.

The University of Windsor Law School (Canada) conducts ADR Certificate Workshops in conjunction with barristers' chambers in London.

Basic training considerations

At present there is little agreement in the UK on what the mediation training content and methodology should be. In most models, training is conducted by experienced practising mediators and not by theoreticians. Training courses are offered mainly by providers of mediation services, both public and private.

Basic components to mediator training

In terms of the training content, the basic components are:

- theories of conflict, models of negotiation, the mediation process and the legal rules affecting mediation practice;

---

36 Oxford Institute of Legal Practice *Post-graduate Certificate and Diploma in Family Mediation Information*.
37 R Mays and B Clark *ADR in Scotland*, The Scottish Office, 1999.

- communication, mediator intervention and negotiation skills; and
- standards and ethics.

Role-playing and simulations are important ingredients of mediation training.[38] Besides providing a forum for skills development, role-plays provide an experiential basis for reflecting on theory and principles. In an article on mediator training, Power suggests that too strong a reliance on training in techniques moulds the mediator in the style of the trainers, and argues for education of an independent, reflective and adaptive practitioner; she recommends that 'principled adaptability' be built into the education of mediators.[39]

Most mediation training, other than family training, does not include material relevant to the substantive content of the disputes in which the trainees might become involved. Examples of substantive knowledge would be the law of torts for personal injury mediations. There is thus an assumption that training will produce *facilitative* and not *evaluative* mediators, though the assumption is not always borne out in practice. It would be feasible to develop the substantive content to suit the trainees, so that those from the helping professions are provided with a legal framework and those from legal backgrounds with basics in psychology. Not all mediation trainees need to develop the same skills and there may be a need to make up for the shortcomings in participants' previous education.[40] Training should aim to provide better ways of appreciating the subtleties of process and subjective ethics than the mere articulation of standards.[41]

Some argue that absence of assessment is justified on the grounds that:

- the 'threat' of appraisal can undermine a rich educational experience;
- assessment might discourage attendance at training and reduce community understanding of mediation;
- the criteria for performance-based assessment are educationally complex and have yet to be perfected;[42]
- assessment is premature and of little significance after only a short period of training; and
- most of those attending training will not practise as mediators but will be able to use the knowledge and skills in many other contexts.

Where it is carried out, assessment provides an opportunity for trainers to inform participants whether or not they are competent in the process and skills of mediation. Assessment is also a response to the requirement of some mediation service

---

38 For a 'Mediator Assessment Form' used for mediation simulations by the UTS Centre for Dispute Resolution, see (1994) 1 *CDRJ* 157–65.

39 M Power 'Educating mediators metacognitively' (1992) 3 *ADRJ* 214 at 215. See also D Cruickshank 'Training mediators: moving towards competency-based training' in K Mackie (ed) *A Handbook on Dispute Resolution: ADR in Action*, Routledge, New York, 1991, at p 248.

40 J Folberg and A Taylor *Mediation: a comprehensive guide to resolving conflicts without litigation*, Jossey-Bass, San Francisco, 1984, at p 238.

41 G Walker 'Training mediators: teaching about ethical concerns and obligations' (1998) 19 *MQ* 33. See also H Astor and C Chinkin 'Mediation training and ethics' (1991) 2 *ADRJ* at pp 205–23.

42 See the (US) National Institute for Dispute Resolution *Performance-based assessment: a methodology for use in selecting, training and evaluating mediators*, Washington DC, 1995.

providers that those applying for accreditation should have received a 'satisfactory' grading at their training. The Society for Professionals Engaged in ADR ('SPIDR') in the US recommends that training should be assessed by performance, rather than paper credentials.[43]

Clinical training

Clinical training and learning through observation, which are common in other occupations, are problematic in mediation because of the private and confidential nature of the process. However, co-mediation and pupil mediation provides a useful vehicle for the clinical training of probationary mediators.

Continued training

Continuing training, audits and other forms of performance-based training are usually required as a basis for accreditation and continuing professional development. Intermediate and advanced level training courses focus on further skills development, additional theory of conflict management, interdisciplinary perspectives on mediation, and problematic issues in standards and ethics. They also provide opportunities for critical reflection on mediation experiences.

Specialist training

Some mediation training has a specialist orientation, for example, training provided to mediators who deal with family mediation. Specialist training allows for substantive issues and problems unique to the relevant fields or organisations to be dealt with in greater detail.

Training for lawyers and advisers

Standards and quality in mediation are also dependent on the skills and understanding of those who refer disputants to mediation and who participate in and advise them during the process. There is now specialist training for lawyers and others performing these roles. This training takes the form of continuing education workshops and seminars. There are also courses on representing clients in mediation.

Education in mediation

It is important to distinguish between training and education in mediation. The terms are often used interchangeably in the literature and in practice. They are, however, not the same. Mediation training is skills-based and focuses on providing dispute resolution skills for users, and technical alternative dispute resolution (ADR) process skills for mediators and advisers of users, such as lawyers. It involves improving communication and negotiation skills, learning about the mediation

---

43 SPIDR Commission *Qualifying neutrals: the basic principles*, SPIDR 1989; and S Press 'Court-connected ADR: policies and issues' *FORUM*, 1995, No 25, at pp 8–10.

process and developing mediation techniques. It is usually competency-based and of longer duration than mediation education. Examples are conflict management and communication training, mediation user training, mediation advocacy training and mediator training.

Mediation education, on the other hand, provides the contextual background and framework to understanding the advantages and limitations of mediation. It is often an on-going process of increasing awareness about conflict itself and potential choices in conflict management and resolution. It may take the form of mediation marketing programmes, where the purpose is to convince potential users to make use of mediation. It may also take the form of awareness programmes, which may touch on what mediation is, how it can be used, when it may be appropriate and where to gain access to mediation services.[44] The Legal Aid Franchise Quality Assurance Standard (Solicitors) 2000, for example, requires all advisers working on Legal Services Commission funded family cases to have an understanding of family mediation and to attend discussion forums and briefing events.

With the increase in the number of mediation training providers and more promotional efforts on their part, it is getting increasingly common for people to be trained as mediators when they may probably never serve as such. This is wasteful and unfortunate, and may cause trainees some dissatisfaction. It is therefore crucial for learning objectives to be determined right from the start. This is so that appropriate forms of training or education can be provided and dispute resolution knowledge and skills that are to be imparted can be matched to the needs of different groups of individuals. That way, only people who may eventually serve as neutrals will undergo mediator training.[45]

Accreditation

The term 'accreditation' implies that an occupational group or public body recognises that an individual has successfully completed a prescribed course of education or training and meets certain levels of performance.[46] In a regulated practice, accreditation may be legally necessary to provide the particular service or to receive benefits, such as promotion and marketing, from the accrediting body. Ongoing accreditation might require continuing education, competency training and skills audits, failing which the accreditation may be withdrawn. Accreditation also implies that the accrediting body has some form of control and discipline over those accredited.

In the UK there currently is no national system of accreditation for mediators. Issues of training and accreditation have been left to mediation organisations themselves, some of which have acted as 'accreditors' for the purpose of their organisations. The term 'accredited mediator' has justification if that accreditation requires training,

---

44 See generally C Constantino and C Merchant *Designing Conflict Management Systems: a guide to creating productive and healthy organisations*, Jossey-Bass, San Francisco, 1996, at pp 134–49, for a discussion on the need to draw a distinction between training and education, and on the proper design of ADR training and education.

45 Ibid.

46 On the differences between accreditation, registration, certification and licensing, see NSW Law Reform Commission 'Training and accreditation of mediators' (1991) 67 *LRC* 35.

assessment, ongoing training, fulfilling audit requirements, and minimum practical experience for continued accreditation. It is a misnomer if only minimal training, without assessment, is required and there are no continuing requirements.[47]

The absence of uniform standards for accreditation has led to the present situation in the UK, where different criteria are being applied.

Mediation Standards in the UK

Concerns

In the 1997/98 Annual Report of the Lord Chancellor's Advisory Committee on Legal Education and Conduct, the Committee recorded its aim to review the standards of education, training and conduct of mediation service providers, initially focusing on family mediation.[48] Genn in her study of the Central London County Court Mediation Pilot highlighted concerns about the quality of mediators.[49] Genn's study of the Central London County Court Mediation Pilot revealed particular concern by solicitors and parties over the accountability and ethics of mediators. In addition, the study revealed that there is no consistency in the view held by mediators on issues like ethics and accountability.[50] Mediation organisations have their own training and accreditation criteria and codes of conduct. Not only are there differences in approach between mediation organisations in different subject areas, like commercial, family and community mediation, but also between organisations in the same field, as will become apparent in the outline below.

Civil/commercial mediation

England and Wales

The Academy of Experts, the ADR Group, the Centre for Dispute Resolution, the Commercial Mediation Centre and the Law Society of England & Wales have developed Codes of Conduct for mediators. The Academy's Code applies to mediators on the Academy's Register of Mediators. The ADR Group's and the Centre for Dispute Resolution's Codes apply to mediators in any mediation conducted under the auspices of those bodies respectively. The Commercial Mediation Centre's Code covers the conduct of mediators appointed by the Centre to resolve a dispute. In accordance with the Guide to the Professional Conduct of Solicitors,[51] solicitors who offer mediation services should comply with the relevant

---

47 J Wade refers to a form of 'whispering accreditation' in terms of which the mediation network, including trainers, mediators and legal advisers, establishes an informal system of 'accreditation', based on experience, reputation, performance and gossip.
48 Lord Chancellor's Advisory Committee on Legal Education and Conduct *Annual Report 1997–98*.
49 H Genn *Central London County Court Mediation Pilot: Evaluation Report*, LCD Research Series, No 5/98, at p 143.
50 H Genn, ibid, at p vii.
51 See Principle 22.04 in the *Guide to the Professional Conduct of Solicitors* (8th edn) 1999

code of practice. The Law Society's Code of Conduct for civil/commercial mediation recommends that solicitors offering civil/commercial mediation should comply with that Code.

Standards are also contained in mediation agreements used by a range of mediation organisations[52] and in the mediation rules and procedures of mediation organisations.[53] A number of courts also issue guidance for mediations conducted in cases before those courts.[54]

The following basic criteria governing mediator conduct are set out in the various Codes, mediation agreements and mediation rules and procedures:[55]

- the mediator should be competent, by having sufficient knowledge of the process and, in some cases, the subject matter of the dispute in question;
- the mediator should be available to the extent required to enable him or her to conduct a mediation expeditiously;
- the mediator should ensure that the parties' participation in the mediation is voluntary;
- the parties, and in some cases the mediator, should have the power to terminate the process if necessary;
- the mediator is required to conduct a mediation fairly and even-handedly and there should be no circumstances which give rise to doubts about the mediator's impartiality or independence;
- the mediator must maintain neutrality and cannot impose a settlement on the parties, although some rules allow a mediator, with the consent of the parties, to make a non-binding evaluation;
- the mediator cannot act in certain cases of conflict and, in other cases, should provide full disclosure to the parties and only proceed with the consent of the parties;[56]
- the fact that a mediation takes place, anything said in caucus sessions and information given in or arising out of a mediation is confidential unless the parties agree otherwise, the information is already in the public domain, the life or safety of any person is at risk, if the law requires disclosure or to enforce a contract;

---

which refers to the Codes of Practice in Annex 22A and B, and reminds solicitors that they are still subject to the rules and principles which govern solicitors' conduct generally when they mediate. If a complaint is made against a solicitor mediator, the Office for Supervision of Solicitors are likely to see adherence to the Law Society's Code of Conduct in mediation as evidence of good practice.

52 For example, the Academy of Experts, the ADR Group, the Centre for Dispute Resolution, the Commercial Mediation Centre and the Institute of Civil Engineers. See also Parts I and II.

53 For example, the Academy of Experts, the Centre for Business Arbitration, The Centre for Dispute Resolution, the Chartered Institute of Arbitrators, the City Disputes Panel, the Commercial Mediation Centre, the Center for Public Resources, the Institute of Civil Engineers, the International Chamber of Commerce, the London Court of International Arbitration, the Royal Institution of Chartered Surveyors and the World Intellectual Property Organisation. See also Parts I and II.

54 For example, the Commercial Court, the county court and the Patents Court.

55 The criteria or principles of mediation are examined in more detail in Part I.

56 The Law Society's Code is most stringent in providing that a solicitor mediator should not act if there is any circumstance which constitutes actual or potential conflict.

- no information produced for or used in a mediation can be used as evidence in later proceedings over the dispute, and the mediator cannot be called as a witness;
- a mediator should be concerned with the fairness of the process, rather than the outcome, although in some cases an exception is made if a party is unrepresented and the proposed agreement is unconscionable;
- in some cases, third party interests are required to be considered by the mediator;
- generally, the mediator cannot provide legal advice, although with the consent of the parties a mediator may be able to give a non-binding evaluation;[57]
- although a mediator may advertise, most Codes require that advertising to be professional and accurate;
- mediators are required to maintain professional indemnity insurance.

The table on page **440** shows the criteria applied by different mediation organisations.

Scotland and Northern Ireland

The Law Society of Scotland has produced a Code of Conduct for solicitor mediators in Scotland. In Northern Ireland the Law Society's general Code of Conduct for solicitors applies to solicitor mediators, for instance, in relation to conflicts of interest.

Community mediation

Mediation UK, the umbrella organisation for community mediation organisations in the UK, seeks to ensure that community mediation services are of the highest possible standard. Standards for community mediators apply when they mediate, but also govern their relationship with other mediators, their mediation service and other agencies. The criteria in Mediation UK's Standards for Mediators are outlined below:

- The ethical framework for a mediation focuses on voluntary participation; confidentiality; the mediator's impartiality, fairness, neutrality and competence; and the mediator refraining from providing advice.
- The mediation process should be structured in such a way as to ensure voluntary participation, collaboration, creativity, openness and identification of the parties' interests.
- Mediators should be aware of the standards, practise their skills through regular mediations, and provide and receive support and supervision.[58]
- Mediators should know the steps required to prepare for a mediation, how to conduct a mediation and what to do after a mediation has been completed.[59]

Mediation UK has also developed standard requirements for community mediation services. The standards cover management, service delivery, personnel and

---

57 The Law Society's Code is underpinned by the concept that solicitor mediators must not give advice to parties in mediation, either individually or collectively.
58 See the next part on Training in this chapter.
59 For more detail see Part II on process.

Organisations and their Documentation

Criteria	Academy of Experts – Agreement to Mediate	Academy of Experts – Guidance notes for mediators	Academy of Experts – Guidelines for mediation	Academy of Experts – Code of Conduct	ADR Group – Agreement to Mediate	ADR Group – Professional Code of Conduct	Centre for Business Arbitration (CBA) – Mediation Rules	Centre for Dispute Resolution (CEDR) – Model Mediation Agreement	CEDR – Model Mediation Procedure	CEDR – Code of Conduct	Chartered Institute of Arbitrators (CIA) – Rules of the Consumer Dispute Resolution Scheme	Commercial Mediation Centre (CMC) – Appointment of Mediator Agreement	CMC – Mediation Rules & Procedures	CMC – Code of Conduct	City Disputes Panel (CDP) – Mediation Rules	Centre for Public Resources (CPR) – Mediation Procedure for business disputes in Europe	Institution of Civil Engineers (ICE) – Conciliators' Agreement	ICE – Conciliation Procedure	International Chamber of Commerce (ICC) – Rules of optional conciliation	London Court of International Arbitration (LCIA) – Mediation Procedure	World Intellectual Property Organisation (WIPO) – Mediation Rules	Law Society of England & Wales – Code of Practice for civil/commercial mediation	Courts – Patents County Court Mediation Rules	Courts – Commercial Court ADR guidance notes
Competence of mediator	✓	✓		✓		✓			✓	✓		✓		✓		✓						✓		✓
Voluntary participation by the parties	✓	✓		✓	✓	✓	✓		✓	✓			✓	✓		✓	✓					✓		
Disclosure by mediator of apparent or actual conflicts of interest	✓			✓		✓			✓	✓	✓	✓	✓	✓		✓				✓		✓		
Impartiality	✓			✓	✓	✓		✓	✓	✓	✓	✓		✓		✓			✓	✓	✓	✓		
Neutrality	✓			✓	✓		✓	✓	✓	✓	✓		✓			✓			✓		✓	✓	✓	
Fairness	✓							✓	✓	✓			✓	✓		✓	✓		✓			✓	✓	
Third party interests						✓				✓				✓								✓		
Confidentiality	✓			✓	✓	✓	✓	✓	✓	✓	✓	✓		✓		✓	✓	✓	✓	✓	✓	✓	✓	
Privilege	✓			✓	✓			✓	✓	✓	✓			✓		✓	✓	✓	✓	✓	✓	✓	✓	
Legal advice					✓												✓	✓				✓		
Recommendations by mediator	✓				✓		✓	✓	✓		✓		✓	✓	✓	✓					✓	✓		✓
Mediator liability	✓	✓							✓			✓	✓		✓	✓				✓	✓			
Professional indemnity insurance				✓				✓														✓		
Advertising by the mediator				✓		✓						✓		✓								✓		

premises. Community mediation services must also demonstrate that they provide sound training and good support for mediators. Mediation UK provides a voluntarily accreditation scheme for community mediation services. It has also set up an advisory service to offer support to community mediation services working towards accreditation. The Mediation UK standards for community mediation services cover:

- the basic principles, which include neutrality and independence of mediators, confidentiality and financial accountability to investors;
- sound management, including adherence to a governing document, a management committee, effective financial systems and record keeping, monitoring of user satisfaction and evaluation of the work of the service;
- responsibility to the community evidenced by a non-discriminatory selection of mediators and by ensuring affordability of services;
- responsibility to clients by ensuring that competent and well-trained mediators are selected for each case and that a system for handling complaints is available;
- responsibility to workers for the service, by providing supervision, support and training, together with a procedure for complaints handling and for disciplining workers, where necessary.

Family mediation

Overview

The UK College of Family Mediators acts as regulator for professional family mediation organisations that are on their approval list and whose members apply for membership of the College. The College does not provide mediation training itself, but accredits training programmes offered by other family mediation organisations. The College hopes to receive statutory powers to regulate and discipline its members.

In England, Wales, Scotland and Northern Ireland there is a wide range of family mediation organisations, with their own standards, codes of practice and disciplinary procedures, although in many cases these mirror those of the UK College of Family Mediators. In addition, in each of England and Wales, Scotland and Northern Ireland, the Law Society regulates lawyer family mediators. The Law Society of England & Wales and of Scotland have also developed codes of practice for lawyer family mediators. Lawyer family mediators are also covered by their professional indemnity insurance if they act as mediators as part of their practices. A lawyer family mediator may, however, also be a member of a family mediation organisation, for example, Family Mediation Scotland (FMS), in addition to the UK College of Family Mediators, which can lead to conflicting standards. This dilemma has led to a debate on the need to standardise standards, although in Scotland, for example, the view is that lawyer family mediators are already accountable to the Law Society and, accordingly, they should not be accountable to other bodies as well.[60]

---

60 B Clark and R Mays 'Regulating ADR: the Scottish experience' (1996) 5 *Web JCLI*.

In comparison, in the Republic of Ireland, the Mediators Institute Ireland (MII) is a regulatory body for accredited mediators, and has statutory recognition. Mediators who are not members of the Institute may practise, provided that they do not refer to themselves as accredited mediators.

Standards for family mediators

The following criteria provide an outline of the standards for family mediators:[61]

- parties' participation in mediation is voluntary and they may discontinue a mediation at any time and, in some cases, a mediator may also terminate the process;
- parties' agreement is required to the terms and conditions of the mediation at the outset; the mediator manages the mediation, although he or she is guided by the parties' wishes; the mediator is not obliged to verify information disclosed; and the mediator can advise on a party's need for further information, on the need for external advice and when a proposed agreement is unlikely to be accepted by a court;
- parties should be given the option of consulting a solicitor before reaching a binding agreement;
- the mediator is required to consider whether a conflict of interests exist and the parties' informed consent is required if there is a conflict of interest;
- a mediator cannot impose his or her views about the merits of the case on the parties;
- information disclosed during the mediation is confidential and privileged unless the parties agree otherwise, there is an order from a court, the disclosure relates to facts regarding property or finance, or if a child is suffering or is likely to suffer harm;
- the mediator is required to consider the needs and interests of a child; and the mediator is required to take appropriate action if a child is suffering or is likely to suffer harm;
- power imbalances must be considered by mediators and steps taken to redress any power imbalances;
- a mediator should screen for domestic violence;
- a mediator is required to have appropriate knowledge, mediation practice and continuing professional development, and professional indemnity insurance;
- in terms of advertising, solicitor mediators are required to abide by any restrictions in solicitors' conduct rules.

UK College of Family Mediators' Standards

In relation to the terms and conditions of a mediation, the College's Standards require the parties' agreement at the outset, preferably in writing when there are financial and property issues involved. The mediator is required to explain that his or her role is not to verify information disclosed by a party in the mediation, and cannot guarantee Child Support Act calculations. Although the parties may discontinue a mediation at any time, the College's Standards provide that a mediator

---

61 See also Part I.

can discontinue the mediation if there is fear by one party of violence by the other. The mediator is required to explain to the parties that, in legal proceedings, there can be disclosure of facts, which have been identified in the mediation, relating to property or finance. The involvement of children in the mediation, if appropriate, needs to be discussed with the parties. The mediator is required, by virtue of the UK College's Standards, to be trained to involve children in the mediation if he or she intends to do so. Training in domestic violence screening is compulsory for members of the UK College of Family Mediators. Finally, the College's mediators are required to abide by the complaints procedures of the College.[62]

Standards of other family mediation organisations in England and Wales

The Law Society's Code of Practice for family mediation is voluntary. It provides that the terms and conditions of the mediation should be agreed with the parties, usually in writing. The mediator has autonomy over the conduct of the mediation. A solicitor family mediator cannot act if there is an actual or potential conflict of interest. Although a mediator's personal view should not be given on the merits of a case, the Code acknowledges that a solicitor family mediator may make a comment which is more favourable to one party. The Code provides that financial information provided in the mediation is open information. Privilege does not apply if there is or is likely to be harm to a child or if public policy or the rules of evidence render privilege inappropriate. The Code requires a mediator to consider with the parties measures for the child if the child is suffering or is likely to suffer harm.[63]

The Solicitors' Family Law Association (SFLA) has adopted the Law Society's Code of Practice.[64] National Family Mediation (NFM) and Family Mediators' Association (FMA) comply with the UK College of Family Mediators' Code.[65]

Law Wise has its own Code of Practice, which has been approved by the UK College of Family Mediators. The Code provides that parties may discontinue a mediation at any time. The mediator can provide the parties with legal information, including contact lists. The mediator can also help the parties to identify the information which would be useful for the parties to obtain, and may also suggest possible solutions for the dispute. The Code provides that a mediator must not have acted in another

---

62 See UK College of Family Mediators *Standards and Code of Practice*, 1998; *Directory and Handbook 1999–2000*; and *Creating the firm foundation for a growing profession*.

63 See Law Society of England & Wales *Code of Practice for Family Mediation*; *Standards for accreditation, re-accreditation and supervision/consultancy in family mediation*; and *Guidelines for use by solicitors in the conduct of ancillary relief proceedings*.

64 See Solicitors' Family Law Association *Mediation rules for consultants*; *Mediation selection of applicants for training, practice and accreditation process*; *Mediation, training, accreditation and re-accreditation: appeals procedure*; and *Mediation training for lawyers*.

65 In relation to National Family Mediation, see National Family Mediation *National Core Training Programme*; *What is Mediation?*; *Annual Report*, 1998. In relation to Family Mediators' Association, see Family Mediators' Association *Policy document on selection, recruitment, training and professional practice supervision and consultancy*; *Guidelines to current policy: Domestic violence, child protection, direct consultation*; *Guidelines to training, policy and entry requirements for courses*; and *Training to mediate on all issues in separation or divorce*.

capacity for a party, unless all the parties are informed of this and consent to the mediator's continued involvement. The Code reminds the mediator that the possibility of reconciliation should be kept under review.[66] Law Wise has a complaints procedure, which may result in disciplinary action against mediators, ranging from a caution to reprimand or suspension from the approved list of mediators, with the conditions for re-admittance through to being struck-off that list. Such a finding would be advised to the UK College of Family Mediators if the mediator is also a member of the College.

Standards of other family mediation organisations in Scotland

In Scotland the two main organisations, which set the standards for family mediators, are Family Mediation Scotland (FMS) and Comprehensive Accredited Lawyer Mediators (CALM). FMS adheres to the UK College of Family Mediators' Code although its own Code makes some additional recommendations. A mediator must not act as advocate for a party in the mediation but should also recognise that he or she is not an adjudicator or arbitrator. If information is given by the mediator to a solicitor for one of the parties, that information must also be passed on to the solicitor for the other party. The mediator should aim to reach an agreement in the best interests of the children.[67]

CALM adheres to the Scotland Law Society's Code, although it also has its own Code of Conduct. CALM accredited members are solicitors who are also accredited by the Law Society of Scotland. Accordingly, they are regulated by the Law Society and are disciplined according to the procedures which operate for solicitors in Scotland. CALM's Code provides that a mediator must terminate the mediation if financial information is not disclosed or if the parties are untruthful or abusive. The mediator is required to advise the parties to seek independent legal advice. All communications to the parties' solicitors must be given to both in the same way. A mediator has a duty to safeguard children and this duty overrides the duty of confidence. If an agreement reached in mediation is unfair to a party or is not just, the mediator should alert the parties to whether it is appropriate to continue with the mediation. The Code also requires mediators to undergo training, continue practice and comply with the Law Society's continuing professional development requirements.[68]

Standards of other family mediation organisations in Northern Ireland

Family mediation organisations in Northern Ireland are affiliated to one of the family mediation organisations in England and Wales, for example, NFM, FMA or the UK College of Family Mediators. Relate, for example, is affiliated to NFM and is a member of the UK College of Family Mediators.

---

66 See Law Wise *Code of Practice for Law Wise family mediation*; *Disciplinary and Grievance Procedures*; and *Law Wise family mediation training programme for accreditation*.
67 See Family Mediation Scotland *Registration Procedures*; *National Training Course Information Pack*; *Procedures on Evaluation of Training Mediators*; and *Selection and contracting procedures*.
68 See Comprehensive Accredited Lawyer Mediators *Code of Practice for Members of CALM*.

Standards for family mediation services

Standards set by UK College of Family Mediators

The UK College of Family Mediators has a set of standards for family mediation services in relation to premises, supervision, file review and treatment of employees.[69]

Standards set by other family mediation organisations in England and Wales

National Family Mediation (NFM) has developed quality assurance standards for family mediation services, which wish to gain affiliation with NFM. NFM has a team of trained auditors who monitor the quality of standards.[70]

The Legal Aid Board, as it was then called, developed standards for family mediation franchises. In February 1997 the Board published a document, incorporating its approach, called the 'Draft Code of Practice and Draft Family Mediation Franchise Specification'.[71] The standards have been revised since then. The standards are based on those of the UK College of Family Mediators, the SFLA, the NFM, FMA, BALM and the Law Society. The standards were drafted in light of the requirements set out in the Family Law Act 1996,[72] and provide that the following provisions should be included in the code of practice for franchisees:

- voluntary participation by the parties;
- identification of fear of violence or other harm;
- reconciliation should be kept under review;
- each party should be informed about the availability of independent legal advice; and
- the parties should be encouraged to consider the welfare of their children.

Compliance with the Board's standards is mandatory in the case of family mediators contracted to supply family mediation services.[73] The standards for family mediation franchises set out requirements in relation to the franchise representative; premises; child protection procedures; consultation with children; welfare benefits; status enquiries; insurance; business plans; management structure; supervision; file management; intake; mediation process; outsourcing; financial management; management of employees; complaints and documents and other materials.

Standards set by family mediation organisations in Scotland

Family Mediation Scotland regulates family mediation services through affiliation requirements, which provides standards for selection, training and supervision of mediators by the Service.[74]

---

69 See UK College of Family Mediators *Standards and Code of Practice*, 1998; *Directory and Handbook 1999–2000*; and *Creating the firm foundation for a growing profession*.
70 See National Family Mediation *National Core Training Programme*; *What is Mediation?*; *Annual Report*, 1998.
71 Legal Aid Board *Franchise in Family Mediation Services* 1997.
72 Family Law Act 1996, s 27.
73 A number of organisations in London, Cambridge, Birmingham, Cardiff, Manchester, Northamptonshire and Bristol were contracted for the purpose of providing funded family mediation.
74 See Family Mediation Scotland *Registration Procedures*; *National Training Course*

Comparison with the Republic of Ireland

The Mediators Institute Ireland (MII) accredits training courses and admits members to the Institute. A licence from the Institute to practise as a mediator requires compliance with the Institute's Code of Ethics and Practice. That Code requires mediators to disclose any potential conflicts of interest and any prior and professional relationships with any of the parties. The parties are required to consent if the mediation is to be recorded and the parties need to be told who will listen to the recording and when that recording will be destroyed. The Code provides an exception to confidentiality if information is being used solely for training, supervision or teaching purposes. A mediator is required to be aware of a child's psychological needs and the effect of divorce on children. A mediator is also required to consider whether negotiations in the mediation are likely to be balanced and whether one party is being intimidated by the other.[75]

The Institute has a complaints procedure, which involves, at the first stage, a meeting between the complainant and the member, facilitated by the Institute's Accreditation Board. The dispute is mediated if there is no agreement at that meeting. The Accreditation Board may make an adjudication and sanctions may be imposed on a mediator if a complaint is upheld.[76]

The content of mediation standards

There are two broad categories of provisions in most codes of conduct for mediators: those relating to ethical duties and those relating to other practices and standards expected of mediators. The distinction is not always easy to draw. Folberg and Taylor refer to ethical limitations as the 'do nots' of the process, while standards comprise a positive statement of what is morally and socially expected from the process of mediation and the mediators.[77] An implication of the distinction is that breaches of ethical duties (for example, the impartiality requirement) could be sufficiently serious to have the mediated settlement set aside, whereas variance from other standards (for example, on the ground rules of the mediation process) are not so serious and would not be sufficient to have the agreement invalidated.[78] However, this approach could provide an open invitation to parties who develop reservations about their mediated agreements to scrutinise the conduct of their mediator in order to provide an excuse to get out of the agreement. An alternative approach would be to regard mediators' breaches of ethical duties in the same light as those of lawyers, which do not undo the work they have done but may lay them open to actions in negligence.

Information Pack; *Procedures on Evaluation of Training Mediators*; and *Selection and contracting procedures.*

75 See Mediators' Institute Ireland *Code of ethics and professional conduct for family mediators.*

76 Mediators' Institute Ireland *Complaints Procedure.*

77 J Folberg and A Taylor *Mediation: a comprehensive guide to resolving conflicts without litigation*, Jossey-Bass, San Francisco, 1984, at p 250.

78 G Sammon 'The ethical duties of lawyers who act for parties to a mediation' (1993) 4 *ADRJ* 190–1.

Mediator functions and skills

In some mediator standards and mediation procedures, there is an attempt to describe the mediation process and to list the functions of mediators. The list usually includes assessing the suitability of the matter for mediation, making arrangements for the mediation meeting, ensuring that all parties are fully informed of the nature and purpose of mediation, providing structure and control throughout the mediation meeting, promoting interest-based bargaining among the parties, assisting communication, assisting each party to be realistic, encouraging written documentation of the settlement agreement (or lists of agreed and non-agreed issues), assisting the parties to draw up settlement agreements and terminating the mediation when appropriate. The enumeration of these functions provides a checklist for mediators and could serve to promote consistency in mediation practice. On the assumption that mediating parties actually consult mediator standards, the list of functions could also serve to educate them about the process.[79] It may serve to ensure that they have realistic expectations of mediation and appreciate its strengths and limitations. Many of the mediator functions, however, are worded at levels of generality that do not provide much precision on their own.

Some of the mediator functions listed in the standards and mediation procedures constitute relatively objective features of the process, for example informing the parties as to its nature and purpose and providing control throughout the mediation. Other functions are less objective, for example acting as the 'agent of reality', which is difficult to define and delineate. The standards avoid referring to the specific interventions that mediators can make and contain no reference to the subjective judgments which mediators are obliged to make. Some functions imply specific interventions. For example, the function of facilitating negotiations and communication requires a range of verbal, visualisation, listening and non-verbal skills, and the ability to intervene appropriately by way of summarising, reframing, questioning and drafting. The reality-testing function implies the ability to confront parties on the practicality of substantive proposals, the durability of settlement arrangements, and the feasibility of alternative dispute processing methods. The promotion of interest-based bargaining functions requires interventions appropriate to shift disputants away from positional claims to underlying interests. However, all these orthodox functions can be pursued through a wide range of different interventions, and the extent to which they are pursued will depend on the particular model of mediation in question, the stage of the mediation, and the attributes of the mediator. These contingencies serve to limit the potential for the standards to impart consistency in mediation practice and to educate the parties about the process.[80]

The following example illustrates the difficulties. Where standards impose an obligation on mediators to ensure that parties are informed of the importance of having all the necessary information available, is this duty discharged by advising the parties of this? Is there a duty where the mediator knows that full disclosure is not being

---

79 Some mediation guidelines require parties to be given a copy of the guidelines. Others require an orientation session prior to the mediation to advise the parties on the process. In all cases it might be suspected that clients dissatisfied by the mediation process 'discover' the standards after the mediation to justify their assumption that the mediator's conduct was the reason why no settlement was reached.

80 G Vickery Guidelines for Mediators, unpublished LLM paper, Bond University, Australia, 1993, at p 11.

made? Is there a duty to promote an equal understanding of the information provided before an agreement is reached? If this question is answered in the affirmative, there is still no clarity on what procedural interventions would be required to achieve this objective. It is also consistent with the philosophical assumptions of mediation to allow parties to make decisions based on their commercial interests or emotional needs in the knowledge that not all the facts are on the table or that full disclosure has not been made. The 'self-determination' principle in mediation entails that standards should not be so rigid that they undermine party control.

Ethical standards for mediators

There are many potential ethical issues in mediation.[81] Article 6 of the ECHR provides that, in determination of civil rights, a fair hearing by an independent tribunal is required.[82] Although mediators have no authority to make binding decisions, they nevertheless have a wide range of practical powers. This power is accentuated when information is disclosed to them on a confidential basis in separate meetings. Instead of a direct professional-client relationship with a single party, the mediator has a dualistic client relationship with parties whose interests are in conflict with each other. Unlike professionals who have partisan roles, mediators are non-partisan operators.[83] Unlike the classic third party intervener in disputes, the umpire, mediators do not stand above the fray. They are privy to the intimacies of the dispute and have to make a range of subjective judgments which influence the outcome, but they cannot impose decisions. A mediator has less authority than an umpire, such as an arbitrator, but in many respects has more power. This raises the following ethical issues:

Neutrality

The terms 'neutrality' and 'impartiality' have been considered earlier in this work.[84] It was suggested that neutrality refers to mediators' prior knowledge about or interest in the outcome of disputes, and impartiality to the way in which they conduct the process and treat the parties. In these senses, neutrality is not an indispensable feature of mediation, whereas impartiality is. Some mediator standards use the terms in these senses, and others use them interchangeably. Others again refer to neutrality, in the sense used here, as independence.

In relation to neutrality, the mediation rules of UK ADR organisations provide that a mediator should not act if he or she has a financial or personal interest in the result of a mediation.[85] A solicitor mediator also should not act in cases involving issues on which he or she or a member of his or her firm have at any time acted for any of the

---

81 See H Astor and C Chinkin 'Mediation training and ethics' (1991) 2 *ADRJ* 226; H Brown and A Marriott *ADR Principles and Practice* (2nd edn), Sweet & Maxwell, London, 1999, at Chapter 21; and R Cohen 'Mediation standards' (1995) 6 *ADRJ* 25.
82 The ECHR is discussed in the context of Compulsion in Chapter 9 and Mediation Clauses in Chapter 12.
83 L Riskin 'Towards new standards for the neutral lawyer in mediation' (1984) 26 *Arizona Law Review* 329.
84 See Chapter 1.
85 See, for example, Law Society of England & Wales *Codes of Practice* for both Family Mediation and Civil/Commercial Mediation; UK College of Family Mediators *Code of Practice*; and Commercial Mediation Centre *Mediation Rules and Procedures*.

parties in the mediation.[86] Solicitor mediators and family mediators should withdraw from a mediation if they have acquired confidential information relevant to the dispute or to the parties involved in the mediation from another source or confidential information relevant to another client is likely to be acquired during the mediation.[87] In relation to family mediation, where family mediation services are offered as part of a practice offering other professional services, a family mediator from that practice should not act if a client has received other services from the practice, unless the mediator can show the information given to other professionals of the practice has no bearing on the issues in the mediation.[88] Many standard form mediation agreements, mediation rules and mediator codes of conduct also provide that a mediator should not act for a participant in a mediation in any other professional capacity in relation to the subject matter of the mediation after the mediation.[89] Solicitor mediators and members of their firms cannot act following a mediation for a participant in that mediation in relation to the dispute, the subject of the mediation.[90] Such conflicts issues are likely to be more problematic for large law firms, in particular those which offer mediation as an additional service.

Rules of conduct for solicitor mediators recommend that solicitors should not act, even in cases of potential conflict of interest.[91] The objective of such a provision is to avoid potential breaches of mediators', and lawyers', fiduciary obligations towards their clients and to preserve sound relationships among members of the profession. Even in the case of non-solicitor mediators, if there are any circumstances, which may lead a party in a mediation to perceive a conflict of interest, even if one does not exist, building and maintaining trust with the parties may be difficult. In those circumstances, most mediation rules, standard mediation agreements and mediator codes of conduct provide that a mediator should make full disclosure. Examples of circumstances, which may lead to a perception of a conflict of interest, include:

- a business or professional relationship with a party, an entity associated with a party, or a party's lawyers;[92]

---

86 Law Society of England & Wales *Codes of Practice* for both Family Mediation and Civil/Commercial Mediation; UK College of Family Mediators *Code of Practice*; Commercial Mediation Centre *Mediation Rules and Procedures*; Law Society of Scotland *Code of Conduct for Solicitor Mediators*; and Law Society of England & Wales *Guide to the Professional Conduct of Solicitors* (8th edn) Law Society Publishing, at Chapter 22 on Alternative Dispute Resolution.
87 Ibid; and Legal Aid Board *Family Mediation Quality Assurance Standard*, November 1998.
88 Ibid.
89 For example, UK College of Family Mediators *Code of Practice*; Commercial Mediation Centre *Appointment of Mediator*; Centre for Dispute Resolution *Model Mediation Procedure*; and Law Society of Scotland *Code of Conduct for Solicitor Mediators*.
90 See Law Society *Guide to the Professional Conduct of Solicitors*, op cit, Chapter 22.
91 See, for example, the Law Society of England & Wales *Codes of Practice* for both Civil/Commercial Mediation and Family Mediation.
92 See, for example, Commercial Mediation Centre *Appointment of Mediator*; Center for Public Resources *Mediation Agreement*; Academy of Experts *Guidance Notes for Mediators*; Academy of Experts *Guidelines for Mediation*; and R Mackay and A Brown *Community Mediation in Scotland: a study of implementation*, The Scottish Office Central Research Unit, 1999. In one Australian case, a mediator who was a member of a professional body, which was associated with one of the parties withdrew from the mediation: see Bond Dispute Resolution Centre 'What Skills and Attributes do

- if the mediator or a member of his or her firm has acted for any of the parties in the mediation on issues not relating to the mediation;[93] and
- any personal interest in the outcome of the mediation.[94]

In such cases the aim of disclosure is to receive the parties' confirmation that they are satisfied the factors disclosed do not impact on the mediator's independence. The extent of disclosure would be in keeping with developments in other areas of law and professional practice to treat the obligation as a broad one.[95] Some rules of mediator conduct require the parties to confirm their satisfaction in writing.[96] The need to disclose conflict, whether actual or potential, continues throughout a mediation. Some standard form mediation agreements aim to protect the mediator in cases where there has been a failure to disclose a conflict in the course of mediation.[97] In an Australian case, the mediator was the father-in-law of the judge, who would hear the trial of the case if the mediation were unsuccessful. The mediator had met with this son-in-law the weekend before the trial was due to commence, and informed him that the mediation had been unsuccessful. The court found no bias as the relevant events, together with what was said, had been disclosed to the parties at the first available opportunity.[98]

In relation to family mediation, where family mediation services are offered as part of a practice offering other services, family mediators should ensure that the mediation practice is clear and separate.[99] To ensure that independence is maintained, a court welfare officer who attempts to mediate a family dispute should not write the welfare report for the court if mediation has been unsuccessful.[100]

Impartiality

Unlike neutrality, it is inconceivable that the parties could waive the impartiality requirement without fundamentally altering the nature of the mediation process. Any display of partiality by the mediator would be considered a breach of a basic ethical obligation. There are, however, major practical difficulties in relation to the impartiality requirement provided in mediator standards. Given the confidential nature of mediation, there is little objective evidence on which to assess the alleged

---

Experienced Mediators Possess?' *Bond Dispute Resolution News*, vol 3, October 1999.

93 See Law Society of England & Wales *Codes of Practice* for both Civil/Commercial Mediation and Family Mediation.

94 Ibid.

95 G Vickery Guidelines for Mediators, unpublished LLM paper, Bond University, Australia, 1993, at p 16. This would be particularly where mediation is mandatory. There would also be a concern in private mediations where the mediator's fee is not shared by the parties but paid by one, for example an insurer, or where bulk users of mediation services use the same mediators repeatedly. See H Astor and C Chinkin 'Mediation training and ethics' (1991) 2 *ADRJ*, at p 227.

96 For example, Centre for Dispute Resolution *Code of Conduct*.

97 For example, Centre for Public Resources *Mediation Agreement*; and Commercial Mediation Centre *Appointment of Mediator*. For a wider discussion of mediator liability issues, see the separate section on mediator liability.

98 *Michael John Bates (t/a Riot Wetsuits) v Omareef Pty Ltd* (1998) 1472 FCA.

99 For example, UK College of Family Mediators *Code of Practice*; and Legal Aid Board *Family Mediation Quality Assurance Standards*.

100 See M Roberts *Mediation in Family Disputes: Principles of Practice* (2nd edn), Arena, Hants, England 1997.

partiality of mediators' performances unlike, say, the partiality of arbitrators, which can be assessed in part by examining the arbitration transcript. Allegations of partiality in mediation are likely to result from the unreasonable expectations of one party, or their subjective analysis of what happened. Although impartiality is a pervasive feature in mediator standards, there are likely to be real problems in dealing practically with allegations of partiality.

In relation to outcome

Impartiality of the mediator aims to ensure that the parties can trust the process and the mediator. One way of ensuring that the parties retain autonomy in a mediation is for the mediator to remain impartial regarding the outcome of the mediation.[101] Ensuring impartiality in relation to the outcome extends to ensuring freedom from favouritism or bias.[102] It also requires a mediator to ensure that he or she does not question the basic values of the parties in the mediation, for example, in family mediation, that a mediator accepts that there is a wide range of beliefs and lifestyles.[103]

A mediator needs to be impartial in the sense that the mediator has no authority to arbitrate the dispute or to impose a decision on the parties.[104] Impartiality in relation

---

101 The mediation rules of a wide range of ADR organisations provide for this, for example: the World Intellectual Property Organisation *Mediation Rules*; the London Court of International Arbitration *Mediation Procedure* (which provides that a party to the mediation can object if any circumstances give rise to a doubt as to the mediator's impartiality); the International Chamber of Commerce *Rules of Optional Conciliation* (which provide that a conciliator shall conduct the conciliation process guided by principles of impartiality and equity); the Center for Public Resources *Mediation Agreement*; the Centre for Dispute Resolution *Code of Conduct* (which provides that a mediator must act fairly and impartially); The Academy of Experts *Guidelines for Mediation* (which provide that a mediator must disclose circumstances which are likely to affect the presumption of impartiality); and the Academy of Experts *Guidance Notes for Mediators* (which set out the ten rules of conduct for mediators, including impartiality).

102 The ADR Group *Professional Code of Conduct* refers to this aspect of impartiality as a commitment to serve all of the parties, not just one party, in a mediation. Shapiro, an experienced international mediator in the UK, refers to an example where the mediator, by offering to waive the mediator's fee, in an attempt to assist both parties to bridge the small gap between them, was viewed as biased by the parties.

103 M Roberts *Mediation in Family Disputes: Principles of Practice* (2nd edn), Arena, Hants, England 1997 at p 104; and Center for Dispute Settlement *Parent/Adolescent Training Manual*, November 1987.

104 A fundamental characteristic of mediation, which is provided for in mediation rules and codes of conduct in the UK, for example: Center for Public Resources *Mediation Procedure for Business Disputes in Europe*; Patents Court *Mediation Procedure*; Centre for Business Arbitration *Mediation Rules*; Academy of Experts *Guidance Notes for Mediators*; Academy of Experts *Code of Conduct for Mediators*; Intermediation *Mediation Rules and Rules of Conduct*; Law Society of Scotland *Guidance for Accredited Mediators;* and the *Codes of Conduct* for Family Mediators issued by the Law Society of England & Wales, Law Wise, NFM, FMA and the UK College of Family Mediators. Contrast the view that the activity of mediating is itself a declaration of values as it represents a position on how the dispute will be approached: K Webb 'The Morality of Mediation' in C R Mitchell and K Webb *New Approaches to International Mediation*, Greenwood Press, Westport, 1988; J H Laue 'The Emergence of

to the outcome of a mediation does not mean, however, that a mediator should never make a comment, even if one party may find that comment more acceptable than the other. For instance, mediators frequently comment on the likely consequences of the parties' respective actions in order to reality test their positions. A mediator should always be conscious, when expressing an opinion or making a suggestion, that this should be done in a way which does not impair his or her impartiality, as perceived by the parties. Frequently, comments are made and opinions are proffered in private sessions with each party.[105] A mediator frequently makes suggestions and helps the parties to explore such suggestions. A typical example is where a mediator can see a solution which satisfies all parties' interests.[106] In family mediation, it may be difficult to reconcile the requirement of impartiality with the aim of serving the interests of a child.[107]

It is also common for mediators to encourage some outcomes, whilst resisting others.[108] Such tactics stop short of expressing views on the merits of the dispute, thereby distinguishing mediation from advice, advocacy and arbitration.[109]

The obvious method for ensuring mediator impartiality is to encourage access to independent legal advice ahead of and in the course of a mediation.[110] In some cases, legal advice will be recommended, but will not be sought by a party and the issue becomes whether a mediator should steer the parties towards a settlement which reflects the merits of the dispute, in order to avoid an unjust result prevailing.[111] On one view, the merits are not, in any event, a determining factor for parties in mediation. Personal fairness is usually of greater importance to the parties in

---

Institutionalisation of Third Party Roles in Conflict' in D J Samdole and I Samdole-Staroste (eds) *Conflict Management and Problem Solving: Interpersonal to International Applications*, Frances Pinter, 1987.

105 The Law Society of England & Wales *Code of Practice for Civil/Commercial Mediation*.

106 For example, the mediator may have identified, in private sessions, that there is an overlap in what one party wishes to pay and what the other party wishes to receive, in order to settle the dispute, and the mediator may suggest to a party, as a way of facilitating a resolution, without compromising neutrality or confidentiality, that the timing is right for an offer in the terms discussed privately to be made publicly to another party.

107 For example, if it is not in a child's best interest to continue to see both parents, a mediator may need to persuade the parents of this without compromising neutrality: University of Newcastle upon Tyne Conciliation Project Unit, *Report to the Lord Chancellor's Department on the cost and effectiveness of conciliation in England and Wales*, March 1989, at p 42.

108 R Dingwall and D Greatbatch 'Who is in Charge? Rhetoric and Evidence in the Study of Mediation' (1993) *Journal of Social Welfare & Family Law* 367.

109 The ADR Group's standard form Agreement to Mediate expressly provides that the parties acknowledge that the ADR Group and the mediator do not give legal advice or act as lawyers in the context of the mediation.

110 White Paper *Looking to the Future: Mediation and the Grounds for Divorce*, 1995 Cm 2799, HMSO, London; and Green Paper *Legal Aid: Targeting Need*, 1995 Cm 2854, HMSO, London. Papers affirmed that independent legal advice and assistance should be available before, during and after mediation. See the section on Funding and Mediation in Part III for a further discussion about mediation and legal aid.

111 Justice Lightman *Alternative Dispute Resolution Seminar*, CMS Cameron McKenna, November 1999.

reaching an agreement at mediation.[112] In Australia there has been judicial recognition that the parties' interests in a mediation are as important as an appreciation of their rights.[113] American research supports the view that, where an agreement in a mediation tackles the parties' respective interests, the agreement is more likely to be perceived by the parties as fair.[114] Australian research on family mediation provides additional support.[115] Despite the importance of interests, a mediator will not ignore the merits and will consider the merits at least to the following extent:

- by encouraging the parties to consider the likely outcome at trial;
- by seeking to minimise the potential for further disagreement between the parties, a mediator will aim to ensure that settlement options are workable;[116]
- in family mediation, the mediator may provide the parties with legal information to assist them to understand the principles of the law applicable to the case.[117] Accordingly, family mediators require an understanding of the law relating to interim remedies and enforcement procedures, divorce and financial provision, and adoption.[118] Family mediators need to consider throughout the mediation process whether either party should be given information on suppliers of legal advice.[119] Additionally, a family mediator, who believes that a proposed settlement would not be approved by the court or is unconscionable or inappropriate, would normally inform the parties and either terminate the mediation or refer the parties to their legal advisers.[120]

An exception to the requirement of impartiality occurs when, in the context of commercial and civil mediation, the parties ask the mediator for a recommendation or decision on how the dispute might be resolved. Normally, the mediation rules of ADR organisations provide that the mediator can make a non-binding recommendation or evaluation if the parties request it.[121] Some mediation rules require the

---

112 J Folberg and A Taylor *Mediation: A Comprehensive Guide to Resolving Conflicts without Litigation*, Jossey-Bass, San Francisco, 1984.
113 Gleeson CJ in *Gain v Commonwealth Bank* (16 September 1997, unreported) New South Wales Court of Appeal (Gleeson CJ, Cole JA and Sheppard AJA).
114 J Pearson 'Ten Myths about Family Law' (1993) 27(2) *Family Law Quarterly* 284.
115 S Bordow and J Gibson *Evaluation of the Family Court Mediation Service*, Research Report 12, Family Court Australia, Melbourne, 1994.
116 For example, if the value of consideration is not known at the time of the mediation, the parties may agree to a valuation before a settlement is finalised. If the mediator perceives that there may be a tax problem, for example, with the proposed settlement, the mediator would urge the parties to receive tax advice prior to finalising the settlement agreement.
117 See, for example, the Law Society of England & Wales *Code of Practice for Family Mediation*.
118 L Webley, *A Review of the Literature on Family Mediation*, Report Prepared for the Lord Chancellor's Advisory Committee on Legal Education and Conduct, Institute of Advanced Legal Studies, London, 1998, at p 89.
119 Legal Aid Board *Family Mediation Quality Assurance Standard*, in particular B4.6, which sets out the issues, on which legal advice may be required, including obtaining an injunction or other protective order, interim maintenance, preservation of assets, and disclosure of financial information.
120 The Law Society of England & Wales *Code of Practice in Family Mediation*.
121 For example, Academy of Experts *Guidelines for Mediation*; Centre for Dispute Resolution *Model Mediation Procedure*; City Disputes Panel *Mediation Rules*; Center for Public Resources *Model Mediation Procedure for Business Disputes in Europe*; Commercial Mediation Centre *Mediation Rules and Procedures*; and the Law Society of

mediator to provide the parties with reasons if a recommendation is made.[122] If the parties agree that the mediator's recommendation will be binding, normally the parties will also agree that reference can be made to arbitration or litigation within a certain period of time following the mediator's evaluation.[123]

In relation to process

Another method for ensuring party autonomy in a mediation is for the mediator to conduct the process in a fair and even-handed way.[124] Ensuring fairness in the conduct of the process requires addressing imbalances of power, ensuring that the parties are able to give their informed consent in the process and that there is no coercion operating on a party and providing a structural framework for the mediation, which is fair.[125] Cultural or sex 'identification' is mooted as one way to address these issues. The rationale is that a mediator, who has the same ethnic or religious background and gender as the parties, can better or more easily identify with the parties and vice versa; can correctly interpret signals given by the parties; and can avoid being manipulated by the parties.[126] The obvious difficulty arises when the parties do not share the same ethnic or religious backgrounds and gender.[127] Co-mediation or assistance by a pupil mediator can overcome this difficulty, by ensuring that the ethnic or religious backgrounds or genders of the parties are represented.[128] Alternatively, with appropriate training, a mediator can work effectively with a range of cultural and religious backgrounds and both genders.[129]

The following example illustrates, however, the difficulty that can occur in attempting to ensure fairness and even-handedness:

> 'I felt she was going overboard to be fair to him because she was a woman and did not want to look as though she was ganging up on him with me . . .'[130]

England & Wales *Code of Practice for Civil/Commercial Mediation*.

122 For example, Academy of Experts *Guidance Notes for Mediators*.

123 Otherwise, the recommendation should be in a form that is legally enforceable.

124 See, for example, the Law Society of England & Wales *Code of Practice for Family Mediation*; the UK College of Family Mediators *Code of Practice*; the Law Society of England & Wales *Code of Practice for Civil/Commercial Mediation*; the ADR Group *Professional Code of Conduct*; and the Commercial Mediation Centre *Code of Conduct*.

125 D Pruitt *Negotiation Behavior*, Academic Press, New York, 1981; and D Pruitt and J Rubin *Social Conflict: Escalation, Stalemate and Settlement*, Random House, New York, 1986.

126 S Shah-Kazemi 'Family Mediation and the Dynamics of Culture' *Family Mediation*, vol 6, no 3, at pp 5–7.

127 See R A Bush *The Dilemmas of Mediation Practice: A Study of Ethnical Dilemmas and Policy Implications*, National Institute for Dispute Resolution, Washington DC, 1992 who provides a number of examples.

128 R E Mackay and A J Brown *Community Mediation in Scotland: a study of implementation*, The Scottish Office Central Research Unit, Edinburgh, 1999 cite a community mediation example, where a male party felt that two female co-mediators were taking the side of the other female party.

129 Mediation UK *Training Manual in Community Mediation Skills*, Bristol, 1996; D Gale 'The Impact of Culture on the Work of Family Mediators' (1994) 4(2) *Family Mediation*; and S Goldstein *Cultural Issues in Mediation: a Literature Review*, PCR Working Paper, University of Hawaii, 1986.

130 Keys Young *Research/Evaluation of Family Mediation Practice and the Issue of Violence: Final Report*, Attorney-General's Department, 1996, at p 99.

Tackling power imbalances

Ensuring fairness in the mediation process requires a mediator to identify[131] and counteract power imbalances between the parties, even if no power imbalance is perceived by the parties or it is unacknowledged by them.[132] Codes of practice for family mediators require them to be alert to the likelihood of power imbalances at all times.[133] Accordingly, mediators need to appreciate that power imbalance can arise from a range of factors, including personality attributes, like articulateness; access to information, advice and finance; and the strength or weakness of a party's case.[134]

The issue of power imbalance raises the issue of the position of women in mediation. On one view, women as a group suffer power inequalities and, therefore, are in an unequal position in mediation.[135] Another view is that women are unequal in mediation only if a further power imbalance is present, such as dominance by the other spouse, the other spouse's superior earning power or a lack of advice or negotiation ability. A further view is that, even in those circumstances, it would be 'paternalistic' to refuse mediation to a woman as mediation can empower women.[136]

The existence of power imbalance is demonstrated through manipulation, threats or intimidation.[137] In such circumstances, where the mediation process is likely to become unfair or ineffective, a mediator aims to redress the position in a number of ways:

- by identifying the imbalances and discussing with the parties how best to deal with these issues;[138] and
- by addressing the source of the imbalance, for example, by arranging for information or advice to be provided to the relevant party.[139]

---

131 For a discussion of how family mediators might identify power imbalance, see J Kelly 'A decade of divorce mediation research' (1996) 34(3) *Family and Conciliation Court Review* 373.

132 N Foster and J Kelly 'Divorce Mediators: Who should be Certified?' (1996) 30 *University of San Francisco Law Review*, at pp 667–8.

133 For example, *Codes of Practice for Family Mediators* issued by the Law Society of England & Wales, Law Wise, NFM, FMA, the UK College of Family Mediators and Family Mediation Scotland.

134 J Murray, A Rau, E Sherman *Processes of Dispute Resolution: the Role of Lawyers*, Foundation Press, New York, 1989.

135 A Bottomley 'What is happening to Family Law? A Feminist Critique of Conciliation' in J Brophy and C Smart (eds) *Women in Law*, Routledge, London, 1985.

136 G Davis and M Roberts *Access to Agreement: a Consumer Study of Mediation in Family Disputes*, Open University Press, Milton Keynes, 1988; and C Archbold et al *Divorce in Northern Ireland: Unravelling the System*, Report to the Office of Law Reform, 1999, at p 205. Critics of mediation believe that no technique can empower the dominated spouse in family mediation: Woods 'Mediation: a Backlash to Women's Progress on Family Law Issues' (1985) 19 *Clearinghouse Review* 431.

137 A Ackland *A Sudden Outbreak of Common Sense*, Hutchinson, London, 1990.

138 The Law Society of England & Wales *Code of Practice for Family Mediation*.

139 Ibid; L Webley *A Review of the Literature on Family Mediation*, Report Prepared for the Lord Chancellor's Advisory Committee on Legal Education and Conduct, Institute of Advanced Legal Studies, London, 1998, at p 18; and R A Bush *The Dilemmas of Mediation Practice: A Study of Ethnical Dilemmas and Policy Implications*, National Institute for Dispute Resolution, Washington DC, 1992.

Where the power imbalance cannot be redressed, the mediator will normally bring a mediation to an end, and suggest alternative means for resolving the dispute.[140]

Ensuring informed consent

Fairness of the process of mediation is also premised upon the informed consent of the parties to the process and any agreement reached in the process. An incapacity to comprehend the discussions or to make decisions may occur through depression or other mental problems or an incapacity created by alcohol or drugs.[141]

In commercial mediation, informed consent is usually guaranteed by the presence of lawyers, who advise the parties throughout the process and on any settlement agreement. In family mediation, where lawyers are not typically present, agreements reached in mediation are usually not legally binding, allowing the parties to refer the agreement to lawyers after the mediation.[142] In community mediation, where lawyers are frequently absent but agreements reached in mediation may be legally binding, it has been suggested that the result of the typical mediation is an agreement favouring the interests of the complainant.[143]

The issue arises of the extent to which mediators should intervene to ensure that agreements reached in mediation are based on informed consent.[144] The requirement to maintain confidentiality may, however, result in a party consenting to an agreement without fully informed consent.[145]

Preventing coercion

The existence of pressure to reach or abstain from reaching an agreement undermines the principle of impartiality.[146] The primary responsibility for the resolution of a dispute rests with the parties. A mediator's obligation is to assist them in reaching an informed and voluntary settlement. Although such pressure should not occur, it frequently exists in mediation. A lawyer may, for example, prevent the client from communicating with

---

140 R A Bush *The Dilemmas of Mediation Practice: A Study of Ethnical Dilemmas and Policy Implications*, National Institute for Dispute Resolution, Washington DC, 1992 points to the potential ethical dilemma when discontinuation of the mediation overrides the parties' wishes to continue and loses the potential for settlement.

141 J B Stulberg 'Fairness in Mediation' (1998) 13 *Ohio State Journal on Dispute Resolution*, at pp 936–44. In *Wright v Brockett* 150 Misc 2d 1031 (1991), a settlement agreement reached in mediation was set aside as the conduct of the mediation made informed consent unlikely.

142 C A McEwen, N H Rogers and R J Maiman 'Bring in the Lawyers: Challenging the Dominant Approaches to Ensuring Fairness in Divorce Mediation' (1995) 79 *Minnesota Law Review* 1317; G Davis and M Roberts 'Mediation and the Battle of the Sexes' [1989] *Family Law* p 306; and see the section on termination of a mediation in Part II.

143 N B Gillicuddy 'Factors Affecting the Outcome of Mediation: Third Party and Disputant Behaviour' in Duffy, Grosch and Olczak (eds) *Community Mediation: A Handbook for Practitioners and Researchers,* Guildford, New York, 1991, at p 148.

144 See the section below on mediator neutrality.

145 R A Bush *The Dilemmas of Mediation Practice*, op cit, cites an example, where the rationale for a settlement proposal, disclosed by one party to the mediator in private session, would, if known by the other party, result in a refusal by that party to settle on the terms proposed.

146 S E Merry 'Defining Success in the Neighbourhood Justice Movement' in Momasic and Feeley (eds) *Neighbourhood Justice: Assessment of an Emerging Idea*, Longman, New York, 1982.

the mediator or may pressure the client to accept or reject a settlement.[147] In cases of lawyer coercion, a mediator may, with the consent of the party affected, speak to that party directly and question the party about his or her understanding of the consequences of participation or lack of participation in the mediation.

A mediation also provides scope for the exercise by mediators of coercion, when they step over the line from persuasion to coercion.[148] The study of the Central London County Court Mediation Pilot revealed evidence strongly indicating that the scope for the exercise of coercion by mediators is not absent from mediation, but is 'more or less subtle', depending upon the personality and philosophy of each mediator.[149] It is not clear what would amount to coercion in mediation. While it is clearly incompatible with the assumptions of mediation for mediators to coerce the parties, in the sense of persuading one or the other against their will, or to engage in undue questioning and advocacy, the mediation process is designed to achieve practical settlements with the mediator's assistance. This implies a range of interventions that, in the subjective reality of one or both parties, might appear to involve influence, suggestion, advice or informed opinion. Inevitably the boundary between these interventions and coercion may at times seem indistinct to the parties. Legitimate exertion of pressure by a mediator on the parties in a mediation may include:

- highlighting the costs and other disadvantages involved in resolving the dispute, if an agreement is not reached in the mediation, as a way of exerting pressure on the parties to reach a settlement in the mediation;[150] and
- in family mediation, appealing to a couple's responsibilities to their children, as a means of encouraging reasonableness.

Providing a fair structural framework

There has been a suggestion that when a mediation is conducted solely through separate private sessions, as is common in the case of commercial mediation, the

---

147 R A Bush *The Dilemmas of Mediation Practice: A Study of Ethnical Dilemmas and Policy Implications*, National Institute for Dispute Resolution, Washington DC, 1992 cites an example, where the lawyer refuses to let his client speak to the mediator or the other parties' lawyers, with the consequence that the client is left out of a package deal struck by the other parties with the defendant.

148 J Lewis and R Legard *ACAS Individual Conciliation: a qualitative evaluation of the service provided in industrial tribunal cases*, ACAS, 1999 revealed from a study of ACAS conciliations that respondents perceived pressure from conciliators' need to meet 'settlement targets'.

149 H Genn *The Central London County Court Mediation Pilot: Evaluation Report*, Lord Chancellor's Department Research Series no 5/98, July 1998, at p 143. The study identified a number of examples where a party in mediation felt coerced by the mediator, for example: 'he . . . was more intent on pushing our client into a settlement . . .' and 'he twisted the plaintiff's arm to achieve a settlement . . .' (at pp 113 and 114 respectively).

150 See University of Newcastle upon Tyne Conciliation Project Unit, *Report to the Lord Chancellor's Department on the cost and effectiveness of conciliation in England and Wales*, March 1989, at p 323 where there is an example of a mediator pointing out to the parties that if they didn't agree in the mediation, they would end up in court where the judge would decide, which would please nobody. The lawyers interviewed considered this a form of blackmail: 'it wasn't like that, but the implication was there'. The issue arises whether it is proper for a mediator to make such suggestions, if he or she has no direct knowledge of what the alternative to reaching settlement at the mediation would involve: for example, someone who has no experience of litigation.

parties may not perceive mediator impartiality or process fairness.[151] A perception of partiality can also arise when a mediator spends more time with one party than another in a private session.[152] In two Australian cases, courts have been prepared to consider the duration of a mediation, albeit on the facts of the cases, no procedural unfairness was found.[153]

Confidentiality

Confidentiality is a major ethical requirement in mediation, as it is in the practice of many professions. Most standards affirm that mediators are under a duty to maintain both the confidentiality of the separate meetings, and the overall confidentiality of the mediation. They also refer to possible exceptions to the confidentiality requirement, including where the parties give the mediator permission to make disclosure, where there is a supervening legal requirement to disclose, and where disclosure is necessary to implement and enforce any settlement agreement.

Confidentiality is not absolute.[154] Disclosure may be made by order of the court.[155] Matters which are already public can be disclosed.[156] If the mediator considers that information received in the mediation indicates that the life or safety of a person is or may be at risk, the duty of confidentiality does not apply.[157] An obligation of disclosure may arise where there has been criminal conduct by a party, which may result in an illegal agreement, or where an agreement will be reached on the basis of false information.[158] Some mediator codes of conduct provide that mediators may provide disclosure if they need advice in confidence on any ethical or other question arising in the course of a mediation.[159] In the case of family mediation:

---

151 For example, S Cobb and J Rifkin 'Practice and Paradox: Deconstructing Neutrality in Mediation' (1991) 16 *Law & Social Inquiry* 35.

152 This was the perception of defendants in the mediations, conducted as part of the NHS Mediation Pilot: L Mulcahy et al *Mediating Medical Negligence Claims: An Option for the Future?* NHS Executive, 2000. The Pilot is considered in more detail in the section on Clinical Negligence Claims in Chapter 8.

153 *Commonwealth Bank of Australia v McDonnell* (24 July 1997, unreported) New South Wales Supreme Court (Rolfe J) and *Studer v Boettcher* (1998) NSWSC 524, the mediation had lasted ten hours. The fact that the courts were prepared to explore the duration of a mediation suggests that courts may review an agreement reached in mediation late at night.

154 Scottish Law Commission *Discussion Paper: Confidentiality in Family Mediation*, no 92 provides a useful overview. See also 'Confidentiality in arbitration and mediation' *In-house Lawyer*, March 2000, at p 44.

155 Clarified in mediator codes of conduct. See, for example, the Law Society of England & Wales *Codes of Practice* both Civil/Commercial Mediation and Family Mediation and also the Codes of Practice of a wide range of family mediation organisations, like Law Wise, NFM, FMA, the UK College of Family Mediators and, in the case of Scotland, CALM.

156 Ibid; and also see the Law Society of Scotland *Guidance for Accredited Mediators*.

157 Ibid. National Family Mediation Guidelines provide, in cases where there appears to be danger to a child, that the mediator should advise the parties themselves to seek help from an appropriate agency and, if the parties are not prepared to do this, to report the matter to the parties' solicitors or to social services or court welfare service, if they are already involved.

158 A Bevan *ADR: a lawyer's guide to mediation and other forms of dispute resolution*, Sweet & Maxwell, London, 1992 at p 32.

159 For example, Centre for Dispute Resolution *Code of Conduct*. K Gibson, in his article,

- the financial disclosure on which financial proposals have been reached in mediation is open;
- factual information is open; and
- any information a mediator provides to the adviser of one party must also be given to the advisers of each other party.

Despite these pressures on confidentiality, the duty to maintain it remains one of the most important ethical requirements of mediations. The relevant legal issues which confidentiality raises are considered in the next chapter.

Upholding public policy

Some mediator standards require mediators to act as trustees of public policy in respect of certain matters. For example, mediators in family cases must ensure that the participants consider the best interests of the children and that they understand the consequences for the children of any decision they reach.[160] Where mediators believe that proposed agreements of the parents do not uphold the best interests of the children, they have a duty to inform the parties of this belief and its basis. Such responsibilities undermine the process/content distinction and the notion of mediator neutrality. They do not, however, impose any broad mediator mediator responsibility towards the reasonableness of mediated agreements or the public interest generally.

Other ethical duties

There are numerous other ethical duties that apply to mediators, but are not of unique relevance to the practice of mediation. They include obligations to exercise restraint in publicity and advertising, and to advise about and comply with their fee arrangements.

Unresolved issues

All mediator standards leave issues unresolved. The unresolved issues are a product of the problematic definitions, subtle distinctions and subjective judgments which characterise the practice of mediation. While standards can reduce uncertainty as to professional competence and ethical behaviour, they cannot eliminate it.[161] The following are some of the endemic questions facing mediation theory and practice that are not resolved by the various standards:

- Is the mediator responsible for ensuring substantive fairness of the final settlement?
- Can the mediator assist the 'weaker' party in the negotiation process?
- Should the mediator protect the interests of parties not present at the mediation?

These are complex issues which require a firm conceptualisation of the mediation process and an appropriate theory of ethics.[162] They also require an appreciation of

---

'Confidentiality in Mediation: a moral re-assessment' (1992) *Journal of Dispute Resolution*, 25, recommends a greater discretion on the part of mediators to make disclosure, in particular, to provide a precedent bank so that problems or issues arising in a mediation need not be decided de novo (at pp 54–5).

160 See Chapter 5 on the role of the mediator and the section on Family Disputes in Chapter 8.
161 G Walker 'Training mediators: teaching about ethical concerns and obligations' (1998) 19 *MQ* 33.
162 K Gibson 'The ethical basis of mediation: why mediators need philosophers' (1989) 7 MQ 41. See also the discussion of definitional problems in Chapter 1.

the different factors that are relevant in different areas of mediation practice. Most standards assume the facilitative model of mediation in stipulating, for example, that mediators should not attempt to influence the decision of the parties based on their assessment of the merits of the case. However, much of the confusion in discussions about ethics in mediation is caused by the assumption that key ethical terms are self-evident and universally accepted. In reality much of the normative material on mediator behaviour is written at a high level of abstraction. Before firmer responses can be given to some of the above questions, more descriptive work on what actually happens in the mediation process will be necessary.[163] This is an area in which theoretical principles will have to be driven in part by empirical practice. Many of the issues of subjective ethics which standards leave unresolved will also have to be dealt with in mediator training. Here, professional standards provide a basis for training in mediator ethics,[164] and this training might in turn contribute to clearer statements in guidelines on questions of fairness, neutrality and the use of mediator power.[165] It is also likely that, over time, some standards will be judicially defined and this will provide, for legal purposes, more precision on their scope and extent.

Standardisation and regulation of mediation in the UK

Arguments in favour of standardisation

Given the confidential nature of mediation, and its lack of public scrutiny, standards would go some way to ensuring the accountability of mediation practitioners. Standards would also improve the status and reputation of mediation in the community, and provide the community with information on what to expect of a mediator. Standards would provide mediation service providers with objective criteria against which to assess competency and to provide a measure of consistency. Standards also have an internal function to promote consistency, competency and quality.

In Australia, NADRAC has, in its 2000 Discussion Paper on Standards, expressed the view that it considers that the development of standards would permit promotion of the objectives of mediation, minimise dissatisfaction with its operation, promote mediation services and mediator accountability and promote the use of mediation. NADRAC considers that its approach is consistent with international developments, in particular, the work being done by the USA Society of Professionals in Dispute Resolution ('SPIDR') in devising basic and advanced level competencies for mediators.[166]

---

163 C Dreise *Mediation: the political management of stories*, unpublished LLM dissertation, Bond University, 1993.
164 G Walker 'Training mediators: teaching about ethical concerns and obligations' (1998) 19 *MQ* 33.
165 H Astor and C Chinkin 'Mediation training and ethics' (1991) 2 *ADRJ* at p 231. The New South Wales Law Reform Commission *Alternative dispute resolution – training and accreditation of mediators*, Discussion Paper 21, 1989 at p 23 recognises that ethical violations are more likely to result from ignorance and poor training than from intent.
166 NADRAC *The Development of Standards for ADR: Discussion Paper*, March 2000, at p 26; and SPIDR Progress Committee on Credentials *Competencies and Qualifications (3CQ): Progress Report*, September 1999.

Arguments against standardisation

In the US, where the debate over standards has raged for over a decade, commentators have noted that there is little similarity amongst approaches to standards, even for mediation in similar contexts, like commercial, community or family mediation.[167] Political or self-interest barriers to the development of uniform standards, even within the same mediation subject areas, have become evident. In the commentary to the Uniform Mediation Act by the drafting committee in the US, it was acknowledged that no consensus could be identified in law, research or commentary as to the standards that would achieve effectiveness or fairness in mediation.[168]

The same conclusion was reached by a study in Scotland, where a number of respondents agreed that there was no single approach to mediation training and practice that could be applied across all subject areas and that, accordingly, training should be tailored to suit the requirements of individual subject areas:[169]

'. . . the variant legal, technical, social and emotional issues involved in differing needs and perceptions of the parties . . . may dictate a divergence of approach.'[170]

Accordingly, the concern is that it may be impossible to draft standards which would be applicable to every type of mediation. There are also concerns that uniform standards will create a straight-jacket, stifling creativity and flexibility.[171] Shapiro warns that standards are 'keyed to the minimum'.[172]

Alongside these issues is the concern that, by professionalising mediation through standards, it will become an elite activity, marginalising volunteer and community mediators, in turn limiting competition in the field.[173] In the United States, for example, the concern has been that lawyer mediators will monopolise mediation through standards. Roberts has questioned the propriety of this, given that mediation is not mainstream legal practice.[174]

Content of standards

It is useful to avoid high levels of abstraction in devising standards. In terms of assisting mediators to deal with dilemmas in mediation, examples are useful in

---

167 See, for example, M Rogers and C McEwan *Mediation: Law Policy & Practice*, Lawyers Co-operative, Rochester New York, 1989.
168 Drafting Committee on the Uniform Mediation Act *Notes by the Drafting Committee on the Uniform Mediation Act*, 1 June 1999.
169 R Mays and B Clark *ADR in Scotland*, The Scottish Office, 1999.
170 Ibid.
171 SPIDR Commission *Qualifying neutrals: the basic principles*, SPIDR 1989; and R Mays and B Clark *ADR in Scotland*, op cit.
172 *The Lawyer*, 19 April 1999.
173 M Liebmann (ed) *Community and Neighbour Mediation*, Cavendish Publishing Limited, London, 1998, at p 214.
174 S Roberts 'The Lawyer as Mediator' [1995] *Family Law* 637. See also M Roberts *Mediation in Family Disputes: Principles of Practice* (2nd edn), Arena, Hants, England 1997, at p 66 where she considers that the 'carefully-nurtured development over many years of mediation as a distinct and autonomous professional activity' could be damaged.

standards.[175] It is useful to recognise that standards serve a number of purposes, from guiding the conduct of a mediation through to developing a sense of responsibility by mediators towards their profession and promoting public confidence in mediation. Accordingly, standards should include:

- a definition of mediation;
- an outline of the role of a mediator;
- a description of the mediation process;
- an understanding of the mediator's responsibilities to the process and the parties.

The Canadian Forum on Dispute Resolution suggested an inter-disciplinary approach, building different levels of skill and specialisation around core competencies of mediation practice.[176] The approach is consistent with proposals by NADRAC in its 2000 Discussion Paper on Standards in Australia that standards should be classified into the following areas, with certain core competencies:[177]

- Appropriate knowledge, which includes knowledge about the nature of conflict, the relevance of culture to dispute resolution, negotiation processes and strategies, forms of communication, the legal/social/economic contexts of disputes and mediation procedure.
- Relevant skills, which includes assessment of suitability for mediation, gathering and using information, defining a dispute, communication skills, managing the mediation process, managing the interaction between the parties, creative negotiation strategies, impartiality and consolidating an agreement between the parties.
- Ethics, including accurate promotion of service, effective participation by the parties, appropriate methods of eliciting information from the parties, effective control of the mediation process, maintenance of impartiality, neutrality and confidentiality, and ensuring appropriate outcomes.[178]

Standards for mediation organisations should not only relate to the training and quality control of their mediators, but also to ensuring that their own structure, procedures, complaint systems and fee structures are of good quality, non-discriminatory and transparent.[179] The Lord Chancellor's Department has suggested that a quality mark could be developed for mediation services.[180]

Method for developing standards

The determination of what is required by way of standards requires wide consultation, from ADR organisations, Law Societies and Bar Councils, judges, solicitors

---

175 R A Bush *The Dilemmas of Mediation Practice: A Study of Ethnical Dilemmas and Policy Implications*, National Institute for Dispute Resolution, Washington DC, 1992.
176 Canadian Forum on Dispute Resolution *Report*, 1995.
177 NADRAC *The Development of Standards for ADR: Discussion Paper*, March 2000, at pp 33–50.
178 SPIDR Commission *Qualifying neutrals: the basic principles*, SPIDR 1989:
'[a mediator] should be aware . . . of public expectations but should have the ability to see . . . right and wrong without difficulty or hesitation . . . [there are] many ethical dilemmas for neutrals . . .'
179 Lord Chancellor's Department *ADR Consultation Paper*, November 1999.
180 Ibid.

and barristers, academics, corporate and community leaders and the public.[181] The view of NADRAC, which has recently issued a Discussion Paper on Australian ADR standards is that:

'. . . no one body, organisation, association or governmental agency should attempt to impose standards unilaterally . . .'[182]

They cite the reason for this on the basis that standards should balance the needs and interests of the parties and providers of mediation services with those of the wider society. In addition, NADRAC makes the point that consultation will need to be on-going as standards will need to adapt were circumstances require it, so that consultation will lead to a continuous raising of standards over time.[183]

In the UK a Joint Mediation Forum, which includes representatives from commercial,[184] community[185] and family[186] mediation organisations, has been established and is developing a standard code of conduct for mediators, together with standard training standards.[187]

Attainment and maintenance of standards

Education, training and accreditation are required to ensure that standards are attained and maintained. SPIDR in the US considers that attainment and main-tenance of standards should be a shared responsibility of the mediation community, at least in the early development of mediation.[188] NADRAC in Australia also considers that parties who use mediation services, mediators, mediation service providers, industry associations, educational institutions and government should be involved in the process of attainment and maintenance of standards, although it considers that mediation service providers have the major responsibility.[189] NADRAC considers that the role of mediation service providers in the context of the maintenance of standards requires them to:

- develop codes of conduct for mediators;
- have management systems to monitor the performance of mediators;
- provide initial and continuing development training for mediators;
- monitor feedback on mediators from parties in mediation;

---

181 J Parke 'Lawyers as negotiators: Time for a code of ethics?' (1993) *ADRJ* 26.
182 NADRAC *The Development of Standards for ADR: Discussion Paper*, March 2000, at p 51.
183 Ibid, at p 52.
184 Centre for Dispute Resolution, ADR Group and the Academy of Experts.
185 Mediation UK.
186 UK College of Family Mediators.
187 The Law Society of England & Wales ADR Working Party has withdrawn from the Forum as it considers that the differences in mediation practice, for example in the context of commercial and family mediation, do not lend themselves to uniform standards. There have been three failed attempts in Australia to set up an umbrella mediation organisation.
188 SPIDR *Ensuring Competence and Quality in Dispute Resolution Practice*, April 1995, at p 3.
189 NADRAC *The Development of Standards for ADR: Discussion Paper*, March 2000, at pp 63–4 and 75.

- provide mediators with supervision and evaluation;[190]
- keep a record on the outcomes of mediation; and
- carry out research and evaluation.[191]

Enforcement of standards

There are two potential implications to standardisation.[192] The first implication is that standards provide a basis for making and assessing complaints by mediation consumers. Complaints-handling requires procedures for investigation and discipline. Mediation clients should be able to complain to the standard-setting body about unprofessional conduct, and a professional conduct committee should be able to investigate the matter and take disciplinary steps, including temporary suspension or permanent removal of the offender from the relevant panel of mediators. The following issues arise:

- procedures to be adopted for the investigation of complaints against mediators;
- sanctions to be imposed for breaches of mediator codes of conduct, such as reprimand, financial penalties, naming and shaming, or suspension or expulsion from practice;
- redress available for aggrieved parties, including apologies, refunds of fees, damages and corrective advertising.

Although mediation service providers and traditional legal avenues of redress are the likely mechanisms by which enforcement will be achieved, the issue also arises whether there should be an independent agency, external to the mediation industry, like an ombudsman, to provide an avenue for complaints against both mediators and mediation service providers.[193] Complaints against solicitor mediators can be directed, in any event, to the relevant Law Society and, in the case of barrister mediators, to the relevant Bar Council. In the case of court-based mediation, the issue arises whether complaints could be referred to a procedure connected to the relevant court. The UK Joint Mediator Forum proposes to provide an umbrella organisation for commercial, community and family mediators throughout the UK, which will be called the Mediation Council. Commercial, community and family mediation will have three representatives each on the Council, and the final three will be co-opted from other interested parties. It is proposed that the Council will consider complaints against mediation organisations.

The second implication of standardisation is in relation to the legal liability of mediators and redress for an aggrieved party. This is dealt with in the next chapter. The status of mediator standards is relevant to the level of the duty of care required of mediators.[194] Where standards are stated to be binding on mediators, a deviation

---

190 Peer support and feedback enables mediators to learn from each other in order to develop their skills. It is suggested that peer feedback is essential in order to maintain mediators' trust in the mediation process: D Bryson 'Guidelines for ADR practitioner peer support and development' (1998) 1(1) *ADR Bulletin* 12.
191 Ibid, at pp 76–80.
192 H Astor and C Chinkin 'Mediation training and ethics' (1991) 2 *ADRJ* at pp 237–40.
193 Ibid.
194 G Vickery Guidelines for Mediators, unpublished LLM paper, Bond University, Australia, 1993, at p 12.

from the relevant provision may render the mediator liable to a charge of unprofessional conduct, whereas a guideline provision entails a more tentative professional standard. It should be noted, in respect of both implications, mediator standards contain a potential tension. While they promote confidentiality in the interests of mediation consumers, the enforcement of that principle serves to restrict the extent to which there can be external surveillance of mediator conduct. This restriction will affect consumer complaints, investigative procedures, malpractice actions and market choices. This is part of the duality of ethical standards: whereas they are promoted as serving the interests of clients and society, they can restrict accountability through confidentiality requirements and enhance professional power and self-control through the use of indeterminate language.[195]

Regulation

Lord Irvine, in a speech in late 1998, confirmed the need for standards and objectives, both from the point of view of the mediation profession and of mediation users.[196] The Lord Chancellor's Department ADR Consultation Paper raised the issue of whether regulation of the mediation profession is required, whilst recognising that regulation should not stifle innovation or competition in a developing field.[197]

There are different types of regulation, ranging from the most restrictive, licensing, through to the least restrictive, certification, whereby qualifications are recognised, but an exclusive right to practise is not conferred. Another approach is to regulate only in the case of mandatory mediation schemes. An independent body could oversee the training, accreditation and standards of mediators to whom matters are compulsorily referred for mediation. But even in that case there should be on-going review and evaluation to ensure that the training and standards are appropriate.

The idea of regulation has both supporters and opponents.[198] Those in favour of regulatory tendencies argue that regulation will provide better standards and safeguards for consumers, enhance the status of mediation, improve the legitimacy of the service in the eyes of potential users, and provide some protection for practitioners. Those against regulation argue that it interferes with the market choice of consumers to engage whoever they wish to provide the service,[199] that it inevitably favours existing practitioners at the expense of consumers and potential practitioners, and that it creates a closed shop, monopolistic conditions and increased

---

195 On this theme, in relation to professions generally, see R Abel *The Legal Profession in England and Wales*, Blackwell, Oxford, 1988, at pp 29–31.
196 Lord Irvine *Speech at the Centre for Dispute Resolution ADR Conference*, 11 November 1998, available at http://www.open.giv.uk/lcd/speeches/1998
197 Lord Chancellor's Department *ADR Consultation Paper*, November 1999. See also The Law Society ADR Working Party *ADR – Report prepared by Henry Brown for the Courts and Legal Services Committee*, The Law Society, London, 1991 ('The Brown Report').
198 See, for example, Lord Chancellor's Department *ADR Discussion Paper: Summary of responses*, August 2000.
199 Consumer choice, it is argued, can be better informed by the publication of mediators' qualifications, experience and areas of expertise, and by the education of prospective users of mediation services.

costs. In relation to mediation and other forms of dispute resolution, there are other specific arguments against regulation: it is inconsistent to provide formal controls over an informal process; regulation will take over an 'alternative' system and hand it to professionals; there is as yet insufficient expertise to determine safeguards for training and practice; and there is no demonstrable harm to mediation consumers to justify regulation.

NADRAC, in its 2000 Discussion Paper on ADR Standards in Australia, concluded that self-regulation or quasi-regulation is more appropriate than explicit government regulation for the ADR community in Australia as they determined that there is currently no strong public interest concern to be remedied. For example, enquiries made of Australian law societies and legal ombudsmen revealed virtually no complaints about the way lawyers practise ADR. NADRAC considered that government regulation is required in a limited context, where ADR is mandated by government in some way.[200]

Of the 59% of respondents to the Lord Chancellor's ADR Discussion Paper who addressed the issue of regulation, 37% favoured self-regulation of ADR in the UK, whereas 22% saw a role for government in regulation.[201]

---

200 NADRAC *The Development of Standards for ADR: Discussion Paper*, March 2000, at pp 91–8.
201 Lord Chancellor's Department *ADR Discussion Paper: Summary of responses*, August 2000, at para 82.

12

Legal Issues in Mediation

The Shadow of the Law

All mediation takes place, to a greater or lesser extent, in the shadow of the law.[1] Legal rules, principles and procedures affect, or potentially affect, the way in which mediations are conducted, the behaviours of mediating parties and mediation outcomes. The extent to which the law casts a shadow over mediation depends on many factors:

- whether it is private or court-connected mediation;
- whether the dispute being mediated is of a kind which could be litigated in court;
- whether there are clear legal precedents relating to the dispute;
- whether the mediation takes place during the course of litigation;
- the extent to which lawyers prepare for and participate in the mediation;
- whether a particular mediator focuses on formal rights or underlying interests; and
- whether or not there is a requirement for the mediation outcome or procedure to be reported back to a court or tribunal.

Formally, parties in mediation do not forfeit any of their legal rights and remedies. Where there is no settlement at mediation, and there are legally recognised rights involved, each side can go on to enforce its rights through appropriate judicial procedures. Where there is a settlement at mediation, legal rights and obligations are always affected to some degree. Where the mediation produces a binding agreement, that agreement will supersede the parties' prior rights, unless there are grounds on which a court could invalidate it. Where a mediated agreement is turned into a consent order of court, it can be enforced with the full authority of the state.

There are also indirect ways in which mediation might affect rights and remedies. Generally, the period within which an action must be commenced before a claim becomes time-barred is not extended by the commencement of mediation, so the parties must take the necessary precautions to preserve their legal rights. Moreover, as is shown below, some disclosures which parties make in mediation meetings may be used to their detriment in subsequent legal proceedings. Thus, while parties generally enter mediation with the intention of reserving their legal rights and remedies, mediation may result in those rights being directly or indirectly affected.

This chapter deals with some of the legal issues relating to mediation.[2] It also deals with some of the ways in which the mediation process is being shaped and defined

---

1   On this theme, see the section on mediation and the shadow of the law in Chapter 2.
2   A Kumar and R Muttath 'Enforceability in mediation', paper delivered on 27 March 1999

by the law of England and Wales. In many areas, there has been no statutory treatment of or judicial pronouncement on issues pertaining to mediation, and it is only possible to express an opinion on how the law might deal with them over time. In these areas, changing views on social policy and the public interest will shape the legal contours of the mediation process.

Mediation Clauses

Nature and purpose

Mediation clauses are found in contracts and are designed to either trigger the mediation process in the event of a breakdown in the operation of the contract, or require the parties to consider resolving potential differences, disputes, and disagreements through mediation. There are several reasons for using such clauses.[3] They confront contracting parties with the reality that they may have to face conflicts in the future operation of the agreement. They allow the parties to select and define their own dispute resolution system, for example mediation followed by litigation or arbitration, and to choose in advance either a specified individual or a mechanism for selecting an individual to act as a neutral. They also prepare the parties psychologically on the use of alternative dispute resolution (ADR) processes. They attempt to avoid, at the time the contract breaks down, a conflict over the method of dealing with a resulting dispute. And they pre-empt the problem of a party being concerned that it will be 'showing weakness' by recommending mediation in the heat of a dispute.[4] Mediation clauses are particularly advisable in complex contracts, such as joint venture agreements, which are intended to endure over a long period of time under fluctuating circumstances where the contracting parties will be in a continuing relationship.[5] American research has also indicated that parties participating in mediation pursuant to a mediation clause reach a settlement as frequently as those who agree to mediate when a dispute occurs.[6] Some commentators argue that ADR clauses result in cases, which have precedential value, being diverted from courts, thereby reducing the court's ability to reinforce standards.[7]

---

at the Second Conference on Alternative Dispute Resolution: Mediation – yesterday's ideas, today's techniques, National University of Singapore, *Conference proceedings*, at p 71. The paper discusses enforceability issues surrounding agreements to mediate, mediated settlement agreements and confidentiality in mediation.

3   H Astor and C Chinkin *Dispute Resolution in Australia*, Butterworths, Sydney, 1991, at pp 193–210; M Ahrens and G Witcombe *Australian Dispute Resolution Handbook*, Australian Commercial Disputes Centre Ltd, Sydney, 1992, at p 1; and S Henderson *The Dispute Resolution Manual*, DataLegal Publications, Spring Hill, 1993, at pp 118–19.

4   In the future the inclusion of mediation clauses may have to be specifically considered by lawyers when drafting contracts in order to avoid professional negligence claims. See also the section on the duties of lawyers representing clients in mediation below.

5   See M Pryles 'Dispute resolution clauses in contracts' (1990) 1 *ADRJ* 116–24.

6   J Brett, Z Barsness and S Goldberg 'The effectiveness of mediation: an independent analysis of cases handled by four major service providers' (1996) 12 *Negotiation Journal* 259.

7   For example, E Rolph, E Moller and L Peterson *Escaping the courthouse: private ADR in Los Angeles*, The RAND Institute of Civil Justice, 1994.

Organisations providing private mediation services have drafted standard mediation clauses for use in agreements. The basic elements of the clauses of a number of organisations are set out in a table later in this section. These clauses generally stipulate that if any disputes should arise over the performance of a contract, the parties will refer the matter to mediation. There are variations in the complexity of mediation clauses. Some merely provide for the involvement of an agreed mediator, who can design and control all aspects of the process. Others specify in detail the features of the mediation process (including the relevant timetables to be followed), or incorporate by reference a prescribed mediation procedure contained in a separate document. Some clauses provide for only mediation, while others provide for a sequence of dispute resolution methods, such as negotiation, followed by mediation, followed by arbitration. Some clauses refer all disputes to mediation, while other clauses refer only enumerated categories of disputes.

Customised clauses can be drafted where those of the service-providers or professional associations are not suitable. A number of drafting considerations arise. A preliminary consideration is which ADR process should be adopted. A particular type of ADR may be more appropriate than others for particular kinds of disputes,[8] although it is common for an ADR clause to provide a dispute resolution procedure, which escalates from low cost interest-based processes through to higher cost rights-based procedures. A typical clause begins with negotiation, followed by mediation or some other form of non-binding ADR, with litigation or arbitration as the fall-back, if ADR fails to resolve the dispute. In order to determine the most appropriate escalation procedure, it is necessary to consider the contract in question; to identify the types of disputes that might occur in the life of that contract; to consider the most appropriate dispute resolution procedure for disputes of that kind; and to incorporate those procedures into the clause. A further preliminary issue will be the method for selection or appointment of the neutral, and whether the processes will be administered by an organisation and, if so, which organisation. The costs of the ADR process and the issue of legal costs should also be addressed. In the case of international contracts, governing law and jurisdiction clause should also be considered.

Enforceability of mediation clauses

Many mediation clauses are voluntarily complied with by the parties. This truism is important to bear in mind in any investigation of their enforceability at law. Nevertheless, the question arises as to whether mediation clauses are legally enforceable in cases where one party fails to comply with the relevant terms. In the US, courts have enthusiastically enforced ADR clauses.[9] Although few UK court decisions shed light on this issue, the approach of courts in jurisdictions like Australia may provide a useful indicator of the issues which are likely to be relevant to a consideration of enforceability. There is no legislative basis for enforcing such

---

8   For example, expert determination is commonly used for rent reviews; mediation is used increasingly for insurance disputes; and adjudication is statutorily-mandated for certain construction contract disputes.

9   *McKay v Ashland Oil Inc* 120 FRD 43; *Arabian A M Oil Co v Scarfone* 119 FRD 448; and *DeValk Lincoln Mercury Inc v Ford Motor Co* 811 F 2d 326.

clauses and their enforceability is only now being determined by the courts in terms of general contractual principles. By contrast, the law on the enforceability of arbitration clauses is based on legislation which has been interpreted by the courts and is now well established.[10] The differences between arbitration and mediation limit the relevance of the law on arbitration clauses to that on mediation clauses. The first difference is that arbitration is regulated by statute and the enforceability of arbitration clauses is now grounded in legislation. Second, arbitration involves a well-defined procedure, understood by users and the courts, which is not the case with newer ADR processes such as mediation. Third, it is relatively easy to ascertain whether a party has complied with an arbitration clause, but relatively difficult to establish compliance with a mediation clause. Finally, arbitration guarantees an outcome in the form of the arbitrator's binding award, so that forcing parties into the process will not be an exercise in futility as might be the case with mediation. In the light of these differences, it might be anticipated that the courts will be less likely to enforce mediation clauses than arbitration clauses. However, similar policy considerations affect the courts' approach to both kinds of clauses, involving a balancing of the parties' autonomy to agree on their own dispute resolution method with the rights of persons to bring matters to court if they so wish.

The following six issues are relevant to the enforceability of mediation clauses.[11]

Does a mediation clause survive the termination of an agreement?

Contracts can be terminated in a number of ways, for example through frustration or where one party repudiates the agreement and the other side accepts the repudiation. The question arises as to whether, in these circumstances, an otherwise valid mediation clause survives the termination of the contract. General contractual principles would suggest that, although no further contractual performance is required of the parties after termination, the contract remains on foot for the purposes of enforcing a dispute resolution clause.[12] There is no reason of policy why a mediation clause should not be severable and survive the termination of the main agreement.

A different issue may arise where one party wishes to enforce a dispute resolution clause and the other party claims that the contract containing the clause was void *ab initio*. In relation to arbitration clauses, under English common law, the courts considered the matter from the angle of whether the claim that the contract was void ab initio necessarily entailed a denial that there was any agreement to arbitrate.[13] Examples of such situations included cases of non est factum or denial that there was a concluded agreement. In the context of arbitration clauses, since the decision in

---

10 See generally Mustill and Boyd *Commercial Arbitration* (2nd edn) 1989.
11 D Spencer 'Uncertainty and incompleteness in dispute resolution clauses' (1995) 2 *CDRJ* 23. See also J Lee 'The enforceability of mediation clauses in Singapore' (1999) *SJLS* 229.
12 *Heyman v Darwins Ltd* [1942] AC 356; and see *Chitty on Contracts* (26th edn), para 1701.
13 *Harbour Assurance Co (UK) Ltd v Kansa General International Insurance Co Ltd* [1993] QB 701, CA.

Harbour Assurance Co (UK) Ltd v Kansa General Insurance Co Ltd,[14] notwithstanding allegations that the underlying contract is void, the parties are presumed to have wanted their disputes resolved by arbitration. The clause is capable of surviving the invalidity of the contract in which it is contained, so that an arbitrator would have the jurisdiction under the arbitration clause to determine the initial validity of the contract.[15] The underlying principle is that the agreement to arbitrate is collateral to the main agreement and is therefore able to stand on its own. Under the common law doctrine of separability or autonomy of an arbitration clause, a contract containing an arbitration clause is treated as comprising two separate contracts: (1) the main contract which concerns the commercial obligations of the parties; and (2) a collateral contract[16] to resolve by arbitration future disputes of the nature specified in the arbitration clause. In respect of arbitration the position has been confirmed by statute in England, Wales and Northern Ireland. Section 7 of the Arbitration Act 1996 provides:

'unless otherwise agreed by the parties, an arbitration agreement which forms or was intended to form part of another agreement (whether or not in writing) shall not be regarded as invalid, non-existent or ineffective, and it shall for that purpose be treated as a distinct agreement.'

These principles may be extended to other dispute resolution clauses. It may be argued that as a mediation clause derives its authority from the agreement of the parties, it is severable from the main contract and should be enforced by the courts even where it is alleged that the main contract is void.[17]

Is the mediation clause sufficiently certain?

Clauses in contracts will be void for uncertainty where it is difficult to ascertain the particular rights or obligations of the parties. The law declines to enforce contractual clauses which leave open certain matters to be agreed on in the future.[18] This issue can arise in the following contexts:

Agreements to agree or negotiate

Because it is uncertain as to what terms will be agreed to, or whether the parties will even reach agreement, either party could walk away from an 'agreement to agree' without breaching any obligations. Where a mediation clause makes the occurrence of the mediation dependent on the future wishes of one party ('there will be a

---

14 *Harbour Assurance Co (UK) Ltd v Kansa General International Insurance Co Ltd* [1993] QB 701, CA.
15 Ibid, at 459, 463 and 469.
16 *Bremer Vulkan Schiffbau und Maschinenfabrik v South India Shipping Corpn Ltd* [1981] 1 Lloyd's Rep 253 at 259; *Paal Wilson & Co A/S v Partenreederei Hannah Blumenthal (The 'Hannah Blumenthal')* [1983] 1 Lloyd's Rep 103 at 117.
17 R Giles 'Severability of dispute resolution clauses in contracts' (1995) 14 *The Arbitrator* 38; and D Spencer 'Uncertainty and incompleteness in dispute resolution clauses' (1995) 2 *CDRJ* 23 at 28.
18 *Ridgway v Wharton* (1857) 6 HL Cas 238; *Hillas and Co Ltd v Arcos Ltd* [1932] All ER Rep 494; and *Courtney & Fairbairn Ltd v Tolaini Bros (Hotels) Ltd* [1975] 1 WLR 297.

mediation if X or Y agrees to it'), it will not provide sufficient certainty to be enforceable.[19] This sort of provision is effectively an agreement to agree about mediation, which is too uncertain to be effective and confer any rights. The English courts extended this principle[20] by refusing to enforce agreements to negotiate on certain matters in the future, on the grounds that these arrangements are no different from 'agreements to agree'.[21]

In *Courtney & Fairbairn Ltd v Tolaini Bros (Hotels) Ltd*[22] Lord Denning stated:

'. . . the law . . . cannot recognise a contract to negotiate . . . the reason is because it is too uncertain to have any binding force . . . when there is a fundamental matter left undecided and to . . . negotiation, there is no contract.'[23]

The House of Lords in *Walford v Miles*[24] confirmed that an agreement to negotiate is not enforceable as the court cannot determine the obligations with sufficient certainty and cannot assess compliance.

The issue arises whether other forms of non-binding ADR, in particular mediation, are equivalent to negotiation. In the Australian case, *Coal Cliff Collieries Ltd v Sijehama Pty Ltd*,[25] the New South Wales Court of Appeal considered that such ADR clauses equate to agreements to negotiate, although Kirby P had considered that a contract to negotiate could be enforceable in certain circumstances. Giles J in the New South Wales Supreme Court case, *Hooper Bailie Associated Ltd v Natcon Group Pty Ltd*,[26] considered that it was necessary to distinguish between a contract to negotiate and a contract to mediate. In that case the parties had agreed not to go to arbitration until 'conciliation' had concluded. The plaintiff sought a stay of the arbitration proceedings instituted by the defendants on the grounds that the defendants had not complied with the conciliation requirement. One of the issues raised was whether the agreement to conciliate was sufficiently certain as to the conduct required of the parties. In granting the stay, the court found that it was certain. Giles J found that:

'. . . opponents of enforceability contend that it is futile to seek to enforce something which requires the co-operation and consent of a party when co-operation and consent cannot be enforced; equally they say that there can be no loss to the other party if for want of co-operation and consent, the consensual process would have led to no result . . . the proponents of enforceability contend that this misconceives the objectives of alternative dispute resolution . . . what is enforced is not co-operation and consent, but participation in a process from which co-operation and consent might come.'[27]

---

19 *Minister for Main Roads for Tasmania v Leighton Contractors Pty Ltd* (1985) 1 BCL 381.
20 *Courtney & Fairbairn Ltd v Tolaini Bros (Hotels) Ltd* [1975] 1 WLR 297; and *Walford v Miles* [1992] 2 WLR 174.
21 See Lord Ackner in *Walford v Miles*, supra, at 181, where he held that 'the concept of a duty to carry on negotiations in good faith is inherently repugnant to the adversarial position of [negotiating] parties'. However, English courts have held that clauses which provide that the parties 'agree to use their best endeavours . . .' do not lack the necessary certainty for enforcement, as to which see n 45.
22 [1975] 1 All ER 716.
23 See also *Mallozzi v Carapelli SpA* [1976] 1 Lloyd's Rep 407.
24 [1992] 1 All ER 453.
25 (1991) 24 NSWLR 1.
26 (1992) 28 NSWLR 194.
27 Ibid at 206.

Giles J did not follow the English authorities because he considered that 'the law in New South Wales in relation to contracts to negotiate is not so uncompromising'.[28] Encouraged by US authorities, Giles J concluded that:

> 'an agreement to . . . mediate is not to be likened . . . to an agreement to agree . . . nor is it an agreement to negotiate . . .'[29]

In the more recent case, *Con Kallergis v Calshonie*,[30] Hayne J considered that an agreement to negotiate would be enforceable, provided that the process specified has an identifiable end, as opposed to a requirement in a contract to negotiate to achieve agreement, which would be unenforceable. The focus of the clause should, on that analysis, be on the process, and the agreement to negotiate should be a stage in that process.

In any event, the English view that agreements to agree or to negotiate are unenforceable for lack of certainty may have been weakened by the House of Lords in *Channel Tunnel Group Ltd v Balfour Beatty Construction Ltd*.[31]

Procedure for the mediation

In order to avoid a mediation clause being held too uncertain, and therefore unenforceable, a mediation clause should also be carefully drafted and, in particular, should address the procedural aspects of the mediation process. In the Australian case *Hooper Bailie*[32] the Supreme Court of New South Wales considered that the mediation clause should set out the steps to be followed in the conduct of the mediation or that it should clearly incorporate by reference the rules or guidelines which do this.[33] In *Hooper Bailie* a solicitor's letter that set out the procedure to be followed in a mediation rendered, the court found, the mediation agreement enforceable as the letter set up a 'clear structure' for the mediation.[34]

A word of caution, however, was given in the Australian case, *Elizabeth Bay Developments Pty Ltd v Boral Building Services Pty Ltd*,[35] where Giles J found that the mediation clause in question was not sufficiently certain to be enforceable as the clause provided that the parties were to attempt to settle disputes by mediation 'administered by' a particular ADR organisation, but did not either set out the procedure for the mediation in the clause or clearly incorporate by reference the rules or guidelines for mediation issued by that organisation. In addition, the clause required the parties to sign a mediation agreement when a dispute arose, but it did not identify the agreement. Giles J found that, in requiring the parties to sign an unknown mediation agreement, which was not referred to in the clauses, and which could conflict with the mediation guidelines of the ADR organisation, this arrangement exhibited a lack of certainty as to the procedure which they should follow in

---

28 (1992) 28 NSWLR 194 at 208.
29 Ibid at 207.
30 (1998) 14 BCL 201.
31 [1993] AC 334, followed in *Cott UK Ltd v FE Barber Ltd* [1997] 3 All ER 540. These cases are discussed further below.
32 (1992) 28 NSWLR 194.
33 In that case, care should be taken if there is an 'entire agreement' clause in the agreement: see, generally, *Inntrepreneur Pub Co v East Crown Ltd* [2000] 2 Lloyd's Rep 611 (Chancery Division, Lightman J), for a consideration of 'entire agreement' clauses.
34 (1992) 28 NSWLR 194 at 209.
35 (1995) 36 NSWLR 709.

mediation. This approach was taken despite the fact that, on the concession of both parties, the dispute resolution clause impliedly incorporated the guidelines of the ADR organisation, which provided a detailed procedure for mediation. The judge held that the clause could not be saved by the guidelines, because the guidelines required the signing of a mediation agreement which was not identified in the clause. The mediation clause did not itself lay down a procedure for the mediation.

Spencer points to the incongruity between this judgment and that in the *Hooper Bailie* case, both of which were given by the same judge.[36] In the *Hooper Bailie* case the clause on its own was uncertain, but it was found to be enforceable because of a letter from the plaintiff's solicitor which set out the procedural features of the proposed conciliation. In the *Elizabeth Bay Developments* case there was a six page mediation appointment agreement, and four pages of mediation guidelines, yet these were not regarded as sufficient to supply the required certainty. It is submitted that the certainty requirement was satisfied on the facts of this case and that in similar future circumstances courts should find mediation clauses enforceable.

Agreement to agree on procedure

The further issue, identified in the Australian case law, is that, in relation to the mediation process to be followed by the parties, there should be no stage in that process which requires the parties to agree on a course of action before the process can proceed further. For example, in case the parties cannot agree on the selection of a mediator, the mediation clause, or the mediation rules or guidelines incorporated by reference into the clause, need to specify a nominated third party who will make the appointment.[37] In the *Elizabeth Bay* case[38] the mediation process stipulated by the parties was considered by the court to be:

> '. . . open-ended, indeed unworkable, because the process . . . would come to an early stop when, prior to the mediation it was asked what the parties had to sign and the question could not be answered . . .'

A recent Australian case, *Aiton Australia Pty Ltd v Transfield Pty Ltd*,[39] examined this issue, in relation to a dispute resolution clause, which did not refer to the apportionment between the parties of the mediator's fees and other expenses. The court considered that the apportionment of these costs was not so obvious an arrangement that it could go without saying, or be implied, and whilst it was common practice for these costs to be shared equally by the parties, there were too many options which the parties could have intended. The court found that, since the parties would have to reach their own agreement on this issue, the lack of this information rendered the mediation clause too uncertain to be enforced.

---

36 D Spencer 'Uncertainty and incompleteness in dispute resolution clauses' (1995) 2 *CDRJ* 23 at 33.

37 It is important to ensure that the third party specified offers this service: *Cott UK Ltd v FE Barber Ltd* [1997] 3 All ER 540.

38 (1995) 36 NSWLR 709 at 715.

39 (1999) NSWSC 55020 of 1999, 1 October 1999, where, on an application for a stay of proceedings, the defendant, Transfield, claimed that the contracts which formed the basis of Aiton's claim contained a dispute resolution clause which had to be followed prior to either party commencing proceedings. The clause required the parties 'to make diligent and good faith efforts to resolve disputes in accordance with the provisions of the sections before either party commences mediation, legal action or the expert resolution process, as the case may be'.

Good faith

Lord Ackner in *Walford v Miles*[40] stated that:

'. . . the concept of a duty to carry on negotiations in good faith is inherently repugnant to the adversarial position of the parties when involved in negotiations. Each party to the negotiations is entitled to pursue his . . . own interests so long as he avoids making a mis-representation . . .'

In the Australian case, *Hooper Bailie*,[41] Giles J said:

'. . . there is a necessary tension between negotiation, in which a party is free to, and may be expected to, have regard to self interest rather than the interests of the other party and maintenance of good faith.'

If an agreement to negotiate 'in good faith' may not be enforceable, an agreement to mediate 'in good faith' may suffer the same fate. Decisions in Australia have not been consistent. In *Elizabeth Bay*[42] the court held, in relation to a mediation clause, which required a commitment to attempt 'in good faith' to negotiate, that the clause was too uncertain in meaning to be enforceable. By comparison, Hayne J in *Con Kallergis v Calshonie* considered that the obligation to act in good faith or reasonably in mediation is an obligation that is certain.[43] Another approach, adopted by Einstein J in *Aiton Australia Pty Ltd v Transfield Pty Ltd*,[44] considers that, as the concept of good faith depends on the wording used and the circumstances of each case, although it is undesirable to formulate a list of indicia suggesting compliance or non-compliance with the obligation to mediate in good faith, a framework could be provided in order to ensure sufficient certainty in the use of the phrase, for example:

- to undertake a mediation, which process should be defined; and
- to undertake to have an open mind in that process, in particular, a willingness to consider proposals put forward by a party or the mediator, and a willing-ness to put forward options for resolution of the dispute.

Einstein J considered that good faith mediation does not require the parties to make concessions which are not in their interests, and certainly would not require the parties to reach an agreement. He concluded that the requirement to mediate in good faith is enforceable, provided that it does not amount to an agreement to reach agreement. Despite the more recent Australian willingness to accept good faith clauses, the position in England is uncertain.[45]

---

40 [1992] 2 WLR 174 at 181–2 (with whom the other members of the House of Lords agreed).
41 (1992) 28 NSWLR 194 at 209.
42 (1995) 36 NSWLR 709.
43 *Con Kallergis v Calshonie* (1998) 14 BCL 201 at 211–12.
44 *Aiton Australia Pty Ltd v Transfield Pty Ltd* (1999) NSWSC 55020 of 1999, October 1999, at 156. See also 'Case comment: good faith in mediation – certainty and enforcement' (2000) 17(2) *Build LM* 8.
45 It is suggested that a distinction should be made between a requirement to 'negotiate in good faith' with that 'to use best endeavours', as the latter case obliges a party, for instance, to be available for the negotiations, whereas the former may oblige a party, for example, not to take an unreasonable position in those negotiations: A G Guest et al (eds) *Chitty on Contracts*, General Principles Volume, Sweet & Maxwell, London, 1994, at pp 148–9. Other than the issue of enforceability, drafters should also consider whether the

In summary, on the issue of certainty, it is submitted that the approach in *Hooper Bailie* upholding a mediation clause shows a realistic appreciation of the nature of the mediation process and should be preferred. It is supported by expressions of local judicial policy in favour of mediation.[46] It is also supported by the long-standing attitude of some judges in foreign jurisdictions, in response to claims that general dispute resolution clauses are ambiguous and uncertain, that they will do everything possible to give effect to the intention of the parties, unless it appears that a clause is so devoid of meaning that no particular intention can be attributed to the parties.[47] It is also in accordance with modern business practice, as it is no longer unusual for commercial agreements to contain clauses which require the parties, in the event of a dispute, to negotiate and endeavour to settle the dispute themselves.

The *Hooper Bailie* decision has been relied upon as the authority for the enforceability of mediation clauses in Australia, subject to certain requirements. The decision required mediation clauses to set out with sufficient certainty a procedural framework within which the parties are to operate. The requirements in the circumstances of that case included the procedure for the appointment of the neutral, procedural matters, the possibility of legal representation, information exchange, and evidential matters. The framework must also provide 'sufficient certainty' as to the conduct required of the parties who participate in the mediation.[48]

Is the mediation clause complete?

Although it has not been raised in the cases, the question arises as to whether a mediation clause could be held invalid because it is incomplete. This is closely related to the question of certainty. General contractual principles will cause an agreement to be void for incompleteness where it makes no reference to an important part of the transaction. In *Triarno Pty Ltd v Triden Contractors Ltd*[49] the dispute resolution clause made provision for binding expert determination, but without reference to the procedures to be followed or the rights of the parties in the process. The court held that it had no jurisdiction to construct the procedures to be followed. Courts are also not inclined to imply terms into contracts in relation to procedures to be followed.[50] These principles could be extended to mediation clauses,[51] but it is submitted that greater use of and familiarity with mediation should cause courts to be less concerned about the problem of incompleteness.

---

sort of information likely to be imparted at mediation is capable of misuse by anyone present and provide for necessary safeguards. See V Vann 'Confidentiality in court sponsored mediation: disclose at your own risk?' (1999) 10 *ADRJ* 195.

46 See Chapter 7, section on Courts and Mediation.

47 For example, *Aztec Mining Co Ltd v Leighton Contractors Pty Ltd* (14 February 1990 and 23 February 1990, unreported) Supreme Court of Western Australia (Murray J); and R Charlton 'Case Note' (1990) 1 *ADRJ* 104–6.

48 B Sordo 'Law Society of NSW Review of the Guidelines for solicitor mediators and the dispute resolution model clause' (1993) 4 *ADRJ* 307; R Angyal 'Law Society revises ADR clause to enhance enforceability' (1993) 31 *Law Society Journal* 71 at 73.

49 (1992) 10 BCL 305.

50 D Spencer 'Uncertainty and incompleteness in dispute resolution clauses' (1995) 2 *CDRJ* 23 at 30.

51 D Spencer, ibid, at 24.

Does the mediation clause attempt to oust the jurisdiction of the courts?

It is a basic constitutional principle that the courts are accessible to all persons where a dispute is legally justiciable, and it is not possible to exclude by agreement an individual's right to pursue remedies through the courts. This would be the case where a contract provided that an ADR process such as mediation was an exclusive alternative to litigation. It would be regarded as against public policy to attempt to oust the jurisdiction of the courts in this way and the clause would be unenforceable.

In relation to clauses specifying arbitration as the method of dispute resolution, the courts required in the past that they be in so-called *Scott v Avery*[52] form in order to be enforceable. A *Scott v Avery* clause provides that the parties will first refer specified disputes to arbitration before instituting court proceedings. Arbitration is thus 'a condition precedent' to the commencement of legal proceedings. While it is against public policy to attempt to oust the jurisdiction of the courts, it is possible for parties to covenant that no right of action will accrue until a third party has arbitrated on the matter. Thus at common law the courts balanced the intentions of the parties and public policy by enforcing only certain kinds of arbitration clauses. Nowadays, courts have statutory powers to stay proceedings brought in breach of an arbitration clause.[53]

There is no comparable legislation regulating mediation clauses, and the amount of case law is limited. In *Allco Steel (Queensland) Pty Ltd v Torres Strait Gold Pty Ltd*[54] the Queensland court examined the enforceability of contract clauses requiring disputing parties to comply with an ADR process, referred to as 'conciliation', as a condition precedent to commencing litigation. Master Horton held that the clause in question was unenforceable because it purported to override the principle against the ousting of the courts.[55] As regards the court's jurisdiction to stay proceedings, it was held that both parties had taken up positions 'which effectively rule out the possibility of compromise and conciliation'. As no useful purpose would be served by compelling the parties to comply with the clause, the court would not grant a stay.

While this judgment did not uphold the conciliation clause, it implies that if it had not contravened the non-ousting principle it would have been enforceable. This view was taken by the English High Court in *Halifax Financial Services Ltd v Intuitive Systems Ltd*,[56] where it was prepared to consider the principle, although it declined to order a stay of proceedings in that case as it did not consider that, as a matter of construction, the mediation clause in question was a condition precedent to the issue of proceedings. The court was persuaded to this conclusion by the fact that the ADR procedures in that case would only be triggered if one of the parties issued a written notice to the other.[57] In addition, escalation within the ADR procedure was not compulsory, but at the option of either party.[58]

---

52 (1856) 5 HL Cas 811; 10 ER 1121.
53 Arbitration Act 1996, s 9.
54 Supreme Court of QLD, 2742 of 1989 (12 March 1990, unreported) (Master Horton).
55 On the authority of *Anderson v G H Mitchell & Sons Ltd* (1941) 65 CLR 543.
56 [1999] 1 All ER (Comm) 303.
57 The relevant portion of the clause was: '. . . senior representatives of the parties will, within 10 Business Days of a written notice from either party to the other, meet . . . and attempt to resolve the dispute without recourse to legal proceedings'.
58 The further relevant portion of the clause was: '. . . if the dispute is not resolved as a result

Are there other policy considerations affecting the enforceability of mediation clauses?

An agreement to mediate cannot oust the right to adjudication, provided by the Housing Grants, Construction and Regeneration Act 1996.[59] The Unfair Contract Terms Act 1977 exposes clauses in contracts to scrutiny for reasonableness where either a party to the contract is a consumer or the clause appears in a party's standard contract. The Act seeks to prevent making a liability or its enforcement subject to onerous conditions. Since s 13 of the Act indicates that an arbitration clause is not an onerous condition, it is difficult to see how a mediation clause would be considered onerous. In contrast, the Unfair Terms in Consumer Regulations 1999 provide wider protection, exclusively for the benefit of consumers, and indicate that hindering a consumer's right to take legal action could be considered unfair.[60] Some argue that a mediation clause could fall foul of Article 6 of the ECHR, incorporated into UK law by the Human Rights Act 1998, as it prohibits restrictions on access to courts within a reasonable time, although it is submitted that the considerations applicable to ousting the court's jurisdiction (supra) are equally relevant, as are those discussed in the context of compulsion to mediate in Chapter 9.[61]

Article 6 also imposes a requirement of procedural fairness, which raises the issue of whether a dispute resolution clause could be defeated on the grounds that it fails to uphold the requirements of procedural fairness. In *Aztec Mining Co Ltd v Leighton Contractor Pty Ltd*,[62] a dispute resolution clause provided, inter alia, for reference to an independent expert who was required to follow certain expedited procedures before giving a binding decision. It was submitted by the plaintiff that the prescribed procedure was inappropriate for the complex dispute in question and should be struck down as offending the fundamental requirements of fairness. The procedure allowed the parties to make submissions to the expert, to be consulted on matters of procedure, and to be legally represented. The court declined to strike it down and held that there was nothing preventing either party from seeking redress in court over allegations of error or impropriety by the expert. In *Elanay Contracts v The Vestry* (30 August 2000) the Article 6 requirement that a party should have a reasonable opportunity to present its case was found (per HHJ Harvey QC) to have no application to adjudication on the basis that an adjudicator's decision is not a final determination. As mediation does not involve any determination by a mediator, Article 6 is unlikely to provide a basis for requiring procedural fairness in mediation.

---

of such a meeting, either Party may . . . propose to the other . . . that structured negotiations be entered into with the assistance of a . . . mediator . . .'
59   In *R G Carter Ltd v Edmund Nuttall Ltd* (21 June 2000, unreported) HHJ Thornton QC determined that a mediation clause cannot undermine the right of any party to refer a dispute to adjudication 'at any time' (s 108). See the section on Construction Disputes in Chapter 8 for further detail about the statutory adjudication scheme.
60   Arbitration clauses in consumer contracts are unfair where these relate to a claim which does not exceed £5,000: Unfair Arbitration Agreements (Specified Order) 1999, SI 1999/2167 and Arbitration Act 1996, s 91. In Joined Cases C-240/98 and C-244/98 *Oceano Grupo Editorial SA v Quintero* (27 June 2000, unreported), the European Court of Justice held that a jurisdiction clause in a consumer contract is unfair unless individually negotiated.
61   For further consideration of the human rights issue, see Chapter 9 and Ethical Standards in Chapter 11.
62   Supreme Court of WA, 1109 of 1990 (23 February 1990, unreported) (Murray J).

There are several policy arguments which favour the enforceability of mediation clauses which do not undermine the principle against ousting the courts' jurisdiction.[63] Where the clear intention of the parties is merely to postpone the commencement of litigation until another dispute resolution process has been attempted, the courts should give effect to that intention by upholding the contract.[64] Favourable attitudes towards ADR options also support the enforceability of such clauses.[65] The changing nature of public policy is found in a series of measures taken by the government and the courts to promote the use of mediation as a means for resolving commercial, social and community disputes.[66] Moreover, it is submitted that some of the reasoning behind the decisions upholding arbitration clauses can be applied to other dispute resolution clauses.[67]

Drafting mediation clauses

Although mediation clauses are now used regularly, it is clear that the law on their enforceability is not yet settled. From the decided cases, it appears that drafters of mediation clauses should be attentive to the following factors: [68]

(a)   mediation clauses should be clear and certain in their own right, or it should be possible to derive certainty from extrinsic documents expressly referred to in the clauses;

(b)   they should be complete and comprehensive;

(c)   they should specify the procedures to be followed by the parties in setting up and undertaking the mediation, with some reference to the identity of the mediator, the responsibility for payment of the mediator's fees and the timetables to be followed;

(d)   alternatively, they should incorporate by reference the mediation procedure of an organisation providing;

(e)   they should uphold the non-ouster principle by stipulating that the parties should first submit their dispute to mediation before they institute court proceedings; and

(f)   they should be wary of provisions requiring participation in good faith.[69]

Utilising these criteria, the table below provides a snapshot of the range of the standard mediation clauses drafted by UK mediation organisations:

---

63   In other countries courts have enforced clauses providing for dispute resolution processes other than arbitration. See the American cases analysed in H Astor and C Chinkin *Dispute Resolution in Australia*, Butterworths, Sydney, 1991, at pp 209–10. See H Brown and A Marriott *ADR Principles and Practice* (2nd edn), Sweet & Maxwell, London, 1999, at pp 117–25.

64   *Public Authorities Superannuation Board v Southern International Developments Corpn Pty Ltd*, NSW Supreme Court, 17896 of 1987 (19 October 1987, unreported) analysed in H Astor and C Chinkin, op cit, at pp 198–202.

65   On judicial policy towards mediation, see generally Chapter 7.

66   See generally Chapter 7.

67   R Angyal 'Enforceability of alternative dispute resolution clauses' (1991) 2 *ADRJ* 32.

68   For a full list of considerations with regard to commercial contracts, see A Hood 'Commercial contracts, lawyers and alternative dispute resolution: a proactive habit' (1998) 9 *ADRJ* 129; R Angyal 'Enforceability of agreements to mediate' in G Raftesath and S Thaler (eds) *Cases for Mediation*, Sydney LBC Information Services, 1999, at p 1.

69   See R Angyal, op cit, at p 9.

Mediation Organisation	Is mediation a pre-condition to any other step?	Are procedures for the mediation incorporated?	Is there a fall back in case the parties cannot agree on a particular issue?	Is there a 'good faith' requirement?
Academy of Experts[70]	Parties agree to submit their dispute to expert determination, mediation or such other recognised alternative dispute resolution process *as they shall agree is appropriate*	The mediation is conducted in accordance with the rules, guidance and code of conduct produced by the Academy[71]	Appointment of the mediator is made by the Academy in the absence of agreement between the parties, although the parties can select another appointing authority[72]	No
The ADR Group[73]	Although the parties agree to resolve the dispute through mediation, *if a party does not wish to participate in the mediation, the next step in the dispute resolution process can be taken*	The mediation is conducted *under the auspices of the ADR Group*, and the clause does not refer to or incorporate the mediation procedures	The Chartered Institute of Arbitrators or the Law Society appoints a mediator in the absence of agreement between the parties, although the parties can select another appointing authority[74]	Yes
Centre for Dispute Resolution[75]	Standard clause provides that parties agree to attempt mediation. The parties may select an additional paragraph, specifying that no other step is to be taken until the mediation is terminated. The Centre's Model Mediation Procedure (incorporated by reference) provides that litigation/ arbitration is possible unless the parties agree otherwise[76]	The Centre's Model Mediation Procedure is incorporated by reference[77]	The Centre will appoint the mediator and decide any other point in the absence of agreement between the parties on the issue[78]	No

70 See *Atkins Court Forms and Precedents*, ADR Volume, at p 65 for the wording of the Academy's clauses.
71 See Chapter 7.
72 The Academy's mediation rules, guidance and mediation agreement should also be reviewed to check whether, in the case of any 'agreement to agree' provisions in those documents, a fall back has been provided or, in the absence of that fall back, to consider providing for this in the contract.

Chartered Institute of Arbitrators[79]	The parties agree not to progress arbitration for a certain period of time to allow an attempt to be made at mediation	Mediation is stipulated to be in accordance with the relevant mediation scheme[80]	The Institute appoints the mediator where the parties cannot agree[81]	No
City Disputes Panel[82]	The parties agree to refer the dispute to mediation before any other step is taken	Mediation is to be conducted in accordance with the City Disputes Panel Mediation Rules then in force[83]	The Centre appoints the mediator where the parties cannot agree on the appointment[84]	Yes
Commercial Mediation Centre[85]	The parties agree to refer disputes to mediation	Mediation is conducted in accordance with the Mediation Rules and Procedures of the Centre in effect at the date of the agreement[86]	The Centre appoints a mediator from the Centre's panel if the parties do not agree on an appointment[87]	No

73 See *Atkins Court Forms and Precedents*, op cit, at p 67 for the wording of the Group's clauses.

74 The ADR Group's mediation rules and mediation agreement should be reviewed to check whether, if the parties need to agree any aspect, there is a fall back provision in the case of a failure to agree.

75 See Centre for Dispute Resolution *Model ADR Contract Clauses*.

76 Accordingly, if the parties do not intend this to occur, this portion of the Model Mediation Procedure should be deleted or, as suggested in the Centre's *Model ADR Contract Clauses*, a further paragraph should be added to the mediation clause, specifying that this portion of the Model Mediation Procedure only applies if the opening presentations have been made and the mediator has seen each party for at least one hour.

77 See Parts I, II and Chapter 11 for further detail about the content of the Model Mediation Procedure.

78 The Centre suggests that a further paragraph can be added to the mediation clause, stating that the parties can vary the provisions in the Model Mediation Procedure by agreement as a way of avoiding any lack of fall back provision.

79 See *Atkins Court Forms and Precedents*, ADR Volume, at p 68.

80 For further information about the mediation schemes, see the sections on Mediation Organisations in Chapter 7 and on Consumer Disputes in Chapter 8.

81 The terms of the scheme, for example, should be reviewed, to ascertain whether there are any provisions, which require the parties to agree procedures, in circumstances where there is no fall back in the case of a failure to agree.

82 See City Disputes Panel *Members' Briefing*, 17 November 1997, for the Panel's dispute resolution clauses.

83 See Parts I and II, and Chapter 11 for further information about the content of the rules.

84 The Panel's rules and mediation agreement should be reviewed in order to ensure that no provisions require the parties to agree on procedures, in circumstances where there is no fall back provision, in case the parties fail to agree.

85 See Commercial Mediation Centre *Suggested contract provisions*.

86 See Parts I and II, and Chapter 11 for an outline of the content of the rules.

87 The Centre's mediation rules and mediation agreement should also be reviewed to

Law Society of Northern Ireland	Mediation *does not prevent the parties from commencing or pursuing litigation or arbitration*	The clause specifies that the ADR procedure is that established by the Law Society	The procedure would need to be reviewed to ensure that there are appropriate fallback provisions	Yes
London Court of International Arbitration[88]	Parties agree to mediate	The mediation is conducted in accordance with the Court's mediation procedures in force at the date of referral to mediation[89]	The Court appoints a mediator if the parties cannot agree[90]	No
World Intellectual Property Organisation[91]	Disputes are submitted to mediation	Mediation is conducted in accordance with the Organisation's mediation rules[92]	The Organisation can appoint the mediator in case of failure to agree between the parties[93]	No

It would appear, therefore, that the Academy's and ADR Group's mediation clauses are not in *Scott v Avery* form. If *Elizabeth Bay* is any guide, the ADR Group's clause does not specifically refer to or incorporate a mediation procedure. Although all the clauses provide a fall back in the case of a failure by the parties to agree on the appointment of a mediator, the rules, procedures and mediation agreements of the various organisations would need to be checked in case there are other provisions which require the parties to reach an agreement, as in the case of apportionment of mediator fees, but do not specify what is to happen if the parties cannot reach agreement. Those rules, procedures and mediation agreements also need to be checked to ensure that the parties can determine when the required procedure has been concluded. In the cases where reference is made to a good faith requirement, the Australian cases would suggest that specifying what is meant by this

---

ascertain whether there are any procedures which need to be agreed by the parties, and in respect of which there is no fall back provision in case the parties fail to agree.

88 London Court of International Arbitration *Recommended Clauses*, available at http://www.lcia-arbitration.com.

89 This may create some difficulty as it is the procedure existing at the date of the dispute, not the date of the agreement that is relevant.

90 The mediation procedure should be reviewed in order to ensure that any aspects which need to be agreed between the parties provide for a fall back provision, in case of failure to agree. Hence, the difficulty, as it is the procedure at the time of the dispute, not the agreement, which is referred to.

91 World Intellectual Property Organisation *Recommended contract clauses and submission agreements*, 1997.

92 See Parts I and II, and Chapter 11 for an outline of the content of the rules.

93 The Organisation's mediation rules should be reviewed in order to check whether other aspects of the procedure require agreement between the parties and provide for a fall back provision in case of failure to agree.

requirement, at least to show that it does not impose an agreement to reach agreement, is desirable.

Complying with mediation clauses

There is as yet no firm authority on the question of what is required of the parties in order for them to comply with the obligations in an enforceable mediation clause. It could be argued that they need to attend the mediation meeting, to disclose information to the other side, to follow the procedural directions of the mediator, to engage in constructive negotiations and to remain at the mediation until there is good cause to terminate it. In addition it might be argued that the parties should act in good faith and reasonably. However, some of these requirements would involve difficult subjective judgments to be made by outsiders to the mediation and there are other areas, such as communicating constructively and effectively, where it would be difficult to define their obligations clearly. In some situations it would be easier to deduce that parties had acted in bad faith or unreasonably, for example in sitting mute throughout the mediation, than that they had acted in good faith and reasonably. There are also practical difficulties in establishing proper compliance with mediation clauses, caused by the private and confidential nature of the process. Nevertheless, there is no reason in principle why courts or other agencies cannot, in an appropriate case, determine whether a party has complied with his obligations under the mediation clause. Each case would, of course, depend on its own facts.

In *Elizabeth Bay Developments Pty Ltd v Boral Building Services Pty Ltd*[94] the court commented on a provision that the parties would 'enter into this mediation with a commitment to attempt in good faith to negotiate towards achieving a settlement of the dispute'. Giles J had difficulties with the 'good faith' requirement, not so much in relation to ascertaining the presence or absence of good faith, but more in relation to 'the tension between negotiation, in which a party has regard to self-interest rather than the interest of the other party, and the maintenance of good faith'.[95] This approach seems to overlook the differences between unassisted, adversarial negotiations and mediated negotiations which have the potential to shift the parties towards collaborative, interest-based bargaining. As has been shown in this text, the involvement of a trained mediator can constructively transform negotiations in many ways.

Australian and English courts have not had problems with clauses requiring parties to exercise their 'best endeavours';[96] this term has been held not to impose an infinite obligation, but merely conscientious and reasonable action. It is submitted that in the light of increasing use of mediation clauses, should a dispute arise as to a party's obligation under a mediation clause, the courts will be able to develop criteria for the satisfactory compliance with obligations arising from them. For example, in an

---

94 Supreme Court of NSW, 55093/4 (1995) 26 NSWLR 709 (Giles J).
95 See *Hooper Bailie Associated Ltd v Natcon Group Pty Ltd* (1992) 28 NSWLR 194 at 209; *Coal Cliff Collieries Ltd v Sijehama Pty Ltd* (1991) 24 NSWLR 1 at 26–7; and *Walford v Miles* [1992] 2 WLR 174.
96 For example, in relation to obtaining building approvals: *Hawkins v Pender Bros Pty Ltd* [1990] 1 Qd R 135. See n 45.

Australian case based on the Native Title Act,[97] the Native Title Tribunal discussed the requirement to negotiate in good faith and found that the totality of the circumstances would be considered to determine whether or not the parties approached the negotiations with an open mind and a genuine desire to reach a settlement.[98]

Remedies for breach of mediation clauses

Where there has not been proper compliance with a mediation clause, one or other of the parties will be in breach of contract. This raises the question of what remedies there are for the breach of a mediation clause.[99] Following are the potential remedies warranting consideration:

Stay of proceedings

A stay of proceedings involves a court refusing to accept a matter for trial in the light of special circumstances raised by the defendant. Courts have a statutory power to stay proceedings brought in breach of an arbitration clause, but that power does not extend to mediation.

Courts also have a discretionary power to stay proceedings where there is a dispute resolution clause which is 'nearly an immediately effective agreement to arbitrate, albeit not quite'.[100] For example, an expert determination clause, although not an arbitration clause, has been found to come close to it.[101] In *Cott UK Ltd v FE Barber Ltd*,[102] Hergarty J explained that: [103]

> '. . . in light of the changing attitudes of our legal system, the court plainly has a jurisdiction to stay under its inherent jurisdiction, where the parties have chosen some alternative means of dispute resolution.'

Accordingly, in order for the court to exercise the discretionary power, the parties must have chosen a binding alternative dispute resolution procedure, which would not normally encompass processes like negotiation, mediation or early neutral evaluation.[104]

Apart from those powers, courts can also require compliance with certain procedures, which are condition precedent to litigation or arbitration.[105] This does not mean that a court would not have jurisdiction to hear a case: instead, in the

---

97 *Western Australia v Taylor* (1996) 134 FLR 211. The Native Title Act is an example of Australian legislation that imposes an obligation to engage in good faith negotiations.

98 D Spencer 'Case Note: complying with a requirement to negotiate in good faith' (1998) 9 *ADRJ* 226; and P Mead 'ADR agreements: good faith and enforceability' (1999) 10 *ADRJ* 40. See the section on Reasonableness of Conduct in Chapter 10.

99 M Shirley 'Breach of an ADR clause – a wrong without a remedy?' (1991) 2 *ADRJ* 117.

100 *Channel Tunnel Group Ltd v Balfour Beatty Construction Ltd* [1993] AC 334.

101 Ibid.

102 [1997] 3 All ER 540, following the earlier decision in *Channel Tunnel Group Ltd*, supra.

103 However, Hegarty J held that there were good grounds for refusing the stay based on the facts of the case. See J Lee 'Enforcing an ADR clause: Cott UK Ltd v Barber Ltd' [1999] *SJLS* 257 for a discussion of the case.

104 *Halifax Financial Services Ltd v Intuitive Systems Ltd* [1999] 1 All ER (Comm) 303.

105 *Scott v Avery* (1865) 5 HL Cas 811, 10 ER 1121.

appropriate case, it would enable the court to grant a stay. The appropriate case, in the context of mediation, would be where the mediation clause makes the mediation a condition precedent to commencing litigation or arbitration, that is, the mediation clause must be in *Scott v Avery* form.[106]

Courts have an inherent jurisdiction to stay proceedings,[107] and an additional, more general, discretion to stay proceedings in order to encourage settlement between the parties.[108] It would be possible, on this basis, for a court to stay an action to encourage the parties to attempt mediation, in circumstances where there was a mediation clause, even if it was not in *Scott v Avery* form. In the Australian case of *Hyslop v Liverpool Hospital*[109] the apparent unwillingness of the parties to make the ADR process work entailed that there was little likelihood of a successful resolution. As the court had no confidence that a stay would lead to an efficient and speedy resolution through the alternative procedure, it declined to exercise its discretion in the defendant's favour. In *Allco Steel (Queensland) Pty Ltd v Torres Strait Gold Pty Ltd*[110] a stay was also refused, inter alia, because the court considered that it would have been an exercise in futility to refer the matter to conciliation. That general discretion raises issues over art 6 of the European Convention on Human Rights, although an Australian case might give an indication of how courts might approach the matter. In *Townsend and Townsend v Coyne*,[111] Young J considered that a stay could be granted in three exceptional circumstances, where:

(a) there is an inadequate presentation of the case;
(b) it is provided for by statute; and
(c) there is an abuse of process.

In the case, the owners of the property in question were seeking to remove caveats which had been placed on land title at the 'eleventh hour' and injunction proceedings were necessary to allow settlement to take place. On these facts, there was no abuse of process to warrant the stay being granted.

Of all the potential remedies, a stay is the most feasible option where one party is in breach of a valid mediation clause. This adds to the reasons for courts to be open to granting stays in appropriate circumstances. Policy considerations support the grant of stays where the parties have freely given their consent to a mediation clause and there are no overriding considerations of public interest or private harm. However, courts will have to engage in a difficult balancing act. Should plaintiffs be obliged to participate in a process which could provide, but cannot guarantee an outcome but at a potentially higher costs and at a later date of resolution? Where courts give

---

106 Compare civil law countries, such as France, where the parties' agreement to mediate is effective as a matter of contract, eg *Peyrin v Société Polyclinique des Fleurs* (unreported, but see case comment (1997) Arb 63(4) 302).
107 For example, Supreme Court Act 1981, s 49(3) in the case of the High Court and Court of Appeal; and County Courts Act 1984, s 76 in the case of county courts (*Gore v Van der Lann* [1967] 2 QB 31). In the case of county courts, the High Court and the Court of Appeal, CPR, r 3.1(2)(f) also allows courts the power to stay proceedings generally or until a specified date/event to effect case management.
108 CPR, r 26.4.
109 Supreme Court of NSW, 3905 of 1987 (14 October 1987, unreported) (Hodgson J).
110 Supreme Court of QLD, 2742 of 1989 (12 March 1990, unreported) (Master Horton).
111 Supreme Court of NSW Equity Division, 002023/95 (26 April 1995, unreported) (Young J).

preference to the former interests by granting a stay, they would be indirectly enforcing the mediation clause.

Specific performance

Specific performance is a remedy for breach of contract in which the court orders a contracting party to carry out the obligations agreed to, for example for a vendor to make delivery of a specific commodity to a purchaser. Specific performance is an equitable remedy which is ordered in the discretion of the court. In relation to mediation clauses, the question arises as to whether a court could order a party to participate in a mediation. There are a number of potential problems in relation to the grant of this remedy. Specific performance will not be ordered where there is a close personal relationship between the parties and it would be difficult for the court to supervise performance, as is the case with mediation. Equitable principles also decree that the courts will not issue futile orders or orders which they cannot enforce. A court is also unlikely to order specific performance where the supervision of performance would be impossible.[112] However, if damages would be an inadequate remedy the courts could, on equitable principles, consider an order for specific performance.

Damages

An award of damages is another possible remedy for the breach of a mediation clause. Damages in contract are designed to put plaintiffs in the position they would have been in had the defendant carried out its contractual obligations. A major difficulty in relation to mediation clauses is that it is only possible to speculate on what position the plaintiff would have been in had the mediation clause been complied with. It is not only uncertain whether there would have been a successful outcome, but the terms of that outcome are impossible to determine. Moreover, the injury flowing from a breach might be so unique that damages could not constitute an adequate remedy.[113] A mediation clause could include a genuine pre-estimate of damages which would be suffered by either party in the event of a breach. Provided that such a pre-estimate did not constitute a penalty, this arrangement might allow an action for liquidated damages. However, there are likely to be difficulties in obtaining a court award of damages for breach of a mediation clause.

Non-binding mediation clauses

In the legal view of the world, the value of mediation clauses is measured mainly in terms of their enforceability in law. However, even if mediation clauses are not enforceable by the courts, they can still serve useful purposes and there might be advantages in including them in agreements.[114] The parties may agree, in full awareness of enforceability problems, on a clause which requires them to consider mediation at the time when a dispute arises.[115] The inclusion of such clauses will

---

112 R Angyal 'Enforceability of agreements to mediate' in G Raftesath and S Thaler (eds) *Cases for Mediation*, Sydney LBC Information Services, 1999, at p 7.
113 M Shirley 'Breach of an ADR clause – a wrong without a remedy?' (1991) 2 *ADRJ* 117 at 118.
114 M Pryles 'Dispute Resolution Clauses in Contracts' (1990) 1 *ADRJ* 116 at 118.
115 See, for example, Academy of Experts clause, in table above.

focus attention on the possibility of a non-litigious remedy, and within a particular industry there may be powerful extra-legal inducements to comply with them. Moreover, a party who suggests settlement of a dispute through negotiation or mediation might be suspected of having a weak case, which is less likely to be the case where the party seeks to activate an existing dispute resolution clause.[116]

Agreements to Mediate

Most private mediators require parties to sign a contract, here called an Agreement to Mediate, before they commence work on the mediation. Most Agreements to Mediate deal with the appointment of the mediator, the conduct and procedure of the mediation, matters of confidentiality, the roles of the parties and mediator, the mediator's fee arrangements, and matters of liability and indemnity. Terms can also be implied into Agreements to Mediate. Because of the many different views and understandings of the essential nature of mediation and the mediator's position, it is advisable for the Agreement to Mediate to make some reference to the roles and functions of the mediator. The mediator may, for example, be required to perform multiple functions, including some beyond the scope of those normally associated with mediation.[117] It is also advisable for the Agreement to Mediate to refer to the procedures which will be followed, or to incorporate standard rules developed by mediation organisations providing mediation services. Another issue which should be dealt with in the Agreement to Mediate is the status of agreements reached at the mediation. In one Australian commercial mediation, agreement was reached by the parties but was not reduced to writing and there was later a dispute as to whether it was a term of the mediation that agreement would not be final until it was in written form.[118]

If the mediator does not comply with the Agreement to Mediate, either party might have a remedy for breach of contract. However, to pursue this remedy the party would have to institute legal proceedings, which is what it was attempting to avoid in the first place. This strategy would also not assist in resolving the original dispute.[119] The parties may therefore wish to specify the grounds and procedures for removal of the mediator in the Agreement to Mediate.

Disclosure and Evidence

The litigation process allows each party to secure the disclosure of documents and other information in the possession of the other party. This is designed to assist the parties in the preparation of their respective cases and to avoid surprises at trial.

---

116 M Pryles 'Dispute Resolution Clauses in Contracts' (1990) 1 *ADRJ* 116 at 119.
117 The CEDR Model Mediation Procedure recognises that the parties may agree to a non-binding evaluation. In an Australian example, the mediator in a construction case can act as mediator or conciliator, to conduct a mini-trial, and to make recommendations to the parties: 'J Tyrril, New ADR Agreement' (1993) 31 *Australian Construction Law Newsletter* 26–9.
118 The mediator was subpoenaed to testify as to the terms and conditions of the mediation. See also below, on enforcement of mediated settlement agreements.
119 H Astor and C Chinkin *Dispute Resolution in Australia*, Butterworths, Sydney, 1992, at p 203.

Where there is a dispute over access to specific documents or information, the court can, in appropriate circumstances, order its production and exchange. Generally speaking, mediation does not provide the same legal mechanisms for ensuring the disclosure of relevant information. Even in 'institutionalised' forms of mediation, the mediator is given no power to order the disclosure of documents. This is consistent with the voluntary nature of mediation.

It should be noted that there may be situations where a material non-disclosure of information may vitiate a mediated settlement agreement. Examples include situations where the non-disclosure distorts a positive assertion so as to make it a misrepresentation, where the agreement requires uberrima fides, and where a fiduciary relationship exists between the contracting parties. Although the legal validity of a mediated agreement may be challenged on these grounds, such a remedy only operates after the mediation and is less attractive than legal mechanisms for ensuring disclosure before the mediation takes place.

As regards evidence at the mediation meeting, the question arises as to whether the formal rules of evidence enforced by courts and tribunals have any application in mediation. The rules of evidence are designed to promote reliability, fairness and quality in the presentation of documents and oral testimony to courts. They exclude some categories of evidence on policy grounds and compel witnesses to testify on what they have heard and seen themselves and not to report on what they have heard from others. In mediation there are no restrictions on what parties can say or on which documents they can produce. As regards the breadth of 'evidence', mediation has a very broad notion of relevance. As regards the accuracy of evidence, mediation does not exclude hearsay evidence, as mediation is not concerned with resolving issues of fact or assessing credibility. In other words, the formal rules of evidence do not apply to mediation.

Confidentiality in Mediation

The role of confidentiality in mediation

Mediation is often promoted as being confidential and privileged. The confidentiality of mediation is justified in terms of several factors.[120] The first is that it makes mediation attractive to potential users who wish to avoid publicity, and increases the willingness of parties to enter into it in the knowledge that any disclosures cannot be used against them subsequently. The second is that confidentiality can make mediation more effective by encouraging the parties to be frank and to disclose their real needs and interests, which promotes the prospects of settlement. The third is that it protects the reputation of mediators and reinforces their impartiality by excluding them from pressure to make disclosures during or after the mediation. In reality, however, mediation is not as confidential as it is sometimes claimed to be.

There are two levels of confidentiality in the mediation process. The first is in relation to the separate meetings between mediators and the individual parties.[121] Here it is

---

120 F Crosbie 'Aspects of confidentiality in mediation: a matter of balancing competing public interests' (1995) 2 *CDRJ* 51.
121 See Institute of Civil Engineers *Conciliation Procedure*; Centre for Business Arbitration

claimed that confidentiality induces candour and frankness and provides a safe environment for each party to reveal and reflect on their fundamental concerns.[122] This confidentiality obligation constrains only the mediator and the relevant party or parties can waive their rights.[123] The second is in relation to the mediation process as a whole, in respect of which both the mediator and the parties have obligations.[124] This confidentiality is designed to prevent publicity for mediation proceedings and to avoid adverse consequences for the parties in respect of disclosures they might have made. Confidentiality problems could arise in three sets of circumstances:[125]

(a) where one of the parties to the mediation attempts to refer to what transpired in the mediation for use in a court or other setting outside the mediation;

(b) where a third party, including a court or tribunal, seeks disclosure through the mediator or a party or by attempting to access mediation documents; and

(c) where the mediator wishes to disclose on a voluntary basis.

As a matter of law, practice and policy, confidentiality in mediation is not a straightforward matter.[126] Here the subject is looked at in terms of common law privileges, contractual principles, equitable doctrines and statutory regulation.

Common law privileges

Without prejudice privilege

Generally, at common law, oral and written statements made on a 'without prejudice' basis during negotiations towards the settlement of a dispute are inadmissible in subsequent court proceedings relating to the same subject matter.

The rationale for this privilege is the desirability of resolving disputes and minimising litigation, as well as a recognition that such communications have little probative value, but are highly prejudicial. In *Cutts v Head*, Oliver LJ explained the rationale in the following way:

'. . . the parties should be encouraged as far as possible to settle their disputes without resort to litigation. They are not to be discouraged by the knowledge that anything that is said in the course of such negotiations (and that includes . . . as much of the failure to reply to an offer as an actual reply) may be used to their prejudice in the course of the proceedings. They should . . . be encouraged freely and frankly to put their cards on the table.'[127]

---

and Mediation *Rules*; and ADR Group *Agreement to Mediate*. On the nature and functions of separate meetings, see Chapter 4.

122 See, for example, H Astor 'Mediation in intra-lesbian disputes' (1999) 20 *Melbourne University Law Review* 953.

123 Some mediators stipulate in their mediation agreement that the mediator has a discretion to disclose any information revealed in the separate meetings.

124 For example, Centre for Dispute Resolution *Code of Conduct*.

125 M Shirley and W Harris 'Confidentiality in court-annexed mediation – fact or fallacy?' (1993) 13 *Queensland Lawyer* 221 at 223.

126 For another discussion on the extent of the confidentiality in mediation, see L Harman, 'Confidentiality in mediation' in G Raftesath and S Thaler (eds) *Cases for Mediation*, Sydney LBC Information Services, 1999, at p 29; and Atkin Chambers 'Confidentiality in arbitration and mediation' (2000) 14 *Commercial Law Journal* 2.

127 [1984] Ch 290 at 306.

The House of Lords, in *Rush & Tompkins Ltd v Greater London Council*, reinforced the public policy consideration of encouraging litigants to settle their disputes rather than to litigate them. Lord Griffiths explained:

'... the without prejudice rule renders inadmissible in any subsequent litigation connected with the same subject matter proof of any admissions made in a genuine attempt to reach a settlement ... It goes without saying that admissions made to reach a settlement with a different party within the same litigation are also inadmissible whether or not settlement was reached with that party ... The public policy that applies to protect general nego-tiations from being admissible in evidence should also be extended to protect those negotiations from being discoverable to third parties ...' [128]

Several propositions may be canvassed about the without prejudice privilege:

(1) The privilege only applies to communications made when there is a dispute or there are ongoing negotiations between the parties.

(2) The privilege may only be claimed by the parties to the without prejudice negotiations and their solicitors. If a party took no part in the without prejudice negotiations, either personally or through an agent, he cannot claim the privilege.

(3) Where the negotiations conducted without prejudice lead to a settlement, the agreement that results from a mediation is not itself privileged,[129] unless the agreement is incorporated in another document. Subject to Scottish legis-lation, in the context of family mediation, discussed below, parties can agree that reference to documentation used in the mediation will be precluded, even after a settlement has been reached.[130] Accordingly, a mediator should remind the parties that, unless the mediation agreement provides otherwise, privilege does not extend to the provisions of any settlement agreement and that the extent of disclosure of the resulting settlement is best provided for in the agreement itself.[131]

(4) Correspondence that is not marked 'without prejudice' may nevertheless be privileged if it forms part of a course of without prejudice negotiations, for instance, where some of the communications were marked 'without prejudice'. However, where there is no evidence that the parties wrote or intended the correspondence to be written on a without prejudice basis, and there is a dispute as to whether the parties intended the negotiations to be without prejudice, the correspondence may not be protected by the without prejudice privilege in the absence of a without prejudice marking.

---

128 [1989] AC 1280 at 1299.

129 *Rush & Tompkins Ltd v Greater London Council* [1989] AC 1280, [1988] 3 All ER 737, although the discussions which led to that outcome would remain confidential and without prejudice.

130 Centre for Dispute Resolution *Model Mediation Procedure* provides that 'all information produced for or arising out of a mediation, including the agreement reached, is confidential except as necessary to enforce that agreement'. The International Chamber of Commerce *Rules of Optional Conciliation* provide that 'the agreement reached is confidential unless its execution requires disclosure'; the Commercial Mediation Centre *Appointment of Mediator* states that 'other than the final agreement, information prepared for or given in the mediation can only be used for the mediation'; and the City Disputes Panel *Mediation Rules* provide that 'all information is confidential, except disclosure necessary to enforce the agreement reached'.

131 See, for example, the Law Society England & Wales *Code of Practice for Civil/Commercial Mediation*.

(5) Conversely, a without prejudice marking does not necessarily render a document privileged. Where the privilege is challenged, the court may examine the document to determine whether the conditions for the privilege to apply do in fact exist.[132]

(6) Even if the contents of without prejudice correspondence are not admissible in evidence, the fact that such correspondence existed is admissible to show that negotiations had taken place, and is the subject of disclosure.[133]

(7) The issue arises whether an offer made in the course of without prejudice discussions is admissible on the issue of costs. Robert Walker LJ in *Unilever v Procter & Gamble* considered, in the light of *Cutts v Head* and *Calderbank v Calderbank*, that it was not.[134] He did not accept arguments that, in such a case, the offer is not sought to be used as an admission of liability. Whilst acknowledging that the public policy aspect of the without prejudice rule was not concerned with the admissibility of statements which are relevant otherwise than as admissions, he considered that practical difficulties would occur if it was necessary to dissect identifiable admissions and withhold protection from the rest of a without prejudice communication, unless there is a special reason to do so, and that accordingly the concept of admissions should be given a wide meaning to include all matters disclosed or discussed in the without prejudice discussions. As Robert Walker LJ had referred to Part 44 of the Civil Procedure Rules ('CPR'), which allows courts to have regard to the conduct of the parties before and during proceedings on the issue of costs, he was not persuaded that this Part allowed offers made in the course of without prejudice discussions to be taken into account on the issue of costs. CPR, Part 36 governs the effect of without prejudice offers on the costs issue, and CPR, r 48.7(3) provides that disclosure of privileged material may be ordered by a court when considering a wasted costs order.

Australian case law has confirmed that the without prejudice privilege applies to mediation,[135] even if a mediation is conducted for the purpose of resolving only part of a dispute.[136] The rationale is that parties would be disinclined to agree to mediate where information obtained during the mediation could later be used against them in litigation if the mediation were unsuccessful. Although the UK case law has not specifically confirmed that the without prejudice privilege applies to mediation,[137] as a form of negotiation or attempt to settle a dispute, it falls clearly within the contemplation of the without prejudice rule. Standard form mediation agreements also typically provide that the mediation shall be conducted on a without prejudice basis.[138]

---

132 *South Shropshire District Council v Amos* [1987] 1 All ER 340.

133 *Parry v News Group Newspapers Ltd* [1990] 140 NLJR 1719.

134 [2000] FSR 433; *Cutts v Head* [1984] Ch 290 per Oliver and Fox LLJ; and *Calderbank v Calderbank* [1976] Fam 93.

135 *AWA Ltd v Daniels (t/a Deloitte Haskins & Sells)* (1992) 7 ACSR 463 (Rolfe J and Rogers CJ).

136 *Lukies v Ripley (No 2)* (1994) 35 NSWLR 283.

137 *Instance v Denny Bros Printing Ltd* [2000] 05 LS Gaz R 35 raised issues of mediation confidentiality, as to which see the next section. Lloyd J avoided deciding the third party point decided in the Australian *Village Nine* case on the basis that the entities in question, although not parties to the negotiations, were 'related or connected to them'.

138 The City Disputes Panel *Mediation Rules* provide that 'mediation is conducted on the same basis as without prejudice negotiations in an action in the courts of England and

The privilege is not, however, absolute and resort may be had to without prejudice material for a variety of reasons where the justice of the case requires it. The privilege may not apply where provision is made, expressly or impliedly, for the parties to report progress to outside constituents, for example, in the mediation of public policy disputes where there is a need to report to and involve outsiders to the mediation. The privilege, in relation to mediation, will also be subject to all the common law and statutory limitations,[139] which provide a number of exceptions to the privilege.[140] The public interest may justify admissibility, for example, in cases of impropriety by a party, such as lack of good faith, misrepresentations, defamation, threats or blackmail.[141] The privilege would not ordinarily apply where the communication indicates that any person is suffering or likely to suffer serious harm.[142] Considerations of child welfare also override the rule protecting privileged communications.[143] The rules of evidence can also render the privilege inapplicable.

Wales or Scotland or Northern Ireland'; The London Court of International Arbitration *Mediation Procedure* provides that the 'mediation process, negotiations, statements, documents prepared for mediation are confidential and covered by the without prejudice privilege'; the Centre for Business Arbitration *Mediation Rules* state that 'without consent, no party or the mediator can use anything said during the mediation or any information concerning or obtained in the course of the mediation outside the mediation'; the ADR Group's *Agreement to Mediate* provides that 'documents and information produced for or given in the mediation is confidential and shall be used only for the mediation'; the World Intellectual Property Organisation *Mediation Rules* state that 'unless agreed by the parties, there can be no introduction into evidence of any views expressed in relation to settlement, and in admissions made in the course of the mediation, any proposals made by the mediator and any willingness to accept any proposal'; the Institute of Civil Engineers *Conciliation Procedure* provides that 'conciliation proceedings are without prejudice . . . nothing disclosed may be used as evidence in subsequent proceedings'; the International Chamber of Commerce *Rules of Optional Conciliation* state that 'parties will not in any later proceedings introduce any views expressed in relation to possible settlement and any proposals put forward by the conciliator'; the Commercial Mediation Centre *Mediation Rules* and *Procedure* provide that 'any information in a mediation will not affect the rights or prejudice the position of the parties in any subsequent litigation'; the Chartered Institute of Arbitrators *Rules of the Consumer Dispute Resolution Scheme* set out that the 'conciliator cannot be required to disclose any information obtained in the mediation'; and the Centre for Dispute Resolution *Model Mediation Procedure* provides that 'all information provided for the mediation is 'without prejudice' and not admissible as evidence or discoverable in any litigation or arbitration relating to the dispute'.

139 See Criminal Evidence Act 1898 and Civil Evidence Act 1968 for statutory exceptions.
140 For a detailed discussion of common law exceptions, see Robert Walker LJ in *Unilever plc v Procter & Gamble Co* [1999] 2 All ER 691; and to D Foskett *The Law and Practice of Compromise* (4th edn), Sweet & Maxwell, London, 1996.
141 *Re Daintrey, ex p Holt* [1893] 2 QB 116; *Kitcat v Sharp* (1882) 48 LT 64; *Rush & Tompkins Ltd v Greater London Council* [1989] AC 1280, [1988] 3 All ER 737 at 1300; *Forster v Friedland* (10 November 1992, unreported), Court of Appeal, Civil Division, Transcript no 1052 at p 5; *W v Egdell* [1990] Ch 359; and see generally Foskett *The Law and Practice of Compromise* (4th edn), Sweet & Maxwell, London, 1999, at p 152. But not to prove that what was said at trial is untrue: see *UYB Ltd v British Railways Board* [2000] 43 LS Gaz R 37, CA.
142 See, for example, the Law Society of England & Wales *Code of Practice the Civil/Commercial Mediation* and also for *Family Mediation*.
143 In the Australian case, *Hutchings v Clarke* (1993) 113 ALR 709, an admission by a

As the privilege belongs to the parties jointly, it can be waived by the parties expressly or otherwise in legal proceedings,[144] in which case a mediator could be compelled to testify.[145]

The law in this area is not static. The readiness of the courts to extend the scope of the without prejudice privilege in appropriate circumstances has potential implications for mediation. In *Lukies v Ripley (No 2)*,[146] the parties entered negotiations with the aim of reducing the scope of litigation, rather than with the aim of settling the dispute. The court extended the without prejudice privilege to cover this situation. This judgment has relevance for what is referred to in this book as 'scoping mediation'.

There is some controversy as to whether the without prejudice privilege is available against interested parties other than those to a negotiated agreement, particularly where they are parties in the same dispute. This situation may arise in a multi-party mediation where some parties have reached agreement without the knowledge of others, and the latter seek access to information about the mediation to assist them in preparing for litigation. It may, for instance, arise in a construction dispute where the main contractor reaches a mediated settlement with the owner, and sub-contractors subsequently apply to court for disclosure of information about the weight which their claims carried in the mediation in order to further their claims against the contractor.

In *Rush & Tompkins Ltd v Greater London Council*,[147] the House of Lords, in a case with similar facts (except that the settlement was arrived at through without prejudice negotiations instead of mediation), held as follows:

(1) The application of the without prejudice rule was not dependent on the use of the phrase 'without prejudice', and if it was clear from the surrounding circumstances that the parties were seeking to compromise the action, evidence of the content of the negotiations would, as a general rule, not be admissible at the trial and cannot be used to establish an admission or partial admission.

(2) Without prejudice correspondence entered into with the object of effecting the compromise of an action remained privileged after the compromise had been reached and, accordingly, the correspondence between the owner and the main contractor was inadmissible in any subsequent litigation connected with the same subject matter, whether between the same or different parties, and was protected from subsequent discovery even by other parties to the same litigation.

---

father during a without prejudice settlement discussion that his motives for seeking custody was to avoid paying child support was admissible.

144 For example, when a document or part of a document is deployed in an interim application or at trial: see *Great Atlantic Insurance Co v Home Insurance Co* [1981] 1 WLR 529; *Derby & Co Ltd v Weldon (No 10)* [1991] 1 WLR 660; *and Somatra Ltd v Sinclair Roche & Temperley (a firm)* [2000] 1 WLR 2453, per Waller J, and available at http://uk.law.com/cgi-bin/gx.cgi

145 *Re D (minors)* [1993] 1 FLR 933; C Tapper *Cross and Tapper on Evidence* (9th edn), Butterworths, London, 1999, at pp 467–70; and D Parker and L Parkinson 'Solicitors and Family Conciliation Services: Basis for Professional Co-operation' (1985) 15 *Family Law* 273.

146 (1994) 35 NSWLR 283.

147 [1989] AC 1280, [1988] 3 All ER 737.

(3) Following from this, the sub-contractors were not entitled to discovery of the without prejudice correspondence which had passed between the owner and the main contractor.

The most recent Australian decision, on the without prejudice privilege, extended the principle to prevent disclosure of documents, provided in a mediation, as against a party who did not participate in the mediation.[148]

An illustration of the limitations on the without prejudice privilege is provided by the Australian case of *AWA Ltd v Daniels (t/a Deloitte Haskins and Sells)*, supra. This matter was referred to mediation by the trial judge, Rogers CJ (Comm Div), with the consent of the parties, after 12 days of trial. The mediation was unsuccessful and was followed by two interlocutory judgments. AWA Ltd had brought proceedings against its auditors for allegedly failing to audit its accounts properly. In the mediation process AWA Ltd disclosed the existence of a document containing a full indemnity for its directors in respect of the legal proceedings. When litigation resumed, the auditors served a notice to produce on AWA Ltd to obtain the indemnity deed, and AWA Ltd relied on the fact that the mediation had been conducted on a without prejudice basis. Rolfe J examined the relevant authorities and competing policy considerations and held that the privilege did not apply as the auditors were only seeking to prove a fact which was referred to in the mediation.

On a broad reading, this judgment implies that evidence as to something discussed or disclosed at a mediation meeting will not be excluded where it can be proved by independent evidence before a court or tribunal. Source documents will not be protected from discovery where these are referred to in mediation. A party may serve a notice to admit, an interrogatory, or a notice for disclosure in respect of admissions made or documents disclosed, although the actual statement made at mediation cannot itself be referred to. So merely because facts are referred to or documents are produced in mediation does not render them inadmissible if they are otherwise admissible. As Shirley and Harris point out, if a party approaches a mediation as a pre-trial fishing expedition and its opponent makes revelations of fact, there is nothing to prevent the strategic use of the information to the disclosing party's detriment at trial.[149]

When the hearing in the *AWA Ltd v Daniels* case resumed, the auditors sought to tender in evidence the indemnity deed which AWA Ltd had produced. When this was opposed, the trial judge ruled the document admissible, but approached the matter differently from Rolfe J. Rogers CJ found that the prior High Court judgments were not directly applicable, but came to the same conclusion as Rolfe J on the grounds that the evidence showed that the auditors were aware of the existence of the deed before the mediation, and that it could, and should, have been disclosed previously by AWA Ltd. This approach limits the precedent value of the

---

148 *Mercantile Mutual Custodians Pty Ltd v Village/Nine Network Restaurants & Bars* [1999] QCA 276, Court of Appeal, Queensland where Byrne J cited English case law in support, in particular Lord Griffiths in *Rush & Tompkins Ltd v Greater London Council* [1989] AC 1280 at 1305, Professor Leonard in *The New Wigmore* (at 3:67) and Hobhouse J in *Prudential Assurance Co Ltd v Fountain Page Ltd* [1991] 1 WLR 756 at 771. Leave to appeal to the High Court was refused: High Court of Australia, 21 June 2000.

149 M Shirley and W Harris 'Confidentiality in court-annexed mediation: fact or fallacy?' (1993) 13 *QLD Lawyer* 221 at 223.

judgment to its peculiar facts. Rogers CJ, moreover, conceded that on other facts he would have been more inclined to extend protection by finding the privilege applicable. He also said that the position might be different if the evidence sought to be admitted is of an objective fact about which the party has no inkling or which would not ordinarily come to the knowledge of that party in the normal course of litigation and the existence of which was only revealed by a statement made in the course of and for the purpose of the mediation.

Legal professional privilege

Generally, confidential communications made between a lawyer and his client are privileged if they arose in the course of and for the purpose of giving or obtaining legal advice. Communications made between the client and third parties may also attract privilege if the communications were made for the dominant purpose of obtaining legal advice in connection with on-going litigation.[150] The policies behind this privilege are to allow clients and their lawyers to speak freely, with confidence and trust, and without fear of being forced to disclose the nature of their confidential communications, and to encourage the use of lawyers by disputing parties.

As the foundation of this privilege extends from the principle that a client should be entitled to obtain legal advice in confidence, for a document to attract this privilege, the party asserting the privilege must prove that the dominant purpose of the communications was to obtain legal advice.[151] A strong suggestion of any other equal or more dominant purpose than to seek legal advice would, in itself, be fatal to a claim for privilege in respect of the document.

This privilege, like the without prejudice privilege, is subject to exceptions.[152] It does not apply to any communication made in furtherance of any illegal purpose.[153] Nor does it apply to any fact observed by the lawyer showing that a crime or fraud has been committed since the commencement of the lawyer's involvement. The privilege is intended for the protection of the client, so the lawyer may disclose the communications with his client's express consent. It can also be waived by a party making an intended or unintended disclosure,[154] and if the client brings a claim against his lawyer in respect of the advice.[155]

Legal professional privilege applies in relation to judicial, administrative and other proceedings in which persons can be compelled to produce information. It has been suggested that the first limb of the privilege, communications created for the purpose of giving or obtaining legal advice, would attach to work prepared by lawyers for

---

150 *Greenough v Gaskell* (1833) 1 My & K 98 at 103; and *Crompton (Alfred) Amusements Machines Ltd v Customs and Excise Comrs* [1972] 2 QB 102.
151 *Waugh v British Railways Board* [1980] AC 521, where the House of Lords rejected the High Court of Australia's 'sole use' test in *Grant v Downs* (1976) 135 CLR 674 in favour of Barwick CJ's approach in that case.
152 For example, *Derby & Co Ltd v Weldon (No 7)* [1990] 1 WLR 1156.
153 *R v Cox and Raitton* (1884) 14 QBD 153.
154 *Guiness Peat Properties Ltd v Fitzroy Robinson Partnership (a firm)* [1987] 2 All ER 716.
155 *Ridehaulgh v Horsefield* [1994] Ch 205.

clients in mediation.[156] Policy should also support an extension of the privilege to mediation as this acknowledges a broader conception of justice than that provided by litigation. It can also be argued that the second limb should apply to court-connected mediation.

In the context of mediation, the question arises as to whether the disclosure to the mediator of documents such as legal opinions, which would otherwise be privileged, could constitute such a waiver. This could be a problem where mediation rules and agreements allow the mediator to call for documents from the parties. If it does amount to a waiver, the other side could demand the production of the documents if the mediation was unsuccessful and the matter went to trial. One basis for arguing that the privilege is waived is that the mediator is, for some purposes, the agent of each party, but this argument would be difficult to sustain. The better view is that the parties make disclosure to mediators for only a limited purpose, namely to assist them to facilitate the decision-making process, and this should not amount to a waiver of the privilege. Public policy would also support the retention of the privilege in these circumstances, since the contrary approach would unravel the confidentiality for both parties and place mediators in invidious positions.

Marital privilege

In relation to family mediation in the UK, privilege was initially accorded to communications between a mediator and the parties where the purpose of the communication was designed to effect a reconciliation of the parties.[157] The privilege attached to family conciliators because they were attempting reconciliation and not because of their standing as conciliators,[158] the rationale being that there can be no chance of reconciliation unless the parties are able to talk with frankness to the conciliator and with complete confidence that what they said would not be disclosed.[159] As the privilege was a form of public interest privilege, the public interest being the preservation of marriage, the privilege could be overridden by another public interest, such as the protection of a child.

Lord Hailsham LC suggested that the categories of public interest privilege are not closed and alter over time as social conditions develop.[160] In 1971 a Practice Direction issued by the President of the Family Division of the High Court provided that both reconciliation and conciliation negotiations should be legally privileged.[161] A further Practice Direction in 1982 provided that discussions at conciliation appointments before a registrar and at private meetings with the court welfare officer should be privileged.[162] These Practice Directions did not, however, extend privilege to conciliation that was not part of court proceedings. Although the Booth Committee recommended that conciliation in family disputes should be absolutely

---

156 F Crosbie 'Aspects of confidentiality in mediation: a matter of balancing competing public interests' (1995) 2 *CDRJ* 51.
157 *Henley v Henley* [1955] 1 All ER 590n; *Theodoropoulos v Theodoropoulos* [1963] 2 All ER 772; and *Pais v Pais* [1970] 3 All ER 491.
158 Sir Jocelyn Simon P in *Theodoropoulos v Theodoropoulos*, supra.
159 Denning LJ in *McTaggart v McTaggart* [1948] 2 All ER 754.
160 *D v NSPCC* [1978] AC 171 at 230.
161 Practice Direction [1971] 1 All ER 894.
162 Practice Direction [1982] 3 All ER 988.

privileged,[163] it was only in 1993 that case law clarified the issue of privilege in family mediation where reconciliation was not an issue, by extending privilege to mediation where reconciliation was not the purpose of the negotiations, provided that the discussions related to matrimonial disputes over children in proceedings under the Children Act 1989.[164] The privilege is subject to the public interest in protecting the child's interests.[165] It would not apply, therefore, where the maker of the statement has caused or is likely to cause harm to a child.[166] In relation to communications in family mediation relating to matters other than children and reconciliation, the general without prejudice privilege will need to be relied upon.

Codes of family mediator practice typically provide that family mediators should ensure that parties agree that any factual disclosure made in the mediation with a view to resolving any other issue, for instance, relating to property and finances, may be disclosed in legal proceedings.[167]

In Scotland, protection in family mediation is afforded by statute, and is discussed further below.

A privilege for mediation or mediators?

At present the law extends the without prejudice privilege only to the parties in mediation. The mediation process enjoys no privileges over and above the other common law and statutory privileges. However, the categories of privilege are not closed, and the breadth of existing categories can be extended. Currently there is also no specific privilege for mediators, and there is no authority for extending the without prejudice privilege to those, such as mediators, who assist negotiations between parties.[168] The traditional view is that mediators have no sufficient interest to afford them this benefit. This means that, in the absence of any statutory or contractual protection, mediators would be compellable witnesses and would have little protection if subpoenaed. Although mediation agreements may provide that the parties will not call the mediator, or that the mediator cannot act as a witness in any action over matters in dispute following the mediation,[169] in one Australian case,

---

163 Booth Committee *Report of the Committee on Matrimonial Causes*, HMSO, London, 1985, para 4.60.

164 *Re D (minors)* [1993] 1 FLR 933, where the Court of Appeal considered the issue of privilege, in a case where a mother wished to file evidence from a psychologist who had mediated between her and the father of the child.

165 Compare *Re E C (Disclosure of Material)* [1996] 2 FLR 123, were disclosure made in proceedings relating to children, admitting to causing the death of a child, was not disclosed to the police. The court found that the public interest in promoting disclosure outweighed other interests.

166 *Re D (minors)*, supra. See also C Tapper *Cross and Tapper on Evidence*, op cit, at pp 470–1.

167 For example, Codes of Conduct issued by the Law Society of England & Wales, Law Wise, NFM, FMA, the UK College of Family Mediators and CALM (Scotland).

168 In Helen Garner's book, *The First Stone: some questions about sex and power*, Picador, Sydney, 1995, the author refers to a conciliator involved in an allegation of sexual harassment who was subpoenaed and gave evidence in a criminal trial without any apparent question of privilege being raised. In the UK the Law Reform Committee has not supported a privilege for court welfare officers who conciliate: *16th Report*, at paras 39 and 40.

169 The International Chamber of Commerce *Optional Conciliation Rules* provide that the

notwithstanding such an agreement, the mediator was subpoenaed to attend a court hearing and was required to testify.[170] An English district judge took the opposite view in *Bezant v Ushers Brewer* (Bristol County Court, Stuart Brown DJ, 1997). In Belgium, Sweden and Italy, a lawyer who has acted as a mediator is able to invoke confidentiality provisions in subsequent litigation; however, non-lawyers who act as mediators may be required to testify about what occurred in the mediation. In Germany, parties can agree not to call the mediator as a witness, and that agreement will be upheld in civil courts and in arbitrations, but not in administrative and criminal courts.

The policies underlying other privileges could be extended to mediators.[171] One argument in favour of extending privilege is that it would avoid credibility conflicts between the parties and mediators.[172] In the US, courts have used the public interest rationale to allow a mediator to object to testifying.[173] US commentators justify the approach on the basis that it is essential to the proper functioning of mediation.[174] One of the implications of extending the privilege to mediators is that the consent of both the mediator and the parties would be required to waive the privilege.

As regards mediators' notes, in *Knight v Truss-Michaelis and Truss-Michaelis*[175] the plaintiff applied for an order that the Legal Aid Office of Queensland provide for inspection all books, records, files and notes in its possession with respect to a mediation conference held on its premises. The mediator had specifically advised the parties at the commencement of the mediation that his notes would not be made available to them. However, the plaintiff's application was based on the argument that a compromise had been reached at the mediation and that access to the documents was necessary to confirm the fact and terms of the compromise on which the plaintiff wanted to sue. In granting the order, Pratt DCJ acknowledged that disclosure would 'strike at the very heart of the mediation system', but he held that here it was necessary to use the evidence to explain the intention of the parties to the written compromise. One way of avoiding the consequences of this approach would be to make it a condition of mediation that any agreement reached will not be

---

parties 'will not call the conciliator as a witness in any later proceedings unless agreed between them'; the Academy of Experts *Code of Conduct* provides that the mediator 'must refuse to act as a witness, advocate or adviser for any party in any later action over matters in dispute in the mediation'; the ADR Group *Agreement to Mediate* sets out that the parties 'cannot subpoena . . . the mediator to testify or produce records, notes or information in later proceedings'; the Centre for Dispute Resolution *Model Mediation Procedure* provides that the mediator 'cannot be called as a witness, consultant, arbitrator or expert in any litigation or arbitration in relation to the dispute'; and the Center for Public Resources *Model Mediation Procedure for Business Disputes in Europe* provides that the mediator 'cannot be a witness, consultant or expert in any proceeding relating to the subject matter of the mediation'.

170 *Commonwealth Bank of Australia v McDonnell* (24 July 1997, unreported) New South Wales Supreme Court (Rolfe J).

171 See the statement of policy in *Rush & Tompkins Ltd v Greater London Council* [1989] AC 1280, [1988] 3 All ER 737 at 739.

172 See H Brown and A Marriott *ADR Principles and Practice* (2nd edn), Sweet & Maxwell, London, 1999, at pp 501–4.

173 For example, *NLRB v Macaluso* 618 F 2d 51 (9th Cir 1980).

174 J McCrory 'Confidentiality in mediation of matrimonial disputes' (1988) 51 *MLR* 442.

175 (14 April 1993, unreported) District Court of QLD (Pratt DCJ); and G Clarke et al 'Dispute Resolution' (1993–4) *Queensland Annual Law Review* 78–9.

enforceable until it has been reduced to writing and signed by the parties.[176] This has indeed been the approach adopted in the UK by a number of mediation organisations.[177]

The wider issue is whether there is or should be privilege attaching to the whole mediation process.[178] There are a number of arguments in favour of this approach. The willingness of parties to attempt a mediation is often attributed to its without prejudice nature. This characteristic encourages a candid flow of information in mediation.[179] Critics suggest that a degree of scrutiny encourages good faith negotiations and discourages attempts to use the process cynically, although some mediation programmes in the US have reported high settlement rates, even in the absence of privilege.[180] Developments in relation to the public interest privilege could have implications for mediation. This privilege[181] excludes otherwise relevant evidence from being admitted in court proceedings if its disclosure would be prejudicial or injurious to the public interest. Traditionally this privilege has been restricted to matters of national security or the proper running of government at the highest level. However, the categories of public interest privilege are not closed and can change over time according to prevailing views of the public interest. There have been extensions of the privilege to government matters well removed from the highest levels of state, provided there has been a public interest in suppressing information which outweighs the public interest in disclosing it.[182]

Every State in the United States, except Delaware, has now adopted some form of mediation privilege.[183] The rationale for this development has been that public confidence in and the voluntary use of mediation will expand if people have confidence that statements made in mediation will not be disclosed in the context of other processes. Even if a mediation privilege is accepted the issue arises whether all kinds of mediation should be treated in the same way. Some argue that, since there is a greater public interest in protecting certain kinds of mediation over others, privilege rules which may be appropriate for one type of mediation may not be appropriate for another.[184]

---

176 Ibid. See also the section above on the 'without prejudice' privilege.
177 For example, the CEDR *Mediation Agreement* provides that no settlement reached in the mediation will be binding until it has been reduced in writing and signed by or on behalf of the parties.
178 Booth Committee *Report of the Committee on Matrimonial Causes*, HMSO, London, 1985; and Law Commission *Family Law: the Grounds for Divorce*, Law Commission no 192, October 1990.
179 W D Brazil 'Protecting the Confidentiality of Settlement Negotiations' (1988) 39 *Hastings Law Journal* 1955; and M L Prigoff 'Toward Candor or Chaos: the Case of Confidentiality in Mediation' (1988) *Seton Hall Legislative Journal* 1.
180 L Ray et al (eds) *ABA Dispute Resolution Directory*, 1983, at pp 145–50.
181 Technically, it is an immunity, not a privilege, which cannot be waived by the parties because it is public-interest based.
182 See C Tapper *Cross and Tapper on Evidence* (9th edn) Butterworths, London, 1999, at pp 472–509.
183 See Center for Public Resources *Alternatives* 1999, vol 17(1), at p 17.
184 K Gibson 'Confidentiality in Mediation: a moral re-assessment' (1992) *Journal of Dispute Resolution* 25 at 43; and A Kirtley 'The Mediation Privilege: Transformation from Theory to Implementation – Designing a Mediation Privilege to protect Mediation Participants, the Process and the Public Interest' (1995) *Journal of Dispute Resolution* 1 at 8–10 and 16–18.

Contractual protection of confidentiality

Mediation agreements typically include confidentiality provisions,[185] the breach of which may give rise to an action for breach of contract.[186] Even if it is not explicit in the agreement between the parties, confidentiality may be implied.[187]

Although confidentiality agreements are persuasive as to the party's intent, courts may not necessarily uphold such agreements. In a 1999 decision, *Instance v Denny Bros Printing Ltd*,[188] the High Court upheld the confidentiality clause in the Centre for Dispute Resolution ('CEDR') Model Mediation Procedure.[189] In the United States, courts have been willing to see confidentiality provisions in mediation agreements upheld as they foster the public policy in favour of mediation.[190]

In general terms, public policy favours the enforcement of confidentiality clauses in agreements.[191] These clauses seem to provide significantly broader scope than is provided by the privileges under the law, but it is likely that some of the limitations on the privileges under the law would also be imposed on confidentiality clauses where these are not already written into the Agreement to Mediate. There would also be limitations on the kinds of remedies which could be achieved for breaches of such undertakings.

The terms of a mediation agreement or confidentiality agreement between the mediator and the parties should set out clearly the intention of the parties in relation to confidentiality and, in particular, should specify:

- the parts of the mediation process to which the obligation of confidentiality attaches;
- the type of information subject to confidentiality;
- the person able to assert confidentiality and the person against who confidentiality can be asserted;

---

185 As do mediation rules and codes of conduct, for example: World Intellectual Property Organisation *Mediation Rules*; Patents Court *Mediation Procedures*; Institute of Civil Engineers *Conciliator Agreement*; International Chamber of Commerce *Rules of Optional Conciliation*; ADR Group *Code of Conduct*; Commercial Mediation Centre *Code of Conduct*; Academy of Experts *Code of Conduct* and *Guidance Notes for Mediators*; and UK College of Family Mediators *Code of Practice*.
186 *Lamb v Evans* [1893] 1 Ch 218.
187 In relation to arbitration, see *Ali Shipping Corpn v Shipyard Trogir* [1998] 1 Lloyd's Rep 643 where the Court of Appeal found that confidentiality was an implied contract term. Compare the Australian position: *Esso Australia Resources Ltd v Ploughman* (1995) 128 ALR 391 where the Australian High Court did not consider that there was a general duty of confidence in arbitration.
188 [2000] 05 LS Gaz R 35, supra.
189 The Commercial Court in Brussels (Tribunal de Commerce – Mons et Bruxelles, 1999/13-559) has also upheld the confidentiality provisions in a Centre for Dispute Resolution mediation clause, by ordering the parties to remove from subsequent arbitration proceedings in the same matter all references to the mediation: Centre for Dispute Resolution *Resolutions*, Issue no 24 at p 2.
190 K Brown 'Confidentiality in Mediation: Status and Implications' (1991) 2 *Journal of Dispute Resolution* 307 at 320–2.
191 F Crosbie 'Aspects of confidentiality in mediation: a matter of balancing competing public interests' (1995) 2 *CDRJ* 51 at 70.

- any exceptions to confidentiality; and
- the obligations of the mediator both during and after the mediation in relation to information received in confidence during the course of the mediation.

There are also ways in which confidentiality may, intentionally or unintentionally, be circumvented. For example, once information is imparted within the mediation process in joint session, the information will be known to all parties, who may use that information without necessarily disclosing it.[192]

Equitable remedy for breach of confidence

In equity persons who receive information in circumstances of confidence cannot make unauthorised use of the information. Where there is no remedy in contract, a court may be willing to exercise equitable jurisdiction to grant relief against an actual abuse, or a threatened abuse, of confidential information.[193] The elements that have to be satisfied for this equitable remedy to be available are:[194]

(1) the information to be protected must have the necessary quality of confidence about it;

(2) that information must have been imparted in circumstances importing an obligation of confidence;

(3) there must be an unauthorised use of the information to the detriment of the party who originally communicated it; and

(4) where the claimant is a private individual, there is actual or potential detriment.

Normally, actions for breach of confidence involve situations such as an employment relationship in which an employee uses the employer's trade secrets for his or her own benefit. It could apply to mediation on the ground that confidential information is received by mediators only on the limited basis that it be used to allow them to perform their functions effectively. There would be a breach of confidence where mediators used the information for purposes other than assisting the mediation, or where they merely disclosed it to a third party without authorisation. Unlike most breach of confidence situations, it is less likely that information disclosed in mediation would be commercially valuable. In the event of a breach, the affected party could seek injunctive relief, and where the mediator used the information for his or her own benefit he or she could be ordered to make restitution of any profits acquired. Damages are also possible in appropriate circumstances. Where the information relates to complicity in fraud or criminal activity by the

---

192 For example, if a spouse admits in a mediation to having various bank accounts, the other spouse may call him or her at trial to produce details of those accounts: see the UK College of Family Mediators *1999/2000 Directory and Handbook*, Sweet & Maxwell, London 1999, at p A99. By way of further example, if in the course of a mediation, a legally-aided client's solicitor admits that his or her client's case is weak on an issue, the other party's lawyer may notify the funders in an attempt to have the funding withdrawn.

193 *Saltman Engineering Co Ltd v Campbell Engineering Co* [1963] 3 All ER 413n; and *Fraser v Thames Television Ltd* [1984] QB 44.

194 *Coco v A N Clark (Engineers)* [1969] RPC 41; and *A-G v Guardian Newspapers Ltd (No 2)* [1988] 3 All ER 545.

relevant party, the mediator may have a 'public interest' defence in disclosing such information to the relevant authorities.[195]

Statutory protection of confidentiality

Many statutes dealing with mediation protect the confidentiality of mediation through privilege and secrecy provisions. These provisions reinforce the common law position. Statutory provisions on privilege generally provide that mediation is confidential and that evidence of anything said or of any admission made in a mediation meeting is not admissible in any proceedings before any court, and that documents prepared for the purposes of or in the course of a mediation are likewise not admissible in evidence. The provisions normally contain one or more exceptions to the general grant of privilege.[196]

In Scotland, protection for family mediation is afforded by the Civil Evidence (Family Mediation) (Scotland) Act 1995. The protection applies to family mediation relating to:

- residence of a child;
- contact with a child;
- a child's up-bringing;
- matters relating to a child's welfare;
- issues arising out of the breakdown or termination of a marriage, including all financial disputes.[197]

The protection is only available if the mediation is conducted by a person accredited as a family mediator by an organisation approved by the Lord President of the Court of Session in Scotland.[198] The Act also lists the following exceptions to the general rule of inadmissibility:

- information as to any contract entered into during the mediation;
- information as to what occurred during the mediation, where it relates to the subject matter of a challenge to any contract which is entered into during the mediation;
- where the participants (other than the mediator) agree;
- in relation to any related children's hearings, adoption proceedings and other proceedings involving children concerning the child's care or protection.[199]

In relation to employment disputes, ss 133 and 134 of the Employment Protection (Consolidation) Act 1978 provide that any information given to a conciliation officer in the performance of his or her duties, shall not be admissible in evidence.

In the US, statutes mandate confidentiality in local rules for required participation in Federal Court mediation programmes.[200] In Australia also, mediations conducted as part of a court-annexed mediation scheme are normally governed by legislation and court

---

195 *Initial Services Ltd v Putterill* [1968] 1 QB 396; and *Francome v Mirror Group News-papers Ltd* [1984] 2 All ER 408.
196 Children Act 1989, s 1 provides that the best interests of a child may require disclosure.
197 Civil Evidence (Family Mediation) (Scotland) Act 1995, s 1.
198 Ibid.
199 Ibid, s 2.
200 Alternative Dispute Resolution Act 1998, s 652(d). Confidentiality statutes in the United States include the Alabama Code, Alaska Statutes, Arizona Revised Statutes Annotated,

rules, which address the issue of confidentiality, as are mediations conducted under other legislative schemes.[201] Some statutes require mediators to take an oath of secrecy, and most statutes identify some or all of the following exceptions to confidentiality:[202]

- with consent of the person from whom the information was received;
- as required by law;
- where there are reasonable grounds for believing that disclosure is necessary to protect a person from injury or property from damage;
- to report the commission of an offence;
- to inform a court that the mediation took place and whether an agreement was reached;
- where reasonably required for research, provided that the parties' identities are not revealed.

Some of the deficiencies identified in Australian legislation include the failure to address issues of disclosure to the world at large, the use which may be made of information, and sanctions for breach.

Confidentiality and conflict of interests

The Australian case of *Frank Stephen Wolf v Adelle Grivas*[203] illustrates one of the unintended consequences of mediation confidentiality for lawyers. The facts of the

---

Arkansas Code Annotated, California Codes, Colorado Revised Statutes, Connecticut General Statutes, Delaware Code Annotated, Florida Statutes and Florida Statutes Annotated, Georgia Code Annotated, Hawaii Revised Statutes, Idaho Code, Illinois Revised Statues, Indiana Code and Indiana Code Annotated, Iowa Code, Kansas Statues Annotated, Kentucky Revised Statutes Annotated, Louisiana Revised Statutes Annotated, Maine Revised Statutes Annotated, Maryland Code Annotated, Massachusetts General Laws, Michigan Compiled Laws, Minnesota Statues, Missouri Revised Statutes, Montana Code Annotated, Nebraska Revised Statutes, Nevada Revised Statutes, New Hampshire Revised Statues Annotated, New Jersey Revised Statutes, New Mexico Statutes Annotated, New York Statutes, North Carolina General Statutes, North Dakota Century Code, Ohio Revised Code Annotated, Oklahoma Statutes, Oregon Revised Statutes, Pennsylvania Consolidated Statutes Annotated, Rhode Island General Laws, South Carolina Code Annotated, South Dakota Co-defined Laws Annotated, Tennessee Code Annotated, Texas Codes Annotated, Utah Code Annotated, Vermont Statutes Annotated, Virginia Code Annotated, Washington Revised Code, West Virginia Code, Wisconsin Statutes and Wyoming Statutes. For details of the areas covered by the statutes, see http://www.stanford.edu/group/sccn/mediation

201 For example, the Retail Leases Act (NSW) protects statements or admissions made in the course of mediation over a retail lease dispute (s 69) and the Native Title Act (NSW) protects words spoken or acts done at a native title mediation (s 45). The Dispute Resolution Centres Act 1990 (QLD) provides that privilege attaches to anything said or any admission made in a mediation (including defamation), and to any document prepared for the purpose of, or in the course of, a mediation session (including defamatory material), except if all participants consent to admissibility or where it is necessary to prevent or minimise the danger of injury to any person or damage to any property: ss 36 and 37. The Mediation Act 1997 (ACT), by way of further example, makes inadmissibility subject to the exceptions set out in the Evidence Act 1995 (Cth): s 9.

202 For example, Dispute Resolution Centres Act 1990 (QLD), s 37; and Mediation Act 1997 (ACT), s 10.

203 ACT Family Court, No CA 1440 of 1986 (11 August 1994, unreported) (Finn J).

case were somewhat complex. During the course of a custody hearing between a former husband (A) and wife (B), A's solicitor disclosed to the court that she had a vague recollection of having acted as a pro bono mediator at the Canberra Mediation Centre ten months previously between one of the husband's witnesses (F) and F's former husband. F was the ex-wife of B's current fiancé and was to give evidence about the fiancé's alleged behavioural problems with children in support of A's claim that B should not be granted custody. The solicitor had no independent recollection of the mediation, which had been conducted subject to a standard confidentiality agreement. The solicitor undertook to have no further part in the hearing as far as F's evidence was concerned but B applied for the solicitor (and her barrister) to be restrained from further acting for A. The court had to decide the issue of whether A's lawyer should be dismissed on the grounds that she may have gained information or insight about B's fiancé when she acted as mediator between him and his ex-wife (F). The court emphasised that, in exercising its discretion, it would ensure that justice was done and appeared to be done in the circumstances. While there was a perceived risk of injustice to the wife B if the solicitor continued to act, this was outweighed by other factors if she was removed: increased costs for A, increased delay for both A and B, the fact that any information available to the solicitor from the mediation was already available to A through F, who was a competent witness in the case, and the fact that the solicitor had undertaken to leave the court when F or F's former husband gave evidence and to refrain from discussing the evidence of either until the case was determined. The solicitor was allowed to continue acting in the case. However, the court emphasised that in circumstances such as these the mediator owed a duty of confidence to both F and F's former husband and that it could restrain a lawyer who owed a duty of confidence under a mediation agreement from continuing to act in a case involving one or both parties to the mediation. A broader concern was expressed by Finn J about conflict of interest issues:

'I am concerned that as solicitors and barristers become increasingly involved in alternative dispute resolution procedures, such as mediation, the likelihood of problems such as the one that has arisen in this case, arising in future cases must exist. In my view the legal professional bodies will need to consider putting in place procedures that avoid as far as possible situations arising which can undermine public confidence in either the legal system, or in alternative dispute resolution procedures.'

There is also a concern that lawyers acting for a party in a mediation may gain knowledge which could be used against the other party in later proceedings. While the problems are in fact no greater than conflict of interest issues facing lawyers in other contexts, confidentiality and conflict of interests issues will require attention as mediation becomes a permanent feature of the legal landscape.[204] The basic principles which emerged from *Prince Jefri Bolkiah v KPMG (a firm)* [1999] 2 AC 222 were:

- consideration is required to be given to whether there is increased risk of disclosure or misuse of a former client's confidential information; and
- the risk should be real, rather than fanciful or theoretical, but need not be substantial.

The case confirmed that a solicitor may act against a former client, even one in respect of whom the solicitor's firm holds confidential information, if the client

---

204 Lawyers should have regard to the guidelines in the Professional Conduct of Solicitors eg: 8th edn, Law Society of England & Wales, 1999.

consents or, in the absence of consent, so long as it can act consistently with obligations of confidence or other fiduciary duty owed to the client.[205]

In the case of mediators, mediation agreements usually stipulate that a mediator cannot undertake work for or against a party in relation to the dispute on account of confidential information which will have been imparted to the mediator in the course of the mediation.[206] Law Society Codes of Practice for Mediators provide that solicitor mediators should withdraw from a mediation if they have acquired confidential information relevant to the dispute or the parties in the mediation from another source or when confidential information relevant to another client is likely to be acquired during the mediation.[207]

Confidentiality policy and practice

It is clear that the law on confidentiality in mediation is complex, unclear in parts, and yet to be fully developed. The extent of confidentiality in mediation involves a balancing of competing interests. On one hand, there is an interest in promoting and encouraging the settlement of disputes outside the court system and in protecting emerging ADR processes such as mediation. On the other hand, there is an interest in disputing parties obtaining full disclosure between themselves, and in courts and tribunals having the best access to evidence and information, regardless of what has transpired in mediation. The principle of sanctity of contract supports the maintenance of confidentiality where the parties have committed themselves to it. If, however, the confidentiality is too wide, it will sterilise too much evidence and seriously undermine the trial process. If the confidentiality is too narrow, it will discourage parties from entering mediation and from using their best endeavours to settle once there.[208] A balance is required between supporting mediation, on one hand, and not freezing litigation or upholding illegality, on the other. This balance is not an easy one to achieve. Australian courts have acknowledged the need for further consideration of the policy underlying the mediation confidentiality question.[209]

It has been suggested that the exceptions to confidentiality are so numerous that they almost erode confidentiality, as it applies to mediation.[210] The legal complexities

205 See also R S G Chester et al 'Conflicts of interest, Chinese walls and changing business of the law' *Business Law International*, 2 January 2000, p 35.

206 The Law Society of England & Wales *Code of Practice for Civil/Commercial Mediation*. The Center for Public Resources' *Mediation Agreement*, takes the position one step further by prohibiting the mediator from working on any matter for or against a party in a mediation for a period of six months following the mediation unless all the parties consent. For an outline of the American position in relation to subsequent representation, see *Barajas v Oren Reality and Development Co*, 57 Cal App 4th 209. See also the section on Neutrality in Chapter 11.

207 Law Society of England and Wales *Guide to Professional Conduct of Solicitors* (8th edn) Law Society Publishing, at Chapter 22 on ADR; and Law Society of Scotland *Code of Conduct for Solicitor Mediators*. See also the section on Neutrality in Chapter 11.

208 L Boulle 'Confidentiality and the mediation process' (1992) 3 *ADRJ* 272.

209 Rogers J in *AWA Ltd v Daniels (t/a Delloite Haskins and Sells)* (1992) 7 ACSR 463 at 469.

210 L R Freedman and M L Prigoff 'Confidentiality in Mediation: the need for Protection' (1986) 2 *Ohio State Journal on Dispute Resolution* 37 at 40.

relating to the confidentiality of mediation necessitate caution in the promotion and explanation of the mediation process. Sweeping assurances about 'watertight' privacy and confidentiality in mediation are not a wise strategy for practising mediators. It is recommended that mediators advise the disputants before them that there may be limitations on the extent to which courts will protect communications made during mediations. Ultimately there is an important issue of credibility and legitimacy at stake for the mediation movement. As there are undoubted limitations to the confidentiality principle, these should be dealt with as clearly as possible before the commencement of mediation.

Confidentiality and other participants in mediation

As witnesses, experts, supporters and other persons who might be present at mediation meetings are not parties to the Agreement to Mediate, or to confidentiality undertakings in the settlement agreement, it is necessary to ensure their commitment to confidentiality in other ways. Mediators deal with this by asking 'outside' parties to sign confidentiality undertakings before entering the mediation room. Organisations providing mediation services may have standard undertakings which have to be signed by all participants who are not party to the Agreement to Mediate.

Enforcement of Mediated Settlement Agreements

Court order or contract?

If the parties record their settlement agreement as an order of a court[211] or if the mediator is appointed an arbitrator for the purpose of issuing a consent award,[212] the

---

211 For example, the Central London County Court Mediation Pilot, *Form MD9* Report to the Court, sets out a range of options:
   • that by consent, the claim be withdrawn;
   • that by consent, there be judgment for a specified sum with no order as to costs or costs agreed at a specified figure or to be taxed if not agreed;
   • that by consent, all proceedings are stayed upon the terms set out in the schedule to the Report.
   In Scotland, family mediated agreements may be formalised through a Minute or Joint Minute of Agreement.
   A range of statutes in Australia provide, in the context of court-referred mediations, that the court can provide an order giving effect to an agreement reached after mediation, upon the mediator filing with the court a certificate confirming the agreement reached: for example, Supreme Court of QLD Act 1991, s 110 and District Court Act of QLD Act 1967, s 105.
212 For example, the Academy of Experts *Guidance Notes for Mediators*, and the Institute of Civil Engineers' *Conciliation Procedure* provide that the mediator can be appointed as an arbitrator to issue a consent award. See also C Newmark and R Hill 'Can a mediated settlement become an enforceable arbitration award?' (2000) 16(1) *Arbitration Int* 81.

settlement is immediately enforceable and a court may provide summary judgment. In some cases mediating parties applying for consent orders may have to supply additional evidence before receiving the court's validation, for example, where the parties to a divorce make unusual arrangements for the custody of their children, the court may require the parties to provide evidence to satisfy it that such arrangements are in the best interests of the children. Such evidence allows the court to vet the agreement in terms of family law norms.

Otherwise, enforcement will depend on whether the settlement agreement is a legally enforceable contract between the parties. If a party does not abide by the terms of a binding settlement agreement, the other party cannot pursue the original course of action, but can sue on the settlement agreement.[213] Damages for breach, specific performance or an injunction are possibly remedies in cases on non-compliance with the terms of a mediated settlement agreement. The rules of law applicable to those remedies, including rules relating to causation, remoteness and the duty to mitigate loss, would be relevant.

In relation to an agreement reached through ACAS conciliation, the Trade Union Reform and Employment Rights Act 1993 provided that written compromise agreements had the effect of ousting the jurisdiction of the tribunal, provided that independent legal advice on the effect of the proposed agreement had been received by the employee from a lawyer, who was insured in accordance with the requirements in the Act. The Employment Rights (Dispute Resolution) Act 1998 has clarified the insurance requirements, and stipulates that the advice can be provided by an independent adviser.

Without prejudice bar?

Even though the mediation is conducted on a without prejudice basis, once an agreement is reached, it becomes open.[214] This issue has been considered by courts in Australia, specifically in the context of mediated settlement agreements. The Farm Debt Mediation Act renders inadmissible a 'document prepared . . . in the course of, or pursuant to, a mediation session'. It was argued that the provision extended to any agreement reached in mediation, with the effect that the agreement was protected by privilege. In *State Bank of New South Wales v Freeman*,[215] Badgery-Parker J found that an agreement reached at mediation might be regarded as a document which comes into existence after, not in the course of or pursuant to, a mediation session. Rolfe J in *Commonwealth Bank of Australia v McDonnell*[216] agreed, recognising that, otherwise, the parties could reach agreement at a mediation and later refuse to abide by it on the basis that its admissibility is precluded.

---

213 For this reason, frequently a term is included in the settlement agreement that, in case of non-compliance, the parties' rights in respect of the original course of action are re-instated.
214 Sometimes referred to as 'the open face of a mediation': P Martin 'Good Practice Guidelines' in UK College of Family Mediators *1999/2000 Directory and Handbook*.
215 (31 January 1996, unreported), New South Wales Supreme Court.
216 (24 July 1997, unreported), New South Wales Supreme Court.

Privity issues

The Contracts (Rights of Third Parties) Act 1999 sets out the circumstances in which a third party has a right to enforce a contractual term, even though not a party to the contract in question.[217] Section 1 provides a two-limb test:

- where the contract expressly provides; or
- where the contract purports to confer a benefit on the third party unless it appears on a true construction of the contract that the contracting parties did not intend to do so.

The third party need not have been in existence at the time the contract was made. Certain contracts, like employment and carriage of goods contracts, are excluded from the ambit of the Act. The effect of the Act is that courts may award to the third party all the remedies for breach, which would be available to the contracting parties.

Variation and rectification issues

In the case of a mediated settlement, recorded as an order of the court, the court has power to alter the order to correct an accidental slip or omission.[218] A consent order can also be rectified in a fresh action upon the same grounds as would enable a court to rectify an agreement, like mutual mistake.[219]

In an action for rectification of an agreement, English law makes admissible the previous negotiations of the parties and their declarations of subjective intent.[220] Where a third party has a right under the Contracts (Rights of Third Parties) Act 1999 to enforce a contractual term in a contract, to which it is not a party, s 2 of the Act provides that the contracting parties cannot, by agreement, vary the contract in a way which affects the third party's right without the consent of the third party, unless the express terms of the agreement or a court allow for this.

Grounds for evading settlement terms

Mediated agreements are subject to normal contractual principles as regards their validity and review. Notwithstanding practical problems caused by the confidentiality principle, mediated agreements can be reviewed and invalidated at common law if there are vitiating factors that render the agreement, or a part of it, either void or voidable, or which allow the court to order the rescission of the agreement.

---

217 The Act implemented the recommendations of the Law Commission in its Report on *Privity of Contract: Contracts for the benefit of third parties*, Law Com No 242 (1996).
218 For example, Civil Procedure Rules, r 40.12.
219 *Huddersfield Banking Co Ltd v Henry Lister & Sons Ltd* [1895] 2 Ch 273.
220 *Investors Compensation Scheme Ltd v West Bromwich Building Society* [1998] 1 WLR 896.

No binding contract reached

Obligations in a mediated agreement will not bind if the agreement is unenforceable as no binding contract was reached.[221] Whether a mediated agreement is binding on the parties requires consideration to be given to the following questions:

- Was it intended to be final and binding?
- Does it contemplate that further terms will be agreed?[222]
- Does it require execution of documents by way of formality?

The essential requirements for a binding contract are:

- intention to create legal relations;
- certainty of terms;
- consideration or a deed;
- in some cases, certain formalities are also required.[223]

The intention of the parties is ascertained objectively from the circumstances. For example, if the parties act as if the original dispute still exists, they may provide evidence that no binding agreement was intended. Alternatively, commencement of performance provides contrary evidence.[224] In relation to certainty of the terms, a term may be implied into an agreement if the term is reasonable or necessary to give business efficacy to the contract, or it is obvious that it goes without saying or is capable of clear expression and does not contradict any express terms of the contract.[225] The parties may leave terms to be agreed by a third party or some other mechanism without falling foul of uncertainty of terms.[226] In complex commercial disputes, parties may record heads of terms at the mediation, but will agree to prepare a more formal document, recording the agreed terms, subsequently. The nature of such an agreement may fall into one of three categories:

---

221 Memoranda of Understanding reached in the course of family mediation, as outlined above, are not binding until formalised by the parties' lawyers or by order of the court. A court will be influenced by any agreement reached by the parties unless it is unfair to one of the parties; is not in the best interests of children; or if the facts on which it is based, are incorrect. Any agreement on financial and property matters will be judged against that which would be considered reasonable according to law. Agreements reached in community mediation, although not intended to be binding, may have legal consequences.

222 In some cases, there might be no intention to be legally bound, as in *May and Butcher Ltd v R* [1934] 2 KB 17n; whereas, in other cases, the remaining terms can be ascertained by applying the standard of reasonableness, as in *Foley v Classique Coaches Ltd* [1934] 2 KB 1.

223 For the formalities required in different contexts, for instance, agreements involving the disposition of an interest in land, see D Foskett *The Law and Practice of Compromise* (4th edn), Sweet & Maxwell, London, 1996.

224 *G Percy Trentham Ltd v Archital Luxfer Ltd* [1993] 1 Lloyd's Rep 25; and see *DMA Financial Solutions Ltd v Baan UK Ltd*, 28 March 2000, reported in *New Law Digest* 3 May 2000 (Chancery Division).

225 *The Moorcock* (1889) 14 PD 64; *Shirlaw v Southern Foundaries (1926) Ltd* [1939] 2 KB 206; *Morton v Morton* [1942] 1 All ER 273; and *Liverpool City Council v Irwin* [1977] AC 239.

226 It may be appropriate, when drawing up an agreement, to provide for any ambiguity in that agreement is to be resolved by the mediator. On this issue, generally, see *Hillas and Co Ltd v Arcos Ltd* [1932] All ER Rep 494; (1932) 147 LT 503.

- the parties may intend to be immediately bound even if some of the detail of the arrangement still needs to be worked out;[227]
- performance of a term is conditional upon the execution of the formal document;
- the parties do not intend to be bound until the formal document is executed.[228]

In relation to consideration, mutual promises provide adequate consideration for each other and the release of a bona fide claim also constitutes adequate consideration.

In a recent English case, *DMA Financial Solutions Ltd v Baan UK Ltd*,[229] the High Court considered the issue of whether negotiations, albeit not in the context of a mediation, had resulted in a concluded contract. The court referred to the following factors in support of its finding that the negotiations resulted in a concluded contract:

- the negotiators had actual or ostensible authority to commit the parties to a contract;
- the negotiations were such that the parties might become contractually bound in the course of them before the execution of a written agreement;
- the negotiations were not conducted on a 'subject to contract' basis;
- there was no evidence that the parties would not be bound until a formal written agreement was signed;
- there was no usage in the industry in issue that agreements were never binding until drawn up and signed (in fact, in the IT industry it was not unusual for agreements to be binding before the documents were produced);
- the agreement did not omit any crucial element;
- all the matters raised in the negotiations were agreed in one way or another; and
- by commencing performance.

Agreements to mediate in civil/commercial cases usually contain a clause stating that any agreement reached in the mediation will be binding when reduced to writing and signed by both parties.[230] A mediator does not usually draft a memorandum in a family mediation or an informal agreement in a community mediation on the basis that these constitute a binding agreement.

Rescission on account of an 'unjust factor'

A party may attempt to escape its obligations under a mediated settlement agreement by claiming fraud, undue influence, unconscionability, duress,[231] lack of capacity or authority to contract,[232] or illegality,[233] with a view to having the mediated settlement

---

227   *First Energy (UK) Ltd v Hungarian Institutional Bank Ltd* [1993] 2 Lloyd's Rep 194.
228   *Winn v Bull* (1877) 7 Ch D 29.
229   28 March 2000, reported in *New Law Digest* 3 May 2000 (Chancery Division).
230   For example, Centre for Dispute Resolution *Model Mediation Procedure*.
231   That Australian courts (*Commonwealth Bank v McDonnell* (24 July 1997, unreported) New South Wales Supreme Court (Rolfe J) and *Studer v Boettcher* (1998) NSWSC 524) have been prepared to explore the duration of a mediation, which suggests that courts may review an agreement reached in mediation late at night.
232   Solicitors attending settlement discussions on behalf of parties were found to at least have ostensible authority to bind their clients to a settlement: *Waugh v HB Clifford & Sons Ltd* [1982] Ch 374; and *Von Schulz v Morriello* (1998) QCA 236.
233   *Miller v Karlinski* (1945) 62 TLR 85 and *Kok Hoong v Leon Cheong Kweng Mines Ltd* [1964] AC 993. In *Eco Swiss China Tine Ltd v Benneton International* [1999] 2 All ER (Comm) 44, the European Court of Justice determined that the competition rules of the

agreement set aside. The remedy is equitable, and its application discretionary.[234] Where the mediated settlement has been recorded as an order of the court, it may be set aside upon the same grounds as would enable the court to set aside an agreement. As in the case of variations, the Contracts (Rights of Third Parties) Act 1999 places restrictions on rescission, where it affects a third party, who has a right to enforce a term of that contract by virtue of the Act.

Two Australian examples provide an insight into the kind of circumstances which may give rise to a claim that the mediated settlement agreement should be set aside on account of an unjust factor. In *Gillford Pty Ltd v Burdon Pty Ltd*[235] the claimant sought to have a mediated agreement set aside on account of purportedly fraudulent misrepresentations made by a party in the mediation about its assets and liabilities. On the facts, the court did not find that the claim had been made out, and declined the relief sought. In *Abriel v Westpac Banking Corpn*[236] a party to a mediated agreement claimed that it had done so on account of duress, which occurred when its lawyers withdrew from the mediation, and the other party took unfair advantage of that disadvantage. The court declined an application to strike out the claim, stating that, although the claim is novel, it could not be concluded that it was doomed to failure. In such a case, consideration needs to be given to whether the party protested at the time, had an alternative course of action open, and was independently advised. Commercial pressure to settle a case is unlikely to constitute duress.[237]

Cross border considerations

Issues of jurisdiction arise, as in the case of any agreement. Where the parties to a mediated agreement are from different jurisdictions, it is prudent to include a governing law and jurisdiction clause in the agreement. In an attempt to promote mediation, the Portuguese Government is reported to be attempting to secure cross-border recognition of mediation agreements.[238]

'Cooling off' periods

In the context of a legislative scheme for mediation in Australia between farmers and their creditors, the Farm Debt Mediation Act (NSW) 1998 provides, as a mechanism for avoiding enforcement disputes, a cooling off period, which commences when the mediated agreement is entered into and ends on the fourteenth day afterwards, or as agreed between the parties. During this period, the agreement can be rescinded, although if a party has received a benefit under the agreement in the meantime, a claim for compensation, adjustment or accounting is possible.

EC Treaty can lead to the annulment of decisions of private dispute resolution bodies, even if national law does not apply domestic competition rules to private dispute resolution bodies. Although in that case the parties had resolved their dispute through arbitration, all private settlements are subject to EU competition rules.

234 *Spence v Crawford* [1939] 3 All ER 271 at 288 per Lord Wright; and *Cheese v Thomas* [1994] 1 WLR 129 at 137 per Nichols VC.

235 20 April 1995, Federal Court of Australia, NSW Registry, General Division (No AG79 of 1994 FED No 169/95) (Lockhart J).

236 [1999] FCA 50, a judgment of the Federal Court of Australia, NSW Registry (Branson J).

237 *Atlas Express Ltd v Kafco* [1989] QB 833.

238 *The Law Society Gazette*, 9 March 2000, at p 9.

Legal Liability of Mediators

The basis of mediator liability

A significant form of accountability for mediators is the possibility that legal proceedings may be brought against them.[239] As at the time of writing, there are no known cases in the UK where legal proceedings have been brought against mediators. This may be due partly to the relative novelty of formal mediation in the UK. The users of mediation may therefore be uncertain about what to expect. It may also be due partly to the existence of immunities against liability for mediators. Mediators are not decision-makers. It has been argued that the fact that mediation allows parties to make final decisions renders it difficult to establish a link between any 'damage' and the conduct of the mediator.[240] Nevertheless, as with all other providers of professional services, it is not inconceivable that proceedings may be brought against mediators by aggrieved disputants or third parties.

Courts will be faced with competing policy considerations in relation to the liability of mediators. On one hand, the widespread concerns about litigation and the increasing endorsement of mediation alternatives will incline the law to shield mediators from too onerous a form of liability. Liability could dissuade individuals from serving as mediators, particularly when the remuneration is modest or the service is provided by volunteers. There is no direct correlation between levels of remuneration and mediation skill – some of the best-trained mediators work for community or volunteer services, and for them exposure to liability would provide a double disadvantage. On the other hand, there is the view that mediators should be subject to stringent standards of liability. The existence of civil liability would have a beneficial impact on the behaviour of mediators, and on the quality of mediation services, and on the overall development of standards. The fact that mediation is a private dispute resolution process already attracts criticism relating to the potential for shielding malpractice and unfair mediated agreements, and too narrow a basis of liability would further insulate it from societal norms.

There are three types of situations in which parties might seek to hold mediators liable. The first is where they feel that they could have settled on substantially better terms than they did during the mediation. The second is where they feel that they could have done better had they not settled at all during mediation. The third is where, regardless of the outcome, they feel aggrieved about some aspect of the mediation procedure. It is notionally easier to find a basis for liability in respect of procedural matters than it is in respect of substantive matters, particularly where the mediator draws a clear process/content distinction and there are legal advisers in the mediation or there is scope for independent legal review.

---

239   See A Chaykin 'Mediator liability: a new role for fiduciary duties?' (1984) 53 *University of Cincinnati Law Review* 731; A Chaykin 'The sultans of swap: defining the duties and liabilities of American mediators' (1986) 99 *Harvard Law Review* 1876; A Chaykin 'The liabilities and immunities of mediators: a hostile environment for model legislation' (1986–7) 2 *Ohio State Journal on Dispute Resolution* 47; A Lynch 'Can I sue my mediator? – Finding the key to mediator liability (1995) 6 *ADRJ* 113.

240   A Lynch, ibid, at 124.

Liability in contract

Mediators are potentially liable if they breach the mediation contract between themselves and the parties. A contract to mediate can be written, verbal or implied. Many mediation service providers have standard form contracts which deal with, or incorporate by reference, the procedures to be followed in the mediation meeting, the roles and responsibilities of the mediator and the disputants, fees and costs arrangements, methods of terminating the agreement, and matters of privacy and confidentiality. Such contracts may also incorporate by reference mediation standards or codes of conduct, which then become terms of the mediation agreement. Commentators argue that an obstacle to contractual relief for breach of an express term is that mediation organisations normally draw up mediation agreements, with their own protection in mind.[241] The availability of legal advice to the parties would be a factor, which discounts this concern.[242] Commentators point to another obstacle to contractual relief, being that mediation agreements are traditionally vague.[243] As mediation becomes more established, however, this problem is also likely to disappear.[244]

Terms may also be implied in a mediation contracts if:

- to do so would be reasonable;
- it is necessary to give the agreement business efficacy;
- it is so obvious that it goes without saying;
- it is capable of clear expression; and
- doing so does not contradict an express term.[245]

An example is an implied term that the mediator will perform with reasonable skill and care. Difficulty arises when attempting to determine the standard that a mediator must reach in order to perform his or her role. The traditional standard implied is reasonable skill and care, and reasonableness is assessed by examining the standard of care that is considered the norm in the field in question.[246] At this stage there are few norms in relation to the profession of mediation, in particular since mediation is a flexible process and an individual mediator's style influences the process. Mediator codes of conduct help to identify what is regarded as reasonable skill and care, and for this reason are examined in some detail in this book.[247] In the case of complaints against solicitor mediators, in particular, adherence to the Codes of Mediator Practice recommended by the Law Society is likely to be considered as evidence of good practice.[248] But following an industry norm, for example, would not preclude liability from being incurred if the standards followed by the industry as a whole are

---

241 A A Chaykin 'Mediator Liability: A New Role for Fiduciary Duties?' (1984) 53 *Cincinnati Law Review* 731 at 738.
242 A Lynch 'Can I Sue My Mediator? Finding the Key to Mediator Liability' (1995) *Australian Dispute Resolution Journal* 113.
243 A A Chaykin 'Mediator Liability: a New Role for Fiduciary Duties?' op cit, at 737.
244 A Lynch 'Can I Sue My Mediator? Finding the Key to Mediator Liability', op cit, at 114.
245 For example, *BP Refinery (Westernport) Pty Ltd v Hastings Shire Council* (1978) 52 AJLR 20.
246 For example, *Bolan v Friern Hospital Management Committee* [1957] 1 WLR 582.
247 A A Chaykin 'The Liabilities and Immunities of Mediators: A Hostile Environment for Model Legislation' (1986–7) 2 *Ohio State Journal on Dispute Resolution* 47 at 63.
248 Principle 22.04 of the *Guide to the Professional Conduct of Solicitors* (8th edn) Law Society Publishing,1999.

deemed to be lacking.[249] In the case of mediation, the standard of care expected of a mediator is still a somewhat indeterminate norm.

A mediator will be in breach of the mediation contract where he or she fails to perform an obligation in accordance with the applicable standard of care. Mediators should also be careful not to make representations[250] as to the likely outcome of a trial, for example, by representing that the mediation will provide a more favourable outcome than litigation. A mediator could be found liable for breach of a contractual promise if the outcome does not materialise. As a precaution, mediation agreements may provide that no promises as to the result of the mediation or litigation are implied.[251] Where there is a breach, one or both parties will prima facie be entitled to damages. However, the onus is on the party concerned to prove actual loss or damage to establish that it was caused by the mediator's conduct. Damage will be regarded as too remote where it did not arise naturally out of the breach or it was not in the contemplation of the parties. Damages in contract are compensatory, not punitive, and are designed to put the parties in the position in which they would have been had the contractual obligation been carried out. Damages may include expenses incurred as a result of the breach, out-of-pocket expenses incurred in preparing for the mediation, and consequential losses.

There are likely to be several difficulties in establishing a claim for damages based on a mediator's breach of contract. The first relates to establishing a breach. This would not be problematic in cases involving, for example, a breach of the confidentiality or conflict of interest provisions. It would be more difficult to establish a breach by reason of negligence or on the ground that the mediator did not provide the quality of performance required by the contract. In the case of mediators, it is difficult to define reasonable standards of behaviour, although the development of mediator standards will facilitate this task to some extent. The second difficulty relates to causation, that is, the party must establish that it was the mediator's determinative decisions that amounted to negligence, for example in not acting as the agent of reality, that was the cause of any damage.[252] Another difficulty arises in the calculation of damages, which would require an assessment of what the outcome of the mediation would have been had the breach not occurred. This would be highly speculative, given the uncertainty over the terms of a settlement, or even whether there would have been an agreement had the mediator performed all his or her duties. A final obstacle to contractual liability is the use of immunity clauses that exclude mediators from any liability in the performance of their obligations. These clauses are found in many mediation agreements, and are considered later in this section.

Liability in tort

Negligence actions are used to hold professionals such as doctors, solicitors or auditors liable towards their clients and to obtain compensation for injured parties.

---

249 *Edward Wong Finance Co Ltd v Johnson, Stokes & Master* [1984] AC 296.
250 See Misrepresentation Act 1967, s 2 and *Chitty on Contracts* (27th edn) at para 6-037.
251 J Folberg and A Taylor *Mediation – a comprehensive guide to resolving conflicts without litigation*, Jossey-Bass, San Francisco, 1988, at pp 281–2.
252 As to causation, generally, see *Monarch Steamship Co Ltd v Karlshanns Oljefabriker (A/B)* [1949] AC 196.

They can be based on a negligent act or omission relating to the special skills and knowledge expected of professionals, or to a negligent mis-statement that causes economic loss. In the case of mediation, a negligence action could emanate from a party who is subsequently dissatisfied with a deal struck at mediation and attributes this loss to the negligence of the mediator. This party must establish the basic elements of negligence:

- a duty of care owed by the mediator to the aggrieved party;
- a breach of this duty by failure to exercise the standard of care required of a mediator;
- actual loss or damage sustained by the party; and
- a causal connection between the negligent act and the loss.

Approaches to liability in tort tend to reflect the realities of economic and social forces and, in the context of professional negligence, to be responsive to the nature of the client/professional relationship. In relation to the duty of care owed by mediators, courts would look for a relationship of proximity between the mediator and client on which to base a duty of care to avoid foreseeable injury. In the case of liability for negligence, the initial consideration is whether the mediator owes a duty of care to the parties, having regard to proximity, reasonable foresight of damage and whether it is just and reasonable to impose a duty of care.[253] Where advice is given, proximity may exist. In the mediation context, a mediator does not normally give advice to a party, although a mediator may expose himself or herself to liability if advice is provided, whether actually or inadvertently, or if a settlement agreement or heads of terms are drafted by the mediator. To avoid these risks, a mediator would normally recommend to the parties to seek independent legal advice. It could also be argued that, since not all mediators have the same training or level of expertise (for instance, compare a highly-paid commercial, with a volunteer community, mediator), it would be not be just and reasonable for mediators to be subject to the same duty of care.[254] Ultimately, courts will consider whether a reasonable person would foresee that negligence might cause damage, and whether there are countervailing reasons of policy why there should be no duty of care. Several factors will be relevant here, such as evidence of reliance placed by the court upon the mediator; the social and policy considerations as to where the loss should fall; and the fact that mediation is not yet a recognised profession.

As regards the standard of care required of a mediator, the test is that of reasonableness in the circumstances. Mediator standards, mediation agreements and legal writings provide an initial basis for determining relevant standards of reasonable service. If mediators purport to have special skills or knowledge in particular subject areas, they may, if they express their views on those subject matters, be held to a higher standard of care. The circumstances of the parties, such as their level of education or lack of legal representation, will also be relevant to the question of reasonableness. However, there is little agreement on what a competent mediator should do or refrain from doing. At this stage in the development of mediation practice, it could still be difficult to say whether a mediator had fallen below the accepted minimum level of professional practice expected of reasonably competent

---

253 Lord Bridge in *Caparo Industries plc v Dickman* [1990] 2 AC 605 at 617–19.
254 A Stickley 'Pinning Civil Liability upon a Mediator: a lost cause of action?' (1998) 19 *Queensland Lawyer* 95.

mediators. In *Michael Hyde & Associates Ltd v J D Williams and Co Ltd*, the Court of Appeal stated that, where a profession embraces different views of acceptable practice, competence should be measured by the lowest acceptable standard.[255]

A major obstacle to recovery against a mediator is the requirement that actual damage must have been sustained which would not have been sustained but for the negligent conduct of the mediator. It would have to be established that it was the conduct of the mediator, and not the actions of the parties, which caused, or materially contributed to, the injury. But how can one know what the other party or parties would have done, or failed to do, had the mediator not acted in the way alleged? Unlike parties who are injured by the negligence of a motor vehicle driver, parties in a mediation are not passive victims but active participants in a dynamic process in which causation is a highly complex issue. While a party may be able to show that he or she would not have settled on those terms but for the mediator's conduct, it would be extremely difficult for him or her to show that the other party would have agreed to a different settlement had the mediator done all that he or she was charged with not doing. As Lynch observes: 'Untangling the causative link is an extremely complex and perhaps unachievable process'.[256] Further, where the parties are legally represented during the mediation or where the alleged damages are incurred after the mediator had advised the parties to seek independent legal advice, it would be almost impossible to fix the causative blame on the mediator. On the other hand, any mediator who drafts a settlement agreement at the end of the mediation could be subject to the requirement that the draft be an accurate reflection of what was agreed to. Whether damage was caused by the conduct of the mediator was considered in the US case of *Lange v Marshall*, [257] where the court dismissed an action for negligence against the mediator on the grounds that he failed to negotiate a better settlement for the plaintiff as the plaintiff could not prove a causative link between the outcome and the mediator's actions.

A further problem relates to the calculation of damages. In the law of torts, damages are awarded to put plaintiffs in the position that they would have been in had the tort not been committed. The nature of the mediation process makes this a highly speculative calculation. It will be difficult for a party to establish his or her actual loss by reference to what might have been obtained by resolution of the dispute at court or arbitration.

In practice, a claim for damages is likely to be based on an alleged negligent mis-statement which caused a party economic loss, for example, if they entered into a contract which was less profitable than the contract they would have entered into had the mis-statement not occurred.[258] However, liability for negligent mis-statements is, for a range of policy reasons, more restrictive than liability for other acts or omissions. It would have to be established that the party relied on the mediator and

---

255 (2000) Times, 4 August. In the context of mediation, the application of this test is nevertheless problematic as it is not clear whether it should be the lowest acceptable standard for mediators generally, or whether it should be the lowest acceptable standard for the particular type of mediation in issue. As standards develop, and mediation matures, the problem will be reduced.

256 A Lynch 'Can I Sue My Mediator? Finding the Key to Mediator Liability' (1995) *Australian Dispute Resolution Journal* 113 at 123.

257 622 SW 2d 237 (Mo Ct App 1981).

258 According to the line of cases from *Hedley Byrne & Co v Heller & Partners Ltd* [1964] AC 465.

that the mediator knew or ought to have known that his or her words would cause the reliance.[259] Notionally, this would be easier where the party had particularly requested information and advice and his or her reliance was reasonable in the circumstances, or where there was a special relationship between the mediator and the parties which generated this reliance. If the mediator had expressly disclaimed responsibility for the accuracy of a particular statement, or indicated that its substance should be independently verified by the parties, for instance by saying 'don't take my word for it', the disclaimer of responsibility would be a factor weighing against a finding of liability. The Misrepresentation Act 1967, s 2 (1) introduced a statutory claim for damages for negligent misrepresentation, although the obstacles outlined above would still apply. The benefit of an action under the Act is that it places the onus on the defendant to prove that he or she had reasonable grounds to believe, and did believe, that the representation was true. Fraudulent misrepresentation would occur if a mediator makes a statement, knowing it to be false, with the intention that it should be acted upon by a party in the mediation, and that party suffers loss by acting in reliance on the statement.[260]

While some writers suggest that negligent malpractice may be the most likely basis for a liability claim against mediators, there would be a number of practical difficulties in establishing a claim where a party is unhappy with the mediated outcome. This is partly because of the fact that the 'exact contours of the relationship between the mediator and client are highly individualised and variable, depending upon the dispute involved and the services that the mediator has agreed to provide.[261] It is difficult to see why a mediator, who receives much less specific training than those in professions typically liable for malpractice, should face equal standards of care. For a mediator to be accountable for the substantive terms of a mediated agreement, there would need to be a redefinition of the mediator's role, that is, controlling not only the process but also the outcome.

Fiduciary obligations

Another potential source of liability for mediators is the possibility of a fiduciary obligation towards the parties. Fiduciary obligations allow rights and duties to the

---

259 *Hedley Byrne & Co v Heller & Partners Ltd* [1964] AC 465 at 486 per Lord Reid:
   '... a reasonable man, knowing that he was being trusted or that his skill and judgment were being relied on, would ... have three courses open to him. He could keep silent or decline to give the information or advice sought; or he could give an answer with a clear qualification that he accepted no responsibility for it or that it was given without that reflection or enquiry which a careful answer would require; or he could simply answer without any such qualification. If he chooses to adopt the last course he must ... be held to have accepted some responsibility for his answer being given carefully, or to have accepted a relationship with the enquirer which requires him to exercise such care as the circumstances require.'
   See also *Henderson v Merrett Syndicates Ltd* [1995] 2 AC 145; and *Esso Petroleum Co Ltd v Mardon* [1976] QB 801.
260 *Bradford Third Equitable Benefit Building Society v Borders* [1941] 2 All ER 205; *Pan Atlantic Insurance Co Ltd v Pine Top Insurance Co Ltd* [1995] 1 AC 501; and *Barton v County NatWest Ltd* [1999] Lloyd's Rep Bank 408.
261 A A Chaykin 'Mediator Liability: A New Role for Fiduciary Duties?' (1984) 53 *Cincinnati Law Review* 731 at 736.

parties to be enforced in the absence of contractual obligations or a recognised standard of care.[262] A fiduciary relationship must exist to found a claim:

'A fiduciary is someone who has undertaken to act for or on behalf of another in a particular matter in circumstances which give rise to a relationship of trust and confidence. The distinguishing obligation of a fiduciary is the obligation of loyalty. The principal is entitled to single-minded loyalty of his fiduciary.'[263]

Fiduciary obligations are 'flexible enough to cover many of the almost unimaginable number of contexts in which clients need protection'.[264] The principal can sue for breach of fiduciary duties without having to prove that loss occurred and the problems with causation and remoteness which exist in tort and contract are absent. The law of fiduciary duties imposes a strict liability; it is no defence that the client has suffered no loss or detriment or that the mediator acted in good faith. Whether a fiduciary relationship arises is a question of fact in each case.

In relation to mediation, it may be argued that the close relationship of trust between the mediator and the parties gives rise to fiduciary obligations owed by mediators. The general principle would be that the mediator has an obligation not to abuse the trust reposed in him or her, either to the detriment of those relying on the mediator's skill or for his or her own benefit. One commentator identifies three fiduciary obligations owed by mediators to their clients: even-handedness and lack of bias, trustworthiness and diligence; he suggests that these duties might be breached if a mediator failed to provide important facts that could have influenced the parties' decision to enter into a transaction, created an atmosphere where one party felt coerced into accepting a proposal, communicated with one party secretly, or deceived the parties as to his or her credentials and experience.[265] The confidential nature of the mediator/client relationship would also produce an equitable duty of confidence. Thus, where one party reveals information of a confidential nature to the mediator, the mediator cannot use the information without that party's consent. In the US, for example, a mediator owes a duty to the parties to ensure that the mediation process is fair and, accordingly, a mediator could be liable if there is breach of that duty.[266]

However, there are other considerations which may make the traditional fiduciary relationship inapplicable to mediation. One problem relates to the extent of the mediator's power to influence the parties' affairs. Many approaches to mediation deny any such power, though the reality of much mediation practice is that mediators do exercise influential powers in relation to the disclosure of information, the conduct of negotiations, and the operation of mediation. Another problem in relation to the possible fiduciary duties of a mediator is that a fiduciary may not act for two

---

262 *Henderson v Merrett Syndicates Ltd* [1995] 2 AC 145 at 372 per Lord Browne-Wilkinson:

'The existence of a contract does not exclude the co-existence of concurrent fiduciary duties (indeed the contract may well be their source) . . .'

263 Millett LJ in *Bristol and West Building Society v Mothew* [1998] Ch 1.

264 A A Chaykin 'Mediator Liability: A New Role for Fiduciary Duties?' (1984) 53 *Cincinnati Law Review* 731 at 736.

265 Ibid.

266 G Hufnagle 'Mediator Malpractice Liability' (1989) 23 *Mediation Quarterly*, at pp 33–36.

beneficiaries in the same transaction;[267] and likewise, a mediator cannot owe separate duties to parties whose interests are in conflict. It would be impossible for a mediator to simultaneously fulfil fiduciary obligations to all the parties present at a mediation who have conflicting interests.[268] This is unlike traditional fiduciary models, such as solicitor and client or agent and principal, where the fiduciary cannot place himself or herself in a position of conflict of duty. Lynch suggests that if mediators do not have fiduciary obligations towards the parties, it might be argued in the alternative that a mediator has a duty to the mediation process, that is, to prevent abuses of the process by the parties.[269] This would include the duty of impartiality, the duty of non-coerciveness and the duty of thoroughness. As a matter of policy, however, the courts may be reluctant to apply the fiduciary relationship to the mediation context because, although each situation would be assessed on its merits, holding that all mediators, regardless of their professional expertise, compensatory arrangements and institutional settings, are fiduciaries may deter entry into the mediation field or induce practising mediators to accept disputes only from high-paying customers.

Other forms of liability

Liability for breaching other professional standards

Professionals such as psychologists and lawyers, when acting as mediators, remain liable for breaches of their own professional standards. Conversely, mediators might incur liability if during the course of the mediation they trespass into professional areas in which they are not licensed to practise. In an American case,[270] a mediator was successfully sued by the local bar association on the ground that his mediation practice involved him in the unauthorised practise of law. In 1993, a South African court granted an injunction against a family mediator for similar reasons.[271]

Liability to third parties

The question arises as to whether mediators may be liable where a party to the mediation harms an outside party in circumstances where the mediator could have attempted to prevent the harm from occurring. In an American case,[272] a psychotherapist was found to have been negligent when he failed to warn a female student of his patient's threats to murder her. It could be argued that this principle should be extended to mediators. However, apart from difficulties relating to causation and remoteness, the relationship between mediators and parties differs from that between psychotherapists and patients (which includes some responsibility for controlling patients' conduct).

---

267 A Lynch 'Can I Sue My Mediator? Finding the Key to Mediator Liability' (1995) *Australian Dispute Resolution Journal* 113 at 117.
268 Thus, the CEDR *Model Mediation Procedure*, for example, provides that the mediator and the Centre are not agents of, or acting in any capacity for, any of the parties.
269 A Lynch 'Can I Sue My Mediator? Finding the Key to Mediator Liability' (1995) *Australian Dispute Resolution Journal* 113 at 118.
270 *Werle v Rhode Island Bar Association* 755 F 2d 195 (1st Cir 1985).
271 Unreported decision.
272 *Tarasoff v Regents of the University of California* 17 Cal 3d 425, 551 P 2d 334 (1976).

Criminal liability

There is a possibility of mediators being held criminally liable where their own conduct makes them parties to fraud or the commission of a statutory offence, or where they conspire with the parties to commit a criminal act. This liability would be determined according to the general principles of criminal law.

Non-enforceability of agreements

Another form of accountability in mediation derives from the fact that the principles of contract law and equity may serve to make some mediated agreements unenforceable. In cases of undue influence, duress or an unconscionable bargain, while there may be no liability for the mediator concerned, any agreement reached at mediation may be set aside by a reviewing court.

Judicial review of mediators' actions

This form of review is not available in respect of private mediations as those mediating are not part of the administrative branch of government. They have potential application where mediation is provided by a government agency. Even here there is likely to be limited scope for review. For there to be judicial review, there must be a reviewable 'decision' of the relevant official or authority. Most of the matters determined by mediators during the course of a mediation would not constitute 'decisions' for purposes of review since they do not directly affect the parties' rights. Possible exceptions to this might be the termination of the mediation meeting, or the filing of an adverse report on one of the mediating parties, both of which could prejudice the parties' rights. Decisions made during the intake stages of mediation may also constitute 'decisions', for example a refusal to take on a mediation where it is requested by one party. Generally, however, there is not likely to be extensive judicial review of the actions of mediators.

Mediator immunity

Contractual exclusions

Standard mediation agreements usually contain an exclusion clause, providing mediators with immunity. Some clauses exclude all liability,[273] whereas other clauses provide a more limited exclusion.[274] The efficacy of an exclusion of mediator liability

---

273 For example, the Academy of Experts *Guidelines for Mediation* provide that the mediator will not be liable for any act or omission arising out of the mediation.

274 For example, the Commercial Mediation Centre *Mediation Rules and Procedures* provide that a mediator is not liable save for the consequences of fraud or dishonesty; the Centre for Dispute Resolution *Model Mediation Procedure* provides that the mediator will not be liable for any act or omission unless done in bad faith; the World Intellectual Property Organisation *Mediation Rules*, Intermediation *Mediation Rules* and *Rules of Conduct* and the London Court of International Arbitration *Mediation Procedure* all provide that a mediator will not be liable except in cases of deliberate wrong-doing; the Center for Public Resources *Model Mediation Agreement for Europe*

clause has not been tested in the UK. It is likely that, as with other types of exclusion clauses that:

- such clauses must be clear and unambiguous;
- the burden will be on a mediator to show that the clause, on its true construction, covers the obligation or liability which it is alleged to exclude;
- in the absence of clear words, the parties to a mediation agreement would not be taken to have intended that an exemption clause should apply to the consequences of a mediator's negligence;[275] and
- any doubt or ambiguity would be resolved against the mediator seeking to rely on it.[276]

A mediator who acts outside the scope of the mediation agreement could not rely on an exclusion clause.[277] Where a party to a mediation agreement is a consumer, or if the exclusion clause is a standard term in a mediation agreement, which has not been negotiated, ss 2, 3 and 11 of the Unfair Contract Terms Act 1977 provide that the exclusion or restriction of liability is assessed against the requirement of reasonableness, having regard to the circumstances at the time the agreement was made.[278] The Unfair Terms in Consumer Contracts Regulations 1999 may provide an additional source of redress for a consumer.[279]

There are competing policy considerations behind the extension of immunities to mediators. One of the justifications is that many mediators are volunteers or mediate as a form of social service and are paid very low rates of remuneration. Immunity can also be said to have social utility as far as the development and promotion of mediation are concerned. However, there are also arguments against the extension of wide immunities to mediators. They deny recourse to parties damaged by negligent practice. That would be especially invidious where the mediation is mandatory and the parties are required to fund it themselves.[280] Consumer interests would be better protected if there were no immunities, with mediators holding insurance coverage and being indemnified by the institutions for which they provide services.

---

and its *Model Mediation Procedures for Business Disputes in Europe* provide that a mediator will not be liable except for wilful misconduct or gross negligence.

275 Buckley LJ in *Gillespie Bros & Co Ltd v Roy Bowles Transport Ltd* [1973] QB 400 at 419; May LJ in *Lamport & Holt Lines Ltd v Coubro, The Raphael* [1982] 2 Lloyd's Rep 42 at 49; and Hobhouse J in *Caledonia Ltd v Orbit Valve Co* [1994] 1 WLR 221 at 232.

276 *Chitty on Contracts* (27th edn), at paras 14.05–14.019.

277 Compare with fundamental breach: *Suisse Atlantique Société d'Armement Maritime SA v N V Rotterdamsche Kolen Centrale* [1967] 1 AC 361; reaffirmed in *Photo Production Ltd v Securicor Transport Ltd* [1980] AC 827.

278 Schedule 2 provides guidelines for assessing reasonableness, including the strength of the bargaining positions of the parties; whether the party could have entered into a similar agreement with other persons, without the exemption clause; and whether the party knew or ought to have known of the existence of the term.

279 The Regulations (see regs 4–6) apply to a consumer who enters into a standard term agreement with a supplier of services in the course of a business (which could catch a mediator and mediation organisation, provided that the mediation service is supplied in the course of a business). A standard term will be regarded as unfair if it causes a significant imbalance in the parties' rights and obligations under the contract, to the consumer's detriment. The indicative list of unfair terms, in Schedule 2 of the Regulations, includes restrictions on legal remedies.

280 This situation is currently not present in the UK.

The trend towards mediator immunity assumes that the role of mediators in dispute settlement is of such a nature that the judicial/arbitral immunity should be extended to them. A judge's absolute immunity from liability is considered necessary in order for the law to be administered independently, without fear, and with finality. Review by an appeal court constitutes an alternative to bringing proceedings against a judge. This immunity has been partially extended to arbitrators who, like judges, are decision makers but in a predominantly private capacity. Arbitration Act 1996, s 29 provides an arbitrator with immunity, except for fraud. Some argue that since mediators neither perform an adjudicatory function nor have any decision-making role, no immunity should exist. The argument has weight given that adjudicators under the Housing Grants Construction and Regeneration Act have no immunity. Perhaps it may be desirable to establish a 'modest threat of liability'[281] which represents the middle ground between permitting the mediator too much licence, on the one hand, and regulating the system too stringently, on the other.

Professional indemnity insurance

Where there are grounds for mediator liability and no general immunity exists, mediators may be exposed to damages awarded in favour of aggrieved parties. This may necessitate the procuring of professional indemnity insurance for mediators. Insurance cover is a requirement in many mediator codes of practice.[282] It is necessary to check that the policy covers work as a mediator.[283] Some mediation organisations arrange cover for their members.[284] Solicitor mediators are covered by their firm's insurance, provided that they act as a mediator in their capacity as a member of the firm.[285]

Statutory immunity for mediators?

Statutory immunities against civil liability for mediators are rare. In so far as court-based mediation is conducted by a judicial officer, mediation would be treated as part of his or her judicial duties, and would not be liable to be sued. For example, a Commercial Court judge conducting an early neutral evaluation in accordance with the Court's Practice Direction would be protected.

The issue arises whether statutory immunity should be provided to mediators. Debate in Australia, for example, has raised issues over whether immunity, if it is to be granted, should be limited, for example, to mediators with formal accreditation or mediators who provide court-referred mediation.[286]

---

281 A A Chaykin 'Mediator Liability: A New Role for Fiduciary Duties?' (1984) 53 *Cincinnati Law Review* 731.
282 For example, the Codes of Conduct of the Law Society of England & Wales, Law Wise NFM, FMA and the UK College of Family Mediators.
283 NFM and FMA Codes of Practice require the cover to be approved by those organisations.
284 For example, ADR Group, Centre for Dispute Resolution and FMA.
285 Law Society of England & Wales *Code of Practice* in both Family Mediation and Civil/Commercial Mediation; and Principle 22.01 of the *Guide to the Professional Conduct of Solicitors* (8th edn), Law Society Publishing, 1999.
286 New South Wales Law Reform Commission *Discussion Paper: Alternative Dispute Resolution – Training and Accreditation of Mediators*. The Commission had concluded

Statutory immunity exists in Australia for mediators performing functions by virtue of court mediation schemes and limited immunity protects mediators attached to community justice centres. In the case of the former, statutes afford mediators the same protection and immunity as a judge has in performing the functions of a judge.[287] In the latter case, statutes afford mediators immunity for anything done in good faith in the execution of their statutory duties.[288]

In a March 2000 Discussion Paper in Australia, the following reasons were advanced for providing facilitative mediators with immunity:

- it allows mediations to be conducted according to a case's circumstances;
- liability might deter the valuable social development of mediation;
- low rates of pay for some mediators;
- if mediators operate under the control of an organisation, there is some guarantee of standards being maintained.[289]

Legal Liability of Lawyer Representatives in Mediation

Should lawyers advise clients of the mediation option?

In the case of family disputes, the Solicitors' Family Law Association (SFLA) Code of Practice requires its members to make clients aware of the mediation option if they consider mediation appropriate. The Law Society of England & Wales has issued guidelines for solicitors in the conduct of ancillary proceedings, which endorse the SFLA Code. Where a party involved in a family dispute is legally-aided, the solicitor for that party would be required to explain the requirement for a meeting with a mediator in order to discuss whether a mediation is appropriate, unless the case is exempted from the relevant provisions in the legal aid legislation.[290]

In the case of other civil/commercial mediation, solicitors interviewed for the Central London County Court Mediation Pilot did not consider that they were obliged to inform their clients of mediation even if an offer to mediate had been made by the court.[291] Solicitors' Practice Rule 15 and Solicitors' Client Care Code

---

that a general immunity for civil liability was not warranted or feasible and that mediators found to be either unethical or incompetent should be held responsible.

287 For example, Family Law Act 1975 (Cth), s 19M.

288 For example, Community Justice Centres Act 1983 (NSW), s 27.

289 NADRAC *The Development of Standards for ADR: Discussion Paper*, NADRAC, March 2000.

290 For more information, see the section on Funding and Mediation in Chapter 9. See also part (c) in *Legal Aid Franchise Quality Assurance Standard (Solicitors)*, June 2000.

291 One solicitor interviewed referred to the difference of opinion at his firm, where some of the lawyers considered that the information from the court about mediation should at least be sent to the client, whereas others disagreed (H Genn *The Central London County Court Mediation Pilot: Evaluation Report*, Lord Chancellor's Department Research Series no 5/98, July 1998, at p 37). Some solicitors stated that they threw the mediation

require solicitors to give 'the best information possible' to clients on the implications of starting litigation.[292] Given the provisions in the CPR and Court Guides encouraging ADR, and the promotion of ADR by courts, it may not be long before an English solicitor is criticised, sanctioned with costs or interest or even found negligent if ADR has not been discussed.[293] Scottish commentators suggest that, as mediation is used more frequently in practice, failure to advise clients about it will, at least, constitute inadequate professional services.[294]

In comparison, with the judicial separation in Ireland in 1989, solicitors were required to notify their clients about mediation services.[295] The Family Law (Divorce) Act 1996 provides that, in the context of separation or divorce, solicitors shall upon receipt of instructions discuss with their clients how mediation might help and shall provide clients with the names and addresses of mediators.[296]

In New South Wales, Australia in 1991 it was suggested that it should be mandatory for lawyers to bring mediation to the attention of parties early in proceedings.[297] The main argument against the proposal was that the imposition of the duty would result in practitioners feeling constrained in providing written advice about options to each client in order to protect against any allegation that the duty had not been complied with.[298]

Writers have suggested that it would be unwise to exclude the possibility of a lawyer being sued in negligence for failing to advise his or her client as to the availability and nature of mediation.[299] In an Australian text on legal ethics, Ross leaves unanswered the question of whether the lawyers' obligations to act with due competence and care extend to advising clients about non-litigation options.[300] Lawyers are not responsible for mere errors of judgment in relation to matters of law

---

materials received from the court in the bin, and others reported that they had advised clients to reject the court's mediation offer (H Genn, ibid). One firm of solicitors wrote to the court when the Pilot had commenced, advising that it would not recommend to their clients acceptance of the court's mediation offers (H Genn, ibid, at p 38).

292 See Chapter 7 for CPR provisions and court requirements in relation to and attitudes towards ADR; *Dyson and Field v Leeds CC* (22 November 1999); and Academy of Experts *Answers to frequently asked questions about mediation*. The Law Society of Northern Ireland has warned solicitors that it may be negligent to fail to advise on the possibility of ADR: *ADR—coming to terms in business*.

293 Academy of Experts *Answers to frequently asked questions about mediation*. The Law Society of Northern Ireland has also warned solicitors that it may be negligent to fail to advise on the possibility of alternative dispute resolution: *ADR – Coming to terms in Business*, The Law Society of Northern Ireland pamphlet.

294 M Stone *Representing clients in Mediation*, Butterworths 1998, at p 94.

295 L Webley *A review of the literature on family mediation: prepared for the Lord Chancellor's Advisory Committee on Legal Education and Conduct*, Institute of Advanced Legal Studies, 1998, at p 29.

296 Family Law (Divorce) Act 1996, s 7.

297 C Chinkin and M Dewdney 'Settlement Week in New South Wales: An Evaluation', *Australian Dispute Resolution Journal*, vol 3, May 1992 no 2, at p 93.

298 T McFarlane 'Should there be a duty to advise of ADR?' (1993) *Litigation Lawyer* 11.

299 See G Sammon 'The ethical duties of lawyers who act for parties to a mediation' (1993) 4 *ADRJ* 190 at 193; and G Robertson 'The Lawyer's Role in Commercial ADR' (1987) 61 *LIJ* 1148: 'it is now incumbent on the lawyer to stop shopping just in the corner shop, where only litigation is available, and to take clients through the shopping centre, where a whole range of ADR techniques is available'.

300 S Ross *Ethics in Law – Lawyer's Responsibility and accountability*, Butterworths,

and discretion, unless they are errors which no reasonably informed and competent member of the profession should have made,[301] or where the standard of care expected of members of the profession is not met. Arguably, as more becomes known about mediation and other ADR options, the more likely it is that a lawyer who fails to advise on them will be found liable. This may in fact be another reason for advocates of mediation to support the arguments advanced by writers for 'ADR' to stand for 'Appropriate Dispute Resolution'.[302] A case may possibly be made for lawyers to be legally obliged to consider 'alternative' options for dispute resolution but a more compelling one can be made for them to consider 'appropriate' options for their clients. Judicial policy is clearly changing in this area and it is too early to predict the exact contours of lawyers' legal duties in relation to mediation.

In relation to mediation representation

The issue, which arises specifically in relation to the conduct of lawyers during a mediation, is that costs orders can be used to penalise parties where they or their lawyers fail to participate reasonably and co-operatively in the mediation process.[303] In a recent, unreported example, an English Mercantile Court judge enquired about the conduct of the lawyers in a mediation, on an application for security for costs, which had been adjourned to enable a mediation to be attempted. The mediation was not successful and the judge sought to enquire into the conduct of the parties or their lawyers in the mediation, following an allegation by one party that the other had attended the mediation in bad faith and that the lawyers were obstructive and unco-operative. Although the judge ultimately excluded this evidence for the purpose of determining the application, the case nevertheless shows the potential willingness by English judges to consider lawyer behaviour in mediation. This may occur more frequently in light of CPR, r 44, which provides that a court can take account, when giving consideration to costs, of the conduct of the parties, including during any settlement attempts. Rule 44 is discussed in more detail in Chapters 7 and 9. This could have important implications for the future behaviour of parties and their lawyers in mediation.

In relation to mediation settlements

Immunity?

The general principle, that an advocate is immune from a claim for damages for negligence arising out of anything done or omitted in the course of conducting a case in court, was established by the House of Lords in *Rondel v Worsley*.[304] In *Saif Alis v Sydney Mitchell & Co*[305] the House of Lords recognised that the principle would extend to work intimately connected with the conduct of a case in court. The Court

---

Sydney, 1979, at pp 343–4.
301 Ibid, at pp 194–5.
302 For more discussion on this point, see for example J Lee 'The ADR Movement in Singapore' in K Tan (ed) *The Singapore Legal System*, 1999, at pp 414–16.
303 See Chapter 9 for detailed discussion about relevant circumstances.
304 [1969] 1 AC 191.
305 [1980] AC 198.

of Appeal in *Kelley v Corston*[306] considered application of the principle in the context of settlement, finding that immunity extended to settlements, which were subject to or required court approval, as in the case of family and probate matters, and to settlements, made on the steps of the court, and embodied in a consent order. Although on the basis of *Kelley* a range of mediated settlements might have been caught by the immunity, the House of Lords has recently abolished the immunity.[307]

Negligence issues

Claims of negligence against a legal representative, in the context of a settlement at mediation, might be made on the following grounds:

- that he or she negligently advised the client to accept a settlement in the mediation;[308] or
- that he or she negligently failed to achieve settlement in the mediation.[309]

In the first case, courts are reluctant to review an assessment made by a lawyer in advising settlement as so many subjective matters pertain to the assessment, for example an assessment by the lawyer of the client's likely credibility if the matter were to be tried and of the strengths and weaknesses of the evidence:

> 'Settlements are to be encouraged as a matter of policy so it would be a discouragement if a party had to justify them in detail.'[310]

Courts will not interfere unless it can be seen that the view the lawyer took was such as no reasonable lawyer could have taken in the circumstances.[311] In an Australian case, *Studer v Boettcher*,[312] a client claimed that his solicitor had been negligent by failing to make a proper assessment of the respective cases and in turn negligently advised him to enter into a settlement at mediation. The court decided the case on the evidence, finding that the client made the decision to settle at the end of the day, albeit one that he did not like:

> 'Like many litigants who believe fervently in their own position, it is a matter of disappointment when they realise their best interest is served in solving the matter, even if they were not enamoured by the terms.'[313]

The case shows that the presence of an experienced mediator does not insulate an agreement from subsequent challenge. It highlights the need for mediators to ensure

---

306 [1998] QB 686; compare *Griffin v Kingsmill* [1998] PIQR P24.
307 *Arthur J S Hall & Co v Simons, Barratt v Woolf Seddon, Cockbone v Atkinson Dacre & Slack, Harris v Scholfield Roberts & Hill* (conjoined appeals) [2000] 3 All ER 673. Given the decision, views on whether the principle extended to solicitors or other advocates is not material. In any event, Courts and Legal Services Act 1990, s 62 provides that a person who provides legal services in relation to any proceedings shall have the same immunity from liability for negligence as if he were a barrister. It does not provide an independent immunity, but tracks the immunity, if any, for barristers.
308 *Biggin & Co Ltd v Permanite Ltd* [1951] 2 KB 314.
309 *Allied Maples Group Ltd v Simmons & Simmons* [1995] 1 WLR 1602.
310 *J Sainsbury plc v Broadway Malyan (a firm)* (1998) 61 Con LR 31, High Court; and *DSL Group Ltd v Unisys International Services Ltd* (1994) 41 Con LR 33 at 39–43.
311 *Atwell v Michael Perry & Co* [1998] 4 All ER 65.
312 [1998] NSWSC 524.
313 Young J.

that the parties themselves are consenting on an informed basis to mediated settlements.[314]

Although the courts might not provide redress, the Office of Supervision of Solicitors might. In one recent English case, a client had agreed to terms of settlement, although not in a mediation, without being properly advised by his solicitor on the amount of costs which would have to be met out of the settlement sum.[315]

In relation to the second case, one issue is whether, and if so to what extent, a solicitor has a duty to persuade reluctant clients of the advantages of a settlement. In *Struder*, although the issue did not arise for decision, Young J usefully commented:

'Certainly 30 or 40 years ago, in an era when legal advisers were expected to take a paternalistic role, it is clear that it was the duty of counsel and solicitors to put pressure on clients to do what the lawyers believed was sensible and in the clients' interest ... I believe it is still appropriate for solicitors to put pressure on clients to do what is, in the lawyer's view, in the clients' own interests. Of course, there must come a point where the client is just behaving as an automaton and if the matter gets to that point then the solicitor should know that he or she should not proceed at least without an independent person speaking to the client to make sure that the client understands ...'

It may be that the need for a 'paternalistic' approach is greater in the case of an inexperienced client who expects that his solicitor will take a broader view of the scope of his retainer and of his duties than in the case of an experienced client.[316]

The second issue relates to causation. When it is alleged that the lawyer's negligence consists of an omission to achieve settlement, consideration is required of what the client would have done if the lawyer had recommended settlement, which is a matter of inference to be determined from all the circumstances.[317] The client's evidence that he would have settled in mediation may not be believed, particularly if there is compelling evidence that he would not have done so.

---

314 Issues of confidentiality were not discussed in the case. The terms of settlement appear in the judgment.
315 The case is outlined in *The Litigation Letter*, November 2000, at p 111.
316 *National Home Loans Corpn plc v Giffen Couch & Archer (a firm)* [1998] 1 WLR 207.
317 *Allied Maples Group Ltd v Simmons & Simmons* [1995] 1 WLR 1602.

13

Themes and Trends in Mediation Practice

Themes in Mediation Practice

From innocence to experience, and beyond

Most new social practices, from psychotherapy to financial advising, display similar patterns in their initial establishment and early development. There tends to be a first phase of innocence, during which there is an optimistic and idealised vision of the new practice and an enthusiastic conviction in its capacity to deal with both individual and societal concerns and issues in better ways than ever before. During this phase there are high profile practitioners, messiah figures and zealous converts, travelling prophets from abroad, miracle stories, and uncritical popular acceptance. As innocence turns to experience, there is a reactive phase during which there is a sceptical and at times hostile critique of the new practice, more exacting standards are demanded of it than of traditional practices, there are horror stories and disappointments, the messiah's fall from grace, and there is a renunciation of foreign intrusions. Finally there is a pragmatic phase, during which there is a more measured understanding of the practice's strengths and shortcomings. It comes to be recognised and organised and takes its place as a conventional pursuit along with its associates and competitors. These phases do not occur in a neat sequential order and a new practice may display characteristics from all three phases at one time.

In the UK there have been no wild or extravagant claims made about mediation being a 'panacea'. Nor is there widespread scepticism, cynicism or dissatisfaction arising from exaggerated claims. Rather there is a growing appreciation of mediation and acceptance of it as an option. This may be due partly to the fact that the UK has had the advantage of learning from the experiences of countries with more mature mediation movements.

From supply to demand

Mediation in the UK has tended to be supply-driven. Initiatives have come from the courts, government, and a number of professional, trade and community organis- ations. However, these initiatives are not based on any substantial evidence of demand for mediation services. Much of institutionalised mediation is therefore a product of encouragement from 'outside' bodies.

This issue has generated questions about whether government and community legal advice centres should be doing more to increase awareness amongst the public at large; and whether law societies and law schools should be doing the same in relation to lawyers. It has been suggested that ADR information centres, run either by government or the voluntary sector, could provide information about ADR at an early stage in disputes in the UK.[1] The Lord Chancellor's Department booklet, 'Resolving disputes without going to court', has taken the first step to help make the public more aware of the possibilities that ADR can offer. The booklet has been made available though courts, citizens advice bureaux, law centres, libraries and business links and connect centres in England and Wales. The Scottish Courts Administration has produced a similar publication for Scotland. Respondents to the Lord Chancellor's ADR Discussion Paper consider that it is also important for the public to 'get a real feel' for mediation, rather than merely reading about it, and have suggested public workshops, seminars and videos.[2] A recent English television documentary has focused on the scope and benefits of family mediation. In Australia, New Zealand and Canada, the solution adopted to allow the public to 'get a real feel' for mediation included 'Settlement Weeks', whereby courts invited litigants to refer their cases to mediation, with positive results seen in all those jurisdictions. The programmes increased public awareness of mediation, and also promoted its use amongst the legal profession.

There are some signs of increasing demand for mediation from actual users. The commercial community shows signs of requiring information and advice on ADR options from lawyers and other advisers, and some private sector enterprises are sending employees to mediation training to assist them make informed decisions on whether to use mediation, and if so how to use it to best effect. The bulk users of the courts, insurers and governments, are also showing signs of resorting to mediation. There is increasing use of mediation clauses in contracts. There are also indications that in areas where legal advice was limited and litigation was never a feasible option, such as in disputes within voluntary associations, schools and other basic communities, there is a greater appreciation that mediation might be appropriate. There is at present some demand for mediation but the mediation movement is far from being transformed into a demand-driven one. There is also more discernment among repeat users of mediation, and their advisers, as to which models of mediation, and which mediator styles, might be suitable for their purposes.

The issue of suitability for mediation has raised the concern that government might specify the circumstances in which mediation should be considered inappropriate. If mediation were understood by lawyers and the public, there should be no need for such a measure. Responses to the Lord Chancellor's ADR Discussion Paper suggest alternative approaches to the issue of testing suitability, including further pilot schemes and customer satisfaction surveys.[3]

---

1   C Archbold et al *Divorce in Northern Ireland: unravelling the system*, Report to the Office of Law Reform, HMSO, 1999, at p 210.
2   Lord Chancellor's Department *ADR Discussion Paper: Summary of responses*, August 2000, at para 34. The Law Society in QLD Australia achieved success in raising public awareness of mediation through a video, featuring a local television celebrity, which was distributed throughout law centres and schools. One respondent to the Lord Chancellor's *ADR Discussion Paper* recommended that a story line including mediation should be included in a soap opera in the UK.
3   Lord Chancellor's Department *ADR Discussion Paper: Summary of responses*, op cit, at para 26.

Ultimately, the issue is whether mediation should continue to be voluntary and whether courts should impose sanctions on parties for failing to consider or attempt mediation. Should government legislate to either require or encourage mediation and, if so, should it be in certain contexts, as in Australia?[4]

From the margins to the centre

Mediation in the UK is becoming more 'institutionalised'. Institutionalisation denotes that mediation has shifted from an unregulated position on the margins of society towards more formal, centralised and regulated forms of practice. Instead of having an uncoordinated, organic development, mediation's progress has been controlled and coordinated by a wide range of public and private institutions. This has distorted the 'alternative' nature of mediation, bringing it into the mainstream of courts, organisational structures and complaints-handling procedures. Inevitably this has rendered mediation a more formal, rigid and bureaucratic process than it would have been on the margins. However, this has also had benefits in terms of consistency, economies of scale, standards setting, promotion and marketing, training and accountability.

From practice to profession

There are also indications that mediation has been rapidly 'professionalised'. The traditional professions are characterised by three features: a sustainable claim to exclusive technical competence in a field, a service ideal, and a sense of community,[5] though professionalism is itself undergoing considerable change, and, some would say, decline.[6] In its present stage of development, mediation can only go some way towards claiming exclusive technical competence, and not to the same extent as the traditional professions. The service ideal, in the sense of devotion to clients' interests over and above personal profit, is evident in some mediation contexts, particularly among volunteer or poorly-remunerated mediators. As regards the community aspect, of which corporate control is a feature, there is as yet no uniformity of organisation and accountability within the mediation movement. Moreover, the current absence of sustained demand for mediation services does not warrant full-time occupation in the field, a necessary feature of professional status. One of the other hallmarks of professional development is increasingly sophisticated forms of training and accreditation and the contemporary mediation movement has achieved some progress in these areas. The development of standards and codes of conduct,

---

4   In Australia, for example, mediation is statutorily mandated in the case of retail tenancy (Retail Leases Act 1994 NSW), strata schemes management (Strata Schemes Management Act 1996 NSW), and farm debt (Farm Debt Mediation Act 1994) disputes.

5   H Wilensky 'The professionalisation of everyone?' (1964) *The American Journal of Sociology* 137; and J Sammons *Lawyer professionalism*, Carolina Academic Press, North Carolina, 1988, at pp 3–12. See also D Weisbrot *Australian Lawyers*, Longman Cheshire, Melbourne, 1990, at p 4

6   Perhaps the increasing recognition of the advantages of mediation and ADR by lawyers heralds a revival of professional traditions in law. See T Morgan 'The fall and rise of professionalism' (1983–4) 18 *University of Richmond Law Review* 451 at 466.

as is occurring in the UK, is another hallmark of professionalisation.[7] Normally standards appear towards the later stages in the development of professional status, after the emergence of training systems, university-based qualifications and national professional organisations. In the UK, they have developed relatively early in the genesis of the mediation movement.

It is not, however, inevitable that mediation will develop a separate professional identity, as there are other countervailing pressures. The established professions have a record of attempting to colonise new practices and using them to supplement their existing services. They may therefore claim that mediation can be accommodated within their existing practices and organisations. Contemporary economic pressures and boundary disputes between existing professions may also increase the temptation to co-opt mediation. There are thus strong forces militating against any claim by the mediation movement for exclusivity and the market control of mediation services.[8] The professionalisation tendencies may also be resisted by agencies that take the approach that mediation should be provided by trained laypersons. Community mediation in particular is influenced by a philosophy of de-professionalisation.[9] Here it is felt that the new practice should be autonomous of existing professions and vested interests, and that it should develop as a community movement and not as another service creeping towards professionalism. There are thus pressures pushing and pulling mediation practice in different directions. The indications are that for some time into the future mediation will constitute both a non-professionalised service with some community roots and a supplementary service for existing professions, including lawyers. It may in the future develop into an autonomous professional discipline.

Pressures on Mediation

There are a number of pressures on modern mediation which are likely to affect its development. These pressures emanate from a variety of sources, and sometimes conflict with one another. Some of these pressures are described below.

The pressure for 'effectiveness'

A perceived weakness of mediation is that it does not guarantee an outcome. As such, pressure may be imposed on the system to increase the likelihood of settlements. This pressure may come from government and state agencies who fund mediations and require finality in order to demonstrate 'efficiency' in the various mediation services. It may come from mediation users who commit resources to mediation but still face the costs of litigation or other forms of dispute resolution if there are no settlements. It may also come from professional advisers who refer

---

7   H Wilensky 'The professionalisation of everyone?' (1964) *The American Journal of Sociology* 137 at 145. Wilensky suggests that in new or doubtful cases, the formal code of ethics may mark the beginning of a push for professional status.
8   D Weisbrot *Australian Lawyers*, Longman Cheshire, Melbourne, 1990, at p 5.
9   See for example Faulkes 'The modern development of alternative dispute resolution in Australia' (1990) 1 *ADRJ* 61 at 61–8.

clients to mediation and are concerned about client dissatisfaction if there are no settlements. It may further come from those within the mediation movement who wish to make it more attractive in the face of perceived competition from other dispute resolution processes. Finally pressure may come from mediators who are intent on improving their reputation by developing quantitative indicators of their effectiveness. The cumulative effect of these pressures may lead to more changes in the practice of mediation to increase the likelihood of settlements. An example is the placing of structural pressure on *facilitative mediation* and the shifting towards *settlement* and *evaluative mediation* in which mediators become more directive, interventionist and outcome-oriented. Med-arb is another manifestation of this trend.[10]

The pressure for efficiency

Consumerism, quality management and economic rationalist pressures are demanding efficiency as well as effectiveness from mediation. It has been suggested that instead of relying on large administrative infrastructures, mediation should be provided through less expensive private services on a user-pays basis. The efficiency pressures demand fewer resources for intake, screening, pre-mediation preparation, use of advisers, lengthy mediations, and multiple mediation meetings. They also demand costs estimates, quotations and fixed fee mediations. Respondents to the Lord Chancellor's ADR Discussion Paper have stated that they would like to see studies comparing the costs of cases proceeding to trial with the costs of cases that have settled through an ADR process, using data from courts, lawyers, insurers and the Legal Services Commission. The pressures for quicker, cheaper and otherwise more efficient services are also being experienced by other professions and occupations, but in the case of a new practice such as mediation they are likely to have a formative effect on its shape and nature.

The answers to these questions also impact on the funding of mediation. Respondents to the Lord Chancellor's ADR Discussion Paper recommended, as funding alternatives, tax incentives, court fee changes and fixed price ADR.

The pressure for returning to basics

While the pressures for effectiveness and efficiency are widespread, there is a countervailing pressure for mediation to retain its authenticity by returning to basic principles and ideals. For those to whom mediation encapsulates an alternative philosophy of community interaction, there is pressure for mediation to retain and reinforce its participatory, empowering and relationship-building qualities. This movement highlights the multiple benefits of mediation other than settlement, and rejects the emphasis on quantifying mediation effectiveness only in terms of settlement rates. It emphasises that settlement rates are only one indicator of the effectiveness of mediation, and that efficiency is often measured only in short-term and easily quantifiable criteria. It expresses the concern that current pressures will lead to mediation becoming legalised and judicialised, as has occurred with many

---

10 Such a trend may, however, be seen as a response to user demands.

administrative tribunals and the arbitration process. A related, but more radical, pressure comes from those who argue that mediation should be a transformative process.[11] Transformative mediation has as its objectives recognition, forgiveness and reconciliation among the disputing parties; it is as much about changing people as it is about resolving disputes. This involves complex additions to the mediation process and evidences a second wave of mediation idealism.

The pressure for quality and standards

Consumerism and quality management pressures are also demanding high standards and accountability in the mediation movement. The questions are demanding: should mediators be allowed to provide recommendations? What type of training and continuing professional development should mediators undergo? What standards should mediators adhere to? What are the ethical and other dilemmas which mediators face and how should these be resolved? Should there be statutory clarification of confidentiality of mediation? How are mediation services to be regulated, if at all? How should quality be assured? How should mediation services be priced?

This implies increased organisation and regulation of mediation, the setting of standards, and responsive systems of complaints-handling where there are allegations of aberrant mediator behaviour. The pressure extends to the demand for survey studies, investigations and inquiries into mediation practice and mediator conduct. There is also currently a high degree of pressure for increasing the amount and quality of mediation education and training and for tightening and standardising accreditation requirements.

The pressure for fairness, justice and rights

Because of its close connection to the justice system, there may be pressures for mediation to comply with standards of due process and procedural fairness. Here it may face the prospect of having its procedures scrutinised and evaluated by the courts themselves, which have in the past imposed their own procedural values on other systems of dispute resolution, such as arbitration. There may also be pressures on mediation to uphold substantive rights and fairness, in the form of legal entitlements, industry standards and community norms. This is particularly evident where one party is less powerful than another, and it could be further accentuated by additional forms of mandatory mediation. The pressure for normative conformity will also come from those who wish to evaluate mediation in terms of conventional standards of dispute settlement. However, it overlooks the value of interest-based dispute resolution and the scope which mediation affords the parties to make decisions about their situation in terms of their own subjective needs.

---

11 R A B Bush 'The promise of mediation – responding to conflict through empowerment and recognition' (1994) 41 *Florida Law Review* 253; and K Cloke *Mediation: revenge and the magic of forgiveness*, Center for Dispute Resolution, Santa Monica, California, 1990.

The pressure of mixed mediation motives

There is pressure for mediation to be a versatile and multi-purpose process. People using mediation have many different motives. Concerns have often been expressed that mediation might be used by parties to litigation as a 'fishing expedition'. Modern systems of disclosure are designed to ensure that full information is disclosed to parties during the pre-trial process, but these systems are often clumsy, expensive, time-consuming and conflict-inducing. Face-to-face meetings in mediation can provide an opportunity for information gathering, for investigating bottom lines and negotiating tactics, and for otherwise assessing litigation tactics. Insurers and other defendants may use it to elicit information and to question and evaluate the demeanour and credibility of claimants, and where it suits their interests may bypass the system and proceed to litigation. Where it is used primarily for this purpose, mediation will become a strategic forum in which risk management decisions can be tested. This is one example of the range of factors which will motivate parties to use mediation.

Future Mediation Adaptations

The mediation movement may possibly respond to these conflicting pressures in a variety of ways, including the following.

Fast track mediation

Fast track mediation will involve attempts to abbreviate aspects of the mediation process in the interests of efficiency.[12] This is likely to be done by trying to comply with its essentials more quickly and succinctly. Fast track mediation is likely to involve prior telephonic and e-mail contacts, the gathering of information through the completion of standard forms, the written identification of concerns and issues, and a very brief mediator's opening and party statements. Attempts will be made to keep the negotiations focused on the issues, with the mediator playing a relatively directive role. It may also make use of 'standard issue' packages suitable for the relevant subject-matter.

Standard issue mediation

Efficiency will also be promoted through 'standard issue' mediation. Mediators who are experienced in the substantive areas of particular disputes are able to predict the kinds of issues which will arise in mediation. Standard lists of issues can expedite the mediation process by providing an initial framework for the parties, which can be supplemented by them where necessary. These can also be used to reassure the parties that the mediator is conversant with issues in the relevant area. Standard issues could be developed for family, personal injury, employment and other disputes.

---

12 A Vergis and D Crosly 'Use of fast track mediation in personal injuries litigation' (1994–5) 1 *CDRJ* 265.

Story-telling

One of the process values of mediation is that it allows for direct and flexible participation by the parties. In some cases there are temptations to overlook this feature where it does not seem necessary for reaching a settlement. Where lawyers are present in a personal injury mediation and liability is not in issue, it may appear unnecessary to allow plaintiffs to recount the stories of their accidents and explain how their lives have been affected. Efficiency imperatives might suggest that the mediation should move quickly to technical issues of damages. In many mediators' experience, however, it is useful to allow plaintiffs to relate their stories about the accident and its aftermath so that they feel that they have been allowed to talk about their distress, and be listened to. A plaintiff's spouse, partner or other care-provider can also be allowed to talk about the effects of the accident so that they also experience the equivalent of their 'day in court', however mythical that concept may be. Mediators could pre-empt any negative responses to the story-telling by explaining to insurers and lawyers that it will take place and what its purpose is in conflict management. Developments along these lines would be a response to consumer pressures and the demand to return to 'basic principles' in mediation.

Modified cross-examination

Traditional mediation does not entertain any formal cross-examination of the parties or of witnesses who may be present. This is to prevent adversarial tendencies developing in the negotiations. It is also a recognition of the fact that mediation is not fact-driven and is not well-suited to dealing with conflicts of fact. Nevertheless, there may be a need to elicit further factual evidence, particularly where a claimant has given a deficient, ambiguous or confused account of past events. Here the mediator may invite the claimant to expand on important points or clarify ambiguous statements, but if there is a further need for information, the mediator may invite the solicitor for the defendant to ask questions of clarification through the claimant's own lawyer. This channel of communication would allow the lawyer to screen the questions and to restate them to the claimant, who could deal with them without pressure or intimidation. The same system could be used with valuers, accountants and other experts. This arrangement, which modifies courtroom cross-examination procedures, would contribute to the due process aspects of mediation. An example of the use of modified cross-examination can be found in New Zealand. It is a standard practice in their Employment Tribunal mediations.

Mooting in mediation

The interest-based, as opposed to rights-based, nature of mediation tends to de-emphasise the need for presentations or argumentation on the law. However, a useful function can be served by allowing the lawyers to make 'best case' presentations on the legal rights and obligations of the case, with a short right of reply to each other's presentation. This mooting element could serve several functions in mediation. It could mutually educate the parties and their advisers, help them to assess their alternatives to settlement more realistically, confront them with the legal arguments of the other side, give them a sense of their 'day in court', provide a justification for backing off positional claims, and provide a useful role for lawyers in mediation. It is one way in which mediation might respond to the demand for taking rights seriously. This is also frequently used in many Employment Tribunal mediations in New Zealand.

Rights-based mediation

Where mediation is conducted in the strong shadow of the law there is sometimes a demand for it to be rights-based. This is often the case in the building and construction industry.[13] Instead of requiring creative interest-based outcomes based on the furtherance of their relationship, both parties may want a quick mediated outcome which is more or less in line with their respective legal entitlements. Where this is the case they will select mediators who are experts in the industry and know how the dispute might be settled through arbitration, litigation or a tribunal decision. This situation will place pressure on the mediator to give the parties an expert assessment of the strengths and weaknesses of their positions, which may be difficult to do where there are only limited facts available. How this assessment is provided will depend on the model of mediation and the style of the mediator. This is another way in which mediation may be forced to respond to the demand for rights-based decision-making.

Using expertise in mediation

Another way in which mediation will adapt to the pressure for outcomes that conform to legal, industry or societal standards will be through the increasing use of experts. Experts can be used as co-mediators, for example computer scientists in disputes pertaining to information technology. Mediation can also produce single experts agreed to by the parties to avoid the 'competing experts' syndrome. Where there are competing experts, mediation principles can be used to facilitate their developing lists of agreed issues and to identify the exact basis for points of difference between them. Introducing expertise into mediation will respond to the demands for it to be substantively driven, and will increase the frequency of evaluative mediation.

Knowing when to stop

To improve, the mediation movement will have to respond to different demands, and adapt to them to remain relevant. However, the evolution of mediation has its limits. The movers of mediation must not be afraid to draw the line when it is obvious that some other dispute resolution mechanism is more appropriate to meet certain types of expectations. Modifications should not be allowed to transform the mediation process into an unrecognisable mutant.

Mediation and Problem-Solving

Mediation is both influencing, and being influenced by, broader trends in the conflict management and problem-solving movements. An example of the effects of these

---

13   J Tyrril 'Construction industry dispute resolution – a brief overview' (1992) 3 *ADRJ* 167.

trends on mediation relates to the issue of diagnosis. One of the critical questions in the dispute resolution literature and practice is that of which dispute resolution system is appropriate for which kind of dispute.[14] This question has led to the development of the diagnostic movement which is likely to become increasingly sophisticated over time and involve the introduction of elaborate procedures for deciding whether matters should be referred to fact-finding, problem-definition, issue identification, case appraisal, arbitration, and so on. In relation to mediation, the diagnostic movement will produce sophisticated methods, based on theory and mediation practice, for assessing the suitability of mediation in different circumstances. The diagnostic approach will further indicate which model of mediation, offered by which style of mediator, is appropriate.

Mediation, in turn, is influencing the broader trends in conflict management and problem-solving. Mediation has brought together many existing disciplines and professions and points the way towards a coalescence of professional expertise in the management of conflict. It has also highlighted the need for more study and understanding of the complexities of human behaviour in dealing with conflicts and disputes. It has focused attention on specific areas requiring more extensive treatment, for example the differences and similarities between positional and interest-based bargaining, value maximisation in negotiation, and the meaning of, and alternatives to, adversarial dispute resolution. It has pointed the way, particularly for the legal profession, to the need for reflective practice in all areas of conflict management so that practitioners can systematise and learn from their experiences. It also provides a model which can be deployed in the design of larger dispute resolution systems.[15]

Conclusion

In Part III, Chapter 7 looked at mediation from a historical perspective. It considered how the mediation movement developed and the main players responsible for its development. Chapter 8 examined current mediation practices, which will continue to evolve to meet the needs of the end-users of mediation in the UK. Chapter 11 studied the issues of quality, standards and accountability, which will certainly receive more attention as the mediation movement advances. Modifications to the current situation are likely to be made in response to the different pressures highlighted there. It will also be interesting to observe how the legal issues outlined in Chapter 12 will be resolved in future, either through legislation or court pronouncements. It will also be interesting to see how the policy issues outlined in Chapter 9 are determined, and how the practical issues, set out in Chapter 10, will

---

14 K Kressel et al (eds) *Mediation Research: the process and effectiveness of third party intervention*, Jossey-Bass, San Francisco, 1989, at pp 402–5; J Wade 'In search of new conflict management process – the lawyer as macro and micro problem-solver' (1995) 10 *Australian Family Lawyer* 23–8, 16–25.
15 J David 'Designing a dispute resolution system' (1993–4) 1 *CDRJ* 26; C Constantino and C Merchant *Designing conflict management systems: a guide to creating productive and healthy organisations*, Jossey-Bass, San Francisco, 1996; and K Slaikeu and R Hasson *Controlling the costs of conflict – how to design a system for your organisation*, Jossey-Bass Publishers, San Francisco, 1998.

change the face of mediation practice in the UK. This last chapter has been devoted to the themes and trends of mediation. It will be exciting to follow these changes, which it is hoped will be based not only on theories or anecdotal evidence of what will serve the UK well, but will be premised on practical experience in mediation and systematic research that includes studies of an empirical nature. How mediation in the UK will take shape remains to be seen. The only certainty about its future is change. In the stormy ocean of conflicts, mediation is proving to be a fragile vessel with a hardy crew.

Appendices

1

Mediation Organisations

GENERAL CIVIL/COMMERCIAL MEDIATION ORGANISATIONS

(a) **England and Wales**

Name	Address	Phone	Fax	Email	Website
Academy of Experts	2 South Square, Gray's Inn, London WC1R 5HP	020 7637 0333	020 7637 1893	admin@academy-experts.org	http://www.academy-experts.org/
ADR Chambers (UK) Ltd	1 Knightrider Court London EC4V 5JP	0207 329 4909	0207 329 4903		http://www.adrchambers.co.uk
ADR Group	36–38 Baldwin St, Bristol BS1 1NR	0117 9467180		adrgroup@admet.co.uk	http://www.admet.co.uk
Arab-British Chamber of Commerce	6 Belgrave Square, London SW1X 8PH	020 7235 4363	020 7245 6688		
Association of Northern Mediators	Goodbard House, Infirmary St, Leeds LS1 2JS	0113 2469129	0113 2467518		
Centre for Business Arbitration	11 Old Square, Lincoln's Inn, London WC2A 3TS	020 7491 9697		arbitration@lincolns-inn.com	http://www.arbitration.lincolns-inn.com
Centre for Dispute Resolution (CEDR)	Princes House, 95 Gresham St, London EC2V 7MA	020 7600 0500	020 7600 0501	mediate@cedr.co.uk	http://www.cedr.co.uk
Commercial Mediation Centre	Chancery House, 53–64 Chancery Lane, London WC2A 1QU	020 7430 2222	020 7430 2022	mediation@btinternet.com	
Consensus Mediation	York House, 89 York St, Norwich NR2 2AP	01603 665 845	01603 633 996	mediate@consensus.uk.com	http://www.consensus.uk.com

Dispute Resolution Ltd	5 Cheviot Drive, Thornbury, Bristol BS35 2YA	01454 281244	01454 281911	dan@dispute-resolution.ltd.uk	http://www.dispute-resolution.ltd.uk
Dispute Mediation	AMC House, 12 Cumberland Avenue, Park Royal, London NW10 7QL	020 8838 0022	020 8965 0229	enquiries@disputemediation.co.uk	
In Place of Strife	58 High St, Harrington, Northampton NN6 9NU	01536 418205		stops@mediate.co.uk	http://www.mediate.co.uk
InterMediation	128 Cheapside, London EC2V 6BT	020 7600 4909	020 7600 6396	support@intermediation.com	www.intermediation.com
International Dispute Resolution Centre	8 Breams Buildings, Chancery Lane, London EC4A 1HP	0207 405 6500			http://www.idrc.co.uk
Littleton Mediation	Littleton Chambers, 3 King's Bench Walk North, Temple, London EC4Y 7HR	020 7797 8600	020 7797 8699	clerks@littletonchambers.co.uk	
London Court of International Arbitration (LCIA)	Houlton House, 161–166 Fleet St, London EC4A 2DY	020 7936 3530	020 7936 3533	lcia@lcia-arbitration.com	http://www.lcia-arbitration.com
London Mediation Service	Lee & Pembertons, 45 Pont St, London SW1X 0BX	020 7589 1114	020 7589 0808	law@leepem.co.uk	
Panel of Independent Mediators (PIMS)	The Panel Administrator, Ocean House, 24 Great Tower St, London EC3R 5AQ	020 7917 1745	020 7917 1746		

Name	Address	Phone	Fax	Email	Website
Reading Dispute Resolution Centre	1 London St, Reading, Berkshire RG1 4QW	01189 509609	01189 502704		
The Workitout Resolution Company	63 Lincoln's Inn Fields, London, WC2A 3LW	020 7692 5502	020 7831 6843		http://www.workitout.co.uk

(b) Scotland

Name	Address	Phone	Fax	Email	Website
Mediation Bureau	Alderstone House, Kirkton South, Livingston, EH54 7AW	01506 641 7818	01506 417843		http://www.academy-experts.org/

BANKING/FINANCE MEDIATION ORGANISATIONS

Name	Address	Phone	Fax	Email	Website
City Disputes Panel (CDP)	8 Breams Buildings, Chancery Lane, London EC4A 1HP	020 7440 7373	020 7440 7374		

COMMUNITY MEDIATION ORGANISATIONS

(a) England and Wales

Name	Address	Phone	Fax	Email	Website
Cardiff Mediation	Unit 2, St Clair Court, 3–11 West Bute St, Cardiff CF10 5EN	02920 316800	02920 316801	Cardiff@mediation.freeserve.co.uk	

| Mediation UK | Alexander House, Telephone Avenue, Bristol BS1 4BS | 0117 9046661 | 0117 9043331 | mediationuk@mediationuk.org.uk | http://www.cix.co.uk/~mediationuk/ |

(b) Scotland

Name	Address	Phone	Fax	Email	Website
Community Mediation Dundee	49 Meadowside, Dundee, Scotland DD1 1EQ	01382 206406			
Edinburgh Community Mediation Project	27 York Place, Edinburgh EH1 3HP	0131 5572101	0131 5572102		
Fife Community Mediation Scheme	24 Hill St, Kirkaldy, Fife, Scotland KY1 1HX	01592 593133	01592 593133		
Livingston & District Community Mediation Service	St Kenneth's Community Resource Centre, Ogilvie House, Sinclair Way, Livingston, Scotland EH54 8HL	01506 435118			

(c) Northern Ireland

Name	Address	Phone	Fax	Email	Website
Mediation Network for Northern Ireland	128a Great Victoria St, Belfast BT2 7BG	01232 438614	01232 314430	info@mediation-network.org.uk	http://www.mediation-network.org.uk

COMPUTER MEDIATION ORGANISATIONS

Name	Address	Phone	Fax	Email	Website
The British Computer Society	1 Sanford St, Swindon, Wiltshire SW1 1HJ	01793 417417	01793 480270	alewis@bcs.org.uk	http://www.bcs.org.uk/

CONSTRUCTION AND PROPERTY MEDIATION ORGANISATIONS

Name	Address	Phone	Fax	Email	Website
The Association of Consulting Engineers	Alliance House, 12 Caxton St, London SW1	020 7222 6557			http://www.bcs.org.uk/
The British Institute of Architectural Technologists	397 City Road, London EC1	020 7278 2206			
The Institution of Civil Engineers	1 Great George St, London SW1P 3AA	020 7222 7722	020 7222 7500		
The Landscape Institute	6–8 Barnard Mews, London SW11 1QU	020 7350 5200	020 7350 5201	mail@l-i.org.uk	http://www.li.org.uk
National House-Building Council	Buildmark House, Boycott Avenue, Old Brook, Milton Keynes, Bucks	01908 691888	01908 678575		
Royal Institute of British Architects	Construction House, 56–64 Leonard St, London EC2	020 7251 0791			

The Royal Institution of Chartered Surveyors (RICS)	Surveyor Court, Westwood Way, Coventry CV4 8JE	0207 2227000	0207 3343800	infor@rics.org.uk	www.rics.org.uk
	9 Manor Place, Edinburgh EH3 7DN	0131 2257078	0131 2263599		

CONSUMER MEDIATION ORGANISATIONS

(a) The Chartered Institute of Arbitrators

Name	Address	Phone	Fax	Email	Website
Chartered Institute of Arbitrators	24 Angel Gate, City Road, London EC1V 2RS	020 7837 4483	020 7837 4185	71411.2735@compuserv.com	http://ourworld.compuserv.com/arbitrators

(b) Ombudsmen

Name	Address	Phone	Fax	Email	Website
Banking Ombudsman	South Quay Plaza, 183 Marsh Wall, London E14 9SR	020 7404 9944		www.obo.org.uk	
Building Societies Ombudsman	Millbank Tower, Millbank, London SW1P 4XS	020 7931 0044	0207 931 8485	5blgsocombudsman@easynet.co.uk	
Pensions Ombudsman	11 Belgrave Road, London SW1V 1RB	020 7834 9144	020 7821 0065		
Insurance Ombudsman	135 Park St, London SE1 9EA	020 7902 8100	020 7902 8197	complaint@theiob.org.uk	http://www.theiob.org.uk

Financial Services Authority	25 The North Colonnade, Canary Wharf, London E14	020 7676 0824	020 7676 9712	clare.boyle@fsa.gov.uk	
National Consumer Credit Federation	98/100 Holme Lane, Sheffield SG4J 1W	0114 2348101	0114 2348101		
Qualitas	Maxwell Road, Stevenage SG1 2EW	01438 316100	01438 315800	qualitas@ttlchiltern.co.uk	
Personal Investment Authority Ombudsman	Hertsmere House, Hertsmere Road, London E14 4AB	020 7216 0016	020 7712 8742		
Mail Order Traders' Association		01704 563787	01704 55111247	malcolmlandau@compuserv.comm	
Scottish Motor Trade Association	3 Palmerston Place, Edinburgh EH12 5AF	0131 2253643	0131 2200416		

(c) Consumer Advice Organisations

(i) **England and Wales**

Name	Address	Phone	Fax	Email	Website
Advice Services Alliance	4 Deans Court, St Paul's Churchyard, London EC4V 5AA	020 7236 6022	020 7248 3367	asa@cwcom.neg	
Consumers' Association	2 Marylebone Road, London NW1 7DF	020 7830 6000	020 7830 7600	which@which.net	

Name	Address	Phone	Fax	Email	Website
National Association of Citizens' Advice Bureaux	Myddleton House, 115–123 Pentonville Road, London N1 9LZ	020 7833 2181	020 7833 4362	consultancy@nacab.org.uk	
National Consumer Council	20 Grosvenor Gardens, London SW1W 0DH	020 7730 4369	020 7770 0191	infor@ncc.org.uk	
Central Cardiff Citizens' Advice Bureau	71 Bridge St, Cardiff CF1 2EE	02920 398676			

(ii) Scotland

Name	Address	Phone	Fax	Email	Website
Citizens' Advice Scotland	26 George Square, Edinburgh EH8 9LD	0131 6670156	0131 6684359		
Scottish Consumer Council	Royal Exchange House, 100 Queens St, Glasgow G1 3DN	0141 2265261	0141 2210731		http://www.scotconsumer.co.uk

(iii) Northern Ireland

Name	Address	Phone	Fax	Email	Website
Central Belfast Citizens' Advice Bureau	6 Callender St, Belfast BT1 5BN	02890 243196	02890 312336		

EMPLOYMENT MEDIATION ORGANISATIONS

Name	Address	Phone	Fax	Email	Website
Advisory, Conciliation and Arbitration Service (ACAS)	27 Wilton St, London SW1X 7AZ	020 7210 3613	020 72103708		
Employment Advisory Specialists				employment@eas-challis.co.uk	

ENVIRONMENT MEDIATION ORGANISATIONS

Name	Address	Phone	Fax	Email	Website
The Environment Council	212 High Holborn, London WC1V 7VW	020 7836 2626	020 7242 1180	info@envcouncil.org.uk	www.the-environment-council.org.uk

FAMILY MEDIATION ORGANISATIONS

(a) England and Wales

Name	Address	Phone	Fax	Email	Website
British Association of Lawyer Mediators (BALM)	The Shooting Lodge, Guildford Road, Sutton Green, Guildford GU4 7PZ	01483 235000	01483 237004	a.logan@cableon.co.uk	
Family Law Consortium	2 Henrietta St, London WC2E 8PS	020 7420 5000	020 7420 5005	flc@tflc.co.uk	www.tflc.co.uk
Family Mediators' Association (FMA)	46 Grosvenor Gardens, London SW1W 0EB	020 7881 9400	020 7881 9401	hmc@globalnet.co.uk	www.familymediators.co.uk

Name	Address	Phone	Fax	Email	Website
Family Mediation of Cardiff	4th floor, St David's House, Wood St, Cardiff CF1 1ES	02920 229692			http://members.aol.com/fmcardiff
National Family Mediation (NFM)	9 Tavistock Place, London WC1H 9SN	020 7383 5993	020 7383 5994	general@nfm.org.uk	http://www.nfm.u-net.com
Professional Development & Training (PDT)	17 Whitefriars, Sevenoaks, Kent TN13	01732 453227	01732 464133		
Relate	Herbert Gray College, Little Church St, Rugby CV21 3AP	01788 573241	01788 535007		
Solicitors' Family Law Association (SFLA)	PO Box 302, Orpington, Kent BR6 8QX	01689 850227	01689 855833	106002.3040@compuserv.com	

(b) Scotland

Name	Address	Phone	Fax	Email	Website
CALM (Comprehensive Accredited Lawyer Mediators)	42 Carden Place, Aberdeen AB1 1UP	01224 621622	01224 621623		
Family Mediation Scotland (FMS)	127 Rose St, South Lane, Edinburgh EH2 4BB	0131 2201610	0131 2206895		
Family Mediation Borders	PO Box 13753, Peebles, EH45 8ZP	01721 724170			

Family Mediation Central Scotland	16 Melville Terrace, Stirling FK8 2NE	01786 472 984		Familymediationcentral @scotlandf.freeserve.co.uk
NCH Action for Children Dumfries & Galloway FMS	51 Newall Terrace, Dumfries DG1 1LN	01387 263185		
NCH Action for Children Family Mediation Fife	30 North St, Glenrothes, KY7 5NA	01592 751095		
Family Mediation Grampian	27 Huntly St, Aberdeen AB10 1TJ	01224 630050		
Family Mediation Highland	62 Academy St, Inverness IV1 1LP	01463 712100		
Family Mediation Lothian	37 George St, Edinburgh EH2 2HN	0131 2264507		
Family Mediation Orkney	43 Junction Rd, Kirkwall, Orkney KW15 1AR	01856 870571		
Shetland Family Mediation	PO Box 1, Yell, Shetland ZE2 9UH	01957 766266		
Family Mediation Tayside	132a Nethergate, Dundee DD1 4ED	01382 201343	01382 201865	
Family Mediation Western Isles	The Bridge Community Centre, Bayhead, Isle of Lewis HS1 2DU	01851 706868		
Family Mediation West	1 Melrose St, Glasgow G4 9BJ	0141 3322731		

(c) Northern Ireland

Name	Address	Phone	Fax	Email	Website
Family Mediation Service	76 Dublin Road, Belfast BT2 ZHP	02890 323454	02890 315292	gerald.clark@relate-n-ireland.com	

(d) Republic of Ireland

Name	Address	Phone	Fax	Email	Website
Family Mediation Service	5th floor, Irish Life Centre, Lower Abbey St, Dublin 1				
Mediators' Institute Ireland (MII)	13 Royal Terrace West, Dun Laoghaire, Dublin	00353 12845277	00353 12800259		

(e) Throughout the United Kingdom

Name	Address	Phone	Fax	Email	Website
UK College of Family Mediators	24-32 Stephenson Way, London NW1 2HX	020 7391 9162	020 7391 9165	liz.walsh@btinternet.com	http://www.ukcfm.co.uk

OVERSEAS MEDIATION ORGANISATIONS

Name	Address	Phone	Fax	Email	Website
American Arbitration Association (AAA)	140 West 51st St, New York 10020	001 212 4844000	001 212 7657274		http://www.adr.org
Center for Public Resources (CPR)	366 Madison Avenue, New York 10017	001 212 9496490	001 212 9498859		
International Chamber of Commerce (ICC)	38, Cours Albert 1er, 75008, Paris, France	00 331 49532828	00 331 49532933	arb@iccwbo.org	www.iccwbo.org
World Intellectual Property Organisation (WIPO)	34 Chemin des Colombettes, 1211 Geneva 20, Switzerland	00 41 223389111	00 41 22740370	arbiter.mail@wipo.int	http://arbiter.wipo.int

2

Useful Websites

www.cpr.com
Website for the Center for Public Resources (CPR) Institute for Dispute Resolution

www.abanet.org/dispute
The website for the American Bar Association Section on Dispute Resolution

http://www.igc/apc.org/nespidr/links.htm
Useful resource links compiled by the Society for Professionals Engaged in ADR (SPIDR)

http://www.mediate.com/organise/newsletters
Dispute resolution journals in the US

http://www.amic.org/
Website of the Arbitration and Mediation Institute of Canada

http://canada.justice.gc.ca/Orientations/Methodes/index_en.html
Site of the Department of Justice Canada Dispute Resolution Project

http://www/austlii.edu.au/au/other/acdc
Site of the Australian Commercial Disputes Centre

http://www.tsonline.co.uk
ADR materials available through the Lord Chancellor's Department website

http://search3.open.gov.uk/cgi-bin/empower
ADR materials available through the UK Government information website

http://www.open.gov.uk/civjustice
Website of the Civil Justice Council which has an ADR sub-committee

http://www.open.gov.uk/lcd/consult/civ/just/adr
Lord Chancellor's Department ADR Consultation Paper

www.legalservices.gov.uk
Community Legal Service website

http://interlex.droit-eco.u-nancy.fr/braudo/arbmed/base/Index.html
French conciliation, mediation and arbitration site

http://findlaw.com/01topics/11disputeres/index.html
FindLaw site on dispute resolution, arbitration and mediation

http://www.hg.org/adr.html
Hieros Gamos site on alternative dispute resolution

http://www.mediate.com/articles/boskey.cfm and http://www.trincoll.edu/~rtoomey/adr.htm/
Comprehensive ADR websites

http://adrr.com/
Contains a substantial number of materials on alternative dispute resolution and mediation

http://www.adrworld.com/
Covers the latest developments in alternative dispute resolution

http://www.interarb.com/vl/pages/
Library of arbitration, ADR, mediation, conciliation and other dispute resolution materials

http://www.crinfo.org/
A conflict resolution information service

http://www.batnet.com/oikoumene/tacr/html
A site which specialises in alternative dispute resolution, especially in relation to technical disputes

http://www.igc.org/conflictnet/
A network of people dedicated to the promotion of alternative dispute resolution

http://www.culma.wayne.edu/CMHER/Cybercampus.html
The 'Resolve-it College' virtual campus, an experimental way of sharing higher educational alternative dispute resolution ideas and resources

http://leflaw.com/general.html
A legal site which can be searched for alternative dispute resolution articles

http://www.medrisk.com
A website for those interested in mediation in the medical healthcare field

http://www.mediationworks.com/inted.html
The site contains resources for the prevention, management and resolution of work place conflicts and disputes in business, government, healthcare and non-profit organisations

http://www.gsm.mq.edu.au/conflict/homepage.htm
Topics focus on negotiation, mediation, grievance procedures, complaints handling, trade disputes and deep-rooted conflict

http://www.batnet.com/oikoume/tacr/html
The Global Arbitration & Mediation Association internet directory of arbitrators, mediators and dispute resolution organisations

http://www.cfcsc.dnd.ca/links/intrel/confli.html/
Organisations and institutes involved in peace and conflict resolution

http://www.expert4law.com/
Website listing of arbitrators, mediators, private judges, special masters, ombudsmen, settlement officers, family law mediators and other ADR service providers

www.mediates.com/drsguest/html
List of US dispute resolution specialists

www.adrc.com/
List of US alternative dispute resolution centres

http://www.icg.org/icg/issues/crtrain/
Training, certification and degree-granting programmes in conflict resolution

3

Further Reading List

(See Bibliography for materials referred to in text)

Acland, Andrew   *Resolving disputes without going to court: A consumers' guide to alternative dispute resolution*, Century Business Books, 1995

Alfini, J   'What happens when mediation is institutionalised: To the parties, practitioners and host institutions' (1994) 9 *Ohio State Journal on Dispute Resolution* 30

The Alternative Newsletter, a quarterly newsletter, which summarises alternative dispute resolution cases, conferences, articles, books and legislation from around the world, although with a US emphasis

Angyl, Robert   'The enforceability of agreements to mediate in Australia: Walford v Miles not followed' (1994) 3 *Arbitration and Dispute Resolution Law Journal* 176

Ap Cynan, R   'Why train lawyers as mediators?' (1993) 90(36) *Law Society Gazette* 2

Arbitration & Dispute Resolution Law Journal, which provides a range of articles on mediation and other ADR developments world-wide, although with a UK emphasis

Arens, P   'Recent trends in German jurisdiction: the transfer of political and administrative duties of the courts' in S Shetreet (ed) *The role of courts in society*, Martinus Nijhoff, Dordrecht, 1988

Astor, H   'Violence and family mediation policy' (1994) 8(1) *Australian Journal of Family Law*

Bacharach, Samuel and Lawler, Edward   'Power of dependence and power paradoxes in bargaining' (1986) *Negotiation Journal* 167

Bishop, G et al   *Divorce reform: a guide for lawyers and mediators*, FT Law & Tax, London, 1996

Bocow, Lawrence and Wheeler, Michael   *Environmental dispute resolution*, Plenum, New York, 1984

Brazil, W   'A close look at three court-sponsored ADR Programmes: why they exist, how they operate, what they deliver and whether they threaten important values' (1990) *U Chi L F* 303

Buerhring-uhle, C   'The IBM-Fujitsu Arbitration: a landmark in innovative dispute resolution' (1991) 2 *Am Rev Intl Arb* 113

Burley-Allen, M   *Listening: the forgotten skill*, John Wiley & Sons, 1982

Bush, R A B   'Dispute resolution alternatives and the goals of civil justice: jurisdictional principles for process choice' (1984) 4 *Wisconsin Law Review* 893

Brian, P   'Reclaiming professionalism: the lawyer's role in divorce mediation' (1994) 28 *Family Law Quarterly* 193

Brunet   'Questioning the quality of alternative dispute resolution' (1987) 62 *Tulane Law Review* 1

Cadogan, Ian and Lewis   'Richard Resolving insurance disputes without going to court' (1991) *Solicitors Journal* 135

Carpenter, S and Kennedy, W *Managing Public Disputes*, Jossey-Bass, San Francisco, 1988

Center for Public Resources (CPR) 'Special Issue: ADR in the courts' (1991) 9 *Alternatives*

Christie, N 'Conflicts as property' (1977) *Bristol Journal of Criminology*

Cloke, K *Mediation: revenge and forgiveness*, Center for Dispute Resolution, Santa Monica, California, 1990

Coates, Robert and Gehm, John "An empirical assessment' in Martin Wright and Bert Galaway (eds) *Mediation in criminal justice: victims, offenders and community*, Sage Publications Ltd, London, 1989

Cormick, G 'Intervention and self-determination in environmental disputes: a mediator's perspective' (1982) *Resolve* 260

Crowfoot, J and Wondolleck, J *Environmental Disputes: community involvement in conflict resolution*, Island Press, Washington, 1991

Davis, G *Partisans and Mediators: the resolution of divorce disputes*, Oxford University Press, Oxford, 1988

Delago et al 'Fairness and formality: minimising the risk of prejudice in alternative dispute resolution' (1985) *Wisconsin Law Review* 1359

Deutsch M *The resolution of conflict*, Yale University Press, Newhaven, 1973

Dingwall, R and Eekelaar, J (eds) *Divorce mediation and the legal process*, Oxford University Press, Oxford, 1988

Donovan et al *ADR Practice Book*, Wiley Law Publications, 1990

Duquesnel, Joseph *Client satisfaction survey: a consumer evaluation of mediation and investigative services*, Report to Judicial Council of California, March 1991

Edelman, P 'Institutionalising dispute resolution alternatives' (1984) 9 *Justice System Journal* 134

Eisenberg, Melvin 'Private ordering through negotiation: Dispute settlement and rule making' (1976) 89 *Private Law Review* 637

Eekelaar, J M and Katz, S N (eds) *The resolution of family conflict: comparative legal perspectives*, Butterworths, Toronto

Erlanger et al 'Participation and flexibility in informal processes: cautions from the divorce context' (1987) 21 *Law & Society Review* 585

Felstiner, William 'Influences of social organisation on dispute processing' (1974) 9 *Law & Society Review* 63

Fine, E S (ed) *ADR and the courts: a manual for judges and lawyers*, Butterworths, New York, 1987

Fiss, O 'Against Settlement' (1984) 93 *Yale Law Journal* 1073

Folberg, J and Milne, A (eds) *Divorce Mediation: theory and practice*, Guildford Press, New York, 1988

Forester *Planning in the face of conflict: mediated negotiation in local land use permitting processes*, Lincoln Institute for Land Policy, 1986

Galanter, M and Cahill, M 'Most cases settle: judicial promotion and regulation of settlements' (1994) 46 *Stanford Law Review* 1339

Geffner, R and Mildred, P 'Mediation and child custody in abusive relationships' (1990) 8 *Behav Science & the Law* 151

Genn, H *Hard bargaining: Out of court settlements in personal injury actions*, Clarendon Press, Oxford 1987

Gibson, K 'Confidentiality in mediation: A moral reassessment' (1992) *Journal of Dispute Resolution* 25

Goldberg, S et al 'Designing an effective dispute resolution system' in J Wilkinson (ed) *Donovan Leisure Newton and Irvine ADR Practice Book*, Wiley, New York, 1991

Goodpaster, Gary 'Rational decision-making in problem-solving negotiation: Compromise, interest, evaluation and cognitive error' (1993) 8 *Ohio State Journal on Dispute Resolution* 299

Green 'A heretical view of a mediation privilege' (1986) 2 *Ohio State Journal on Dispute Resolution* 1

Greenhalgh, Leonard 'Relationships in negotiations' (1987) 3(3) *Negotiation Journal* 235

Gulliver, Philip *Disputes and negotiations: A cross-cultural perspective* Academic Press, New York 1979

Harrington, Christine *Shadow Justice: The ideology and institutionalisation of alternatives to court*, Greenwood Press, Westport, 1985

Haynes, J 'Mediation and therapy: an alternative view' (1992) 10 *Mediation Quarterly* 21

Hibberd, P and Newman, P *ADR and adjudication in construction disputes*, Blackwell Science, Oxford, 1999

Katz, L 'Enforcing an ADR clause – are good intentions all you have?' (1988) 26 *Am Bus L J* 575

Kelly, J 'Mediation and psychotherapy: distinguishing the difference' (1983) *Mediation Quarterly* 33

Kelly, J 'Dispute systems design: a family case study' (1989) 4 *Negotiation Journal* 373

Kelly, J 'Power imbalances in divorce and interpersonal mediation assessment and intervention' (1995) 13(2) *Mediation Quarterly*

Kirkpatrick 'Should mediators have a confidentiality privilege?' (1985) 9 *Mediation Quarterly* 85

Kolb, Deborah *When talk works: Profiles of mediators*, Jossey-Bass, San Francisco 1994

Krivis, Jeffrey 'On-line mediation: An option when distance separates parties' (1998) *American Bar Association Dispute Resolution Magazine*

Lange, M and Aitkin, R *Report on outcomes of mediation: Comprehensive Accredited Lawyer Mediators*, November 1997

Lewis, Richard 'The private settlement of disputes between insurers' (1984) 134 *New Law Journal* 947

Macfarlane, Julie *Rethinking Disputes: the mediation alternative*, Cavendish Publishing, London, 1997

Macfarlane, Julie *Dispute resolution: Readings and case studies*, Emond Montgomery Publications, Toronto, 1999

Matthews, R (ed) *Informal Justice?* Sage, London, 1988

Martindale-Hubbell International *International arbitration and dispute resolution directory 2000*

McCarthy 'The role of power and principle of Getting to Yes' (1984) 1 *Negotiation Journal* 59

McCrory, J P 'Environmental mediation – another piece for the puzzle' (1981) 6(1) *Vermont Law Review*

McCrory, J P 'Confidentiality in mediation of matrimonial disputes' (1988) 51(4) *Modern Law Review*

McEwen, Craig 'Competence and quality' (1993) *Negotiation Journal* 313

Mediation Quarterly, a useful journal focusing on mediation, although with an emphasis on the US

Moller, E et al *Private dispute resolution in the banking industry*, RAND 1993

Moody, S R and Mackay, R E *Greens Guide to alternative dispute resolution in Scotland*, Sweet & Maxwell, Edinburgh, 1995

Moore 'Practical strategies for the phases of mediation' (1987) 16 *Mediation Quarterly* 1

Morris, C 'The trusted mediator: ethics and interaction in mediation' in J Macfarlane (ed) *Rethinking Disputes: the mediation alternative*, Cavendish Publishing, London, 1997

Myers, Selma and Filner, Barbara *Mediation across culture: A handbook about conflict and culture*, Amherst Educational Publishing, 1994

National Consumer Council *A–Z of Ombudsmen: a guide to Ombudsman schemes in Britain and Ireland*, 1997

Nelle, A 'Making mediation mandatory: A proposed framework' (1992) 7 *Ohio State Journal of Dispute Resolution* 287

Phillips and Piazza 'The role of mediation in public international disputes' (1983) 34 *Hastings Law Journal* 1231

Raiffa, Howard *The art and science of negotiation*, Harvard University Press, Cambridge, 1992

Riskin, L. L 'Towards new standards for the neutral lawyer in mediation' (1984) 26 *Arizona Law Review*

Riskin, L L (ed) *Divorce mediation: readings*, American Bar Association, Washington, 1985

Roberts, Marian 'Who is in charge? Reflections on recent research on the roles of the mediator' (1992) 5 *Journal of Social Welfare and Family Law* 372

Rubin, J and Brown, B *The social psychology of bargaining and negotiation*, Academic Press, New York 1975

Rubin, J 'A causerie on lawyers' ethics in negotiations' (1975) 35 *La L Rev* 577

Sander, Frank *Mediation: A selected annotated bibliography*, The American Bar Association Special Committee on Dispute Resolution, 1984

Saposneck, D T (ed) 'Applying family therapy perspectives to mediation' (1986–7) 14 *Mediation Quarterly*

Saposneck, DT *Mediating Child Custody Disputes*, Jossey-Bass, San Francisco, 1983

Schiffer, Richard 'The use of mediation in resolving disputes in electronic data interchange' (1990) 6(2) *Computer Law and Practice* 55

Shaw 'Divorce mediation: some keys to the process' (1985) 9 *Mediation Quarterly* 27

Sherman, Edward 'Court-mandated alternative dispute resolution: What form of participation should be required' (1993) 46 *FMU Law Review* 2079

Silbey, Susan and Merry, Sally 'Mediator settlement strategies' (1986) 8(1) *Law and Policy* 7

Slaikeu, Karl   *When push comes to shove: A practical guide for mediating disputes*, Jossey-Bass, 1995

Smith, R   *Achieving Civil Justice: appropriate dispute resolution for the 1990s*, Legal Action Group, London, 1996

Stulberg and Merry   'Design requirements for mediator development programs' (1987) *Hofstra Law Review* 499

Susskind, L   'Environmental mediation and the accountability problem' (1981) 6 *Vermont Law Review* 1

Susskind, L and Cruikshank, J   *Breaking of the impasse: Consensual approaches to resolving public disputes*, Basic Books, New York 1987

Trubek et al   'The costs of ordinary litigation' (1983) 31 *UCLA L Rev* 72

Twining, W   'Alternative to what? Theories of litigation, procedure and dispute settlement in Anglo-American jurisprudence: some neglected classics' (1993) 56 *Modern Law Review* 380

Umbreit, Mark and Coates, Robert   'Victim-offender mediation: a review of research in the United States' in G Davies et al   *Making amends: mediation and reparation in criminal justice*, Routledge, Chapman & Hall, New York, 1992

Vidmar   'Assessing the effects of case characteristics and settlement forum on dispute outcomes and compliance' (1987) 21 *Law & Society Review* 155

Videos: *Improving negotiation power* (Roger Fisher); *Applying the mutual gains approach to negotiating with a hard bargainer* (Max Bazerman and Lawrence Susskind); and *Competitive and co-operative modes of negotiating* (Gerald Williams), all available from the Harvard Programme on Negotiation.

Walker, J et al   *Mediation: the making and remaking of co-operative relationship – an evaluation of the effectiveness of comprehensive mediation*, Relate, Newcastle-upon-Tyne, 1994

Wald, P   'Negotiation in Environmental Disputes: a new role for the courts?' (1985) 10 *Colum J of Envtl L* 1

Welton et al   'The role of caucusing in community mediation' (1988) 32 *Journal of Conflict Resolution* 181

Weise, R   'The ADR Program at Motorola' (1989) 5 *Negotiation Journal* 381

White   'Machiavelli and the Bar: ethical limitations on lying in negotiation' (1980) *Am B Foundation Res* 926

Wright, M and Galaway, B (eds)   *Mediation and Criminal Justice*, Sage Publications, London, 1989

York, S   *Practical ADR Handbook* (2nd edn), Sweet & Maxwell, London, 1999

Bibliography of Principal Works

ABA News 'Governments should create "cyber-tribunal" says report' *Legal Week*, 20 July 2000, p 9

Abel, R (ed) *The politics of informal justice, vol 1*, Academic Press, New York, 1982

Abel, R *The Legal Profession in England and Wales*, Blackwell, Oxford, 1988

Abel R L 'Conservative conflict and the reproduction of capitalism: The role of informal justice' (1981) *International Journal of the Psychology of Law* 9

Aberdeen City Council 'Noisy neighbours is top complaint' *Aberdeen Press and Journal*, 9 April 1999, p 3

Academy of Experts *Answers to frequently asked questions about mediation; Code of Conduct and Guidance Notes for Mediators; Expert Training for Experts and Dispute Resolvers; Guidelines for Mediation; Resolving your Dispute by Mediation;* and *The Language of ADR—An International Glossary*

ACAS *ACAS's work in 1998*, ACAS 1998

ACCC *Benchmarks for dispute avoidance and resolution—A guide*, Sydney, 1997

Access to Justice Committee *Access to Justice—an action plan (The Sackville Report)*, 1994

Acland, A *A sudden outbreak of common sense*, Hutchinson, London, 1990

Adjudicator's Office *Annual Report 1997*

Adler, P 'Resolving public policy conflicts through mediation: the Water Roundtable' (1990) 1 *Australian Dispute Resolution Journal* 69

Adler, P et al 'The ideologies of mediation' (1988) 10 *Law and Policy* 335

ADR Group *Agreement to Mediate*; and *Professional Code of Conduct for Mediators*

Advisory Group On Citizenship *Education for citizenship and the teaching of democracy in schools*, Qualifications and Curriculum Authority, 1998

Ahrens, M and Witcombe, G *Australian Dispute Resolution Handbook*, Australian Commercial Disputes Centre Ltd, Sydney, 1992

Akasen, G 'Legal considerations in using arbitration clauses to resolve future problems which may arise during long-term business agreements' (1972–3) 28 *Business Lawyer* 595

Alcorn, D 'Mediation and the psychologically injured plaintiff' (1996) 1 *Queensland University of Technology Law Journal* 162

Alexander, E R 'The re-definition of cognitive conflict: Effects of various types of communication' (1979) 23 *Journal of Conflict Resolution* 120

Alexander, R 'Family Mediation: friend or foe for women?' (1997) 8 *Australian Dispute Resolution Journal* 255

Alexander, R 'Family Mediation under the microscope' (1999) 10 *Australian Dispute Resolution Journal* 18

Alfini, J 'Summary jury trial in State and Federal Courts' (1989) 4 *Ohio State Journal on Dispute Resolution* 213

Allen, J D 'Teamwork at Terminal 5' (1997) *Construction News* 4

Allen, S 'Complaints rocket 40% to record level' *The Law Society Gazette*, 21 April 1999

Allen, S 'Mediation plan' *The Law Society Gazette*, 8 December 1999, p 4

Allen, S 'Unnecessary Caution' *The Law Society Gazette*, 30 March 2000, p 30

Allen, S 'County court claims fall' *The Law Society Gazette*, 20 July 2000

Allen, T 'CEDR unveils strategic PI initiative' *Resolutions*, Issue No 25, p 4

Allen, T and H *Draft competencies for lawyers in mediation*, CEDR, 2000

Altobelli, T 'Are you getting enough? Marketing mediation' (1993) *ADR Bulletin* 113

American Bar Association *Standards of Practice for Lawyer Mediators in Family Disputes*, Washington DC, 1984

Amy, D *The politics of environmental mediation*, Columbia University Press 1987

Angel, A 'The use of arbitration clauses as a means for the resolution of impasses in the negotiation of, or during the life of, long-term contractual relationships' (1972–3) 28 *Business Lawyer* 589

Angyal, R 'Enforceability of alternative dispute resolution clauses' (1991) 2 *Australian Dispute Resolution Journal* 32

Angyal, R 'Law Society revises ADR clause to enhance enforceability' (1993) 31 *Law Society Journal* 71

Angyal, R 'Enforceability of agreements to mediate' in G Raftesath and S Thaler (eds) *Cases for Mediation*, Sydney LBC Information Services, 1999

Anstey, M *Negotiating Conflict: insights and skills for negotiators and peacemakers*, Juta & Co, Kenwyn, South Africa, 1991

Anstey, M *Practical peacemaking—a mediator's handbook*, Juta & Co, Kenwyn, South Africa, 1993

Antes, J et al 'Is a stage model of mediation necessary?' (1999) 16 *Mediation Quarterly* 287

Archbold, C et al *Divorce in Northern Ireland: unravelling the system*, Report to the Office of Law Reform, HMSO, 1999

Ardagh, A and Cumes, G 'Lawyers and mediation: beyond the adversarial system?' (1998) 9 *Australian Dispute Resolution Journal* 72

Armstrong, M 'ADR and the public interest in personal injury' [1994] *Journal of personal injury litigation* 178

Astill, F *On alternative significances of definition in dispute resolution*, Paper presented at Australasian Law Teachers' Conference, Canterbury, New Zealand, October 1993

Astor, H Position Paper on Mediation and violence against women, prepared for the Australian National Committee on Violence against Women (NCVAW), 1991

Astor, H 'Elizabeth's story: mediation, violence and the legal academy' (1997) 2 *Flinders Journal of Law Reform* 13

Astor, H 'Mediation for intra-lesbian disputes' (1997) 20 *Melbourne University Law Review* 953

Astor, H 'Rethinking neutrality: a theory to inform practice' part 1 (2000) 11 *Australian Dispute Resolution Journal* 73 and part 2 (2000) 11 *Australian Dispute Resolution Journal* 145

Astor, H and Chinkin, C 'Mediation training and ethics' (1991) 2 *Australian Dispute Resolution Journal* 227

Astor, H and Chinkin, C *Dispute Resolution in Australia*, Butterworths, Sydney, 1992

Atkin Chambers 'Confidentiality in arbitration and mediation' (2000) 14 *Commercial Law Journal* 2

Aubert, V 'Competition and dissensus: two types of conflict in conflict resolution' (1963) 7 *Journal of Dispute Resolution* 26

Auerbach, J *Justice without law*, Oxford University Press, New York, 1983

Augsburger, D *Conflict Mediation across Cultures*, Westminster/John Knocks Press, Kentucky, 1992

Axelrod, R *The evolution of co-operation*, Basic books, New York, 1984.

Ayer 'Isn't there enough reality to go around? An essay on the unspoken promises of our law' 53 *New York University Law Review* 457

Baldwin, J *Monitoring the rise of the small claims unit: litigants' experiences of different forms of adjudication*, Institute of Judicial Administration, University of Birmingham, 1998

Bandler, R and Grinder, J *Reframing: neuro-linguistic programming and the transformatting of meaning*, Real People Press, Moab Utah, 1982

Banking Ombudsman *Annual Report 1998*

Banwell Report, HMSO, May 1967

Bar Council Committee on ADR (Chaired by Lord Justice Beldam) *Bar Council Report*, 1991

Beal, B *On-line mediation: has its time come?* Paper presented at Cyberweek 2000 Conference (available at http://www.disputes.net/cyberweek2000/ohiostate/beal/htm)

Beattie, S 'Is mediation a real alternative to law? Pitfalls for Aboriginal participants' (1997) 8 *Australian Dispute Resolution Journal* 57

Beed, T et al *The role of conciliation*, Civil Justice Research Centre and Law Foundation of NSW, Sydney, 1990

Bellow, G and Moulton, B *The lawyering process: negotiation*, Foundation Press, Mineola, New York, 1981

Berlin, R 'Mediation: sharing vs instructing' (1998) 53 *Dispute Resolution Journal* 48

Bevan, A *ADR: a lawyer's guide to mediation and other forms of dispute resolution*, Sweet & Maxwell, London, 1992

Billinghurst, T 'Benefits of mediation' (1999) 55(9) *Magistrate* 264

Bindman, V 'IT body targets domain name abuse' *The Law Society Gazette*, 19 May 1999, p 18

Bingham, G *Resolving environmental disputes: a decade of experience*, The Conservation Foundation, 1986

Blackshaw, I 'Is mediation the answer?' (2000) 3(4) *Sports Law Bulletin* 2

Blair, A 'Mediation: preparing and presenting' (2000) 22 *Corporate Counsel* 60

Blegvad, B 'Commercial Relations, Contract and Litigation in Denmark: A discussion of Macaulay's Theories' (1990) 24 *Ohio State Journal on Dispute Resolution* 390

Bok, D 'A flawed system' (1983) *New York State Bar Journal* 8

Bolton, R *People skills: how to assert yourself, listen to others and resolve conflicts*, Simon and Schuster, Brookvale, New South Wales, 1987

Bond Dispute Resolution Centre 'What Skills and Attributes do Experienced Mediators Possess?' *Bond Dispute Resolution News*, vol 3, October 1999

Bond Dispute Resolution Centre *Reflections on conflicts—lessons learned*, Survey results, October 1999

Booth Committee *Report of the Committee on Matrimonial Causes*, HMSO, London, 1985

Bordow, S and Gibson, J *Evaluation of the Family Court Mediation Service*, Family Court of Australia, Research and Evaluation Unit, 1994

Borno, Z 'Looking guilt in the face' *Bristol Evening Post*, 26 April 1999

Bottomley, A 'What is happening to Family Law? A Feminist Critique of Conciliation' in J Brophy and C Smart (eds) *Women in Law*, Routledge, London, 1985

Boulle, L 'Confidentiality and the mediation process' (1992) 3 *Australian Dispute Resolution Journal* 272

Boulle, L 'Testing the Mettle: Queensland's First Settlement Week' (1992) 3 *Australian Dispute Resolution Journal* 1

Boulle, L 'Emerging standards for lawyer mediators' (1993) 23 *Queensland Law Society Journal* 575

Boulle, L 'Mini-trial' in The Laws of Australia, 1997

Boulle, L and Hwee Hwee, T *Mediation: principles, process, practice*, Butterworths, Singapore, 2000

Bowen, Bradshaw and Pottinger 'Research to monitor the Cleveland Family Conciliation Service' *Teeside Polytechnic Papers in Law & Society*, 1986, No 1

Bowers, J 'Taking the harass out of harassment' *The Times*, 18 January 2000

Bowsher, P 'The Technology and Construction Court before and after the Woolf Civil Procedure Reforms' (2000) 1 *International Arbitration Law Review* 19

Brazil, W D 'Protecting the Confidentiality of Settlement Negotiations' (1988) 39 *Hastings Law Journal* 1955

Brett, J and Goldberg, S 'Mediator-advisers: a new third party role' in M Bazerman and R Lewicki (eds) *Negotiating in Organisations*, 1983

Brett, J et al 'The effectiveness of mediation: an independent analysis of cases handled by four major service providers' (1996) 12 *Negotiation Journal* 259

Bristol Evening Post Editorial 'Police chief backs funding a project to cut shoplifting' *Bristol Evening Post*, 16 April 1999

Broad, A 'Tackling the legal loopholes' *Post Magazine supplement*, 28 October 1999, p 5

Brooker, P 'Survey of construction lawyers' attitudes and practice and the use of ADR in contractors' disputes' (1999) 17(6) *Construction management and economics*

Brown, H and Marriott, A *ADR Principles and Practice* (2nd edn), Sweet & Maxwell, London, 1999

Brown, J and Ayres, I 'Economic rationales for mediation' (1994) 80 *Virginia Law Review* 323

Brown, K 'Confidentiality in Mediation: Status and Implications' (1991) 2 *Journal of Dispute Resolution* 307

Bryant, G 'The movement towards procedural informalism in North America and Western Europe: A critical study' in R Abel (ed) *The Politics of Informal Justice, vol 1*, Academic Press, New York, 1982

Bryant, G 'Privatisation in the new market for disputes: a framework for analysis and a preliminary assessment' (1992) 12 *Studies in Law, Politics and Society* 367

Bryson, D 'Mediator and advocate: conciliating human rights' (1990) 1 *Australian Dispute Resolution Journal* 136

Buchanan, T 'Fighting fire with mediation' *Resolutions*, Issue No 23, p 7

Buckley, R P 'The applicability of mediation skills to the creation of contracts' (1992) *Australian Dispute Resolution Journal* 227

Budnitz, M E 'Arbitration and disputes between consumers and financial institutions: a serious threat to consumer protection' (1995) 10(2) *Ohio State Journal on Dispute Resolution* 271

Building Societies Ombudsman *Annual Report 1999; Guide for Applicants*, 1999

Burns, K 'Whose party is it anyway? The role of the insured in the mediation process' (1999) 1(8) *ADR Bulletin* 102

Burton, J *The conflict series, vol 3: Readings in Management and Resolution*, St Mary's Press, New York, 1990

Burton, J W *Resolving deep-rooted conflict: a handbook*, University Press of America, Lanham, Maryland, 1987

Bush, R A B *The dilemmas of mediation practice: a study of ethnical dilemmas and policy implications*, National Institute for Dispute Resolution, Washington DC, 1992

Bush, R A B and Folger, J P *The Promise of Mediation: Responding to Conflict through Empowerment and Recognition*, Jossey-Bass, San Francisco, 1994

Butlin, I 'Outcome measures in all issues mediation' (2000) 30 *Family Law* 212

Cameron 'Community Mediation in New Zealand: A pilot project' (1988) *Journal of Social Welfare Law* 284

Cameron, J and Dupuis, A 'The introduction of school mediation to New Zealand' (1994) 24 *Journal of Research and Development in Education*

Campbell, D and Summerfield, P (eds) *Effective Dispute Resolution for the International Commercial Lawyer*, Kluwer, Boston, 1989

Canadian Forum on Dispute Resolution *Report*, 1995

Cappelletti, M 'Alternative Dispute Resolution Processes within the Framework of the World-wide Access to Justice Movement' (1993) 56(3) *Modern Law Review* 288

Cardiff Mediation *Annual Report 1997–98*

Carnevale, P and Pegnetter, R 'The selection of mediation tactics in public sector disputes: a contingency analysis' (1985) 41 *Journal of Social Issues* 65

Carnevale, P et al 'Contingent mediator behaviour and its effectiveness' in K Kressel et al (eds) *Mediation Research: the process and effectiveness of third party intervention*, 1989

Carnevale, P J et al 'Mediator Behaviour and Effectiveness in Community Mediation' in Duffy, Grosch and Olczak (eds) *Community Mediation: A Handbook for Practitioners and Researchers*, Guildford, New York, 1991

Carr, F et al 'The Untapped Potential of ADR in the Construction Industry' (1995) *Federal Lawyer* 32

Carr, F *Partnering: Dispute Avoidance—The Army Corps of Engineers Way*, American Arbitration Association, 1993

Castrey, R T and B P 'Timing: A mediator's best friend' (1987) *Mediation Quarterly* 16

Center for Dispute Settlement *Institute of Judicial Administration and State Justice Institute National Standards for Court-connected Mediation Programs*, Washington DC, 1992

Center for Dispute Settlement *Parent/Adolescent Training Manual*, November 1987

Center for Public Resources *Mediation Agreement*

Center for Public Resources *Mediation Procedure for Business Disputes in Europe*

Center for Public Resources 'An ADR arena suits Davids and Goliaths' *Alternatives*, vol 12, No 2, February 1994

Center for Public Resources *Law Firm ADR: 1994 survey findings*, CPR, New York, 1994

Center for Public Resources *Banking Industry Program*, Center for Public Resources, New York, 1997

Center for Public Resources *Program to resolve employment disputes*, CPR, 1998

Center for Public Resources 'ADR and the 21st Century Law Firm' *Alternatives*, vol 16, No 2, March 1998

Center for Public Resources 'ADR briefs' *Alternatives*, vol 16 No 11, December 1998

Center for Public Resources 'Survey shows ADR savings', *Alternatives*, vol 16, No 11, December 1998

Center for Public Resources 'ADR briefs' *Alternatives*, vol 17, No 6, June 1999

Centre for Business Arbitration *Mediation Rules*

Centre for Dispute Resolution *Resolutions*, Issue nos 22, 24 and 26

Centre for Dispute Resolution *Model ADR Contract Clauses*

Centre for Dispute Resolution *Model Mediation Procedure and Guidance Notes*

Centre for Dispute Resolution *Code of Conduct*

Centre for Dispute Resolution 'Millennium Accord industry focus groups' *Resolutions*, No 22

Centre for Dispute Resolution 'Accountants must take note of ADR' *Resolutions*, Issue no 18, Winter 1997

Centre for Dispute Resolution *Bulletin: Launch of continuing professional development for CEDR mediators*, January 1999

Centre for Dispute Resolution *Time-Limited Mediations*, Boughton, March 1999

Centre for Dispute Resolution 'The value and use of time in mediation' *Resolutions*, Spring 1999

Centre for Dispute Resolution *Press Releases*, 24 February 1999, 26 April 1999, August 1999, July 2000

Centre for Dispute Resolution *Press Release: CEDR Commercial Mediation Statistics April 1999–March 2000*, CEDR, July 2000

Centre for Dispute Resolution *Press Release: New survey warns clients want better mediation advice*, 9 June 1999

Centre for Dispute Resolution 'Lawyers say mediation is weak' *The Lawyer*, 14 June 1999

Centre for Dispute Resolution *Mediation—boxing clever*, Press Release, 6 July 1999

Centre for Dispute Resolution *Court-referred ADR: A guide for the judiciary*, Centre for Dispute Resolution, September 1999.

Centre for Dispute Resolution Charities Unit *Mediation*, CEDR 1999

Centre for Dispute Resolution/Pinsent Curtis *Dispute Resolution Survey: initial analysis paper*, CEDR, March 2000

Centre for Dispute Resolution *Civil Justice Audit*, April 2000

Chambers & Partners *Chambers Guide to the Legal Profession*, Chambers & Partners Publishing, London, 2000

Chancery Division *Chancery Guide*, 1999

Charity Commission *Charities and Contracts: a guide for smaller charities entering into contracts to provide services on behalf of public bodies*, Document CC37, October 1998

Charles, S 'Natural justice and ADR' (1986) *Law Institute Journal* 1079

Charlton, G 'Preliminary conferences: a quality control tool for mediators' (1997) 8 *Australian Dispute Resolution Journal* 114

Charlton, R and Dewdney, M *The Mediator's Handbook—skills and strategies for practitioners*, The Law Book Company, Sydney, 1995

Chartered Institute of Arbitrators *The consumer dispute resolution scheme; The rules of the consumer dispute resolution scheme; Suggested clause for inclusion in consumer contracts; Arbitration and the consumer; General information handbook; Guide to arbitration.*

Chaykin, A 'Mediator liability: a new role for fiduciary duties?' (1984) 53 *University of Cincinnati Law Review* 731

Chaykin, A 'The liabilities and immunities of mediators: a hostile environment for model legislation' (1986–7) 2 *Ohio State Journal on Dispute Resolution* 47

Chaykin, A 'The sultans of swap: defining the duties and liabilities of American mediators' (1986) 99 *Harvard Law Review* 1876

Chester, R S G et al 'Conflicts of interest, Chinese walls and changing business of the law' *Business Law International*, 2 January 2000

Chia, H and Chu, S 'Mediating across cultures—are we supplementing our cultural values through mediation?' *The Alumnus*, July 1999

Chornenki, G 'Mediating commercial disputes: exchanging "power over" with "power with"' in J Macfarlane (ed) *Rethinking disputes: the mediation alternative*, Cavendish Publishing, London, 1997

City Disputes Panel *Mediation Rules*

City Disputes Panel *Members' Briefing*, 17 November 1997

Civil Justice Reform Group *Review of the Civil Justice System in Northern Ireland: Interim Report*, April 1999

Civil Procedure Pre-Action Protocols *Clinical Negligence Protocol*

Clark, B and Mays, R 'Regulating ADR: the Scottish experience' (1996) 5 *Web JCLI*

Clark, E 'Arbitration, dispute resolution and the worldwide web' *The Arbitrator*, August 1997

Clarke S et al *Court-Ordered Civil Mediation in North Carolina: an evaluation*, State of Justice Institute, 1995

Clarke, F *Court-ordered mediation in NYC*, reported at http://www.adrr.com/adr4

Clarke, G and Davies I 'Mediation—when is it not an appropriate dispute resolution process?' (1992) 3 *Australian Dispute Resolution Journal* 70

Clarke, S 'Community justice and victim-offender mediation' in Ohio State University College of Law (ed) *Court reform Implications of Dispute Resolution*, Ohio State University, 1995

Cloke, K *Mediation: revenge and the magic of forgiveness*, Center for Dispute Resolution, Santa Monica, California, 1990

Cobb, S and Rifkin, J 'Practice and paradox: deconstructing neutrality in mediation' (1991) 16 *Law and Social Inquiry* 3

Cohen, R 'Mediation standards' (1995) 6 *Australian Dispute Resolution Journal* 25

Cohen, R *Students Resolving Conflict: peer mediation in schools*, Goodyear Books, USA, 1995

Commercial Court Committee *Meeting Note*, 14 July 1997

Commercial Court *ADR Orders in the Commercial Court—Guidance Notes for Litigants an their Lawyers*

Commercial Court *End of Year Statement 1993–1994*

Commercial Court *Working Party on ADR First Report*, 1996

Commercial Court *ADR Working Party Second Report*, 1998

Commercial Court *Commercial Court Guide*

Commercial Mediation Centre *Appointment of Mediator; Mediation Rules and Procedure; Mediator Code of Conduct; Suggested contract provisions*

Comprehensive Accredited Lawyer Mediators (CALM) *Code of Practice for Members of CALM*

Condliffe, P *Conflict Management—a practical guide*, TAFE Publications, Abbotsford, Victoria, 1991

Condlin, R 'Bargaining in the Dark: the normative incoherence of lawyer dispute bargaining role' (1992) 51 *Maryland Law Review* 1

Connelly, S 'Looking to the future: family mediation in the Republic of Ireland' (1999) 17(7) *ILT* 106

Connolly, P D 'By good disputing shall the law be well known' (1975) 49 *Australian Law Journal* 685

Constantino, C and Merchant, C *Designing Conflict Management Systems: a guide to creating productive and healthy organisations*, Jossey-Bass, San Francisco, 1996

Cooley, J 'Mediation and joke design: resolving the incongruities' (1992) 2 *Journal of Dispute Resolution* 250

Cork, G 'ADR brings high interest returns in financial disputes—the Credit Union Dispute Reference Centre' (1998) 1 *The ADR Bulletin* 35

Corne, P 'Judicial conciliation in Japan' (1993) 4 *Australian Dispute Resolution Journal* 139

Cornes, D 'All change for adjudication' *Construction Law*, July 2000, p 6

Costello, E J 'To mediate or not to mediate?' (1997) *Arbitration and Dispute Resolution Law Journal* 25.

Coulson, R 'Dispute management under modern construction systems' (1983) 46 *Law & Contemporary Problems* 127

CPR Alternatives *Special Issue: ADR in the Courts*, vol 9, No 7, July 1991

CPR Alternatives *Winter Meeting: Mediating among Judges*, vol 16, No 2, March 1998

CPR Alternatives *Special Supplement*, vol 17, No 4, April 1999

CPR Alternatives *ADR and the Courts: Now and in the Future*, vol 17, No 5, May 1999

CPR Institute for Dispute Resolution *Questions to assess ADR suitability regarding consensual ADR*

Crawford, A 'Justice de proximité—the growth of "houses of justice" and victim-offender mediation in France' (2000) 9(1) *Social & Legal Studies* 29

Crosbie, F 'Aspects of confidentiality in mediation: a matter of balancing competing public interests' (1995) 2 *Commercial Dispute Resolution Journal* 51

Cruickshank, D 'Training mediators: moving towards competency-based training' in K Mackie (ed) *A Handbook on Dispute Resolution: ADR in Action*, Routledge, New York, 1991

Davenport, P 'What is wrong with mediation' (1997) 8 *Australian Dispute Resolution Journal* 133

Davet and Bogoch 'Fixed Fight or Free-For-All?' (1980) 7 *Brit J Law & Society* 36

David, J 'Designing a dispute resolution system' (1994) 1(1) *Commercial Dispute Resolution Journal* 27

David, J and Anderson, T *Grievance management in the New South Wales Public Sector*, 1995

Davidson, P 'No dispute over ADR success' *The Lawyer*, 25 October 1999, p 12

Davies, G and Lieboff, J 'Reforming the civil litigation system; streamlining the adversarial framework' (1994) 14(10) *Proctor* 10

Davies, G 'Mediation and the Courts—Inspiration or Desperation: 9 Questions which must be Answered', Paper presented at 29th Australian Legal Convention, September 1995

Davies, M et al *Promoting Mediation, Research and Policy Planning Unit, Report of our Study of the Bristol Law Society's mediation scheme in its preliminary phase*, Research Study No 21, The Law Society, 1996

Davies, P 'Restorative Justice' (2000) 56(6) *Magistrate* 170

Davies, R 'Negotiating personal injury cases: A survey of the attitudes and beliefs of personal injury lawyers' (1994) 68 *Australian Law Journal* 734

Davis, A and Salem, R 'Dealing with power imbalances in the mediation of interpersonal disputes' (1984) 6 *Mediation Quarterly* 17

Davis, D and Roberts, M *Access to Agreement: a Consumer Study of Mediation in Family Disputes*, Open University Press, Milton Keynes, 1988

Davis, D and Roberts, M 'Mediation in the battle of the sexes' (1989) *Family Law* 306

Davis, G 'Monitoring publicly-funded mediation' (1997) *Family Law* 591

Davis, G 'Insolvency proceedings in the age of Woolf' (2000) 1 *Insolvency Law* 33

Davis, G and Bader, K   'In-court mediation: The consumer view, Parts I and II' *Family Law*, vol 15, No 3

Davis, G and Roberts, M   *Access to Agreement: a Consumer Study of Mediation in Family Disputes*, Open University Press, Milton Keynes, 1988

Davis, G and Roberts, M   'Mediation and the Battle of the Sexes' (1989) *Family Law* 306

Davis, G et al   *A preliminary study of victim-offender mediation and reparation schemes in England and Wales*, Research Planning Unit, Paper 42, London HMSO, 1987

Davis, R   'Negotiating personal injury cases: a survey of the attitudes and beliefs of personal injury lawyers' (1994) 68 *Australian Law Journal* 734

Dawson, M   'Non-consensual alternative dispute resolution: pros and cons' (1993) 4 *Australian Dispute Resolution Journal* 173

de Bono, E   *Lateral thinking: a textbook of creativity*, Penguin Books, Sydney, 1970

de Bono, E   *Conflicts: a better way to resolve them*, Penguin Books, Sydney, 1985

de Jersey, P   'ADR—a decade later: still not "mere gimmickry"', Speech delivered at the LEADR Annual General Meeting, 21 October 1998

Deloitte and Touche   *1993 Survey of general and outside counsel*, Deloitte and Touche, 1993

Department of Employment   *Prosperity through skills*, London 1993

Department of the Environment, Transport and the Regions (DETR)   *Sites of special scientific interest: Better management and protection, Consultation Paper*, 10 September 1998

Department of the Environment, Transport and the Regions (DETR)   *High hedges: Possible solutions*, Consultation Paper, September 1999

Department of Trade and Industry   *Modern Markets: confident consumers*, White Paper, DTI, London, 1999

Department of Trade and Industry   *The regulation of conditional access services for digital television*, final consultation paper on detailed implementation proposals, 1999

Department of Trade and Industry   *White Paper on Competitiveness*, DTI 1999

Dewdney, M and Charlton, R   'Editorial' (1992) 3 *Australian Dispute Resolution Journal* 211

Dewdney, M et al   *Continuing development in mediation within the legal system and evaluation of the 1992–3 Settlement Week in New South Wales*, Law Society of NSW, 1993

Dickens, L and Cockburn, D   'Dispute settlement institutions and the courts' in R Lewis (ed) *Labour law in Britain*, Basil Blackwell, Oxford 1986.

Dignan, J   *Repairing the damage*, University of Sheffield, 1992

Dignan, J   *Community Mediation Service General Survey 1995*, University of Sheffield, Sheffield, 1995

Dignan, J et al   *Neighbour Disputes: comparing the cost and effectiveness of a mediation and alternative approaches*, Centre for Criminological and Legal Research, University of Sheffield, 1996

Dignan, J and Sorsby, A   *Resolving Neighbour Disputes through Mediation in Scotland*, Scottish Office, 1999

Dingwall, R and Greatbatch, D   'Who is in Charge? Rhetoric and Evidence in the Study of Mediation' (1993) *Journal of Social Welfare & Family Law* 367

Douglas, A   *Individual Peacemaking*, Columbia University Press, New York, 1962

Down, C   'Crying Woolf? Reform of the adversarial system in Australia' (1998) 7 *Journal of Judicial Administration* 213

Doyle, M   *Advising on ADR: the essential guide to appropriate dispute resolution*, Advice Services Alliance, London, 2000

Drafting Committee on the Uniform Mediation Act   *Notes by the Drafting Committee on the Uniform Mediation Act*, 1 June 1999

Dreise, D   *Mediation: the political management of stories*, unpublished LLM dissertation, Bond University, 1993

Duckers, J   'Woolf at door over Mediation Reform: Lawyers in fear of losing fees' *Birmingham Post*, 17 September 1999

Edelman, A et al   *Partnering*, IWR ADR Series no 4, 1991

Edelman, L et al   'Internal Dispute Resolution: The transformation of civil rights in the work place' (1993) 27(3) *Law & Society Review* 497

Edelman, P   'Institutionalising dispute resolution alternatives' (1984) 9(2) *Justice System Journal* 134

Editorial   (1993) 4 *Australian Dispute Resolution Journal* 255

Effron, J   'Alternatives to litigation: factors in choosing' (1989) 52 *Modern Law Review* 480

Egan, G   *The skilled helper: a systematic approach to effective helping* (5th edn) Brooks/Cole Publishing, Pacific Grove, California, 1994

Eisenberg, M   'Private ordering through negotiation: dispute settlement and rulemaking' (1976) 89 *Harvard Law Review* 637

Elliott, D   'Med-arb: fraught with danger or ripe for opportunity' (1996) 62(3) *Arbitration* 175

Elliott, M   'The role of facilitators, mediators and other consensus building practitioners' in L Susskind et al (eds) *The consensus building handbook—a comprehensive guide to reaching agreement*, Sage Publications, California, 1999

Ellison, R   'The pensions seer' (1999) 28(10) *Pensions World* 58

Ennis, C   'Mediation, construction and Woolf' (2000) 5(1) *C & EL* 8

Environment Council   *Press Releases*, 7 December 1998, 15 January 1999, 3 February 1999, 1 June 1999 and 16 November 1999

Environment Council   *Annual Review 1999*

Environment Council   *Background and case studies*

Environment Council   *Stakeholder Dialogue—the Environment Council Approach*

Environment Council   *Stakeholder Dialogue in Action—case study: The Brent Spar Dialogue Process*

EOCD   *Recommendation of the EOCD Council concerning guidelines for consumer protection in the context of electronic commerce*, 1999

Erlanger, H et al   'Participation and flexibility in informal processes: cautions from the divorce context' (1987) 21 *Law & Society Review* 585

European Commission   *Cost of legal barriers to consumers in the Single Market*, Com (98) 13 Final (14 February 1996)

European Commission   *Out of court bodies responsible for the settlement of consumer disputes*

European Commission   *Recommendation on the principles applicable to the bodies responsible for out of court settlement of consumer disputes*, 28 December 1997 (98/257/EC)

European Commission   *Towards greater efficiency in obtaining and enforcing judgments in the European Union*, Com (97) 609 Final (26 November 1997)

European Commission Communication   *Out of court settlement of consumer disputes*, COM (1998) 198 Final

Family Mediation Borders   *Annual Report 1999*

Family Mediation Central Scotland   *Annual Report 1999*

Family Mediation Lothian   *16th Annual Report 1999*

Family Mediation Scotland   *Annual Reports 1989* and *1999*

Family Mediation Scotland (FMS)   *Code of Conduct; Information Pack; Registration procedures; National Training Course Information Pack; and Procedures and evaluation of training mediators; Statistical returns; Selection and contracting procedures;* and *Making arrangements after separation or divorce*

Family Mediation Service of Northern Ireland   *Annual Report 1996*

Family Mediation Tayside   *Annual Report 1998–9*

Family Mediators' Association (FMA)   *Mediation Practice Manual; Directory of FMA trained mediators listed by County; Supervisor/consultant directory; Policy Document on selection, recruitment, training and professional practice supervision and consultancy; Guidelines to training policy and entry requirements for courses; Training Courses—guide and information; Training to mediate on all issues in separation or divorce; Your training questions answered; Support for people facing separation or divorce; Annual Report; Mediator Code of Conduct; Guidelines to current policy:* and *Domestic violence, child protection, direct consultation*

Fatchett, D   *Creating and expanding opportunities for preventing conflict*, Launch of Carnegie Commission's Report on preventing deadly conflict, 8 January 1998

Faulkes, W   'The modern development of alternative dispute resolution in Australia' (1990) 1 *Australian Dispute Resolution Journal* 61

Faulkes, W   'Pursuing the best ends by the best means' (1985) 59 *Australian Law Journal* 457

Faulkes, W   'The dispute resolution industry—defining the industry and establishing competencies' (1994) *Australian Dispute Resolution Journal* 285

Feer, M   'On "Toward a new discourse for mediation: a critique of neutrality"' (1992) 10 *Mediation Quarterly* 173

Felstiner, W   'Influences of Social Organisation on Dispute Processing' (1974) 9 *Law & Society Review* 69

Felstiner, W et al   'The emergence and transformation of disputes: naming, blaming and claiming' (1980–1) 15 *Law & Society Review* 631

Field, R   'The use of litigation and mediation for the resolution of custody and access disputes: a survey of QLD Family Law Solicitors' (1996) 7 *Australian Dispute Resolution Journal* 5

Filipowski, B A   'The Response of Business to the Challenges of ADR', unpublished paper, Sydney, 28 August 1992

Financial Services Authority and Financial Services Ombudsman Scheme   *A joint consultation paper: Consumer Complaints and the new single ombudsman scheme*, FSA, November 1999

Fine, N and Macbeth, F   *Playing with fire: Training for the creative use of conflict*, Youth Work Press, 1992

Finer Report   *Report of the Committee on One Parent Families*, Cmnd 5629, HMSO, London, 1974

Fisher, J and Blondel, M   *Couples mediation: a forum and a framework*, NSW Marriage Guidance, 1993

Fisher, R   'Negotiating power—getting and using influence' (1983) 27 *American Behavioural Scientist* 149

Fisher, R   'Why not contingent fee mediation' (1986) *Negotiation Journal* 11

Fisher, R   'He who pays the piper' (1987) 6(1) *Corporate Counsel Review* 75

Fisher, R and Brown, S   *Getting together: building a relationship that gets to yes*, Business Books, Boston, 1988

Fisher, R and Ertel, D   *Getting ready to negotiate: the Getting to Yes Workbook*, Penguin Books, New York, 1995

Fisher, R and Ury, W   *Getting to Yes: Negotiating an Agreement without giving in* (rev edn) Hutchinson Books, Boston, 1992

Fisher, R et al   *Getting to Yes: Negotiating an Agreement without giving in* (2nd edn) Houghton Mifflin, Boston, 1991

Fiss, O   'Against Settlement' (1984) 93 *Yale Law Journal* 1073

Fix, M and Harter, P J   *Hard cases, vulnerable people: an analysis of mediation programs at the multi-door courthouse of the Superior Court of the District of Columbia*, The Urban Institute and State Justice Institute Washington, 1992

Flanagan, P   'Payback for victims of crime' *The Mirror*, 18 November 1999

Flanders   'Modelling Court Delay' (1980) 2 *Law and Policy* 305

Fleischmann, E and Bussin, N   *The institutionalisation of ADR: a case study of the Ontario Insurance Commission*, Toronto, 1996

Fleming, J   'First "no settlement, no fee" offer for commercial mediation clients' *The Law Society Gazette*, 8 June 2000

Fleming, J   'Former Eversheds lawyer claims a first in on-line mediation' *The Law Society Gazette*, 20 April 2000, p 20

Fleming, J   'Lawrence Graham is dispute resolver for Internet Bank' *The Law Society Gazette*, 3 August 2000

Fleming, J   'UN banking for mediation plans' *The Law Society Gazette*, 11 May 2000

Flood, J and Caiger, A   'Lawyers and Arbitration: the Juridification of Construction Disputes' (1993) 56 *Modern Law Review* 412

Folberg, J and Taylor, A   *Mediation—a comprehensive guide to resolving conflicts without litigation*, Jossey-Bass, San Francisco, 1988

Folger, J and Poole, M   *Working through Conflict: a communication perspective*, Scott Foresman, Glenview, Illinois, 1984

Ford, Judge   *The Patents Court ADR Programme*, 1996

Fordham, J   'Med-ex: an interesting variation on the ADR theme', *Resolutions*, Issue no 26, Summer 2000

Foskett, D   *The Law and Practice of Compromise* (4th edn), Sweet & Maxwell, London, 1996

Foster, N and Kelly, J   'Divorce Mediators: Who should be Certified?' (1996) 30 *University of San Francisco Law Review* 667

Fracassini, C   'Independent watchdog for lawyers proposed' *The Scotsman*, January 1999

Freedman, L R and Prigoff, M L   'Confidentiality in Mediation: the need for Protection' (1986) 2 *Ohio State Journal on Dispute Resolution* 37

Frisby, S   'Mediating an environmental dispute' (1999) 1 *Proctor* 23

Fuller, L   'Mediation—its forms and functions' (1970–71) 44 *Southern California Law Review* 305

Fulton, M   *Commercial Alternative Dispute Resolution*, The Law Book Company, Sydney, 1989

Galanter, M   'Why the "haves" come out ahead: Speculation on the limits of legal change' (1974) 9 *Law & Society Review* 95

Galanter, M   'Reading the Landscape of Disputes: What we know and don't know (and think we know) about our allegedly contentious and litigious society' (1983) 31 *UCLA Law Review* 4

Galanter, M   'Worlds of deals: using negotiation to teach legal process' (1984) 34 *Journal of Legal Education* 268

Galanter, M   'Quality of Settlements' (1988) *Mo J Dispute Resol* 55

Galanter, M   'The emergence of the judge as a mediator in civil cases' (1996) 69(5) *Judicature* 257

Galanter, M and Lande, J   'Private Courts and Public Authority' (1992) 12 *Studies in Law Politics & Society* 393

Gale, D   'The Impact of Culture on the Work of Family Mediators' (1994) 4(2) *Family Mediation*

Gardner, N   'Mediation helps to mend fences' *Sunday Times*, 25 January 1998

Garner, C   'Churches go for training on how to stop disputes becoming unholy rows' *The Independent*, London, 5 October 1999, p 3

Garner, H   *The First Stone: some questions about sex and power*, Picador, Sydney, 1995

Garwood, F   *The Scottish Scene*, UK College of Family Mediators, Issue 1, Summer 1997

Gee, T and Urban, P   'Co-mediation in the family court' (1994) 5 *Australian Dispute Resolution Journal* 42

Gellman, R   *A brief history of the Virtual Magistrates Project: the early months*, Paper presented at NCIAR Conference, 22 May 1996 (available at http://mantle.sbs.umass.edu/vmag/GELLMAN.htm)

General Council of the Bar   *The Beldam Committee Report of the Committee on ADR*, 1991 ('The Beldam Committee Report')

General Council of the Bar   *The Heilbron/Hodge Committee Report of the Committee on ADR*, 1993 ('The Heilbron Report')

Genn, H   *Hard Bargaining: out of court settlement in personal injury actions*, Clarendon Press, Oxford 1987

Genn, H   *The Central London County Court Pilot Mediation Scheme: Evaluation Report*, University College London, 1998, LCD Research Series No 5/98

Georges, R   *Dispute settlement in Cyberspace*, 23 March 1998 (www.futurelawyer.com/display)

Gettlin, R   'IRS pilot mediation program helps resolve DuPont case' *SPIDR News*, vol 20, No 2, 1996, p 7

Gibson, K   'The ethical basis of mediation: why mediators need philosophers' (1989) 7 *Mediation Quarterly* 41.

Gibson, K 'Confidentiality in Mediation: a moral re-assessment' (1992) *Journal of Dispute Resolution*, 25

Gilbert & Tobin 'Domain names: A view from the antipodes' *Mondaq Business Briefing*, 25 May 1999

Giles, R 'Severability of dispute resolution clauses in contracts' (1995) 14 *The Arbitrator* 38

Gillicuddy, N B 'Factors Affecting the Outcome of Mediation: Third Party and Disputant Behaviour' in Duffy, Grosch and Olczak (eds) *Community Mediation: A Handbook for Practitioners and Researchers*, Guildford, New York, 1991

Gilson, R J and Mnookin, R H 'Disputing through Agents: Co-operation and conflict between lawyers in litigation' (1994) *94 Columbia Law Review* 504

Glasser, C 'Civil Procedure and the Lawyer—the adversary system and the decline of the orality principle' (1993) 56 *Modern Law Review* 307

Goh, B 'Culture: the silent negotiator' (1999) 2(2) *The ADR Bulletin* 19

Goldberg, S et al *Dispute Resolution: Negotiation, mediation and other processes* (2nd edn) Little Brown & Company, 1992

Goldberg, S et al (eds) *Dispute Resolution: Negotiation, Mediation and other Processes* (3rd edn) Aspen Law and Business, New York, 1999

Goldstein, S *Cultural Issues in Mediation: a Literature Review*, PCR Working Paper, University of Hawaii, 1986

Gonfors, M 'Mediation—a romantic ideal or a workable alternative' in H Messmer and H U Ottoc *Restorative justice on trial—pitfalls and potentials of victim-offender mediation: international research perspectives*, Kluwer Academic Publishers, Boston, 1992

Gottman, J M *Marital Intervention: Experimental Investigations*, Academic Press, New York, 1979

Graham, G 'Former advisers settle B&C' *Financial Times*, 8 January 1999

Graham, M 'Solicitor and own-client costs disputes: the new regime' (1999) 4 *Proctor* 32

Granat, R *Creating an environment for mediating disputes on the internet*, Paper presented at NCAIR Conference, 22 May 1996

Green Paper *Access of consumers to justice and the settlement of disputes in the Single Market*, 1992

Green Paper *Legal Aid: Targeting Need*, 1995 Cm 2854, HMSO, London.

Green, E 'Corporate ADR' (1986) 1 *Ohio State Journal on Dispute Resolution* 203

Greenfield, R D and Burt, C O 'ADR in shareholder suits: Old wine in a new bottle' (1993) 135(2) *New Jersey Law Journal* 17

Gregorczuk, H 'The appropriateness of mediation in international environmental disputes' (1996) 7 *Australian Dispute Resolution Journal* 47

Grillo, T 'The mediation alternative: process dangers for women' (1991) 100 *Yale Law Review* 1545

Grose, S and Alford, W 'The dispute resolution project: peer mediation in schools' in D Bagshaw (ed) *Second international mediation conference: mediation and cultural diversity*, 18–20 January 1996, Group for Mediation Studies, University of South Australia outlines the results of an evaluation of peer mediation in Australia

Guest, A G et al (eds) *Chitty on Contracts, General Principles Volume*, Sweet & Maxwell, London, 1994

Gulbenkian Foundation *Children and violence: A report of the commission on children and violence*, 1995

Gulliver, P H *Disputes and Negotiations: a cross-cultural perspective*, Academic Press, New York, 1979

Gurry, F 'The Dispute Resolution Services of WIPO' (1999) *Journal of International and Economic Law* 385

Hager, M and Pritchard, R 'Hither the deal mediators' (1999) 10(10) *ICCLR* 291

Hall, J *Resolving disputes between parents, schools and LEAs: some examples of best practice*, Department of Education and Employment, London, October 1999

Hall, T 'Billington v North Staffordshire Hospital NHS Trust' (2000) 6(2) *C Risk* 71

Halliburton, R 'London Mediation Scheme wins legal aid funds worth £20,000' *The Law Society Gazette*, 13 August 1997

Hamilton, J 'Protecting Confidentiality in Mandatory Mediation: lessons from Ontario and Saskatchewan' (1999) 24 *Queens' Law Journal* 561

Harbridge, R 'Dispute Resolution Procedures in New Zealand Employment Contracts' *AMINZ Newsletter*, September 1996

Harman, L 'Confidentiality in mediation' in G Raftesath and S Thaler (eds) *Cases for Mediation*, Sydney LBC Information Services, 1999

Harrington, C 'De-legalisation Reform Movements' in R Abel (ed) *The Politics of Informal Justice, vol 1*, Academic Press, New York, 1982

Harrington, C 'The Politics of Participation and Non-participation in Dispute Processes' (1984) 6(2) *Law & Policy* 203

Harrington, C and Merry, S 'Ideological Production: the making of community mediation' (1988) 22(4) *Law & Society Review* 709

Harris, D and Veljanovski, C 'Remedies under contract law: designing rules to facilitate out of court settlements' (1983) 5 *Law & Policy Quarterly* 1997

Harris, W 'Consumer disputes and ADR' (1993) 4 *Australian Dispute Resolution Journal* 238

Haynes, J *Divorce Mediation: a practical guide for therapists and counsellors*, Springer Publishing, New York, 1981

Haynes, J 'Mediation and therapy: an alternative view' (1992) 10 *Mediation Quarterly* 21

Haynes, J *The fundamentals of family mediation*, State University of New York Press, Albany, 1994

Headstart *Tackling bullying*, London 1996

Hegland, K 'Why teach trial advocacy? An essay on never ask why' in *Humanistic Education in Law*, Monograph III, 1982

Henderson, S *The Dispute Resolution Manual*, DataLegal Publications, Spring Hill, QLD, 1993

Herman, A H *Law v Business: business articles from the Financial Times 1983–1988*, Butterworths, London, 1989

Herriott, A M 'ADR—a threat to democracy?' (1994) 19 *Alternative Law Journal* 75

HM Treasury Central Unit on Procurement *Disputes Resolution*, CUP No 50

Hobbes, T *Leviathan*, Everyman Edition, 1962

Hodson, D *The Family Law Act: Where now?* Paper presented at UK College of Family Mediators' Annual Conference, 1 July 1999

Hodson, P 'Mediation: an alternative to trust litigation' (2000) 6(10) *Trusts and Trustees* 11

Hoffman, D 'ADR: An opportunity to broaden the shadow of the law' (1994) 21 *Human Rights* 20

Hood, A 'Commercial contracts, lawyers and alternative dispute resolution: a proactive habit' (1998) 9 *Australian Dispute Resolution Journal* 129

House of Commons Health Committee 6th Report 1998–99 Session, *Procedures related to adverse clinical incidents and outcomes in medical care*, 23 November 1999

House of Commons Select Committee on Health *Appendices to the Minutes of Evidence*, 23 November 1999

House of Commons Select Committee on Health *Minutes of Evidence*, 12 July 1999

Hufnagle, G 'Mediator Malpractice Liability' (1989) 23 *Mediation Quarterly* 33

Humphries, M 'Insolvency Mediation and ADR' (1999) 65 *Insolvency Bulletin* 7

Hunt, B 'Legal risk management' (1999) 18(6) *Litigation* 19

Hunter, R and Leonard, A 'Sex discrimination and alternative dispute resolution: British proposals in light of international experience' *Public Law*, Summer 1997

Hurley, D *Paper to Arbitrators' Institute New Zealand*, 1994

ICSID *Rules of Procedure for Conciliation*

INCORE (Initiative on Conflict Resolution and Ethnicity) *Mediation in Practice*

Ingleby, R *Why not toss a coin? Issues of quality and efficiency in Alternative Dispute Resolution*, Paper presented at the AIJA 9th Annual Conference, 1991

Ingleby, R 'ADR's claims "unproven"' (1992) 27 *Australian Law News* 7

Ingleby, R 'Compulsion is not the answer' (1992) 27 *Australian Law News* 17

Ingleby, R 'Court sponsored mediation: the case against mandatory participation' (1993) 56 *Modern Law Review* 441

Ingleby, R *In the ball park: alternative dispute resolution and the courts*, Australian Institute of Judicial Administration, Melbourne, 1991

Institute of Civil Engineers *Conciliation Procedure*

Insurance Ombudsman Bureau *Annual Report 1999*

InterMediation *START ADR Protocol: Endorsement of Principles;* and *Mediation Rules and Rules of Conduct*

International Chamber of Commerce *Rules of Optional Conciliation*

Jaynes, G L 'Dispute Review Boards' (1993) *International Construction Law Review* 159

Jeffrey, M I 'Accommodating negotiation in environmental impact assessment and project approval processes' (1987) 4 *EPLJ* 244

Katsh, E et al *E-commerce, e-disputes and e-dispute resolution*, 2000 (http://www.disputes.net/cyberweek2000)

Katz, L V 'Compulsory ADR and Voluntarism: Two-headed monster or two sides of the coin?' (1993) *Journal of Dispute Resolution* 1

Keefe, R and Rheaume, W 'Pre-Dispute Planning for Business' (1993) 48 *Arbitration Journal* 39

Keilitz, S 'Civil dispute resolution processes' in Ohio State University College of Law (ed) *Court Reform Implications of Dispute Resolution*, Ohio State University, 1995

Kelly, J 'A decade of divorce mediation research' (1996) 34(3) *Family and Conciliation Court Review* 373

Kendall, J *Expert Determination* (2nd edn) FT Law & Tax, London 1996 (3rd edn due in 2001)

Kendall, K 'Expert determination: its use in resolving art and antiquity disputes' *Art Antiquity & Law*, vol 2, Issue 4, December 1997, p 325

Kennedy 'How the law school fails' 1 *Yale Law & Society Review* 71

King, D 'Specialists in family law resolution' (1999) 10 *Australian Dispute Resolution Journal* 63

King, K 'But I'm not a funny person—the use of humour in dispute resolution' (1988) 4 *Negotiation Journal* 119

Kingston Friends Workshop Group *Step by step: Towards resolving bullying in schools*, 1996, video

Kirtley, A 'The Mediation Privilege: Transformation from Theory to Implementation— Designing a Mediation Privilege to protect Mediation Participants, the Process and the Public Interest' (1995) *Journal of Dispute Resolution* 1

Kolb, D *The Mediators*, MIT Press, Cambridge, Massachusetts, 1983

Kolb, D 'To be a mediator: expressive tactics in mediation' (1985) 41 *Journal of Social Issues* 11–26

Kolb, D and Silbey, S 'Enhancing the capacity of organisations to deal with disputes' (1990) *Negotiation Journal* 297

Kovach, K 'Costs of mediation: whose responsibility?' (1997) 15 *Mediation Quarterly* 13

Kressel, K 'Clinical implications of existing research on divorce mediation' (1987) 1 *American Journal of Family Therapy* 69

Kressel, K and Pruitt, D 'Themes in the mediation of social conflict' (1985) 41 *Journal of Social Issues* 179

Kressel, K and Pruitt, D 'Conclusion' in K Kressel et al (eds) *Mediation Research: the process and effectiveness of third party intervention*, Jossey-Bass, San Francisco, 1989

Kressel, K et al (eds) *Mediation Research: the process and effectiveness of third party intervention*, Jossey-Bass, San Francisco, 1989

Kritzer, H 'Adjudication to settlement: Shading in the gray' (1986) 70 *Judicature* 161

Kritzer, H *Let's make a deal: Understanding the negotiation process in ordinary litigation*, University of Wisconsin Press, Madison, Wisconsin 1990

Krivis, J   'Mediating in Cyberspace' *Alternatives*, vol 14, No 10

Kumar, A and Muttath, R   'Enforceability in mediation', paper delivered on 27 March 1999 at the Second Conference on Alternative Dispute Resolution: Mediation—yesterday's ideas, today's techniques, National University of Singapore, Conference proceedings

Kumar, W   'Opportunities for mediation' *Chartered Surveyor Monthly*, vol 7, No 4, January 1998, p 59

Kurien, G   'Critique of Myths of Mediation' (1995) 6 *Australian Dispute Resolution Journal* 43

Lampen, J   *Conflict Busters: the young people's guide to mediation in schools*, Ulster Quaker Peace Education Project, 1997

Landes, W and Posner, R   'Adjudication as a Private Good' (1978) 12 *Journal of Legal Studies* 235

Latham Report   HMSO, July 1994

Laue, J H   'The Emergence of Institutionalisation of Third Party Roles in Conflict' in D J Samdole and I Samdole-Staroste (eds) *Conflict Management and Problem Solving: Interpersonal to International Applications*, Frances Pinter, 1987

Law Commission   *Report on Privity of Contract: Contracts for the benefit of third parties*, Law Com No 242 (1996)

Law Commission   *Shareholder Remedies Report*, No 246

Law Commission   *Shareholder Remedies*, Consultation Paper, No 142

Law Commission   *The Grounds for Divorce*, Law Commission No 192, HMSO, London

Law Reform Committee   *16th Report*

Law Society (NSW)   'Telephone advice and mediation service for resolving discrimination/harassment problems' (1998) 36(1) *Law Society Journal (NSW)* 77

Law Society of England & Wales ADR Working Party   *ADR—Report prepared by Henry Brown for the Courts and Legal Services Committee*, The Law Society, London, 1991 (The Brown Report)

Law Society of England & Wales   *Code of Practice for Family Mediation; Training standards for family mediation; Standards for accreditation, re-accreditation and supervision/consultancy in family mediation; and Guidelines for use by solicitors in the conduct of ancillary relief proceedings*

Law Society of England & Wales   *Code of Practice for Civil/Commercial Mediation; and Training Standards for civil/commercial mediation*

Law Society of England & Wales   *Guide to the Professional Conduct of Solicitors* (8th edn), Law Society Publishing

Law Society of England & Wales   *England and Wales—the international choice for dispute resolution*

Law Society of New South Wales   *Charter for mediation practice—A guideline to the rights and responsibilities of participants*, 1997

Law Society of Northern Ireland ADR   *The crucial psychological point; ADR's Place in the Course of Litigation; and Dispute Resolution Service*

Law Society of Northern Ireland Dispute Resolution Service   *Agreement to Mediate*

Law Society of Northern Ireland   *Press Release: coming to terms in business—Law Society offers new mediation service*, 13 January 1993

Law Society of Scotland   *Code of Conduct and Guidance for Accredited Mediators; Code of Conduct for Solicitor Mediators*

Law Society of Scotland   *Response to the Access to Justice Consultation Paper*, August 1998

Law Wise   *Code of Practice for Law Wise family mediation; Disciplinary and Grievance Procedures; and Family mediation training programme for accreditation*

Lax, D A and Sebenius, J K   *The manager as negotiator: Bargaining for co-operative and competitive gain*, Free Press, New York, 1986

Lee, J   'The ADR movement in Singapore' in K Tan (ed) *The Singapore Legal System* (2nd edn), Singapore University Press, Singapore, 1999

Lee, J   'The enforceability of mediation clauses in Singapore' (1999) *SJLS* 229

Leeds Mediation and Reparation Service   *Annual Report 1992*
Legal Aid Board   *Franchise in Family Mediation Services*, 1997
Legal Aid Board   *Family Mediation Quality Assurance Standard*, November 1998
Legal Aid Board   *A new approach to funding civil cases: Report to the Lord Chancellor*, October 1999
Legal Aid Board   *Guidance for solicitors and mediators involved in the pilot implementation of Part III of the Family Law Act 1996*, 1999
Legal Week National News   'NHSLA announces mediation audit' *Legal Week*, 20 July 2000
Leitch, M   'The politics of compromise: a feminist perspective on mediation' (1986–7) 14–15 *Mediation Quarterly* 163
Lerman, L   'Lying to Clients' (1990) *University of Pennsylvania Law Review* 659
Lesnick, M and Ehrmann, J   'Selected strategies for managing multi-party disputes' (1987) 16 *Mediation Quarterly* 21
Levitt, M   'Kilometer 101: oasis or mirage? An analysis of third party interest in international mediation' (1997) *Mediation Quarterly* 155
Lewis, J and Legard, R   *ACAS Individual Conciliation: a qualitative evaluation of the service provided in industrial tribunal cases*, ACAS, 1999
Lewis, J   *The role of mediation in family disputes in Scotland: report of a research study*, The Scottish Office Central Research Unit, Edinburgh, 1999
Liebmann, M (ed)   *Community and Neighbour Mediation*, Cavendish Publishing Limited, London, 1998
Lightburn, E   'Mediation in international construction disputes' (2000) 17(1) *ICL Rev* 207
Lim, L and Liew, C   'Community mediation—cultural roots and legal heritage', paper presented at conference Mediation—yesterday's ideas, today's techniques, National University of Singapore, 27 March 1999 and published in *Conference Proceedings*
Lim, L Y   'An analysis of intervention techniques in mediation' (1998) 9 *Australian Dispute Resolution Journal* 196
Lim, R and Carnevale, P   'Contingencies in the Mediation of Disputes' (1990) *Journal of Personality and Social Psychology* 259
Limbury, A   'Compulsory ADR before commencing proceedings?' *The ADR Bulletin*, vol 1, No 2, June 1998
Lin, L   'Impact of cultural differences on dispute resolution' (1996) 7 *Australian Dispute Resolution Journal* 197
Lind, E A et al   'In the eye of the beholder: tort litigants' evaluations of their experience in the civil justice system' (1990) 24(4) *Law & Society Review* 953
Lipsky, D and Seeber, R   *The use of ADR in US corporations*, Cornell University School of Industrial and Labor Relations, Foundation for the Prevention and Early Resolution of Conflict (PERC) and Price Waterhouse LLP, New York, 1997
Lockey, J   'Providing a little reinsurance' (2000) 14(21) *The Lawyer* 33
London Court of International Arbitration   *Mediation Procedure*
Lord Chancellor's Department   *Looking to the Future: mediation and the grounds for divorce*, London, HMSO, 1993
Lord Chancellor's Department   *White Paper: Modernising Justice—the Government's plans for reforming Legal Services and the Courts*, 1998
Lord Chancellor's Department   *Conditional Fees Consultation: summary of responses to the Lord Chancellor's Department Consultation Paper*, July 1998
Lord Chancellor's Department   *Quicker Settlement through Mediation*, 28 July 1998
Lord Chancellor's Department   *Consultation Paper: Access to justice with conditional fees*, 1998
Lord Chancellor's Department   *Consultation paper: Conditional Fees—Sharing the Risks of Litigation*, 1999
Lord Chancellor's Department   *ADR Discussion Paper*, November 1999
Lord Chancellor's Department   *ADR Discussion Paper: Summary of Responses*, August 2000
Lord Woolf   *Access to Justice: Interim Report*, June 1995
Lord Woolf   *Access to Justice: Final Report*, July 1996

Loughran, N and Cameron, L   *Edinburgh Mediation Project: final report*, Edinburgh, May 1998

Lynch, A   'Can I Sue My Mediator? Finding the Key to Mediator Liability' (1995) *Australian Dispute Resolution Journal* 113

Maatman   'The future of summary judgment in the Federal Court' (1988) 21 *J Marshall L Rev* 455

Macaulay, S   'Non-contractual Relations in Business: a preliminary study' (1963) 28(1) *American Sociological Review* 55

MacCoun, R J et al   *ADR in Trial and Appellate Courts*, RAND, Santa Monica, 1992

Mackay, R E and Brown, A J   *Community Mediation in Scotland: a study of implementation*, The Scottish Office Central Research Unit, Edinburgh, 1999

Mackay, R E and Brown, A J   'Legal issues in community mediation' (1999) 2 *Jur Rev* 87

Mackie, K   'Negotiation and Mediation: from Inelegant Haggling to Sleeping Giant' in K Mackie (ed) *A Handbook on Dispute Resolution*, Routledge, London, 1991

Mackie, K   'ADR in Europe—lessons from a classic US case' (1992) 5 *EIPR* 183

Mackie, K   'Expert mediators—not experts as mediators: CEDR replies' *Resolutions*, Issue No 16

Mackie, K et al   *Commercial Dispute Resolution: an ADR Practice Guide*, Butterworths, London, 1995

Mackie, K et al   *The ADR Practice Guide: Commercial Dispute Resolution*, Butterworths, London, 2000

Mackintosh, J   'Mediator option for financial wrongdoers' *Financial Times*, 17 August 2000

Maggiolo, W   *Techniques of Mediation*, Oceana Publications, New York, 1985

Maher, F   'All is fair in mediation' *The Lawyer*, 27 March 2000

Manchester Development Educational Project   *The School Issue: a practical guide to successful whole school change*, Manchester Metropolitan University, 1993

Manley, M   'Mediation in libel cases?' *Solicitors' Journal*, 24 March 2000, p 268

Mann, L C   'Mediation of Civil Cases' (1990) 67 *Detroit Law Review* 531

Marlow, L   'The rule of law in divorce mediation' (1985) 9 *Mediation Quarterly* 5

Marsh, S R   *Materials from 5th Annual ADR Institute of the State Bar of Texas*, 1993

Marshall, J   'Mediation Week 1996 reviewed' (1996) *Lawtalk*, Issue 486

Marshall, T and Merry, S   *Crime and accountability*, London HMSO, 1990

Marshall, T and Walpole, M   *Bringing people together: mediation and the reparation projects in Great Britain*, Research & Planning Unit, Paper 33, London HMSO, 1985

Marshall, T F   'Neighbour Disputes: Community Mediation Schemes as an alternative to Litigation' in K Mackie (ed) *A Handbook of Dispute Resolution: ADR in Action*, Routledge, London, 1991

Martin, P   'Good Practice Guidelines' in UK College of Family Mediators, *1999/2000 Directory and Handbook*

Maslow   *Motivation and Personality*, 1954

Mason, Sir Anthony   'Mediation and art disputes' *Art Antiquity & Law*, vol 3, Issue 1, March 1998, p 31

Mayer, B   'Dynamics of power in mediation and negotiation' (1987) 16 M*ediation Quarterly* 75

Mays, R and Clark, B   *ADR in Scotland*, The Scottish Office, 1999

McAllister, B   Paper presented at conference on 'Promoting justice and peace through reconciliation and co-existence', American University, Washington DC, 20 February 1999

McCarthy, P   *Mediation in divorce: are lawyers needed?* Annual Research Conference, The Law Society, London, 1996.

McCarthy, P and Walker, J   'Mediation and divorce law reform: the lawyers' view' (1995) 25 *Family Law* at 361–8

McCarthy, P and Walker, J   'Involvement of lawyers in the mediation process' (1996) 26 *Family Law* at 154–8

McCarthy, P and Walker, J   *Evaluating the long term impact of family mediation: report to the Joseph Rowntree Foundation*, Relate Centre of Family Studies, University of Newcastle upon Tyne, 1996

McCarthy, P and Walker, J   *The role of lawyers in family mediation*, Family Studies Report No 2, September 1996

McCarthy, P et al   *Lawyers in family mediation*, Report to the Law Society, 1996

McClintock, C (ed)   *Experimental Social Psychology*, 1972

McCormick, M   'Confronting social injustice as a mediator' (1997) 14 *Mediation Quarterly* 293

McCrory, J   'Confidentiality in mediation of matrimonial disputes' (1988) 51 *Modern Law Review* 442

McEwen, C and Maiman, R   'Small Claims Mediation in Maine: an empirical assessment' (1981) 33 *Maine Law Review* 237

McEwan, C and Maiman, R   'Coercion and consent: a tale of two court reforms' (1988) 10(10) *Law & Policy* 3

McEwan, C and Milburn, T   'Explaining a paradox of mediation' (1993) 9 *Negotiation Journal* 23

McEwen, C A   'Bring in the Lawyers: Challenging the Dominant Approaches to Ensuring Fairness in Divorce Mediation' (1995) 79 *Minnesota Law Review* 1317

McFarlane, T   'Should there be a duty to advise of ADR?' (1993) *The Litigation Lawyer* 11

McGarvie J, R E   'Judicial responsibility for the operation of the court system' (1989) 63 *Australian Law Journal* 79

McGhie, S   'Battling over the bug: Y2K and US court cases' *Computers & Law*, December 1999/January 2000, p 22

McPheeters, C   'Leading horses to water: may courts which have the power to order attendance at mediation also require good faith negotiation?' (1992) *Journal of Dispute Resolution* 377

Mead, P   'ADR agreements: good faith and enforceability' (1999) 10 *Australian Dispute Resolution Journal* 40

Mediation UK (ed)   *Victim-Offender Mediation Conference Papers*, Mediation UK, 1994

Mediation UK   *Annual Reports 1992–1998*

Mediation UK   *Standards*

Mediation UK   *Mediation Digest*, No 3, 1996

Mediation UK   *Peer mediation: It's good to listen*, 1996

Mediation UK   *Restorative justice: Does it work? Digest of current research on victim-offender mediation and conferencing*, December 1997

Mediation UK   *Training Manual in Community Mediation Skills*

Mediation UK   *Mediation Works! Conflict resolution and peer mediation*, Manual For Secondary Schools and Colleges, 1998

Mediators' Institute Ireland (MII)   *Code of Ethics and Professional Conduct for Family Mediators; Complaints Procedure;* and *Accreditation of Professional Mediators in Ireland*

Meggs, G   'Issues in divorce mediation—methodology and ethics' (1993) 4 *Australian Dispute Resolution Journal* 198

Meltsner, M   'The jagged line between mediation and couples therapy' (1993) 9 *Negotiation Journal* 261

Menkel-Meadow, C   'The Transformation of Disputes by Lawyers: what the dispute paradigm does and does not tell us' (1985) *Journal of Dispute Resolution* 31

Menkel-Meadow, C   'For and Against settlement: uses and abuses of the mandatory settlement conference' (1985) *UCLA Law Review* 485

Menkel-Meadow, C   'Pursuing settlement in an adversary culture: A tale of innovation co-opted or "the law of ADR"' (1991) *19 Florida State University Law Review* 1

Menkel-Meadow, C   'Lawyer Negotiations: Theories and realities—what we learn from mediation' (1993) 56 *Modern Law Review* 361

Menkel-Meadow, C   'Towards another view of legal negotiations: the structure of problem-solving' (1993–4) *University of California Law Review* 754

Mentzel, K E   'Judging the fairness of mediation: a critical framework' (1990) 1 *Mediation Quarterly* 3

Merry, S   'Mediation in non-industrial societies' in K Kressel et al (eds) *Mediation Research: the process and effectiveness of third party intervention*, Jossey-Bass, San Francisco, 1989

Merry, S E   'Defining Success in the Neighbourhood Justice Movement' in Momasic and Feeley (eds) *Neighbourhood Justice: Assessment of an Emerging Idea*, Longman, New York, 1982

Middleton, Sir Peter   *Report to the Lord Chancellor: Review of civil justice and legal aid*, Lord Chancellor's Department, September 1997

Mintzberg, H   *The nature of managerial work*, Harper & Row, New York, 1973

Mizzi, A   'Solve disputes on-line' *The Law Society Gazette*, 12 February 2000, p 5

Mizzi, A   'Euro law reform call' *The Law Society Gazette*, 15 June 2000

Mnookin, R   'Why negotiations fail: an examination of barriers to the resolution of conflicts' (1993) 8 *Ohio State Journal on Dispute Resolution* 235

Mnookin, R and Kornhauser, L   'Bargaining in the shadow of the law' (1979) 88 *Yale Law Journal* 950

Moloney, L et al   *Managing differences: federally-funded family mediation in Sydney—outcomes, costs and client satisfaction*, Attorney-General's Department, 1996

Momasic, R   'Mediation as an alternative to adjudication—Rhetoric to Reality in the neighbourhood justice movement' in Momasic and Feeley (eds) *Common Neighbourhood Justice: Assessment of an emerging idea*, Longman, New York, 1982

Moody, S   'An Overview of ADR in Scotland' in Moody and Mackay (eds) *Green's Guide to ADR in Scotland*, Sweet & Maxwell, 1995

Moore, C   *The mediation process: practical strategies for resolving conflict*, Jossey-Bass, San Francisco, 1996

Morgan, T   'The fall and rise of professionalism' (1983–4) 18 *University of Richmond Law Review* 451

Morley, I and Stephenson, G   *The Social Psychology of Bargaining*, George Allen & Unwin, London, 1977

Morris, P E   'The Banking Ombudsman' (1992) 2 *Lloyds Maritime & Commercial Law Quarterly* 227

Morse, E A   'Mediation in debtor/creditor relationships' 20 *University of Michigan Law Journal* 606

Mowatt, J   'Some thoughts on mediation' (1998) 105 *South African Law Journal* 727

Moynihan, Justice   *Case Appraisal*, QLD Supreme Court Report, Spring Quarter 1997

Mulcahy, L   'The devil and the deep blue sea? A critique of the ability of community mediation to suppress and facilitate participation in civil life' (2000) 27(1) *J Law & Soc* 137

Mulcahy, L et al   *Mediating medical negligence claims: an option for the future?* NHS Executive, 2000

Mulcahy, N   'Conciliation and race complaints' (1992) 3 *Australian Dispute Resolution Journal* 21

Mullaly, M   'Atlantic dispute sets ADR record' *Legal Week*, 21 January 1999

Mullaly, M   'Queen's Bench suffers one-third drop in claims' *Legal Week*, 20 July 2000

Munoz, E   'ADR in local government—using dispute resolution to resolve planning disputes' (1998) 1(2) *ADR Bulletin* 24

Murray, J et al   *Processes of Dispute Resolution: the Role of Lawyers*, Foundation Press, New York, 1989

Mustill and Boyd   *Commercial Arbitration* (2nd edn) 1989

Myers, F and Wasof, F   *A meeting in the middle—a study of solicitors' and mediators' divorce practice*, Scottish Executive, 2000

NACRO   *Reducing conflict: Building communities*, NACRO, 1999

NADRAC   *The Development of Standards for ADR: Discussion Paper*, March 2000

Napier, C   'The resolution of commercial environmental disputes using mediation' (2000) 11(2) *ICCLR* 49

National Consumer Council   *Annual Review 1999*

National Consumer Council   *Seeking Civil Justice*, National Consumer Council, London, 1995

National Consumer Council   *Settling consumer disputes*, 1996

National Family Mediation (NFM)   *Annual Reports* and *Annual Statistics Returns*

National Family Mediation (NFM) *Model Agreement to Mediate*
National Family Mediation (NFM) *National Core Training Programme; What is Mediation?*
National Family Mediation (NFM) *Mediator Code of Conduct;* and *Steps towards competent service practice in all issues mediation*
National Family Mediation (NFM) *Changing the picture for the better*
National Institute for Dispute Resolution (NIDR) *Performance-based assessment: a methodology for use in selecting, training and evaluating mediators*, Washington DC, 1995
National Society for Clean Air and Environmental Protection *National Noise Survey 1999*, NSCA,1999
Naughton QC, P 'ADR Comes in from the Cold' (1995) *New Law Journal* 145
Nergård, T B 'Solving conflicts outside the court system' (1993) 33(1) *British Journal of Criminology* 81
New South Wales Law Reform Commission *Alternative dispute resolution—training and accreditation of mediators*, Discussion Paper 21, 1989
Newman, P 'Mediation-arbitration: can it work legally?' (1994) 60(3) *Arbitration* 173
Newman, P 'Partnering: with particular reference to construction' *Arbitration*, February 2000
Newmark, C and Hill, R 'Can a mediated settlement become an enforceable arbitration award?' (2000) 16(1) *Arbitration Int* 81
Nierenberg, J and Calero, H *How to read a person like a book*, Thorsons Publishers, Wellingborough, Northamptonshire, 1980
Northamptonshire Adult Reparation Bureau *Annual Report 1992*
NSW Law Reform Commission 'Training and accreditation of mediators' (1991) 67 *LRC* 35
Nupen, C 'Mediation' in P Pretorius (ed) *Dispute Resolution*, Juta & Co, Kenwyn, South Africa, 1993

O'Reilly, M and Mawdsley, M 'The management of disputes: a risk approach' (1994) *Australian Dispute Resolution Journal* 260
O'Sullivan, J 'Neighbour disputes are damaging your health' *The Independent*, 6 September 1999, p 6
Oakes, R *An analysis of early neutral evaluation in the United States District Court for the Eastern District of California*, Spring 1991 (unpublished work, California State University, Sacramento 1991)
OECD *Recommendation of the OECD Council concerning Guidelines for consumer protection in the context of electronic commerce*, OECD 1999
Office of Fair Trading *Consumer Redress Mechanisms*, November 1991
Office of Fair Trading *Raising standards of consumer care*, 1998
Office of Law Reform *Divorce in Northern Ireland: a better way forward*, Consultation Paper, Office of Law Review, December 1999
Office of Law Reform *Public Benefit and the Public Purse: legal aid reform in Northern Ireland*, The Office of Law Reform, 1999
Office of Telecommunications *Proposed new dispute resolution procedures for fixed telecommunications*, Consultation Document, September 1999
Omar, P J 'ADR in French company law' (1999) 10(2) *ICCLR* 75
Oxford Institute of Legal Practice *Post-graduate Certificate and Diploma in Family Mediation Information*
Oyre, T *Med-arb: The Interface between Mediation and Arbitration*, at http://www.arbitrators.org/materials/articles

Palmer, M and Roberts, S *Dispute processes: ADR and the primary forms of decision making*, Butterworths, London, 1998
Paratz, D *Mediation—a user's guide*, Australian Commercial Disputes Centre, 1992
Parke, J 'Lawyers as negotiators: Time for a code of ethics?' (1993) *Australian Dispute Resolution Journal* 26
Parker, D and Parkinson, L 'Solicitors and Family Conciliation Services: Basis for Professional Co-operation' (1985) 15 *Family Law* 273

Passow, S 'Y2K claims bugging you?' *The Times*, 30 November 1999

Patents County Court *Mediation Procedure*

Paton, A 'SIF's mediation support is vital' *The Lawyer*, 17 November 1998

Patterson, L 'A Scottish perspective on adjudication' *Construction Law*, March 2000, p 6

Pearson, J 'An evaluation of alternatives to court adjudication' (1982) 7 *Justice System Journal* 420

Pearson, J 'Ten Myths about Family Law' (1993) 27(2) *Family Law Quarterly* 284

Pearson, J 'Family Mediation' in Ohio State University Law School (ed) *Court Reform Implications of Dispute Resolution*, Ohio State University, 1995

Pearson, J and Thoennes, M 'Divorce Mediation Research Results' in Folberg and Milne (eds) *Divorce Mediation: Theory and Practice*, Guildford Press, New York, 1988

Pearson, J et al 'The decision to mediate: profiles of individuals who accept and reject the opportunity to mediate contested child custody and visitation issues' (1982) 6 *J Divorce* 1

Pease, A *Body language: how to read others' thoughts by their gestures*, Sheldon Press, London, 1981

Pengilley, W 'Hidden agendas and other matters' (1993) 4 *Australian Dispute Resolution Journal* 53

Perritt, H *Dispute resolution in cyberspace: Demand for new forms of ADR*, Paper presented at Cyberweek 2000 (available at http://www.disputes. net/cyberweek2000/ohiostate/perritt/.htm)

Persky, J 'Pareto's Law' (1992) 6 *Journal of Economic Perspectives* 181

Peters, T and Waterman, R *In search of excellence: lessons from America's best run companies*, Harper Collins, New York, 1993

Peto, H 'In Pursuit of truth and justice' (1999) 18(6) *Litigation: The Journal of Contentious Business* 2

Phillips, H 'Advocacy in Mediation' (1994) 64 *ALJ* 384

Pike, A 'Dispute Review Boards' (1993) *International Construction Law Review* 467

Plapinger, E and Shaw, M *Court ADR—elements of program design*, CPR Institute for Dispute Resolution, New York, 1992

Plapinger, E and Stienstra, D *ADR and settlement in the Federal District Courts: a sourcebook for judges and lawyers*, Federal Judicial Centre and CPR Institute for Dispute Resolution, 1996

Policy Studies Institute *Conditional fees well established but questions about fairness remain*, Press Release, 1997

Polywka, S 'Mediation: life after the NHS Pilot Scheme?' (2000) 6(1) *C Risk* 25

Posner, R *The Federal Courts: Crisis and Reform*, Harvard University Press, Cambridge, 1985

Posner, R 'The summary jury trial and other methods of ADR: Some cautionary observations' (1986) 53 *University of Chicago Law Review* 366

Posner, R *Economic Analysis of Law*, Little Brown, Boston, 1986

Post Magazine, Legal Supplement 'Woolf overview—not so traditional now', *Post Magazine*, 28 October 1999

Power, M 'Educating mediators metacognitively' (1992) 3 *Australian Dispute Resolution Journal* 214

Press, S 'Court-connected ADR: policies and issues' (1995) 28 *Forum* 5

Price, M 'Comparing victim-offender mediation program models' (1995) 6(1) *VOMA Quarterly*

Price, M 'Victim-offender mediation: The state of the art' (1996) 7(3) *VOMA Quarterly*

Prigoff, M L 'Toward Candor or Chaos: the Case of Confidentiality in Mediation' (1988) *Seton Hall Legislative Journal* 1

Prindable, P 'Is mediation an alternative in commercial lease dispute resolution?' (1994) 5 *Australian Dispute Resolution Journal* 99

Pringle, K 'Aboriginal mediation: one step towards empowerment' (1996) 7 *Australian Dispute Resolution Journal* 253

Prior, A 'What do the parties think?' (1993) 4 *Australian Dispute Resolution Journal* 99

Pritchard, J (ed) *The Legal 500: the clients' guide to UK law firms*, Bath Press, 2000

Pritzker, D 'Regulation by consensus: negotiated rulemaking in the United States' (1994–1995) 1 *Commercial Dispute Resolution Journal* 217

Provine, D *Settlement strategies for Federal District Court Judges*, Federal Judicial Center, Washington DC, 1986

Provine, D 'Justice à la carte: on the privatisation of dispute resolution' (1992) 12 *Studies in Law, Politics & Society* 345

Pruitt, D and Olczak, P 'Beyond hope—approaches to resolving seemingly intractable conflict' in B Bunker and J Rubin (eds) *Conflict Co-operation and Justice*, Jossey-Bass, San Francisco, 1995

Pruitt, D *Negotiation Behavior*, Academic Press, New York, 1981

Pruitt, D and Rubin, J *Social Conflict: Escalation, Stalemate and Settlement*, Random House, New York, 1986

Pryles, M (ed) *Dispute Resolution in Asia*, Kluwer Law International, The Hague, 1997

Pryles, M 'Dispute resolution clauses in contracts' (1990) 1 *Australian Dispute Resolution Journal* 116–24

Queens Bench Division (Commercial Court) *Practice Note*, 7 June 1996 [1996] 3 All ER 383

Quine et al *Community Mediation of Disputes between Neighbours*, The Grubb Institute, London, 1990

Radford, E and Glaser, P 'The psychology of mediation' in P Pretorius (ed) *Dispute Resolution*, Juta & Co, Kenwyn, South Africa

Raiffa, H *The Art and Science of Negotiation*, Belkap Press of Harvard University Press, Cambridge, Massachusetts, 1982

Raitt, F 'Domestic Violence and Divorce Mediation' (1996) 18(1) *Journal of Social Welfare and Family Law* at 11–20

RAND Corporation *An evaluation of mediation and early neutral evaluation under the Civil Justice Reform Act*, Institute for Civil Justice, 1996

Randolph, P 'Scepticism about mediation' (2000) 150 *New Law Journal* 565

Ray, L 'The multi-door courthouse idea: building the courthouse of the future . . . today' (1985) 1(17) *Ohio State Journal on Dispute Resolution* 7

Ray, L and Kestner, P *The multi-door experience: dispute resolution and the courthouse of the future*, Standing Committee on Dispute Resolution American Bar Association, Washington DC, 1988, II-4

Ray, L et al (eds) *ABA Dispute Resolution Directory*, 1983

Redmont 'The transactional emphasis in legal education' 26 *Journal of Legal Education*

Reikert, J 'ADR in Australian Commercial Disputes: Quo Vadis?' (1990) *Australian Dispute Resolution Journal* 31

Relate Northern Ireland *Annual Report 1997*

Relate *Annual Review*, 1999

Renouf, E 'The uneasy sixth stage of mediation' (1992) 3 *Australian Dispute Resolution Journal*

Resnik, J 'Managerial Judges' (1982) 96 *Harvard Law Review* 76

Resnik, J 'Failing Faith: Adjudicatory Procedure in Decline' (1986) 53 *University of Chicago Law Review* 494

Resnik, J 'From "cases" to "litigation"' (1991) 54(3) *University of Chicago Law Review* 5

Ricci, I *Mom's House, Dad's House: making shared custody work*, Collier Macmillan Publishers, London, 1982

Richards, C 'The Expertise of Mediating' (1997) *Family Law* 52

Richards, L 'Pupil pioneers could banish bullies' *Evening Chronicle*, 11 March 1998, p 22

Rickman, N 'The impact of plaintiff finance on personal injury litigation: An empirical analysis' (1999) 5 *Litigation Funding*

Riekert, J 'Alternative Dispute Resolution in Australian Commercial Disputes: Quo Vadis? (1990) 1 *Australian Dispute Resolution Journal* 22

Rifkin, J 'Mediation from a feminist perspective: promise and problems' (1994) 2 *Law and Inequality* 21

Rifkin, J et al 'Toward a new discourse for mediation: a critique of neutrality' (1991) 9 *Mediation Quarterly* 151

Rifkin, R et al *Social conflict: escalation, stalemate and settlement* (2nd edn), McGraw Hill Inc, New York, 1994

Riskin, L 'Mediation and Lawyers' (1982) 42 *Ohio State Law Journal* 29

Riskin, L 'Towards new standards for the neutral lawyer in mediation' (1984) 26 *Arizona Law Review* 329

Riskin, L 'Mediator Orientations: Strategies and techniques' (1994) 12(9) *Alternatives* 111

Roberts, M *Access to Agreement: a Consumer Study of Mediation in Family Disputes*, Open University Press, Milton Keynes, 1988

Roberts, M 'Systems or selves? Some ethical issues in family mediation' (1992) 10 *Mediation Quarterly* 11

Roberts, M *Mediation in Family Disputes: Principles of Practice* (2nd edn), Arena, Hants, England 1997

Roberts, M *Mediation in Family Disputes* (2nd edn) Arena, Aldershot, Northhamton, 1997

Roberts, S *Order and dispute: an introduction to legal anthropology*, Penguin Books, Sydney, 1979

Roberts, S 'Mediation in family disputes' (1983) 46 *Modern Law Review* 537

Roberts, S 'Toward a minimal form of alternative intervention' (1986) 11 *Mediation Quarterly* 25

Roberts, S 'Three models of family mediation' in R Dingwall and J Eekelaar (eds) *Divorce Mediation and the legal process*, 1988

Roberts, S 'ADR and Civil Justice: an Unresolved Relationship' (1993) 56(3) *Modern Law Review* 452

Roberts, S 'The Lawyer as Mediator' [1995] *Family Law* 637

Robertson, G 'The Lawyer's Role in Commercial ADR' (1987) 61 *LIJ* 1148

Robertson, M 'Is ADR part of a movement towards consumer-orientated legal services?' *ADR Bulletin*, vol 1, no 1, May 1998

Robinson, G *Victim-offender mediation: limitations and potential*, Oxford Centre for Criminological Research, University of Oxford, 1996

Robinson, G and Devine, D *Family Mediation Services: Data on the Service April 1992/March 1993*, Northern Ireland Family Mediation Service, 1994

Roche, M and Joychild, F *The Human Rights Act—Discrimination in focus*, Institute for International Research, 1994

Rodgers, P 'ADR should be made compulsory says Irvine' *Legal Week*, 11 November 1999, p 6

Rogers, N and C McEwan *Mediation: Law Policy & Practice*, Lawyers Co-operative, Rochester New York, 1989

Rogers, N and Salem, R *A Student's Guide to Mediation and the Law*, Matthew Bender, New York, 1987

Rolph, E et al *Escaping the courthouse: private ADR in Los Angeles*, The RAND Institute of Civil Justice, 1994

Rose, M 'More law firms turn to mediation as a way to settle negligence claims' *The Law Society Gazette*, 6 May 1999

Rose, M 'OSS backlog plans' *The Law Society Gazette*, 11 August 1999

Ross, S *Ethics in Law—Lawyer's Responsibility and accountability*, Butterworths, Sydney, 1979

Rowe, M 'Options, functions and skills: what an organisational ombudsman might want to know' (1995) 11 *Negotiation Journal* 103

Rubin, J and Sander, F 'When should we use agents? Direct versus representative negotiation' (1988) 4 *Negotiation Journal* 395

Sallmann, P A 'Managing the business of Australian High Courts' (1992) 2 *Journal of Judicial Administration* 80

Sammon, G 'The ethical duties of lawyers who act for parties to a mediation' (1993) 4 *Australian Dispute Resolution Journal* 190

Sammon, G 'What to expect from an external review under the FOI Act' (1998) 8 *Proctor* 16

Sammons, J *Lawyer professionalism*, Carolina Academic Press, North Carolina, 1988

Samuels ACJ, Gordon J 'The Economics of Justice' (1991) 1 *Journal of Judicial Administration* 114

Sander, F E A 'Varieties of dispute processing' (1976) 70 *Federal Rules Decisions* 11

Sander, F E A 'Alternative methods of dispute resolution: An overview' (1985) 4 *University of Florida Law Review* 1

Sander, F E A and Goldberg, S B 'Fitting the forum to the Fuss: A user friendly guide to selecting an ADR procedure' (1994) *Negotiation Journal* 55

Sander, F and Rubin, J 'The Janus Quality of Negotiation: Deal making and dispute settlement' (1988) 4 *Negotiation Journal* 109

Saposnek, D 'The value of children in mediation: a cross-culture perspective' (1991) 8(4) *Mediation Quarterly*

Saposnek, D T *Mediating child custody disputes: a systematic guide for family therapists, court counsellors, attorneys and judges*, Jossey-Bass, San Francisco, 1983

Sarat, A 'Alternatives in dispute processing' (1976) 10(3) *Law & Policy* 339

Sarat, A and Felstiner, W 'Law & Social Relations' (1988) 22 *Law & Policy*

Saunders, H 'We need a larger theory of Negotiation: the importance of pre-negotiating phases' (1985) *Negotiation Journal* 249

Schuck, P H 'The role of judges in settling complex cases: The Agent Orange example' (1986) 53 *University of Chicago Law Review* 337

Schuck, P H *Agent Orange on trial: mass toxic disasters in the courts*, The Belknap Press of Harvard University Press, Cambridge, 1986

Scottish Consultative Council On The Curriculum *Sharing Strategies: ideas for integrating a key aspect of the European dimension into the curriculum*, 1995

Scottish Law Commission *Discussion Paper: Confidentiality in Family Mediation*, no 92

Scottish Office *Consultation paper: Access to justice beyond the year 2000*, 1998

Scottish Office *News Release: McLeish outlines proposed reforms to Scotland's Civil Legal Aid system*, 27 March 1998

Scutt, J A 'The privatisation of justice: power differentials, inequality and the palliative of counselling and mediation' (1988) 11 *Women's Studies International Forum* 503

Seaman, N *Fair shares? Barriers to equitable property settlements*, Women Legal Services Network, Canberra

Semple, D 'When it really does pay to talk' *The Herald (Glasgow)*, 17 November 1999, p 16

Serventy, N 'Understanding shame in mediation and dispute resolution' (1998) 9 *Australian Dispute Resolution Journal* 150

Shadbolt, R A 'Resolution of construction disputes by dispute review boards' (1999) 16(1) *International Construction Law Review* 101

Shaefer, N 'New tenants promise to be good neighbours' *The Northern Echo*, 18 March 1999, p 6

Shah-Kazemi, S 'Family Mediation and the Dynamics of Culture' *Family Mediation*, vol 6, no 3, pp 5–7

Shapiro, D 'Expert mediators—not experts as mediators' *Resolutions*, Issue No 16, p 4

Shapiro, D 'Training neutrals' *New Law Journal*, 21 March 1997

Shapiro, D 'Bridge building: examining recent developments in ADR in the UK' *Axiom*, June 1998

Shapiro, D 'Alternative Dispute Resolution under the new Civil Rules: some guidelines for lawyers and judges' (1999) 18(7) *Litigation—the Journal of Contentious Business* 1

Shapiro, D 'Pushing the envelope—selective techniques in tough mediations' (2000) *ADRLJ* 117

Shapiro, D et al 'Mediator Behaviour and the outcome of Mediation' (1985) 41(2) *Journal of Social Issues* 101

Shavell, S 'Alternative dispute resolution: an economic analysis' (1995) *Journal of Legal Studies* 1

Shenkar, O and Ronen, S 'The cultural context of negotiations: the implications of Chinese interpersonal norms' (1987) 23(2) *The Journal of Applied Behavioural Science* 266

Shepley, C 'Mediation in the Planning System' *Planning Inspectorate Journal*, Issue 7, Spring 1997

Sherman, E 'Court-mandated ADR: what form of participation should be required?' (1993) 46 *SMULR* 2079

Shillito, R 'Mediation in libel actions' (2000) 150 *NLJ* 122

Shirley, M 'Breach of an ADR clause—a wrong without a remedy?' (1991) 2 *Australian Dispute Resolution Journal* 117

Shirley, M and Harris, W 'Confidentiality in court-annexed mediation—fact or fallacy?' (1993) 13 *Queensland Lawyer* 221

Siddle, H 'Family mediation pilot project' *The Law Society Gazette*, 21 July 1999, p 31

Siddle, H 'Family upheaval' *The Law Society Gazette*, 7 July 1999, p 14

Silbey, S 'Mediation Methodology' (1993) 9 *Negotiation Journal* 349

Silbey, S and Merry, S 'Mediator settlement strategies' (1986) 8 *Law and Policy* 7

Simkin, W E *Mediation and the dynamics of collective bargaining*, Bureau of National Affairs, Washington DC, 1971

Singer, R 'The rolling stones revisited: exploring the concept of user satisfaction as a measure of success in ADR' (1994) *Australian Dispute Resolution Journal* 77

Skiffington, L 'There must be a better way: alternative dispute resolution' [1997] *ELB* 24

Skinner, A *Bullying: an annotated bibliography of literature and resources*, Youth Work Press, 1996

Slaikeu, K and Hasson, R *Controlling the costs of conflict—how to design a system for your organisation*, Jossey-Bass Publishers, San Francisco, 1998

Slattery, M J 'The Spedley mediation from the inside' (1993) *Bar News* 23

Smart, C *The problem of rights in feminism and the power of law*, Routledge, London 1989

Smith, J 'Can the advantages of ADR procedures be transposed to a judicial forum?' (1993) 4 *Australian Dispute Resolution Journal* 298

Smith, Q and Monaghan, A 'Diplomatic Defamation' (2000) 2(15) *Legal Week* 119

Smith, V et al *Peer Mediation Scheme: how to use peer group mediation effectively in junior and middle schools*, Bristol Mediation 1995

Social & Community Planning Research *Report of interim findings of research into the role of mediation in family law cases in Scotland*, 1997

Society of Professionals in Dispute Resolution (SPIDR) *Qualifying neutrals: the basic principles*, 1989

Society of Professionals in Dispute Resolution (SPIDR) *Mandated participation and settlement coercion: Dispute resolution as it relates to the courts*, 1991

Society of Professionals in Dispute Resolution (SPIDR) *Ensuring Competence and Quality in Dispute Resolution Practice*, April 1995

Society of Professionals in Dispute Resolution (SPIDR) *Progress Committee on Credentials Competencies and Qualifications: Progress Report*, September 1999

Society of Professionals in Dispute Resolution (SPIDR) *Report and Recommendations of the Society of Professionals in Dispute Resolution Environment/Public Sector Critical Issues Committee*

Solicitors Indemnity Fund *ADR settlement achieves major savings*, Press Release, 22 June 1999

Solicitors' Family Law Association (SFLA) *Mediation rules for consultants; Mediation selection of applicants for training, practice and accreditation process; Mediation, training, accreditation and re-accreditation: appeals procedure; Mediation training for lawyers; The new ancillary relief pilot scheme; Divorce procedure; Good practice regarding the service in the family law context; Good practice note on procedure in domestic violence cases; Courses in all issues mediation; Specialist accreditation scheme 1999; Association Rules; Family Mediation magazine; and Review magazine*

Solomon, L D and J S 'Using alternative dispute resolution techniques to settle conflicts among shareholders of closely held corporations' (1987) 22 *Wake Forest Law Review* 105

Solomon, M   *Case Flow Management in the Trial Court*, Commission on Standards of Judicial Administration, 1973

Solomon, M   *Case Flow Management in the Trial Court Now and for the future*, American Bar Association, 1987

Somerville, R   'Mediation and the planning tribunal' (1996) *Lawtalk*, Issue 486

Sordo, B   'Law Society of NSW Review of the Guidelines for solicitor mediators and the dispute resolution model clause' (1993) 4 *Australian Dispute Resolution Journal* 307

Sordo, B   'The lawyer's role in mediation' (1996) 7 *Australian Dispute Resolution Journal* 20

Sowerby, W   'The proposal that the court be empowered to order parties to mediation' (1996) *DRB* 16

Spencer, D   'Uncertainty and incompleteness in dispute resolution clauses' (1995) 2 *Commercial Dispute Resolution Journal* 23

Spencer, D   'Communication between mediator and judge leads to finding of bias' (1997) 8(4) *Australian Dispute Resolution Journal* 308

Spencer, D   'Case Note: complying with a requirement to negotiate in good faith' (1998) 9 *Australian Dispute Resolution Journal* 226

Spencer, D   'Liability of lawyers to advise on alternative dispute resolution options' (1998) 9 *Australian Dispute Resolution Journal* 292

Spooner, A   'Woolf offers solution for business disputes' *Birmingham Post*, 22 October 1999, p 22

Sports Dispute Resolution Panel   *Rules for arbitration, mediation procedure and rules for an advisory opinion*, SDRP, October 1999

Starbuck, S   'Shipping can no longer afford to shun mediation' (2000) 10 *M Advocate* 26

Stein, P   *Legal institutions—the development of dispute settlement*, Butterworths, London, 1984

Stickley, A   'Pinning Civil Liability upon a Mediator: a lost cause of action?' (1998) 19 *Queensland Lawyer* 95

Stone, D et al   *Difficult conversations—how to discuss what matters most*, 1999

Stone, M   *Representing clients in Mediation*, Butterworths 1998

Street, L   'Binding and non-binding expert appraisal' (1990) 1 *Australian Dispute Resolution Journal* 133

Street, L   'The court system and alternative dispute resolution procedures' (1990) 1 *Australian Dispute Resolution Journal* 5

Street, L   'Representation in commercial mediation' (1994) *Australian Dispute Resolution Journal* 256

Street, Sir Laurence   'The Courts and mediation—a warning' (1991) 2 *Australian Dispute Resolution Journal* 203

Street, Sir Laurence   'Agreed structure for dispute resolution: AMA v Department of Health' (1994) *Australian Dispute Resolution Journal* 185

Street, Sir Laurence   'Mediation and the judicial institution' (1997) 71 *Australian Law Journal* 796

Stubbs, M and Tow, D   'Australian tests for mediation benefits' *Planning* No 1123, 16 June 1995, p 10

Stulberg, J B   *Taking charge/managing conflict*, Lexington Books, Lexington, Massachusetts, 1987

Susskind, L   'Environmental mediation and accountability problem' (1981) 6 *Vermont Law Review* 1

Susskind, L   'Multi-party public policy mediation: a separate breed' *American Bar Association Dispute Resolution Magazine*, Autumn 1997 edition

Susskind, L and McMahon, G   'The theory and practice of negotiated rulemaking' (1985) 3 *Yale Journal of Regulation* 133

Susskind, L et al (eds)   *The Consensus Building Handbook—a comprehensive guide to reaching agreement*, Sage Publications, California, 1999

Sutton, P   'Woolf's reforms: a curate's egg?' *The Times*, 26 October 1999

Swallow, M   'London Courts lose out as litigants head for regions' *The Lawyer*, 24 May 1999

Symonds, G 'Mediation: Contributing to socially inclusive schools' *Mediation* (Mediation UK publication), Autumn 1999, p 5

Tan, N and Lim, K 'Community mediation—models for practice' paper presented at conference Mediation—yesterday's ideas, today's techniques, National University of Singapore, 27 March 1999 and published in *Conference Proceedings*

Tapper, C *Cross and Tapper on Evidence* (9th edn) Butterworths, London, 1999

Tattum, D and Lane, D (eds) *Bullying in schools*, Trentham Books, 1989

Taylor, A 'Toward a comprehensive theory of mediation' (1981) 19 *Conciliation Courts Review* 1

Taylor, A 'Concepts of neutrality in family mediation: contexts, ethics, influence and transformative process' (1997) 14 *Mediation Quarterly* 215

Taylor, D 'Press Release' *World Cargo News*, April 1999

Taylor, V and Pryles, M 'The cultures of dispute resolution in Asia' in M Pryles (ed) *Dispute Resolution in Asia*, 1997

Terrell, T 'Rights and Wrongs in the Rush to Repose: on the Jurisprudential Dangers of Alternative Dispute Resolution' (1987) 36(2) *Emory Law Journal* 541

Thoennes, M and Pearson, J 'Predicting outcomes in divorce mediation: the influence of people in process' (1985) 41(2) *Journal of Social Issues* 115

Thomas, R 'Vialli starts £1.5m libel case in Rome' *Guardian*, London, 14 April 1999

Thompson, B 'Small Taxation Claims Tribunal' (1997) 6 *Proctor* 16

Thornton, M 'Mediation policy and the State' (1993) 4 *Australian Dispute Resolution Journal* 230

Threadgold, S 'Legal Expenses: Meditating on mediation' *Post Magazine*, 7 October 1999, p 26

Thurgood, R 'Mediator intervention to ensure fair and just outcomes' (1999) 10 *Australian Dispute Resolution Journal* 142

Tillet, G *Resolving conflict—a practical approach*, Sydney University Press, Sydney, 1991

Timmis, C 'Litigation' *Legal Business*, March 1999

Touval, S and Zartman, I 'Mediation in international conflicts' in K Kressel et al (eds) *Mediation Research: the process and effectiveness of third party intervention*, Jossey-Bass, San Francisco, 1989

Tractenberg, P 'Court-appointed mediators or special masters: a commentary' (1988) 12 *Seton Hall Legislative Journal* 81

Tsang, L 'Separating the issues' *The Law Society Gazette*, 21 July 1999, p 22

Turner, M 'Computer contract disputes' (1997) 8(3) *Computers & Law*

Turner, M 'Mediation of computer contract disputes' (1997) 7(6) *Computers & Law*

Twining, W 'Alternative to what? Theories of litigation, procedure and dispute settlement in Anglo-American jurisprudence' (1993) 56 *Modern Law Review* 380

Tyrril, J 'Construction industry dispute resolution—a brief overview' (1992) 3 *Australian Dispute Resolution Journal* 167

Tyrril, J 'New ADR Agreement' (1993) 31 *Australian Construction Law Newsletter* 26–9

UK College of Family Mediators *1999/2000 Directory and Handbook*, Sweet & Maxwell, London, 1999

UK College of Family Mediators *Standards and Code of Practice; Training Standards; Policies and Standards of the UK College of Family Mediators—objects and functions of the College; Family Mediation: working to cover the emotional and financial costs of separation and divorce; Creating the firm foundation for a growing profession; Family Mediation Gazette*

UK College of Family Mediators *Precedents* ('Open Statements of Financial Information'; 'Memorandum of Understanding'; 'Guidelines on Memorandum of Understanding and Conflict of Interest')

Umbreit, M S *Victim meets offender: The impact of restorative justice in mediation*, Criminal Justice Press, New York, 1994

Umbreit, M S and Roberts, A W   *Mediation of criminal conflict in England: An assessment of services in Coventry and Leeds*, Centre for Restorative Justice and Mediation, School of Social Work, University of Minnesota, 1996

UNCITRAL   *Conciliation Rules*

University of Newcastle upon Tyne Conciliation Project Unit   *Report to the Lord Chancellor's Department on the cost and effectiveness of conciliation in England and Wales*, March 1989

Ury, W et al   *Getting disputes resolved: designing systems to cut the cost of conflict*, Jossey-Bass, San Francisco, 1986

Ury, W   *Getting past no: negotiating with difficult people*, Business Books, London, 1991

UTS Centre for Dispute Resolution   'Mediator Assessment Form' (1994) 1 *Commercial Dispute Resolution Journal* 157–65

Vann, V   'Confidentiality in court-sponsored mediation: disclosure at your own risk?' (1999) 10 *Australian Dispute Resolution Journal* 195

Vergis, A and Crosly, D   'Use of fast track mediation in personal injuries litigation' (1994–5) 1 *Commercial Dispute Resolution Journal* 265

Verkaik, R   'Commercial Court imposes ADR order to end De Lorean battle' *The Law Society Gazette*, 19 November 1997, p 10

Verkaik, R   'Survey finds city firms turn to mediation for negligence cases' *The Law Society Gazette*, 15 July 1998, p 8

Verkaik, R and Lindsay, R   'Freemasons in an unbrotherly feud over old lodge' *The Independent*, London, 26 July 1999

Vickery, G   'Guidelines for Mediators', unpublished LLM paper, Bond University, Australia, 1993

Virgo, J and Ryley, P   'Mediation, penalties and enforcement' (2000) 13(3) *Compliance Monitor* 269

Wade, J   'Lawyers and mediators: what each needs to learn from and about the other' (1991) 2 *Australian Journal of Dispute Resolution* 159

Wade, J   'Forms of power in family mediation and negotiation' (1994) 6 *Australian Journal of Family Law* 40

Wade, J   'My mediator must be a QC' (1994) 5 *Australian Dispute Resolution Journal* 161

Wade, J   'Strategic interventions used by mediators, facilitators and conciliators' (1994) 5 *Australian Dispute Resolution Journal* 292

Wade, J   'In search of new conflict management processes: the lawyer as macro and micro diagnostic problem solver' (1995) 10(2) *Australian Family Lawyer* 23

Wade, J   'In search of new conflict management processes: Part II' (1995) 10(3) *Australian Family Lawyer* 16

Wade, J   'The last gap in negotiations—why is it important? How can it be crossed?' (1995) 6 *Australian Dispute Resolution Journal* 93

Wade, J   'Forever bargaining in the shadow of the law—who sells solid shadows? Who advises what, where, when?' (1998) 12 *Australian Journal of Family Law* 256

Wade, J et al   'Mediation—the terminological debate' (1994) 5 *Australian Dispute Resolution Journal* 204

Wahrhaftig, P   'Nonprofessional Conflict Resolution' in J Palenski and H Launer (eds) *Mediation Conflicts and Challenges*, Charles C Thomas, 1986

Walker, G   'Training mediators: teaching about ethical concerns and obligations' (1998) 19 *Mediation Quarterly* 33

Walker, J   *Violence and conflict resolution in schools*, Council for Cultural Co-operation, Council of Europe, Strasbourg, 1989

Walker, J (ed)   *Information meetings and associated provisions of the Family Law Act 1996* (First, second and third interim reports to the Lord Chancellor's Department, 1998 and 1999)

Walker, J (ed)   *Summary of research in progress*, Lord Chancellor's Department, 1999

Walker, J et al *An evaluation of comprehensive mediation services for divorcing couples*, Social Policy Research Findings, No 48, Joseph Rowntree Foundation, York, 1994

Wall, J A and Rude, D E 'Judges' mediation of settlement negotiations' (1987) 72(2) *Journal of Applied Psychology* 234

Wall, J and Lynn, A 'Mediation: a current review' (1993) 37 *Journal of Conflict Resolution* 160

Wall, V and Dewhurst, M 'Mediator Gender: Communication differences in resolved and unresolved mediations' (1991) 9(1) *Mediation Quarterly* 63

Walton, R and McKersie A *A Behavioural Theory of Labour Negotiation*, 1965

Watkin, T 'Set Launches Mediation Business' *The Lawyer*, 12 April 1999

Webb, K 'The Morality of Mediation' in C R Mitchell and K Webb *New Approaches to International Mediation*, Greenwood Press, Westport, 1988

Webley, L *A review of the literature on family mediation: prepared for the Lord Chancellor's Advisory Committee on Legal Education and Conduct*, Institute of Advanced Legal Studies, 1998

Weigand, S 'A just and lasting peace: supplanting mediation with the ombuds model' (1996) 12(1) *Ohio State Journal on Dispute Resolution* 95

Weisbrot, D *Australian Lawyers*, Longman Cheshire, Melbourne, 1990

Welbank, M et al *Mediation in the Planning System*, DETR, London, May 2000, p 11

Welton, G et al 'The role of caucusing in community mediation' (1988) 32 *Journal of Conflict Resolution* 181

Weston, M 'Domain names—disputes and resolution: Part 1' (2000) 16(4) *CLSR* 224

Wheeler, S 'Lawyer involvement in commercial disputes' (1991) 18 *Journal of Law and Society* 241

Whissler, P L 'Mediation and adjudication in the small claims court: the effects of process and case characteristics' (1995) 29 *Law & Society Review* 323

White Paper *Looking to the Future: Mediation and the Grounds for Divorce*, 1995 Cm 2799, HMSO, London

Whiting, R 'The single-issue, multiple-issue debate and the effect of issue number on mediated outcomes' (1992) 10 *Mediation Quarterly* 57

Wicks, R 'Mediating clinical negligence claims' (2000) 3 *Medical Litigation* 8

Wilensky, H 'The professionalisation of everyone?' (1964) *The American Journal of Sociology* 137

Wilikens, W et al *Out-of-court dispute settlement systems for e-commerce: report of exploratory study*, Joint Research Centre, Italy, 2000

Williams, G *Legal Negotiation & Settlement*, West Publishing Co, Minneapolis, 1983

Williamson, S 'The silent revolution in dispute resolution' (1994) 68 *Law Institute Journal* 10–11

Wilson, B 'Mediation scheme for nightmare neighbours: bid to solve residents' rows' *The Journal (Newcastle)*, 10 April 1998, p 23

Wilson, B 'Mediating "single issue" disputes' (2000) 30 *Family Law* 664

Wimmer, A M 'The jolly mediator: some serious thoughts about humour in mediation' (1994) 10 *Negotiation Journal* 193

Winfield, M *Far from wanting their day in court: Civil disputants in England and Wales*, National Consumer Council, London, 1996

Winner, M 'Is the research on mediation providing the answer?' (2000) 30 *Family Law* 138

Winner, N 'Capacity to Mediate' *Family and Mediation*, vol 7, no 2

WIPO Arbitration and Mediation Centre *The centre and its services; WIPO Mediation Rules; Guide to WIPO Mediation; Publications List*

Wissler, R L 'A close look at settlement week' (1998) 4 *Dispute Resolution Magazine* 28

Wolski, B 'The role and limitations of Fisher and Ury's model of interest-based negotiation in mediation' (1994) 5 *Australian Dispute Resolution Journal* 210

Wolski, B 'Voluntariness, consensuality and coercion: in defence of mandatory mediation' unpublished LLM paper, Bond University, 1994

Wood, B 'Mediators' Institute Ireland' *Family Mediation* vol 4, No 3, at p 10

Wood J, J R T 'Case Management in the Common Law Division of the Supreme Court of New South Wales' (1991) 1 *Journal of Judicial Administration* 71

Woods 'Mediation: a Backlash to Women's Progress on Family Law Issues' (1985) 19 *Clearinghouse Review* 431

Woodward, S 'Panels prevent damaging disputes' (1999) 10(10) *Construction Law* 28

World Intellectual Property Organisation (WIPO) *Mediation Clauses; Agreement to mediate; Mediation Rules; and Guide to mediation; and Recommended contract clauses and submission agreements*

Yaqoob, T 'Peacemaker in a war of words: New mediation service launches to settle neighbour disputes' *The Sentinel*, 10 October 1998, p 12

Young, K *Research/Evaluation of Family Mediation Practice and the Issue of Violence: Final Report*, Attorney-General's Department, 1996

Zaki, S 'Competition reforms could swamp courts' *Legal Week*, 15 June 2000

Zariski, A 'Lawyers and dispute resolution: what do they think and know (and think they know)? Finding out through survey research' (1997) 4(2) *E Law—Murdoch University Electronic Journal of Law*

Zilinskas, A 'The training of mediators: is it necessary?' (1995) 6 *Australian Dispute Resolution Journal* 55

Zuckerman, A A S 'Quality and Economy in Civil Procedure—the case for commuting correct judgments for timely judgments' (1994) 14(3) *Oxford Journal of Legal Studies* 535

Index

All references are to page numbers